Consequences of Complicity in International Relations

Dimitris Liakopoulos

Consequences of Complicity in International Relations

Dimitris Liakopoulos

W. B. Sheridan Law Books

Academica Press
Washington~London

Library of Congress Cataloging-in-Publication Data

Names: Liakopoulos, Dimitris, author. |
Title: Consequences of complicity in international relations / Dimitris Liakopoulos
Description: Washington : Academica Press, 2020. | Includes references.
Identifiers: LCCN 2020941807 | ISBN 9781680531374

Dedicated to Irene and Sofia

Contents

CHAPTER 1

The consequences of complicity

1.1. Introduction

The case of complicity once completed in all its elements gives rise to the legal consequences provided for in the second and third part of the draft articles on the responsibility of the State and the corresponding provisions of the draft articles on the responsibility of international organizations. The treatment of this profile is indeed conditioned by the lack of what is in our knowledge, data of the practice, so that in the following pages, some hypotheses will be formulated essentially based on the regulatory framework just mentioned. Moreover, if the provisions of the two projects constitute a necessary element in the reconstruction of the legal relationship determined by the accessory event, is also necessary to take into account the peculiarities of the unlawful case under consideration. It must be remembered that this is a crime distinct from the main circumstance which distinguishes complicity from other hypotheses of concurrence in the violation of international law, such as correctness. In the situation contemplated by articles 16 ARSIWA and 14, 58 DARIO include two illicit facts related to each other but distinct from them. In the case of co-imputation, on the other hand, a plurality of subjects contributes to the realization of a single illicit fact. The distinction assumes particular importance for the determination of the legal consequences of each insolvency case. The 2001 project specifically deals only with the claim exercisable by the State injured by an unlawful event attributable to several States. Art. 47 ARSIWA, placed among the provisions relating to the invocation of the responsibility of a State, establishes that "where several States are responsible for the same internationally wrongful act, the responsibility of each State may be invoked in relation to that act." As is clear from the literal datum, the aforementioned provision refers unequivocally to the situation of correction only.[1] The injured party in this

[1]According to the comment of art. 47 "the situation can arise where a single course of conduct is at the same time attributable to several States and is internationally wrongful for each of them" ARSIWA, par. 3. In argument see: S. WITTICH, Joint tort feasors in

case "can hold any responsible State for the wrongful conduct as a whole."[2] Although the comment of art. 47 determine that "the responsibility of each State may be separately inked by an injured one in the sense of article 42"[3] and that the analogy with the civil law institute of joint and several liability "must be applied with care."[4] It is evident that at least in principle the injured party would have the right to demand repair without distinction from one or the other author of the illicit act. [5] The position of the

---

investment law, in C. BINDER, U. KRIEBAUM, A. REINISCH, S. WITTICH, International investment law for the 21st century, op. cit., pp. 716ss. S. BESSON, La pluralitè d'États responsable. Vers une solidaritè international?, op. cit., pp. 31ss. J. CRAWFORD, State responsibility. The general part, op. cit., pp. 334ss. P. D'ARGENT, Reparation, cessation, assurances and guarantees of non repetition, in A. NOLLKAEMPER, I. PLAKOKEFALOS, Principles of shared responsibility in international law. An appraisal of the state of the art, op. cit., pp. 228ss. A. ORAKHELASHVILI, Division of reparation between responsible entities, in J. CRAWFORD, A. PELLET, S. OLLESON, K. PARLETT, The law of international responsibility, op. cit., pp. 658ss. C.J. TAMS, Countermeasures against multiple responsible actors, in A. NOLLKAEMPER, I. PLAKOKEFALOS, Principles of shared responsibility in international law. An appraisal of the state of the art, op. cit., pp. 312ss. In practice art. 47 was examined precisely with regard to a case of joint imputation of the same conduct. See the arbitral sentence in eurotunnel case: The Channel Tunnel Group Ltd and France-Manche S.A. v. The Secretary of State for Transport of the Government of Great Britain and Northern Ireland and le Ministre de l'èquipement, des transports, de l'amènagement du territoire, du tourisme et de la mer du Gouvernement de la Rèpubliqe française, partial award, 30 January 2007. For further analysis see: F. MESSINEO, Attribution of conduct, in A. NOLLKAEMPER, I. PLAKOKEFALOS, Principles of shared responsibility in international law. An appraisal of the state of the art, op. cit., pp. 71ss. The twin provision contained in art. 48 DARIO reproduces in the first paragraph the content of art. 47 ARSIWA but in the second it seems to set up a sensibly different regulation based on the notion of subsistence responsibility, which can be invoked by the injured party "insofar in the invocation of the primary" responsibility has not led to reparation. The comment to this provision does not help to clarify the relationship with article 47 ARSIWA. It is stated that articles 14-18 and 58-62 can be ascribed, at least in principle, to the category of "joint responsibility of an international organization with one or more States (DARIO, par. 1). The same comment then illustrates as an example of subsidiary responsibility the hypothesis envisaged by article 62. It seems that in terms of consequences the 2011 Project places complicity and co-imputation on the same level. It demonstrates in the following developments of the text that the solution indicated by article 48 DARIO constitutes only one of the hypotheses of distribution of the reparation obligations between accompliced State and author of the main fact, which in any case the two offenses in question remain legally distinct."

[2]ARSIWA, par. 2.

[3]ARSIWA, par. 7.

[4]ARSIWA, par. 3.

[5] S. WITTICH, Joint tortfeasors in investment law, in C. BINDER, U. KRIEBAUM, A. REINISCH, S. WITTICH, International investment law for the 21st century, op. cit., pp. 716ss. S. BESSON, La pluralitè d'États responsable. Vers une solidaritè international?, op. cit., pp. 31ss. P. D'ARGENT, Reparation, cessation, assurances and guarantees of non

accomplice subject and except for very precise hypotheses which will be discussed later, is distinguished from that of the principal author not only from the point of view of the qualification of the conduct but also with regard to its consequences, since the two offenses concur in different measure to cause the injury of the injured party.

The accessory fact gives rise to a secondary juridical relationship between the subject who carries it out and the injured party parallel to the one between it and the author of the main unlawful act. The opinion that the report in question should qualify as a "recntsähnlichen Beziehung"[6] due to the contribution made by the accomplice to the violation of a primary obligation of which it should also be addressed as provided by art. 16 b) ARSIWA. In this way, the author of the accessory act "tritt somit weningstens indirekt in eine Rechtsbeziehung zum verletzten Staat"[7] tried to prove that the legal title on which the responsibility of the accomplice is based is entirely independent of that which qualifies the main act and is constituted precisely by the customary norm contained in articles 16 ARSIWA and 14, 58 DARIO. This rule while indirectly contributing to protecting the legal good of the primary rule violated by the principal author, maintains its own autonomy with respect to the latter.[8] Regardless of any consideration regarding the condition set by letter. b) of art. 16 ARSIWA (and the analogous DARIO provisions) we can therefore affirm with the support of the majority doctrine,[9] that the illicit fact of complicity

---

repetition, in A. NOLLKAEMPER, I. PLAKOKEFALOS, Principles of shared responsibility in international law. An appraisal of the state of the art, op. cit., pp. 238ss.

6A. FELDER, Die Beihilfe im Recht der völkerrechtlichen Staatenverantwortlichkeit, op. cit., pp. 275ss.

7A. FELDER, Die Beihilfe im Recht der völkerrechtlichen Staatenverantwortlichkeit, op. cit., H.P. AUST, Complicity in international law, op. cit., pp. 272ss, examines this position by redeeming the merit of having highlighted that the peculiarities of the unlawful case regulated by art. 16 ARSIWA have a decisive influence on the secondary legal relationship. The conclusion reached by the author is that the illegality of the accessory fact gives rise to the consequences regulated by the 2001 project thanks to the fact that art. 16 can be considered "a transformative provision in the realm of secondary rules" (page 273).

8See also: B. REINALDA, B. BERBEEK, Autonomous policy making by international organizations, ed. Routledge, London & New York, 1998, pp. 4ss.

9V. LANOVOY, Complicity and its limits in the law of international responsibility, op. cit., pag. 263 which Felder commented that: Questionable whether, formally speaking, legal consequences can attach to the complicit actors "telle quelle." J. QUIGLEY, Complicity in internationale law. A new direction in the law of state responsibility, op. cit., pp. 125ss. P. D'ARGENT, Les rèparations de guerre en droit international public. La responsabilitè internaitonale des États à l'èpreuve de la guerre, ed. Bruylant, Bruxelles, 2002. P. D'ARGENT, Reparation, cessation, assurances and guarantees of non repetition, in A. NOLLKAEMPER, I. PLAKOKEFALOS, Principles of shared responsibility in international law. An appraisal of the state of the art, op. cit., S. WITTICH, Joint tortfeasors in investment law, in C. BINDER, U. KRIEBAUM, A. REINISCH, S. WITTICH,

gives rise to a secondary, distinct juridical relationship. It is the case to reiterate it from that which involves the author of the main fact. The comment to art. 16 ARSIWA, moreover, seems to confirm what has just been pointed out where is stressed that the obligations envisaged by the second part of the same project[10] are incumbent on the accomplice.

The considerations carried out up to this point induce to exclude moreover that the responsibility of the accomplice can be invoked by subjects different from the injured party, according to the scheme of art. 48, par. 1 ARSIWA and 49 DARIO. Even in the hypothesis that the accessory fact facilitates the violation of an erga omnes partes or obligation, a State not directly injured could exercise the faculties provided for by the provisions in question exclusively with respect to the principal author. Only the latter in fact would be attributable to the violation of an obligation "owed to a group of States including that of and (...) established for the protection of a collective injector of the group" or "owed to the international community as a whole."[11] The only obligation violated by the accomplice would in any case be the one established by articles 16 ARSIWA and 14, 58 DARIO which, however, is not suitable in our opinion to establish legal situations for subjects other than the injured party. Similar considerations could be valid outside the liability regime in relation to the hypothesis referred to in art. 60 VCLT. [12] The aid or assistance in the substantial violation of a treaty in our opinion does not legitimize the parties to the suspension or extinction of the latter with respect to the accomplice. Also in this case the accessory deed does not include any breach of the agreement. The references to the exceptio inadimpleti contractus found in international jurisprudence[13] are mostly

International investment law for the 21st century, op. cit., pp. 715ss. B. GRAEFRATH, Complicity in the law of state responsibility, op. cit., pp. 380ss.

[10]ARSIWA, par. 10.

[11]ARSIWA, par. 1. V. LANOVOY, Complicity and its limits in the law of international responsibility, op. cit., pp. 292ss.

[12]B. GRAEFRATH, Complicity in the law of state responsibility, op. cit., pp. 384ss.

[13]See the sentence of 2 February 1923 decided by the Swiss federal court in king Lepeshkin case, judgment of 28 January 1926 made by the cour de Paris in the Renault et Sociètè des Usines Renault case Renault v. Sociètè Rousky Renault according to which there exists a right of Resolution of the Conventions of the Hague of 1096: "En vertu de la clause rèsolutoire qui est expresse ou sous-entendue dans les traitès." The sentence of 7 October 1949 rendered by the district Court of Rotterdam in the king Tatarko case. The sentence of 27 March 1950 issued by the Frankfurt Court of appeal in the security for costs (Switzerland) case. In this regard, all that can be said is that if one considers the single treaty decomposable into bilateral relations, one will be faced with a normal bilateral treaty and therefore with the possibility of a reaction as an individual exception, while where the single treaty is considered not to be broken down into bilateral relations, there is still the possibility of a solution envisaged or obtained interpretatively from the treaty.

formulated in sufficiently broad terms to include also forms of reaction to a violated breach. For example, in this regard, the separate opinion of judge Hudson in the Deviation of the waters of the Meuse case which configures the existence of "an equity where two parties have assumed an identical or a reciprocal obligation which is engaged with a continuing non-performance of that obligation by the other party (...)."[14]

Following the approach of the two projects-which notoriously reflects the reconstruction proposed by Ago in his third report[15] and followed by the majority of doctrine-we will examine in first paragraphs of this section, the content of the juridical relationship in question, verifying the existence in the head of the accomplice of the obligation of termination of the conduct and to provide guarantees of non-repetition and of the obligation to repair.[16] With regard to the latter, our assessments will

---

[14]PCIJ, Publications, Serie A/B, p. 4, p. 77 where the judge refers separately to the exception non adimpleti contractus, noting that: "It is so just, so equitable so universally recognized that it must be applied in international relations also." The judge Altamira then denied that the principle could be applied in the present case because the obligations that emerged would not have had a sinallagmatic nature (paragraphs 39-43). The configurability of the exception inedimpleti contractus in international law was confirmed by the arbitral tribunal in the context of ICSID in the Klöckner Industire-Anlagen GmbH and others v. Republic of Cameroon case of 21 October 1983, in ICSID Reports, vol. 2, p. 9 par. 63, in which the question of the unlawfulness of the breach was not explicitly addressed. A. ZIMMERMANN, C.J. TAMS, K. OELLERS-FRAHAM, The Statute of the International Court of Justice. A commentary, op. cit.

[15]R. AGO, Troisième rapport sur la responsabilitè des États. Le fait internationalement illicite de l'État, source de responsabilitè internationale, op. cit., par. 43.

[16]According to Anzilotti, first of all in international doctrine, the failure to comply with an international obligation always corresponds to the emergence of a new juridical relationship between the State which is responsible for the fact and the one towards which the existed duty can demand reparation. D. ANZILOTTI, La responsabilitè internationale des Etats à raion des dommages soufferts par des ètrangers, in Revue Gènèrale de Droit International Public, 1, 1906, pp. 152ss. Anzilotti was not the first to take up the principles that identified with regard to the consequences of the international crime only in their general features, but his configuration of the obligation to repair was subsequently widespread and exercised a decisive influence on the subsequent doctrine. J. PERSONNAZ, La rèparation du prèjuice en droit international public, ed. Sirey, Paris, 1939: "Se concretisent dans le devoir de rèparation, et des conditions dans lequelles cette dernière sera effectuèe (...)." J. SPIROPOULOS, Die Haftung der Staaten für "indirekten Schaden" aus völkerrechtlichen Delikten, in Niemeyers Zeitschrift für Völkerrecht, 35, 1925-1926, pp. 60ss. G. SALVIOLI, La responsabilitè des États et la fixation des dommages-intèrêts par les tribunaux internationaux, in Recueil des cours, ed. Brill, Bruxelles, vol. 28, 1929, pp. 238ss. R. LAIS, Die Rechtsfolgen völkerrechtlicher Delikte, Dunker & Humblot, Berlin, 1932. L. REITZER, La rèparation comme consèquence de l'acte illicite en droit international, ed. Sirey, Paris, 1938, pp. 32, 116ss. P.A. BISSONNETTE, La satisfaction comme mode de rèparation en droit international, Imprimerie Granchamp, Genève, 1952. L. BOTTIGLIERO, Redress for victims of crimes under international law, ed. Springer,

be based essentially on causal efficiency with respect to the injury suffered by the injured party. In the last paragraphs we will instead evaluate the configurability of self-protection measures against the complicit subject.

1.2. The content of liability relationship determined by the accessory event. The obligation to terminate the conduct at the expense of the accomplice State

The "first" consequence of the unlawful act[17] is regulated by art. 30 a) ARSIWA (which corresponds to art. 30 a) DARIO), based on "the State responsible for the internationally wrongful act under an obligation (...) to cease that act, if it is continuing." As noted by the rapporteur Arangio-Ruiz, the obligation of cessation is ascribable to the category of consequences of the offense only in a broad sense, placing itself conceptually as "outside the framework of reparation in a proper sense,"[18] according to an approach expressly shared in the practice of arbitration Court awarding the dispute concerning the Rainbow Warrior case. [19] According to ILC the duty to interrupt the unlawful act fulfils the function of safeguarding "the continuing validity and effectiveness of the underlying primary rule" and even indirectly the collective interest "in the preservation of a reliance on, the rule of law,"[20] so that the ratio of art. 30

Leiden, 2004. R. BERNHARDT, Decision of international courts and tribunals and international arbitrations, ed. Elsevier, Amsterdam, New York, Oxford, 2014. E.F. BAUER, Die Völkerrechtswidrige Entführung, Duncker & Humblot, Berlin, 1968, pp. 92ss.

[17]ARSIWA, par. 4.

[18]G. ARANZIO-RUIZ, Preliminary report on state responsibility, UN Doc. A/CN.4/416 & Corr. 1&2 and Add.1 & Corr. 1, in Yearbook of International Law Commission, vol. II, art. 22. Only in more recent times has the doctrine concerned itself with the obligation to cease conduct as an autonomous consequence of the fact. See for example: O. CORTEN, The obligation of termination, in J. CRAWFORD, A. PELLET, S. OLLESON, K. PARLETT, The law of international responsibility, Oxford University Press, Oxford, 2010, pp. 545ss. V. BAILLY, The cessation of acte illicite en droit international, LGDJ, Paris, 2015. The doctrine either does not consider the remedy in question or more often tends to bring it back to restitutio in integrum: K. STRUPP, Das Völkerrecht Delikt, op. cit., pp. 210ss. J. PERSONNAZ, La rèparation du prèjudice en droit international public, op. cit., pp. 84ss. B. GRAEFRATH, Responsibility and damage caused, in Recueil des cours, op. cit., pp. 84ss. It should be noted that in practice it is not easy to trace a clear dividing line between the obligation to terminate and the return in a specific form.

[19]Case concerning the difference between New Zealand and France concerning the interpretation or application of the two agreements concluded on 9 July 1986 between the two States, that are related to the problems arising from the Rainbow Warrior Affair, 30 April 1990, in Recueil des Sentences Arbitrales, vol. XX, pp. 215ss, par. 113.

[20]ARSIWA, par. 5. O. CORTEN, The obligation of cessation, in J. CRAWFORD, A.

a) is probably reconstructed in light of art. 29 according to which the consequences of the offense do not affect the effectiveness of the primary obligation violated by the responsible State.[21] It is clear that with respect to the mode of operation of secondary rules the termination carries out a function that could be defined as preventive to the extent that on the one hand it prevents the emergence of reparative claims in relation to the part of the offense avoided as a result of the interruption of the harmful conduct[22] and by the other prevents the aggravation of the prejudice suffered by the injured party.

What we want to underline for the purposes of our investigation is that in the hypothesis of complicity the obligation to terminate is functional to the content of the intermediate provision of art. 16 ARSIWA and 14, 58 DARIO constituting a necessary corollary. In other words, from art. 30 a) an obligation arises for the assistant State consisting in the immediate interruption of the behaviour which integrates the material element of complicity. In this regard, some considerations based on the peculiarities of the obligation established by art. 30 a) ARSIWA and the similar arrangement of the DARIOs. First of all, the obligation of termination incumbent on the accomplice operates independently of the parallel one (possibly) pending on the author of the main unlawful act. Secondly, given that it arises automatically regardless of the claim exercised by the injured party,[23] it can be said that the cessation obligation arises at the very moment in which the accessory event is integrated and obviously once the main fact is realized. A clarification is essential. The obligation to terminate, however, only in the event of a permanent or an instantaneous tort is repeated or likely to be repeated "on a series of occasions."[24] If the first notion does not raise particular interpretative difficulties, as is sufficient to refer to art. 14 ARSIWA,[25] the second category of offense mentioned in the commentary to art. 30 a) appears

PELLET, S. OLLESON, K. PARLETT, The law of international responsibility, op. cit., pp. 545ss.

[21]C. CRAWFORD, State responsibility. The general part, op. cit., pp. 464ss.

[22]G. ARANZIO-RUIZ, Preliminary report on state responsibility, op. cit., par. 22.

[23]G. ARANZIO-RUIZ, Preliminary report on state responsibility, op. cit., par. 41. R. KOLB, The international law of state responsibility, op. cit., pp. 151ss. J. CRAWFORD, State responsibility. The general part, op. cit., pp. 465ss.

[24]ARSIWA, par. 3.

[25]Permanent or continuous offenses must be understood based on art. 14, ar. 2 ARSIWA behaviour that lasts "(…) over the entire during which the act continues and remains not in conformity with the international obligation." R. AGO, Septième rapport sur la responsabilitè internationale (suite), op. cit., pp. 38ss, par. 28. F. DI STEFANO, Fait continu, fait composè et fait complexe dans le droit de la responsabilitè internationale, in Annuaire Français de Droit International, 52, 2006, pp. 4ss.

more problematic.[26] The comment to art. 15 ARSIWA seems to understand by the notion of repeated offense what in ECtHR jurisprudence is defined as practice incompatible with ECHR, namely: “An accumulation of identical or analogous breaches which are sufficiently numerous and interconnected to amount not merely to isolated incidents or exceptions but to a pattern or system.”[27] It is clear that art. 30 a) may apply to the accessory event only on condition that the latter falls into one of the two categories indicated by ILC. Thirdly, the project clarifies that the cessation obligation is imposed as much on the unlawful Commission,[28] as on the omissive one, a conclusion which was already reached by the Arangio-Ruiz[29] subsequently confirmed by the arbitration sentence rendered in the Rainbow Warrior case.[30]

These observations allow to adhere to the orientation for which art. 30 a) applies to the ancillary event that is permanent.[31] Although in our opinion this condition can only be seen in the hypothesis of a problem in which the accessory event is concomitant with the main one. In any case the duty of termination could be particularly effective in the event that the accomplice’s conduct is omissive.

1.3. (Follows) The obligation to offer insurance and guarantees of non-repetition

Art. 30 b) codifies a further consequence of the unlawful act, that is to say the obligation on the part of the State responsible for providing “appropriate assurances and guarantees of non repetition, if circumstances so require.”[32] This rule is commonly considered applicable where the conditions exist, including the unlawful act referred to in art. 16 ARSIWA

---

[26]J. CRAWFORD, State responsibility. The general part, op. cit., pp. 463ss. O. CORTEN, The obligation of cessation, in J. CRAWFORD, A. PELLET, S. OLLESON, K. PARLETT, The law of international responsibility, op. cit., pp. 548ss.

[27]ECtHR, Ireland v. United Kingdom of 18 January 1978, par. 159.

[28]ARSIWA, par. 2.

[29]G. ARANZIO-RUIZ, Preliminary report on state responsibility, op. cit., par. 42, where the rapporteur bases his deduction on the circumstance that the omission would by definition be a permanent offense to the extent that “is protracted beyond the date within which such an obligation (de faire) is performed.”

[30]Rainbow Warrior Affair, op. cit., par. 113.

[31]A. FELDER, Die Beihilfe im Rect der völkerrechtlichen Staatenverantwortlichkeit, op. cit., pp. 276ss. H.P. AUST, Complicity in international law, op. cit., pp. 274ss. P. D’ARGENT, Reparation, cessation, assurances and guarantees of non repetition, in A. NOLLKAEMPER, I. PLAKOKEFALOS, Principles of shared responsibility in international law. An appraisal of the state of the art, op. cit., pp. 215ss. V. LANOVOY, Complicity and its limits in the law of international responsibility, op. cit., pp. 266ss.

[32]V. LANOVOY, Complicity and its limits in the law of international responsibility, op. cit.,

and 14, 58 DARIO. The consequence in question would automatically operate in all the hypotheses of complicity, because "of the threat that unsanctional complicity poses to the international legal order as a whole"[33] the guarantee of non-repetition. This would therefore have a fundamental preventive function. From a general point of view, the purpose of these guarantees is to strengthen for the future the fulfilment of the violated primary obligation, preventing the repetition of the violation. In our opinion the nature of the consequence in question imposes an assessment of the circumstances of the case and more precisely of the risk of reiteration of the circumstances of the case and more precisely of the risk of repetition of the unlawful fact under consideration. It seems to us to exclude that the claim of the injured State founded on art. 30 b) always complies with general international law.[34]

The consequence under examination, unlike the obligation of termination, does not operate automatically, since it must be the subject of a specific request by the aggrieved party[35] and, above all, has an exceptional character, as can be deduced from the literal tenor of the provision.[36] Although it is not limited to the continuous fact,[37] the obligation to offer non repetition guarantees does not operate in relation to all the illegal cases, but as mentioned only with respect to those "which appear more likely to be repeated."[38] The exceptional nature of the guarantees of

---

[33]V. LANOVOY, Complicity and its limits in the law of international responsibility, op. cit., pp. 267ss.

[34]It must be considered that the customary nature of the obligation under examination has been consolidated to the adoption of the 2001 Project also thanks to ICJ jurisprudence and to a opinio juris partly deducible from the silence of States regarding the provision proposed by the ILC. In this sense see: S. BARBIER, Assurances and guarantees of non-repetition, in J. CRAWFORD, A. PELLET, S. OLLESON, K. PARLETT, The law of international responsibility, Oxford University Press, Oxford, 2010, pp. 554ss. Even in recent times there was a substantial divergence of views in doctrine. If some supported the customary nature of the guarantees of non-repetition. In this sense see: B. STERN, A plea for "reconstruction" of international responsibility based on the notion of legal injury, in M. RAGAZZI, International responsibility today. Essays in memory of Oscar Schachter, Martinus Nijhoff Publishers, Leiden, Boston, 2005, pp. 104ss. A. ZIMMERMANN, C.J. TAMS, K. OELLERS-FRAHAM, The statute of the International Court of Justice. A commentary, op. cit.

[35]R. KOLB, The international law of state responsibility, op. cit., pp. 152ss.

[36]ARSIWA, par. 13. See also: J. CRAWFORD, State responsibility. The general part, op. cit., pp. 44ss. S. BARBIER, Assurances and guarantees of non-repetition, in J. CRAWFORD, A. PELLET, S. OLLESON, K. PARLETT, The law of international responsibility, op. cit., pp. 552.

[37]J. CRAWFORD, State responsibility. The general part, op. cit., pp. 469, which underlined the difference from this point of view with the obligation of termination.

[38]G. ARANGIO-RUIZ, State responsibility revisited. The factual nature of the attribution of conduct to the state, op. cit. G. ARANZIO-RUIG, Second report on state responsibility

non-repetition, moreover, is confirmed by the debates that took place within the ICL still on the eve of the adoption of 2001 Project. The president of the editorial Committee, Gaja underlined that the measure in question does not constitutes "a necessary part of the legal consequences of all internationally worn-out acts," although its introduction in the article should be seen as a useful policy.[39] The preventive function carried out by art. 30 b) occurs only in limited hypotheses. And in fact, even taking into account only the practice concerning the non-repetition guarantees arranged in the jurisdictional context, after the LaGrand case,[40] a certain reluctance on the part of ICJ to accept questions related to the measure in question[41] is shown. The case concerning the construction is proof of the wall in the occupied Palestinian territory, where ICJ has avoided ruling on

---

A/CN.4/425 Corr 1 and Add 1& Corr. 1, 1980, vol. II.

[39]In Yearbook of International Law Commission, vol. I, 2001, p. 15.

[40]ICJ, LaGrad case (Germany v. The United States of America), judgement 27 June 2001, in ICJ Reports, 2001, pp. 499ss. The dispute concerned the violation by the United States of the obligation provided by art. 36 of the Vienna Convention on Consular Relations of 1963 to inform the German consular authorities of the arrest and subsequent death sentence of two German citizens. Germany claimed that the United States offered guarantees of non-repetition of the offense both general and specific. The central aspect of the affair was represented by the American admission of the violation of the Convention of 1963. The ICJ considered that the German claim considered to be satisfied by the commitment assumed by the United States to adopt measures to promote respect for the Convention, even in part of the own local authorities and that in the specific case of new sentences to severe penalties of German citizens that occurred in violation of the Convention on consular relations, the United States should have allowed the review of convictions. Also in the decision concerning the dispute over the application of the Bermuda II Agreement (arbitration award of 30 November 1992 in the dispute between the United States and United Kingdom and Ireland of North) it seems certain that the arbitration panel understood both notions in the sense inspired by the French legal tradition. The conduct obligations seem to coincide with a "best efforts obligation" or with an obligation to make an effort. Less clear is what the Court intends an obligation for result. The qualification of the obligation imposed by art. 10, par. 2 as an obligation of result is linked as emerges from a passage of the sentence previously reported to its mandatory force. It does not seem reasonable to understand this in the sense of a binding forum understood in a formal sense since it certainly does not have the remaining part of the exhortative value disposition, is to be understood in our opinion in the light of an overall reading of the decision as a rule that imposes an obligation to succeed. The Iran-United States Court makes use of the expressions obligation of conduct and obligation for result in A15/A24 (award n. 590, par. 95) case makes use of the notion of result obligation to point out that greater flexibility is allowed to United States with regard to the mode of implementation of a certain obligation, which would not require the maintenance of a precise conduct indicated in the standard itself.

[41]S. BARBIER, Assurances and guarantees of non-repetition, in J. CRAWFORD, A. PELLET, S. OLLESON, K. PARLETT, The law of international responsibility, op. cit., pp. 555ss.

Israel's obligation to offer guarantees of non-repetition and that concerning mutual assistance in criminal matters in which the same orientation has been maintained.[42]

We can argue that the provision contained in art. 30 b) is applicable to the unlawful act regulated by art. 16 ARSIWA and 14, 58 DARIO, once the risk of reiteration is ascertained. Two observations apply in this regard. On the one hand, it does not seem that the obligation in question is conditioned by the seriousness of the unlawful fact, as could be deduced from the reference made by art. 48, par. 2 b) ARSIWA to this kind of consequences. ICJ's case-law appears to testify in the sense indicated. In the LaGrad case, rather than the gravity of the infringement, the seriousness of the prejudice suffered by the individual in whose defense the appellant State is concerned became more important. Further confirmation seems to be derived from the advisory opinion on the construction of a wall in the occupied Palestinian territory where ICJ has not ruled on the guarantees pursuant to art. 30 b) ARSIWA although it has detected the violation of a fundamental principle of the order to that of self-determination of peoples. Similar considerations can be formulated with regard to more recent cases in which claims of guarantees of the type in question have been advanced as a result of offenses not covered by art. 40 ARSIWA.[43] It is useful to remember that in our opinion the case of complicity does not include a serious violation of general international law even when accessing an unlawful erga omnes. But this circumstance does not exclude the fact of the accomplice from the list of offenses for which it requests non-repetitive assurances. On the other hand, it should be noted that ICJ's reluctance to arrange such measures and in general the caution with which they are required in practice is probably related to a presumption of good faith the order to the future behaviour of the author of the offense. In the case of jurisdictional immunities of the ICJ State, it stated that: "As a general rule, there is no reason to state that a State has been declared weary by the Court will repeat that act or conduct in the future, since its good faith must be presumed."[44] It does not seem risky to

---

[42]Certain questions of mutual assistance in criminal matters (Djibouti v. France), judgment of 4 June 2008, in ICJ Reports, 2008, par. 17. A. ZIMMERMANN, C.J. TAMS, K. OELLERS-FRAHAM, The Statute of the International Court of Justice. A commentary, op. cit.

[43]As for example the declaration of ministry of defence of the Federal Republic of China in relation to the violation by the United States of the exclusive economic zone of the South China Sea: "We demand the United States (...) take effective measures to prevent a recurrence of such incidents."

[44]State jurisdictional immunities (Germany v. Italy: Greece intervening), judgments of 3 February 2012, in ICJ Reports, 2012, pp. 154, par. 138. A. ZIMMERMANN, C.J. TAMS, K. OELLERS-FRAHAM, The Statute of the International Court of Justice. A commentary,

assume that this presumption could operate to a lesser extent in the hypotheses of complicity whose subjective element as we have seen can also take the form of fraud. Which by definition constitutes the antithesis of good faith.

The evaluations carried out up to this point lead to the conclusion that, when the secondary relationship between accomplice and injured party occurs. The expected consequence can be configured by art. 30 b), where there is a well-founded risk of reiteration of the illegal conduct in question. It can be added that in the assessment of the circumstances of the case, two factors could be determined. On the one hand the intensity of the subjective element of complicity in the assumption that the demonstration of the illicit intent on the part of the accomplice could reduce the presumption of good faith normally recognized to the responsible State, on the other the entity of the prejudice suffered by the injured party under the double profile of the prejudice suffered due to the accessory conduct and of the reasonably foreseeable one in case of reiteration thereof.

1.4. Obligation to repair

According to the 2001 Project: "International law attributes to the responsible State new obligations and in particular that to make reparation for the harmful consequences flowing from that act."[45] This finding applies to all international offenses and those regulated by art. 16 ARSIWA and 14, 58 DARIO. The provision that applies to the hypotheses of complicity examined in this work is art. 31 ARSIWA.

Examination of this profile requires two preliminary observations. First of all, the obligation to repair is at least in principle conditioned by the existence of a prejudice. This is a notoriously very broad concept, since it includes "both material and moral damage."[46] This circumstance arises on the occurrence of the unlawful act,[47] leads us to not exclude the possibility that the prejudice is well implicit in the very notion of illicit fact, as claimed in part of the doctrine.[48] It should also be remembered that the injured party plays a notoriously central role in determining the existence of the prejudice itself and in particular the moral one. ILC as we will see later stated that satisfaction is directed to the repair of prejudices "arising from the very fact of the breach of obligation, irrespective of its

op. cit.

[45]ARSIWA, p. 87, par. 2.

[46]ARSIWA, p. 91, par. 5.

[47]ARSIWA, p. 91, par. 5.

[48]B. STERN, A plea for "reconstruction" of international responsibility based on the notion of legal injury, in M. RAGAZZI, International responsibility today. Essays in memory of Oscar Schachter, op. cit., pp. 564ss.

material consequences for the State concerned."[49] The ILC editorial Committee still shortly before the adoption of the definitive project signalled a substantial coincidence between moral damage and notion of legal prejudice that arises from the simple violation of an obligation.[50] From a substantive point of view, the notion of legal prejudice remains under the regime of international responsibility despite of what is noted by the rapporteur Crawford. It is not located in the final draft of 2001 and consequently in that of 2011 on the responsibility of international organizations.[51] Secondly, the ancillary and the main conduct concur to cause a single prejudice on the part of the injured party, even though they integrate two distinct illicit facts.

In this regard, the problem that needs to be addressed here relates to the way in which the obligation to repair due to the accomplice is asserted. In this regard, it must be considered that in general terms, where there is a plurality of distinct offenses, is necessary to determine the causal link between each of them and the prejudice suffered by the injured party.[52]

On this point both projects have a limited usefulness. The comment of art. 16 ARSIWA, clarifies that if the etiological connection between accessory and main fact is qualifiable in terms of conditionality "the injury suffered can be concurrently attributed to the assisting and the acting State."[53] If this condition is fulfilled, the repair should take place following the model of joint and several responsibility,[54] notoriously difficult to apply in the international order.[55] In all other hypotheses, the complicit State "should not necessarily be held to indemnify the victim for all the consequences of the act, but only for those which, in accordance with the principles States in part two of the articles flow form its own conduct."

The need arises on the one hand to verify in which circumstances the distribution of the reparative consequences between main and

---

[49]ARSIWA, p. 106, par. 3.
[50]In Yearbook of International Law Commission, vol. I, p. 388, par. 16.
[51]J. CRAWFORD, State responsibility. The general part, op. cit., pp. 487ss.
[52]P. D'ARGENT, Reparation, cessation, assurances and guarantees of non repetition, in A. NOLLKAEMPER, I. PLAKOKEFALOS, Principles of shared responsibility in international law. An appraisal of the state of the art, op. cit., pp. 222ss.
[53]ARSIWA, p. 67, par. 10, which is referred as "strangely enough." See also: P. D'ARGENT, Reparation, cessation, assurances and guarantees of non repetition, in A. NOLLKAEMPER, I. PLAKOKEFALOS, Principles of shared responsibility in international law. An appraisal of the state of the art, op. cit., pp. 228ss.
[54]J. QUIGLEY, Complicity in international law. A new direction in the law of state responsibility, op. cit., pp. 105ss.
[55]J.E. NOYES, B.D. SMITH, State responsibility and the principle of joint and national liability, op. cit., pp. 258ss. V. NOLLKAEMPER, D. JACOBS, Shared responsibility in international law. A conceptual framework, op. cit.

accomplice is configurable and on the other to determine the methods of the distribution itself. There are two factors that in our opinion combine to resolve the issue on the one hand, the causal link between illicit fact and prejudice. As regards the first profile, is known that the application of principles in the matter of causality can take place only on the basis of the facts and circumstances of the individual case, making it impossible to search for universally valid formulas for all causal relationships. This finding highlighted by ILC in the comment of art. 31 ARSIWA,[56] applies a fortiori with regard to the consequences of complicity where, before examining the link between unlawful act of the accomplice and prejudice of the injured party, is necessary to determine the one between accessory fact and main unlawful act.

In general terms, the juridical procedure relating to the aetiological nexus is based on the presumption of normality and predictability,[57] so that the link in question is deemed to exist where the normal course of events indicates that the prejudice must be considered as a logical consequence of a given fact, i.e. a consequence of which the author of the conduct should and could have foreseen.[58] The notion of proximate cause is essentially based on this presumption and constitutes the general criterion based on the comment of art. 31 ARSIWA that allows to determine "a sufficient causal link which is not too remote."[59] However, in the hypothesis of complicity this criterion could be unsuitable to determine the portion of prejudice attributable to each and the two responsible subjects. It has been considered[60] to be able to use for this purpose some theoretical models elaborated by the doctrine with regard to the plurality of events that are related to the same prejudice. This is the cumulative and complementary intervention of several causes.

In the first situation there are two causes, none of which is in itself capable of determining the prejudice that rather derives from their convergence. In the context of complicity with this model the hypothesis highlighted by ARSIWAs in the comment of art. 16, in which the accessory fact constitutes a sine qua non of the main fact. A circumstance of this type in which the injured party is unable to demonstrate which portion of the

[56]ARSIWA, PP. 92-93, par. 10.

[57]B. BOLLECKER-STERN, Le prèjudice dans la thèorie de la responsabilitè internationale, op. cit., pp. 192ss.

[58]G. SALVIOLI. La responsabilite des Etats et la fixation des dommages et interets par les tribunaux internationaux, in Recueil des cours, ed. Brill, Bruxelles, vol. 28, 1929, pp. 251ss.

[59]P. D'ARGENT, Reparation, cessation, assurances and guarantees of non repetition, in A. NOLLKAEMPER, I. PLAKOKEFALOS, Principles of shared responsibility in international law. An appraisal of the state of the art, op. cit., pp. 222ss.

[60]B. BOLLECKER-STERN, Le prèjudice dans la thèorie de la responsabilitè internationale, op. cit., pp. 267ss.

injury is attributable to the accomplice's action. "It is difficult to argue that the aid is not responsible for the whole of the harm inflicted by the principle."[61] In these cases the difference between complicity and joint responsibility ends with the disappearance at the moment of determination of the legal consequences of the respective insolvency cases.[62] In this context, the reference[63] to the theory of equivalence of the conditions for which all causes have an equivalent effect is correct. In particular if these are two illicit facts attributable to two different subjects, the injured party may demand reparation indifferently from the one or on the other side of those responsible.[64]

The model of complementary intervention refers to the hypothesis in which several causes concur to determine that "amalgame indifferenciè que consitue le dommage global." In this case is possible to break down the prejudice and assign each share-part to the concurrent causes. In our investigation this model can be applied to the situation in which the accessory event has contributed significantly but not conditionally to the realization of the main act. The two authors will be obliged to provide the repair but each according to a proportionate proportion[65] to their causal

---

[61] J. QUIGLEY, Complicity in international law. A new direction in the law of state responsibility, op. cit., pp. 128ss.

[62] S. WITTICH, Joint tortfeasors in investment law, in C. BINDER, U. KRIEBAUM, A. REINISCH, S. WITTICH, International investment law for the 21st century, op. cit., pp. 715ss.

[63] P. D'ARGENT, Reparation, cessation, assurances and guarantees of non repetition, in A. NOLLKAEMPER, I. PLAKOKEFALOS, Principles of shared responsibility in international law. An appraisal of the state of the art, op. cit., pp. 232ss.

[64] B. BOLLECKER-STERN, Le prèjudice dans la thèorie de la responsabilitè internationale, op. cit., pp. 270ss.

[65] C. PERELMAN, Le raisonnable et le dèraisonnable en droit, in Archives de Philosphie du Droit, 29, 1978, pp. 35ss. J. DELBRÜCK, Proportionality, Encyclopedia of Public International Law, 1984, pp. 396ss. G. BRAIBANT, Le principe de proportionnalitè, in Mèlanges offerts à M. Waline. Le juge et le droit public, LGDJ, Paris, 1974, pp. 298ss. E. GRABITZ, Der Grundsatz der Verhältnismäßigkeit in der Rechtsprechung des Bundesverfassungsgerichts, in Archiv des öffentliches Recht, 98 (4), 1973, pp. 568ss. F. OSSENBÜHL, Rechtliche grundfragen der Erteilung von Schulzeugnbissen, Duncker & Humblot, Berlin, 2019, pp. 51ss. According to the authors, the theme of guilt is somewhat controversial, while a hierarchy of offenses from the point of view of gravity does not seem to be reconstructable or at least does not seem to be possible to go beyond as would be necessary for the purpose of proportionality of the bipartition between ordinary and international crimes. The quantification of the coercion employed constitutes an almost insurmountable problem, particularly when it is necessary to measure the economic or political strength as such, that is to say independently of the patrimonial effects. A retaliation should be considered proportionate only if it is implemented within the limits of what is strictly necessary for the attainment of the repair. To us it seems understood as a limit to the exercise of peaceful individual and collective countermeasures. Proportionality

contribution in the injury.[66] The theoretical model under consideration is reflected in the notion of concomitant causes already elaborated, albeit in an embryonic form by the most recent doctrine[67] and object of investigation by the penultimate rapporteur of ILC on international responsibility, Arangio-Ruiz. This is the situation in which the unlawful act has a decisive but not exclusive role in the causation of the prejudice that must be considered as the outcome of concomitant causes. In these cases "to hold the author State liable for full compensation would be neither equitable nor in conformity with a proper application of the causal link criterion."[68] As is well known, this solution was not found in the final 2001 draft where it states that it incorporates the orientation of speaker Crawfordr,[69] that the practice "do

---

is an extra-juridical criterion that States can consider and even impose in the negotiation and which can express a fair or reasonable way to settle a dispute by interested States or interpreter. It does not seem from this point of view that it deserves an excessive dramatization if it is placed in the whole context of the regime of the exercise of peaceful countermeasures as emerges from the practice. It seems to us that the absence in practice of referring to proportionality is not accidental and can be explained precisely in the light of the general context in which international life takes place. The reprisals would not be subject to proportionality and indeed in the past, even those armies could be considered as particularly serious. We can refer within this framework to peaceful countermeasures, since the latters consisting in an armed reaction to offenses different from the armed attack. These are already illicit, while the armed reactions to an armed attack or the legitimate defense on the contrary are subject to the proportionality requirement. Peaceful countermeasures are subject to a time limit in the sense that they must be removed as soon as the crime that led to its implementation ceases. Different or worsening distortions or inequities from the ordinary ones that are assailed every day deriving from the unequal political power in the hands of the States. The circumstance that States do not react with disproportionate countermeasures can be understood in any sense in the absence of high clues in the pure and simple sense that they feel free to react more or less heavily, also taking into account the economic and ideological cost incurred for the counter-measures adopted. The interpretation that we consider to be proportionate or disproportionate to what happens according to its own criterion considers a proportionate reaction at the same time, according to its own idea of proportionality and which then draws the consequence that the idea of proportionality is inherent in the facts or reasonableness with which facts would come true.

[66]P. D'ARGENT, Reparation, cessation, assurances and guarantees of non repetition, in A. NOLLKAEMPER, I. PLAKOKEFALOS, Principles of shared responsibility in international law. An appraisal of the state of the art, op. cit., pp. 224. B. GRAEFRATH, Complicity in the law of state responsibility, op. cit., pp. 380ss.

[67]G. SALVIOLI, La responsabilite des Etats et la fixation des dommages et interets par les tribunaux internationaux, op. cit., pp. 245ss. C. EAGLETON, The responsibility of states in international law, The New York University Press, New York, 1928, pp. 203ss.

[68]G. ARANGIO-RUIZ, State responsibility revisited. The factual nature of the attribution of conduct to the state, op. cit. G. ARANZIO-RUIG, Second report on state responsibility, op. cit, p. 269.

[69]J. CRAWFORD, Third report on state responsibility, Doc. A/CN.4/507 and Add. 1-4th, in Yearbook of International Law Commission, vol. II, 2000, parr. 31, 34. J. CRAWFORD,

not support the reduction or mitigation of reparation of concurrent causes, except in cases of temporary fault."[70] It seems that outside the hypothesis in which the accessory event is the condition of the main one, ILC completely excludes that an obligation of reparation may arise at the head of the State.[71]

It is therefore difficult in our opinion to understand how the thesis of the punitive end of reprisals is compatible with the generally recognized relevance of the requirement of proportionality if we consider that in the latter criterion the idea of excluding the arbitrary element seems to be innate (exercised by the reacting subject) or in any case of unexpected and exemplary that in some way should distinguish a punitive behaviour. Nor is it clear why the reacting subject should warn if it is asking for a repair. The subject deemed offender as in general is admitted if he really raises a penalty and reacts by way of example. It may in fact be that in certain circumstances exemplarity is guaranteed precisely by reacting immediately or even reacting in a disproportionate manner (according to a hypothetical third-party arbitrator), which with those criteria should proceed to such investigations. These problems arise in domestic law where in fact the penalty is proportional to the offense and at least in a state of law does not depend on the individual arbitrariness that can in the international order, given its "anarchy" they do not find adequate accommodation. Retaliation would have a reparative purpose if on the one hand it explains why the reaction should be proportional or should be preceded by procedural activities, constituting the repair a sort of objective yardstick of these requirements. On the other hand it is on a par with the punitive purpose, to objections about the greater or lesser extent of the notion of accepted reparation. The fact that today is affirmed that the reprisals or countermeasures have as an end the cessation of the illicit or its effects could for example be understood as a confirmation of the reparative aim since the cessation of the offense has always been considered a form of reparation. The cessation of the offense does not

---

State responsibility. The general part, op. cit., pp. 495ss.

[70]ARSIWA, par. 12.

[71]The comment of art. 16 affirms that in cases where that internationally wrongful act would clearly have occurred, the responsibility of the assisting State will not extend to compensating for the act itself, ARSIWA, p. 66, par. 1. The English version of the comment seems to refer only to compensation, and is used by art. 36 to describe the compensation. The French text refers more clearly to the obligation to reproduce in its entirety "c'est ainsi qe dans le cas où fait en question se serait de toute manière produit, sa responsabilitè ne siètandra pas à la rèparation du prèjudice causè for le fait lui-même (...)." The reading of this part of the commentary based on the French text would seem to be preferable in fact from the approach taken by the ILC under the direction of the Crawford rapporteur to the causal link between the illicit and the prejudice of the injured party.

constitute a form of reparation but rather the simple fulfilment of the primary obligation that is not fulfilled. Similar disquisitions are almost always only theoretical. The identification of this relief is worth the critical sense from the works regarding the future of ILC on international responsibility and the passage from the initial essentially punitive to an essentially re-integrationist approach based above all on the purpose of obtaining the cessation of the offense, while admitting that in what measure there is always in the exercise of counter-measures a punitive intention. This should presumably be identified when the offense against which the reaction is directed appears to have been carried out with guilt, or with malice, or when is a crime and in any case the only aspect to come into relief in relation to the purpose or function of the countermeasures, that is, as much de jure condito as de jure condendo the repairing ones. States, in fact, although they agree on the fact that others have stopped, they must revoke the already adopted countermeasures or refrain from adopting them, they do not consider themselves bound to react to the achievement of an end or to the adoption of certain suitable measures to achieve it. It seems to us that the temporary nature and timeliness of peaceful countermeasures cannot be confused or identified either with the existence of an internationally relevant purpose or with the existence of a teleological type of proportionality.

Nevertheless it seems to us that the solution indicated by the speaker Arangio-Ruiz is at least from a theoretical point of view, applicable to the hypothesis in which the accessory fact has contributed significantly but not decisively to the realization of the main crime. In the situation that we are examining the concomitant causes are constituted by illicit facts, of which the international law has an interest in effectively enforcing the legal consequences. The two cases cited by the rapporteur Crawford and ILC to exclude the configurability of concomitant causes seem irrelevant. In the Corfu strait case in which ICJ charged all the repercussions to Albania[72] is too peculiar to be indicative of the profiles we are dealing with. It should be remembered that in the case in question the absence from the litigation procedure of the State allegedly responsible for the main unlawful act weighed. The diplomatic and consular personnel of the United States in Tehran case, is not relevant for the purposes of our reasoning since one of the causes in competition in that affair was attributable to the action of private individuals. As noted by the doctrine in both cases the offense of the State deemed responsible had been carried out after the concurrent causes had occurred,[73] i.e. explaining the greater

[72]J. CRAWFORD, State responsibility. The general part, op. cit., pp. 496ss.

[73]S. WITTICH, Compensation, in Max Planck Encyclopedia of Public International Law, 2008, par. 18.

(causal) proximity to the prejudice of the former than the latter.

In this context, we believe we can also apply a third theoretical model to the complicity situation, that of the exclusive intervention in which a purely apparent competition of causes is hypothesized, so that only one factor among those (apparently) in competition is equipped with causal efficiency with respect to the prejudice suffered by the injured party.[74] In our case, if we assume that the factor in question is solely the main unlawful fact, the causal contribution of the accessory fact will only be apparent. This hypothesis is expressly foreseen in the comment to art. 16 ARSIWA in which ILC clarifies that: "The assistance may have been a non-incidental factor in the Commission of the primary act, may have contributed only to a minor degree, if to all the injury suffered."[75] In our opinion, in this circumstance only the juridical prejudice that as said can be considered subsistent due to the sole Commission of the unlawful act in question must be taken into account.

As we have mentioned, in addition to the causal link, another factor constituted by the subjective element of the accessory fact is important in identifying the reparation due the accomplice State. The problem of the different levels of guilt in the international offense has a considerable influence on the nature and extent of the reparation due the responsible State.[76] Similarly, according to the rapporteur Arangio-Ruiz, there is no doubt as to the relevance of the fault in determining the legal consequences of an unlawful event. It is the presence of fault not essential for an act to cross the threshold reparating the lawful form the unlawful. The legal consequences of an act which has passed that threshold are the same whether or not any fault (dolus included) is present in any degree. If the intentionality of the fact does not affect the quantum of compensation, it seems certain that a subjective attitude of this type can determine the invocation of satisfaction instead of the repair by equivalent (dommages-intèrêts / Entschädigung). It should be noted that the project in which the fault has a notoriously marginal position, refers to this profile in art. 39 (nemo commodum capere potest de sua own injuria),[77] relating to the

---

[74]P. D'ARGENT, Reparation, cessation, assurances and guarantees of non repetition, in A. NOLLKAEMPER, I. PLAKOKEFALOS, Principles of shared responsibility in international law. An appraisal of the state of the art, op. cit., pp. 223ss. B. BOLLECKER-STERN, Le prèjudice dans la thèorie de la responsabilitè internationale, op. cit., pp. 293ss.

[75]ARSIWA, p. 67, par. 10.

[76]L. OPPENHEIM, International law. A treatise, Longmann Green & Co., London, 1955, pp. 354ss.

[77] The norm in establishing a decadence from the power to invoke responsibility establishes a iuris mechanism, which constitutes a special applicative hypothesis of the general principle nemo potest as contra factum proprium often indicated through the reference to the Anglo-Saxon theory of estoppel (W. FRIEDE, Das Estoppel-Prinzip im Völkerrecht, in

reduction of the reparation payable by the injured State in the event that the latter has contributed negligence to its injury.[78]

In the case of complicity, the intensity of the subjective element and its suitability to influence the reparative consequences must be taken into account, although is in our opinion excessive to believe that the intentionality of the accessory fact may lead to a mutation of the causal

---

Zeitschrift für ausländisches Recht und Völkerrecht, 5, 1935, pp. 545ss. W. FRIEDMAN, The changing structure of international law, Columbia University Press, Columbia, Princeton, 1973, pp. 198ss. N.A. GREEN, International law. Law of peace, Macdonald & Evans, London, 1973, pp. 22ss. A.D. MCNAIR, The law of treaties, Oxford University Press, Oxford, 1961, pp. 486ss. I. SEIDL-HOHENVELDERN, L'ordre public international et la fraude à la loi-Luer importance en droit international public, in Mèlanges offerts à Jacques Maury, ed. Sirey, Paris, 1960, pp. 475ss).The nemo potest as a contra factum proprium rule corresponds to a real norm of closure of the international order whose typical preclusive effect does not meet exceptions related to the particular nature of the septum of concretely elation issues, placing itself as an impassable limit to the exercise of any active subjective legal situation including those arising in the area of state responsibility (S. ROSENNE, The law and practice of the international Court, ed. Brill, Dordrecht, Boston, 1985, pp. 324ss.). In any case, it is emphasized that the duty of consistency in conduct cannot only directly provide the substantial discipline of certain social relations, but can manifest itself as in the case of the prohibition of the mutatio libelli or in certain forum prorogatum opoteses to mention some of its possible applications. With regard to the first, it is sufficient to consider that on the basis of a consolidated a general principle of law recognized by civilized nations pursuant to art. 38, lett. c) of the ICJ Statute in the international trial, as well as the internal one. The parties are prohibited from proposing new questions with respect to those initially sent to the judge, which are not justified by the thesis. Questions and exceptions were however presented by the counterpart. As for the forum prorogatum, this is an exceptional procedure for the attribution of international arbitration jurisdiction that is independent of the existence of a valid, initial compromise between the counter-States. This procedure is characterized by the unilateral referral to the tribunal by one of the parties in quarrel, of the relative right of action followed by the acceptance of the counterparty of the jurisdiction of the arbitrator, with the consequence of definitively rooting this last the potestas decidendi. However, such acceptance can also be deduced from the simple conduct of the respondent State in the Court that is completely incompatible with the will to object to the arbitrator's incompetence, as in the case in which this State has no objection to the lack of jurisdiction. Requirements for the protection of custody impose in this case the application of the allegans contraria non audiendus est rule which will result in the loss of the right for the State to invoke the defect of the Court of appeal as a consequence of the behaviour previously observed, a conclusion corroborated by that part of the old doctrine that brings the discipline of the forum prorogatum to the estoppel (P. STILLMUNKES, Le "forum prorogatum" devant la court permanente de justice internationale e la court internationale de justice, in Revue Gènèrale de Droit International Public, 35, 1964, pp. 676ss. A. ZIMMERMANN, C.J. TAMS, K. OELLERS-FRAHAM, The Statute of the International Court of Justice. A commentary, op. cit.

[78] B. STERN, The obligation to make reparation, in J. CRAWFORD, A. PELLET, S. OLLESON, K. PARLETT, The law of international responsibility, Oxford University Press, Oxford, 2010, pp. 570ss.

link that relates this conduct to the principal.[79]

1.5. (Follows) The various forms of reparation that the injured party can demand from the accomplice State

The considerations made in the previous paragraph allow us to review the various forms of repair indicated by art. 34 ARSIWA (corresponding to article 34 DARIO). The first of them is known as constituted by the resitutio in integrum, whose purpose is based on art. 35 ARSIWA, to restore "the situation which existed before the wrongful act was committed." The primacy of this form of reparation,[80] is motivated by the need to prevent the responsible State from benefiting from the illicit fact, merely paying a sum as a repair for equivalent.[81] From a general point of view, restitutio appears to be difficult to apply. In addition to the hypothesis in which it can be reasonably unexecuted,[82] the restitutio may well be materially impossible, so as expressly provided for by art. 35. Turning to the case of complicity, part of the doctrine observes that in principle there are no reasons to prevent from setting up an obligation to repay the complicit State.[83] Others, on the other hand, probably consider more reasonable that the case of complicity constitutes one of those "typical" cases in which simply "restitution is not available."[84] In effect, if one looks at what in practice is the object of restitution, such as for example "the release of persons wearily appointed or the return of ownership wrongly seized,"[85] is easy to understand how such measures cannot be requested to the accomplice State, but rather to the principal author, i.e. the subject who normally exercises the necessary control over

[79]P. D'ARGENT, Reparation, cessation, assurances and guarantees of non repetition, in A. NOLLKAEMPER, I. PLAKOKEFALOS, Principles of shared responsibility in international law. An appraisal of the state of the art, op. cit., pp. 227ss, which is affirmed that: "The knowledge of the facts will not only influence the apportionment in a situation of complementarity causes, but it may also eventually change that qualification into a cumulative causes situation."

[80]C. GRAY, The different forms of reparation: compensation, in J. CRAWFORD, A. PELLET, S. OLLESON, K. PARLETT, The law of international responsibility, Oxford University Press, Oxford, 2010, pp. 589ss.

[81]R. KOLB, The international law of state responsibility, op. cit., pp. 155ss.

[82]R. KOLB, The international law of state responsibility, op. cit., pp. 156ss.

[83]A. FELDER, Die Beihilfe im Rect der völkerrechtlichen Staatenverantwortlichkeit, op. cit., pp. 276ss.

[84] H.P. AUST, Complicity in international law, op. cit., pp. 277ss. V. LANOVOY, Complicity and its limits in the law of international responsibility, op. cit., pp. 282ss.

[85]ARSIWA, p. 96, par. 1.

goods or persons whose restitutio it claims.

For what concerns the compensation settled by art. 36 ARSIWA, that is to say the most frequent form of reparation in the practice of international relations,[86] can only reaffirm to itself what has been said in the previous paragraph, namely that the evaluation must be made on a case by case basis. In principle, taking into consideration the models of causal competition illustrated above, the injured party could make its claim for compensation, considered as a whole, against the accomplice State or as an alternative to the principal author, but only in the hypothesis attributable to the cumulative intervention model of the various causes. The application of art. 36 is expressly excluded a fortiori, in the third hypothesis, that of the exclusive intervention in which there is only an apparent causal competition and the role of the accomplice is limited to facilitating the main conduct. It cannot be excluded in the second hypothesis, the one included in the complementary intervention, in which the accessory event is not a condition of the main one, but contributes significantly to the realization of the latter. In these cases the application of art. 36 may not be easy as is necessary to quantify the portion of injury attributable to the cause determined by the accessory event.

The compensation claim against the accomplice is subjected, in any case to the general conditions set by art. 36 ARSIWA. First of all it is interesting to underline that the mentioned provision takes as its object the repair of direct and indirect damage[87] and not the generic prejudice, where the difference between the two notions is more marked than the one claimed by the Crawford.[88] This damage must be susceptible to economic evaluation.[89] The reference to the loss of profit and the importance attributed to "actual damage to property and persons,"[90] attributes to the

---

[86]ARSIWA, p. 99, par. 2.

[87]It seems to us that the injured State in order to be recognized as the holder of a possible right to pecuniary reintegration of the damage arising from the violation of international obligations in its confiscations, can only be considered as a unit in its diminished patrimonial capacity and in its assets and specifically interceded damaged by another's anti-juridical behaviour. It does not seem to us admissible that the identification of a general principle in the matter of compensation may proceed by separating the economic relevance of individual interests from the purely ideal or moral one of the damages that can affect the goods and interests that directly affect the State. And this independently of the notion that we want to accept the State as a subject of the international order. It should be pointed out that an equivalent reparation obligation by equivalent can be said to exist as a general consequence of the international offense only if it can be demonstrated that a claim in this sense is made by the injured State following the violation of any international obligation, customary or contractual that has caused an economic prejudice to the State or its citizens.

[88]J. CRAWFORD, State responsibility. The general part, op. cit., pp. 486ss.

[89]ARSIWA, p. 96, par. 1. S. WITTICH, Compensation, op. cit., par. 10.

[90]ARSIWA, P. 99, par. 1.

notion in question an obviously financial connotation that involves the application of specific rules relating to the calculation of the compensation sum,[91] per se problematic even in simple cases in which there is a single illicit fact. And this is the most important aspect of ascertaining this type of prejudice, as a result of a very rigorous application of the causal standards.[92]

It must be assumed that the compensation by the accomplice is configurable in the hypothesis of the cumulative intervention of causes, which occurs when the accessory event is a condition of the main one. The case attributable to the complementary intervention appears more complex. Although it is not excluded in theoretical terms that the reparation of the damage is proportional to each of the concomitant causes, is undeniable that this occurs in the case of compensation only if the interpreter is able to clearly distinguish the various causal links from time to time. Otherwise is reasonable to assume that the compensation will be borne entirely by the principal author,[93] who in such a circumstance will not be able to

---

[91]R. KOLB, The international law of state responsibility, op. cit., pp. 159ss.

[92]H.P. AUST, Complicity in international law, op. cit., pp. 278ss, highlights the difficulties of compensation for damage to the accomplice, but does not exclude configurability at least from a theoretical point of view.

[93]To a similar conclusion, although based on a different reasoning, we find: V. LANOVOY, Complicity and its limits in the law of international responsibility, op. cit., pp. 284ss. This author excludes the possibility of a compensation obligation for the accomplice by mentioning to confirm this deduction the ICJ sentence in the case concerning the application of the genocide Convention of February 2007. In that circumstance the ICJ considered it necessary to ascertain "a sufficiently direct and certain causal nexus between the wrongful act, the respondent's breach of the obligation to prevent genocide, and the injury suffered by the applicant." Since the Court cannot (...) regard as proven a causal nexus between the respondent's violation of its obligation of prevention and the damage resulting from the genocide at Srebrenica, financial compensation is not the appropriate form of reparation for the breach of the obligation to prevent obligation (par. 462). In this regard, two observations can be made. First, the illicit fact attributed to Serbia was recognized by the ICJ in violation of the obligation to prevent genocide, based on art. III e) of the same convention. If the ICJ reached this conclusion based on the violation of the obligation of prevention, then according to the cited author: "It is safe to assume that a similar reading would apply to complicity." In reality, the inverse deduction formulated by H.P. AUST, Complicity in international law, op. cit., pp. 283-284, the orientation of the ICJ was conditioned in that case by the omissive character of the offense in question that notoriously presents greater difficulties when determining its causal efficiency on a given injury. The author's complicity consists mainly of a given bias. The author, on the other hand, consists mainly of commissive behaviours, which normally do not raise the difficulty just indicated. In the second place, in our opinion the considerations already made regarding the peculiarity of the case under examination and in particular the erroneous exclusion of the omissions from the list of accessory facts and the essentially penal connotation of the concrete case judged by the ICJ, which make the case not very exemplary for the purposes of our investigation. A. ZIMMERMANN, C.J. TAMS, K.

benefit from any reduction of the damage. It remains firm in accordance with articles 31 and 34 ARSIWA which in this case the author of the accessory event will bear the obligation to provide the injured party with a repair that may be carried out in another form.

The last form of reparation to be examined is the satisfaction regulated by art. 37 ARSIWA under which the responsible State "is under an obligation to give satisfaction for the injury caused by that act insofar as it cannot be made good by restitution or compensation" specifying, in par. 2 that: "Satisfaction may consist in an acknowledgement of the breach, an expression of regret, a formal apology or another appropriate modality." It is to be shared the opinion that satisfaction is the most appropriate form of reparation in most cases of complicity.[94] The reasons for this deduction are many. First of all, the subject of the provision pursuant to art. 37 is not the damage, according to the meaning given by art. 36 but the prejudice, which the ILC ultimately seems to understand as a legal prejudice.[95] In this sense, the statement contained in the comment to art. 37, for which the satisfaction provides to repair a prejudice that arises due to the illicit fact considered in itself, also on the basis of a presumption regarding the existence of the causal link. In the same way it seems relevant the act that the project configures the remedy contemplated by art. 27 as a residual, i.e. relating to prejudices that do not fall within the scope of the previous provisions. To deduce that satisfaction concerns only intangible damages that are not susceptible to economic evaluation.[96]

Secondly, the role that the injured party plays in this context must be underlined. From a general point of view, the repair often takes place in function of the negotiation between the perpetrator of the crime and the injured party, on the basis[97] of the claim exercised by the latter in relation to the form of reparation which it considers most appropriate, so that it can be considered that "the injured State is here dominus negotii."[98] It seems

OELLERS-FRAHAM, The Statute of the International Court of Justice. A commentary, op. cit.

[94]H.P. AUST, Complicity in international law, op. cit., pp. 285. V. LANOVOY, Complicity and its limits in the law of international responsibility, op. cit., pp. 286ss.

[95]C. HOSS, Satisfaction, in Max Planck Encyclopedia of Public International Law, 2011, par. 10.

[96]ARSIWA, p. 106, par. 2. It should be noted that according to a part of the doctrine the function of satisfaction does not end with the typically restorative one, since in some cases it may well assume an affective connotation. In this sense see: W. WYLER, A. PAPAUX, The different forms of reparation. Satisfaction, in J. CRAWFORD, A. PELLET, S. OLLESON, K. PARLETT, The law of international responsibility, Oxford University Press, Oxford, 2010, pp. 625ss.

[97]C. GRAY, Judicial remedies in international law, op. cit., pp. 6ss.

[98] R. KOLB, The international law of state responsibility, op. cit., pp. 149ss. B. GRAEFRATH, Responsibility and damage caused, op. cit., pp. 71ss, for which the injured

to us that this observation, moreover, is validated by art. 43 ARSIWA,[99] applies a fortiori where a legal asset such as the dignity and burden of the aggrieved State and the relative discretion available to the latter in complaining of a prejudice comes to the fore.

1.6. Conclusions regarding the content of the liability relationship between accomplice State and injured party

The unlawful fact provided for by articles 16 ARSIWA and 14, 58 DARIO gives rise to a new legal relationship between accomplice State and injured party. First of all, we saw that the author of the fact in question is subjected on the one hand to the obligation to interrupt the conduct if it is continuous and on the other to offer guarantees of non-repetition, if there is a risk of repeating the accessory fact.

The accomplice State is obliged to fulfil the obligation of reparation enshrined in art. 31 ARSIWA. The application of this norm to the situation determined by complicity is to be carried out starting from a premise. In the presence of a plurality of distinct offenses, is necessary to determine the causal link between each of them and the prejudice suffered by the injured party. We evaluated three hypotheses, corresponding to as many theoretical models relating to the concurrence of causes. In the first the accessory fact is characterized by being condicio sine qua non of the main one. In this case, as the 2001 Project clarifies, the injured party will have the right to address its reparatory claim regardless of the principal author or the accomplice. The second hypothesis is that in which the accessory event contributes significantly but not conditionally to the

---

party has "a remarkable discretionary power affecting the contents of the duty of reparation." In the same orientation see also: L. REITZER, La rèparation comme consèquence de l'acte illicite en droit international, op. cit., pp. 134ss.

[99]In this sense see: Y. KERBRAT, The interaction between the forms of reparation, in J. CRAWFORD, A. PELLET, S. OLLESON, K. PARLETT, The law of international responsibility, Oxford University Press, Oxford, 2010, pp. 573ss. This is the central disposition of the framework of the consequences of the unlawful act, entitled: "Notice of claim by an injured State." According to par. 1 the injured party that intends to enforce the responsibility of the state responsible for the crime "shall give notice of its claim to that State." The second paragraph makes it clear, in unequivocal terms, that through the notification the injured State can specify "the conduct that is responsible for taking into account the worn out act, if it is continuing," but above all "what form of reparation should take in accordance with the provisions of part two." In the same orientation see also: J. PEEL, Notice of claim by an injured state, in J. CRAWFORD, A. PELLET, S. OLLESON, K. PARLETT, The law of international responsibility, Oxford University Press, Oxford, 2010, pp. 1032, which is affirmed that "in general, it is the prerogative of the injured State to elect the form of reparation to be provided by the responsible State."

realization of the main crime. In this circumstance, the two authors will be obliged to provide the repair but each according to a share proportional to their causal contribution in the injury. The third hypothesis is that in which the role of the accomplice can be defined as a mere facilitation with respect to the main conduct. In this case the obligation to repair will be by means of satisfaction.

As for the forms of reparation, we have seen that restitutio in integrum[100] constitutes in the case of complicity an obligation that is difficult to carry out by the accomplice State. The compensation then subject to a rigid application of the criterion of causality, as well as to certain rules relating to the exact determination of the sum due as compensation. The application of these parameters could prove to be impractical in several cases attributable to the case of complicity. In such circumstances, satisfaction may represent the most appropriate form of repair of the injury suffered by the injured party.

1.7. The implementation of international responsibility in the complicit State Counter-measures against the accomplice State

The regulation of counter-measures is regulated by the third party of ARSIWAs and by IV part, DARIOs. Both are opened with a block of provisions concerning the invocation of responsibility (articles 42-48 ARSIWA and 43-50 DARIO). The central provision is to this concern contained in articles 42 ARSIWA and 43 DARIO for which the necessary legal title "to invoke the responsibility of another State" or "of another international organization" is primarily assigned to the State or international organization affected by the unlawful conduct. The notion of an aggrieved party[101] relevant with reference to the case of complicity can be found in our opinion in lett. a) of the two provisions cited, concerning the hypothesis in which the violated obligation exists only with respect to the party that invokes the responsibility. In other words, we are in the framework of a bilateral obligation although established by a rule of

[100]The material damage has no consistency and autonomy with respect to the anti-court behaviour, that is, respect to the violation as such. With the consequence that, on the other hand, the different examples of refunds cannot in any case be considered as many forms of reparation of a real damaging event caused by the violation. They seem rather to target the same anti-juridical behaviour. They intervene on the violated or unfulfilled obligation that determine the cessation of violation and performance of the due service.

[101] G. GAJA, The concept of an injured state, in J. CRAWFORD, A. PELLET, S. OLLESON, K. PARLETT, The law of international responsibility, Oxford University Press, Oxford, 2010, pp. 942ss.

general international law codified by articles 16 ARSIWA and 14, 58 DARIO. In the case of complicity, two specular legal situations are established, in relation to the specific case in question. On the one hand the obligation not to assist the unlawful act of others, on the other the subjective right not to suffer accessory behaviour to the principal offense. We have already clarified that there are no elements to consider that the responsibility of the accomplice can also be invoked by subjects other than the injured party, for example, due to the nature of the primary rule violated by the principal author.

Having made this clarification, is necessary to understand whether the subject injured by the accessory unlawful act has the right to resort to forms of self-protection and the particular counter-measures. Since the two projects do not provide any specific indication in this regard and that the case of complicity qualifies on the basis of articles 16 ARSIWA and 14, 58 DARIO as an unlawful fact it must be inferred that the issue is governed by the general provisions on counter-measures contained in articles 49-53 ARSIWA and 51-56 DARIO. There are no structural reasons to exclude the configurability of counter-measures in the hypothesis in question, at least from a theoretical point of view.[102] The substantial absence of praxis leads to the formulation of some hypotheses which take into account on the one hand the nature and role of the counter-measure in today's international order and on the other the peculiarities of the accessory fact.

The 2001 project, like the one on the responsibility of functional entities, does not contain a precise definition of counter-measures,[103] but merely uses a decidedly broad concept. The term indicates in the two instruments cited "measures that would be contrary to the international obligation of an injured towards the responsible State, if they were not taken by the former in response to an internationally wrongful act by the latter in order to procure cessation and reparation."[104] From a general point of view these are exceptional measures, as shown by the literal tenor of art. 49 ARSIWA,[105] whose adoption is subject to certain preventive obligations,

[102]H.P. AUST, Complicity in international law, op. cit., pp. 288. V. LANOVOY, Complicity and its limits in the law of international responsibility, op. cit., pp. 293ss.

[103]J. CRAWFORD, State responsibility. The general part, op. cit, pp. 685ss.

[104]ARSIWA, p. 128, par. 1. In argument see also: A.L., SICILIANOS, Les rèactions dècentralisèes à l'illicite. Des contremesures à la lègitime dèfense, LGDJ, Paris, 1990. D. ALLAND, Justice privèe et ordre juridique international. Etude thèorique des contre-mesures en droit international public, ed. Pedone, Paris, 1994. D. ALLAND, The definition of countermeasures, in J. CRAWFORD, A. PELLET, S. OLLESON, K. PARLETT, The law of international responsibility, Oxford University Press, Oxford, 2010, pp. 1135ss.

[105]According to art. 49, par. 1 ARSIWA: "An injured State may only take countermeasures against a State which is responsible for an internationally wrongful act in order to induce that State to comply with its obligations under part two." According to the comment to this

regulated by the same project in art. 52 and well established in international practice.[106] It is also believed that the use of counter-measures has become "fairly rare,"[107] probably due to the validity of the various international liability regimes with respect to which the general regulations have a residual nature.

1.8. (Follows) Problematic aspects of the counter-measures taken against the accomplice State

The question of counter-measures against the complicit State raises at least two problematic profiles, closely related to each other. The first is known that the use of countermeasures presupposes the ascertainment of the unlawful situation by the injured party itself, which has the prerogative "d'aprecier raisonnablement et de bonne foi les situations et les règles qui le mettent en cause."[108] It is important to note

---

provision the use of the "only" adverb would indicate "the limited and exceptional nature of countermeasures," ARSIWA, p. 128, par. 2. The notion of integral obligations comes to the fore only for some particular categories of obligations erga omnes and it does not seem to be able sic et simpliciter fit to all types of the treaties to which it has been referred. It seems difficult to reconstruct the existence of integral obligations outside the specific agreements. It would perhaps have been more appropriate to provide for a power of withdrawal for each contracting party since the sustainment of a treaty concerning disarmament is aimed at rearmament of the State concerned and this activity would hinder the renewed application of the treaty.

[106]Y. IWASAWA, N. IWATSUKI, Procedural conditions, in J. CRAWFORD, A. PELLET, S. OLLESON, K. PARLETT, The law of international responsibility, Oxford University Press, Oxford, 2010, pp. 1149ss.

[107] C.J. TAMS, Countermeasures against multiple responsible actors, in A. NOLLKAEMPER, I. PLAKOKEFALOS, Principles of shared responsibility in international law. op. cit., pp. 312ss.

[108]Affaire du lac lanoux, Espagne v. France of 16 November 1957, in Recueil des Sentences Arbitrales. Vol. XII, p. 310, par. 16, the known lack in international law of authoritative and superordinate procedures for ascertaining the right constitutes the reason why each State that considers itself injured may, after having ascertained the alleged violation, proceed with the adoption of countermeasures. See in argument: C. LEB, Cooperation, the law of transboundary water resources, Cambridge University Press, Cambridge, 2013. H. KELSEN, Unrecht und Unrechtsfolge im Völkerrecht, in Zeitscrhift für öffentliches Recht, 1932, pp. 482ss. The author had rejected Anzilotti's first theory/position (D. ANZILOTTI, La responsabilité internationale des Etats à raison des dommages soufferts par des ètrangers, op. cit.) With respect to the content of international responsibility, claiming that the consequence of the the international offense was not the obligation of reparation but the sanction (Zwangsakt), intended precisely as a reaction of the injured State through the application of coercive measures against the offender. Position that has been adopted in the past also by others in international doctrine (A. GOMEZ-ROBLEDO VERDUZCO,

Concepto de responsabilidad internacional del Estado segùn Hans Kelsen, in Boletin Mexicano de Derecho Comparado, 62, 1985, pp. 66ss. A. CARLEBACH, Le problème de la faute et sa place dans la norme du droit international, op. cit., pp. 4ss. C. GRAY, Is there an international law of remedies?, in British Yearbook of International Law, 56, 1985, pp. 27ss. A.V. FREEMAN, The international responsibility of states, ed. Longman, London, 1970. R.W. TUCKER, Principles of international law, Holt, Rinehart and Winston, New York, 1966, pp. 16ss). In the international legal system, since there is no institution responsible for imposing such coercive measures on individuals, the sanctions would consist of reprisals and the war to which the State which claims to be the victim of an unlawful act unilaterally applies. The Austrian author draws attention to the fact that the secondary obligation of reparation in the execution of which the content of international responsibility should be exhausted could in turn be violated, thus giving rise to an unbroken chain of new obligations unfulfilled only if the act coercive is interpreted as the true consequence of the crime, the juridical succession of premises and consequences can find a conclusion in itself. Kelsen asserts the impossibility of reconstructing an obligation of reparation in general international law before and independently of the agreement between the interested States in consideration of the lack in the international order of organs which can in any case and obligatorily fix the content and the amount of the repair. When there is no objective request that establishes the extent of the reparation in relation to a concrete case, then it must be admitted that a repair obligation cannot exist at least with regard to its content without the consent of the offender State. There is need for an agreement between the State that violated the primary obligation and the injured State to constitute the obligation of reparation imposed on the former. The extent of the repair as it is not directly established by the same international objective law is agreed on the basis of the agreement between the States concerned. In our opinion, this representation of international responsibility in terms of an opposition between reparation and sanction not only does not correspond to the substance of Kelsen thought but neither is it cogent to grasp how much of it must be accepted for the purpose of determining the nature of the repair of the consequences of international crime. It is entirely secondary in this construction and presents itself as a subsequent problem, then to establish whether the coercive act has the nature of a penalty or a forced execution due to the non-fulfilment of a replacement repair obligation. For Kelsen the repair is not part of the content of the responsibility even in domestic law. On the contrary, the subject who has violated the primary obligation is not considered yet responsible if it can fulfil a secondary substitute obligation, that is because the application of the coercive act that constitutes the content of responsibility becomes possible only when the second obligation has remained unfulfilled. In reality, Kelsen's position is on a different level than an investigation that proposes to positively ascertain in practice the existence or otherwise of a reparative or punitive responsibility or of both types in the international order. Precisely this insistence on the structural characteristics of the legal system rather than on the particular forms that international responsibility can assume is at the same time the main limitation of Kelsen's thesis on the non-existence of an obligation of reparation in international law. If the lack of a function that ensures the verification of the violated obligations by the center undoubtedly constitutes a limitation of international law, it cannot fail to regard both primary and secondary obligations. Despite this limitation, the existence of an international legal order means that the identification in the general right of an obligation to repair is not a problem that may depend on the consensual character that will have the ascertainment of its content in relation to the concrete case. From this point of view Kelsen does not distinguish the problem of the

that this unilateral qualification takes place at the risk and peril of the reacting subject, who may incur liability "for its own wrongful conduct in the event of an incorrect assessment."[109] In our case the risk in question seems particularly evident when we consider that the injured party is called upon to carry out a double qualification. Given the fact that the accomplice is ancillary to the principal one, it must make an assessment in relation to two facts legally distinct, attributable to different subjects, and according to a logical process aimed at determining first the main fact, then the accessory one. Furthermore, the evaluation of the latter must also invest the subjective element which is completely negligible with regard to the main fact. Moreover, it seems doubtful that as a result of this qualification the injured party could take a counter-measure against the complicit State without having previously addressed the same reaction towards the principal author.

Secondly, there is the problem of the object of the counter-measure, that is, of the obligation that the injured party can lawfully violate as a reaction to the accessory event. In this regard, ARSIWA provide some indications in "negative" terms. In addition to the list of unsustainable

---

existence of a specific obligation of reinstatement of the damage to be positively verified on the basis of the analysis of the practice of States and that of the controversy on its content or simply on its amount that could be posed in a manner not different also for the so-called primary obligations, whether they are provided by general or particular law. He proves to be confused between the customary or contractual nature of the obligation to repair and the way (agreement or sentence) with which to resolve a possible dispute on its consistency in the individual concrete case. Obviously we do not exclude the existence of a secondary obligation of reparation, the other relief raised by Kelsen with respect to the dominant doctrine according to which the obligation in question could not constitute the real consequence of international offense since it is susceptible of being in turn disregarded, giving rise to an unbroken series of new obligations violated. The possibility granted to a State to apply self-protection measures to guarantee the respect and execution of its own rights does not mean that the international order cannot abstractly contemplate a particular liability regime for damages, as happens in the internal legal systems. A regime in which the rights and obligations provided by it are extinct to be guaranteed through the application of those same self-protection measures. See also in argument: CH. LEBEN, Les sanctions privatives de droit ou de qualitè dans les organizations internationales spècialisèes, ed. Bruylant, Bruxelles, 1979, pp. 41ss. This seems to be confirmed, in addition to the sentence cited in the text, by the known arbitration ruling in the Air Services Agreement case where the Court stated that "each State establishes for itself its legal situation towards other States," with the precision that "if a situation arises which in one state's view, results in a violation of an international obligation by another State. The first State is entitled, within the limits set by the general rules of international law pertaining to the use of armed force, to affirm its rights through countermeasures." The Air Services Agreements of 27 March 1946, USA v. France, decision of 9 December 1978, in Recueil des Sentences Arbitrales, vol. XVIII, pp. 443, par. 81.

[109]ARSIWA, p. 130, par. 3.

violation obligations as a counter-measure, contained in art. 50, par. 1 it must be pointed out that according to ILC the reaction of the injured State may not take the form of the "reciprocal" counter-measure,[110] consisting in the non-fulfilment of the same obligation violated by the offender or of an obligation connected to this.[111] This data serves to dissolve the knot. The content violated by the accomplice State, in our opinion, is able to condition to some extent the object of the possible countermeasure exercisable by the injured party. The direct parameter with which to assess the accessory fact is constituted by the intermediate standard laid down in articles 16 ARSIWA and 14, 58 DARIO which contributes only indirectly to protecting the legal asset injured by the author of the main fact. As we have seen, the link between the rule in question and content of the primary rule violated by the principal author is configured as functional.

Two solutions can be traced, even in hypothetical terms, depending on whether the choice of the countermeasure is based on the direct parameter or on the legal interest indirectly damaged by the accomplice State, with the clarification that both the criterion of proportionality set by art. 51 ARSIWA. In the first case the evaluation of obligation is considered not to assist in the offense of others, given its essentially instrumental nature. We will have to look at the prejudice suffered by the injured party, or rather that quantitative element which constitutes the first term of the proportionality test imposed by art. 51 and which is reflected in the practice.[112] In adopting the counter-measure, then the injured party will have to evaluate the type of reparation that, according to art. 52 must have previously requested the author of the accessory event together with the portion of prejudice possibly attributable to that State according to the criteria seen in the previous section. The use of counter-measures should not be particularly problematic when the repair takes place on the model of the CEO cumulative intervention of causes or of the complementary model. The same cannot be said with reference to the third model, that of exclusive intervention, in which the contribution provided by the accomplice to the injury appears to be completely negligible. One can ask whether in such circumstances the refusal by the author of the accessory fact to provide adequate satisfaction may give the aggrieved

---

[110]ARSIWA, p. 129, par. 5.

[111]See, W. RIPHAGEN, Sixth report on the content, forms an degrees of international responsibility (part two of the draft articles) and "implementation" (mise en oeuvre) of international responsibility and the settlement of disputes (part three of the draft articles), op. cit.

[112]ICJ, Gabčikovo-Nagymaros Project (Hungary v. Slovakia), judgment, 25 September 1997, in ICJ Reports, 1997, pp. 56, par. 85. A. ZIMMERMANN, C.J. TAMS, K. OELLERS-FRAHAM, The Statute of the International Court of Justice. A commentary, op. cit.

party title to take a counter-measure against it. In principle the literal tenor of art. 52, par. 1 in conjunction with art. 43 does not seem to provide elements for a negative answer. As the commentary suggests to the ARSIWAs, the evaluation must be carried out according to the specific case and above all by applying the principle of proportionality.[113]

The second solution is based on the juridical interest that the accomplice State has indirectly damaged by means of its own conduct. The 2001 Project establishes that the proportionality of the counter-measure must be evaluated also in consideration of certain qualitative elements, "such as to promote the rule of infringing and the seriousness of breach."[114] In this perspective, the injured party could take into account the legal good and the complicit State contributed to the infringement through its own tort. The counter-measure could have as its object an obligation of content similar to that violated by the author of the main crime, provided of course that this obligation does not fall within the list of "obligations not affected by counter-measures" contained in art. 50 ARSIWA.

1.9. Conclusions on the implementation of responsibility of the accomplice State

There are no reasons to exclude the configurability of counter-measures in the context of that particular secondary juridical relationship that is established between the accomplice State and the injured party. This statement of principle must be measured on the one hand with the numerous procedural and substantive conditions, to which the exercise of counter-measures is subordinated from a general point of view and on the other with the peculiarities of the accessory fact itself capable of further limit the use of this form of self-protection. In the hypothesis considered, the injured party must make a preliminary assessment of the illegality not of one but of two facts which, although bound, appear to be legally distinct. Another obstacle could arise with regard to the obligation susceptible to infringement as a counter-measure, given that the violation of the accomplice is simply instrumental to the violation of the primary rule established by the principal author. Emphasis was placed on two possible solutions to the problem. If the normative parameter directly violated by

---

[113]ARSIWA, p. 131, par. 8, where the ILC evaluates, not excluding a priori, the hypothesis in which the offender has rejected a satisfaction request after providing other forms of reparation. It seems to us that it always admits in principle the hypothesis formulated in the text, i.e. the use of countermeasures when satisfaction is the only restorative measure required by the author of the illicit and rejected by them.

[114]ARSIWA, p. 135, par. 6.

the accomplice is taken as selection criterion, that is art. 16 ARSIWA or 14, 58 DARIO then it will be necessary to look at other aspects of the accessory fact and in particular the prejudice that it has contributed to determine. This assessment may not be easy in particular in the hypothesis that the causal link between the accessory event and the prejudice in question is minimal. The second solution is based on the legal good indirectly injured by the accomplice State so that the injured party could take to the breach of an obligation of content similar to that violated by the main fact. In both cases, the requirement of proportionality of the counter-measure rests on them. Although this criterion has relative flexibility, there is no doubt that "disproportionate counter-measures could give rise to responsibility on the basis of the State taking such measures."[115] It does not seem unlikely that the injured party decides to resort to other forms of self-defense even in the hypotheses in which it would have prima facie title to adopt a counter-measure. Often States choose to employ retaliation[116] instead of a counter-measure in the hypothesis that the latter appears "politically impossible or disproportionate and therefore illegal."[117]

1.10. Complicity of States in the illicit fact of an international organization

The notion of international organization is relevant to the present work. The analysis of complicity of States in the unlawful act by international organizations as a case in point presents peculiarities which constitute the reflection of the nature and characteristics of the assisted subject. For this reason it seems to us essential to outline in advance the notion of international organization to which we will refer in the rest of the work.

---

[115]ARSIWA, p. 134, par. 1.

[116]Retaliation can sometimes cause more damage to a State than a countermeasure, as was evidenced by the doctrine that identified the limits of retaliation by clashing with the elementary objection that an act in lawful hypothesis that was subjected to limits would necessarily end up becoming illicit when these limits are exceeded in contradiction with the starting hypothesis. See also in argument: E. ZOLLER, Peacetime unilateral remedies, Martinus Nijhoff Publishers, Dobbs Ferry, New York, 1984. Y. ELAGAB, The legality of non-forcible counter-measures in international law, op. cit., J. ALCAIDE FERNÁNDEZ, Contre-mesures et règlement des diffèrends, in Revue Gènèrale de Droit Intenational Public, 108 (2), 2004, pp. 348ss. T. BUERGENTHAL, S.D. MURPHY, Public international law, West Group, Saint Paul, Minnesota, 2007. B.E. CARTER, P.R. TRIMBLE, A.S. WEINER, International law, Aspen publishers, New York, 2007. F.I. PADDEU, Countermeasures, in Max Planck Encyclopedia of International Law, 2015.

[117]T. GIEGERICH, Retorsion, in Max Planck Encyclopedia of Public International Law, 2011, par. 4. J. CRAWFORD, State responsibility. The general part, op. cit., pp. 698ss.

A study focused on international responsibility requires to include within its scope of investigation exclusively institutional unions characterized by an organic apparatus capable of carrying out activities evaluated by the international order, i.e. consisting in the exercise of rights, powers, faculties or in the performance or violation of obligations established by the same law.

Moreover, the notion of international organization (IO) generally accepted by the doctrine seems to give a central importance to the personality of institutions under consideration. The international organization can be qualified as a voluntary association of subjects of international law constituted by international acts from which an institution arises of a stable nature provided with an internal legal system of its own and equipped with at least one body whose will does not correspond to that of Member States, through which the body itself carries out common purposes of the associates, through the exercise of specific functions conferred by the agreement itself.[118] It is believed that the most relevant aspect is the ownership by the functional entity of a distinct will, or a broad degree of decision-making autonomy with respect to the founding States.[119]

The few instruments that can be useful to reconstruct the notion of international organization that has become established in conventional practice seem to attribute decisive importance to the intergovernmental character of the institutions in question. The VCLT in establishing that its scope of applicability is understood to be extended inter alia, "to any treaty which is the constituent instrument of an international organization and to any treaty adopted within an international organization" (art. 5), specifies that for the "international organization means an intergovernmental

---

[118]M. VIRALLY, Definition and classification of international organizations, in G. ABI-SAAB, The concept of international organization, UNESCO, Paris, 1981, pp. 50ss. J.A. BARBERIS, Nouvelles questiones concernant la perssonalitè juridique internationale, in Recueil des cours, ed. Brill, Brussels, vol. 180, 1983, pp. 216ss. H.G. SCHERMES, N.M. BLOKKER, International institutional law. Unity within diversity, ed. Springer, Leiden, Boston, 2003, pp. 26ss, C. BRÖLMANN, The institutional veil in public international law. International organizations and the law of treaties, Hart Publishing, Oxford & Oregon, Portland, 2007, pp. 20ss, according to which what constitutes qualifying an international organization is the coexistence of three elements: The institution of an international agreement, the faculty of the same to express, by means of at least one of its organs, a will distinct from that of the founding states, its concrete come into being and operate on the basis of international law.

[119]I. SEIDL-HOHENVELDERN, G. LOIBL, Das Recht der Internationalen Organizationen entischliesslich der Supranationalen Gemeinschaften, Heymanns Verlag, Köln, 2000, pp. 4ss. I. BROWNLIE, Principles of public international law, Oxford University Press, Oxford, 2003, pp. 650ss. N. WHITE, The law of international organization, Manchester University Press, Manchester, 2005.

organization" agreement (art. 2, par. 1 (i)). Provision of identical content can be found in art. 2, par. 1, letter i) of the VCLT between States and international organizations and between these latters.

Completely similar definitions can be found in art. 1, par. 1,VCLT on the representation of States in their relations with international organizations of a universal nature and in art. 2, par. 1,VCLT on the succession of state treaties. The definition resulting by VCLT is "traditional but rudimentary,"[120] representing the meager outcome of the process of codification of the law of treaties in the course of which the various rapporteurs have tried to frame legally a phenomenon such as that of international organizations that already at the end of the 1950s showed some problematic, and not even ambiguous, aspects.[121] In his first report the speaker Brierly had proposed a definition of international organization understood as "an association of States with common organs which is established by treaty." This notion does not contain any express reference to the international personality of the institutions in consideration even if in the "inherent nature of treaties and joint expressions of the several will of the parties" and of the circumstance for which "an entity without sovereign organs can have no will."[122] The next rapporteur, sir G. Fitzmaurice had provided a notion that in addition to responding to the opinion of the majority doctrine, it seems to have the merit of completeness,[123] useful in regulatory areas other than treaty law. "The term international organization means a collectively of States established by treaty with a constitution and common organs, having a personality distinct from that of its Member States and being a subject of international law with treaty capacity."[124]

Also during the process of codifying the regime of international responsibility for the State, constant reference was made to the inter-state nature of international organizations. The draft of articles approved in first reading in 1996 in dealing with, albeit marginally, the question of personality of organizations, operates a reference to those "international intergovernmental organizations such as UN, the specialized agencies" on

[120] K. SCHMALENBACH, Article 2, in K. SCHMALENBACH, O. DÖRR, Vienna convention on the law of treaties. A commentary, ed. Springer, Berlin, Heidelberg, 2012, pp. 45ss.
[121] J.L. BRIERLY, Report on the law of treaties, Doc. A/CN.4723, in Yearbook of International Law Commission, 1950, vol. II, pp. 229, par. 39.
[122] J.L. BRIERLY, Report on the law of treaties, op. cit., pp. 230, par. 40.
[123] S. BELLIER, Le recours à l'arbitrage par les organizations internationales, Harmattan, Paris, 2011, pp. 25ss.
[124] G. FITZMAURICE, Report on the law of treaties, UN Doc. A/CN.4./101, in Yearbook of International Law Commission, 1956, vol. II, p. 108.

which subjectivity does not seem to raise doubts.[125] A notion of this type is also found in the comment of art. 57 ARSIWA. It should also be noted that the feature in question has assumed importance for the purposes of distinguishing organizations from non-governmental organizations.[126]

The draft of articles on the responsibility of international organizations presents a much broader notion of organization than that contained in the legal instruments to those mentioned. Art. 2 a) of the definitive project clarifies beforehand that this concept refers to an "organization established by a treaty or other instrument governed by international law and possessing its own international personality (...)."[127] As can be seen from the literal datum in which there is no reference to the intergovernmental nature of the entity, ILC's approach is aimed at taking note of the most recent tendencies of the practice "in which international organizations increasingly tend to have a mixed membership in order to make cooperation more effective in certain areas."[128] In other words, the notion of international organization differs from the traditionally one imposed by ILC itself under the profile and membership which in this instrument is also meant to "entities other than States such as international organizations, territories or private entities."[129] Therefore, DARIOs also apply to those organizations that have a public-private hybrid membership, such as the world tourism organization.

A clarification is essential. The notion of international organization just outlined constitutes a model that the principles can be found in a good number of international organizations, be universal or regional. It seems that EU is hardly attributable to the model in question. Without wishing to enter the chaste debate[130] regarding the applicability

[125]In Yearbook of International Law Commission, 1975, vol. II, p. 89. This is the comment to art. 13 relating to the attribution of conduct carried out by international organization bodies.

[126]In this sense, Resolution n. 288 (X) adopted by the UN Economic and Social Council on 27 February 1950 with reference to the implementation of art. 71 of the Charter, concerning the consultative status of NGOs.

[127]DARIO, p. 10, par. 14.

[128]DARIO, p. 10, par. 14.

[129]DARIO, p. 10, par. 15.

[130]In the light of the analysis carried out and the applicable legal instruments, the position of those who believe that, within the Common Security and Defense Policy (CSDP), the EU acquires a high level of control over the conduct of States seems to be shared. The action of military contingents depends largely on its decisions and those of its organs, particularly of the Council. If such reasoning is followed, it is not entirely unfounded to say that troops taking part in the Union's military operations can be considered as de facto organs of the Organization. However, if we look more closely at the ICTY practice that used the overall control criterion and the approach adopted on the subject by the ILC, it emerges that the constitutive element of the subordination of individuals or non-state

entities to the State remains substantially within the limits of a hierarchical relationship between the two parties. It follows that the hierarchical subordination to the will of the State constitutes one of the characterizing aspects of the de facto organs. If we transfer this concept to CSDP, we can see that such a hierarchical characterization in the relationship between EU and Member States or third parties participating in the missions is unfounded from a legal point of view, since they are two international law actors placed on the same "level," although profoundly different from each other. In other words, it is hardly conceivable, in our opinion, to be able to detect, within the framework of a CSDP military operation, that subordination of the Member State (or third party) to the will of the Union which instead seems to be a fundamental element to configure an individual or a group as a de facto organ of a State. In our opinion, the contingents taking part in CSDP's military operations cannot therefore qualify as EU bodies pursuant to article 6 of the 2011 Project. The application of this provision is, therefore, excluded with reference to the attribution of unlawful conduct during CSDP operations. The absence of specific provisions that configure the state contingents as organs of the Organization when acting in the context of CSDP operations can be explained by the awareness of the risks associated with the Commission of violations of international law and, consequently, perhaps also by the will of to ensure that, first and foremost, States must respond on the international level to any illegal conduct. On the other hand, emphasis should be placed on the large, and in some ways inexplicable, asymmetry between the 2001 Project and the 2011 one regarding the regulation of the question of the attribution of conduct. From the above analysis, in our opinion, a "deficient" regulatory framework emerges, in which the (few) provisions regarding the attribution of conduct of the 2011 Project do not seem sufficient in order to regulate the different situations that can in practice occur with reference to the increasingly complex practice of international organizations. See in argument: P.C. CAMMAERT, B. KLAPPE, Authority, command and control in United Nations-led peace operations, in T. GILL, D. FLECK (eds.), Oxford University Press handbook of the international law of military operations, Oxford University Press, Oxford, 2010, pp. 262ss. The "effective control" test was used by the North Rhine-Westphalia Court of Appeals in the Rheinland-Pfalz case, it appears to us that the only case decided by a court concerning the responsibility for offenses committed during a CSDP mission in particular with regard to the question of the attribution of conduct to the European Union or to the sending States-Administrative Court of Cologne (VG Köln), Ali Mohamed Aw-Dahir v. Germany, Az 25 K 4280/09, judgment, 11 November 2011. The case was then decided in the second degree by the Court of administrative appeal of North Rhine-Westphalia, Az. 4 A 2948/11, 18 September 2014 to decide in on which entity (EU, UN or Germany) to attribute a violent conduct of international obligations to respect human rights. The judges, in particular, considered Germany responsible for violating the rules that sanction the prohibition of torture and inhuman and degrading treatment for having transferred some Somali pirates to Kenya in order to bring them to trial, after they had been arrested by the German ship "Rheinland-Pfalz" acting under the EUNAVFOR operation. The Court found that there were no grounds for setting up an assignment of conduct to EU under article 7 of the 2011 Project, stating that the organization did not have "effective control" over the transfer of pirates. The judges came to this conclusion by adopting an "exclusionary" reasoning and asserting that the decision to transfer these subjects to Kenya was taken exclusively by the German authorities, which also had "operational" control over all the phases of this transfer. The Court also appears to be leveraging the "causal" aspect, since it claims that the transfer of pirates was a direct consequence of German decision not to put these individuals on trial

to the organization of the rules codified in DARIOs, it seems clear to us that it has such characteristics to distinguish it in a decisive manner, the model has been referred to.[131] Not surprisingly, in the most recent literature, studies focusing specifically on the international EU responsibility have appeared.[132] It is well known that in the field of Common Foreign and Security Policy (CFSP) the Union operates substantially like a common international organization.[133] Clarification is important because at least in principle,[134] some operational activities carried out by EU within the CFSP, such as peace-keeping missions, are substantially attributable to the general model.[135]

---

on their territory. In essence, the judges considered that the EU did not have "effective control" over the transfer based on the actual circumstances of the fact, according to the provisions of the commentary to article 7, since, although operating in the context of a conduct operation under the aegis of EU, the German vessel had taken orders exclusively from its own national authorities, which also controlled the transfer. M. LARSEN, Attribution of conduct in peace operations: the "ultimate authority and control" test, in The European Journal of International Law, 19 (3), 2008, pp. 510ss. J. D'ASPREMONT, The law of international responsibility and multilayered institutional veils: The case of authorized regional peace-enforcement operations, SHARES Research Paper n. 24, 2013, pp. 13ss.

[131]The first element in this sense is undoubtedly represented by the presence in the EU system of a jurisdictional body with exclusive jurisdiction in relation to the interpretation and application of the EU law and of international law within the same organization. It should be considered that the violation of community obligations by a Member State can only lead to the ascertainment of the same by the CJEU following the outcome of an infringement procedure and if the conditions for an action with ex-contractual liability are present. In other words, within this order it is excluded that a Member State can act autonomously to enforce the non-fulfilment of a community obligation put in place by another Member State. In the same way, the consequences of this default are accurately disclosed by the founding treaties and are subject to CJEU decisions.

[132]A. DELGADO CASTELEIRO, The international responsibility of the European Union. From competence to normative control, Cambridge University Press, Cambridge, 2016.

[133]B. TAXIL, Notions, sources et règimes de responsibilitè, in E. LAGRANGE, J.M. SOREL, Droit des organizations internationales, LGDJ, Paris, 2013.

[134]G. MARHIC, Le règime de responsabilitè des opèrations de paix de l'unione europèenne. Quelles règles applicables?, in Revue Belge de Droit International, 46, 2013, pp. 137ss, for which the responsibility for the offenses committed by the peace forces of the Union would be regulated by art. 340 TFEU with which the organization would have established a liability regime with characteristics that would in any case converge with those co-established by the ILC in the DARIO.

[135]E. PAASIVIRTA, P. J. KUIJPER, Does one size fit all? The European Community and the responsibility of international organizations, in Netherlands Yearbook of International Law, 36, 2005, pp. 169-226. C. LECK, International responsibility in United Nations peacekeeping operations: Command and control arrangements and the attribution of conduct, in Melbourne Journal of International Law, 10, 2009, pp. 346ss. R. BUCHAN, UN peacekeeping operations: When can unlawful acts committed by peacekeeping forces be attributed to the UN?, in Legal Studies, 32 (2), 2012, pp. 284ss. T.D. GILL, D. FLECK,

1.11. International organizations' extent of personality

In the notion of subject of the international order the question of imputation of the manifestations of will in which the exercise of the subjective right or the juridical power deriving from the international norms is resolved, as the activities that constitute the fulfilment or violation of obligations arising from the same rules.[136]

This premise is generally considered sufficient to hold that the general principles regarding international responsibility are applicable to those international organizations that present the characteristics of subjects

The handbook of the international law of military operations, Oxford University Press, Oxford, 2011, pp. 523ss.

[136] The question of the imputation of the manifestations of will and of the unlawful acts of the subjects according to an apportionment which is commonly defined as normative for which it would be possible to include in the general international law a complex of secondary rules concerning the imputation of the illicit fact. See in argument: L. CONDORELLI, C. KRESS, The rules of attribution: General considerations, in J. CRAWFORD, A. PELLET, S. OLLESON, K. PARLETT, The law of international responsibility, Oxford University Press, Oxford, 2010, pp. 221ss. The ILC in the codification of the regulatory regime of responsibility adhered to this approach, already the speaker Ago has observed that: "The attribution à l'Etat du comportement adopte en fait par des êtres physiques est nècessairement basèe sur des donnèes juridiques, et non pas sur la reconnaissance d'un lien de causalitè naturelle (...)." R. AGO, Troisième rapport sur la responsabilitè des États. Le fait internationalement illicite de l'État, source de responsabilité internationale, op. cit., art.5, par. 106, p. 245, the project approved in first reading in 1996 and art. 4 of the definitive one of 2001 establishes that a given illicit attitude is attributable to the State under international law, according to an orientation that was then confirmed in ARSIWA (art. 4). The attribution of the unlawful remains a mere factual operation on the basis of the link and behaviour of the State, that is to say on the basis of historical-sociological causality (and therefore factual) and not on criteria determined by international law confirming a position already supported by the aforementioned doctrine. The misunderstanding would arise from the idea that international law regulates imputation on the basis of the domestic law of each State. The data itself is not a necessary nor a sufficient condition, given that the conduct of the so-called de facto organs and that the mere circumstance that an individual is a de jure organ is not sufficient to justify the attribution. The only difference between de jure and de facto organs is that only for the former it can be presumed to save the effectiveness of their conduct referable to the State. International law plays a limited role in solving the imputation problem although it cannot be denied the existence of an essential nucleus of rules that seems to be inspired by the need for certainty and stability in international relations. For further analysis see: G. TOWNSEND, State responsibility for acts of de facto agents, in Arizona Journal of International and Comparative Law, 14, 1997, pp. 662ss. S. SILVERBURG, International law. Contemporary issues and future developments, ed. Routledge, London & New York, 2018.

of the international order.[137] The subjectivity of functional entities is the logical prerequisite for their international responsibility and is confirmed in the aforementioned art. 2, lett. a) DARIO.[138]

The investigation of the contractual will of the founding States is decisive for the purposes of ascertaining the functions, powers and competences[139] assigned to the entity. Moreover, since the international organizations remain alive as long as the assumption of their institution

---

[137]C. EAGLETON. International organization and the law of responsibility, in Recueil des cours, ed. Brill, Bruxelles, vol. 77, 1950, pp. 324ss. E. JIMENEZ DE ARECHAGA, International responsibility, in M. SØRENSEN, Manual of public international law, Macmillan & Co, London, New York, 1968, pp. 532ss, which is affirmed that: "There is a general presumption that the principles concerning international responsibility in inter-state relations apply, mutandis mutandis to international organization, though certain modifications are a necessary consequence of the inherent character of such institutions." In the same orientation: K. GINTHER, international organizations, responsibility, in Encyclopedia of Public International Law, 1983, pp. 162ss. W. MENG, Internationale Organizationen im Völkerrechtichen Deliktsrecht, op. cit., pp. 324ss. I. BROWNLIE, Principles of public international law, op. cit., pp. 686ss. A. PELLET, L'imputabilitè d'èventuels actes illicites. Responsabilitè de l'OTAN ou des États membres, in C. TOMUSCHAT, Kosovo and the international community: A legal assessment, ed. Brill, The Hague, 2002, pp. 194ss. T. STEIN, Kosovo and international community. The attribution of possible internationally wrongful acts: Responsibility of NATO or of its Member States?, in C. TOMUSCHAT, Kosovo and the international community: A legal assessment, ed. Brill, The Hague, 2002, pp. 182ss. M.N. SHAW, International law, Cambridge University Press, Cambridge, 2008, pp. 120ss. Also the ICJ before the ILC started the codification of the responsibility of international organizations seemed to adhere implicitly to this approach. See, Difference relating to immunity from legal process of a special rapporteur for the Commission on human rights, advisory opinion of 29 April 1999, in ICJ Reports, 1999, pp. 89, par. 66. A. ZIMMERMANN, C.J. TAMS, K. OELLERS-FRAHAM, The Statute of the International Court of Justice. A commentary, op. cit.

[138] G. GAJA, First report on responsibility of international organizations, UN Doc. A/CN.4/532, p. 105, par. 15, which is affirmed that: "Logically a study on responsibility of international organizations should consider all the organizations that are subjects of international law."

[139]P. D'ARGENT, La personnalitè juridique internationale de l'organization internationale, in E. LAGRANGE, J.M. SOREL, Droit des organizations internationales, LGDJ, Paris, 2013, pp. 439ss. T. GAZZINI, Personality of international organizations, in J. KLABBERS, Å. WALLENDAHL, Research handbook on the law of international organizations, Edward Elgar Publishers, Cheltenham, 2001, pp. 34ss. A.S. BARROS, C. RYNGAERT, J. WOUTERS, International organizations and member state responsibility. Critical perspectives, ed. Brill, Bruxelles 2016, pp. 11ss. M. VIRALLY, La notion de fonction dans la thèorie de l'organization internationale, in G. ABI-SAAB, La communautè internationale. Mèlanges offerts à Charles Rousseau, ed. Pedone, Paris, 1974, pp. 278ss, for which the competence of organization "dèsigne l'objet même de la fonction, c'est-à-dire le champ ouvert à son activitè et les conditions auxquelles cette activitè peut s'yu dèployer," which the notion of power is identified with a: "Peut faire l'organization dans son domain de compètence."

exists, that is to say the consent of pre-existing subjects,[140] it should be noted that their international personality is of a derivative nature and not originating, in the same way as the state one. To affirm that a non-state entity with a legal personality means that it possesses certain capabilities provided for by the law, capacities that are different under the double formal and substantial profile, compared to the state ones. This affirmation seems to be confirmed by ICJ's jurisprudence, and this is a very important element.[141] It has until recently,[142] addressed the preliminary question of international subjectivity only with regard to UN or at most specialized institutions. In the advisory opinion on the reparation of damages suffered in the UN service it concluded that "the organization is an international person. That is not the same thing as saying that is a State, which it certainly is not, or that its legal personality, rights and duties are the same as those States (…), whereas a State possesses the totality of international rights and duties recognized by international law, the rights and duties of an entity such as the organization must depend upon its purposes and functions as specified or implied in its constituent documents and

[140]C. FOCARELLI, International law as social construct. The struggle for global justice, Oxford University Press, Oxford, 2012, pp. 178ss, which the author observed that the international organizations: "Are voluntarily created by States, persisting in life and dissolved when their Member States so decide."

[141]M. MENDELSON, The definition of international organization in the International Law Commission's current project on the responsibility of international organizations, in M. RAGAZZI, Responsibility of international organizations. Essays in memory of Sir Ian Brownlie, Martinus Nijhoff Publishers, Leiden, Boston, 2013, pp. 384ss. The universal vocation of the UN and of the specialized institutes would have played in the opinion of this author a central role in ICJ's argument in all the consultative procedures in which the question of subjectivity came into relief: For these reasons, the considerations about the objective personalities of the UN are not ipso facto extensible to other international organizations, unless they present characteristics similar to those posed by the ICJ. In the same orientation see also: I. SEIDL-HOHENVELDERN, Die völkerrechtliche Haftung für Handlungen internationaler Organizationen im Verhältnis zu Nichmitgliedstaaten, in Österreichische Zeitschrift für öffentliches Recht, 11, 1961, pp. 498ss, the universal character of the UN, together with the breadth of its material skills, played a decisive role in the reasoning of the ICJ. I. SEIDL-HOHENVELDERN, Liability of member states for acts or omissions of an international organization, in S. SCHLEMMER-SCHULTE, K.U. TUNG, Liber amicorum F.I. Shihata. International finance and development law, ed. Springer, The Hague, Boston, New York, 2001, pp. 732ss.

[142]At least until 2012 when the ICJ also dealt incidentally with the question of the personality of the global mechanism established by the Convention on desertification of 1996, judgment n. 2967 of the administrative tribunal of the international labour organization upon a complaint filed against the international fund for agricultural development, in ICJ Reports, 2012, p. 10ss. A. ZIMMERMANN, C.J. TAMS, K. OELLERS-FRAHAM, The Statute of the International Court of Justice. A commentary, op. cit.

developed in practice."[143] In this regard, judge Ago noted in his individual opinion related to the advisory opinion given by ICJ regarding the interpretation of the Agreement of 25 May 1951 between WHO and Egypt,[144] which "une organization internationale est, comme un Etat, un sujet de droit international, mais possèdant une capacitè juridique internationale restreinte et surtout, à la diffèrence de l'Etat, elle est un sujet dèpourvu de toute base territoriale."[145] Contrary to the state one, the spectrum of competences of an international organization is not general but is governed by the principle of specialty as ICJ itself reiterated in the opinion on the lawfulness of the use of nuclear weapon during an armed conflict of 1996.[146] From this principle it follows that the acts adopted by an organization outside its sphere of competence must be considered as having no legal effects.[147]

The internationalist doctrine is almost unanimous in admitting the inequality between State and functional subjectivity, [148] generally

---

[143]Reparation for injuries suffered in the service of the UN, in ICJ Reports, 1949, pp. 179-180. It must also be added that internal jurisprudence has long settled on the different nature of the functional personality resulting from the State. In this sense also: G. ARANGIO-RUIZ, The federal analogy and UN Charter, in the European Journal of International Law, 1, 1997, pp. 16ss. The principal objective of the author was to point out the improper nature of any comparison between international organizations and inter-individual phenomena associated with domestic law and on the other to deny the thesis of the presumed over-ordering of the organization with respect to Member States, excluding an evolution of the international organization phenomenon in a federal sense, and absorbing state sovereignty, such as to entail a structural change, even partial, of the joint system of coexistence between the powers. A. ZIMMERMANN, C.J. TAMS, K. OELLERS-FRAHAM, The Statute of the International Court of Justice. A commentary, op. cit.

[144]Interpretation of the agreement of 25 March 1951 between the WHO and Egypt, advisory opinion, in ICJ Reports, 1980, p. 73. A. ZIMMERMANN, C.J. TAMS, K. OELLERS-FRAHAM, The Statute of the International Court of Justice. A commentary, op. cit.

[145] A. ZIMMERMANN, C.J. TAMS, K. OELLERS-FRAHAM, The Statute of the International Court of Justice. A commentary, op. cit.

[146]Legality of the use by a state of nuclear weapons in armed conflicts, advisory opinion, in ICJ Reports, 1996, p. 16, par. 25. A. ZIMMERMANN, C.J. TAMS, K. OELLERS-FRAHAM, The Statute of the International Court of Justice. A commentary, op. cit.

[147] P. KLEIN, Les compètences et pouvois de l'organization internationale, in E. LAGRANGE, J.M. SOREL, Droit des organizations internationales, LGDJ, Paris, 2013, pp. 721ss.

[148]The functional or derivative and secondary nature of the personality of international organizations is supported by majority doctrine. See in particular: R. BINDSCHEDLER, International organizations, general aspects, in Encyclopedia of Public International Law, 1992, pp. 1299ss. A. REINISCH, Developing human rights and humanitarian law accountability of the Security Council, in American Journal of International Law, 95 (4), 2001, pp. 858ss. P. SANDS, P. KLEIN, Bowett's law of international institutions, Sweet & Maxwell, London, 2009. I. SEIDL-HOHENVELDERN, G. LOIBL, Das Recht der Internationalen Organizationen entischliesslich der Supranationalen Gemeinschaften, op.

classifying the former as originating, the latter as derivative or secondary. The principal attribute of the international personality of the State is notoriously constituted by the sovereignty, which bears the selves a set of at all peculiar active and passive juridical situations.[149] The fundamental property of personality of an international organization lies in the notion of function,[150] which "constitue sa justification and cells of tout son activité, sa ratio, aux deux sens du terme, raison d'être et limitation."[151] It must also be emphasized that by virtue of a well-established practice,[152] the transfer of competence from a State to an international organization does not relieve the former of the fulfilment of obligations materially falling within that specific sphere of competence.[153] This leads some of the doctrine to believe that Member States "demeuren titualires des

---

cit., pp. 472ss. P. REUTER, Droit international public, op. cit., pp. 224ss. P. DAILLER, M. FORTEAU, A. PELLET, Droit international public, op. cit., pp. 643ss. S. SUR, Les organizations internationales. Dynamiques et dèsenchantement, in Revue Gènèrale de Droit International Public, 116, 2012, pp. 668ss.

[149]Sovereignty is notoriously assumed to be a fundamental parameter from which it follows that it is the holder of both the rights and obligations, such as shown in the arbitration ruling of 4 April 1928 on the case relating to the island of Palmas to protect within the territory object of sovereignty, the rights of other States.

[150]G. CAHIN, La variètè des fonctions imparties aux organizations internationales, in E. LAGRANGE, J.M. SOREL, Droit des organizations internationales, LGDJ, Paris, 2013, pp. 678ss. P. D'ARGENT, La personnalitè juridique internationale de l'organization internationale, in E. LAGRANGE, J.M. SOREL, Droit des organizations internationales, op. cit., pp. 454. The distinction in question was at the basis of the VI report presented by P. Reuter at the ILC on the law of treaties between States and international organizations or between international organizations. P. REUTER, Sixième rapport sur la question des traitès conclus entre États et organizations internationales ou entre deux ou plusiers organizations internationales, UN Doc. A/CN. 4/298, in Annuaire de la Commission du Droit International, 1977, vol. II, p. 127ss, par. 25.

[151]M. VIRALLY, Le principle de rèciprocitè dans le droit international contemporain, op. cit., pp. 291ss. J. KLABBERS, The transformation of international organizations law, op. cit., pp. 9ss.

[152]A leading case was presented in Melchers & Co v. Federal Republic of Germany case of 9 February 1990, n. 13258/87 where the European Commission of human rights has inaugurated the orientation for which the transfer of powers to an international organization does not in itself apply to exclude state responsibility on an equal footing with the ECHR in order to exercise the powers that have been transferred to the functional body under consideration.

[153]I. BROWNLIE, The responsibility of states of the acts of international organizations, in M. RAGAZZI, Responsibility of international organizations. Essays in memory of Sir Ian Brownlie, Martinus Nijhoff Publishers, Leiden, Boston, 2013, pp. 361ss, which the author has cited the Waite and Kennedy v. Germany case. It was ruled by ECtHR on 18 February 1999. It is affirmed that: "Whilst the context is that of human rights, the principle invoked would seem to be general in its application. A State cannot avoid responsibility by creating an international organization (...)."

comètences dont ils ont transfèrè l'exercice à une organization internationale."[154]

For the purposes of our investigation it seems relevant the relationship that de jure subsists between organizations and Member States where is observed that the membership relationship by definition characterized by a certain degree of legal stability means that the process of forming the will of the entity even if formally independent it cannot be considered entirely original on a factual and substantive level. As has been opportunely noted, this constitutes the most marked discrepancy between state and functional subjectivity, since it is a matter of kind and not merely of degree.[155] It should be added in this regard that the relationship of belonging to an international organization provides in some cases different legal positions of the individual Member States for what concerns the formation of the organs and the adoption of the relative resolutions giving rise to a suitable instrument to express on a permanent basis and automatic way the prevailing social forces in the international community. The decision of the General Assembly to ask ILC to prepare a tool for codifying the responsibility of international organizations and the inclusion in the same instrument of a discipline aimed at regulating state responsibility in "connection with the act of an international organization and on the other the responsibility of an internal organization in connection with the act of a State."[156]

1.12. Functions of international organizations. Subdivision into conceptual instrumental categories to a study on international responsibility

The study of complicity of States in the offense of international organizations requires that a summary of activities carried out by the organizations in the fulfilment of functions for which they were established must be traced, even if summarily. The number of existing international organizations makes it easy to imagine the way to precisely describe each of these activities. It seems appropriate to proceed through

[154] P. KLEIN, Les compètences et pouvois de l'organization internationale, in E. LAGRANGE, J.M. SOREL, Droit des organizations internationals, op. cit., pp. 720ss.
[155] R. SADURSKA, C. CHINKIN, The collapse of the international Tin Council. A case of state responsibility?, op. cit., pp. 888, no functional body is able to perform its statutory functions without the active participation and involvement of the Member States, a circumstance to which the author assumes that "is unrealistic to claim that an international organization is an entity independent from the States which created it."
[156]DARIO, p. 35ss, p. 89ss.

the analysis of conceptual categories within which the activities of functional bodies can be traced. In pursuit of the goals assigned to it, the international organization carries out a wide range of functions. According to the prevailing doctrine approach, which seems preferable for limited purposes, a study on international responsibility can be divided into regulations and operational or executive. The accepted bipartition founded on the assumption for which all those functions that are not strictly and exclusively normative,[157] can be considered operative, imposes two clarifications. First of all it should be noted that at the origin of the operational function the preliminary exercise of a regulatory function, given that the former always takes place as a result of the adoption of certain legal acts which constitute its normative basis. Secondly, even though it necessarily carries a certain degree of simplification of the legal reality.[158] This categorization may be useful, in order to frame the context within which the principal behaviour of an international organization may take place.[159] All the activities of the organizations are

---

[157] I. JOHNSTONE, Law making through the operational activities of international organizations, in The George Washington International Law Review, 40, 2008, pp. 88ss. P. F. LAVAL, Les activitès opèrationnelles, du conseil à l'administration international du territoire, in E. LAGRANGE, J.M. SOREL, Droit des organizations internationales, LGDJ, Paris, 2013, pp. 767ss. R. BINDSCHEDLER, International organizations, general aspects, op. cit., pp. 1302ss, which distinguished between "legislative and executive" the principal functions of international organizations. P. SANDS, P. KLEIN, Bowett's law of international institutions, op. cit., they substantially adhere to this approach: In addition to the jurisdiction or quasi-jurisdictional function, the authors identify two categories of functions. The legislative or regulatory and the executive or administrative ones. He also adheres to this approach: S. BELLIER, Le recours à l'arbitrage par les oganisations internationales, op. cit., pp. 137ss, where it notes that only organizations that perform predominantly operational functions resort to arbitration for the purpose of resolving conflicts of which they are parties. Instead, G. CAHIN, La variètè des fonctions imparties aux organizations internationales, in E. LAGRANGE, J.M. SOREL, Droit des organizations internationales, op. cit., pp. 671ss, in addition to the regulatory function (règulation) it is possible to identify four other functions. That of permanent discussion forum, consisting in making available to "an internationale societè fundamentalel conflictuelle les cadres et the instruments d'une multilateral, permanent et universelle," which however does not seem to be relevant for the purposes of international responsibility, that of administration recognizable for example in the management of non-autonomous territories, the function of providing financial assistance or services and the peacekeeping one.

[158]Correctly the ILC rapporteur on relations between States and international organizations notes that: "Given the wide variety of functions entrusted to international organizations (...) any classification will necessarily be inadequate." See, L. DÍAZ-GONZÁLEZ, Fourth report on relations between states and international organizations (second part of the topic), UN Doc. A/CN/424/Corr.1., in Yearbook of International Law Commission, vol. II. pp. 153ss, par. 36.

[159]Another part of the doctrine includes among the activities within which international

subject to international law which governs them through normative parameters that can now be found among the customary norms among those that are conventional for the institution. Art. 3 DARIO establishes as a general rule that "very internationally wrongful act of an international organization of international responsibility of that organization." The instrument in question does not refer to the types of conduct of international organizations unless specified in art. 4 that it may be of a commissive or omissive nature and that from a subjective point of view it may be carried out by any organ or agent of the organization in the performance of its functions. This means that in principle the unlawful behaviour can take place within the framework of any activity, contrary to what is expected and imposed by an international obligation of the institution. In this sense, depose the combined provisions of articles 5, 6 and 10 of the project.

1.13. The regulatory function

The primary function of international organizations is certainly the normative one, i.e. to determine if not to direct the guidelines of Member States in the matters of competence of the same entity. For the purposes of this investigation, the irrelevant indirect regulatory function that is notoriously carried out in promoting the adoption of juridical acts having collective efficacy, stimulating Member States to carry out a normative activity that otherwise would not be undertaken by them.[160] Confining ourselves to the direct regulatory function with which the body participates in the processes of juridical production of the international order, it must be emphasized that in this framework the adoption by the international organizations of legal acts is of central importance. This defined formal function is articulated through the various decision-making processes governed by the treaties of the same bodies and aimed at the adoption of acts the different legal: a) Acts with binding effectiveness; b) acts with binding effect only with regard to Member States that have

---

organizations may engage in international offenses even the activities carried out by the administrative agents of the same bodies. See for example: G. ZAGEL, Responsibility of international organizations for international law, in Sudebnik, 11, 2006, pp. 652ss. In our opinion, the need to illustrate the offenses of international organizations prevents us from dwelling on the conduct of administrative agents that only rarely produce effects outside the internal organization of the same bodies. Even if this order is not in any way comparable to the state regulations for our purposes, it is advisable to limit the scope of the investigation to the obligatory relationships that bind the institution with respect to other subjects of the international order.

[160] G. ULESTEIN, Les activitès normatives de l'organization internationale, in E. LAGRANDE, J.M. SOREL, Droit des organizations internationales, LGDJ, Paris, 2013, pp. 746ss.

accepted or contributed to their adoption; c) non-binding acts. The direct regulatory function also includes the agreements concluded by organizations with other subjects of the international order and in some ways also their participation in the formation process of the norms of general international law.[161] The notion of a normative function, therefore, must be understood in its broadest sense, that is, as that set of activities with which the international organization creates or contributes to creating institutive norms for a wide range of subjective legal situations in their head including faculties and powers, or acts capable of producing at least legally relevant effects.

The first category of acts to which reference is made is constituted by the third-degree of sources or with centralized training, that is to say from the documents adopted by international organizations that are likely to create subjective legal situations for the recipients, thus giving rise to the exercise of a particular form of international public authority,[162] or even international legislation.[163] What comes to the fore is therefore the suitability of the act to impose on Member States to maintain or not to hold a determined behaviour or to pursue certain results, the nomen juris of the act. Among the acts of the type considered, is certainly worth mentioning, in addition to some acts of secondary EU law,[164] some resolutions adopted by UN bodies in the same way as the Statute of this organization. These are the Resolutions with which by virtue of art. 17 of the Charter, the General Assembly approves the budget of the institution and above all the decisions taken from the Security Council on the basis of art. 41 of Chapter VII, in addition to those provided by art. 94, par. 2 which attributes to this

---

[161]G. CAHIN, Le coutume internationale et les organizations internationales: L'incidence institutionnelle sur le proessus coutumier, ed. Pedone, Paris, 2001.

[162]A. VON BOGDANDY, P. DANN, M. GOLDMANN, Developing the publicness of public international law. Towards a legal framework for global governance, in German Law Journal, 9, 2008, pp. 1381ss, the notion of public authority was intended "as the legal capacity to determine others and to reduce their freedom, i.e. to their uniltaterally legal or factual situation" with the clarification that the exercise of this public authority can assume a binding circumstance which is realized when the deed "modifies the legal situation of a different legal subject without its consent (...)."

[163] G. ULESTEIN, Les activitès normatives de l'organization internationale, in E. LAGRANDE, J.M. SOREL, Droit des organizations internationales, op. cit., J. WOUTERS, C. RYNGAERT, T. RUYS, G. DE BAERE, International law. A european perspective, Bloomsbury, New York, 2018.

[164]According to art. 288 TFEU. For further analysis see: A. HATJE, J.P. TERHECHTE, P.C. MÜLLER-GRAFF, Europarechtswissenschaft, ed. Nomos, Baden-Baden, 2018. J. SCHWARZE, V. BECKER, A. HATJE, J. SCHOO, EU-Kommentar, ed. Nomos, Baden-Baden, 2019. M. KELLERBAUER, M. KLAMERT, J. TOMKIN, Commentary on the European Union treaties and the Charter of fundamental rights, Oxford University Press, Oxford, 2019.

body the power to adopt measures to oblige an unsuccessful Member State before a sentence of ICJ to fulfil what is imposed by the same sentence. It is hardly necessary to point out that even specialized UN institutions have, in limited cases, the power to adopt legally binding acts. By way of example, reference can be made to the normative activity carried out by the International Civil Aviation organization established by the Chicago Convention on 7 December 1944. The Council pursuant to art. 43 of the aforementioned Convention constitutes one of the main organs of the organization together with the Assembly.[165] It carries out the obligatory functions consisting in the adoption by a majority of two thirds (art. 90) of norms and recommended practices that in accordance with art. 54 merge into the Annexes or Annexes to the Agreement.[166] The forecast that most interests us in this session is represented by art. 12 which regulates the power of the organization in the matter of overflight of the international sea with respect to which the Member States are bound by a categorical obligation of conformity. The recommendations adopted by the International Labor Organization pursuant to art.19, par. 6 b) are binding between the binding deeds, even if they contain less stringent obligations than those described by its Constitution given that the Member States have the obligation to "bring the recommendation before the authority or other authorities with which to compete in the matter of the enactment of legislation or other action."[167] In reality the problematic indicated did not at this stage take on a central importance. The forms of the reactions allowed and the identification of the subjects authorized to implement them did not fall within the ILC priorities. The members of the latter simply confined themselves to anticipating any issues related to the introduction of the concept of international crimes, which would have had to find a more adequate forum for discussion in the context of the work, concerning the consequences of the international crime. The prospect of some form of involvement of the UN in the planned regime of crimes

---

[165]The Council is made up of 36 Member States elected by the Assembly chosen from among the most important states in the field of air transport, including: 1.The States of chief importance in air transport; 2.The States not otherwise included which make the largest contribution to the provision of facilities for international civil air navigation and 3.The States not otherwise included whose designation will insure that all the major geographic areas of the world are represented on the Council (art. 50, lett. b).

[166]A. MALINTOPPI, La fonction normative de l'OACI, in Revue Gènerale de l'Air, 10, 1950, pp. 1050ss.

[167]R. AGO, Huitième rapport sur la responsabilitè des États. Le fait internationalement illicite de l'État, source de responsabilité internationale, op. cit., p. 45, par. 92, Ago had clearly ruled out that the Commission of an international offense could give rise to a new legal reaction between the state author of the violation and the international community understood as a formal entity with an autonomous apparatus with respect to its members.

should have been appropriately deepened only the follow-up which partly explains the poor formalization of the proposals put forward in this first period. It appeared as a necessary guarantee for the acceptance of the notion indicated by the States. In this regard it was recalled that at the very acceptance of the notion of jus cogens, in the codification of the law of treaties, one had arrived only thanks to the simultaneous introduction of the jurisdiction mandatory by the ICJ on the subject.[168] This reference also explains the substantial favour already manifested in this phase for the provision also in this sector of a mandatory recourse to the judicial regulation.

Secondly, it is necessary to point out the institutional acts that acquire binding efficacy only with regard to Member States that have expressly accepted the prescriptive content. The provisions of art. 7 of the Pact of the League of Arab States according to which "majority decisions shall be binding only upon those states which have accepted them." In some cases the acceptance mechanism can operate tacitly as is the case with the international health regulations adopted by WMO World Assembly under the terms of art. 22 of the Statute of this organization.[169] The procedure of adoption of the act is based on the opting-out technique by virtue of which states that do not intend to participate in a given resolution are allowed not to assume the obligations deriving from it. Without it is useful to prevent the adoption of the act. In this case, however, it can be said that health regulations can be classified as simplified agreements rather than unilateral acts of the organization.

The third category of institutional acts, decidedly predominant from a quantitative point of view, is constituted by the Recommendations.[170] Terms with which normally reference is made to non compulsory acts.[171] This typology includes some Resolutions adopted

[168] C. GINTHER, K. ZEMANEK, Völkerrecht zwischen normativen Anspruch und politischer Realität. Festschrift für Karl Zemanek zum 65. Geburtstag, Duncker & Humblot, Berlin, 1994, pp. 320ss. J. CRAWFORD, Chance, order, change. The course of international law, ed. Brill, Bruxelles, 2014.

[169] "(...) Regulations adopted pursuant to article 21 shall come into force for all members after due notice has been given of their adoption by the health assemble except for such members as may notify the director general or rejection or reservations within the period stated in the notice."

[170] Except for the cases in which the term designates acts having compulsory efficacy as in the case of certain recommendations of the WMO.

[171] M. VIRALY, La valeur juridique des recommanations des organizations internationales, in Annuaire Français de Droit International, 2, 1956, pp. 66ss., which the author affirmed in negative sense that "pas son absence de force obligatoire. Tout au plus accepte-t-on de lui recconnaître une valeur politique, ou même simplement morale; ce qui, dans l'essprit de beacoup et lmalgrè les protestations de convenance est encore une façon de s'exriment purement nègative."

by General Assembly and UN Security Council on the subject of peacekeeping pursuant to articles 10-14 and 36-41 of the Statute of the organization. Assuming as a valuation parameter the legal nature of the deed, it can be noted that the recommendation is a manifestation of a desire to solicit from the recipient the implementation of a determined passive or negative conduct to be carried out in the international order or, if necessary, in the whole of the state system. The recommendation, which in most cases can be qualified as a legally relevant fact, takes on the characteristics of the legal fact in very specific circumstances. In the first case the recommendations are taken as a mediated point of reference to be integrated with other elements that are necessarily different for the determination of indirect juridical effects, that do not derive directly and immediately from the act considered itself. In this regard, the up-west African opinion is known where judge Lauterpacht proposed the thesis according to which: "The persistent disregard" of a series of recommendations by a UN Member State would be such as to integrate the violation of obligation to cooperate in good faith with the organization descending from the founding treaty of the same.[172]

But the type of Recommendation that is relevant in our investigation is that pertaining to the category of legal fate. According to a part of the doctrine to this category, the resolutions through which the UN Security Council should fulfil the conditions set forth in art. 39 of the Charter urges the adoption by the States that are recipients of measures involving the use of armed force. The act in question would more precisely result in an authorization whose legal effect consists in the suspension of the prohibition of the use of force in international relations contained in art. 2, par. 4 of the UN Charter.[173] The legal effect of which is discussed is configured as direct since is produced immediately following the completion of the formative process of the resolution while sharing the common non-mandatory efficacy would still be separate acts with first the

[172]Voting procedure on questions relating to reports and petitions concerning the territory of South West Africa, advisory opinion of June 7th 1955, in ICR reports, p. 90ss, par. 120.

[173]The notion of authorization in international law does not seem to depart in a decisive way from that obtainable from the general theory of the legal act. The authorization is included in the category of legal acts at the time of completion and which is conditioned by the faculty of exercising a power with which the addressee of the same act is invested. In other words, the purpose of the authorization is to remove the provisions set forth by law for the performance of other legal acts or for the performance of certain activities. The UN Security Council on which pursuant to art. 24 of the organization's Statute is incumbent on the main responsibility of maintaining peace and internal security, removing by means of the authorization the legal obstacle to the exercise by the Member States of the juridical power to impose the armed force upon evaluation to borrow the words used by the doctrine with reference to the internal law of utility and the appropriateness of this exercise in the particular case.

Council limits itself to exhorting States to behave in a lawful way, while with the second is in an illegitimate manner.

1.14. Operational functions

In addition to regulatory activities, a certain number of activities that can be defined as operational are to be found in practice and law of international organizations. They generally consist in the performance of material conduct aimed at the pursuit of objectives which by their nature require a concrete execution in the international social reality or the intervention within individual national communities, sometimes even replacing the territorial State. These activities take on a variable content based on the statutory purpose that the institution intends to pursue. International organizations with technical or political competence put in place material conduct aimed, for example, at protecting refugees from technical assistance in food maintenance of peace and international security up to territories' administration.

The object of this work is to divide the operational activities following an instrumental criterion with respect to profiles of international responsibility that will be addressed in the following chapters; so that due to the subjects involved in the implementation of these operations we would distinguish between: a) Activities carried out by the international organization using only its own resources;[174] b) activities for which the organization delegates the performance to third parties, private individuals or other legal entities, particularly states or other international organizations; c) activities carried out by the organization in competition with other subjects.

To the first category are ascribable the operations that the

[174]ICJ with the Affaire des pêcheries case decided on 18 December 1951, in ICJ Reports, 1951, pag. 116, the ICJ has assessed the international lawfulness of the institution by Norway of a fishing zone off the coast, reserved for the citizens of that Scandinavian country but which the United Kingdom considered instead open to the exploitation of fishing vessels of any nationality. The ICJ decided the dispute in favour of Norway so that it had no way to take into consideration the request for repair by the United Kingdom; but once its rights have been recognized, it does not appear that the Oslo government has insisted on repeating his request for reparation, defined by his own representatives, as hypothetical and as an extremely novel one (ICJ, Mèmoires, op. cit., p. 722). In the same orientation is the Fisheries case jurisdiction (United Kingdom v. Iceland), merits, judgment, ICJ Reports 1974, p. 3. Fisheries jurisdiction (Federal Republic of Germany v. Iceland), merits, judgments, ICJ Reports, 1974, p. 175, "(...) Or with fishing vessels registered in the Federal Republic of Germany or with their fishing operations by threat or use of force are unlawful under international law, and that Iceland is under an obligation to make compensation (...)" (par. 144). A. ZIMMERMANN, C.J. TAMS, K. OELLERS-FRAHAM, The Statute of the International Court of Justice. A commentary, op. cit.

institution carries out through its own institutional apparatus using its organs and agents that is respectively "any person or entity which has that status in accordance with the rules of the organization" and "an official or other person or entity, other than an organ, which is charged by the organization to carrying out or helping to do this, one of its functions, and thus through whom organization's acts."[175] Consider that the notion of organ of the organization must be understood here as such as to include also the subsidiary one and those that have been the object of a loan to an organization by one or more States.

The second category concerns the operational activities for which the entity has decided to delegate the execution to Member States or third parties. According to a common approach,[176] at least two groups of activities of the type considered can be identified. The former includes the so-called outsourcing phenomena which are essentially contractual in nature, to which the international organization operates "or perform specific tasks, and/or provide related services, based on specified terms and conditions."[177] Although initially limited only to non-essential services (for example the provision of interpreters), irrelevant from an external point of view to the entity, the outsourcing has gradually extended also to peace-keeping operations,[178] initially with regard to purely technical and instrumental aspects but to status inherent also to the exercise of certain police activities, entrusted to private companies "afin d'obvier aux rèticenses des Etats censès lui fournir des continents."[179] This group also includes contracts concluded by the UN in the context of territorial administrations such as health or food. In the same way we can mention the contracts concluded by the World Bank in the context of the fight against corruption.[180] It is hardly necessary to point out that similar negotiating figures could give rise to some questions those the identification of the applicable law. There is no doubt that, at least in principle, private conduct would be attributable to the delegating

---

[175]Art. 2, c) and d) DARIO.

[176]P. F. LAVAL, Les activitès opèrationnelles, du conseil à l'administration international du territoire, in E. LAGRANGE, J.M. SOREL, Droit des organizations internationales, op. cit., pp. 790ss.

[177]Joint Inspection Unit. The challenge of outsourcinf for the United Nation systems, JIU/REP/9774, 1997, p. 1, par. 2.

[178]D. MEYER, Les contrats de fourniture de biens et services dans le cadre des opèrations de maintien de la paix, in Annuaire Français de Droit International, 42, 1996, pp. 79ss.

[179]P. JACOB, La mise en oeuvre des normes et opèratons de l'organization internationale, in E. LAGRANDE, J.M. SOREL, Droit des organizations internationales, op. cit., pp. 884ss.

[180]L. BOISSON DE CHAZOURNES, E. FROMAGEAU, Le mècanisme de sanction de la Banque mondiale contre la fraude et la corruption. Le droit administratif global comme outil d'èlaboration et de consolidation d'une procèdure, in C. BORIES, Un droit administratif global?, A global administrative law? ed. Pedone, Paris, 2012, pp. 262ss.

organization in terms of international responsibility.[181]

The second group of delegated activities involves only subjects of international law. The most significant example is undoubtedly the operations aimed at maintaining peace and involving the use of armed force carried out by Member States, subject to Security Council's authorization.

In some circumstances the organization acts in the international social reality in competition with third parties. These activities can also be divided into two sub-categories. On the one hand operations and international organization are carried out in collaboration with private subjects, on the other those performed jointly with States and/or with other international organizations. The first aspect is the collaboration between UN agencies responsible for humanitarian assistance and some non-governmental organizations.[182] In such hypotheses a private public hybridization is recorded in functions carried out by the international organizations. This is part of the framework of the Code for global public-private partnership, a concept which means more or less institutionalized forms of cooperation that involve subjects of international and private order on an equal footing in pursuit of public interest ends through privatistic management tools and techniques. Much more relevant, having regard to the subject of this study, is the second of the two sub-categories mentioned, namely that which is realized when an international organization carries out together with other subjects of the international order certain activities preordained to the pursuit of objectives which normally they are of general interest to the international community. The territorial administration of Kosovo established by the UN Security Council can be mentioned with the Resolution 1244 of 10 June 1999[183]

---

[181]P. JACOB, La mise en oeuvre des normes et opèrations de l'organization internationale, in E. LAGRANDE, J.M. SOREL, Droit des organizations internationales, op. cit., pp. 886ss.

[182]J. CROWE, K. WESTON-SCHEUBEL, Principles of international humanitarian law, op. cit.,

[183]A. SCHWABACH, Yugoslavia v. NATO, Security Council Resolution 1244 and the law of humanitarian intervention, in Syracuse Journal of International Law and Commerce, 27 (1), 2000, pp. 92ss. W. MOORMAN, Humanitarian intervention and international law in the case of Kosovo, in New England Law Review, 37, 2002-2003, pp. 776ss. D.H. ALLIN, Unintended consequences. Managing Kosovo independence, in What status for Kosovo?, Chaillot paper, Institute for Security Studies of WEU, October 2001. W.H. LUERS, Choosing engagement. Uniting the U.N with U.S interests, in Foreign Affairs, 79, 2000. S.H. BARNES, The contribution of democracy to rebuilding post-conflict societies, in American Journal of International Law, 95 (1), 2000, pp. 1ss. W.S. BETTS, N. CARLSON, G. GISVOLD, The post-conflict transitional administration of Kosovo and the lessons-learned in efforts to establish a judiciary and rule of law, in Michigan Journal of International Law, 22, 2001. M.G. BRAND, Institution-building and human rights

and Kosovo independence.[184] This administration was based on two pillars.

---

protection in Kosovo in the light of UNMIK legislation, in Nordic Journal of International Law, 70, 2001. J.R. CROOK, The fiftieth session of the UN Commission on human rights, in American Journal of International Law, 90 (1), 1994. M.S. ELLIS, The consequence of the Kosovo conflict on Southeastern Europe, in The International Lawyer, 34, 2000. A. GERSON, Peace building: The private sector's role, in American Journal of International Law, 95, 2001. O. KORHONEN, International governance in post-conflict situations, in Leiden Journal of International Law, 14 (3), 2001, pp. 3 ss. M.J. MATHESON, United Nations governance of post conflict societies, in American Journal of International Law, 95, 2001. N. MAZIAU, L. PECH, L'administration internationale de la Bosnie-Herzègovine: Un modale pour le Kosovo?, in Civitas Europa, 2000. W.M. REISMAN, Kosovo's antinomies, in American Journal of International Law, 93 (4), 1999. A. SCHNABEL, Kosovo and the challenge of humanitarian intervention: Selective indignation, collective action and international citizenship, United Nations University Press, Tokyo, 2000. C. STAHN, International territorial administration in the former Yugoslavia: Origins, development andchallenges ahead, in Zeitschrift für ausländisches öffentliches Rechts und Völkerrecht, 61, 2001. R. ZACKLIN, Beyond Kosovo: The United Nations and the humanitarian intervention, in Virginia Journal of International Law, 41, 2001. M.S. ELLIS, Y. DOUTRIAUX, T.W. RYBACK, Justice and diplomacy resolving contradictions in diplomatic practice and international humanitarian law, Cambridge University Press, Cambridge, 2018. B. GLAD, C. DOLAN, Striking first. The pre-emption and preventive war doctrines and the reshaping of US foreign policy, ed. Springer, Berlin, 2016. S. ALLEN, D. COSTELLOE, G. FITZMAURICE, The Oxford handbook of jurisdiction in international law, Oxford University Press, Oxford, 2019. M. ODELLO, R. PIOTROWIC, International military missions and international law, ed. Brill, Bruxelles, 2011, pp. 136ss.

[184]E. MILANO, The Security Council and territorial sovereignty: The Case of Kosovo, in International Community Law Review, 12, 2010, pp. 172ss, for our analysis we are particularly interested in the position of ICJ through the advisory opinion of 22 July 2010, Conformitè au droit international de la dıclaration unilatırale d'indıpendance relative au Kosovo. See also: the declaration of judge Tomka (par. 2 ss.); the separate opinions of judges Keith (par. 5 ss.) and Sepΰlveda-Amor (par. 2 ss.);the dissenting opinions of judges Bennouna (spec. par. 13 ff.), Koroma (par. 2 ss.) and Skotnikov (par. 1 ss.). The ICJ is therefore back on the interpretation of relations between art. 12 and 96, an issue that had already been addressed in the previous consultative opinion on the construction of the wall in the occupied Palestinian territory. On that occasion, it had stated that a request for an opinion does not constitute a recommendation of the General Assembly on a dispute or a situation (i.e. an act strictly covered by the limit laid down in article 12). The ICJ, however, had long paused to demonstrate how in practice the scope of art. 12 had gradually been scaled down, given the tendency shown by the Council and the Assembly to deal with the same issues in parallel, albeit with regard to different profiles. This practice (which was also carried out in the management of the construction of the wall even before the request for an opinion) was to be considered, in the opinion of the Hague judges, fully compatible with the rule indicated. Based on these reflections, it was felt that the position taken by ICJ in that forum about the irrelevance of art. 12 for the purpose of ascertaining its advisory competence was not applicable mutatis mutandis to the case of the declaration of independence of Kosovo, but only concerned the hypothesis in which, before the adoption of the request for an opinion, the General Assembly had already dealt with, in parallel with

One of a civil nature, consisting of the UNMIK subsidiary UN body, the other of a military nature constituted by the KFOR mission authorized with the same Resolution by the Security Council but established directly and at least by one point view of NATO. UN's activity in East Timor at the end of the 1990s could also fall within this framework with Resolution 1264 of 15 September 1999, the Security Council authorized: "(..,.) The establishment of a multinational force under a unified command structure (INTERFET)" with the task among others to support the activity that was carried out in this period by the UN through UNAMET (United Nations Mission in East Timor).[185]

---

the Security Council, of the question submitted to the ICJ (a situation not evidently found in the present case, given that, as stated above, the definition of the final political status of Kosovo did not appear on the agenda of the General Assembly). The objection is linked to a misinterpretation of the reasoning developed by ICJ in the advisory opinion on the construction of the wall. The further arguments advanced regarding the interpretation of art. 12 concerned in fact the real function of the provision, and which in fact establishes, for the situation of the Kosovo, the return to the initial unilateralism of the 1999 humanitarian intervention, ultimately marking the failure of the attempt at multilateral and collective management launched, not without contradictions, with Resolution 1244 (1999).

[185]O. ENGDAHL, Multinational peace operations forces involved in armed conflict: Who are the parties?, in K.M. LARSEN, C. GULDAHL COOPER, G. NYSTUEN, Searching for a "principle of humanity" in international humanitarian law, Cambridge University Press, Cambridge, 2013, pp. 256ss. P.M. OLSON, A NATO perspective on applicability and application of international humanitarian law to multinational forces, in International Review of Red Cross, 95, 2013, pp. 654ss.

CHAPTER 2

Complicity of States in the offense of international organizations: Regulatory framework

2.1. Introduction

The case of States' complicity of in the illicit fact of general organization examined by the party before this work. The 2011 project codifies this standard in art. 58 par. 1 perfectly reproducing the provisions of art. 16 ARSIWA and par. 2 includes a safeguard clause. The normative analysis carried out in the first part must be considered valid also in relation to the situation that we are going to investigate further with particular reference to case elements and causal link that links the incident to the main crime. The material element will be determined according to the circumstances by a behaviour that may be per se lawful or unlawful and in this latter hypothesis commissive or omissive. Similarly, the subjective element will have to be reconstructed case by case with the specification that also in this hypothesis some presumptions will operate in order to know the circumstances of the main fact.

The object of this understanding is the analysis of some specific profiles of state complicity in the offense of international organizations in addition to those illustrated in the first part. These peculiarities exclusively concern the hypothesis included in the field of art. 58, in which the accomplice State is a member of the organization responsible for the main crime. This is the condition set by lett. b) of art. 58, par. 1 for which is required that the author of the accessory event be bound by the same primary obligation violated by the international organization receiving assistance. Secondly, we will examine the complicity of States in the violation by the body of obligations that protect essential legal assets of the international community as a whole.

2.2. States' complicity in the violation of international organizations contractual obligations of which they are members

The considerations set out in Chapter 2 should be applied to exclude the possibility that the customary norm on matters of complicity suffers the condition formulated by ILC within the codifying provisions of the same rule. Even if its adherence to general international law is admitted, the requirement in question would not preclude the configurability of the case under consideration in the hypothesis in which a State facilitates the organization of which is a member in breach of a contract agreement obligation, and independently from the organization itself.

The condition sub lett. b) of art. 58, par. 1 DARIO could indeed be read through a more flexible hermeneutic criterion than the one used with regard to the analogous disposition of ARSIWAs that takes into account the nature of functional entities and their relationship with Member States. For this reason it could be argued that the treaties in burn fall within those "obligations opposable to the assisting" State[186] with respect to which, according to ILC, the scope of the rule on complicity should be limited. In our opinion the position of States with respect to the treaties concluded by the organization of which they are members cannot be qualified in terms of total extraneousness. The following considerations apply.

The problem, which is by no means new, has been the subject of attention in various locations. The work carried out by the Institut de Droit International deserves to be mentioned, which in 1973 was under the direction of R.J. Dupuy of the question of "application des règles du droit international gènèral des traitès aux accord internatonaux conclus par les organizations internationales."[187] According to rapporteur's opinion the agreements concluded by the international organizations and among them those that possess "une compètence de dècision obligatoire" cannot be considered as res inter alios acta by the Member States providing that such agreements are concluded by the institution within the limits of one's material competence.[188] Therefore the initial resolution provision provided in art. 10, which "un accord conclu lègalement par une organization international engage juridiquement tous ses membre."[189] The wording of this article has been considered incompatible with the general

---

[186]J. CRAWFORD, Second report on state responsibility, op. cit., pp. 50ss, par. 183.

[187]In Annuaire de l'Institut de Droit International, vol. 55, p. 214ss.

[188]H.J. GEISER, Les effets des accords conclus par les oganisations internationales, ed. PeterLang, Berne, Las Vegas, 1977, pp. 140ss.

[189]In Annuaire de l'Institut de Droit International, vol. 55, p. 316.

principles of treaty law that prevent Member States from being bound by agreements concluded by the organization of which they are members since it acts internationally as an independent subject with respect to them. For these reasons, art. V of the Resolution adopted at the Rome session establishes that the agreements concluded by an international organization do not entail obligations on the part of Member States with the specification that this "ne prèjuge pas les obligations qui peuvent rèsulter d'un tel accord pour les Etats membres soit des règles pertinentes de l'orgnisation, soit d'une norme de droit international gènèral."[190]

The topic was also partially discussed in ILC during the drafting of the treaty law agreement between States and international organizations and between international organizations (VCLT II). The ILC had proposed an article (art. 36 bis) according to which three conditions had to be met in order for a treaty concluded by an organization to create rights and obligations for its Member States: Consent from the parties to the agreement by all members of the organization. Such consent was brought to the attention of the other party.[191] The provision was known to originate from the sixth report that the speaker Reuter presented to ILC in 1977. It is based on the fundamental consideration that the principle pacta tertiis nec nocent nec prosunt is essentially founded on "the sovereignty and independence of States."[192] He believed that the characteristics of functional bodies other than those of States would have imposed greater flexibility in the application of the same principle to the treaties concluded by the functional bodies.[193] According to this approach the VCLT of 1969 had been modeled on sovereign subjects the new codifying instrument should have regulated the subject of treaties concluded by functional institutions. Precisely the search for greater flexibility led the speaker to question himself on the possibility of identifying "a single situation intermèdiaire entre le statut de partie et celui de tiers."[194] The States

---

[190] J. SALMON, Quelques des lacunes en droit, op. cit., pp. 338ss.

[191] Draft articles on the law of the treaties between states and international organizations or between international organizations with commentaries, in Yearbook of International Law Commission, 1982, vol. II, part 2, p. 17ss, p. 43.

[192] Report of the International Law Commission on the work of its Eighteenth session, 4 May-19 July 1966, Official records of the General Assembly, Twenty first session, Supplement n. 9 (A/6309/Rev.1), Doc. A/CN.4/191, in Yearbook of International Law Commission, vol. II, p. 177, p. 226.

[193] P. REUTER, Sixième rapport sur la question des traitès conclus entre États et organizations internationales ou entre deux ou plusiers organizations internationales, op. cit., p. 129, par. 10, which is affirmed that: "En effet, telle applicaton ou telle consèquencce qui ne tiendrait qu'au dèsir de sauvegarder la souverainetè et l'indèpendance des États pourrait ne pasêtre nècessaire pour le cas des organizations internationales."

[194] P. REUTER, Sixième rapport sur la question des traitès conclus entre États et organizations internationales ou entre deux ou plusiers organizations internationales, op.

participating in the diplomatic Conference held in Vienna in 1986 decided not to include this provision in the final text of the Convention, preferring to leave the question substantially unresolved. Art. 74, par. 2 establishes that the provisions of the Convention do not prejudice any issue that could arise regarding a treaty regarding international organization's responsibility. The following par. 3 also leaves unresolved the question that could arise regarding the determination of obligations and rights of an international organization's Member States towards a treaty to which that organization is a party.

The question was debated in doctrine[195] and resolved at DARIO in art. 62 with regard to the much broader problem of the eventual Member States responsibility deriving from the only bond of membership, that is

---

cit., p. 131-132, par. 19.

[195]J.P. RITTER, La protection diplomatique à l'ègard d'une organization internationale, op. cit., pp. 444ss. I. PERNICE, Die Haftung internationaler Organizationen und ihrer Mitarbeiter-dargetellt am "Fall" des internationalen Zinnrates, in Archiv des Völkerrechts, 26, 1988, pp. 419ss. C. AMERASNIGHE, Liability to third parties of member states of international organizations: Practice, principle and judicial precedente, in American Journal of International Law, 85, 1991, pp. 273ss. M. HARTWIG, Die Haftung der Mitgliedstaaten für internationale Organizationen, ed. Springer, Berlin, 1993, pp. 290ss. R. HIGGINS, Problems and process. International law and how we use it, in Oxford University Press, Oxford, 1994, pp. 47ss. P. KLEIN, La responsabilitè des organizations internationales dans les ordres juridiques interne set droits de gens, op. cit., pp. 516ss. In the opinion of another part of the doctrine, the non-existence of a rule of general international law of this type does not necessarily translate into the exclusive responsibility of functional bodies. On the one hand, the tendency of the international community to do not completely exempt States from liability for offenses committed by the entity. In this spirit see: M. HIRSCH, The responsibility of international organizations toward third parties. Some basic principles, Martinus Nijhoff Publishers, Dordrecht, Boston, London, 1995, pp. 102ss. On the other hand, it would be erroneously wrong to infer from the personality of the organizations the exclusive responsibility of the same. W. WENGLER, Völkerrecht, op. cit., pp. 178ss, given that they are derived entities and not originating from the international element. Although is added in the internal law lacks a rule similar to that which in the internal legal systems allows the constitution of a limited liability company, it can be argued that in principle there is a subsidiary liability to the Member States of the organization. H.T. ADAM, Les organismes internationaux spècialisès, LGDJ, Paris, 1965, pp. 130ss. In the same spirit of orientation see also: W. MENG, Internationale Organizationen im Völkerrechtichen Deliktsrecht, op. cit., 325ss. H.G. SCHERMERS, International institutional law, ed. Brill, Leiden, 1980, pp. 780ss. I. BROWNLIE, The responsibility of states of the acts of international organizations, in M. RAGAZZI, Responsibility of international organizations. Essays in memory of Sir Ian Brownlie, op. cit., pp. 362ss. C. TOMUSCHAT, The international responsibility of the European Union, in E. CANNIZZARO, The European Union as an actor in international relations, Wolters Kluwer, Deventer, 2002, p. 178ss. H. VAN HOUTTE, International law and community treaty-making, in Northwestern Journal of International Law & Business, 3, 1981, pp. 633ss.

to say regardless of any form of competition of the States themselves in the offense of the functional entity. For the purposes of our investigation limited to the hypothesis whose Member State helps or assists the institution in the non-fulfilment of a conventional obligation of the latter, is sufficient to observe that the problem of the relative efficacy of the treaties sets itself the very peculiar terms where it comes into the relation between functional body and Member States is relevant. It is undeniable that the latter cannot be considered part of the agreement concluded by the organization with third parties. Nevertheless it does not seem that their legal position can be qualified in terms of absolute extraneousness with respect to the obligatory relationship regulated by such a treaty. The contrary opinion would result from a premise founded on a radical conception of the personality of international organizations, given that "à coup sûr, les Etats membres ne sont pas des tiers par rapport aux accord à sa charte constitutive."[196] In other words, the agreement concluded by an international organization cannot qualify as res inter alios acta compared to Member States. The membership relationship cannot "se dèsintèresser des accords que l'organization conclut et qui peuvent avoir pur eux des consèquences diverses, d'ordre financier, notamment."[197] It seems significant that this consideration is also shared by that part of the doctrine which denies the configurability of a subsidiary responsibility of Member States for the unlawful act of the organization. The position taken on this point by R. Higins, rapporteur of the Institut de Droit International on the responsibility of international organizations is interesting. With specific reference to the agreements concluded by the international organizations, the rapporteur notes that: "While they are not parties to such treaties, they are not parties to the sense that are engaged in the implementation of such treaties."[198] Among these acts are certainly in our opinion those consisting in facilitating the breach of the treaty by the entity.

It does not seem entirely unreasonable to assume that the treaty

[196] P. REUTER, Premier rapport sur la question des traitès conclus entre États et organizations internationales ou entre deux ou plusieurs organization internationales, op. cit., pp. 375ss.

[197] The doctrinal orientation in support of the exclusive responsibility of the organization was also accepted by the Institut de Droit International which adopted during the Lisbon session of 1995 a Resolution on which: There is no general rule of international law whereby Member States are, due solely to their membership, liable, concurrently or subsidiarily, for the obligations of an international organizations of which they are members," (Annuaire de l'Institut de Droit International, vol. 66, 1966, p. 445). The final report of Committee accountability of international organizations of International Law Association arrives at a substantially similar solution, ILA, Berlin Conference (2004), Accountability of international organizations, Final report, pp. 26ss.

[198] In Annuaire de l'Institut de Droit International, vol. 66, 1995, p. 284.

concluded by the organization is capable of producing the consequences for the Member States in terms of guarantees of a correct execution of the conventional obligation.[199] In this regard, some considerations apply to the order of non-inclusion of art. 36 bis in the final text of the Vienna Convention of 1986.[200] The provision proposed by the rapporteur Reuter that for the placement within the Convention should have been an exception if not a clarification of the rule concerning the ineffectiveness of treaties towards third parties.[201] This had aroused a wide debate within the ILC,[202] which would have had no reason to exist if the impartiality of Member States had settled in traditional terms. Despite the wide debate during the diplomatic conference it was often pointed out that the Member States could not conceptually be placed in a position of third party with respect to the treaty itself, at least in a de jure condendo perspective. According to the opinion of the Dutch delegate Riphagen, Member States would be considered: "Third parties in law, but not in fact,"[203] while in the

---

[199]M. HARTWIG, Die Haftung der Mitgliedstaaten für internationale Organizationen, op. cit., pp. 298ss, which, while excluding that the members may consider a form of subsidiary liability due to the fact of the organization, points out that the guarantee of the correct execution of the contractual obligations assumed by the international organization can also be read in the light of the organization's funding obligations incumbent on the States that are part of it. The author takes care to specify that "Dies besagt nin nicht, daß die Zahlungsverpflictungen der Mitgliedstaaten gegenüber der Internationalen Organization unmittelbare Rechte von Dritten begründen (...) Die obige Argumentation führt nicht zu einer primären, gleichrangigen Verpflichtung der Mtgliedstaaten gegenüber der Organization erweisen sich vielmehr als Mittel der Deckung für die Verbindlichkeiten der Organization, aud das auch dritte Völkerrechtssubjekte zurückgreifen können" (pag. 299). In the same orientation see also: A. PELLET, International organizations are definitely not states. Cursory remarks on the ILC articles on responsibility of international organizations, in M. RAGAZZI, Responsibility of international organizations. Essays in memory of Sir Ian Brownlie, Martinus Nijhoff Publishers, Leiden, Boston, 2013, pp. 49ss. P. PALCHETTI, Exploring alternative routes: The obligation of members to enable the organization to make reparation, in M. RAGAZZI, Responsibility of international organizations. Essays in memory of Sir Ian Brownlie, Martinus Nijhoff Publishers, Leiden, Boston, 2013, pp. 303ss.

[200]C. BRÖLLMANN, The 1986 Vienna Convention on the law of treaties: The history of draft article 26 bis, in J. KLABBERS, R. LEFEBER, Essays on the law of treaties. A collection of essays in honour of Bert Vierdag, ed. Brill, The Hague, 1998, pp. 122ss.

[201]P. DAILLER, Article 74 (Convention de Vienne de 1986), in O. CORTEN, P. KLEIN, Les Conventions de Vienne sur le droit des traitès. Commentaire article par article, ed. Bruylant, Bruxelles, 2006, pp. 2634ss.

[202]As stated in the commentary to the draft articles on the law of treaties between States and international organizations: "Article 36 bis is unquestionably the one that has aroused most comment, controversy and difficulty, both in and outside the Commission" (Draft articles on the law of treaties between States and international organizations or between international organizations with commentaries, op. cit., p. 43).

[203]UN Conference on the law of treaties between States an international organizations or between international organizations, Vienna, 18 February-21 March 1986, Official records,

opinion of the UN delegate Szasz: "It would be most desirable if, in the situation contemplated in article 36 bis, Member States of international organizations designed to be considered third parties to a treaty."[204] It should be noted, however, that the failure to include art. 36 bis in the final text of the 1986 Convention did not translate at all into the unconditional adherence to the thesis of the extraneousness of Member States with respect to the contract agreement concluded by the organization when, rather in a safeguard clause art. 74, par. 3 which does not exclude the emergence in the aforesaid States of any rights and obligations "under a treaty to which organization is a party."[205]

Precisely a comprehensive consideration of the aforementioned provision has led the most careful doctrine to call into question the third party claim regarding the execution of conventional obligations concluded by the organizations to which they are members. The inclusion or art. 74, par. 3 of the definitive text of the Convention constitutes an argument in itself sufficient to exclude in the hypotheses under examination, the applicability of the norms of the Vienna Convention in the hypotheses under examination. The applicability of the norms of the Vienna Convention relating to the efficacy of treaties towards third States (articles 34-36.)[206] Moreover, art. 74 was introduced by the plenary Committee at the diplomatic Conference on the initiative of three international

---

summary of the plenary meetings and of the meetings of the Committee of the whole, vol. I, p. 141.

[204]UN Conference on the law of treaties between States and international organizations or between international organizations, op. cit., p. 164.

[205]P. DAILLER, Article 74 (Convention de Vienne de 1986), in O. CORTEN, P. KLEIN, Les Conventions de Vienne sur le droit des traitès. Commentaire article par article, ed. Bruylant, Bruxelles, 2006, pp. 2636ss, for which par. 74, eliminates the risk of interpreting the suppression of art. 36 bis or in the sense of having to consider "systèmatiquement" the Member States of an international organization as third parties with respect to the treaty concluded by it. In our opinion, substantially similar considerations apply to the debate that took place during Rome's session of the Institut de Droit International. The failure to approve art. 10 of the Resolution proposed by the rapporteur Dupuy, led the Institute to adopt a solution that was certainly more "prudent" but at the same time open, not excluding that general international law more accurately governed the effects agreed upon by the organizations at random with their Member States.

[206]PH. MANIN, La Convention de Vienne entre Etats et organizations internationales ou entre organizations internationales, in Annuaire Français de Droit International, 32 (1), 1986, pp. 454ss. R. HEUSA VINAIXA, Algunas consideraciones sobre el Convenio de Viena de 1986 sobre Tratados celebrados entre Estados y organizaciones internaconales o entre organizaciones internacionales, in Revista Española de Derecho Internacional, 41, 1989, pp. 65ss. G. GAJA, A "new" Vienna Convention on treaties between states an international organizations: A critical commentary, in British Yearbook of International Law, 58, 1987, pp. 264, there is some incongruity in considering the Member States totally as "third States" when often the international organization only acts under the latters direct control.

organizations of a universal character and above all holders of important capacities in the panorama of functional bodies, namely the International Monetary Fund, United Nations and International Labour Organization.[207] In the perspective of these organizations the project of art. 36 bis gives "special emphasis on international organizations because it touched on the vast subject of relationships between organizations and Member States."[208] The failure to include the provision cited in the definitive text of the agreement has therefore led IMF, ILO, UN to propose an intermediate solution which was then merged into art. 74, par. 3 which did not exclude expressis verbis the emergence of certain obligations of Member States of international organizations. In the same venue, the then European economic community expressed a significant orientation, believing that: "The legal fiction that an international organization is, as such, separate and distinct from its Member States cannot be carried to the extreme validly concluded by the organization to which they belong. Such attitude could actually be interpreted as a philosophical approach based upon the concept that an international organization constitutes an independent sovereign entity, possessing original powers, just like the national States."[209] It is in this perspective that some data deriving from international practice must be framed. During the oral phase of the Fisheries jurisdiction (Spain v. Canada) case,[210] Spain stated before the ICJ: "Nous ne prètendons pas invoquer la qualitè d'Etat tiers de l'Espagne par rapport à l'accord entre le Canada et la Communautè (res inter alios acta) pour faire la istinction entre les deux diffèrendes. En tant qu'Etat membre de la communautè europèenne, l'Espagne a suivi la nègociation de l'accord et a votè favorablemente au sesin du conseil pour le signer et y consentir car elle croit fermement que la coopèration multilatèrale est la mèthode adèquate pour règler les graves problèemes de gestion et de onservation que posent les dènommès stocks chevauchant."[211]

207UN Conference on the law of treaties between states an international organizations or between international organizations, Vienna, 18 February-21 March 1986, op. cit., pp. 71, p. 78.

208 This is the opinion of the delegate of ILO during the 19th meeting of the plenary Committee at the diplomatic Conference. UN Conference on the law of treaties between States and international organizations or between international organizations, Vienna, 18 February-21 March 1986, op. cit., p. 142.

209Report of the International Law Commission on the work of its thirty-third session (4 May-24 July 1981) Annex II, Doc. A/36/10, Official records of the General Assembly, thirty-sixth session, supplement n. 10, p. 202.

210Fisheris jurisdiction (Spain v. Canada), jurisdiction of the Court, judgment, in ICJ Reports, 1998, pp. 432ss. A. ZIMMERMANN, C.J. TAMS, K. OELLERS-FRAHAM, The Statute of the International Court of Justice. A commentary, op. cit.

211A. REMIRO BROTONS, in Plaidoire Spanish of 9 June 1998 (Fisheries jurisdiction, verbatim records, p. 42, par. 9).

It seems reasonable to conclude that the requirement set by art. 58, par. 1 b) DARIO must be considered satisfied even in the case of assistance provided by a State to the violation of a treaty of which only the organization is a party. Moreover, this deduction applies regardless of the merely factual circumstance for which the Statute of the body authoring the main fact provide for clauses limiting the responsibility of Member States,[212] or on the contrary relating to the extension of the contractual obligations to the same States. The instituting act of an international organization like any other international treaty does not produce ultra part effects.[213] These provisions and in particular those which exclude any kind of responsibility of Member States of the organization are for third parties res inter alios acta.[214] Otherwise, the States that establish an international organization would be entitled to exclude their responsibility towards third parties regardless of the existence of a rule of general international law operating in this sense.[215]

---

[212]Articles of agreement of the international finance corporation, adopted a Washington on 25 May 1955 and emended on 27 June 2012, which in art. II (membership and capital), section 4 (limitation on liability) was established that "no member shall be liable, by reason of its membership, for obligations of the corporation (…)."

[213]G. GAJA, Fourth report on responsibility of international organization, op. cit., pp. 122, par. 87.

[214]P.C. SZASZ, The law and practices of the International Agency for Atomic Energy, Wien, 1970, pp. 989ss. M. HARTWIG, Die Haftung der Mitgliedstaaten für internationale Organizationen, op. cit., pp. 158ss.

[215]M. HIRSCH, The responsibility of international organizations toward third parties. Some basic principles, op. cit., pp. 104ss, on the contrary: H.G. SCHERMERS, Liability of international organizations, in Leiden Journal of International Law, 1, 1988, pp. 6ss. These observations also apply to the statutory provisions which extend the particular obligations contracted by the Institution to the Member States. Consider for example art. 216, par. 2 TFEU on the basis of affirming the agreements concluded by the Union bind its institutions and Member States. The letter of this rule led part of the doctrine especially in the past to affirm that EU Member States should be held responsible on the international level in the hypothesis of violation of an agreement concluded by the Union. See in argument: P. PESCATORE, Les relations extèrieurs des Communautès europèennes, in Recueil des cours, ed. Brill, Bruxelles, 1961, pp. 134ss. In the same spirit of orientation see also: M.J. HAHN, G. SCHUSTER, Le droit des Etats membres de se prèvaloir en justice d'un accord liant la Communqutè: l'invocabilitè du GATT dans l'affaire Rèpublique fèdèrale d'Allemagne contre Conseil de l'Unione europèenne, in Revue Gènèrale de Droit International Public, 99, 1995, pp. 378ss. The widely prevailing opinion attributes to the law in question a scope essentially internal to the Community structure simply by compiling the obligation of the Member States to respect the agreements concluded by the Union of the same obligations of the community. This obligation should be read in the light of the principle of loyal cooperation enshrined in art. 4, par. 3 of the TEU. See in argument: P. LACHMANN, The international legal personality of the European Communities: Capacity and competence, in Leiden Journal of International Law, 3, 1984, pp. 12ss. P. COUVREUR, Reflexions sur la portèe et les effets de l'engagement conentionnel externe

If the proposed evaluations are not groundless, it must be assumed that art. 58 DARIO applies a fortiori also to the complicity of States in the non-fulfilment by the organization of an obligation deriving from an agreement. That is, an agreement concluded by international organizations together with their Member States,[216] to nothing revealing the distinction that is also important for other profiles of responsibility between mixed agreements containing indications about the distribution of obligations between organization and Member States,[217] and agreements that do not bear no such clause.[218] In both cases the complicit State of the breach would be bound to the treaty assumed as a parameter of evaluation of the main crime, a circumstance that art. 58, par. 1 b) assumes a sufficient condition of operation of the standard.

2.3. Complicity of States in unlawful erga omnes of international organizations of which they are members

The general rule on the matter of complicity also operates with regard to the competition in the violation of mandatory rules establishing

---

de la CEE, in Melanges Tryol Serra, Madrid, 1986, pp. 330ss. A. CONZE, Die völkerrechtliche Haftung der Europäischen Gemeinschaft, ed. Nomos, Baden-Baden, 1987, pp. 68ss. H. KRÜCK, Völkerrechtliche Verträge im Recht der Europäischen Gemeinschaften, ed. Springer, Berlin, 1977, pp. 126ss. A. GESLIN, Rèflexions sur la repartition de la responsabilitè entre l'organization internationale et ses États membres, in Revue Gènèrale de Droit International Public, 109, 2005, pp. 570ss. E. NEFRAMI, Les accords mixtes de la Communautè Europèenne aspects communautaires et internationaux, ed. Bruylant, Bruxelles, 2007, pp. 562ss. M. HARTWIG, Die Haftung der Mitgliedstaaten für internationale Organizationen, op. cit. pp. 163ss. F. LUSA BORDIN, The analogy between states and international organizations, op. cit.

[216] E. NEFRAMI, Les accords mixtes de la Communautè Europèenne aspects communautaires et internationaux, op. cit.

[217]Consider the solution adopted by Annex IX to the UN Convention on the Law of the Sea which is known to be open to accession by international organizations pursuant to art. 305, par. 1, lett. f) on the basis of the combined provisions of articles 5 and 6 of this conventional instrument at the time of the signing or accession an international organization must indicate by means of a declaration the matters governed by the agreement with respect to which it has received the relative competences from the Member States; the latter are required to deposit a declaration of similar content.

[218] For example, the interregional framework agreement between the European community and the MERCOSUR signed in Madrid on 15 December 1995, which establishes in art. 32 the southern municipality which on one side means the community or its Member States or the community and its Member States (...) and on the other MERCOSUR or its Member States according to the treaty establishing the southern municipality. For further details see: H. MCCOUBREY, J. MORRIS, Regional peacekeeping in the post-cold war era, Kluwer Law International, The Hague, London, Boston, 2000, pp. 228ss.

obligations erga omnes. Confining ourselves to the hypothesis in which the accomplice State is a member of the organization responsible for the main fact, it seems to us that in some cases the material element of the case may be supplemented by a specific omissive fact. In fact, in the international legal order, there are some rules that mainly concern environmental protection, which require States to monitor potentially illegal or harmful activities carried out by the organizations to which they belong. In our opinion, if the omission were characterized by the subjective element and could facilitate the violation of regulations concerning environmental protection, it could in principle be a form of complicity within the meaning of art. 58 DARIO.

The material element in the hypothesis considered must be analyzed in the light of rules established for the environmental protection. We refer in particular to those regulatory regimes aimed at regulating international responsibility deriving from the exploitation of sea bottoms placed beyond state jurisdictions and the extra-atmospheric space in which the moon and other celestial bodies are to be understood.[219] The regime of responsibility for space law differs in some aspects from that of general international law. While in relation to the responsibility of the State for deeds of private individuals, according to the general principles the State responds only if it has failed to adopt the necessary measures to prevent the offense for the international law of space it responds regardless of the existence of an omission. Furthermore and always in derogation from the general principles the attribution of responsibility to the State is independent of the assumption of imputability constituted by the fault of the agent and does not know causes of exclusion with the exception of the guilt of the subject injured by setting up a hypothesis of objective liability in this sense. In this case the liability for wrongdoing depends on the content of the material rules applicable to the use of aerospace means including the "protests" of States in relation to the transit of space objects in the atmospheric space above their territory does not necessarily imply that they consider in any case lawful this transit.

In both cases mentioned above, the notion of common heritage of humanity understood as the "matèrialisation de l'intrerêt commun de l'humanitè dans des espaces, biens et être vivants dèterminès"[220] is

---

[219]L. CONDORELLI, L'imputation à l'Etat d'un fait internationalement illicite: solutions classiques et nouvelles tendances, op. cit., pp. 121ss.

[220]A.C. KISS, La notion de patrimoine commun de l'humanitè, in Recueil des cours, ed. Brill, Bruxelles, vol. 175, 1982, pp. 243ss. W. RIPHAGEN, The international concern for the environment as expressed in the concepts of the "common heritage of mankind" and of "shared natural resources," in M. BOTHE, Trends in environmental policy and law, Gland, Switzerland, 1980, pp. 343ss. R. WOLFRUM, The principle of the common heritage of mankind, Zeitschrift für ausländisches Recht und Völkerrecht, 53, 1983, pp. 314ss. A.

highlighted. It is well known that the soil and subsoil of the high seas give rise to a distinct area, the international area of sea-beds which, pursuant to art. 136 of the Montego Bay Convention constitutes "the common heritage of mankind."[221]

Similarly, the notion of common heritage is fully applied in the regulation of activities conducted by States and international organizations in the outer space and in celestial bodies.[222] The 1967 Treaty already contains a substantial reference to the notion under consideration where it establishes as a general principle that the exploitation and use of extra-atmospheric space "shall be the province of all mankind" (art. 1). It should be noted in this regard that the combined provisions of articles IV of 1967 Treaty and XXII of 1972 Convention induces to qualify the juridical regime of such spaces as common heritage of the humanity with the specification that according to part of the doctrine some norms of the 1967 Treaty among which art. IV would be included among the norms of jus cogens.[223] What has been found so far is expressly confirmed in art. 11 of the 1979 Treaty which regulates the activities of the moon on the basis of which: "The moon and its natural resources are the common heritage of mankind."

The set of rules aimed at the discipline and protection of the common heritage of humanity falls into the category of international norms capable of imposing on States obligations towards the international community itself. Moreover, the existence of erga omnes obligations in the field of environmental protection is confirmed by some normative data of no minor importance. First, the Charter of economic rights and duties of States which, in the context of Chapter III, provides for two provisions, articles 29-30 relative to the common responsibilities of States towards the international community among which a prominent role is attributed to the protection, preservation and enhancement of the environment for present and future generations. Secondly, it must be remembered that the draft

---

KISS, State responsibility and liability for nuclear damage, in Denver Journal of International Law and Policy, 35 (1), 2006, pp. 68ss. G. LAMMERS, New developments concerning international responsibility and liability for damage caused by environmental interferences, in The Hague Yearbook of International Law, 20, 2007, pp. 88ss.

[221] J. VOGLER, The global commons: Environmental and technological governance, Wiley, New York, 2000. R. O'KEEFE, World cultural heritage: Obligations to the international community as a whole?, in International and Comprative Law Quarterly, 53, 2004, pp. 190ss. V. VADI, Cultural heritage in international investment law and arbitration, Cambridge University Press, Cambridge, 2014, pp. 100ss. C. FORREST, International law and the protection of cultural heritage, ed. Routledge, London & New York, 2012, pp. 51ss.

[222] A.C. KISS, La notion de patrimoine commun de l'humanitè, op. cit., pp. 152ss.

[223] L. CONDORELLI, Z. MÉRIBOUTE, Some remarks on the state of international law concerning military activities in outer space, in Indian Yearbook of International Law, 6, 1975, pp. 17ss.

articles on state responsibility approved on first reading in 1996 included among the categories of international crimes also the serious violation of an international obligation of essential importance for the preservation and safeguard of human environment.

Among the due diligence obligations relating to environmental protection, it seems to us that a fundamental role is played by art. 139 of Convention of Montego Bay.[224] This provision regulates the responsibility of States with regard to the activities carried out in the international area of the seabed, in which the responsibility for pollution is also included. Paragraphs 2 and 3 of the law provide for States to supervise and for individuals or organizations activities of which they are members to be carried out in accordance with the rules set forth in part XI of the Convention. How was it detected[225] art. 139 imposes on states obligations. According to French formulation: "Il incombe aux Etats parties de veiller à ce que les activitès menèes dans la Zone (…) le soient conformèment à la prèsente partie." The international Court of law of the sea confirmed in an advisory capacity that art. 139 imposes on states parties the Convention of obligations of two diligence,[226] consisting in the preparation of "adequate means to exercise best possible efforts, to do the utmost, to obtain this result." Unlike the provision contained in par. 2,[227] the obligations provided by par. 3 instead incumbent as repeatedly emphasized exclusively on Member States of those international organizations that carry out such activities independently with respect to

224 S. VÖNEKY, A. HÖFELMEIER, Article 139, in A. PROELS, United Nations convention on the law of the sea. A commentary, C.H. Beck, Hart Publishing, München/Oxford, Oregon & Portland, 2017, pp. 968ss.

225 L. CONDORELLI, H. DIPLA, Solutions traditionnelles et nouvelles tendances en matière d'atttributon à l'État d'un fait internationalement illicite dans la convention de 1982 sur le droit de la mer, in A.A.V.V., Le droit international à l'heure de sa codificaton. Études à l'honneur de R. Ago, vol. III, ed. Giuffrè, Milano, 1987, pp. 66ss.

226 ITLOS, Responsibilities and obligations of states sponsoring persons and entities with respect to activities in the area. Request for advisory opinion submitted to the seabed disputes Chamber, case n. 17, 1st February 2011. This is an opinion given on the request of the Council of the international authority of the marine funds in order inter alia to the responsibility of the States Parties to the agreement for the activities carried out by non-state bodies in the area. It should be pointed out that apparently does not specifically concern the content of par. 3 of art. 139 based on the analysis of the article as a whole and the obligations contained in the first two paragraphs, relating to activities conducted by private individuals. Having said this, it seems reasonable to believe that according to an interpretation, both object and teleological, of the norm as established by the Chamber is also valid with reference to paragraph 3, whose placement appears in a particularly significant systematic perspective.

227 The par. 2 of art. 139 forms a form of joint liability for the international organization and its Member States limited to the hypotheses of damages arising from the activities they carry out jointly in the international seabed area.

said States. The responsibility of Member States for breach of the due diligence obligation governed by par. 3 does not absolve the organization of international liability deriving from the possible violation of obligations imposed on it by the strength of paragraphs 1 and 2 of art. 139 on the basis of which the provisions of part XI of the agreement governing the activities carried out in the international area of sea-beds are imposed on both categories of subjects expressly contemplated by the law, namely the States that are parties to the Convention and the international organizations of which they are members.[228]

Due diligence duties also seem to be found in the 1967 Treaty on space where is configured through the combined provisions of articles VI and XIII, the obligation of States to guarantee that the organization of which they are members fulfils the obligations provided by the treaty itself. This interpretation seems to be confirmed by the declaration of principles relating to the remote sensing of the earth from the extra-atmospheric space of 3 December 1986. According to art. XIV of treaty principle on space, each State has the obligation to ensure that all the remote-sensing

---

[228] The relationship between the conventional provisions of the type considered and the regime of liability regulated by general international law must be understood in the light of the combined provisions of articles 235, par. 1 and 304 of the Convention on the Law of the Sea. The first rule that is inscribed in part XII dedicated to the protection and preservation of the marine environment establishes that the responsibility of the States in this sector in which the convention governs a series of obligations both material and accessory (i.e. due diligence duties) is governed by general international law. This is a peculiar form of dynamic reference to customary law which requires the investigator to carry out an investigation not only to detect normative data on the subject but also to ensure coordination with the various evolutionary sectors of the law international, among which we believe the responsibility of the functional bodies. By virtue of art. 304 set out in the sixteenth part of the agreement between the general provisions, the rules therein laid down regarding the liability for damages "without prejudice to the application of existing rules and the development of other rules regarding responsibility and liability under international law." The law in question has aroused great interest on the part of the doctrine since it establishes the complementary nature of the norms of the Convention with respect to general international law. Art. 304 indicates that the purpose of the agreement is not to regulate an alternative liability regime with respect to the ordinary one, but a complementary regime aimed at a cumulative application of the law to the general regulations in the context of international tort. For further analysis see: N.L. HORBACH, P.H. BEKKER, State responsibility for injurious transboundary activity in retrospect, in Nordic International Law Review, 72, 2003, pp. 328ss. R. LEFEBER, Transboundary environmental interference and the origin of state liability, ed. Brill, The Hague, 1996. A.E. BOYLE, State responsibility and international liability for injurious consequences of acts not prohibited by international law. A necessary distinction?, in International and Comparative Law Quarterly, 39 (1), 1990. pp. 5ss. J.G. MERRILLS, International dispute settlement, Cambridge University Press, Cambridge, 1999. R. BRATSPIES, Transboundary harm in international law, Cambridge University Press, Cambridge, 2006.

activities carried out in the space are conducted in accordance with the rules of international law "irrespective of whether such activities are carried out (...) through international organizations to which such States are parties."[229] The position of obligations of the type considered by Member States of international organizations active in the field of space exploration probably originates from the circumstance for which these organizations are not entitled to adhere to the instruments stipulated to protect the extra-atmospheric space. The 1967 Treaty, for example, is open to the signing of States only according to what follows from the provision of art. XIV.

It seems that a rule of general international law has been formed which imposes on States the obligation to exercise due diligence so that the activities carried out by international organizations (or by private individuals) do not result harmful and are not carried out in violation of environmental standards. These, initially reconstructed with reference to the marine environment only, can be extended by analogy to the protection of the extra-atmospheric space and the environment considered as a whole. It operates according to the mechanism of art. 139, par. 3 of the Convention on the Law of the Sea, attributing to States in the hypotheses there are analyzing the duties/powers of control over the activities possibly carried out by the international organizations in the spaces considered. The violation of the general rule just outlined implies that the responsibility of States arises out of an omissive conduct, consisting in not having prepared the measures imposed by the necessary diligence[230] and in not having prevented the violation by the body of which they are members of obligations preordained to the environmental protection.

It does not seem entirely unreasonable to believe that the same rule operates with regard to the protection of legal assets of a similar nature to that examined up to now. We refer to the protection of fundamental human rights which is equally objective and payable by the international community as a whole. In other words, it can be argued that Member States of international organizations have the obligation to ensure that they do not commit fundamental human rights violations in the performance of their duties.

In the light of what was noted in previous paragraphs, it can be hypothesized that an omissive offense of the type considered could

---

[229]Declaration of principles relating to remote sensing of the earth from outer space, UN Doc. 41/65, 3th of December 1986.

[230]L. CONDORELLI, L'imputation à l'Etat d'un fait internationalement illicite: solutions classiques et nouvelles tendances, op. cit., pp. 140ss. F. ORREGO VICUÑA, Le règime d'exploration et d'exploitation, in R.J. DUPUY, D. VIGNES, Traitè du nouveau de la mer, ed. Economica, PaResolution Bruxelles, 1985, pp. 552ss.

integrate the material element of complicity, should it prove to be suitable for facilitating or significantly contributing to an infringement of erga omnes obligations by an international organization. It will be necessary for the accessory fact to be configured that Member States have a subjective attitude consisting at least in the awareness of circumstances in which the main fact attributable to the organization has occurred.

The effort to build a system of non-prohibitive primary norms regarding environmental damage seems to constitute more a work of progressive development of international than of codification of existing law. In general international law the dichotomy between illicit and non-illicit constitutes the rules and even if some conditional authorization rules were deemed to exist they appear to be the product of customs established with a long historical process. It was inevitable to include this matter (of environmental damage) in the historical/juridical ILC path as a product of flexible and non-prohibitive norms in primary rules, highlighting that such obligations, in order to be really effective, require a connection and a welding point on the responsibility which must constitute the ultimate guarantee of the whole system of the primary obligations of a parallel guarantee of each of these obligations. The obligation of reparation escapes the traditional framework in the responsibility for wrongdoing as a secondary obligation deriving from the violation of prohibitive rules on prevention and it can only then rely on the concept of risk liability. In our opinion the problem must be set in certain sectors of international law (environmental damage, from technological and industrial activities, cyber espionage,[231] from terrorist activities, and so on) there are real prohibitive

[231]The obligation to establish supervision aimed at knowing the evolution of events within cyberspace would have obvious critical profiles. The State, in fact, in order to fulfil it effectively, should exercise a pressing control of the communications and of the architecture of the national internet, going to configure a real surveillance mechanism on the subjects that access it. This solution appears to be in contrast with the provisions of the corpus of human rights that prescribe the protection of the right to privacy. As reiterated by the Human Rights Council, the normative relevance of the provisions aimed at protecting human rights must also be applied with reference to digital-computer relations (Resolution of 5 July 2012, UN Doc. A/HRC/17/27) it should be pointed out that a general application of the principle of due diligence cannot be excluded with reference to cyber events. According to international law, whenever the State exercises its territorial sovereignty, it will have to behave diligently in order to prevent and suppress unacceptable harmful consequences with reference to other States. Since the management of cyberspace is now considered by almost the unanimity of the international community as a manifestation of the sovereignty of the State over the territory, compliance with the principle of due diligence must be properly guaranteed by the States also in the cybernetic context, specifying the diligence in precise standards of conduct do not yet seem to have materialized in the formation of customary rules specifically applicable to the subject under consideration. The absence of a legislative corpus to realize the general obligation of

diligent conduct reduces the effective relevance of the principle under examination, which, although potentially able to guarantee the imposition of obligations on States aimed at reducing the danger deriving from the world computer-cybernetic. For further analysis see: M. ROSCINI, Cyber operations and use of force, Oxford University Press, Oxford, 2014, pp. 34ss. K. MACAK, Decoding article 8 of the International Law Commission's articles on state responsibility: Attribution of cyber operations by non-state actors, in Journal of Conflict & Security Law, 16, 2016, pp. 406. J.D. OHLIN, K. GOVERN, C. FINKELSTEIN (eds.), Cyber war, law and ethics for virtual conflicts, Oxford University Press, Oxford, 2015, pp. 130ss. K. MACAK, International law and practice, from cyber norms to cyber rules: Re-engaging states as law-makers, in Leiden Journal of International Law, 30, 2017, pp. 883ss, "(...) the absence of a cyber-specific system of rules of international law does not mean that there are no legal rules that would apply to cyber activities (...)." N. TSAGOURIAS, R. BUCHAN, International law and cyber space, ed. Edward Elgar Publishers, Cheltenham, 2015, pp. 66ss, "(...) the State can exercise its prescriptive and enforcement jurisdiction over cyberspace and cyber activities on the basis of nationality and territoriality (...)." S. HERZOG, Revisiting the Estonian cyber attacks: Digital threats and multinational responses, in Journal of Strategic Security, 4, 2011, pp. 52ss. R. BUCHAM, Cyber attacks: Unlawful uses of force or prohibited interventions?, in Journal of Conflict and Security Law, 17, 2012, pp. 214ss. T. RID, R. BUCHANAN, Attributing cyber attacks, in The Journal of Strategic Studies, 38, 2015, pp. 7ss. M. ROSCINI, Evidentiary issues in international disputes related to state responsibility for cyber operations, in Texas International Law Journal, 50, 2015. S. SHACKELFORD, State responsibility for cyber attacks: Competing standards for a growing problem, in Conference on Cyber Conflict Proceedings, 2010, "(...) given what has been demonstrated about the extreme technical difficulties of proving the identity of cyber attacks due to the nature of the Web's architecture, such a standard would in essence give a free pass to state sponsors of cyber attacks (…) without either new techniques such as the probabilistic tracing project (...) or very unsophisticated hackers, effective control would make state responsibility for cyber attacks virtually a non-starter (...)." C. ALLAN, Attribution issues in cyberspace, in Chicago-Kent Journal of International and Comparative Law, 14, 2013. T. PAYNE, Teaching old law new tricks: Applying and adapting state responsibility to cyber operations, in Lewis & Clark Law Review, 20, 2016, pp. 686ss. J.C. WOLTAG, Military cyber warfare: Cross-border computer network operations under international law, ed. Intersentia, London/Antwerp, 2014, pp. 274ss, "(...) the major problem in this regard has been shown to be the insufficient technical capacity to track and trace hostile computer network operations to their source systems. As a consequence the legal attributability of the operation is similarly inadequate (...)." M.N. SCHMITT, In defence of due diligence in cyber space, in Yale Journal Law Forum, 24, 2015, pp. 79ss, "(...) if the territorial State fails to terminate an ongoing non-state cyber operation mounted from its territory against another State, and doing so is practical and reasonable in the circumstances, then the territorial State commits an internationally wrongful act by failing to exercise its obligations under the principle (...)." E. JENSEN, State obligations in cyber operations, in Baltic Yearbook of International Law, 14, 2014. R. KOLB, Reflections on due diligence duties and cyberspace, in German Yearbook of International Law, 58, 2015, 114ss. A. BENDIECK, Due diligence in cyberspace, in Stiftung Wissenschaft und Politik German Institute for International and Security Affairs, ed. Palgrave Macmillan, London, 2016, pp. 12ss. R. BUCHAN, Cyberspace, non-state actors and the obligation to prevent transboundary harm, in Journal of Conflict & Security Law, 21, 2016, pp. 430ss. S.

norms of general international law that prohibit certain state behaviours. In the affirmative case it cannot be doubted that their violation always in the hypothesis of the existence of prohibitive norms will have to be verified if they impose limited obligations or not limited by the concept of diligence. In the first case the violation will result in liability for wrongdoing and fault. In the second one the violation will result in liability for tort and without fault (strict liability or absolute responsibility). In the presence of prohibitive regulations that prohibit certain state behaviours, we remain in the field of tort liability and the only problem is to establish the exact nature of state obligations and the precise form of tort liability.

In this case, the concept of risk liability (or without tort) does not come into play in our opinion. Instead, it can play a role when the lack of prohibitive norms in a certain sector is ascertained and at the same time it also occurs that according to international practice there is also a state liability. The concept of risk liability may become relevant, perhaps in a residual way, when is ascertained that prohibitive regulations exist but such as to impose only a duty of care to the State and at the same time also verify that it incurs responsibility despite having acted diligently. This approach favors an examination about the existence and content of the primary norms existing in a certain sector which are deduced from the praxis and States jurisprudence not only in the pathological hypothesis of their violation but also considering both the conceptual difference between certain dangerous activities and the conduct held by the State in relation to them and the conceptual difference between liability for wrongdoing.

Within this framework the first error is that of confusing between the lawfulness of a certain activity and state conduct held on the occasion of such activity. Once the lawfulness of technological, industrial and environmental activities has been established a priori, they always automatically consider state conduct to be lawful and consequently once the state responsibility has been established or ascertained, are induced to place it as a risk liability. Instead, it must be considered possible at least in hypothesis that the lawfulness of an activity undertaken in a State is accompanied by the unlawfulness of state conduct which does not prevent

---

SHACKLEFORD, S. RUSSELL, A. KUEHN, Unpacking the international law on cybersecurity due diligence: Lessons from the public and private sectors, in Chicago Journal of International Law, 16, 2016, pp. 8ss, "(...) the United States is more voluntary, Germany takes a more regulatory approach featuring a comprehensive cybersecurity policy that has long eluded U.S. policymakers, and China's approach encompasses broader economic and national security efforts (...)." E. JENSEN, E. TALBOT, Cyber sovereignty: The way ahead, in Texas International Law Journal, 50, 2015, pp. 278ss, "(...) as a matter of sovereignty, States have the right to develop their cyber capabilities according to their own desires and resources (...)." E. JENSEN, State obligations in cyber operations, op. cit., pp. 29ss.

certain harmful effects deriving from such activity. In this case the State violates with its conduct prohibitive rules of international law and incurs liability for tort but not for risk.

A second error is to believe that the distinction between liability for wrongdoing and without an offense corresponds to the distinction between liability for and responsibility without fault. Once affirmed or ascertained that the State is responsible for the damage caused even when is not at fault or has used due diligence to prevent it, they are induced to configure this responsibility as risk liability. At least at the conceptual level, it must be held that responsibility without illicit and that on the contrary is only one of the possible forms of liability for wrongdoing. The latter covers not only the due diligence obligations but also those not conditioned by the due diligence that we have defined as performance obligations. The possible existence of result obligations in a certain sector must not lead us to leave the sphere of liability for tort. It is certainly possible at least in hypothesis that in a particular subject there exist prohibitive norms of international law that impose on States an obligation of result. In this case, the State violating these rules will incur liability without fault but for tort. From this it follows that the investigation cannot be limited, in our opinion, to ascertaining that there is a liability of the State even though is not due to fault or lack of care. It must also extend to assessing the nature of the primary obligations in order to establish whether it is a fault-free responsibility or a liability.

To correctly frame the problem about the foundation and role of responsibility without illicit in general international law it is necessary to free oneself from the aforementioned conceptual errors and to shift the perspective from the general question on the configurability or otherwise the responsibility to the specific questions about existence or less of prohibitive norms of international law in certain well-defined sectors and about the exact nature of international obligations established by these rules.

In finis, also in the matter of liability from lawful activities ends up taking on a decisive and preliminary role in investigating the existence or otherwise of certain prohibitive primary norms and about the presence or absence of due diligence in the content of these rules, i.e. research based on conceptual assumptions of general character and from the executive point of view of the general principles of responsibility and formal categories of offenses, to favor instead the examination of the practice in relation to the various material sectors of state obligations in which it detects de facto the concept of diligence.

2.4. Concluding remarks

The case in point of the second part of this work presents a peculiarity to the generic complicity between subjects in the unlawful act, constituted by the membership report which links the accomplice State to the international organization responsible for the main fact. On the basis of this consideration we have examined two profiles with respect to which art. 58 DARIO takes on a specific importance within the framework of the rules on international responsibility. The first relates to the condition set by par. 1, lett. b) of this provision. Like the analogous provision contained in ARSIWA, the case of complicity is conditioned by the recipient in the complicity of obligation violated by the functional body. On this point we had already noted that in general terms this condition does not seem to us to correspond to the State of general international law. In this chapter we have added a further argument centered on the fact that the Member States of an international organization cannot be considered completely extraneous to the contractual obligations of the latter with third parties.

The second profile concerns the concurrence of States in violation by the body of obligations placed to protect the international community as a whole. It was noted that a set of rules of general international law requires States to ensure that institutions to which they belong do not commit violations of rules on environmental protection or legal assets of similar value. In our opinion, the violation of these supervisory obligations may give rise to complicity if the negligence of States under consideration is accompanied by the subjective element examined in Chapter II and is able to facilitate the harmful conduct of national body.

CHAPTER 3

Hypothesis of responsibility and reparation in disputes between individuals and States before the control bodies established by human rights treaties

3.1. Introduction

The attribution of the unlawful conduct to an organization determines, most of the times a gap of jurisdictional protection for the victims. The reparation against the individual may be denied, internally, by the recognition of organizations immunities before the national courts[232] and, on international level, by the absence of control mechanisms established by the human rights treaties. On the other hand, the internal systems of organizations, if existing, often prove inadequate. The attribution of states conduct allows the individual to access the existing jurisdictional control systems at an international level. This possibility has become in recent years far from being theoretical and the organisms seized by individuals have developed increasingly sophisticated solutions.

Taking UN as a reference, the scenarios that can come to the fore are essentially: The force actions established by the Organization and multinational operations under the joint aegis of several Organizations.[233]

The complexity of these contexts is due to the presence in the field of various subjects: The Organization that establishes or authorizes the operation, the State of sending the contingents that makes its organs available temporarily, and, finally, the State that territorially hosts the mission. In the peace operations established by UN,[234] an area to which

[232]N.M. BLOKKER, N.J. SCHRIJNER, Immunity of international organizations, ed. Brill, The Hague, 2015. T. PAJUSTE, The evolution of the concept of immunity of international organizations, in East West Studies, 8, 2017.
[233]D. LIAKOPOULOS, L'ingerenza umanitaria nel diritto internazionale e comunitario, op. cit.
[234]G. MARHIC, Le régime de responsabilité des opérations de paix de l'Union européenne: quelles règles applicables?, in Revue Belge de Droit International, 117 (1), 2013, pp. 44ss.

this analysis is limited, the tasks tend to be distributed as follows: The Organization is responsible for predetermining the mandate and objectives of the operation through the figure of the General Secretary, to whom he hierarchically depends the supreme commander of the mission.[235] The sending States are entrusted with the ordinary activities related to the stationing of the mission on the territory of the host State, including the preparation and training of the military, administrative, and disciplinary functions, as well as the fundamental exercise of jurisdictional functions in criminal matters. The role of the State that hosts territorially the forces instead tends to be rather reduced.[236] That said, assuming that the military contingents employed therein put in place a conduct in violation of rules protecting human rights. The central issue to be resolved concerns, thus, the attribution of said conduct, alternatively or cumulatively, to States of dispatching the contingents and/or to the organization that established or authorized the military operation.[237]

The issue is among the most complex in the field of international liability, as the peculiar organic nature of the agent (the contingents of states made available to the Organization)[238] puts into crisis the use of institutional-regulatory criteria or purely factual for the purpose of attributing the conduct. The contingents used in the operations established by UN are in fact definable, such as "agents doubles," as they are subject to a double "commandement" such that they do not cease to constitute organs of the respective sending States, despite being incorporated in organization's transaction.[239] In principle, the

---

[235]The commander of the mission, in turn, guides the individual national commanders in charge of the corresponding contingents sent by the States through an articulated chain of command. Recruitment of national contingencies is carried out by means of specific supply agreements stipulated between the government of the sending State and the Secretary General (see, for example, UN Doc. S/5575, of 4 March 1964, paragraph 4, as it concerns the United Nations Peacekeeping Force operation in Cyprus (UNFICYP) and the UN Doc. S/RES/743 (1992) of 21 February 1992, paragraph 2 with regard to the UNPROFOR operation).

[236]The supplier State, unlike the territorial one, retains significant powers over the organs made available to the Organization, although the Organization maintains command and operational control of the mission. On the possible complicity of the territorial State in the commission of an offense. See: B. AMRALLAH, The international responsibility of the United Nations for activities carried out by UN peacekeeping forces, op. cit., pp. 69ss.

[237]C. ARCHER, International organizations, ed. Routledge, London & New York, 2014.

[238]J. KLABBERS, Reflections on role responsibility. The responsibility of international organizations for failing to act, in European Journal of International Law, 28 (4), 2017, pp. 1138ss.

[239]"(...) Les casques bleus sont et restent des organes des Etats fournisseurs. Leur lien avec l'Etat national respectif n'est nullement coupé ou mis en sommeil pendant la durée de leur engagement au service de l'ONU." L. CONDORELLI, Le statut des forces de l'Onu et le droit international humanitaire, in Rivista di Diritto Internazionale, 1995, pp. 881ss.

double organic nature should correspond to the possibility of assigning the pipelines simultaneously to sending States and the Organization.

The hypothesis of double or multiple attribution of the conduct was also taken into consideration in the Project of the International Law Commission (ILC) of 2011.[240] The Special Rapporteur of the Project had in fact found, since the first studies, that the illegal conduct should not necessarily to attribute themselves exclusively to a single subject. In this regard, some examples taken from the practice were mentioned, including the bombing of former Yugoslavia by NATO in 1999, attributable both to the Organization, responsible for planning the military operation, and to its Member States, responsible for have it executed.[241] Also the Commentary of the ILC licensed in 2011 does not exclude tout court the possibility of a double (or multiple) attribution of a conduct to States and organizations.[242] It is lacking, however, to indicate with sufficient precision the juridical or factual criteria this can happen. In relation to the conduct carried out by a state body made available to the Organization, both art. 6 of the Project of ILC (relating to the conduct of an organ or an agent of the organization), and art. 7 (relating to the conduct of a state body or organization made available to another organization).[243] While art. 6 is intended to operate when the state body is fully detached and, therefore, incorporated into the structure of organization to the point of making it a

[240]Draft Articles on the responsibility of international organizations, with commentaries, General Commentary, p. 2, par. 3.

[241]V. GAJA, Second Report on responsibility of international organizations, UN Doc. A/CN.4/541 of 2 April 2004, p. 3, par. 7.

[242]Although it may not frequently occur in practice, dual or even multiple attribution of conduct cannot be excluded. Thus, attribution of a certain conduct to an international organization does not imply that the same conduct cannot be attributed to a State; nor does the attribution of conduct to a State rule out the same conduct to an international organization. One could also envisage conduct being simultaneously attributed to two or more international organizations, for instance when they establish a joint organ and act through that organ (see, Draft Articles on the Responsibility of International Organizations, op. cit., p. 16). For further details see: L. CONDORELLI, Le statut des forces de l'Onu et le droit international humanitaire, op. cit. C. LECK, International responsibility in United Nations peacekeeping operations: Command and control arrangements and the attribution of conduct, in Melbourne Journal of International Law, 10, 2009, pp. 360ss. A. NOLLKAEMPER, Dual attribution. Liability of the Netherlands for conduct of dutchbat in Srebrenica, in Journal of International Criminal Justice, 9, 2011, pp. 1148ss. C.A. BELL, Reassessing multiple attribution: The International Law Commission and the Behrami and Saramati decision, in International Law and Politics, 42, 2010, pp. 352ss. S. GROVER, The responsibility to protect: Perspectives on the concepts meaning, property application and value, ed. Routledge, London & New York, 2018.

[243] See in particular: M. MÖLDNER, Responsibility of International Organizations-Introducing the ILC's DARIO, op. cit., pp. 286ss.

de iure organ,[244] art. 7 would be applied in more complex situations, in which the state body does not remain completely detached, but maintains an organic connection with the State, while operating in the context of an organization. This hypothesis therefore seems destined to be applied precisely in relation to the conduct carried out by the military contingents made available by the supplier States in the operations planned by UN.[245]

According to the letter of art.7 ILC, the conduct of the body made available to the organization is attributable to the latter only to the extent that it exercises effective control over such conduct.[246] The provision therefore seems to introduce a criterion of "effective control"[247] which in

---

[244]"(...) When an organ of a State is placed at the disposal of an international organization, the organ may be fully seconded to that organization. In this case the organ's conduct would clearly be attributable only to the receiving organization (...) in (this case), the general rule set out in article 6 would apply" (Draft Articles on the Responsibility of International Organizations, cit., p. 20).

[245]"Article 7 deals with the different situation in which the seconded organ or agent still acts to a certain extent as organ of the seconding State or as organ or agent of the seconding organization. This occurs for instance in the case of military contingents that a State places at the disposal of the UN for a peacekeeping operation, since the State retains disciplinary powers and criminal jurisdiction over the members of the national contingent. In this situation the problem arises whether a specific conduct of the seconded organ or agent is to be attributed to the receiving organization or to the seconding State or organization" (Draft articles on the responsibility of international organizations, with commentaries 2011, cit., p. 20, par. 1).

[246]According to art. 7: "(...) The conduct of an organ of a State or an organ or agent of an international organization that is placed at the disposal of another international organization shall be considered under international law an act of the latter organization if the Organization exercises effective control over that conduct (...)." The provision thus confines itself to establishing the cases in which it is possible to attribute to the organization the conduct of a body which is not de jure fully incorporated into its structure, but which, by virtue of the "effective control" exercised by it over its conduct, acts by engaging the responsibility of the organization itself.

[247]It is beyond the scope of the present inquiry to reconstruct the appropriate elements to establish the notion of "effective control." We merely recall that the CDI had already introduced the concept regarding the behaviour of a body made available to one State by another State (see article 6 ARS, Draft Articles on the Responsibility of the States for Internationally Wrongful Acts, with commentaries 2001, UN Doc. A/56/10 of 10 August 2001). On the identification of the elements used by art. 7 DARIO for the purpose of the attribution of the conduct, see P. PALCHETTI, Attributing the conduct of dutchbat in Srebrenica: The 2014 Judgment of the District Court in the Mothers of Srebrenica Case, in The Netherlands International Law Review, 62, 2015, pp. 279-294, 283-285. P. PALCHETTI, The allocation of responsibility for internationally, committed in the course of multinational operations, in International Review of the Red Cross, 95, 2013, pp. 727-742. According to the author, art. 7 refers to assessments of a legal nature ("the organization must exercise" and "fact organization"). (P. PALCHETTI, Attributing the conduct of dutchbat in Srebrenica, op. cit., pp 284ss). With specific reference to the practice of Organizations v. Report of the Commission of an inquiry established by the Security

itself is not suitable to attribute the conduct, by way of double imputation, to States and organizations.[248] In other words, it allows attributing the conduct exclusively to the organization that receives the body and not the sending State.

The attribution of the same conduct simultaneously to States and organizations is then founded on the basis of other provisions contained in the Draft Articles on Responsibility of States for International Wrongful Acts of 2001 (DRSIWA) and Draft Articles on the Responsibility of International Organizations (DARIO), respectively art. 4 DRSIWA and art. 6 DARIO. Art. 48 DARIO, on the other hand, although it envisages an hypothesis of shared responsibility for the same conduct, is not conferring on the case in question as it concerns the multiple attribution of responsibility but not of conduct.[249]

Another question then is to understand whether the articles

Council Resolution 885 (1993) to investigate armed attacks on UNOSOM II personnel which led to casualties among them, UN Doc. S/1994/653 of 1 June 1994, p. 45, par. 243 and by which it emerges that the exclusion of the responsibility of the UN is the consequence of the lack of exercise of "effective control" by the Organization on the national contingents."

[248]The provision in question: "(...) Does not concern the issue whether a certain conduct is attributable to a State or an international organization, but rather to which entity-the contributing State (...) or the receiving organization-conduct has to be attributed" (see: Draft Articles on Responsibility of International organizations, op. cit., p. 21). In this sense: P. PALCHETTI, Attributing the conduct of dutchbat in Srebrenica: The 2014 judgment of the district court in mothers of Srebrenica case, op. cit., pag. 283 ("(...) This provision only concerns attribution to the receiving organization. The fact that the State retains effective control simply excludes the possibility of attributing the conduct to the organization according to article 7 (...)").

[249]See: L. CONDORELLI, De la responsabilité internationale de l'ONU et/ou de l'État d'envoi lors d'actions de Forces de Maintien de la Paix: l'écheveau de l'attribution (double?) devant le juge néerlandais, in QIL-Questions of International Law, Zoom-in 1 (2014), pp. 3-15 "(...) les casques bleus étaient partant devenus des organes (subsidiaires) ou agents des N.U., leurs comportements étant alors de ce fait même toujours imputables à celles-ci (dans la logique-cette fois-des articles 4 et 5 AREFII), et ce même en cas d'excès de pouvoir ou de violation des instructions reçues (Article 7 AREFII, qui sera ensuite repris mutatis mutandis à l'Article 8 AROI) (...) des cas qui de toute évidence n'ont rien à voir avec celui des FMP, où ces organes des États d'envoi que sont les contingents nationaux sont "transformés" en organes de l'ONU et où l'attribution dépend donc de la relation organique (dans la logique des articles 4 et 5 AREFII, reproduite par la suite dans l'article 6 AROI, mais non pas dans la logique "déviante" de l'article 7 AROI), et non du contrôle effectif quant aux comportements en question" (p. 6 and note 9). In the same spirit also: P. PALCHETTI, Attributing the conduct of Dutchbat in Srebrenica, op. cit., pag. 283, which is declared that: "(...) Whether, and on what legal basis, the conduct of the troops is to be attributed to the sending State should be assessed in the light of the rules of attribution set forth in the articles on the Responsibility of State (ARS) (...) attribution to the State can be justified on the basis of the criterion set forth in article 4 of ARS (...)."

elaborated by ILC on the subject of attribution correspond to general international law. Already during the discussion of the Project several States and organizations had expressed rather divergent positions on the point. Among the observations presented,[250] UN position is particularly significant, as they have always defended the idea that the conduct carried out by the forces employed in peace operations would be exclusively attributable to them.

In support of this assumption, the organization often refers to de jure elements (i.e. the fact that the agents made available by the States "are transformed" into real organs of the Organization)[251] and, with regard to joint operations, also de facto elements (such as the alleged effective control exercised by the Organization on forces).[252] On the other, the concurrent responsibility of the sending States has been recognized only in exceptional circumstances. This is the case, for example, of damage

---

[250] Article 48 leaves therefore open the hypothesis that a conduct is imputable only to a subject, but the responsibility is borne by two. On the verge see: G. GAJA, Special Rapporteur of ILC, Second Report on responsibility of international organizations, UN Doc. A/CN.4/541 of 2 April 2004: "Dual attribution of conduct normally leads to joint, or joint and several, responsibility. However, joint, or joint and several, responsibility does not necessarily depend on dual attribution."

[251] See: International Criminal Police Organization (Responsibility of international organizations. Comments and observations received from international organizations, UN Doc. A/CN.4/556 of 12 May 200, pp. 23-25). "(...) As a subsidiary organ of the UN, an act of a peacekeeping force is, in principle, imputable to the Organization, and if committed in violation of an international obligation entails the international responsibility of the Organization and its liability in compensation" (Letter of 3 February 2004 by the United Nations Legal Counsel to the Director of the Codification Division, A/CN.4/545, sect. II.G). The same position from the General Secretary (UN Doc. A/CN.4/637/Add.1 (2011), p. 14, par. 3). For further details see: D. SAROOSHI, The United Nations and the development of collective security: The delegation by the UN Security Council of its Chapter VII powers, Oxford University Press, Oxford, 1999, pp. 163-166. On the contrary: I. BROWNLIE, The responsibility of states of the acts of international organizations, in M. RAGAZZI, International responsibility today. Essays in memory of Oscar Schachter, ed. Brill, Leiden, 2005, pp. 335ss. V. LANOVOY, Complicity and its limits in the law of international responsibility, op. cit., S. YEE, Towards an international law of co-progressiveness, Martinus Nijhoff Publishers, The Hague, 2014. M.N. SHAW, International law, Cambridge University Press, Cambridge, 2014. A. NOLLKAEMPER, The duality of shared responsibility, in Contemporary Politics, 24 (5), 2018, pp. 528ss.

[252] This is what can be drawn from the position expressed by the General Secretary in the report on the financing of peacekeeping operations drawn up in 1996, in which the international responsibility of the Organization seems to derive from the actual control exercised by it on the conduct of operations in joint venture operations, the responsibility for the conduct of the troops lies in the United States. In the absence of formal arrangements between UN and the United States, the United Kingdom provides the following powers: The UN peacekeeping operations Report of the Secretary-General, UN Doc. A/51/389 of 20 September 1996, pages 6, paragraphs 17 and 18.

caused by contingents to persons and property as a result of gross negligence of the sending State, [253] or of violations of international humanitarian law obligations.[254] Consistent with this approach, the model agreement is to be stipulated between UN and the supplier State for the provision of national contingents providing on the one hand that "the UN will be responsible for dealing with the loss or damage to their property."[255] On the other that "if the loss, damage, death, injury arose from gross negligence or willful misconduct of personnel provided by the government, the latter will be liable for such claims,"[256] thus introducing a distinctly discipline depending on whether the pipelines have been put in place ultra vires or not.

The divergences on the criteria to be applied for the purpose of attributing the conduct in question were not slow to appear even in the decisions made by national and international courts once the Project was adopted. For example, Netherlands domestic courts have used art. 7 DARIO to establish the attribution of the conduct to the State (and not to the organization).

The following analysis is intended to illustrate the current position of ECtHR which, only recently, seems to have admitted the application of the double attribution criterion to the behaviours carried out by the contingents operating in force actions planned by the organizations.

3.2. (Follows) Reconstruction of ECtHR position regarding the problem of conduct attribution

Strasbourg judges in recent years have been called on several occasions to rule on the attribution of the offense to the contracting States operating in force actions instituted or authorized by the UN. ECtHR

---

[253] Financing of the United Nations peacekeeping operations Report of the Secretary-General, op. cit., p. 10, par. 42.

[254] Given the exclusive criminal jurisdiction of the State of nationality and its obligation to ensure respect for international humanitarian law by members of its forces, the General Assembly may wish to consider recognizing the state responsibility of nationality for violations of international humanitarian law by members of its national contingent, and its responsibility in compensation (...) (see: Financing of the United Nations Protection Force, op. cit., p. 11, par. 44).

[255] F. LUSA BORDIN, The analogy between States and international organizations, op. cit.

[256] Contribution Agreement between the UN and the Participating State contributing resources to the Peacekeeping Operation, UN Doc. A/50/995 Annex of 9 July 1996. The use of the terms responsibility (referred to the Organization) and liability (referring to the supplier States) could suggest that the State of nationality of the quota would have only a financial obligation to repay the Organization.

initially ruled out this possibility, although some national courts had long recognized the imputation of the conduct to States of sending troops, as in Nissan case[257] and, more recently, in Bici[258] and Al-Jedda[259] cases decided by the Courts of the United Kingdom. The issue was addressed in the well-known Behrami and Behrami v. France and Saramati v. France, Germany and Norway sentences, still today counted among the most probably discussed precedents of ECtHR jurisprudence.[260] The facts of the case are

---

[257]Nissan v. Attorney general, decided by Queen's Bench Division, in All England Law Reports, 1967, vol. 2, pp. 203ss.

[258]Bici v. Ministry of Defence (Court d'Appeal, Queen's Bench Division, decision of 7 April 2004). The case concerned civil redress for the conduct of the British contingent serving in Kosovo, under the cover of the UN mission. In this circumstance the attribution of the conduct to the UN has never been called into question "[t]he Crown retained command of the British forces notwithstanding that they were acting under the auspices of the U.N. (...)."

[259]House of Lords, R (on the application of Al-Jedda) (FC) (Appellant) v. Secretary of State for Defence (Respondent), sentence of 12 December 2007. It is interesting to note that the British judges have explicitly referred to the DARIO Project. It was common ground between the parties that the government was issued by the International Law Commission in article 7 of its draft articles on the Responsibility of International Organizations. On that occasion, applying art. 7 of the Project and therefore the criterion of effective control foreseen therein it was established that the (alleged) damaging conduct was attributable not so much to the UN as to the British contingent. The British judges had in fact held that: "It could not be said that the United States had been under the effective command and control of the UN, or that the United Kingdom were the Court also ruled on the same case" (see below in this paragraph, to which reference should also be made to details of the case). Bikes v. Ministry of Defense (Court of Appeal, Queen's Bench Division, decision of 7 April 2004). The case concerned civil redress for the conduct of the British contingent serving in Kosovo, under the cover of the UN mission. In this circumstance the attribution of the conduct to the UN has never been called into question "(t)he Crown retained command of the British forces notwithstanding that they were acting under the auspices of the U.N."

[260]ECtHR, Behrami and Behrami v. France, Saramati v. France, Germany and Norway of 2 May 2007. And in the same spirit see also: Milisavljević v. Serbia of 4 April 2017. Al Nashiri v. Romania of 31 May 2018. For further details see: P. DE SENA, M. C. VITUCCI, The European Courts and the Security Council: Between dédoublement fonctionnel and balancing of values, in European Journal of International Law, 20, 2009, pp. 193 ss. A. SARI, Jurisdiction and international responsibility in peace support operations: The Behrami and Saramati cases, op. cit., pp.151-170. C.A. BELL, Reassesing multiple attribution: The International Law Commission and the Behrami and Saramati decision, in International Law and Politics, 42, 2010, pp. 502-547. P. BODEAU-LIVINEC, G.P. BUZZINI, S. VILLALPANDO, ECHR judgment on applicability of European Convention on Human Rights to acts undertaken pursuant to UN Chapter VII operation in Kosovo, in American Journal of International Law, 102, 2008, pp. 323-330. M. MILANOVIC, T. PAPIC, As bad as it gets: The European Court of Human Rights' Behrami and Saramati decision and general international law, in International and Comparative Law Quarterly, 58, 2009, pp. 267-296. P. KLEIN, Responsabilité pour les faits commis dans le cadre d'opérations de paix et étendue du pouvoir de contrôle de la Cour européenne des droits de

known, as is known the international framework in which they are inserted: The so-called "humanitarian" intervention led by NATO in the territory of the Republic of the former Yugoslavia[261] endorsed ex post facto by Resolution 1244 (1999) of the Security Council.[262] In the opinion of ECtHR, the unlawful conduct put in place by UNMIK (i.e. the failure to supervise the de-mining activity) had to be attributed to UN as the agents were subsidiary organs of the Organization. With reference to the conduct of KFOR (the arrest and illegitimate detention of the applicant), the offense was attributed to UN not to sending States, based on the substantially "normative" criterion.[263]

In the opinion of ECtHR, both UNIMIK and KFOR would not have acted on the direct initiative of the supplying States, but on the authority of the Security Council,[264] which would have determined and even directed the disputed conduct due to the ultimate control and the ultimate authority exercised by it.[265] On this basis Behrami and Saramati appeals were declared ratione personae inadmissible.[266] ECtHR declaring

---

l'homme: quelques considérations critiques sur l'arrêt Behrami et Saramati, in Annuaire Français de Droit International, 53, 2007, pp. 43ss. C. TOMUSCHAT, Human rights: Between idealism and realism, Oxford University Press, Oxford, 2014. M.P. MOELLE, The international responsibility of international organizations. Cooperation in peacekeeping operations, Cambridge University Press, Cambridge, 2013.

[261]A. CASSESE, Ex iniuria ius oritur: Are we moving towards international legitimation of forcible humanitarian countermeasures in the world community?, in European Journal of international Law, 10, 1999, pp. 23ss.

[262]Res. 1244 (1999), of 10 June 1999, UN Doc. S/RES/1244 (1999), which established an interim administration for Kosovo (United Nations Interim Adminstration in Kosovo-UNMIK) and which also authorized the UN Member States to establish a military security presence with the substantial participation of the NATO forces, which operated under a unified command and control (Kosovo Force-KFOR). On the relationship and coordination of UNMIK with the current EULEX mission, established within the European security and defense policy.

[263]ECtHR, Behrami, op. cit., par. 143.

[264]ECtHR, Behrami, op. cit., par.123-126, in which the ECtHR ascertains that the disputed conduct falls within the mandate of KFOR and UNIMIK.

[265]ECtHR, Behrami, op. cit., par. 129.

[266]"(...) The Court finds that the UNSC retained ultimate authority and control and that effective command of the relevant operational matters was retained by NATO. In such circumstances, the Court observes that KFOR was exercising lawfully delegated Chapter VII powers of the UNSC so that the impugned action was, in principle, "attributable" to the UN." ECtHR, Behrami, cited above, paragraphs 140 and 141, (emphasis added). Note that the expression "ultimate" control has never been used in the case law of the Court (with the exception of the Matthews case-see below), nor of the ICJ and there is no trace either in the Comments to the international responsibility of States and Organizations. This term has been used by some authors regarding the legitimacy and validity of the delegations of power granted by the Security Council. According to D. SAROOSHI, The United Nations and the development of collective security, op. cit., pp. 163ss.

the appeal ratione personae inadmissible, resolved the case on the basis of the imputation of the unlawful fact to the Organization and thus avoided ascertaining its competence ratione loci, pronouncing itself on the possible extraterritorial extension of states jurisdiction concerned pursuant to art. 1 ECHR.[267]

In the conclusion of ECtHR, in our opinion unconvincing on legal level and worrying about the resulting lack of protection, one could read a clear attitude of deference to the Security Council. In this key some passages of the decisions on the importance of objectives pursued by the Security Council can be interpreted when it acts on ex Chapter VII of the Charter[268] and the function that this political body performs in peace and security management of the entire international community.[269]

The solution adopted in Behrami case was thus criticized because ECtHR was forced to subsequently review its position on the matter, albeit progressively. Some "traces" of Behrami and Saramati can still be found, for example, in the decisions taken at a short distance in Kasumaj v. Greece, [270] Gajic v. Germany [271] and Beric and others v. Bosnia and

---

[267]See also: A. VAN AAKEN, I. MOTOC, The European Convention on Human Rights and general international law, Oxford University Press, Oxford, 2018.

[268]G.I. HERNANDEZ, Beyond the control paradigm? International responsibility and the European Union, in The Cambridge Yearbook of European Legal Studies, 15, 2012-2013, pp. 644ss.

[269]A. SARI, Jurisdiction and international responsibility in peace support operations: The Behrami and Saramati cases, op. cit., pp. 168ss. "The risk that Behrami and Saramati could create a void in the protection of ECHR rights is compounded by the ECHR's rejection of the applicants submissions based on Bosphorus case (...)."

[270]ECtHR, Kasumaj v. Greece of 5 July 2007. "As such, their actions were directly attributable to the UN, an organization of universal jurisdiction fulfilling its imperative collective security objective (...) the Convention cannot be interpreted in a manner which would subject the acts and omissions of Contracting Parties which are covered by UNSC Resolutions [under Chapter VII of the UN Charter] and occur prior to or in the course of such missions, to the scrutiny of the Court" (ECtHR, Behrami, op. cit., par. 149-150-151). According to other authors: "[T]his reference to the imperative peace and security aim to the effectiveness of Security Council action. Court's real interest is focused on the values enshrined in collective security action, more specifically on ensuring public safety and the smooth international administration of Kosovo. More than the formal primacy of UN Security Council obligations, it is the primacy of some UN substantive values that is at stake (...)." In this sense: P. DE SENA, M.C. VITUCCI, The European Courts and the Security Council: Between dédoublement fonctionnel and balancing of values, op. cit., pag. 206.

[271] ECtHR, Gajic v. Germany of 28 August 2007. For further details see: K. MUJEZINOVIĆ LARSEN, The human rights treaty obligations of peacekeepers, Cambridge University Press, Cambridge, 2012. C. FERSTMAN, International organizations and the right for accountability. The remedies and reparations gap, Oxford University Press, Oxford, 2017. D.T. GILL, D. FLECK, The handbook of the international law of military operations, op. cit., M. FINK, Frontex and human rights. Responsibility in

Herzegovina[272] cases. The following year, in Stephens v. Cyprus, Turkey and the UN case, the ECtHR applied the "exclusive and ultimate control" test, specifically referring to Behrami and Saramati jurisprudence, together, however, with that of "effective control," as if to look for a conciliation with what is expressed by the DARIO and, at the same time, a reconsideration of its previous positions.[273]

Only with the Al-Jedda[274] case, concerning the military actions conducted in Iraq authorized by the Security Council in 2003,[275] the ECtHR has inaugurated an approach in evident discontinuity with the previous jurisprudence, gradually opening the way to the use of the criterion of multiple attribution. In the present case, the applicant asked the ECtHR to verify the violation of art. 5 par. 1 ECHR (right to individual freedom), by the British authorities, for having been arrested and detained for more than three years in the Shaibah detention center in Basra, a structure controlled by the British contingent, present in Iraq as a multinational security force authorized by the Security Council in virtue of Resolutions 1511 (2003)[276] and 1546 (2004).[277]

---

multi-actor situations under the CHR and EU public liability law, Oxford University Press, Oxford, 2019.

[272]ECtHR, Beric and others v. Bosnia and Herzegovina of 16 October 2007. B. RAINEY, W. WICKS, C. OVEY, Jacbos, White and Ovey: The European Convention on Human Rights, op. cit.,

[273]ECtHR, Stephens v. Cyprus, Turkey and the UN of 11 December 2008, which is stated that: "(...) The States do not have effective control." See also: L. DOSWALD-BECK, Human rights in times of conflict and terrorism, Oxford University Press, Oxford, 2011. M. LANGFORD, W. VANDENHOLE, N. SCHEININ, Global justice, state duties. The extraterritorial scope of economic, social and cultural rights in international law, Cambridge University Press, Cambridge, 2017, pp. 188ss.

[274]ECtHR, Al-Jedda v. United Kingdom of 7 July 2011. In addition to the issue of attribution, the case is interesting from the point of view of the harmonizing interpretation of Security Council's Resolutions and of the Unions the behaviours carried out under their cover. B. RAINEY, W. WICKS, C. OVEY, Jacbos, White and Ovey: The European Convention on Human Rights, op. cit., C. MCLACHLAN, Foreign relations law, Cambridge University Press, Cambridge, 2014, pp. 334ss. C. MALLORY, European Court of Human Rights. Al Skeini and others v. United Kingdom judgment of 7 July 2011, in The International and Comparative Law Quarterly, 61 (1), 2012, pp. 304ss.

[275]Resolution n. 1511 of 2003, v. UN Doc. S/RES/1511 of 16 October 2003.

[276]A. SWAIN, R. AMER, J. ÖJENDAL, The democratization project. Opportunities and challenges, Anthem Press, London, New York, Delhi, 2011.

[277]The operation in question had been foreseen by the Security Council resolution no. 1511 of 2003, The situation between Iraq and Kuwait (UN Doc. S/RES/1511 of 16 October 2003). The resolution, while authorizing "all necessary means," would not have consented to also implement extra-judicial detention measures. This possibility instead found a more explicit recognition in the subsequent resolution n. 1546, which referred to the text of the letter of the US Secretary of State, in which the internment for imperative reasons of security was expressly indicated among the measures that can be implemented (Resolution

ECtHR, not recognizing the exercise by UN of a control over the conduct, neither by virtue of the "ultimate control" criterion, nor by the "effective control," has attributed the same to the United Kingdom, State of dispatch of the troops, declaring, through the "distinguishing" technique, that the case in question, unlike the Behrami one, was inserted in the context of a mission of force authorized but not established by the Organization.[278]

It is interesting to note that this decision was adopted concurrently with the application by some internal courts of the criterion of double imputation of conduct to the State of sending troops. This refers in particular to cases brought before the Dutch courts Nuhanović and Mustafic v. Netherlands,[279] followed by the Madri of Srebrenica v. Netherlands case, on the same historical facts, but of wider scope.[280] The Dutch decisions originated from the well-known episode of genocide coming to Srebrenica "under the eyes" of the Dutch contingent (Dutchbat) employed in the UNPROFOR peacekeeping operation, conducted under

---

1546 (2004) adopted by the Security Council at its 4987th meeting, on 8 June 2004, UN Doc. S/RES/1546 (2004) of 8 June 2004). For further analysis see: D. LIAKOPOULOS, L'ingerenza umanitaria nel diritto internazionale e comunitario, op. cit. L. HILL-GAWTHORNE, Detention in non-international armed conflict, Oxford University Press, Oxford, 2016, pp. 174ss. K. EPPERT, UN intervention practices in Iraq: A discursive approach to international interventions, ed. Routledge, London & New York, 2019.

[278]The Court on this occasion, citing art. 7 DARIO, as adopted in the first reading by the ILC and some passages of the related commentary, was able to conclude that: "The UN Security Council had neither effective control nor ultimate authority and control over the acts and omissions of foreign troops within the Multi-National Force and that the applicant's detention was not, therefore, attributable to the UN" (ECtHR, Al-Jedda v. United Kingdom, op. cit., par. 85 - 86).

[279]Supreme Court of the Netherlands, the Netherlands (Minister of Defense and Minister for Foreign Affairs) v. Hasan Nuhanović, ruling of 6 September 2013, ILC 2061, which confirmed, in essence, the sentence of the Hague Court of Appeal of 5 July 2011, in reform of the decision of the District Court of 10 September 2008, ILC 1092, par. 4.8.

[280]District Court of The Hague, Mothers of Srebrenica v. The Netherlands, case no C/09/295247/HA ZA 07-2973, decision of 16 July 2014. It should be noted that the appeal was originally presented by the association against the UN to see the civil responsibility of the organization recognized, but the Dutch courts had denied this request, relying on the rules on the immunity of the Organizations. From this case the controversy arose before the judges of Strasbourg on which we will return shortly (European Court of Human Rights, Stichting Mothers of Srebrenica and others v. The Netherlands, appeal No. 65542/12, decision of 11 June 2013). For further analysis see: J. KLABBERS, An introduction to international organizations law, Cambridge University Press, Cambridge, 2015. N. VAN DER HAVE, The prevention of gross human rights violations under international human rights law, ed. Springer, Berlin, 2017. K. GASSELING, The legacy of Srebenica. Potential consequences of reducing liability for troop contributing countries in modern UN peacekeeping operations, in Boston College of International and Comparative Law Review, 40 (2), 2017, pp. 348ss.

the UN aegis.[281] In front of the internal courts, the relatives of the victims of the genocide had asked the Dutch State to be sentenced for civil damages for the behaviour of the Ducthbat[282] and, in particular, following the decision, taken two days after the fall of the enclave of Srebrenica in the hands of the Bosnian Serb army, to have Muslim refugees evacuated from the Potocari, effectively delivering them to their "ethnic cleaners."

In the opinion of the Dutch courts, Dutchbat's conduct[283] was to be attributed to the Netherlands because of the effective control exercised by them, based on a two-way interpretation of art. 7 DARIO together with art. 48,[284] rather questionable.[285] The sending State of the quota responsibility in the opinion of ECtHR should derive from the fact that it has retained the authority in disciplinary matters, as well as the criminal jurisdiction against its own soldiers who have contravened UN orders, a circumstance that should have allow the Dutch State to prevent the occurrence of events in Srebrenica.[286] In other words, Dutch decisions

---

[281]J. WOUTERS, E. BREMS, S. SMIS, P. SCHMITT, Accountability for human rights violations by International Organizations, Oxford University Press, Oxford, 2010, pp. 269-286. R.C. WALL, War in the Balkans. An encyclopedic history from the fall of the Ottoman empire to the breakup of Yugoslavia, ed. ABC-CLIO, California, Oxford, 2014.

[282]It should be noted that before the fall of Srebrenica the Dutch troops had requested an aerial intervention, which however was never authorized for several reasons; among these the fact that: "The UN would be perceived as having entered a war against them, which was not authorised by the Security Council the risk of losing control over the process would imply possible grave consequences for the UN troops (…). The use of air power might endanger the humanitarian mission of UNPROFOR, (...) the fear of Serb reprisals against UN troops" (see also: Report of the Secretray-General Pursuant to General Assembly Resolution 53/35, UN Doc. A/54/549, of 15 November 1999, par. 503).

[283]C. RYNGAERT, I.F. DEKKER, R.A. WESSEL, Judicial decisions on the law of international organizations, Oxford University Press, Oxford, 2016.

[284]"International law in particular article 7 DARIO in conjunction with article 48 (1) DARIO, does not exclude the possibility of dual attribution of given conduct." Supreme Court of the Netherlands, Netherlands (Minister of Defense and Minister for Foreign Affairs) v. Hasan Nuhanović, judgment of 6 September 2013, ILDC 2061, 3.11.2). See also: K. MACAK, Internationalized armed conflicts in international law, Oxford University Press, Oxford, 2018.

[285]As already explained in the previous paragraph, art. 7 allows the imputation of the conduct exclusively to the Organization and not to the sending State of the troops. As for art. 48, the provision seems to regulate the different hypothesis of multiple attribution of responsibility and not of conduct (see, L. CONDORELLI, De la responsabilité internationale de l'ONU et/ou de l'État d'envoi lors d'actions de Forces de Maintien de la Paix, op. cit., pp. 9ss. C. RYNGAERT, Supreme Court (Hoge Raad), State of the Netherlands v. Mustaficn et al., State of the Nethrelands v. Nuhanovic, Judments of 6 September 2013, Netherlands International law Review, 60, 2013, pp. 441-446. A. REINISCH, The Conventions on the privileges and immunities of the United Nations and its specialized agencies. A commentary, Oxford University Press, Oxford, 2016).

[286]"The question whether the State had "effective control" (...) must be answered in view

have emphasized the power that the State had to address orders to its troops, so that they would not complete the acts actually carried out. In this way not only the faculty of giving orders but also the juridical and factual power to prevent the occurrence of the offense was included in the notion of "effective control."[287]

Dutch decisions are mentioned here as a significant precedent which seems to have partially guided ECtHR jurisprudence on the criterion of the double attribution of the conduct.[288] In this regard it should also be mentioned the Jaloud case concerning an incident which occurred following a shoot out triggered by a vehicle and a checkpoint guarded by Dutch military stationed in the Basra region and operating within the framework of the international stabilization mission of Iraq, established by the Security Council with Resolution no. 1483 (2003). In relation to these events, Strasbourg judges seem to have adhered the thesis of conduct double attribution, as a reflection of the agent's double organic garment.[289]

3.3. (Follows) The related problem of extraterritorial state jurisdiction

The ECtHR to ascertain the responsibility of one or more contracting States that have taken part in a force action established or authorized by an organization must verify its competence not only ratione

---

of the circumstances of the case. This does not only imply that significance should be given to the question whether that conduct constituted the execution of a specific instruction, issued by the UN or the State, but also to the question whether, if there was no such specific instruction, the UN or the State had the power to prevent the conduct concerned" (Court of Appeals of the Hague in Nuhanovic v. the Netherlands case, op. cit., par. 5.9).

[287]See, T. DANNENBAUM, Killings at Srebrenica, effective control, and the power to prevent unlawful conduct, in International and Comparative Law Quarterly, 61 (3), 2012, pp. 713-728. According to the author: "When orders are contravened, the relevant levers of control over the conduct are those that impact discipline and obedience to lawful commands. Because in peacekeeping forces those levers are held exclusively by the State. It is the State that has the control most likely to be effective in preventing wrongdoing that contravenes UN orders." See also: K.M. LARSEN, Attribution of conduct in peace operations: The "ultimate authority and control" test, op. cit., pp. 520ss A. NOLLAKAEMPER, D. JACOBS, J.N.M. SCHECINGER, Distribution of responsibilities in international law, op. cit., H. NASU, The UN Security Council's responsibility and the "responsibility to protect," in Max Planck Yearbook of United Nations, 15, 2011, pp. 379ss.

[288]F. DIREK, Responsibility in peace operations: Revisiting the proper test for attribution conduct and the meaning of the "effective control" standard, in Netherlands International Law Review, 61, 2014, p. 1-22. A. MOMIROV, Dutch courts and Srebrenica: Ascribing responsibilities and defending legally relevant relationships, in Netherlands Yearbook of International Law, 63, 2012, pp. 233ss.

[289]ECtHR, Jaloud v. the Netherlands of 20 November 2014.

personae but also ratione loci.[290]

The mere possibility of attributing to a state conduct carried out outside its national borders does not automatically imply the unfolding of its jurisdiction over the situation in question. The attribution of conduct and the exercise of state jurisdiction are, in fact, two clearly distinct questions from a logical and legal point of view: The first concerns the subjective element of the crime, while the second relates to the objective element since the exercise of "jurisdiction" is a prerequisite for considering the obligation to the State to be applicable.[291]

The ascertainment of the existence of states jurisdiction in the cases under examination can result in a problematic operation since the offenses committed in the context of force actions usually take place in areas geographically distant from states territory whose conduct is disputed. Since art. 1 ECHR it requires the contracting States to guarantee the conventional rights "to any person within their jurisdiction," is then necessary to demonstrate the extension of state jurisdiction in an extraterritorial sense.[292]

The existence of states extraterritorial jurisdiction has been recognized by ECtHR in a conspicuous number of cases, essentially attributable to two situations: When there is a control or a state authority on a foreign territory, according to "spatial" model, or when this happens on an individual or a group of individuals, according to "personal" model.[293]

These two basic paradigms have been the subject of continuous extensive interpretations by ECtHR. The "spatial" model was in fact

---

[290] G. ANDREOPOULOS, Better late than never? The evolving responsibility of international organizations, in A. BRYSK, M. STOHL, Contesting human rights, Edward Elgar Publishers, Cheltenham, 2019.

[291]ECtHR, Catan and others v. Republic of Moldova and Russian Federation of 19 October 2012, par. 118. see: T. GAMMELTOFT-HANSEN, J. VEDSTED-HANSEN, Human right and the dark side of globalization. Transnational law enforcement and migration control, ed. Routledge, London & New York, 2016.

[292]P. DE SENA, The notion of "contracting parties' Jurisdiction" under article 1 of the ECHR: Some marginal remarks on Nigro's paper, in Italian Yearbook of International Law, 2010, pp. 75ss. M. MILANOVIC, Extraterritorial application of human rights treaties: Law, principles and policy, Oxford University Press, Oxford, 2011.

[293]M. MILANOVIC, Extraterritorial applications of human rights treaties: Law, principles and policy, op. cit., 2011. R. WILDE, The legal space or espace juridique of the European Convention on Human Rights: Is it relevant to extraterritorial state action?, in European Human Rights Law Review, 2, 2005, pp. 116ss. G. FITZMAURICE, P. MERKOURIS, The interpretation and application of the European Convention of Human Rights. Legal and practical implications, Martinus Nijhoff Publishers, The Hague, 2012. K. DA COSTA, The extraterritorial application of selected human rights treaties, Martinus Nijhoff Publishers, The Hague, 2012.

considered applicable also to hypotheses of jurisdiction in extremis, i.e. in relation to areas of modest size, on the basis of the control exercised over well-defined portions of territory.[294] The application of personal model was instead divided into two further variants: On the one, the situations of de facto control over one or more individuals ("de facto control over a person"), on the other, the situations of control "regulatory authority" ("authority or de jure control over a person.")[295]

With regard to the specific cases in which the state jurisdiction was exercised in an extraterritorial sense due to the operations established or authorized by the organizations, it is possible to identify an evolutionary line that starts from the Banković decision, passing through the Al-Jedda and Al-Skeini cases, up to the most recent Hassan and Jaloud cases. As is known in Banković case, concerning the bombing of the Radio Televizije Srvije building by a missile released by the NATO aeronautical forces in 1999, ECtHR has adopted a rather restrictive view of the territorial scope of ECHR, evoking the idea of an "espace juridique européen," i.e. a space confined exclusively within the regional area bounded by the borders of the contracting States.[296] In Behrami case the ECtHR instead preferred not to rule on the problem of ECHR's ratione loci applicability, resolving the case on the basis of conduct attribution.[297] In Al-Saadoon and Mufdhi v.

---

[294] ECtHR, Medvedyev and others v. France of 29 March 2010, par. 66-67, which is affirmed that "(...) full and exclusive control over the Winner and its crew, at least de facto." See also: Al-Saadoon and Mufdhi v. United Kingdom of 3 July 2009, par. 88, "[t]he Court considers that, given the total and exclusive de facto, and subsequently also de jure, control exercised by the United Kingdom authorities over the premises in question, the individuals detained there, including the applicants, were within the United Kingdom's jurisdiction." See also: G. GIACCA, Economic, social and cultural rights in armed conflict, Oxford University Press, Oxford, 2014.

[295] With regard to the latter category, the Court seems to attach ever more importance, for the purposes of verifying the existence of jurisdiction, to the fact that the conduct of the State has been put in place as "legitimate extraterritorial jurisdiction under international law, or place in a regulatory framework in which the State concerned has assumed responsibility for ensuring public security, or the exercise of other powers relating to sovereignty, outside its territory." ECtHR, Jaloud v. Netherlands, op. cit., par. 152.

[296] ECtHR, Banković and others v. Belgium of 12 December 2001. For further analysis see: R.A. LAWSON, Life after Bankovic: On the extraterritorial application of the European Convention of Human Rights, in Extraterritorial application of the Human Rights Treaties, ed. Intersentia, Antwerp, 2004, pp. 83-123. See from the European Commission on Human Rights: Cyprus v. Turkey of 26 May 1975 and an individual appeal in ECtHR in Loizidou v. Turkey case of 18 December 1996, which the ECtHR declared that: "(...) The responsibility of the Contracting Party may also arise when as a consequence of military action-whether lawful or unlawful-it exercises effective control of an area outside its national territory (...)." For further details see also: J.P. COSTA, La Cour europèenne des droits de l'homme. Des juges pour la libertè, op. cit.

[297] A. SARI, Jurisdiction and international responsibility in peace support operations: The

United Kingdom case, the ECtHR then returned to the issue, progressively moving away from the solution that emerged in the NATO bombing case.[298]

Only with the Al-Jedda and Al-Skeini sentences[299] did ECtHR show that it had overcome the controversial law principles of the Bankovic decision. In particular in the Al-Skeini case, concerning the appeal lodged by six Iraqi citizens for the death of their respective relatives, caused by the British armed forces in some anti-terrorist operations in Iraq in 2003, the ECtHR considered that the United Kingdom had exercised "public powers" as well as control and authority over individuals (therefore according to the personal and not spatial model).[300]

Another interesting fact of the Al-Jedda decision is the concurrent opinion of Rozakis and Bonello judges, who proposed to adopt a functional test to ascertain states jurisdiction, which overcomes the dichotomy between "space" and "personal" model. According to the

---

Behrami and Saramati cases, op. cit., pp. 151-170. According to these authors the jurisdiction ratione loci of the Court should be checked, before dealing with the merit of the issue of attribution, in order to avoid unnecessary investigations if the Court found itself incompetent to know the dispute. Actually the Court, par. 151, seems to hint at the profile of the application in the ECHR space, while basing the whole reasoning on the inadmissibility ratione personae of the appeal: "(...) The impugned acts and omissions of KFOR and UNMIK cannot be attributed to the respondent States and, moreover, did not take place on the territory of those States or by virtue of a decision of their authorities (...)."

[298]ECtHR, Al-Saadoon and Mufdhi v. United Kingdom of 3 July 2009. In the case in question the Court attaches importance to the fact that the UK authorities exercised complete and exclusive control over the detention facilities where they were held to be recurrent. It should be noted that the removal from the principles expressed in Bankovic was already traceable in the various appeals presented against Turkey, including the Issak v. Turkey case, Pad and others v. Turkey and Isaak and Others v. Turkey of 16 November 2004; Pad and others v. Turkey of 28 June 2007; Isaak and Others v. Turkey of 28 September 2006).

[299]ECtHR, Al-Jedda v. United Kingdom, op. cit. Al-Skeini v. United Kingdom of 7 July 2011. For further details see: G. HEATHCOTE, D. OTTO, Rethinking peacekeeping gender equality and collective security, ed. Springer, Berlin, 2014. K. KAMBER, Prosecuting human rights offences: Rethinking the sword function of human rights, ed. Brill, The Hague, 2017. R. REYNOLDS, Human rights in the line of fire: Al-Skeini v. United Kingdom, in Judicial Review, 16, 2011, pp. 340ss.

[300]"It can be seen, therefore, that following the removal from power of the Ba'ath regime and until the accession of the Interim government, the United Kingdom (together with the United States) assumed in Iraq the exercise of some of the public powers normally to be exercised by a sovereign government. In particular, the United Kingdom assumed authority and responsibility for the maintenance of security in South East Iraq. In these exceptional circumstances, the Court considers that the United Kingdom, (...) exercised authority and control over individuals killed in the course of such security operations, so as to establish a jurisdictional link between the deceased and the United Kingdom for the purposes of article 1 of the Convention." ECtHR, Al-Skeini v. the United Kingdom, op. cit., par. 149).

judges, states jurisdiction would subsist whenever the exercise of one of the five functions in which the respect of conventional rights is declined: Refrain from direct violation through their own agents, prevent violations by third parties, investigate violations committed, punish those responsible for them and compensate the victims.[301]

This solution seems to recall the functional conception of state jurisdiction that has long been evoked in doctrine according to which the ECHR contracting States which exercise forms of government power with regard to territories not subject to their sovereignty, appear to be bound to respect the obligations arising from them, to the extent that the exercise of these forms of power is likely to affect the enjoyment of the same rights sanctioned by them, relied upon from time to time the Court. ECtHR decisions seem to be based on the "functional" notion of jurisdiction, particularly the Jaloud case, which represents a definitive overcoming of the Banković jurisprudence.[302] In the jurisprudential framework so far outlined that the possibility of presenting an individual appeal aimed at ascertaining state responsibility that has acted in the context of a military operation established or authorized by an organization must be assessed. Assuming that ECtHR recognizes its ratione personae and loci competence to rule on the case, overcoming the various obstacles related to the profile of attribution and extraterritorial jurisdiction of the State concerned, it remains to be evaluated the concrete repair obtainable by the individual.

3.4. State responsibility for the adoption of internal measures in implementation of obligations deriving from their participation in international organizations

The liability hypothesis addressed by ECtHR concerns the adoption of internal measures by the States to implement obligations deriving from their membership in organizations. In such cases, the mere

[301]ECtHR, Al-Skeini v. the United Kingdom, op. cit., Concurring opinion of judge Bonello, (par. 3 and 10).

[302]ECtHR, Banković and others v. Belgium and others of 19 December 2001. For further details see: E. ROXSTRUM, M. GIBSON, T. EINARSEN, The NATO bombing case (Banković et al. v. Belgium et al.) and the limits of western human rights protection, in Boston University International Law Journal, 23, 2005, pp. 58ss. P.T. COLLINS, Civil-military "legal" relations: Where to from here? The civilian courts and the military in the United Kingdom, United States and Australia, ed. Brill, The Hague, 2018. G. HEATHCOTE, D. OTTO, Rethinking peacekeeping, gender equality and collective security, op. cit.

presence of internal acts with efficacy in the national territory of contracting States was considered a sufficient element to justify the ratione personae and loci admissibility of the appeals. At this juncture the problematic aspect that has arisen did not concern the question of conduct and jurisdiction attribution, but rather the delicate coordination between ECHR and the international obligations deriving from organizations such as UN or EU. In most cases, these were measures implementing the sanctioning regimes envisaged by the two Organizations, which, as already mentioned, raise known issues of (in) compatibility with the protection of human rights.[303]

The question must be analyzed here according to the perspective of responsibility for violation of rights enshrined in ECHR, considering that States, have often found themselves in a situation without (apparent) way out, having to coordinate potentially conflicting international obligations. In assessing the interpretative solutions devised by the States to respect the various commitments assumed at international level, ECtHR was called upon to pronounce, incidentally, on the relations between the "ECHR system" and orders originating from the founding treaties of other international organizations.[304]

From the developed jurisprudence it is possible to identify two distinct situations subject to scrutiny. Firstly, state behaviour called to implement an obligation deriving from an organization, in potential conflict with the ECHR, is highlighted without having had any margin of discretion (par. 6). Secondly, the state that internally carries out the obligation of the Organization has a margin (even a minimum) of maneuver, both in the proper implementation moment and in the previous interpretative phase. The solutions reached by ECtHR in the two distinct hypotheses deserve to be separately analyzed, highlighting then some aspects that we consider critical for both hypotheses.

3.5. (Follows) State responsibility in the absence of a margin of discretion and the doctrine of equivalent protection

The question of state responsibility for the implementation of international obligations conflicting with the ECHR arose for the first time with regard to EU acts, which was not (and still is not) part of ECHR, with

---

[303] L. BOISSON DE CHAZOURNES, M. KOHEN, International law and the quest for Its implementation. Liber Amicorum Vera Gowlland-Debbas, Martinus Nijhoff Publishers, Leiden, 2010, 73-84.

[304] K. DAUGIRDAS, How and why international law binds international organizations, op. cit., pp. 330ss.

consequent ratione personae inadmissibility of any appeals filed against it.[305] In order to reconcile the need of states to respect ECHR and, at the same time, to implement EU acts, ECtHR has developed the well-known doctrine of "equivalent protection."[306] In light of this position, a state party to ECHR that merely implements acts imposed, without any margin of discretion, by an organization is not responsible for ECHR violations if the organization in question ensures a level of protection of fundamental rights at least equivalent to the conventional one. The presumption of non-infringement of ECHR can however be overcome by the proof that, in the specific case, there has been a manifest violation of human rights within the organization itself.

A first trace of the theory under examination is attested already towards the end of the fifties in X v. Federal Republic of Germany case, but it is in M & Co v. Federal Republic of Germany case of 10 June 1958: "(...) If a State contracts treaty obligations and subsequently concluded another international agreement which disables it from performing its obligations under the first treaty it will be answerable for any Federal Republic of Germany (…)," made just a short distance from the historic Solange II ruling of the German Constitutional Court,[307] the version, even if embryonic, of the doctrine of equivalent protection was drafted. On this occasion the Commission, not wishing to question the autonomy of EU system, declared itself satisfied with the level of protection of human rights therein, emphasizing the role played by CJEU in the system of the organization in question. Consequently, the appeal was declared ratione materiae inadmissible.[308]

---

305 L. BOISON DE CHAZOURNES, C. ROMANO, R. MACKENZIE, International organizations and international dispute settlement: Trends and prospects, Martinus Nijhoff Publishers, New York, 2002, pp. 73-88.

306 A.S. BARROS, C. RYNGAERT, J. WOUTERS, International organizations and member State responsibility: Critical perspectives, op. cit., pp. 154ss. E. RAVASI, Doctrine of equivalent protection in human rights protection by the ECtHR and the ECJ, ed. Brill, The Hague, 2017, pp. 24ss.

307 The ECtHR affirmed that: "(...) The Convention does not prohibit a Member State from transferring powers to international organizations. Nonetheless (...) a transfer of powers does not necessarily exclude a state responsibility under the Convention with regard to the exercise of the transferred powers (...) to an international organization is not incompatible with the Convention provided that within that organization fundamental rights will receive an equivalent protection." In the same spirit is the case: M & Co. v. Federal Republic of Germany of 9 February 1990. See also in argument: N.L.A. LORENZ, X. GROUSSOT, G.T. PETURSSON, The European human rights culture. A paradox of human rights protection in Europe?, Martinus Nijhoff Publishers, Leiden, 2013.

308 This decision, as is known, has overturned the previous Solange I, with which the Constitutional Court has claimed the power to review the Community acts of secondary law in the light of German constitutional principles until (as long as, "Solange" in German)

The doctrine of equivalent protection was resumed, a few years later, in Matthews case,[309] where the presumption of equivalence was not applied due to the margin of discretion of the British State in relation to a EU act concerning European Parliamentary elections.[310]

Only with the famous Bosphorus case that the doctrine of protection has been perfected in its various aspects.[311] The case concerned the seizure by the Irish authorities of an aircraft of the Yugoslavian Airlines chartered by the Turkish Bosphorus Airways company, implementing a EU Regulation [312] containing sanctions against the former Federal Republic of Yugoslavia, in play of a Security Council Resolution. [313]

---

the EU had not guaranteed a system of protection of human rights at least equivalent to the national one. In the Solange II decision, however, the Court notes that the observance and protection of human rights guaranteed by the Court of Justice of the European Union was substantially similar to that offered by the German constitutional system (especially with regard to judicial mechanisms). "So long as the European Communities, in particular European Court case law, generally ensure effective protection of fundamental rights (…), the Federal Constitutional Court will no longer exercise its jurisdiction to decide on the applicability of secondary Community legislation (...) and it will no longer review such legislation by standard of the fundamental rights contained in the Basic Law." German Constitutional Court: BverfGE-casw, Solange II, decision n.73, 339 2 BvR 197/83 Solange II, par. f.

[309] C. BANNER, A. THOMSON, Human rights review of state acts performed in compliance with EC law-Bosphorus Airways v Ireland, in European Human Rights Law Review, 6, 2005, pp. 650ss. ECtHR: Heinz v. Contracting States and parties to the European Patent Convention also parties to the European Patent Convention of 15 October 1992, which is stated that: "(...) The procedural safeguards established by the European Patent Convention, pursuant to which the EPO was established, ensured that fundamental rights would receive protection "equivalent" to that provided by the Court."

[310] The act in question, relating to direct elections to the European Parliament of 8 October 1976, excluded the citizens of Gibraltar-and Mrs Matthews among them-from the right to vote. Following this decision, see also the European Court of Human Rights, Senator Lines GmbH v. the 15 Member States of 10 March 2004, where the responsibility of the fifteen States of the Union had been invoked following the decision of the European Court of Justice which rejected the applicant's request to suspend obligation to pay a fine imposed by the European Commission. However, the dispute did not continue, since the Court of First Instance withdrew the fine and the applicant, consequently, lost the status of "victim" of the alleged violation of human rights.

[311] ECtHR, Bosphorus Hava Yollari Turizm ve Ticaret Anonim Sirket Ireland of 30 June 2005. C. RYNGAERT, The European Court of Human Rights approach to the responsibility of member states in connection with acts of international organizations, in International and Comparative Law Quarterly, 60, 2011, pp. 1000ss.

[312] Council Regulation (EEC) No 990/93 of 26 April 1993 concerning trade between the European Economic Community and the Federal Republic of Yugoslavia (Serbia and Montenegro), OJ L 102, 28.4.1993. See also: P. KOUTRAKOS, EU international relations law, Hart Publishing, Oxford & Oregon, Portland, 2015.

[313] Resolution of the Security Council of the United Nations Bosnia and Herzegovina, UN Doc. S/RES/820 (1993) of 17 April 1993, par. 24. For further details see: A.S. KOLB, The

ECtHR, having ascertained the absence of a maneuver margin on the part of the Irish authorities in the application of EU Regulation, confirmed some principles elaborated by the previous jurisprudence,[314] consecrating the principle according to which the State that limits itself to implement the obligations arising from an organization with equivalent protection does not incur violations of ECHR. The Bosphorus decision represents an evolution with respect to previous judgments in that it is added that the "certification of equivalence" recognized to the organization can be denied on the basis of a double verification. The first, of a general and abstract nature, consists in the evaluation of the level overall protection of human rights ensured by the organization concerned; the second, of a specific nature, relates, instead, to the evaluation of measures adopted in the concrete case in order to ascertain that the protection of human rights was not manifestly lacking in the case in question.[315]

UN Security Council member's responsibility to protect a legal analysis, ed. Springer, Berlin, 2017. V.J. PROULX, Institutionalizing state responsibility, Oxford University Press, Oxford, 2016.

314"(...) A state action taken in compliance with such legal obligations is justified as long as the relevant organization is considered to protect fundamental rights, as regards both the substantive guarantees offered and the mechanisms controlling their observance, in a manner which can be considered at least equivalent to that for which the Convention provides." ECtHR, Bosphorus Ireland, op. cit., par. 155.

315"(...) Any such presumption can be rebutted if, in the circumstances of a particular case, it is considered that the protection of Convention rights was manifestly deficient" (ECtHR, Bosphorus v. Ireland, op. cit., par. 156). It is therefore an equivalence of substantive rights and procedural guarantees, i.e. the judicial mechanisms capable of ensuring respect for rights. Therefore, the certification referred to above can only be applied to acts potentially subject to control by the courts of Luxembourg. From this point of view, the "immunizing" effect generated by the doctrine of equivalent protection would be more limited compared to what emerged from the previous jurisprudence (in this sense see: P.J.A. DE HERT, F. KORENICA, The doctrine of the equivalent protection: Its life and legitimacy before and after the European Union's Accession to the European Convention on Human Rights, in German Law Journal, 13, 2012, pp. 884ss). Thus conceived the doctrine of equivalent protection, differs from what was affirmed by the judges of the German Constitutional Court, according to which the presumption that arises following the judgment on equivalent protection would be overcome only by a large-scale lowering of the standards of protection of human rights. For this reason it is allowed to file appeals against national implementations of Union acts before the courts of Strasbourg, where this possibility is precluded by the reasoning of the German courts. Opinion 2/13, Accession of the European Union to the European Convention for the Protection of Human Rights and Fundamental Freedoms, ECJ, 18 December 2014, ECLI:EU:C:2014:2454. D. HALBERSTRAM, "It's the autonomy, stupid!" A modest defense of opinion 2/13 on EU accession to the ECHR, and the way forward, in German Law Journal, 16, 2015, pp. 114ss. P. E. ECKHOUT, Opinion 2/13 on European union accession to the ECHR and judicial dialogue. Autonomy or autarchy, in Fordham International Law Journal, 38 (4), 2015, pp. 964ss. D. LIAKOPOULOS, European integration and its relation with the jurisprudence of European

Court of Human Rights and private international law of European Union, in Homa Publica. Revista Internacional de Direitos Humanos e Impresa, 2 (2), 2018. L. HALLESLOV STORGAARD, European Union law autonomy versus European fundamental rights protection. On opinion 2/13 on EU accession to the ECHR, in Human Rights Law Review, 15 (3), 2015, pp. 487ss. On the one hand, art. 53 does not oblige the States to guarantee a higher level of protection than that of the ECHR, on the other the same CFREU must guarantee the same level of protection of the ECHR so that there is no conflict between the two provisions. Moreover, the CJEU has evoked the specificity of the Union's control system on respect for fundamental rights, in particular the principle of mutual trust in the areas of civil and criminal judicial cooperation, visa, asylum and immigration, namely the area of freedom, security and justice that obliges each Member State to presume respect for fundamental rights by the other Member States and the absence of their jurisdictional powers in the field of foreign and security policy. See also in case: C-168/13 PPU, Jeremy F. of 30 May 2013, ECLI:EU:C:2013:358, published in the electronic Reports of the cases. The CJEU affirmed that: "(...) The absence of the necessary provisions of the framework, it must be that for the implementation of the objectives of the framework to a European Arrest Warrant (...)." In the same spirit see also: CJEU, C-399/11, Stefano Melloni of 26 February 2013, ECLI:EU:C:2013:107; C-396/11, Ministerul Public-Parchetul de pe lângă Curtea de Apel Constanţa v. Radu of 29 January 2013, ECLI:EU:C:2013:39, both of them published in the electronic Reports of the cases. F.M.W. BILLING, The right to silence in transnational criminal proceedings. Comparative law perspectives, ed. Springer, Berlin, 2016, pp. 323ss. C. JANSSENS, The principle of mutual recognition in European Union law, Oxford University Press, Oxford, 2013, pp. 208ss. F. KORENICA, The EU accession to the ECHR: Between Luxembourg's search for autonomy and Strasbourg's credibility on human rights protection, ed. Springer, Berlin, 2015, pp. 282ss. S. MORANO-FOADI, L. VICKERS (eds.), Fundamental Rights in the EU-A matter for two Courts, Oxford University Press, Oxford, 2015. T. LOCK, The future of EU accession to the ECHR after Opinion 2/13: Is it still possible and is it still desirable?, in Edinburgh School of Law Research Paper Series, 2015. F. PICOD, La Cour de justice a dit non à l'adhésion de l'Union européenne à la Convention EDH, in La Semaine Juridique, Édition Générale, 2015, pp. 230, 234. J.P. JACQUÉ, The accession of the European Union to the European Convention on Human Rights and Fundamental Freedoms, in Common Market Law Review, 48 (4), 2011, pp. 995, 1005. S. PEERS, The EU's Accession to the ECHR: The dream becomes a nightmare, in German Law Journal, 16, 2015, pp. 213, 222. E. SPAVENTA, A very fearful Court? The protection of fundamental rights in the European Union after Opinion 2/13, in Maastricht Journal of European and Comparative Law, 22, 2015, pp. 51ss. M. KUIJER, The accession of the European Union to the ECHR: A gift for ECHR's 60th anniversary or an unwelcome intruder at the party?, in Amsterdam Law Forum, 4 (3), 2011, pp. 17-32. C. LADENBURGER, Vers l'adhésion de l'Union européenne à la Convention européenne des droits de l'homme, in Revue Trimestrielle de Droit Européen, 47 (1), 2011, pp. 20-26. T. LOCK, The ECJ and the ECtHR: The future relationship between the two European courts, in The Law and Practice of International Courts and Tribunals, 8, 2010, pp. 375-398. D. ASHIAGBOR, N. COUNTOURIS, I. LIANOS, The European Union after the Treaty of Lisbon, Cambridge University Press, Cambridge, 2012, pp. 109-135. N. O'MEARA, A more secure Europe of rights? The European Court of Human Rights, the Court of Justice of the European Union and EU Accession to the ECHR, in German Law Journal, 12, 2011, pp. 1813-1832. J. POLAKIEWICZ, EU law and the ECHR: Will the European Union's accession square the

These assumptions were then resumed, again with reference to EU, in Michaud case,[316] where ECtHR considered that it should not apply the presumption taking into account states margin of discretion, and, lastly, in Avotiņš v. Latvia case.[317]

The interesting fact is that the Bosphorus solution has become over the years a logical-juridical construction suitable to become a criterion for resolving regulatory conflicts between ECHR and the decisions taken by various organizations, even different from EU. Originating in a spirit of evident self-restraint (that is, to prevent the Strasbourg court from interfering with European system's autonomy), the doctrine under examination has then become an argumentative weapon in

circle?, in European Human Rights Law Review, 6, 2013, pp. 592-605. A. POTTEAU, Quelle adhésion de l'Union Européenne à la CEDH pour quel niveau de protection des droits et de l'autonomie de l'ordre juridique de l'UE?, in Revue Générale Droit International Public, 115, 2011, pp. 77-111. A. TORRES PEREZ, Too many voices? The prior involvement of the Court of Justice of the European Union? in European Journal of Human Rights, 40, 2013, pp. 565-583. L. BESSELINK, M. CLAES, J.H. REESTMAN, A Constitutional moment: Acceding to the ECHR (or not), in European Constitutional Law Review, 11, 2015, pp. 2ss. D. HALBESTRAM, It's autonomy stupid. A modest defense of Opinion 2/13 on EU accession to the ECHR, and a way forward, in Michigan Law Paper 105, 2015. L.H. HALLESKOV STORGAARD, EU law autonomy versus European fundamental rights protection-On Opinion 2/13 on EU accession to the ECHR, in Human Rights Law Review, 15, 2015, pp. 485. J.P. JACQUÉ, CJUE-CEDH: 2-0, in Revue Trimestrielle de Droit Européen, 40 (4), 2014 pp. 823ss. C. KRENN, Autonomy and effectiveness as common concerns: A path to ECHR accession after Opinion 2/13, in German Law Journal, 16 (1), 2015, pp. 147ss. S. LAMBRECHT, The sting is in the Tail: CJEU Opinion 2/13 objects to draft agreement on accession of the EU to the European Convention on Human Rights, in European Human Rights Law Review, 15 (1), 2015, pp. 185ss. M. PETITE, The battle over Strasbourg: The protection of human rights across Europe has suffered a setback, thanks to the Court of Justice of the European Union, in Competition Law Insight, 2015, pp. 10ss. R.A. WESSEL, A. ŁAZOWSKI, When Caveats Turn into Locks: Opinion 2/13 on Accession of the European Union to the ECHR, in German Law Journal, 16, 2015, pp. 179ss. B. DE WITTE, Article 53, in S. PEERS et al. (eds.), The EU Charter of Fundamental Rights, A Commentary, Hart Publishing, Oxford & Oregon, Portland, 2014, pp. 1523-1538. J. MEYER (ed.), Charta der Grundrechte der Europäischen Union, ed. Nomos, Baden-Baden, 2014, pp. 813-826. J.P. JACQUÉ, La Cour de l'Union et l'application de la Charte dans les Etats membres: "Mehr Licht," in European Yearbook on Human Rights, 14, 2014 pp. 125-147.

[316] ECtHR, Affaire Michaud v. France of 6 December 2012. F. TIMMERMANS, Fundamental rights protection in Europe before and after accession of the European Union to the European Convention on Human Rights, in Liber amicorum Pieter Van Dijk, M. Van Roosmalen and others op. cit., pp. 225ss.

[317] ECtHR, Avotiņš v. Latvia of 23 May 2016 and see also: Gasparini v. Italy and Belgium of 12 May 2009. For further details see: D. LIAKOPOULOS, Protection of human rights between European Court of Human Rights and Court of European Union, in International and European Union Legal Matters, 2015.

the hands of the applicants to impute state violations to human rights for acts carried out by the most varied organizations.

The presumption was in fact extended mutatis mutandis to NATO in the Gasparini case,[318] to the European Patent Organization in Klausecker v. Germany case of 2015, at the International Olive Oil Council in the Lopez Cifuentes v. Spain case of 2009 and, again, to other Organizations. However, the most delicate problems in the application of the Bosphorus solution emerged when the ECtHR was called to verify, not without embarrassment, the level of protection of human rights within the UN. For a long time Strasbourg judges have avoided in every way the possibility to pronounce themselves on the point. Indeed, with reference to the obligations arising from the resolutions of the Security Council, ECtHR showed a certain deference towards the UN. It is hardly necessary to recall that in Behrami and Saramati cases the doctrine of equivalent protection was not applied, preferring, on the one hand to attribute the act in question to the Organization, on the other to recall art. 103 of the UN Charter.[319]

In subsequent decisions (Al-Jedda and Nada) the ECtHR has further avoided verifying whether the UN offered protection equivalent to that of the Council of Europe, believing that there was still room for maneuver on States part in interpreting resolutions. The point was instead openly addressed in Al-Dulimi and Montana Management Inc. v. Switzerland case decided by the Chamber of the second section-although the solution to the matter was later revoked by the Grand Chamber decision.[320] With the Al-Dulimi case ECtHR has added an interesting piece to the complex mosaic that outlines the relationship between "ECHR system" and UN.[321]

The case concerned the conduct of Switzerland which, in implementation of Resolution 1483 (2003) of the Security Council, had proceeded to confiscate the assets belonging to the applicants, Mr. Khalaf

---

[318]ECtHR, Behrami and Behrami v. France, Saramati v. France, Germany and Norway, op. cit., and Berić and others v. Bosnia and Herzegovina, op. cit.

[319]S. KITHARIDIS, The power of article 103 of the UN Charter on Treaty obligations. Can the Security Council authorise non-compliance of human right treaty obligations in UN peacekeeping operations?, in Journal of International Peacekeeping, 20 (1-2), 2016.

[320]ECtHR, Al-Dulimi and Montana Management Inc. v. Switzerland of 26 Novembre 2013, postponed to the Grand Chamber exam on 14 April 2014 at the request of Switzerland. For further details see: S. KADELBACH, Al-Dulimi and Montana management Inc v. Switzerlnd (ECtHR), in International Legal Materials, 55 (6), 2016, pp. 1023ss. D. HARRIS, M. O'BOYLE, C. WARBRICK, Law of the European Convention on Human rights, op. cit., pp. 372ss.

[321]The 1518 Committee, created by Security Council Resolution 1518 (2003), replaced the Committee established by Resolution 661 (1990), which imposed a general embargo on Iraq.

M. Al-Dulimi and the Montana Management company he directs. Considered among the financiers of the Iraqi regime of Saddam Hussein, the applicants' names had been included in the list of recipients of sanctions by the 1518 Committee of the Security Council.[322] Mr. Al-Dulimi had challenged the internal deeds of asset freezing before the Swiss Federal Court, which, as a last resort, had opposed a firm refusal to examine the merits of the matter. According to the judges, the acts in question were bound to what was established by the Security Council with Resolution 1483, whose effectiveness should moreover be considered prevailing over any other international obligation possibly in conflict on the basis of art. 103 of the UN Charter. Mr. Al-Dulimi had then attempted to obtain the removal of his name directly from the Security Council's blacklist, first addressing a request for delisting to the Committee and then resorting to the Focal Point intergovernmental mechanism, in both cases with a negative outcome. At this point, the appellants had decided to appeal to ECtHR in order to determine whether Switzerland, by taking the measures to freeze its assets without granting a judicial review of the sanction in question, had violated the fundamental procedural guarantees provided for by article 6 par. 1 ECHR.[323]

Since the adoption of the asset freeze measure had been imposed by the Security Council in such a timely and detailed manner as to leave Switzerland no room for maneuver in the execution phase, the Chamber of the second section, not seeing any margin of harmonization between the various obligations involved, has for the first time (dis) applied the

---

[322]B. SIMMA, D.E. KHAN, G. NOLTE, A. PAULUS, N. WESSENDORF, The Charter of the United Nations, a commentary, Oxford University Press, Oxford, 2012, pp. 1293-1301.

[323]D. LIAKOPOULOS, Equo processo nella Convenzione europea dei diritti dell'uomo e nel diritto comunitario, ed. Cedam, 2007. D. LIAKOPOULOS, Protection of human rights between European Court of Human Rights and Court of European Union, op. cit., on the compatibility of the analogous criterion foreseen by art. 3 of the Swiss law of private international law and art. 6 of the Convention of the ECtHR in the sentence of Naït Liman v. Switzerland of 15 March 2018, par. 208ss, where it is also highlighted the similarity of the norm to the Swiss law with that contained in the Union regulations. For the improper nature of the actual link between the dispute and the court seised pursuant to art. 5 of the ECHR see also the the ECtHR Arlewein v. Sweden case of 1st March 2016, par. 63ss. D. LIAKOPOULOS, Protection of human rights between European Court of Human Rights and Court of European Union, op. cit., ECtHR, Nunes Dias v. Portugal of 10 April 2003. For further details and analysis see: B. RAINEY, W. WICKS, C. OVEY, Jacbos, White and Ovey: The European Convention on Human Rights, op. cit., J.P. COSTA, La Cour europèenne des droits de l'homme. Des juges pour la libertè, op. cit., F. TIMMERMANS, Fundamental rights protection in Europe before and after accession of the European Union to the European Convention on Human Rights, op., cit., pp. 225ss. D. HARRIS, M. O'BOYLE, C. WARBRICK, Law of the European Convention on Human rights, op. cit., pp. 372ss.

presumption of equivalence with reference to the UN system. Therefore, classifying the protection of procedural rights within the 1518 Committee of sanctions as insufficient-and thus excluding the presumption of equivalence the Chamber, with a close majority, judged the respondent State responsible for the violation of art. 6 par. 1 ECHR.[324]

However, this conclusion was contested by Switzerland, which requested the referral of the case to the examination of the Grand Chamber, which instead considered that there was a margin of appreciation for the State and, consequently, did not apply the Bosphorus solution. Therefore, to date, the (dis) application of equivalence presumption with reference to the UN, and the consequent verification of Member States responsibility, has not yet been the subject of a (final) ruling by the Strasbourg judges.

3.6. (Follows) State responsibility in the presence of a margin of discretion

In a second sub-group of decisions always concerning the internal implementation of obligations deriving from their membership in organizations, the ECtHR has instead given importance to the presence of a "margin of discretion" or "maneuver" available to States. In these cases States have been held responsible for not having interpreted, and then implemented, the acts of the Organization in order to avoid a conflict with ECHR.

The "human rights friendly" interpretation of obligations deriving from the organizations initially concerned the resolutions of the Security Council on the use of force and, subsequently, those that imposed the adoption of "targeted" sanctions. The guiding principles on the matter are to be found in the Al-Jeddah decision, which has challenged the suitability of art. 103 of the UN Charter to ensure, tout court, the prevalence of Security Council resolutions on ECHR obligations. On this occasion, the ECtHR sought to compose the potential regulatory conflict on the interpretative level, forcing a "harmonizing" interpretation of the Security Council's resolutions, through the presumption of their compliance with respect to human rights.[325]

It must be said that some years before the CJEU in the last act of the famous Kadi "saga,"[326] concerning the negative impact on human

---

[324]B. SIMMA, D.E. KHAN, G. NOLTE, A. PAULUS, N. WESSENDORF, The Charter of the United Nations, a commentary, op. cit.,

[325]ECtHR, Al-Jedda v. United Kingdom of 7 July 2011, par. 102.

[326]CJEU, joined cases: C-415/05 P, Kadi & Al Barakaat Int'l Foundation v. Council of 8 November 2008, ECLI:EU:C:2008:461, I-6351. For details see: R. UERPMANN-WITTZACK, Rechtsfragen und Rechtsfolgendes Beitritts der Europäischen Union zur

rights of the sanctions imposed by the Security Council, had already shown that it wanted to abandon the use of hierarchical criteria to resolve conflicts of rules, such as art. 103 of the UN Charter and the notion of ius cogens. According to Luxembourg judges the protection of human rights, in particular the respect of the two process guarantees, act, like a balancing with the need for international security, from "preventive counter-limit" to the automatic operation of Security Council Resolution within the EU framework. Parallel to the Kadi saga, even Strasbourg judges, called to rule on the same sanctions, avoided the reference to art. 103 of the UN Charter, claiming from States every possible effort to reconcile only apparently conflicting international obligations.

ECtHR clarified the point in Nada case, concerning the implementation by the Swiss authorities of resolutions of the Security Council which imposed sanctions against Mr. Youssef Nada, an Italian citizen of Egyptian origin accused of financing the Al-Qaeda network. However, while in the Al-Jeddah case the resolution left such interpretive margins as to allow for the harmonization of obligations imposed by the ECHR and the conduct required by the Security Council, in Nada case the resolution was formulated in such an explicit and clear manner as to leave no doubt about the opposition to ECHR. Nevertheless, according to the somewhat forced interpretation of Strasbourg judges, the State would still have retained some discretion, "which was admittedly limited but nevertheless real," in the execution of Security Council resolutions. According to the twisted reasoning of ECtHR, States should interpret the resolutions as meaning that they imply the existence of a margin of maneuver in the implementation phase, such as to avoid collisions with the rights sanctioned by the ECHR. This margin would have allowed the respondent State to adopt internal measures cut to the specific case and respectful of the applicant's human rights.[327]

Based on these premises, ECtHR considered that Switzerland had

---

EMRK, in Europarecht, 2012, pp. 167ss. C. NOWAK, Europarecht nach Lissabon, ed. Nomos, Baden-Baden, 2011. D. CHALMERS, G. DAVIES, G. MONTI, EU law, Cambridge University Press, Cambridge, 2014. J. TILLOTSON, N. FOSTER, Text, cases and materials on EU law, Gavedish Publishing, New York, 2013. M. HORSPOOL, M. HUMPHREYS, EU law, Oxford University Press, Oxford, 2012, pp. 552ss. SATZGER, International and European criminal law, Hart Publishing, Oxford & Oregon, Portland, 2017. T. OPPERMANN, C.D. CLASSEN, M. NETTESHEIM, Europarecht, C.H. Beck, München, 2016.

[327]ECtHR, Nada v. Switzerland of 12 September 2012 (spec. Par. 196). E. DE WET, From Kadi to Nada: Judicial techniques favouring human rights over United Nations Security Council sanctions, in Chinese Journal of International Law, 12, 2013, pp. 787-808. S. SCHMAL, M. BREUER, The Council of Europe: Its law and policies, Oxford University Press, Oxford, 2017. D. STEPHENS, P. BARK, Imagining law. Essays in conversation with Judith Gardam, University of Adelaide Press, 2016.

not (shown to have) made every effort to do so, using the limited room for maneuver available to it. More precisely, the state was condemned for not having mitigated the sanctions imposed by the Committee with internal measures that took into consideration the peculiar health conditions of the applicant, as well as the "geographical" specificity of the case.[328]

In the same spirit of "systematic harmonization" of international obligations, the Al-Dulimi case was set by the Grand Chamber.[329] First of all, it must be said that the important precedents Kadi and Nada made it unlikely an overruling by the Grand Chamber with respect to the solution proposed by the Chamber. However, the long time taken to reach a decision, the only apparent majority with which it was adopted[330] and the full body of competing and dissenting opinions show that the confirmation of the solution adopted by the Chamber was not so obvious. In fact, it stops the condemnation of Switzerland for the violation of art. 6 par. 1, the reasoning of the Grand Chamber judges differs, in part, but significantly, from that of the Chamber in the following fundamental passages.

The first point that deserves attention is the failure to recognize a real "regulatory conflict" between the obligations in question, such as to require the use of hierarchical criteria (such as article 103 of the UN Charter or the notion of ius cogens) or the reference to the theory of equivalent protection.[331] Contrary to what was argued by the Chamber, the Grand Chamber considered that Switzerland maintained a margin of maneuver, if not in the application of the Security Council resolution, at least in its interpretation.[332] Having denied the existence of a regulatory

---

[328]It should be noted that in the Nada case, Switzerland had been called upon to implement the sanctioning measure of the travel ban against the applicant, Youssef Nada, suffering from health problems for which it was necessary to move outside the enclave of Campione d'Italia where he resided. In doing so, Switzerland would have failed to incorporate the sanctions with appropriate acts to respect the principle of proportionality in limiting the rights of the recipient of the sanctions. (ECtHR, Nada v. Switzerland, op. cit., par. 195-196).

[329]ECtHR, Al-Dulimi and Montana Management Inc. v. Switzerland, op. cit.

[330]The decision was voted on with fifteen votes in favor and two against. However, among the fifteen judges, seven, while sharing the conclusion of the sentence, have criticized the reasoning followed and one has partially disagreed.

[331]See the opinion of judge: Pinto de Albuquerque, accepted also from the judges: Hajiyev, Pejchal and Dedov.

[332]ECtHR, Al-Dulimi, op. cit., par. 149. Actually, in the last passages of the sentence in question a reference can be made to the application of the doctrine of equivalent protection. According to the judges of the Grand Chamber "the system applicable in the present case, in compliance with the following form Resolution 1730 (2006), enabling applicants to apply to a "focal point" for the deletion of their names from the Security Council lists, not afford satisfactory protection" (paragraph 153). ECtHR, Al-Dulimi, op. cit., par. 149. On the difference between the margin of discretion in the implementation of the Security Council resolutions and in their interpretation see: S. HOLLENBERG, The diverging

conflict, the Grand Chamber opted for the argumentative model inaugurated with the Al-Jedda case, based on the presumption of compliance of the Security Council resolutions with the human rights protected by ECHR and their harmonious systemic interpretation in the light of ECHR.[333]

Switzerland was therefore disputed that it had chosen an interpretation of Resolution 1483 that was not in accordance with ECHR, as it precluded the recipient of the sanction from being able to appeal to the internal courts to allow a review of measures, as this right was not expressly excluded in Resolution.[334] ECtHR therefore rejected the objection of Swiss government, according to which the indications contained in the resolution to freeze "immediately" and "without delay" the assets of applicants were impeded by any judicial review as they left no room for maneuver to national authorities.

It should be noted, however, that the judicial review that the domestic Courts should have carried out would consist in the opinion of ECtHR in a de minimis poll, limited to excluding only the profiles of arbitrariness in the adoption of freezing measures.

The second aspect of novelty of the sentence with respect to the previous jurisprudence is that national judges have recognized the obligation of a (limited) control on the sanctions in question, focused on the respect of arbitrariness prohibition, as a standard resulting from a balancing "the need to ensure respect for human rights and the imperatives of protecting international peace and security."[335]

3.7. (Follows) Criticisms of the orientations examined

When ECtHR is called upon to rule on the conduct of a state that imposes obligations imposed by an organization it is concerned, first of all, to ascertain the presence or absence of a margin of discretion on the part of States. This verification therefore constitutes the first bifurcation of the

---

approaches of the European Court of Human Rights in the cases of Nada and Al-Dulimi, in International and Comparative Law Quarterly, 64, 2015, pp. 454ss.

[333]ECtHR, Al-Dulimi, op. cit., par. 139-140.

[334]ECtHR, Al-Dulimi, op. cit., par. 146, "where a resolution such as that in the present case, namely Resolution 1483, does not contain any clear or explicit wording excluding the possibility of judicial supervision of the measures taken for its implementation, it must always be understood as authorising the courts of the respondent State to exercise sufficient scrutiny so that any arbitrariness can be avoided."

[335]ECtHR, Al-Dulimi, op. cit., par. 146, which is affirmed that "(...) [t]he obligations on States under Resolution 1483 (2003) were clear and explicit, leaving them no room for discretion (...)."

reasoning usually followed by ECtHR which, if so, carries out a full scrutiny on the possible liability of the State pursuant to ECHR, while, if not, it limits itself to applying the doctrine of equivalent protection.

In this regard, the conclusions reached by ECtHR on the presence of a margin of discretion by States are not convincing. In particular, it raises some doubts about having considered in Nada and Al-Dulimi cases a room for maneuver (albeit subtle), suitable for allowing Switzerland to harmonize (apparently) conflicting obligations. It seems to us that the prescription contained clearly in Security Council's resolutions to freeze "immediately" and "without delay" individuals funds on lists does not leave many alternatives to States.[336] It could even be assumed that it is irreconcilable with a judicial review of sanctions before national courts which, hypothetically, could take several years. Furthermore, it is not clear how the language used by Security Council resolutions leaves such room for maneuver in States, whereas the one used in EU regulations does not allow it, as in Bosphorus case, to implement one of the prerequisites for the application of equivalent protection theory. A "political," but not "legal" answer may perhaps be found in the comitas that ECtHR intends to show to the UN.

With regard to the inadequate distinction between the attribution and jurisdiction profile, we can say that in cases where the obligation descending from the organization leaves no margin of discretion in its interpretation or implementation, ECtHR applies the theory of equivalent protection. It has not yet been sufficiently clarified however for what reasons state conduct, although being an action strongly "bound" to organization's decision, is in any case attributable to State and not to the organization itself, with the consequences that this entails on the plan of admissibility of ratione personae appeal.[337] Recently Sajó judge, in the dissenting opinion expressed in Al-Dulimi case decided by the Chamber, raised the point, believing that, given the absence of a margin of maneuver on the part of Switzerland in implementing the Security Council resolution, the conduct presumably harmful should be attributed to the UN Organization and not to the State. However, this solution was completely rejected by the decision adopted by the majority of ECtHR that, both in

[336]In the case of Al-Dulimi, the existence of such a margin was challenged not only by the defendant State, but also by France and Great Britain as intervening States. According to the British government, "[t]he obligations on the States under Resolution 1483 (2003) were clear and explicit, leaving them no room for discretion (...)" ECtHR, Al-Dulimi, op. cit., par. 119). A partially different argument could apply to the adoption of the sanction of the travel ban, as the implementation of the same would leave a margin of maneuver slightly wider than the measure of freezing funds.

[337]F. HOFFMEISTER, Bosphorus Hava Yollari Turizm ve Ticaret Anonim Sirket v. Ireland. App. No. 45036/98, in American Journal of international law, 100, 2006, pp. 447ss.

Chamber and Grand Chamber decision in Al-Dulimi case, preferred to decide the matter, in continuity with Bosphorus jurisprudence, imputing the act in question to Switzerland without clarifying the reason.

Whenever the problem has arisen, Strasbourg judges have limited themselves to ascertaining the existence of internal measures adopted by the national authorities, which would have entailed the existence of state jurisdiction pursuant to art. 1 ECHR. However, such reasoning seems to us to be questionable both because it does not resolve the central issue, and because it ends up super-imposing the profile of conduct imputation (which may determine the admissibility or not of ratione personae appeal) and state jurisdiction ascertainment pursuant to art. 1 (which determines the admissibility of the ratione loci appeal). On the other, as we will see in the next section, ECtHR does not adequately distinguish the two aspects (attribution and jurisdiction) even in cases where an internal measure is absent.[338]

Even admitting that in cases where a contracting State has limited itself to reproduce with internal measures, without any margin of maneuver, an obligation deriving from the Organization must be attributed to State (and not to the Organization).[339] We believe that ECtHR should have better clarified its position on the point by referring, not so much to dédoublement fonctionne theory, as to DARIO, rarely mentioned in its jurisprudence, especially with regard to provisions contained in Chapter VI, entitled "state responsibility in connection with Organization conduct."[340] In this respect, one of the weakest points of ECtHR jurisprudence is precisely the failure to attempt to reconcile its solutions with the existing general international law on the subject, limit that emerges also in relation to the elaboration of equivalent protection, a theory which we now need linger.

And on the functioning of the equivalent protection and on its non-comparison with the general international law on responsibility? A third criticism concerns the operation of equivalent protection doctrine, one of the pillars on which the approach adopted by ECtHR on the subject of state responsibility connected to organizations acts. This theory and the underlying assumption on which it is based can be moved, first of all, by a radical critique, contesting the premise that every organization must guarantee a standard of protection of human rights at least equivalent to

---

[338]ECtHR, Boivin v. 34 Member States of the Council of Europe of 9 September 2008.

[339]A. CASSESE, Remarks on Scelle's theory of "role splitting" (dédoublement fonctionnel in international law), in European Journal of International Law, 1, 1990, pp. 210ss.

[340]A. NEDESKI, N. NOLLKAEMPER, Responsibility of international organizations "in connection with the acts of States," op. cit., C. RYNGAERT, The European Court of Human Rights approach to the responsibility of Member States in connection with acts of international organizations, op. cit., pp. 997-1016.

the "system" created by the ECHR. While in fact the "ECHR system" was created with the primary task of verifying respect for human rights through a jurisdictional mechanism, there are several organizations that do not have the same purpose and that, therefore, do not have human rights equivalent protection structures (especially jurisdictional). It is worth recalling in this regard that the reasoning underlying the doctrine of equivalent protection is clearly inspired by the Solange I, II and III decisions of the German Constitutional Court (adopted respectively in 1974, 1986 and 2015),[341] which, however, were drafted to resolve relations

---

[341] Maastricht Urteil, BVerfG 89, 1993. For further details see: M. DEVISSER, Constitutional review in Europe: A comparative analysis, Hart Publishing, Oxford & Oregon, Portland, 2013. H. LINDAHL, Fault lines of globalization. Legal order an the politics of a-legality, Oxford University Press, Oxford, 2013. M. WENDEL, Exceeding judicial competence in the name of democracy. The German Federal Constitutional Court's OMT reference, in European Constitutional Law Review, 10, 2014, pp. 264ss. M. HONG, Human dignity, identity review of the European Arrest Warrant and the Court of justice as a listener in the dialogue of Courts: Solange-II and Aranyosi: Bverfg 13 December 2015, 2 BvR 2735/154 Solange III and ECJ (Grand Chamber) 5 April 2006, joined cases C-404715 and C-659/15 PPU, Aranyosi and Căldăraru, in European Constitutional Law Review, 12, 2016, pp. 550ss. E. DUBOUT, Les règles ou principles inhèrented à l'identitè constitutionelle de la France: une supra-constituionnalitè, in Revue Française de Droit Constitionnel, 108, 2010, pp. 452ss. M. BOSSUYT, W. VERRIJDT, The full effect of EU law and of constitutional review in Belgium and France after the Melti judgment, in European Constitutional Law Review, 7, 2011, pp. 356ss. P. GÉRARD, W. VERRIJDT, Belgian Constitutional Court adopts national identity discourse: Belgian Constitutional Court n. 62/2016, 28 April 2016, in European Constitutional Law Review, 13, 2017, pp. 182ss. For a spain see: F. CASTILLO DE LA TORRE, Tribunal constitucional (Spanish Constitutional Court), Opinion 1/2004 of 13 December 2004, in Common Market Law Review, 42, 2005, pp. 1170ss. For Hungary: G. HALMAI, The hungarian national(ist) constitutional identity, in Quaderni Costituzionali, 2017, pp. 152ss. C. HARLOW, P. LEINO, G. DELLA CANNANEA, Research handbook on EU administrative law, Edward Elgar Publishers, 2017. pp. 453ss. P.J.C. ORTIZ, EU treaties and the judicial politics of national courts: A law and politics approach, ed. Routledge, London New York, 2015. A. VON BOGDANDY, M. KOTTMANN, C. ANTPÖHLER, J. DICKSCHEN, S. HENTREI, M. SMRKOLJ, Reverse Solange-protecting the essence of fundamental rights against the Member States, in Common Market Law Review, 49, 2012, pp. 490ss. A. VON BOGDANDY, M. IOANNIDIS, Systemic deficiency in the rule of law: What it is, that has been done, what can be done, in Common Market Law Review, 51, 2014, pp. 60ss. D. KOCHENOV, L. PECH, Monitoring and enforcement of the rule of law in the EU rhetoric and reality, in European Constitutional Law Review, 12, 2015, pp. 514ss. T. KONSTADINIDES, The rule of law in the EU: The internal dimension, Hart Publishing, Oxford & Oregon, Portland, 2017. C. CLOSA, D. KOCHENOV, Reinforcing rule of law oversight in the EU, Cambridge University Press, Cambridge, 2016. M. ADAMS, A. MEUWESE, E. HIRSCH BALLIN, Constitutionalism and the rule of law. Bridging realism and realism, Cambridge University Press, Cambridge, 2017, pp. 423ss. N.W. BARBER, M. CAHILL, R. EKINS, The rise and face of the European constitution, Hart Publishing, Oxford & Oregon, Portland, 2019. F.C. MEYER, From "Solange II to Forever I." The

between two judicial bodies, namely the German Constitutional Court and CJEU. The application of the mutatis mutandis theory to UN, instead, would lead to a confrontation between a judicial (the Court) and a political body (the Security Council), distorting the ratio in question. The functioning of the theory would then be at least circumscribed to the organizations that have the powers to (directly) affect the protection of individual rights and the Bosphorus solution should be proportionally applied. We believe, in other words, that the level of protection guaranteed within an organization should not always and necessarily be equivalent to that of ECHR, but may change according to the organization in question, in a manner proportionate to the powers it exercises actually on individuals.

It is true that, as far as is known, the organizations to which the theory has been directly applied have never explicitly raised these objections and therefore seem somehow to have given acquiescence to the solution given by ECtHR. The UN, for example, does not seem to have publicly challenged the theoretical assumptions of the doctrine. Indeed, many authors often emphasize the ability of the Bosphorus doctrine to resolve normative contrasts in a "diplomatic" way, highlighting the virtuous dialogue that would be created with the organization concerned and the consequent raising of protection standards. In this regard, some important improvements made to the Security Council sanctions Committees, such as the establishment of the Focal Point in 2006 and, even more significantly, the Ombudsman in 2009, are usually referred to.

Even if we admit that we want to share the basic assumption of equivalent protection doctrine, there remain however some perplexities regarding the consequences deriving from the application or non of the equivalence presumption. It has been said that, if the organization concerned protects the rights of individuals in an equivalent manner, state conduct would be removed from the scrutiny of ECtHR. However, ECtHR has not specified that the substantial "immunity" is based on the responsibility that generates the equivalence presumption. Abstractly, this situation seems to recall the functioning of one of the circumstances of exclusion of the offense envisaged by Chapter V of 2001 DRSIWA. The circumstance by which the States acted in implementation of an obligation

---

German Federal Constitutional Court and the European Arrest Warrant (and how the CJEU responded), in New Journal of European Criminal Law, 7, 2016, pp. 278ss. Federal Constitutional Court of Germany, order no. 2735/14 of 15 December 2015. For further analysis see: L. VIOLINI, A. BARAGGIA, The fragmented landscape of fundamental rights protection in Europe, Edward Elgar Publishers, Cheltenahm, 2018, pp. 95ss. S. VOENEKY, G.L. NEUMAN, Human rights democracy and legitimacy in a world of disorder, Cambridge University Press, Cambridge, 2018, pp. 216ss. L.I. GORDILLO, Interlocking constitutions: Towards an interordinal theory of national European and UN law, Hart Publishing, Oxford & Oregon, Portland, 2012.

deriving from an organization with "certification" of equivalent protection, it would then function as a clause of exclusion of state responsibility drawn up, under the lex specialis, for the conventional system of offenses on which ECtHR supervises. If this were indeed the case, the operation of such a clause would, however, deserve to be compared with the existing rules of general international law on the subject.

Similar doubts also arise in relation to consequences that occur in the opposite scenario, namely when the organization does not offer equivalent protection or, while offering it in general terms, in the case in question it is found to be "manifestly insufficient."[342] One of the most obscure points of the doctrine under examination concerns the title of direct or indirect responsibility of States, which, even individually, can be called upon to respond to organizations shortcomings. Chamber's decision in the Al-Dulimi case represented the only example in which the protection within an organization was considered not equivalent to that of ECHR and in which, consequently, priority was given to ECHR with respect to the obligations set by the Organization, holding the state implicitly responsible for not having complied with this priority order. However, the decision did not clarify the responsibility of the respondent State, having regard also to the provisions of DARIO or DRSIWA-including art. 61 DRSIWA, which foresee different possible combinations in terms of attribution of responsibility (or conduct) between States and Organization. The issue is destined, for now, to remain open since the Grand Chamber in the Al-Dulimi case has set its reasoning on other premises. Another topic of discussion dates back to the other tools for resolving regulatory conflicts. In reality, it is now clear from the latest decisions that the ECtHR wants to avoid in any way ruling on the resolution of regulatory conflicts, especially when they concern the incompatibility of ECHR with the obligations contracted by States based on Chapter VII of the UN Charter. If ECtHR, when cornered, recognizes that it is faced with irreconcilable international obligations through interpretations that are also forcibly

---

[342]In this regard, the elements necessary to establish a judgment of equivalence and the contours of the requirement of "manifest insufficiency," threshold, not better defined below which the automatic exclusion of state responsibility is not realized, are not clear. On the point see the concurrent opinion of judge Ress in the Bosphorus decision, in which he suggested using as a guiding criterion for the examination of insufficient evidence the respect that the Court of Justice would have in the future given to the precedents of the Court of Strasbourg and the jurisprudence of the Court of justice not in general, but rather in relation to the intensity of protection of the specific right guaranteed by the ECHR that is allegedly infringed (see: Concurring opinion of judge Ress, para 1-5, in Bosphorus v. Ireland, op. cit). In favour of an assessment in relation to individual cases and not in respect of the overall conformity of the system as a whole, under penalty of nullifying the rationale of the mechanism of individual appeals before the Court.

harmonizing, in light of the choices made so far, it would have two possible options for resolving the regulatory conflict.

The first is the hierarchical definition of the relationships between different legal systems. Useful tools for this purpose are both the supremacy clause contained in art. 103 of UN Charter (with consequent prevalence of ECHR resolutions,)[343] both the notion of ius cogens (with consequent prevalence of the imperative norms of international law on resolutions) and the (dis) application of equivalence presumption (with consequent priority of ECHR on resolutions).

The explicit reference to art. 103 Charter at first sight it would appear to be a precluded path, given the very hard and innumerable criticisms that this solution has attracted in the past,[344] as well as having been abandoned by the Luxembourg judges.[345] However, it must be emphasized that in the last decision on the subject (Al-Dulimi), the capacity of art. 103 was not entirely disavowed to resolve possible regulatory conflicts, as has emerged also in Mothers of Srebrenica case.

The impression is that ECtHR prefers to give priority to Security Council resolutions, and therefore to the value of security in respect of individual human rights,[346] to avoid interfering with the delicate task

---

[343] J.P. COT, A. PELLET, M. FORTEAU, La Charte des Nations Unies. Commentaire article par article, vol. II, ed. Economica, Paris, 2006, pp. 2134-2147. R. LIVOJA, The scope of the supremacy clause of the United Nations, in International and Comparative Law Quarterly, 57, 2008, pp. 583-612. D. BOWETT, The impact of Security Council Decisions on dispute settlement procedures, in European Journal of international law, 5, 1994, pp. 89-101. R. HIGGINS, P. WEBB, D. AKANDE, J. SLOAN, S. SIVAKUMARAN, Oppenheim's international law, Oxford University Press, Oxford, 2018. K.L.H. SAMUEL, N.D. WHITE, Counter-terrorism and international law, ed. Routledge, London & New York, 2017. R.S.J. MARTHA, The financial obligation in international law, op. cit., M.W. DOYLE, Dialectics of a global constitution. The struggle over the UN Charter, in European Journal of International Relations, 18 (4), 2011, pp. 602ss. On the fact that the effect of supremacy covers the resolutions of the Security Council, see International Court of Justice, Montreal Convention Forming the Aerial Incident at Lockerbie (Libya v. UK, Libya v. United States), (Provisional Measures), ICJ, Reports, Opinion of 14 April 1992. On the reading of the art. 103 which is imposed jointly with the articles 1 par. 3, 24 par. 2 and the preamble to the Charter. A. ZIMMERMANN, C.J. TAMS, K. OELLERS-FRAHAM, The Statute of the International Court of Justice. A commentary, op. cit.

[344] ECtHR, Behrami and Behrami v. France, Saramati v. France, Germany and Norway, op. cit.

[345] This is clearly evident from par. 149 of the Al-Dulimi decision taken by the Grand Chamber, which excludes the application of art. 103 for the sole reason that, in the case in question, there was no conflict between international obligations.

[346] Therefore, in light of a joint reading of the articles 1 par. 3, 24 par. 2 and 103 of the Charter, resolutions that deviate from compliance with the aims and principles of the Charter, within the limits of an adequate balance with the need for the maintenance of international security (this last undoubtedly primary objective of the Organization), could

exercised by the Organization in terms of use of force and struggle to terrorism. Whatever the purpose and function of the call made by ECtHR to art. 103, however, it should not be forgotten that, according to a certain interpretation, the provision would impose a priority on Security Council resolutions provided that they were adopted in accordance with the UN purposes and principles, including the respect for human rights.[347]

The possibility, instead, of invoking the notion of jus cogens is precluded by the lack of a firm opinion on the qualification of most of the rights sanctioned by ECHR as imperative norms of international law. In the case of art. 6 ECtHR, for example, this possibility was expressly excluded by ECtHR jurisprudence itself.

After the decision of the Grand Chamber in Al-Dulimi uncertain it is also the future of the (dis) application of the doctrine of equivalent protection, which, as has been correctly pointed out in the doctrine, is an adequate interpretative tool to make a system prevail over other.

A second route would therefore remain open, indeed never clearly explored by ECtHR, namely that of setting the relationship between "ECHR" and "UN system" in dualistic terms, in the same way as an adequate balance between values.[348] Referring to counter-limits theory, the Court could argue that the obligations deriving from States membership to organizations "enter" into the legal systems of ECHR signatory States purged from those parts which conflict with certain rights sanctioned by ECHR, among which it often notes access to justice (a reasoning that we could define "at Kadi I"[349] and, mutatis mutandis, "at 238/2014" of the Italian Constitutional Court).[350] This would mean,

---

be considered invalid and therefore the effect of the supremacy clause referred to in art. 103.

[347]ICJ, Jurisdictional Immunities of the State (Germany v. Italy: Greece intervening), Dissenting Opinion of Judge Cançado Trindade, par. 219, of 3 February 2012. A. ZIMMERMANN, C.J. TAMS, K. OELLERS-FRAHAM, The Statute of the International Court of Justice. A commentary, op. cit.

[348]Looking closely at the Al-Dulimi decision of the Grand Chamber, the Court seems to use, in part, the technique of balancing values, but only in identifying the standard for the review of resolutions by internal courts (i.e. the control of a possible arbitrariness of the sanctions).

[349]CJEU, joined cases: C-415/05 P, Kadi & Al Barakaat Int'l Foundation v. Council of 8 November 2008, op. cit. For details see, R. UERPMANN-WITTZACK, Rechtsfragen und Rechtsfolgendes Beitritts der Europäischen Union zur EMRK, op. cit.

[350]For further details see: G. BOGGERO, The legal implications of sentence no. 238/2014 by Italy's Constitutional Court for italian municipal judges: Is overcoming the "triepelian approach" possible?, in Zeitschrift für ausländisches öffentliches Recht und Völkerrecht, 76, 2016, pp. 204ss. A. CHECHI, Judgment n. 238-2014 (IT. Const. Ct.), in International Legal Materials, 54 (3), 2015, pp. 472ss. M. SCHEININ, The Italian Constitutional Court's judgment 238 of 2014 is not another Kadi case, in Journal of International Criminal Justice,

however, taking a position on some rather delicate aspects. First of all, ECtHR should qualify ECHR's individual provisions as a counter-limit to the implantation of ECHR system and, at the same time, implicitly recognize the existence of profiles of illegality in Security Council resolutions if not give them the qualification of ultra vires acts on the basis of a joint reading of articles 1 par. 3, 24 par. 2 and 103 of the UN Charter. Last but not least, ECtHR should raise "ECHR system" to a galaxy that is autonomous from other legal systems that dot the order of international law.

However, even the "dualistic" road today seems not viable. The final result of this approach would in fact lead to a surgical application of international law contrary to the will of ECHR States Parties[351] and, on closer inspection, to that of ECHR itself which on several occasions repeated that the latter is a tool to be applied not in a "legal vacuum," but in an integrated way with other obligations of international law incumbent on States.[352]

Given the blind alleys to which the various instruments for resolving regulatory conflicts lead (the hierarchical approach, including the non-application of equivalent protection, and the dualistic approach operated with the balancing technique), we believe that in the future the ECHR will be brought to deny at root the existence of a contrast between obligations, forcing increasingly harmonizing interpretations.

Another point of thought is oriented towards the notion of arbitrariness as a new emerging standard of protection. We have seen that in Al-Dulimi case decided by the Grand Chamber, a forced systematic interpretation of Security Council resolutions was chosen, recognizing judges' national legitimacy to review the content of the same in terms of arbitrariness, as a standard resulting from a balance between "the need to

---

13 (3), 2016, pp. 616ss. E. BJORGE, C. MILES, Landmark cases in public international law, Hart Publishing, Oxford & Oregon, Portland, 2017. B.E. CARTER, A.S. WEINER, D.B. HOLLIS, International law, Wolters Kluwer, New York, 2018, pp. 706ss.

[351]"Would result in a dissociation between the different international systems, with the risk that the inability of States to fulfil their obligations according to the respective systems might lead to a weakening of those obligations, whose binding force might no longer be perceived in the same manner that would have the combined effect of minimising the importance of the operations imposed by the Security Council Resolutions under Chapter VII of the UN Charter in order to preserve international peace and security, of encroaching upon the exclusive competence of the Security Council as a political decision-maker, and also of weakening the authority of the judgments of the European Court of Human Rights itself" (ECtHR, Al-Dulimi, op. cit., par. 111).

[352]"As the Court has observed on many occasions, the Convention cannot be interpreted in a vacuum and should so far as possible be interpreted in harmony with other rules of international law of which it forms part," ECtHR, Hassan v. the United Kingdom of 16 September 2014, par. 77.

ensure respect for human rights and the imperatives of protecting international peace and security."[353] ECtHR does not specify what the standard thus identified consists of.

The notion of "arbitrariness" seems to refer to abnormal vices which, resorting to the terminology of administrative law, would lead to the nullity of an act for lack of its essential elements, such as macro deficiencies, errors in proceeding and in facto, as for example oversights cases of homonymy, the latter error also frequent in the practice of the Committees. If this were the case, the new arbitrariness parameter would require the domestic courts to verify the correspondence between the names included in the sanctions lists and applicants' identity, as well as the belonging of the goods to be frozen to these which, for example in Al-Dulimi case, the Swiss courts had indeed done and, moreover, to request and obtain precise information on the case in question. It remains uncertain, however, to what extent the examination of this information may lead to an evaluation of the reasons justifying the inclusion of a name in the list. Even if the judgment of arbitrariness included also some profiles of merit, it would seem that a judicial control comparable to that emerging from the Kadi II[354] decision would have to be excluded. It could then be referenced (but the ECtHR did not specify it at all) to the "international" standard identified by the Ombudsman operating for the Sanctions Committee for individuals associated with Da'esh and Al-Qaeda.[355]

3.8. (Follows) On the failure to consider the international plan and behaviours payable by governments within organizations

First of all, there is a general lack of coordination between national

[353]ECtHR, Al-Dulimi, op. cit., par. 146.

[354]The degree of judicial control over the sanctions referred to by the Al-Dulimi decision does not seem to be closer to the full judicial review supported by the Court of Justice of the European Union in the Kadi II case (see Commission, Council, United Kindom v. Yassin Abdullah Kadi, op. cit., Section 111 ss and 134). The judge of the Union, in conducting his scrutiny of the sanctions challenged, believes, among other things, that he should have access to the information and evidence supporting the reasons for the adoption of the sanction, verifying "the material accuracy the facts brought to trial in the light of such information or elements and assess the probative effectiveness of the latter according to the circumstances of the case and in the light of any comments made in this regard, in particular, by the data subject (...)" (paragraph 124).

[355]According to the procedure adopted by this body the inclusion (and maintenance) of a name in the lists is legitimate if "there is sufficient information to provide a reasonable and credible basis for listing." The procedure used by the Ombudsman of the Sanctions Committee against individuals associated with Da'esh and Al-Qaida.

and international levels, as can be seen by considering, for an instant, the practical implications of the Al-Dulimi judgment. The eventual verification by the national courts of the arbitrary nature of a sanction leads to a coordination between judicial decision and the action of the executive body that must annul or modify the internal provision implementing the measure. However, this would not necessarily translate into a change in the sanction at the international level (within the Committees). It is not to be excluded, from another point of view, that if an internal court were to ascertain the arbitrariness of a sanctioning measure (with consequent interruption or modification of its efficacy), which does not follow the cancellation or modification of the sanction also in the list of relative Committee, there would be serious profiles of international state responsibility for the failure or not exact compliance with Security Council resolutions, as a consequence of the conduct of its judicial bodies.[356] Moreover, any internal decision to cancel or modify the imposed sanction, not followed by a change also within the Committees, would not prevent another UN Member State from adopting the same measure in relation to additional assets present in its territory and therefore the possibility that the judges of the second State will pronounce themselves on the arbitrariness of the sanctions in a different way from those of the former. It would therefore be appropriate for the ECtHR to clarify, even incidentally, whether ECHR States Party, having ascertained the actual arbitrariness of a sanction, should promptly notify the Committee with the aim of erasing their registration. In this way, contradictory behaviours between executive and judiciary and international and national level would be avoided.

A second aspect, connected to the previous one, not specifically addressed by the ECtHR, concerns the positive behaviours that can be demanded by the representatives of governments within the organizations and the pressures that these must be able to exercise therein. In this respect, and with reference to the listing and delisting procedures, it would have been useful to pronounce judgments on the behaviour of the contracting States, not only through their judges, but also through their representatives in the international organization, and in particular by the missions of Permanent States at UN. In the Al-Dulimi case, for example, ECtHR would have had to evaluate more carefully the behaviour of the respondent State in relation to the following aspects: To what extent the State concerned used every reasonable effort to make procedural improvements to the functioning of the Committee;[357] to what extent it was involved in

[356]A. TZANAKOPOULOS, Disobeying the Security Council, Oxford University Press, Oxford, 2011.

[357]In this regard, it should be noted that Switzerland, which has twice been condemned by

the decision-making processes that led to the inclusion of the name in the lists; if and to what extent it was interested in the case of the plaintiffs and proposed and/or supported a request for delisting to the Committee, also through the intergovernmental mechanism of the Focal Point.[358] In this regard, ECtHR should have clarified the possible existence of an obligation for ECHR States Party to take action within the Sanctions Committees, i.e. the framework of the existing procedures for the protection of the individual concerned, in order to obtain the cancellation and/or modification of the restrictive measures, according to a scheme that recalls the exercise of "diplomatic protection."[359]

These considerations clearly highlight the limits of decisions-such as Nada and Al-Dulimi-which require contracting States to fill the protective vacuum inherent in the targeted sanctions regime only at national (and not even international) level. It is certainly true that ECtHR is responsible for assessing the conduct of ECtHR States Parties and not that of international organizations. However, we believe that this limitation would not have prevented it from taking a stronger position with respect to positive behaviours due to governments in these intergovernmental forums.[360]

---

the Court, although it has only been a member of the United Nations since 2002, is part of the group of so-called Like Minded States (which also includes Austria, Belgium, Costa Rica, Denmark, Finland, Germany, Liechtenstein, the Netherlands, Norway, Sweden), who presented concrete proposals for changes to the procedures followed by the Committees to make them more respectful of the procedural guarantees (see last document filed on 12 November 2015 Proposal to the United Nations Security Council by the Group of the Like-Minded States) on targeted sanctions.

[358]In the Al-Dulimi case, the Swiss government (through its permanent mission to the UN), in a letter dated 5 November 2004 addressed to the presidency of the 1518 Committee, had supported the applicant's first delisting request.

[359]See: GC, T-253/02, Ayadi v. Council of 12 July 2006, ECLI:EU:C:2006:200, II-02139. T-49/04, Hassan v. Council and Commission of 12 July 2006, ECLI:EU:C:2006:201, II-00052. For further analysis see: G. ZICCARDI CAPALDO, The pillars of global law, Ashgate Publishing, London, 2013, pp. 295ss.

[360]J.F. FLAUSS, Immunites des organizations internationales et droit international des droits de l'homme, in La soumission des organizations internationales aux normes internationales relatives aux droits de l'homme, in Journée d'études de Strasbourg/Societe Francaise pour le Droit International. Institut International des Droits de l'Homme, ed. Pedone, Paris, 2009, pp. 71-94.

3.9. Other hypotheses of state responsibility in connection with organizations conduct. The jurisprudence on the recognition of organizations immunities

For completeness of investigation further cases should be reported in which the contracting States have been called upon to respond for their own conduct adopted internally and connected to organizations activities. The common datum of these further liability hypotheses is the absence of internal measures to implement obligations descending from organizations.

Two groups of decisions fall into this category: The first concerns the responsibility deriving from membership, that is, the mere belonging of States to an organization;[361] the second, concerns the recognition of organizations immunities by internal courts.

In a number of cases ECtHR was asked to evaluate the decisions of national judges who recognized the immunities due to organizations. This is certainly not a new phenomenon. It involved, initially and to a large extent, labour disputes between Organizations and their employees which remains internal to the State concerned, which is why it is analyzed in this section, unlike the other liability hypothesis.

National courts have been asked to rule on compensation for civil damages arising from the commission of serious human rights violations by organizations. Reference is made to actions undertaken by a large number of applicants, aimed at obtaining compensation for civil damages suffered as a result of UN failure to prevent serious violations of fundamental human rights (think of Mothers of Srebrenica case before Dutch judges) or for violations due to gross negligence (as in Georges case before the US courts connected to the epidemic spread in Haiti), carried out in both cases on a large scale.[362]

The immunities of organizations raise several theoretical questions, but here it exclusively notes the fact that the recognition of immunities deprives individuals of an effective remedy for the violations suffered. The problem is part of the wider debate on the immunities recognized to foreign States and their negative impact on conventionally recognized human rights of a procedural nature. It must be said that the

---

[361]C. DOMINICÉ, Observations sur le contentieux des organizations internationales avec les personnes privées, in Annuaire Français de Droit International, 45, 1999, pp. 623ss.

[362]Georges v. United Nations, no. 15-455 (2d cir. 2016). For further analysis see: E. MADDOCK DILLON, M. DEXTER, The Haitian revolution an the early United States: Histories, textualities, geography, University of Pennsylvania Press, Pennsylvania, 2016. M. GARCIN, The haitian cholera victims complaints against the United Nations, in Zeitschrift für ausländisches öffentliches Recht und Völkerrecht, 75, 2015, pp. 680ss.

ratio of the two immunities is different. In the case of Organizations' immunities are functional in preserving the independence and autonomy necessary to be able to pursue their institutional goals and, therefore, for their proper functioning. In the case of States these norms are the reflection of state sovereignty.[363] However, this does not mean that the recognition of immunities, in both cases, leads to a significant limitation of the rights of the individual. More generally, regardless of compatibility with ECHR, the recognition of States and organizations immunities appears to be less and less compatible with a "modern" conception of international law that values individual interest over (inter) State especially when there are no other remedies available to victims who have suffered serious violations of fundamental norms of international law.

The issue is extremely complex because it clearly sheds light on the tensions between a vision of international law that is still markedly conservative and a more modern one. It is beyond the scope of this research to trace the current balance between the two conflicting forces. We will limit ourselves, therefore, to briefly reconstruct the answers given by ECtHR in light of the ECHR system, dwelling, in particular, on the plots with the theory of equivalent protection.

The leading cases in which ECtHR has concatenated the two reasonings on the recognition of immunities, on the one hand, and on equivalent protection, on the other, are represented by the famous Waite and Kennedy and Beer and Reagan v. Germany[364] decisions. In these cases the applicants contested the legitimacy of decisions with which German courts had granted immunity from jurisdiction to an international Organization (the European Space Agency-ESA), in relation to a dispute concerning labour relations of his non-official staff.

In both cases ECtHR, called upon to resolve the umpteenth regulatory conflict (this time between the rules on immunity and those set to protect procedural rights), discarded the possibility of applying the hierarchical criteria for solving regulatory conflicts, sought a compromise between the two opposing requirements,[365] applying a test of

[363] L. CONDORELLI, Conclusions Generales, in La soumission des organizations internationales aux normes internationales relatives aux droits de l'homme. Journée d'études de Strasbourg/Societe Francaise pour le Droit International. Institut International des Droits de l'Homme, ed. Pedone, Paris, 2009, which the author declared that: "(...) Sont justifiées par des exigences de respect de la souveraineté d'entités indépendantes (...). Il ne saurait en aller de même dans les relations entre les Etats membres d'une organization internationale et celle-ci, puisque l'organization est la créature des Etats et est appelée l'exercer les fonctions que ceux-ci lui ont attribuées au moyen du traité constitutif (...)."

[364] ECtHR, Waite and Kennedy v. Germany and Beer and Regan v. Germany of 18 February 1999.

[365] E. ROBERT, The jurisdictional immunities of international organizations: The balance

proportionality to the limitation and compression of the procedural law in question. What is interesting is that in the cases under consideration the proportionality in the restriction of the right to go to a judge was assessed not so much in relation to the purpose of this limitation (i.e. the good functioning of international organizations), but rather to the existence of alternative ways available to the applicants to assert their reasons.[366] Having ascertained the existence of such alternative mechanisms, ECtHR considered that in Waite and Kennedy and Beer and Reagan cases art. 6 ECHR had not been violated.[367]

The principles of law obtainable from the cases in question seem to have been denied by the recent jurisprudential change attested starting from the Stichting Mothers of Srebrenica v. Netherlands.[368] This decision has been criticized by several parties and, in particular, for the failure to balance the interests at stake and for not having clarified the connection between the purpose of immunities (the proper functioning of the Organization) and the restriction of the right of justice for the victims.

---

between the protection of the organizations interest and individual rights, in Mélanges en l'honneur de Jean Salmon, ed. Bruylant, Bruxelles, 2007, pp. 1445ss. E. CHUKWUEMEKE OKEKE, jurisdictional immunities of states and international organizations, Oxford University Press, Oxford, 2018.

[366] The balancing between the requirements of the rules on immunity and those aimed at protecting human rights is therefore substantiated by a verification of alternative and equivalent remedies to those denied at national level by the application of immunities. In fact, the Court states that "a material factor in granting" means the applicants that had available alternative means to protect their rights under the Convention, ECtHR, Beer and Regan v. Germany, op. cit., par. 58. According to this view, national courts should recognize implicit renunciation whenever the international organizations have not established alternative ways of meeting the need for the right to bring proceedings before a court. There are also those who felt that the non-recognition by the national courts of immunity in favour of the Organizations would constitute a countermeasure to the unlawful.

[367]"Taking into account in particular the alternative means of legal process available to the applicants, it cannot be said that the limitation on their access to the German courts with regard to ESA impaired the essence of their "right to a court" or was disproportionate for the purposes of article 6 § 1 of the Convention," (ECtHR, Beer and Regan v. Germany, op. cit., par. 62-63). As for the verification by the national courts about the existence and effectiveness of alternative remedies, the doctrine is essentially divided between those who support the opportunity for a limited control and those who, instead, wish for an enlarged one. For an overview of the different theories, see: J.F. FLAUSS, Immunites des organizations internationales et droit international des droits de l'homme, op. cit., pp. 85ss. In this regard, it is interesting the opinion of a judge of the Court who, in a case concerning the immunity of foreign States, did not want the mere equivalence of protection, but the identity of the procedural guarantees recognized to the individual (see the dissenting opinion of judge: Loucaides in case Al-Adsani v. United Kingdom of 21 November 2001). See also: E. KWAKWA, Globalization and international organizations, ed. Routledge, London & New York, 2017.

[368]ECtHR, Stichting Mothers of Srebrenica and others v. the Netherlands of 11 June 2013.

The case is linked to the events of the Srebrenica genocide, in relation to which we have already highlighted the role of UN and Dutchbat. The aspect we are dealing with here concerns the recognition of UN immunities in appeals presented by the families of the victims before the Dutch judges. According to Dutch courts, the immunity provided to UN by art. 105 UN Charter[369] would have an absolute character, covering all the acts that fall within the functions of the Organization, such as those committed in the context of peace operations, and would be such as to prevent judges from reviewing the conduct (rectius the omissions) implemented in such contexts. The Dutch courts also refused to investigate whether the recognition of immunities was necessary for the purpose pursued, stating that, otherwise, there would be "enormous consequences on the decision-making power of the Security Council on similar peacekeeping missions (...)."[370]

Finally, in their opinion, the applicability of organizations immunities would not be hindered by the binding nature of the violated rules.[371] The applicants subsequently turned to Strasbourg judges to verify whether the recognition of UN immunity by the Dutch domestic courts had led to a denial of justice and therefore a violation of art. 6 ECHR attributable to the Netherlands.[372]

ECtHR, considered art. 6 expression of a right susceptible to restrictions[373] and recalled the legitimate aim pursued by organizations immunity regulations ("ensuring the proper functioning of such organizations"), referred to the previous Behrami and Saramati, with the consequent recognition of the prevalence of UN Charter obligations on

---

[369]E. KWAKWA, Globalization and international organizations, op. cit.

[370]District court of the Hague, LJN: BF0181, Rechtbank's-Gravenhage, op. cit., par. 5.14.

[371]District Court of the Hague, LJN: BF0181, Rechtbank's-Gravenhage, op. cit., par. 5.14. In this regard, the Dutch courts referred to the jurisprudence of the Court of Strasbourg, which had addressed this issue with respect to the immunity of States (ECtHR, Al-Adsani v. The United Kingdom, op. cit., par. 66). It should be noted that this last case has also had some influence on the decision of the International Court of Justice, Jurisdictional Immunities of the State (Germany v. Italy: Greece intervening), ICJ Reports, 2012, decision of 3 February 2012 and from the ECtHR the Jones v. United Kingdom case of 14 January 2014). Which shows that quite controversial decisions become precedents that feed so many questionable decisions. For further details see: B. LOVE, The International Court of Justice: Jurisdictional immunities of the state (Germany v. Italy: Greece intervening. Jurisdictional immunities of the state (Ger. v. IT. Greece intervening (ICJ), in International Legal Materials, 51 (3), 2012, pp. 564ss. A. ORAKHELASHVILL, Jurisdictional immunities of the state (Germany v. Italy; Greece intervening), in American Journal of International Law, 106 (3), 2012, pp. 610ss.

[372]ECtHR, Stichting Mothers of Srebrenica and others v. the Netherlands, op. cit., par. 139 lett. b).

[373]ECtHR, Stichting Mothers of Srebrenica and others v. the Netherlands, op. cit., par. 154.

other international obligations, pursuant to art. 103. ECtHR has ruled out, however, that it could derive any indication from what was established in the Bosphorus case regarding equivalent protection, since the dispute between applicants and UN was based on the use of force by the Security Council and on the limits which bind the latter when acting on the basis of Chapter VII of the UN Charter. Since with these activities the UN intends to pursue the fundamental purpose of maintaining international peace and security, ECHR, in the opinion of ECHR, could not be interpreted "in a manner in which the acts and omissions of the Security Council to domestic jurisdiction are without UN's consent."[374] Otherwise the States, through their own courts, would interfere with the pursuit of UN "key mission" and, therefore, with the conduct of its military operations.

Having clarified this aspect, ECtHR then addressed the problem of the existence of an exception to the applicability of the rules on immunity if a norm of ius cogens was violated. Having classified as a peremptory norm not only the prohibition of genocide Commission, but also the rule requiring to prevent the latter.[375] ECtHR has found that international practice does not seem to attest to this exception.

Finally, the Strasbourg judges have examined applicants' observation about the total absence of any kind of alternative remedy to the possibility of referring a judge to enforce their own claims. Strasbourg judges did not ignore the fact that, indeed, a forum was lacking to appeal against the conduct carried out by the subjects operating in the UNPROFOR mission.[376] This obvious deficiency, in the opinion of

---

[374]On the content of the obligation of States to prevent the genocide commission v. International Court of Justice, Case Concerning the Crime of Genocide (Bosnia and Herzegovina v. Serbia and Montenegro), ICJ Reports, 2007, Decision of 26 February 2007. See in argument: C. PEGORIER, Ethnic cleansing: A legal qualification, ed. Routledge, London, New York, 2013. A. NOLLKAEMPER, I. PLAKEFALOS, Principles of shared responsibility in international law, Cambridge University Press, Cambridge, 2014. A. ZIMMERMANN, C.J. TAMS, K. OELLERS-FRAHAM, The Statute of the International Court of Justice. A commentary, op. cit.

[375]ECtHR, Stichting Mothers of Srebrenica and others v. the Netherlands, op. cit., par. 158. Therefore, the aforementioned decision of the International Court of Justice on the failure to recognize the immunity of Italian courts against the German State is referred to.

[376]The agreement establishing such military force should have provided, pursuant to art. 48, the establishment of a committee competent to hear these appeals, but the provision was never implemented, nor the competent body set up. See: Agreement on the status of the United Nations Protection Force in Bosnia and Herzegovina of 15 May 1993 (UN Treaty Series I-30006), and in particular art. 48, according to which "(...) any dispute or claim of a private law character to which UNPROFOR organ member thereof is a party and over which the courts of Bosnia and Herzegovina do not have jurisdiction because of any provision of the present agreement, shall be settled by a standing claims Commission to be established for that purpose (...)."

ECtHR, could not, however, be attributable to the Dutch State and therefore the appeal against the Netherlands was considered inadmissible. ECtHR concluded in the sense that the immunity recognized by the Dutch courts to UN served a legitimate and not disproportionate purpose.[377]

The relationship between organizations immunities regulations and individual right of access to justice has recently been addressed in the Klausecker case (concerning the recognition of immunities to the European Patent Organization in a dispute concerning employment relationships with the same).[378] This shows, once again, the different comitas that Strasbourg judges turn to Organizations: Maximum towards UN, reduced for the others.

3.10. State responsibility for the failure to protect individuals affected by the activities of organizations: Hypotheses envisaged

Adopting mainly the perspective of ECHR and the control over it exercised by ECtHR, two hypotheses will be examined. The first concerns Member States responsibility for behaviours adopted within the organization[379] and, in particular, for the omitted or insufficient supervision of the work of its organs. The second concerns, instead, an external behaviour of the State towards the organization, that is the lack of intervention to protect individuals injured by an offense attributable to it. In this second case it is a question of assessing whether the State has diligently worked to induce the responsible organization to repair the prejudice caused to individuals who are under the jurisdiction of that State, regardless the existence of a membership relationship between the latter

---

[377]ECtHR, Stichting Mothers of Srebrenica and others v. the Netherlands, op. cit., par. 165 e 169.

[378]The Court found that the plaintiff, being able to participate in the arbitration procedure to settle the dispute with the Organization, had at his disposal the reasonable alternative remedies for the protection of his procedural rights sanctioned by the ECHR. According to the judges of Strasbrugo: "Having regard to the foregoing, the Court considers that, in having been offered the arbitral procedure in question, the applicant had available to him reasonable alternative means to protect effectively his rights under the Convention" (ECtHR, Klausecker v. Germany of 6 January 2015, par. 76). See also: A. JAKUBOWSKI, K. WIERZYŇSKA, Fragmentation vs. The constitutionalisation of international law: A practical inquiry, ed. Routledge, London, New York, 2016.

[379]In the cases of offenses committed in force operations, behaviours held by the sending States contingents on the national territory of the host State of the mission were highlighted. Likewise, in cases concerning targeted sanctions, the responsibility of the State has been assessed in relation to the internal measures and decisions taken by the executive and judicial bodies.

and the organization in question.[380]

The two hypotheses that we intend to investigate are therefore distinguished from the others analyzed in the previous section since in these cases it is not possible to attribute to States the conduct detrimental to the organization, neither by way of double attribution, nor on an exclusive basis, lacking an internal implementation measure of the obligation arising from the organization. In other words, while in the previously analyzed cases the States answer for a conduct similar, in substance, to that theoretically imputable to organizations. In the cases that we are going to examine now the presumably illicit conduct of the State is autonomous and different from that committed by the organizations, despite this being connected.[381]

The first question concerns the positive nature of the obligations incumbent on States and the parameter of due diligence with which to verify compliance with the purposes of imputation of responsibility to States.[382]

The second regards, instead, the assessment of ECtHR competence pursuant to art. 1 ECHR. Since in the hypotheses under examination there is no internal measure suitable to establish state authority on the individuals concerned, it will be necessary to understand what the connection (the "involvement" to use the expression of ECHR) consists with the illicit fact of the organization necessary for the requirement set by art. 1 ECHR. The question will be addressed and resolved in relation to the two different hypotheses of responsibility analyzed. It is possible from now on to anticipate that this question can be

---

[380]See, C. RYNGAERT, H. BUCHANAN, Member State responsibility for the acts of International Organizations, in Utrecht Law Review, 7, 2011, pp. 132ss.

[381]The situation, from this point of view, is comparable to that already analyzed in Section I, par. 9, where the responsibility of the States for having recognized the immunity to the Organizations was under discussion. However, in the case of the recognition of immunity, the harmful conduct (i.e. national courts decision) was nevertheless carried out internally, which is why it was analyzed in the previous section.

[382]As is well known, the rights enshrined in the ECHR require States not only to refrain from interfering with the enjoyment of the same, but also to work with positive behaviours to ensure their protection, avoiding the occurrence of a certain event or ensuring the pursuit of a certain result. In the jurisprudence of the Court the positive obligations were derived, depending on the case, both from the individual provisions of the ECHR (think of the right to life, the right not to be subjected to inhumane and degrading treatments, the right to have effective remedies, etc.), both by art. 1. In this regard, the provision pursuant to art. 1 "is seen more than ever as the cornerstone of the Convention system, to the point that it constitutes an independent source of general obligations-which are also positive obligations-on States" (J. AKANDJI-KOMBE, Positive obligations under the European Convention on Human Rights. A guide to the implementation of the European Convention on Human Rights, Human Rights Handbook No. 7, Council of Europe Publishing, 2007).

overcome if a functional conception of state jurisdiction has been adopted for a long time evoked in doctrine, consisting in states' power to influence the enjoyment of rights sanctioned by ECHR. By virtue of this conception, the States entitled to intervene against the organization to protect individual interests would have jurisdiction over individuals, both by virtue of special rules of the organization (such are, for example, the procedures that regulate the drafting and keeping of sanctions lists), and according to the rules of general international law (with an action that approaches diplomatic protection).

As far as the first hypothesis is concerned, that is the behaviours payable by the governments within the organizations, it will be inspired by some ECtHR decisions that have addressed the issue of state responsibility due to its belonging to a certain organization (responsibility from membership) (par. 11), in order to draw some general reflections on the conduct payable by government delegates involved in the decision-making processes of organizations (par. 12). After having indicated the general conditions for asserting states' responsibility for the behaviour held within the organization, the reasoning carried out on the behaviours carried out by the permanent representations of States will be applied in the framework of procedures aimed at drawing up and maintaining the lists of individual sanctions adopted by the Security Council (par. 13).

The second hypothesis of responsibility, that for behaviours payable by States in external relations with organizations, has never been addressed by ECtHR. To our knowledge, more generally, ECTHR has never been called upon to directly review the compatibility with ECHR chancellery's contracting State "diplomatic silence" following human rights violations suffered by individuals under its jurisdiction, but committed by another State and/or organization. The ways in which a government manages, or does not relations with other subjects of international law are difficult to control even when they cause direct prejudice to individuals. The foreign policy choices made by States, especially if characterized by a high degree of discretion, tend to escape ECtHR syndicate and, in most cases from the internal courts (typically administrative). However, to a more careful analysis, some passages can be found in some recent decisions of ECtHR which, if properly exploited, could lead the interpreter to a conclusion in the opposite direction (par. 15).

Therefore, it will be necessary to understand if it is reasonable to maintain that the States, under whose jurisdiction the victims of the offenses committed by the organization are located, are or not required to work diligently to ensure that the responsible organization ceases the violation and repairs the prejudice caused (par. 16). In this way, some useful ideas will be obtained to answer the question raised about the hypothetical compulsory state intervention in diplomatic protection against the organization.

3.11. Positive behaviours required by Member States within organizations. Membership responsibility

The first aim is to verify if organization's Member States can be called to answer for their actions and behaviour of their delegates within the organization itself. To this end it is necessary to adopt a broad interpretation of the obligations contained in the treaties on human rights signed by the States. From this point of view, some conventional provisions can certainly be interpreted to the point of imposing certain positive behaviours on the State within the organizations which, if violated, would entail reparation in the ways and forms envisaged by the various conventional reference systems.

The issue has been incidentally touched, as far as ECHR protection system is concerned, in some decisions concerning states' responsibility due to their membership in organizations (the so-called membership responsibility). The interesting fact about this line of decisions is that, unlike the previous ones, the responsibility is attributed to States not because of the internal reproductive measures of the organization act, but for the mere institution of an organization without an equivalent protection system of human rights to the conventional one.

In a first group of cases the applicants complained that the decisions concerning employment relationships adopted by some organizations (Eurocontrol in Boivin[383] and EU in the Connolly case)[384] were detrimental to their rights sanctioned by ECHR.[385] Since no specific action or omission of the agreed States was contested, the appeals before ECtHR were presented without distinction against all organizations Member States in question and, consequently, they were declared ratione personae inadmissible, since the States had not intervened, directly or indirectly, in the proceedings that had led to the contested decisions and,

---

383ECtHR, Boivin v. France and Belgium of 9 September 2008. See also: P. LEACH, Taking a case to the European Court of Human Rights, Oxford University Press, Oxford, 2011. J.A. GREEN, C.P.M., WATERS, Adjudicating international human rights. Essays in honour of Sandy Ghandi, Martinus Nijhoff Publishers, The Hague, 2014.

384This was more precisely the decision taken by the Administrative Court of the Labour Organization in the Boivin case and by the Court of Justice of the European Union in the Connolly case.

385The ECtHR affirmed that: "(...) In the present case the applicant cannot be said to have been "within the jurisdiction" of the respondent States for the purposes of article 1 of the Convention. The Court finds that the alleged violations of the Convention cannot therefore be attributed to France and Belgium" (ECtHR, Boivin v. France and Belgium, op. cit.).

consequently, had not exercised their jurisdiction over the appellants pursuant to art. 1 ECHR.[386] The Rambus[387] and Beygo[388] decisions are also inspired by similar considerations, always concerning labour disputes between individuals and organizations (respectively the European Patent Organization and the Council of Europe).

Partially deviates from the decisions preceding the Kokkelviserij v. Nehterlands case of 5 February 2009,[389] in which the applicant complained that he had not been able to present written briefs after the intervention of EU Advocate General in the context of a proceeding brought before CJEU, and that this would have entailed a violation of art. 6 ECHR. The appellant's request, this time, was examined on the merits given that the proceedings before CJEU originated from a reference for a preliminary ruling raised by the Netherlands. The Kokkelviserij decision, applying the presumption of equivalence in circumstances in which the respondent state intervention was rather limited in scope (consisting precisely in the mere uprising of the preliminary ruling), marked a first evolution with respect to the previous jurisprudence which required an "involvement" of the much larger Member State.[390]

After some time, with Galić and Balgojević v. the Netherlands decisions,[391] ECtHR seems to have wanted to "correct the shot," clarifying that States "involvement" necessary to root the competence of ECtHR must be of a certain relevance and cannot derive from mere "static" factors, such as the fact of host on its national territory the headquarters of an organization from which the allegedly damaging deed came (in the case in

386ECtHR, Rambus Inc. v. Germany of 16 June 2009.

387ECtHR, Beygo v. 46 Member States of the Council of Europe of 16 May 2009.

388ECtHR, Cooperatieve Producentenorganisatie Van De Nederlandse Kokkelvisserij U.A. v. Netherlands of 20 January 2009. See also: A. ROSAS, Balancing fundamental rights in EU law, in Cambridge Yearbook of European Legal Studies, 16, 2014, pp. 348ss.

389T. LOCK, The European Court of Justice and international courts, Oxford University Press, Oxford, 2015.

390In the Bosphorus case the application of the doctrine of equivalent protection seemed to presuppose, as a necessary condition, the adoption on national territory of a measure in execution of the obligation arising from the participation of the State to the Organization (if only to ascertain the jurisdiction of the Court ratione loci and personae). See: ECtHR, Bosphorus Hava Yollari Turizm ve Ticaret Anonim Sirket v. Ireland, op. cit., par. 137, "in the present case it is not disputed that the act about which the applicant company complained, the detention of the aircraft leased by it for a period of time, was implemented by the authorities of the respondent State on its territory following a decision made by the Irish Minister for Transport. In such circumstances the applicant company, as the addressee of the impugned act, fell within the "jurisdiction" of the Irish State, with the consequence that its complaint about that act is compatible ratione loci, personae and materiae with the provisions of the Convention (...)."

391ECtHR, Galić v. the Netherlands and Blagojević v. the Netherlands of 9 June 2009, par. 46.

question it was the United Nations Court for the crimes committed in Former Yugoslavia).[392]

The following month ECtHR confirmed the point in Lopez Cifuentes v. Spain case[393] believing, mutatis mutandis, that Spain could not be called upon to respond to the decision taken by the International Olive Council concerning employment relationships with the plaintiff for the mere fact of hosting the headquarters of the Organization on its territory (in Madrid).

In the cases analyzed so far, however, the "involvement," more or less extensive, of the respondent State had always manifested itself in a conduct adopted on a national level. In this regard, the Gasparini decision is particularly innovative, with which ECtHR has in fact introduced a new hypothesis of state responsibility for defects and structural gaps in the internal procedures of organizations, in the absence of an internal intervention by national authorities.[394] In the case in question, a NATO official contested that the dispute before an internal Commission of the Organization, regarding an increase in the pension contribution, had occurred according to a procedure without the guarantees provided by art. 6 ECHR,[395] complaining, in particular, the absence of a public hearing. The plaintiff reproached Italy (state of nationality) and Belgium (NATO Headquarters) for not having taken the necessary measures to provide the Organization with an internal jurisdictional system compatible with the protection of rights recognized by ECHR. In relation to this finding, ECtHR considered itself ratione personae and loci competent to ascertain the responsibility of both agreed States, to then exclude it in the light of the presence of an equivalent protection system within the Organization.

A first element of interest in the Gasparini decision is the irrelevance for ECtHR of the territorial location of the damaging event for the purposes of the requirement set by art. 1 ECHR. Secondly, it seems appropriate to highlight the assertion that the mere transfer of powers to an organization, without the backing of conventional guarantees, constitutes a source of autonomous and omissive responsibility for Member States.[396] From this it could be inferred states obligation to ensure

[392]In the Galić case, the applicants complained of a lack of judicial protection in the procedures adopted by the UN Tribunal for crimes committed in the former Yugoslavia and summoned the Netherlands as the host State of the aforementioned Court on its territory. This last circumstance was not considered in itself suitable for attributing responsibility to the Netherlands and the appeal was considered inadmissible ratione personae.

[393]ECtHR, Lopez Cifuentes v. Spain of 7 July 2009.

[394]ECtHR, Gasparini v. Italy and Belgium of 12 May 2009.

[395]B. SIMMA, D.E. KHAN, G. NOLTE, A. PAULUS, N. WESSENDORF, The Charter of the United Nations, a commentary, op. cit.

[396]ECtHR, Gasparini v. Italy and Belgium, op. cit., par. 4 and 7.

that the organization of which they are members and to which they devolved certain competences offers an equivalent protection of conventional rights. However, compliance with this guarantee obligation does not end when the organization is set up, but would continue throughout its entire "life," as an obligation to continuously monitor its performance. In this way, ECtHR has in fact "pierce the veil" of the separate and autonomous juridical personality of NATO, in order to consider itself competent to judge on Member States responsibility, in the absence of their specific intervention. However, it is not clarified what the title of indirect or subsidiary responsibility on the basis of which Member States are responsible for an organization's crime.[397]

These innovative guidelines have been confirmed in two recent decisions adopted in 2015 in the lesser known Perez and Klausecker v. Germany cases[398] in which the appellants challenged the defendant State for the violation of the right of access to the court, sanctioned by ECtHR, in relation to labour disputes initiated, respectively, against UN and European Patent Organization.

In the Perez case, the applicant, a former employee of the UN Volunteers program, complained of procedural shortcomings in internal appeals concerning her employment relationship with the Organization before the UN Administrative Court and the Joint Appeals Board (a body of appeal to the internal decisions of the Organization). Of these deficiencies, according to the appellant, Germany should have replied for not having ensured that within the Organization there was a system of resolution of labour disputes equivalent to the standards of ECHR. What is interesting for us is the direct reference to the Gasparini jurisprudence and the consequent confirmation of the hypothesis of Member States responsibility for the lack of diligent monitoring activity within the Organizations.[399]

Excluding Germany's responsibility for the mere fact that the decision of the contested Organization had its effects on German territory (specifically in Bonn, where the applicant's of UN office was working and residing),[400] ECtHR stated that in transferring part of the sovereign powers

---

[397] C.M. BROLMANN, Member States and international legal responsibility. Developments of the institutional veil, in International Organizations Law Review, 12, 2015, pp. 358-381.

[398]ECtHR, Perez v. Germany and Klausecker v. Germany of 6 January 2015.

[399]On the merits, however, the point was not then resolved by the Court, which has declared incompetent to receive the appeal for the non-exhaustion of internal remedies (especially those before the German Constitutional Court).

[400]This was not in itself a circumstance appropriate to consider "the contested act under the jurisdiction of Germany pursuant to art. 1 of the ECHR," referring to the previous Galić and Balgojević v. The Netherlands (ECtHR, Perez v. Germany, op. cit., par. 63). In support

to an international organization of which they are members, the contracting States have a legal obligation to monitor that the rights guaranteed by ECHR receive "equivalent protection" within the organization from that guaranteed by the conventional system.

Even more interesting in this regard is the Klausecker case, concerning a labor dispute between the applicant (a German citizen with a handicap in his hand) and the European Patent Organization which, with a decision then challenged before the International Court Labour Organization (ILO), had decided not to recruit the appellant due to his physical unfitness for the job requested. In this case Germany's responsibility was invoked in relation to two behaviours: For having granted immunity to the European Patent Organization before its domestic courts and for having created an Organization without adequate procedures for resolving labour disputes.[401] On the first point ECtHR concluded that the restriction of the right of access to the judge was legitimate in this case.[402] More interesting for our purposes is the second challenge to Germany, namely to have contributed to creating an organization without adequate procedures for resolving labour disputes. In this regard, ECtHR ruled out that the respondent State exercised its jurisdiction solely because the headquarters of the organization was located in Munich and that the decision had been taken there.[403] However, even in the absence of an "intervention" or "involvement" of the German authorities in the labour dispute,[404] ECtHR confirms what has already been stated in Gasparini, namely that if the applicant explicitly criticizes an equivalent protection defect within the Organization, ECtHR is competent to verify the supervision of the State on the work of the Organization.[405] By expressly taking into account Gasparini (...) the Court

---

of the same conclusion, the Court also noted that there had been no involvement of the German Government, never directly or indirectly intervening at any stage in the labour dispute between Ms Perez and the UN.

[401]The same consideration also applied to the existing procedures within the ILO.

[402] The Court, having ascertained its competence since the conduct in question (i.e. the decision of the German Courts) had taken place under the jurisdiction of Germany and was imputable to it, has implemented the test formulated in the aforementioned Kennedy decision. The Court thus found that the plaintiff, being able to participate in the arbitration procedure to settle the dispute with the Organization, had at his disposal the reasonable alternative remedies for the protection of his procedural rights sanctioned by the ECHR. According to the judges of Strasbourg "(...) [h]aving regard to the foregoing, the Court considers that, in having been offered the arbitral procedure in question, the applicant had available to him reasonable alternative means to protect effectively his rights under the Convention (...)." ECtHR, Klausecker v. Germany, op. cit., par. 76.

[403]ECtHR, Klausecker v. Germany, op. cit., par. 81.

[404]ECtHR, Klausecker v. Germany, op. cit., par. 93.

[405]Guaranteed by the Convention and received within that organization an "equivalent

deducted from the principles developed in the Bosphorus case that, when transferring part of their sovereign powers to an international organization of which they are a member, contracting Parties to the Convention were under an obligation to monitor that the rights would have been "equivalent" to the conventional one.[406]

In the light of the aforementioned cases, it is worth dwelling on the approach adopted by ECtHR in relation to the question of the jurisdiction of the defendant States and the attribution to them of the responsibility for the disputed conduct. In cases where it is not possible to identify an "involvement" of national authorities with respect to the disputed act, since the latter falls exclusively within the juridical sphere of the organization with a separate and autonomous personality, the ECtHR considers the applicants not subject to state jurisdiction. However, the interesting fact is that these appeals are declared ratione personae inadmissible[407] and, therefore, based on the attribution of the unlawful act solely to the Organization.[408]

---

protection" to that secured by the Convention system (ECtHR, Klausecker v. Germany, op. cit., par. 97).

406This judgment was valid in a general way (with reference therefore to the architecture of the Organization), as well as in the concrete case, since the presumption of equivalence was not overcome by the proof of a deficiency. This conclusion is not surprising given that the Court has always found the presence of an adequate level of protection within the various organizations whose actions were called to respond - indirectly - to the Member States agreed.

407"(...) The Court recalls that it recently gave decisions in a number of applications where the impugned decision emanated from an internal body of an international organization or an international tribunal outside the jurisdiction of the respondent States, in the context of a labour dispute that lay entirely within the internal legal order of an international organization that had a legal personality separate from that of its Member States. It was decisive for the respondent States to be held responsible under the Convention in those cases whether the States concerned had intervened directly or indirectly in the dispute, and whether an act or omission of those States or their authorities could be considered to engage their responsibility under the Convention. If that was not the case, the Court considered the applicants not to have been "within the jurisdiction" of the respondent States concerned for the purposes of article 1 of the Convention and therefore declared the applications to be incompatible ratione personae with the provisions of the Convention in this respect" (ECtHR, Klausecker v. Germany, op. cit., par. 92).

408See Practical Guide on Admissibility criteria 2014, of Council of Europe, par. 173, "there are exceptions to the principle that an individual's physical presence in the territory of one of the Contracting Parties has the effect of placing that individual under the jurisdiction of the State concerned, for example where a State hosts the headquarters of an international organization against which the applicant's complaints are directed. The mere fact that an international criminal tribunal has its seat and premises in the Netherlands is not a sufficient ground for attributing to that State any alleged acts or omissions on the part of the international tribunal in connection with the applicant's conviction." In this case we mention also the case: Lopez Cifuentes v. Spain of 7 July 2009, which is affirmed that "the

The two aspects (the existence of jurisdiction and the question of pipelines imputability) end up overlapping in the reasoning of ECtHR, which would seem to make the question of attribution fall into the requirement set by art. 1 of ECHR. It is not clear whether this is due to a conscious view of the two legal issues as parts of the same problem. The impression is that ECtHR prefers to resolve the issue on the basis of the attribution in order not to admit the absence of state jurisdiction on individuals present in their own territory and to recognize, consequently, that the individuals, in these contexts, are under the complete 'jurisdiction' of organizations.

The inclusion of ratione personae applicability profile in art. 1 ECHR, however, seems to us a choice that can be criticized from a methodological point of view. Art. 1 of ECHR seems to us require ECtHR to ascertain exclusively the existence of state "jurisdiction" in a spatial sense, a circumstance that relates to the objective element of the crime, the jurisdiction being a prerequisite for the objective application of conventional obligations. Conversely, the admissibility of ratione personae appeal depends on the question of conduct attribution and therefore concerns the subjective element of the offense, which does not appear to be included in art. 1 ECHR. The attribution, in our opinion, can instead be inferred from an implicit rule, obtainable from the general international law on the subject of illicit that ECtHR is inevitably called to apply when it verifies state responsibility for ECHR violations.[409]

Finally, analyzing the merit of the just mentioned jurisprudence, it is possible to derive some principles of law that are useful to understand whether, and to what extent, states' conduct within the organizations is bound by the limits deriving from the treaties on human rights.

A staple of ECtHR jurisprudence is that States do not free themselves from the obligations they have entered into with regard to human rights simply because they have transferred competences to international organizations.[410] In other words, "when Member States

---

impugned decisions had been taken by an international organization that was not under the jurisdiction of the respondent State, in the context of a labour dispute that fell fully within the legal authority of that organization, which had a legal personality distinct from that of its Member States, including the host country. Accordingly, the alleged violations of the Convention concerning the disciplinary proceedings within the ILC could not be attributed to the host country concerned. As to the possible liability of the ILC, as the organization was not a Contracting Party to the Convention, it could not be held responsible under the provisions thereof: Incompatible ratione personae (...)."

[409] It could also be inferred the rule of competence ratione personae by art. 34 which provides for the possibility for individuals to propose an individual appeal only against the "States Parties" of the ECHR.

[410] "(...) The Court is of the opinion that where States establish international organizations

access international organizations, they do not leave their international law obligations at home."[411] For this reason the transfer of competences to an organization should, in principle, take place with the guarantees provided by the conventional system. In order to impute to the Member State the responsibility for violation of ECHR with respect to an offense exclusively attributable to the organization of which it is a part, ECtHR must ascertain a specific "involvement or intervention" of the contracting State; otherwise the appeal is ratione personae inadmissible, even if directed against all Member States of the organization that adopted the disputed act, by virtue of the screen constituted by the separate and autonomous personality of the entity.[412]

The "involvement" required by ECtHR exists without any doubt when the contracting State has adopted on its national territory internal reproductive measures of the obligations deriving from belonging to the organization.[413] This is true even when the internal action of the national authorities is particularly limited.[414] In addition to these eventualities, ECtHR in Gasparini decision and in decisions that refer to it (Klausecker and Perez) outlined another hypothesis of state responsibility connected to their membership in organizations. In the aforementioned cases, the acts disputed by the appellants (the decisions in the field of labour disputes) were considered attributable exclusively to the organization and the "involvement" of the agreed States did not manifest itself, not even in a "minimal" manner, at national level. Their "involvement" derived rather from the lack of vigilance on respect for human rights in organizations.[415]

---

in order to pursue or strengthen their cooperation in certain fields of activities, and where they attribute to these organizations certain competences and accord them immunities, there may be implications as to the protection of fundamental rights. It would be incompatible with the purpose and object of the Convention, however, if the Contracting States were thereby absolved from their responsibility under the Convention in relation to the field of activity covered by such attribution (...)." ECtHR, Klausecker v. Germany, op. cit., par. 63.

[411]C. RYNGAERT, The responsibility of Member States of international organizations. Concluding observations, in International Organization Law Review, 12, 2015, pp. 516ss.

[412]C. RYNGAERT, The responsibility of Member States of international organizations. Concluding observations, op. cit.

[413]Moreover, as has been observed in legal literature, in these cases the objection raised by the principle expressed by the ICJ in the Monetary Fund case, according to which a Court cannot pronounce in a prejudicial manner on the legal position of a person absent, would be relevant. In the proceeding see: P. PALCHETTI, Litigating Member State responsibility. The monetary gold principle and the protection of absent organizations, in International Organizations Law Review, 12, 2015, pp. 469ss.

[414]ECtHR, Kokkelviserij v. Nehterlands, op. cit.

[415]The "involvement" of the State usually requested derives from the omissive behaviour of the States in this particular international context. It should be noted, however, that this aspect (that is, the failure to monitor States in the Organizations) must be expressly

The interesting aspect is that the control of ECtHR seems to extend, in these cases, to the conduct of States delegates within organizations. This is evident, for example, in Gasparini case, where ECtHR assessed whether the two agreed States were responsible for supporting, within the NATO Atlantic Council, the approval of the regulation on labour disputes of the Organization's officials. The ECtHR, noting that "the two respondent States (Italy and Belgium) had rightly considered, the time they approved the NATO Civilian Personnel Regulations and its annexes, through their permanent representatives on the North Atlantic Council, that the provisions governing the procedure before the Appeals Board guaranteed a fair hearing,"[416] it really seems to judge the behaviour of the permanent representations of States within the Organization. In Klausecker case the control of ECtHR seems to extend, although not explicitly as in the Gasparini case, to Service Regulations adopted by the delegates of Member States (including Germany) of the Organization, as well as to the proposal to start an arbitration to define the dispute with the applicant.

3.12. Theoretical conditions of state responsibility for the conduct of their delegates within the Organizations

The damaging act adopted by the organization must be divisible into several segments that show an autonomous power of States affecting individual rights.

It is necessary first of all that the applicant contest an autonomous conduct assumed by states delegates within the organization and that this, considered individually, has violated an individual right of the applicant. This implies, in other words, carrying out an "unpacking" operation of the complex decision-making processes of the organization, in order to isolate one or more behaviours carried out by state delegates that have contributed to the adoption of the unlawful act by the organization.[417] It is then necessary to verify the existence of state jurisdiction over the segment of activity carried out by the delegates pursuant to art. 1 ECHR.

The evaluation of the existence of a margin of power maintained by the States in the decision-making processes of the organizations can be a problematic operation and, to date, it is a matter still unexplored

criticized by the appellant for the Court to rule on this point.

[416]ECtHR, Gasparini v. Italy and Belgium, op. cit.

[417]This will not be possible, for example, in cases where the damaging conduct consists of a decision of a body of the monocratic organization (for example the UN Secretary), or of experts, in which the representatives of the States have not participated.

by ECtHR.[418] In the hypotheses of responsibility consolidated in the Strasbourg jurisprudence state power over individuals has always been linked to a territorial datum. The applicants were in fact subject to ratione loci state jurisdiction that acted in the context of organizations' activities: Territorial in cases of adoption of internal measures, extraterritorial in offenses committed in the context of force operations. In the case of crimes committed by delegates within the organization, the governing authority exercised by the latter cannot be placed in the territorial or extraterritorial paradigm of jurisdiction, since it takes place in the specific context of the Organization: A juridical space (organization's legal status) which, by definition, does not coincide with states territorial boundaries.[419] Nevertheless, it seems reasonable to assume that States, in this peculiar context, exercise on individuals who can be defined as "regulatory" (such as, for example, the power to propose the inclusion of a name in the sanctions lists). The very identification of some individual portions of authorities exercised independently by States is often sufficient to demonstrate that they, through these portions of power, exercise their jurisdiction over individuals pursuant to art. 1 ECHR, in the terms described above and regardless of a territorial connection with the individuals concerned. Clearly the existence and scope of these powers preserved by states are to be evaluated, case by case, according to the type of act object of dispute.

---

[418]The doubts on the existence of a jurisdiction of the States in relation to the conduct of its delegates within the organizations have not been dispelled in the Gasparini case, where the Court has not justified its jurisdiction, nor ratione loci pursuant to art. 1 of the ECHR, or ratione personae, or has it clarified what are the requirements for identifying the States that can be agreed, as legitimate passive, by the applicants. The Court considered that it was competent to judge the conduct of both Italy (the applicant's nationality) and Belgium (the host State of the organization), but without clarifying what elements of fact or law are rooted in exercise of the jurisdiction of the two States and whether this should take place on the basis of different elements for Italy and Belgium. The position of the two States has therefore been totally equated without further argumentation. The opportunity to clarify the point is then missed in subsequent decisions. In the Klausecker and Perez cases it was in fact agreed only Germany (headquarters of the Organizations involved), which claimed that the contested acts were to be attributed to the Organization and that the appeal was inadmissible ratione personae.

[419]The fact that the conduct detrimental to the delegates can be located in the territory of the State in which the organization is based does not imply that it is the State that exclusively exercises jurisdiction over the positions taken individually by the States within the organizations. Just as it is not relevant that the prejudice suffered by individuals is produced in a certain State, which is often different from the one where the harmful conduct takes place (i.e. the seat of the organization).

3.13. The segment of conduct must refer to a state party to human rights treaties

The attribution of the conduct in the case in question is an operation that does not present particular difficulties. To the extent that the fact disputed by the individual is not the complex act of the organization (attributable to it alone), but a segment of it, is imputable to the State by reason of the organic link existing with the representatives who, acting in the name and on behalf of their State of belonging, they have put in place the segment of the act in question. If it is true that, in some cases, government delegates also act as organs of the Organization, any double organic nature has a functional nature and should therefore be assessed with reference to the specific function exercised by the subject and specific object under dispute.

3.14. (Follows) The segment of conduct must be contrary to contracted obligations

With regard to the objective element of offense, it is necessary to examine the nature and scope of obligations sanctioned by ECHR that burden the delegates, to then verify if the segment of conduct attributable to them is contrary to the same obligations. In this regard, the negative duties deriving from ECHR do not seem to be relevant, as it is unlikely that an action of the delegate is suitable, individually considered, to directly interfere with a conventionally recognized right.

Attention should, in our opinion, be directed instead to the positive guarantee obligations that can be derived from an extensive reading of art. 1 ECHR. From this point of view, there is no great difficulty in affirming, prima facie, that state delegates are called upon to prevent the adoption of decisions by the organization which would entail a violation of the rights of individuals and, in the event of bankruptcy, they are required to terminate the violation itself.[420] In other words, States must, as far as they

[420] There is no provision in the ECHR text, or in the context of intergovernmental cooperation that explicitly States must respect human rights. A different argument could apply with reference to the Pact on economic, social and cultural rights, whose art. 2 par. 1 provides that "each State Party to the Present Covenant shall undertake to take steps, individually and through international assistance and co-operation, especially with the full realization of the rights in the present Covenant by all appropriate measures." On the relevance of the conduct of the States within the economic organizations, such as the IMF and the World Bank. See also: M. LANGFORD, W. VANDENHOLE, M. SCHEININ, W. VAN GENUGTEN (ed. by), Global justice, State duties: The extraterritorial scope of economic, social and cultural rights in international law, Cambridge University Press, Cambridge 2013. E. BAIMU, A. PANOV, Responsibility of international organizations an

can, respect and enforce the fundamental rights provided by ECHR also within the organizations of which they are a part.

As regards the compliance with positive obligations, the central issue to be resolved is the identification of the diligence parameter below which states behaviour is to be considered non-compliant with the contract obligation. The question of due diligence by delegates in organizations has never been addressed explicitly by ECtHR. It could then be cautiously held that the hypothetical standard applicable in the context in question is neither high ("do everything possible for"), nor medium ("carry out any reasonable effort that may be required given the position of the subject"), but rather low ("avoid arbitrary or manifestly unreasonable behaviour"). In this regard, a factor to be taken into consideration is the nature of the primary rule violated, given that the protection of certain rights requires States to ensure more intense and anticipated protection.[421]

Another problem is then to prove the causal link between delegator's omissive behaviour (lack of diligence in supervising the organization's work) and the infringement of rights sanctioned by ECHR. The prejudice concretely suffered by the individual in many cases is the result of the complex act adopted by the Organization, but not of the behaviour of the prodromal delegate to the resolution. However, as we will see in the next paragraph, there are certain behaviours of the representatives of the suitable States, all considered, to produce a violation of the positive ECHR obligations, causing a prejudice in the subjective sphere of individuals.

If this is the case, all that remains is to reconcile the model of responsibility outlined above with the solutions offered by general international law. In this regard, reference could be made to article 61 DARIO, a provision that imposes state responsibility for having circumvented an international obligation (by) using the competence of an organization in the context in which the violated obligation applies. The provision would be destined to operate in the cases under discussion, since the competence attributed to the Organization to adopt a certain complex act, combined with the lack of states diligence in individual phases, leads the organization to perform a fact which, from States' point of view, it would certainly be illegal.

The possibility of identifying profiles of state responsibility for the position taken within the decision-making process of an organization is a hypothesis that has already been taken into consideration by some

---

the World Bank inspection panel: Parallel tracks unlikely to converge?, in The World Bank Legal Review, 2011, vol. 3, pp. 149ss.

421 See: Art. 3 ECHR. C. GRABENWARTER. European Convention on human rights: ECHR, op. cit.

authors, both with reference in general to the vote expressed by the delegates,[422] and with specific reference to the direction given by Member States to the decisions taken by economic organizations.

3.15. The conduct payable by UN Member States representatives in the context of the listing and delisting procedures of sanctions committees

From our point of view, the positive obligations deriving from the conventional rules in question bind states representatives both in the listing and delisting phase. Assuming that the individual has suffered a prejudice deriving from the behaviour of delegates, and therefore intends to agree the sending State before one of the human rights control bodies verify that the conditions indicated in the previous paragraph are present.

First of all, it should be noted that the resolution with which a name is entered or deleted from the lists is the result of a complex decision-making procedure attributable to the Security Council, which, however, can be "unpacked" in many different activities attributable to individual UN Member States. Assuming that the reasons justifying the inclusion of a name in the lists are totally unfounded, it is possible to identify at least five distinct conduct that may entail state responsibility: First, to have designated a natural or legal person; secondly, not to have reported to the Committee any information regarding the individual recipient of the measures which, if revealed, would have led to a different decision by the Committee (therefore they are elements suitable to modify and/or cancel the sanction deriving both from intelligence activities, that from judicial decisions); third, not having promptly activated a cancellation request, despite having the right to do so; fourth, to have objected arbitrarily to the cancellation of a name proposed by other States, thus preventing the Committee from adopting a consensus decision to delist; fifth, and last, not having submitted an exemption request if the reasons for doing so were met.

These pipelines are prodromal fragments or in any case connected to the unlawful decision of the Organization (the inclusion and/or maintenance of the name in a list), but still autonomous and independent

---

[422]Art. 60 affirms that "a State Member of an international organization incurs international responsibility if, by taking advantage of the fact that the organization has competence in relation to the subject-matter of state international obligations, it circumvents that obligation by causing the organization to commit an act that, if committed by the State, would have constituted a breach of the obligation. Paragraph 1 applies whether or not the act in question is internationally wrongful for the international organization (...)."

of it. On the other hand, individual conduct is an expression of a margin of state power over individuals, relevant for the purposes of the notion of jurisdiction pursuant to art. 1 ECHR. It is indeed undeniable that the permanent representation of a State exercises a form of "jurisdiction" over individuals (in the sense of "the suitability of government's powers to permanently influence the enjoyment of rights guaranteed in ECHR")[423] which decides to propose the designation of their name on the list, to arbitrarily oppose the cancellation, not to communicate relevant information, or not to submit a request for cancellation and/or exemption. It does not take into consideration the fact that the harmful conduct is materially carried out outside the territorial boundaries of these States (more precisely in the UN headquarters in New York). What matters is that states delegates, both when they act and when they do not, exercise a significant influence on the prerogatives of individuals who enter for a short time-but in a stable way-into the sphere of power and authority of the government concerned.

Thus conceived, the notion of jurisdiction would not extend to all UN Member States, but exclusively to States that actually have the powers and instruments to affect the rights of individuals based on special rules established by Committees' guidelines. In most cases, the "regulatory" control exercised through the work of state delegates also corresponds to a "territorial" control by state authorities, due to the actual presence of the individual in state territory to which the delegates belong. However, it could also happen that the individual is in a different territory from the State held responsible for the behaviour of its delegates.

We assume, for example, that an Italian citizen and resident has been entered on the list of one of the Committees on the proposal of Sweden, which has acted on the basis of manifestly unfounded information acquired by its intelligence apparatus. Suppose then that, once the total lack of information material has been verified, Sweden has not subsequently activated itself to cancel the registration. In this case Sweden, whose permanent representation acted in concrete in the Headquarters of the Committees in New York, exercised for a certain period of time a jurisdiction over the individual physically present in the territory of another State (Italy). This does not exclude, in principle, that even Italy, as a State of citizenship[424] and therefore entitled to propose a request for

---

[423] F. MARCHADIER, Convention européenne des droit de l'homme et des libertès fondamentales, op. cit., pp. 679-694. C. TEITGEN COLLY, La Convention europèenne des droits de l'homme: 60 ans et après?, op. cit. W.A. SCHABAS, The European Convention on Human Rights: A commentary, Oxford University Press, Oxford, 2015, pp. 1755ss.
[424] J.D. MOUTON, P. KOVÁCS, La concept de citoyennetè en droit international, ed. Brill, The Hague, 2019.

delisting, has exercised jurisdiction over the individual in relation to a different conduct (for example, the failure to request cancellation) and may incur violations of the positive rights sanctioned by the Convention, if it is shown that, aware of the absence of registration, it has failed to take action.

Having ascertained the existence of states jurisdiction with respect to such conduct, state responsibility regarding the two elements of which the crime is composed must be briefly evaluated.

From a subjective point of view, the behaviours highlighted are undoubtedly attributable to States, even in the absence of the adoption of a measure on the national territory, as they are (usually) implemented by one of their bodies: The permanent UN representation. In fact, this conclusion cannot be objected to states representations act as organs of the Organization; as the procedures are conceived, it is clear that the permanent representatives express a point of view of their nationality, which does not bind the organization, but rather-in the case of the request for delisting-is even aimed at opposing it. On the other hand, the choice to propose (or not) a cancellation request, as well as to designate or oppose the cancellation, or simply to keep the Committee informed, is the result of specific instructions that individual governments give to their permanent representatives and of which the States are, in our opinion, called to respond.

From an objective point of view, it is equally easy to agree that the actions and omissions in question commit state responsibility for failure to comply with positive obligations.[425] The five behaviours indicated above seem, prima facie, to be contrary to guarantee obligations, as they do not prevent (or do not put an end to) the violation of rights by the Security Council decision. In other words, the States, through the conduct shown, do not seem to use the margin of power available to them to direct the decision-making process of the Committees in a manner consistent with ECHR. It will then be up to ECtHR to assess, case by case, when the behaviour of the delegates is below the required diligence parameter, which, as already stated, could be relatively low in these circumstances. Member States responsibility could therefore be arbitrariness or the manifest unreasonableness of the behaviour of their delegates or the total absence of even a minimal effort aimed at guiding the Committees in a

[425]On the contrary, it seems more difficult to argue that the conduct of the delegates directly violates the negative obligations arising from the ECHR, as it is unsuitable to interfere, individually considered, with individual rights. The same designation, despite being a positive action carried out by the delegates of the State, does not in itself create a violation of the law illegitimately restricted by the measure. In fact, the designation proposal until it is voted by the Committee is not capable of determining the violation and may not be followed by the final decision of the Organization, which is the act from which the injury actually results.

manner consistent with ECHR.

3.16. (Follows) Elements of practice obtainable from national and international courts jurisprudence in support of the illustrated thesis

The hypothesis outlined above of "unpacking" the unlawful fact of the organization to then attribute single behaviours equally unlawful to Member States seems to find a partial confirmation in some decisions issued by national and international courts. Alongside Gasparini, Perez and Klausecker cases, some decisions must be mentioned which specifically dealt with the activities of delegates in the procedures used by the Sanctions Committees.

First of all, we should mention the aforementioned Ayadi decision of the former Tribunal of First Instance of EU (General Court (GC) in our days), from which it is possible to infer, in a nutshell, a "regional" obligation for EU Member States to promote within the Committees a request for delisting in favour of its own citizens or residents if there are no justified reasons to keep the name on the lists. It is therefore a duty of conduct (the proposal of -and not already obtaining the delisting) which is imposed on the permanent representations of EU Member States within UN. Once the information has been collected and examined, taking into account that the interested parties do not have the right to be heard personally by the Sanctions Committee, EU contacted Member States are obliged to "promptly ensure that the case of interested parties is presented without delay and in fair and impartial manner to the said Committee, to be re-examined, if this is objectively justified in the light of the relevant information provided."[426]

The sentence therefore shows that the choice by state representatives to intervene or not in the context of the procedure for erasing a name from the lists is not the result of total and absolute discretion. This applies to EU Member States which, by promoting a cancellation request within the Sanctions Committees, fully guarantee the right of access to justice, as provided for and interpreted by EU law. It therefore remains to ask whether such behaviours could also derive from

---

[426]The fact that the individual is not personally listened to within the Committees is a trait that still characterizes the procedure existing for all the Committees, even after the establishment of the Focal Point which, as we have mentioned above, is an intergovernmental mechanism. Partially different objections could only apply to the Al-Qaeda Committee and to Da'esh, in relation to which the Ombudsman office was established in 2008.

the contractual obligations concerning the protection of human rights.

Analyzing the jurisprudence of the main international bodies responsible for the control of human rights, in particular ECtHR and the Committee established by the Additional Protocol to the Covenant on Civil and Political Rights, we believe that behaviours similar to those recognized in the Ayadi case are also imposed on states parties to the respective treaties by virtue of positive obligations. On the other hand, the fact that the GC has derived the aforementioned duties of diligence from ECHR (as well as from the respect for human rights resulting from the constitutional traditions common to EU Member States, as established by article 6 TEU)[427] suggests that the same obligations apply at least to Member States of the Council of Europe.

In this respect, the Nada decision issued by the Swiss Federal Court shows that the Ayadi sentence has also had an impact on countries that are not EU members.[428] Referring explicitly to Ayadi sentence, the Court, taking into consideration the behaviour of the Swiss government held before the Committee, stated that Switzerland had the obligation to submit an application for exemption to the Sanctions Committee or, at least, to inform it of the fact that considered the reasons for the designation to be non-existent, due to the filing of the criminal proceedings against Mr. Nada. Even ECtHR, called upon to rule on the responsibility of Switzerland in relation to the same case, faced, albeit incidentally, the question of the behaviours payable by states representatives within the organizations. The decision has already been analyzed with regard to the problem of reconciling apparently conflicting international obligations. The interesting data that we now want to highlight is that ECtHR held Switzerland responsible, not only for not having "mitigated" the harshness of sanctions, given the margin of maneuver it possessed, but also for

[427]For further analysis see: A. HARTKAMP, C. SIBURGH, W. DEVROE, Cases, materials and text on European Union law and private law, Hart Publishing, Oxford & Oregon, Portland, 2017, pp. 282ss. K. LENAERTS, I. MASELIS, K. GUTMAN, European Union procedural law, Oxford University Press, Oxford, 2014, pp. 133ss. M. WIERZBOWSKI, A. GUBRYNOWICZ, International investment law for the 21st century, Oxford University Press, Oxford, 2015. A.H. TÜRK, Judicial review in European Union law, Edward Elgar Publishers, Cheltenham, 2010. L. WOODS, P. WATSON, Steiner & Woods European Union law, op. cit., pp. 37ss E. BERRY, M.Y. HOMEWOOD, B. BOGUSZ, Complete European Union law. Texts, cases and materials, Oxford University Press, Oxford, 2013. G. CONWAY, European Union law, ed. Routledge, London & New York, 2015. F. NICOLA, B. DAVIES, European Union law stories, Cambridge University Press, Cambridge, 2017. J. USHERWOOD, S. PINDER, The European Union. A very short introduction, Oxford University Press, Oxford, 2018.

[428]ECtHR, Swiss Federal Supreme Court, Nada v, SECO of 14 November 2007, para. 9.1. For the text of the sentence: v. Oxford Reports on International Law-ILDC 461 (CH 2007). The case is known, as well as the procedural developments before the Court of Strasbourg.

not having warned Sanctions Committee and Italy (state of nationality of the applicant) of the fact that there were no reasonable suspicions for the imposition of the measure in question.[429] According to ECtHR, if the Swiss State had promptly notified the Italian one, the latter could in turn inform the Sanctions Committee of this circumstance and put it in the position to cancel the name.[430] According to ECtHR reconstructions, the respondent State would instead have limited itself to "suggesting to the applicant to contact the Italian permanent representation to UN, making him moreover present that in that moment Italy was part of the Security Council."[431]

---

[429]The judges of Strasbourg seem to implicitly censor three interesting circumstances of the overall conduct held by the respondent State: First, the fact that Switzerland never advanced a request for exemption to the Sanctions Committee in favour of the applicant; second, that it waited more than four years to inform the Committee that the investigations into Mr Nada had not provided any evidence of his alleged links to Al-Qaeda; third-and particularly relevant-that Switzerland has in no way encouraged Italy to make a formal delisting request. The judges of Strasbourg observe that "[i]n this connection the Court is surprised by the allegation that the Swiss authorities did not inform the Sanctions Committee until 2 September 2009 of the conclusions of investigations closed on 31 May 2005 (...). Observing, however, that the veracity of this allegation has not been disputed by the government, and without any explanation having been given by the latter for such delay, the Court finds that a more prompt communication of the investigative authorities' conclusions might have led to the deletion of the applicant's name from the UN list at an earlier stage, thereby considerably reducing the period of time in which he was subjected to the restrictions of his rights under article 8 (…). However, it does not appear that Switzerland ever sought to encourage Italy to undertake such action or to offer it assistance for that purpose" (ECtHR, Nada v. Switzerland, op. cit., par. 188 and 194). See also the opinion of judge Bratza, accepted also from judges: Nicolau and Yudkiska. "(...) We fully share the view of the Federal Court that, while Switzerland could not itself proceed with deletion, it could at the very least have transmitted the results of the investigation to the Sanctions Committee and have actively supported the delisting of the applicant. With the benefit of the results of its own investigation, it could also have encouraged Italy, as the State of nationality and residence of the applicant, to take steps earlier than July 2008 to request the deletion of the applicant's name. Such measures were not bound to have met with success. There remained, however, a real prospect that they would have resulted in the deletion of the applicant's name and the restoration of his rights (article 8) at a much earlier stage than eventually occurred (...)" (par. 12).

[430]Note that the name of Mr. Nada had been inserted on the initiative of the United States and not of the Switzerland, which therefore could not reproach the conduct of the designation nor even that of the unsuccessful request for deletion since the only State able to take this initiative was Italy (State of citizenship and residence of the applicant). In fact, the Court observes that "Switzerland was neither its State of residence, nor the Swiss authorities were competent to undertake such action" (ECtHR, Nada v. Switzerland, op. cit., par. 194).

[431]The Court has noticed that: "(..) As to the applicant's requests to the Italian authorities with a view to obtaining their support in a delisting procedure, the Federal Department's representative suggested that the lawyer contact the Italian Permanent Mission to the UN,

From the passages reported the behaviours payable by the delegates seem to go well beyond those brought to light until now: Even the States not entitled to submit a cancellation request directly, should keep the Sanctions Committee informed of the information material in their possession, present if an exemption request, and even "encourage" the legitimate State to promote the cancellation request, offering the necessary assistance to the same.

Unfortunately, in Al-Dulimi case, Strasbourg judges did not take the opportunity to comment on the same issues, preferring to attribute to Switzerland the sole responsibility for the internal conduct of its judicial bodies and not for the behaviour of the Swiss representatives to the Sanctions Committee.[432]

This hypothesis of state responsibility does not emerge however only from the conventional system on which ECtHR supervises. The existence of similar obligations, if not more extensive, for government representatives within the Committees can also be found in the jurisprudence of the Committee for Civil and Political Rights (the Committee on Human Rights). In the Sayadi case in particular, the names of the applicants, two citizens of Belgian origin, had been inserted on the proposal of Belgium in the lists of the 1267[433] Committee following the opening of a criminal investigation.[434] However, after some time, the Brussels Court of First Instance had sentenced the Belgian authorities "à demander sous le bénéfice de l'urgence au Comité des sanctions des Nations Unies de radier les noms des demandeurs de la liste et d'en

adding that Italy had, at that time, a seat on the Security Council (...)" (ECtHR, Nada v. Switzerland of 12 September 2012, par. 54 and 194).

[432]This aspect was not addressed perhaps because in this case Switzerland had done everything in its power to fulfil the positive obligations mentioned above, supporting, through its permanent mission to UN, the first request for delisting of the applicant in a letter dated 5 November 2004 addressed to the presidency of the 1518 Committee.

[433]For further details see: D. MOECKLI, S. SHAH, S. SIVAKUMARAN, International human rights law, Oxford University Press, Oxford, 2010, pp. 598ss. C.C. MURPHY, EU counter terrorism law: Pre-emption and the rule of law, Hart Publishing, Oxford & Oregon, Portland, 2012. A.M. SALINAS DE FRÍAS, K. SAMUEL, N. WHITE, Counter terrorism. International law and practice, Oxford University Press, Oxford, 2012.

[434]Committees communication n. 1472/2008: Nabil Sayadi and Patricia Vinck v. Belgium, CCPR/C/94/D/1472/2006, of 29 December 2008. For further details see: A. CIAMPI, Security Council targeted sanctions and human rights, in B. FASSBENDER, Securing human rights?: Achievements and challenges of the UN, Oxford University Press, Oxford, 2011, pp. 123ss. F. KRENC, La Belgique "condamnée" pour la première fois par le Comité des droits de l'homme sur fond de lutte contre le terrorisme: cap sur Genève!, in Journal des Tribunaux, 2009, n. 6367 (24 oct. 2009), pp. 621 ss. M. MILANOVIC, The Human Rights Committee's views in Sayadi v. Belgium: A missed opportunity, in Goettingen Journal of International Law, 3, 2009, pp. 520ss. N.D. WHITE, The law of international organizations, Oxford University Press, Oxford, 2016.

communiquer la preuve aux demandeurs, à peine d'une astreinte de 250 euros par jour de retard, à compter de l'expiration du délai de 30 jours à partir de la signification du présent jugement."[435] Belgium had therefore promptly filed a cancellation request before the Sanctions Committee and, a few months later, national judges had confirmed the groundlessness of accusations against the appellants even in criminal proceedings. However, Belgium had failed to obtain the cancellation of names due to the opposition of one of the permanent members of the Committee (United States). The applicants then addressed a communication to the Human Rights Committee against the United States - declared inadmissible on the grounds that the respondent State had not ratified the Additional Protocol recognizing the competence of the Committee to receive individual communications[436]-and against Belgium, which is was held responsible for violating articles 12 and 17 of the International Covenant on Civil and Political Rights (freedom of movement and protection from attacks on honour and reputation).[437]

The Belgian government was considered primarily responsible for having proposed the inclusion of names in a premature manner on lists, or only after three months of criminal investigations and without sufficient information having been collected. Furthermore, although Belgium was not considered responsible for the failure to delete the name from the list as it did not have the material power to impose such removal on the Committee, it was nevertheless held responsible for maintaining the name on the list, a circumstance that would have involved damage to the image and reputation of the applicant.[438] Human Rights Committee, being moreover aware of the fact that Belgium had sent a cancellation request twice, without success, stated that "although the state party is itself not competent to remove authors' names from the Sanctions Committee's list, the Committee is nevertheless of the view that the state party has the duty to do all it can to have their names removed from the list as soon as possible, to provide the authors with some form of compensation and to make public the requests for removal. The state party is also obliged to ensure that similar violation do not occur in the future."[439] It therefore

---

[435]Nabil Sayadi and Patricia Vinck v. Belgium, op. cit.

[436]The appeal was originally lodged against a group of other States, against which the Committee on Civil and Political Rights instead found that internal remedies had not been carried out, a condition which only came about in relation to Belgium.

[437]For further details see: ICESCR, I. BANTEKAS, L. OETE, International human rights law and practice, Cambridge University Press, Cambridge, 2013, pp. 686ss. B. SAUL, D. KINLEY, J. MOWBRAY, The International Covenant on Economic, Social and Cultural Rights: Commentary, cases and materials, Oxford University Press, Oxford, 2014.

[438]Nabil Sayadi and Patricia Vinck v. Belgium, op. cit., par. 10.13.

[439]Nabil Sayadi and Patricia Vinck v. Belgium, op. cit., par. 12 e 13.

appears that the Committee of Human Rights requires from states parties to the Covenant a particularly high standard of diligence ("do everything possible"). The point was criticized by several partially dissenting judges.[440]

3.17. Some hints about the behaviours payable by governments in external relations with organizations

Attention is now focused on the positions taken by States on international level, no longer within organizations, but in external relations with them. The margin of states power over individuals in this case does not derive from their membership with a particular organization, but from being sovereign subjects of international law who, as such, can act against other subjects such as international organizations. In other words, the exercise of states powers have in international relations to protect individuals is highlighted here.

The States are entitled to (re) act in organizations unlawfulness of different ways and on the basis of different titles, depending on whether the prejudice has affected the rights (especially) of injured State, States other than the injured, or individuals. With regard to states interventions to protect individuals, who roughly assume the guise of a diplomatic action, the various diplomatic, economic and political means that could be used were invoked to assert their grievances against organizations and to demand from them the due repair. Now is the time to verify whether the individual can actually demand the adoption of such measures by the State under whose jurisdiction is located, which does not necessarily coincide with the State of citizenship.

That said, it is noted first of all that in the treaties on human rights there is no conventional provision which expressly imposes on Contracting States the obligation to act internationally with every means to protect the persons subject to their jurisdiction whose rights have been violated by an other subject (state or organization).

With reference to ECHR, the point was confirmed in a well-known story (the Abbasi case)[441] concerning diplomatic protection

---

[440]See the dissenting opinions of judges: Rodley, Shearer and Motoc. "Although it failed to make the argument explicitly, it is evident that the state party has done what it could to secure the authors' de-listing. In so doing it has provided the only remedy within its power (…). For Shearer "the state party has tried to secure the delisting but to no avail. There is no other avenue open to it to correct the mistake that was made. Not can be a remedy where the state party acted in good faith to discharge its obligations under a superior law (...).""

[441]Regina (Abbasi) v. Secretary of State for Foreign Affairs CA (EWCA Civ.) ER (D) 70

decided by the United Kingdom courts.[442] An obligation of action, moreover, cannot be deduced even from general international law: The different openings of opposite sign recorded in practice have not yet crystallized to the point of establishing with certainty the existence of an obligation for States to act in diplomatic protection to enforce the responsibility of another State or another organization.[443] This does not preclude, in our opinion, the possibility of recognizing such an obligation in the hypothesis of offenses in question. In this regard, a fundamental difference between the violations of human rights by organizations and the traditional cases of "mistreatment of foreigners" committed against citizens by a foreign State should be emphasized: While the former occur in state territory of which contests the failure to fulfil positive obligations. In the second case the abuses take place outside the territory (and jurisdiction) of the States called to intervene. Therefore, in cases of crimes committed on state territory, it is precisely the territorial element of violations that leads to assume, until proven otherwise, the existence of a limited state "jurisdiction" on situations object of dispute, with consequent greater possibility for the applicants to demonstrate the effectiveness of the positive obligations deriving from the treaties.

This being the case, the question must therefore be resolved on the interpretative level, investigating whether it is possible to extend the normative scope of the conventional positive obligations so as to derive an obligation for the States to adopt every reasonable measure to protect the rights of the persons under their jurisdiction, including the adoption of diplomatic measures against the subject held responsible (in our case the Organization), such as the invitation to negotiate, or the presentation of complaints and requests for reparation in the appropriate forums, aimed at guaranteeing the enjoyment of rights sanctioned by ECHR.

Some useful ideas could be derived from ECtHR decisions which require States not to repatriate individuals present in their territory to countries where conventionally established rights could be violated. In these cases, the States are asked to take the necessary measures, including those of a diplomatic nature, to prevent the Commission of an offense by other States. ECtHR position with regard to positive obligations due from the contracting States following the violation of human rights perpetrated by another State on its territory is definitely more relevant in this regard.

---

of 6 November 2002. See also: S. JUSS, M. SUNKIN, Landmark cases in public law, Hart Publishing, Oxford & Oregon, Portland, 2017, pp. 258ss.

[442]The reference is to the decision of Abbasi and others v. Secretary of State for Foreign Affairs and others of 6 November 2002, p. 22, par. 79. According to the British courts, there were no provisions of the ECHR which explicitly required their government to act in diplomatic protection for the benefit of one of its citizens.

[443]ECtHR, Tarakhel v. Switzerland of 4 November 2014.

The issue has been dealt with extremely interestingly in Ilaşcu and others v. Moldava and Russia decision. [444] The case concerned the acts carried out by the separatist regime established in the Moldovan region of Transnistria, a case very far from the one under examination, in relation to which ECtHR has been called to face complex problems of jurisdiction and attribution of conduct. The Russian Federation was given responsibility for ECHR's material violations complained of by the applicants (articles 3 and 5), on the assumption of "global" control exercised by it in Transnistria, the region where the violations had occurred. With reference, instead, to the Republic of Moldova, the ECtHR established that it could not be attributed to it the violation of negative obligations, since the State did not exercise an effective control of the territory, while maintaining a jurisdiction over the applicants (essentially due to their physical presence on the national territory). On the basis of this consideration, the Republic of Moldova has been called to respond for the violation of positive obligations, or for not having taken all the necessary measures to ensure compliance with ECHR.[445] In particular, this state would have failed to adopt measures of an economic, diplomatic and political nature aimed at the release of some of the applicants held by the separatist regime. In this regard, ECtHR noted that, during the negotiations between Moldova and separatists, no mention was made of the situation of applicants and - again in this diplomatic forum - no requests had been made to guarantee them the rights enshrined by ECHR. According to Strasbourg judges, if the conduct of the Moldovan authorities here had been "more attentive to the applicants" they would have prevented the violation of applicants rights or at least would have put an end to them.[446]

---

[444]ECtHR, Ilaşcu and others v. Moldova and Russia of 8 July 2004. For further analysis see: J.A. HESSBRUEGGE, The European Court of Human Rights: Catan and others v. Moldova and Russia, in International Legal Materials, 52 (1), 2013, pp. 219ss. H. DUFFY, The war on terror and the framework of international law, Cambridge University Press, Cambridge, 2015. A. NOLLKAEMPER, D. JACOBS, J.N.M. SCHECHINGER, Distribution of responsibilities in international law, op. cit., pp. 283ss.

[445]"Although Moldova did not in fact exercise control in that region, according to the Court, it was considered that it still had "jurisdiction" over that part of the territory, pursuant to art. 1 of the ECHR. This situation, however, according to the Court, "reduce the scope of that jurisdiction" in the sense that the commitment assumed by the contracting State on the basis of the aforementioned article was to be assessed exclusively in light of the positive obligations towards individuals present on that territory."

[446]ECtHR, Ilaşcu and others v. Moldova and Russia, op. cit., par. 350, which "(...) in their negotiations with the separatists, the Moldovan authorities have restricted themselves to raising the question of the applicants' situation orally, without trying to reach an agreement guaranteeing respect for their Convention rights (…). Similarly, the applicants have been deprived of their liberty for nearly twelve years, no overall plan for the settlement of the Transdniestrian conflict brought to the Court's attention deals with their situation, and the

The relevant data of this decision for our initial question is twofold: On the one hand the control of ECtHR on the behaviours kept (rectius not held) by the state authorities in bilateral diplomatic relations with the State responsible for the violations (the Russian Federation); on the other, States' duty is to work diligently and put an end to violations committed in their own territory, but attributable to another person who has temporarily maintained effective control over a given area or over certain people. And this is precisely the point of the decision that interests us, and that is that the territorial State where ECHR's material violations have occurred - even if these are not attributable to it - remains bound to the positive obligations of art. 1 ECHR. In particular, the territorial state is responsible for preventing the offense and, once the violation has already occurred for the hands of others, endeavour to end it by resorting, if necessary, to appropriate diplomatic means.[447]

Regarding "the obligation to protect"[448] the individuals present in their territories, another interesting starting point for our initial question can be obtained from the Guiding Principles on business and human rights elaborated by the UN in the context of the discussion on the duties that are required to States in whose territories multinational business activities are registered.[449] Although the reflections on the duties of territorial States to "respect," "protect" and "guarantee a remedy" have been developed with reference to the harmful activities of private individuals (multinational companies) operating in their territories, the same reasoning could, in our opinion, apply also in relation to the (illicit) activities of intergovernmental organizations. It is then possible to interpret the first principle expressed in the Guiding Principles, according to which "States must protect against human rights abuse within their territory and/or jurisdiction by third parties,"[450] as if to impose the adoption of specific measures to prevent, investigate and end to offenses committed by organizations through "effective policies, legislation, regulations and adjudication." The range of

---

Moldovan government did not claim that such a document existed or that negotiations on the subject were in progress (...)." (par. 348).

[447]ECtHR, Ilaşcu and others v. Moldova and Russia, op. cit., par. 349. The ECtHR has nevertheless admitted that it is not able to indicate the exact content of the diplomatic measures to be adopted, but, nevertheless, to be able to assess the adequacy of those adopted or of their non-adoption.

[448]D. SILANDER, D. WALLACE, International organizations an the implementation of the responsibility to protect, ed. Routledge, London & New York, 2015.

[449]On the three fundamental obligations "to respect," "protect" and "remedy" countries, see the Guiding Principles on Business and Human Rights. Implementing the UN "Protect, Respect and Remedy" Framework, attached to UN Human Rights Council Resolution 17/4 of June 16, 2011, UN Doc. HR/PUB/11/04.

[450]D. SILANDER, D. WALLACE, International organizations and the implementation of the responsibility to protect, op. cit.

"effective policies" could also include diplomatic measures to be adopted with regard to the responsible organization.

3.18. (Follows) State responsibility for the failure to adopt diplomatic measures aimed at requiring the reparation of the offense committed by the organizations on its territory

Law principles that derive from the Ilaşcu decision and the Guiding Principles appear to be applicable, mutatis mutandis, to the present study and, in particular, to the offenses committed in organizations operations of force. Although the situation of the offenses committed by the organizations differs substantially from the peculiar circumstances of the Ilaşcu case (which concerned a secessionist movement and the territorial State, the latter being the only one to have international legitimacy) and those taken into consideration by the Guiding principles on business and human rights (which refer to activities carried out by private parties, i.e. companies). In the hypotheses of offenses under examination there is instead a subject of international law fully legitimized to operate in state territory. However, with a certain abstraction the context under discussion does not differ substantially from the relevant elements of the Ilaşcu case, as well as from the circumstances in which the Guiding Principles are applicable. In fact, in the territory there is an organization that, depending on the activity or mission it performs, exercises more or less intense control over an area or over certain people, while the territorial state maintains a certain "margin" of jurisdiction over the individuals, whose size varies according to the operation carried out by the organization and the powers assigned to it. The limitation of state jurisdiction determines a reduction of the scope of obligations in terms of human rights, which are limited only to the positive ones.

This consideration could also apply to state hosting projects financed by economic organizations which then materialize in violations of human rights. In these cases the imposition of positive obligations on States that territorially host projects can be considered as a just counterpart to some national policy choices. To the extent that the states surrender part of their sovereignty and control over their territory to third parties, this choice cannot completely come back to individuals in the event that these individuals then commit human rights violations.

It follows that on the State that hosts the organization's activities on its territory, the positive obligations to protect human rights continue to be imposed in principle.[451] The territorial states would therefore be required to behave diligently to prevent the occurrence of ECHR violations committed by the organizations and, if they do not succeed, they should nevertheless work to put an end to the violation, resorting, if necessary, to the appropriate diplomatic measures against the organizations (complaints, requests for reparation, guarantee of non-repetition etc.). Before affirming the responsibility of territorial States for failure to intervene to protect individuals under their jurisdiction, it is necessary to verify other profiles. As a preliminary matter, it must be ascertained that the territorial State has effectively maintained even a minimum control of the territory, through the exercise of a limited jurisdiction. Secondly, it is necessary to verify that no liability exclusion clauses for non-compliance with positive obligations are highlighted. In this regard, some circumstances linked to the impossibility (economic and/or political) of the hosting State, organization's mission to fulfil human rights treaties could be decisive. Indeed, such situations become relevant in conventional liability systems only from the angle of derogation or restriction clauses to the provisions therein. As is known, states parties to human rights treaties may resort to waiver clauses in emergency situations, or place the necessary restrictions on the rights enshrined therein, provided that balancing with other needs is in accordance with the requirements of proportionality and necessity. Thirdly, we need to think about the diligence parameter required of States, which could also be relatively low in this context and aimed exclusively at avoiding arbitrary or manifestly unreasonable behaviour.

In these terms it is then possible to hypothesize a control over the adequacy of measures, of a diplomatic nature, adopted by States towards the organization responsible for the offense. Such control seems to us even more necessary given the fact that the actions (or omissions) undertaken internationally by States against the organizations responsible for the

---

[451]In the case, for example, of the spread of cholera epidemic in Haiti, one could reconstruct the positive obligations in question in the light of the Covenant on Civil and Political Rights, which the Republic of Haiti has already signed since 1991, and of the Inter-American ECHR human rights (Pact of San Josè), ratified since 1977, on whose interpretation and application Haiti has recognized since 1998 the jurisdiction of the Inter-American Court of Human Rights. From this perspective, one could therefore ask what was the responsibility of Haiti for not having prevented the spread of the epidemic imported by Nepalese from peacekeepers. It should be ascertained whether Haiti has obtained adequate guarantees from UN on the protocols adopted to prevent the entry of infectious diseases and then, once the violation has occurred, if it has sufficiently guaranteed the rights of the victims under its jurisdiction, asking the Organization to adopt measures to cease and repair the wrongdoing. From the survey carried out in the previous chapter, the fulfilment of the positive obligations on the part of Haiti seems to have been, in this respect, rather unsatisfactory.

crime are often the only forms of available remedy.[452] In the same way, the adoption of internal administrative, legislative or judicial measures, suitable for guaranteeing a remedy for the violations committed on one's own territory, will be evaluated.

In concrete terms it is reasonable to suppose that the States that host organizations activities on their territory, due to the "duty to protect" the individuals under their jurisdiction, must first have obtained guarantees from the organization, through the adoption of protocols or agreements, and the rights of individuals present on their territory are respected. Secondly, territorial States should provide internal procedures capable of "collecting" and assessing the point of view of victims of violations. If they then consider it inappropriate to defend them internationally, since individual interests, although founded, are considered in the concrete case inferior to any conflicting national interests at stake, States would be called upon to offer some form of compensation to the victims (even to an extent symbolic). This line of reasoning, in hindsight, is very close to what is already provided for in the recommended practices referred to in art. 19 of the Diplomatic Protection Project[453] and to what has recently been claimed by some authors as a counterweight to the recognition of immunities of foreign States for serious violations of human rights.[454]

It should also be noted that the existence of internal procedures such as those described, while not constituting a reparation for the prejudice suffered by the unlawful organizations conduct, would represent, for the victims, a partial satisfaction of their individual right of access to justice, and, for the States, a fulfilment of the obligation "(to) remedy" which is imposed in cases of abuses committed on its own territory in the light of the Guiding Principles.

Having said this, the hypothesis state responsibility proposed by

---

[452]We have repeatedly stressed how often the offense of the Organization creates a situation of denial of justice for the victims, if the conduct is exclusively attributable to the organization and there are no internal remedies available to the organizations, nor remedies before the national courts because of immunity. Another question is then to understand to what extent the diplomatic action of the State is an appropriate "alternative" remedy for the victims. See: P. PALCHETTI, Can State action on behalf of victims be an alternative to individual access to justice in case of grave breaches of human rights?, in Italian Yearbook of International Law, 24, 2014, pp. 53ss. A. VON ARNAULD, Völkerrecht, op. cit.

[453]See also: E. DENZA, Nationality and diplomatic protection, in Netherlands International Law Review, 65 (3), 2018, pp. 465ss.

[454]See Access to remedy, in Guiding Principles on Business and human rights, op. cit., which is affirmed that "(...) as part of their duty to protect against business-related human rights abuse, States must take appropriate steps to ensure, through judicial, administrative, legislative and other appropriate means, that when such abuses occur within their territory and/or jurisdiction those affected have access to effective remedy (...)."

us must come to terms with reality and therefore we must ask ourselves if it would lead to significant results in terms of reparation for the victims of violations. In ECtHR jurisprudence this hypothesis emerged in cases where the contracting states actually had the power to prevent the violation of rights protected by ECHR or, at least, to guarantee their cessation. In contrast, the States under whose jurisdiction the victims of the offenses in question are located and are often weak. Collapsing States do not always possess the resources necessary to take preventive and subsequent measures against the responsible organization (or any state agent), such as diplomatic ones. However, these considerations, in addition to adhering to a political and non-juridical merit, will have to be evaluated, on a case-by-case basis, by the body in charge of the control of human rights, given that state responsibility could meet is limited to the violation of an obligation of conduct and not of result. Therefore, only the state that, taking into account all the circumstances of the case, has not held a diligent conduct suitable to prevent the offense and, once verified, to request a repair of the same (but not already to obtain it) will be held responsible.

In identifying the due diligence parameter, different circumstances should be taken into account, first and foremost the skills devolved to the organization and the nature of the allegedly violated rule. Whatever the standard identified by the mechanisms of human rights control, we can cautiously believe that state total "diplomatic inertia" in whose territory the offenses took place must be considered as not conforming to the positive obligations provided for by the treaties if it is the result of a totally arbitrary or manifestly unreasonable decision. We could hypothetically expect even more significant behaviours from States, such as submitting requests for the reparation of victims to the attention of organization, or establishing appropriate diplomatic negotiations to obtain a certain result (which does not necessarily coincide with compensation of an economic nature). What is certain is that States, in order to free themselves from all responsibility, cannot limit themselves to arguing that they did not have effective and/or global control over the part of the territory in which the alleged violations actually occurred, but will have to demonstrate before the control bodies to have behaved in accordance with the standard of due diligence or to have legitimately applied any derogation clauses or restrictions to the conventionally sanctioned rights.

The hypotheses of state responsibility considered here undoubtedly present some limits in terms of results that can be concretely obtained, first of all, the fact that the repair by territorial States could be of limited scope for the victims. However, the arguments developed in this section, read in a de iure condendo perspective, would entail an adequate incentive for the states to put the necessary "pressures" on the responsible subject (the organization), inviting him to fulfil the secondary obligations deriving from the illicit.

3.19. Concluding remarks

The various studies on the responsibility of international organizations often share the same goal, namely that of "bridging" the organizations through the imposition of customary norms and general principles elaborated by states practice without, and sometimes against, the consent of the same. Both the theories that refer to the traditional categories of international law, and those that claim to ignore them, try to apply to organizations, by deduction, norms that ensure the control of their work (respectively from outside or inside), to front a practice of organizations often meager, uneven or not yet settled.

On the other hand, a method of inductive analysis that is limited to the description of "what organizations do and say," would risk condoning the non-virtuous practice of organizations. Furthermore, such an analysis would not lead to significant results given the lack of uniformity between organizations behaviours and would preclude a general and unitary vision, necessary to face the topic in question.

The imposition on organizations of some fundamental principles on the subject of responsibility follows, in our opinion correctly, an axiomatic logic that is independent of the existence of a generally compliant practice of multiple (and multiform) organizations. This applies, for example, to the de jure application of the rule requiring organizations to repair the damage caused by the crime. Another and more complex question is whether the individual, under the rules of general international law, is the recipient of reparation. The secondary obligation of reparation towards individuals, which is intertwined with the primary obligation to guarantee a remedy (or access to justice in the broad sense), should, in our opinion, lie with organizations that exercise a form of "jurisdiction" on individuals, whose thickness would affect the standard of compliance with the norm itself. On the other, it should not be forgotten that the individual right to a remedy, as part of the broader rule that requires respect for the rule of law, is recognized as a fundamental principle by different actors of the international community in an increasingly progressive manner continuous and widespread, so as to constrain even the organizations. Proof of this is the fact that some organizations today recognize the applicability to them of the principles of the rule of law,[455] while they are

[455] M. AVBELJ, J. KOMÁREK, Constitutional pluralism in the EU and beyond, Hart Publishing, Oxford & Oregon, Portland, 2012. K. LENAERTS, Federalism and the rule of law: Perspectives from the European Court of Justice, in Fordham International Law Journal, 33, 2011, pp. 1338ss. I. WEIBUST, J. MEADOWCROFT, Multilevel environmental governance. Managing water and climate change in Europe and North

more reluctant to bind themselves to the whole "package" of customary rules for the protection of human rights. The UN, for example, in addition to promoting the debate on the importance of these issues for Member States, have expressed their willingness, at least in words, to apply the rule of law to their work, despite their attitude does not always seem to go in the same direction.

Some consideration must now be given to the functioning of the two liability regimes that come into play following the Commission of the offenses in question. The first regime governs the responsibility of organizations in light of the general secondary rules of international law drafted by the Commission in the Project adopted in 2011 (DARIO).

The DARIO Project, drawn up along the lines of 2001 DRSIWA, analyzes the liability relationships deriving from the unlawfulness of organizations from a predominantly inter-state perspective. This means that the subjects called upon to implement the consequences of the offense committed by the organizations, in the absence of special rules, are exclusively the states and in infrequent hypothesis, the other organizations. Not recognizing rights for individuals and subordinating the setting in motion of responsibility to States (discretionary) initiative of DARIO, in the opinion of many, would have a reduced application scope, or nothing, in cases of violation of human rights committed by the organizations. According to this line of reasoning, this would cause a significant lack of protection for the victims as they would encounter different difficulties if they wanted to get a remedy and a repair of the prejudice suffered directly from the organizations. In fact, before national jurisdictions the rules on the immunity of organizations are operative, while on international level the control mechanisms established by human rights treaties are not competent to receive direct appeals against the organizations and the internal ones established by the organizations themselves are often inadequate.

The initiatives taken by citizenship states, however, present different limits from the perspective of individuals, above all the traditional discretion exercised by states in these contexts. To complicate the legal framework is added a significant political data. The reference is to the fact that states choice to intervene to protect individuals is often altered, if not coerced, by certain significant political and financial implications. More precisely, the invocation of the responsibility of organizations can be discouraged by the fact that financing and support programs depend on these States hypothetically called to act. It is therefore probable that, in these cases, national interests end up compressing the rights of injured individuals.

America, Edward Elgar Publishers, Cheltenham, 2014. C. PANARA, The sub-national dimension of the EU: A legal study of multilevel governance, ed. Springer, Berlin, 2015.

Furthermore, the typical "one to one" relationship underlying the controversies that arose in the ambit of diplomatic protection is distorted, in the cases under examination, by the fact that behind the responsible organization "more States are hiding." This disparity certainly constitutes a further significant obstacle to the invocation of organization's responsibility.

Examining the practice of offenses committed by the UN, it is clear that, apart from "proceduralized" interventions (such as those provided by the guidelines adopted by the Sanctions Committees), the submission of complaints and the subsequent negotiation of compensation in favor victims are quite rare phenomena and have occurred on the initiative of the economically and politically strongest States.

As is known, the attribution of the unlawful act to States allows individuals to access the jurisdictional control systems established by the treaties on human rights and, consequently, to invoke state responsibility according to a conventional regime. The possibility for the individual to establish a controversy towards the responsible state is undoubtedly a remedy that can lead to a more certain and direct reparation than the one that can be obtained in previously seen disputes.

Through ECtHR jurisprudence a line of demarcation has been traced that marks the internal or international context in which the disputable conduct of contracting States are located. The behaviours manifested internally have been further distinguished according to whether they have been put in place by states within their territorial boundaries (it is the case of internal measures adoption to implement the sanctions imposed by organizations or courts decisions that recognize the immunity to organizations) or in those of a third State (this is the case of the conduct of national contingents employed in force actions established and authorized by UN).

Particular attention was paid to the hypotheses of responsibility for the adoption of internal measures in implementation of obligations deriving from States participating to organizations. The problematic aspect concerned not so much the issues of conduct attribution and the existence of state jurisdiction, but rather the delicate coordination between ECHR and the potentially conflicting international obligations, a task that proved particularly thorny when it came to coordinating Security Council resolutions with conventionally sanctioned rights.

Our investigation has limited itself to detecting the main problems inherent in the two distinct elements of the offense, namely the criterion to be used to attribute the conduct alternatively or exclusively to the sending States and to the organization, and the existence of state jurisdiction in extraterritorial sense, as an objective assumption of (spatial) application of the obligations in question. In these cases the mere presence of acts with efficacy on the national territory of states contractors was considered sufficient to justify ratione personae and loci the eligibility of the appeals.

Our investigation has tried to connect, in a de iure condendo perspective, the two regimes of responsibility analyzed, asking ourselves about the behaviours that could be demanded by States at the international level. More precisely, it was assessed whether the failure to adopt positive behaviours within or against the organizations responsible for the crime could lead to state responsibility for the violation of primary obligations contracted in terms of human rights, with particular reference to those established by ECHR.

Responding to this question in a cautiously positive sense, two hypothetical types of responsibility have been identified: The first concerns the use of state powers that possess in virtue of their membership to address from within the conduct of organizations in a manner consistent with ECHR; the second, instead, concerns the conduct of States that do not intervene from outside against the responsible organization.

As far as the first hypothesis is concerned, a fixed point obtainable from ECtHR's jurisprudence is that the states do not free themselves from the obligations contracted on the subject of human rights simply because they have transferred some competences to international organizations. The transfer of skills should in principle take place with the guarantees provided by the conventional system. If this applies in general, in some recent ECtHR decisions (precisely in Gasparini, Klausecker and Perez cases) the states have been called to respond also for the lack of vigilance on the respect of human rights in organizations, in the absence of internal measures adopted on national territory. The interesting aspect is that in these cases ECtHR judgment has extended to the positive behaviours of states delegates kept within organization's organs.

On the basis of these latest decisions, a possible model was then drawn up aimed at ascertaining state responsibility for the conduct of their delegates involved in the adoption of decisions by the organizations. This model would make it possible to "unpack" the complex act of organizations in violation of human rights (these are usually resolutions), to then verify whether the behaviour adopted individually by state representatives in this context has respected the positive obligations deriving from the treaties on human rights. The multiple and complex issues that may arise in this operation have therefore been highlighted (and partially resolved), including the problem relating to the standard of diligence required for states delegates acting within the organizations and that of the existence of state jurisdiction in relation to a conduct that takes place in the legal space of organizations. In this latter regard, it seems to us that the functional notion of state jurisdiction would make it possible to impute not a widespread responsibility on the part of all Member States of the organization for the fact committed by the latter (which would moreover be precluded by the screen constituted by the autonomous personality of the organization), but a Member State individually responsibility, within the complex of decision-making processes, maintain the substantial power to affect individuals rights.

The conclusions we reached were then lowered in the context of the procedures followed by the Sanctions Committees, in relation to which states delegates exercise significant and autonomous powers. In this regard, some elements of the practice of conventional bodies seem to confirm the functioning of the proposed model, at least in relation to the actions and omissions of the delegates in the framework of procedures relating to the drafting and maintenance of lists of the sanctioned individuals.

With reference instead to the hypothesis of state responsibility, we have concluded that the existence of positive obligations can go so far as to require the adoption of diligent behaviours-both preventive and subsequent-to the State in whose territory the offenses of the organizations are verified. From this point of view, it could then be expected that the territorial State would diligently activate itself so that the organization would repair the injured individuals, establishing appropriate contacts and diplomatic relations with the same and adopting the necessary measures. With regard to state interventions before the Security Council committees, individuals unjustly registered on the lists usually obtain, through the defense of their citizenship, a form of reparation that approaches the restoration of the situation before (i.e. the cancellation from the blacklist). The possibility of obtaining, in addition, an economic compensation for the damages suffered (such as damage to reputation or image) is not provided for in the procedures of the Committees and has never been requested by the States in practice.

Individuals affected by the crimes committed in the force actions established by the organizations, through the negotiations undertaken by their own citizenship States, can obtain, in principle, reparative compensatory measures. However, the practice indicates that the stipulation of global or individual economic compensation agreements is subordinated to the minor or major diplomatic force of victims in relation to the Organization, depending on the granting of compensation, ultimately, from the political will of Member States which, on a case-by-case basis, decide to make the necessary economic resources available.

As regards instead the disputes between individuals and States before the control bodies set up by human rights treaties, the reparation for this viable route basically follows the forms and methods provided for by the conventional reference system and varies according to the disputed conduct to States. In this regard it is good to distinguish the cases according to whether the behaviours attributable to States are in fact similar to those theoretically attributable to organizations or whether they are autonomous, even if connected to the crime of the latter. If in the first case the reparation obtainable by the individual is substantially similar to that achievable in disputes between States and organizations, in the second case the answer is different. To give an example, in the hypothesis in which an international body appealed to by individuals considers a State responsible for having implemented the sanctions imposed by the Security Council in violation of the conventionally sanctioned rights, the reparation obtainable does not consist in being removed from the lists of the Committee, but at most in a judicial review of the internal measure, with consequent cancellation or modification of the same exclusively at national level. On the other hand, the reparation obtainable in the event that the control bodies ascertain state responsibility for the omission of supervision within the organization or for the lack of intervention to protect the individuals affected by the activities of the same is more uncertain.

Finally, with respect to the solutions analyzed so far, a third alternative model to the previous ones is lacking which allows to implement the responsibility of organizations towards individuals. The point deserves to be investigated more in a perspective of widening the present research topic. What, however, it is now possible to detect, at least from an analysis at first sight of the various internal mechanisms established by UN, is that they lack unity and effectiveness, which prevents them from being placed in a special type of liability regime. These mechanisms do not appear to be suitable for guaranteeing the implementation of the Organization's responsibility according to the traditional categories envisaged in the Project, as they often do not provide an effective remedy for the prejudice suffered by individuals. The internal remedies currently operating for the UN seem to fall into the category of accountability systems that aim to ensure compliance with the primary rules of international law (such as the principle of transparency and respect for the rule of law) and not secondary ones.

From this point of view, it is certainly desirable a greater development of such systems in the direction of an "external" control to the work of the organizations through mechanisms that, even if deprived of the sophisticated guarantees of the two process, allow an independent examination of the appeals and eventually provide for remedial measures for the injury suffered. It should also be noted that the consolidation of this third route would prevent States from responding, on the basis of indirect liability claims, to the internal shortcomings of the organizations they are members of and to consider their intervention necessary to protect the injured individuals.

Bibliography

A.A.V.V., Commentary on the second Geneva Convention, Cambridge University Press, Cambridge, 2017.

ABASS, A., Complete international law: Text, cases and materials, Oxford University Press, 2014.

ABASS, A., Consent precluding state responsibility. A critical analysis, in International and Comprative Law Quarterly, 53 (2), 2004, pp. 212ss.

ABELLO GALVIS, R., CAVELIER, G., Derecho internacional contemporaneo, Editorial Universidad del Rosario, Bogotà, 2013.

ABI-SAAB, G., The Appellate Body and treaty interpretation, in M. FITZMAURICE, O. ELIAS, P. MERKOURIS, Treaty interpretation and the Vienna Convention on the Law of Treaties: 30 Years on, Martinus Nijhoff Publishers, Leiden/Boston, 2010, pp. 100ss.

ABI-SAB, G., The uses of article 19, in European Journal of International Law, 10 (2), 1999, pp. 340ss.

ACCIOLY, H., Principles gènèraux de la responsabilitè internationale d'après la docrine et la jurisprudence, Recueil des cours, ed. Brill, Bruxelles, vol. 96, 1959, pp. 354ss.

ACHTEN, N., Compensation claims of individuals for violations of rules on conduct of hostilities. Comment on a judgment of the District Court of Bonn, Germany-LG Bonn 1 0 460/11, 11 December 2013, in Humanitares Volkerrecht, 28, 2015, pp. 35ss.

ACOSTA ESTÉVEZ, J.B., Normas de ius cogens, efecto erga omnes, crimen internacional y la teoria de los circulo concèntricos, in Anuario de Derecho Internacional, 11, 1995, pp. 4ss.

ADAM, H.T., Les organismes internationaux spècialisès, LGDJ, Paris, 1965, pp. 130ss.

ADAM, H.T., Les organismes internationaux spècialisès. Contribution à la thèorie gènèrale des ètablissements publics internationaux, LGDJ, Paris, 1992.

ADAMS, M., MEUWESE, A., HIRSCH BALLIN, E., Constitutionalism and the rule of law. Bridging realism and realism, Cambridge University Press, Cambridge, 2017, pp. 423ss.

AEBERHARD, P., CHAUMET, P.O., Droit et stratègies de l'action humanitaire, ed. Mare & Martin, Paris, 2018.

AGO, R., Le dèlit international, in Recueil des cours, ed. Brill, Bruxelles, vol. 68, 1939, pp. 416ss.

AGO, R., Premier sur la responsabilitè des États-Historique de l'oeuvre accomplie jusqu'ici en ce qui concerne la codification du sujet de la responsabilitè internationale des États, Doc. A/CN.4/217 and Corr. 1 and Add.1, in Annuaire de la Commission du Droit International, 1969, vol. II, pp. 128ss.

AGO, R., Quatrième rapport sur la responsabilitè des États-le fait internationalement illicite de l'État, source de responsabilitè internationale (suite), UN Doc. A/CN.4/264 and Add. 1, in Annuaire de la Commission du Droit International, 1972, vol. II, pp. 27ss.

AGO, R., Troisième rapport sur la responsabilitè des États. Le fait internationalement illicite de l'État, source de responsabilitè internationale, UN Doc. A/CN.4/246 and Add. 1-3, in Annuaire de la Commission du Droit International, 1971, vol. II, p. 209-215, par. 29.

AGUILAR NAVARRO, M., La responsabilidad internacional y la organizacon de la sociedad internacional, in Escuela de funcionarios internacionales, cursos y conferencias, 9 (3), 1955-1956, Madrid, 1957, pp. 157ss.

AHLBORN, C., Remedies against International Organizations. A relational account of international responsibility, in K. WALLENS, Remedies and responsibility for the actions of international organizations, ed. Brill, Hague, 2014, pp. 545ss.

AHLBORN, C., The rules of international organizations and the law of international responsibility and the law of interntional responsibility, in SHARES Research Paper 02 (2011), ACIL 2011-03, pp. 29ss.

AHLBORN, C., The use of analogies drafting the articles on the responsibility of international organizations: An appraisal of the "copy-paste approach," in International Organizations Law Review, 9, 2012, pp. 54ss.

AHLBORN, C., To share or not to share? The allocation of responsibility between international organizations and their member states, in Die Friedens-Warte, 88, 2013, pp. 46ss.

AHLSTRÖM, C., The status of multilateral export control regimes: An examination of legal and non-legal agreements in international cooperation, Iustus Forlag, Uppsala, 1999.

AJIBOLA, B., Dispute resolution by the International Court of Justice, in Leiden Journal of International Law, 21, 1998, pp. 124ss.

AKANDJI-KOMBE, J., Positive obligations under the European Convention on Human Rights. A guide to the implementation of the European Convention on Human Rights, Human Rights Handbook No. 7, Council of Europe Publishing, 2007.

AKEHURST, A., Reprisals by third states, in British Yearbook of International Law, 44, 1970, pp. 4ss.

AKEHURST, M., The hierarchy of the sources of international law, in British Yearbook of International Law, 47, 1975, pp. 274ss.

AKSENOVA, M., Complicity in international criminal law, Oxford University Press, Oxford, 2016.

ALAMUDDIN, A., NABIL JURDI, N., TOLBERT, D., The special tribunal for Lebanon law and practice, Oxford University Press, Oxford, 2014, pp. 64ss.

ALBORN, C., The rules of international organizations and the law of international responsibility, in international organizations Law Review, 8, 2011, pp. 398ss.

ALCAIDE FERNÁNDEZ, J., Contre-mesures et règlement des diffèrends, in Revue Gènèrale de Droit Intenational Public, 108 (2), 2004, pp. 348ss.
ALEXY, H., Völkerrechtliche Praxis der Bundesrepublick Deutschland im jahre 1958, in Zeitschrift für ausländisches Recht und Völkerrecht, 20, 1960, pp. 663ss.
ALLAN, C., Attribution issues in cyberspace, in Chicago-Kent Journal of International and Comparative Law, 14, 2013.
ALLAND, D., Countermeasures of general interest, in European Journal of International Law, 13, 2002, pp. 1232ss.
ALLAND, D., Justice privèe et ordre juridique international. Etude thèorique des contre-mesures en droit international public, ed. Pedone, Paris, 1994.
ALLAND, D., L'interprétation du droit international public, in Recueil des Cours, ed. Brill, Bruxelles, vol. 362, 2012, pp. 216ss.
ALLAND, D., The definition of countermeasures, in J. CRAWFORD, A. PELLET, S. OLLESON, The law of international responsibility, Oxford University Press, Oxford, 2010, pp. 1135ss.
ALLEN, S., COSTELLOE, D., FITZMAURICE, M., The oxford handbook of jurisdiction in international law, Oxford University Press, Oxford, 2019.
ALLIN, D.H., Unintended consequences. Managing Kosovo independence, in What status for Kosovo?, Chaillot paper, Institute for Security Studies of WEU, October 2001.
ALLOTT, P., Eunomia. New order a new world, Oxford, New York, 1990, pp. 325ss.
ALMQVIST, J., ESPOSITO, C., The role of courts in transitional justice. Voices from Latin America and Spain, ed. Routledge, London & New York, 2013, pp. 177ss.
ALONSO, H., Current trends on modes of liability for genocide, crimes against humanity and war crimes, in C. STAHN, L. VAN DEN HERIK (eds.), Future perspectives on international criminal justice, T.M.C. Asser press, The Hague, 2010, pp. 522-524.
ALSTON, P., Non-State actors and human rights, Oxford University Press, Oxford, 2005, pp. 80, and 113ss.
ALVAREZ-JIMENEZ, A., Methods for the identification of customary international law in the International Court of Justice's jurisprudence: 2000-2009, in International and Comparative Law Quarterly, 60, 2011, pp. 681-711.
ALVAREZ, J., The United Nations in the Time of Cholera, in AJIL Unbound, 108, 2014-2015.
ALVAREZ, J.E., International organizations as law-makers, Oxford University Press, Oxford, 2005, pp. 85ss.
ALVAREZ, J.E., Limits of change by way of subsequent agreements and practice, in G. NOLTE, Treaties and subsequent practice, Oxford University Press, Oxford, 2013, pp. 124ss.
AMBOS, K., Der Allgemeine Teil des Völkerstrafrechts: Ansätze einer Dogmatisierung, Duncker and Humblot, Berlin, 2002.

AMERASINGHE, C., Principles of the institutional law of international organizations, Cambridge University Press, Cambridge, 2005, pp. 244ss.
AMERASINGHE, C.F., An assessment of the ILC's articles on the responsibility of international organizations, in M. RAGAZZI (ed.), Responsibility of International Organizations. Essays in Memory of Sir Ian Brownlie, ed. Brill, Bruxelles, 2013.
AMERASINGHE, C.F., Principles of the Institutional Law of International Organizations, Cambridge University Press, Cambridge, 2005, pp. 486ss,
AMERASINGHE, C.F., State responsibility for injuries to aliens, Clarendon Press, Oxford, 1963.
AMERASINGHE, F., Local remedies in international law, Cambridge University Press, Cambridge 2004, pp. 64ss.
AMERASNIGHE, C., Liability to third parties of member states of international organizations: Practice, principle and judicial precedence, in American Journal of International Law, 85, 1991, pp. 273ss.
AMOROSO, D., Moving towards complicity as a criterion of attribution of private conducts. Imputation to states of corporate abuses in the US case law, in Leiden Journal of International Law, 24, 2011, pp. 990ss.
AMRALLAH, B., The international responsibility of the United Nations for activities carried out by U.N. peace-keeping forces, in Revue Egyptienne de Droit International, 17, 1976, pp. 57-82.
ANDENAS, M., BJORGE, E., A farewell to fragmentation. Reassertion and convergence in international law, Cambridge University Press, Cambridge, 2015.
ANDENAS, M.T., Jurisdiction procedure an the transformation of international law. From Nottebohm to Diallo in the International Court of Justice, in European Business Law Review, 23 (1), 2012, pp. 130ss.
ANGELET, N., Droit du pouvoir, pouvoir du droit: Mélanges offerts à Jean Salmon, ed. Bruylant, Brussels, 2007, pp. 94ss.
ANNACKER, C., The legal règime of erga omnes obligation, in Austrian Journal of Public International Law, 46, 1994, pp. 158ss.
ANNACKER, E., Die Durchsetzung von erga omnes Verpflichtungen vor dem Internationalen Gericthshof, D. Kovac Verlag, Hamburg, 1994.
ANZILOTTI, D., Cours de droit international, LGDJ, Paris, 1999, pp. 529ss.
ANZILOTTI, D., La responsabilitè internationale des Etats à raion des dommages soufferts par des ètrangers, in Revue Gènèrale de Droit International Public, 1, 1906, pp. 152ss.
ANZOLA-RORDRÍGUEZ, S.I., Governing through customary international law?, in International Law, Revista Colombiana de Derecho Internacional, 20, 2012, pp. 168ss.
APOLLIS, G., Le règlement de l'affaire du "Rainbow Warrior," in Revue Gènèrale de Droit International Public, 32, 1987, pp. 14ss.
ARABIAN, M.J., KUCH NEGAD, A., BABAE, M., RAMIN NIA, M., Disputes on sovereignty over the islands in the light of international judicial decisions, in International Journal of Humanities and Cultural Studies, 3 (1),

2016, pp. 893ss.

ARAI-TAKAHASHI, Y., Excessive collateral civilian casualties and military necessity, in C. CHINKIN, F. BAETENS, Sovereignty, statehood and state responsibility, Cambridge University Press, Cambridge, 2015, pp. 326ss.

ARAJÄRV, M., The changing nature of customary international law: Methods of interpreting the concept of custom in international criminal tribunals, ed. Routledge, London & New York, 2013.

ARANGIO-RUIZ, G., Customary law: A few more thoughts about the theory of "spontaneous" international custom, in N. ANGELET, Droit du pouvoir, pouvoir du droit: Mélanges offerts à Jean Salmon, ed. Bruylant, Brussels, 2007, pp. 93-10.

ARANGIO-RUIZ, G., The federal analogy and UN Charter, in the European Journal of International Law, 1, 1997, pp. 16ss.

ARANZIO-RUIZ, G., Dualism revisited. International law and interindividual law, in Rivista di Diritto Internazionale, 2004, pp. 985ss.

ARANZIO-RUIZ, G., Fourth report on state responsibility, Doc. A/CN.4/444 and Add.1-3, in Yearbook of International Law Commission, 1992, pp. 35ss.

ARANZIO-RUIZ, G., The normative role of the General Assembly of the United Nations and the Declaration of principles of friendly relations with an appendix on the concept of international law and the theory of international organization, in Recueil des cours, ed. Brill, The Hague, vol. 136, 1972, pp. 42ss.

ARATO, J., Subsequent practice and evolutionary interpretation: Techniques of treaty interpretation over time and their different consequences, in The Law and Practice of the International Courts and Tribunals, 9, 2010, pp. 444ss.

ARATO, J., Treaty interpretation and transformation: informal change in international organizations, in Yale Journal of International Law, 38, 2013, pp. 290ss.

ARCHER, C., International organizations, ed. Routledge, London & New York, 2014.

ARGÉS, J.R., Jus cogens: La actualidad de un tòpico juridico clàsico, Editorial Reus, Madrid, 2019.

ARMSTRONG, D., Routledge handbook of international law, ed. Routledge, London & New York, 2009

ASCENSIO, H., La responsabilitè selon la cour internationale de justice dans l'affaire du gènocide bosniaque, in Revue Gènèrale de Droit International Public, 111, 2007, pp. 298ss.

ASHIAGBOR, D., COUNTOURIS, N., LIANOS, I., The European Union after the Treaty of Lisbon, Cambridge University Press, Cambridge, 2012, pp. 109-135.

ASHLEY DEEKS, S., "Unwilling or unable:" Toward a normative framework for extraterritorial self-defence, in Virginia Journal of International Law, 53 (3), 2012, pp. 484ss.

ASHWORTH, A., HORDER, J., Principles of criminal law, Oxford University Press, Oxford, 2013, pp. 426ss.

AUST, A., Handbook of international law, Cambridge University Press, Cambridge, 2010, pp. 230ss.

AUST, A., Modern treaty law and practice, Cambridge University Press, Cambridge, 2007.

AUST, H.P., Article 2 (5), in B. SIMMA, D.E. KHAN, G. NOLTE, A. PAULUS, The charter of the United Nations. A commentary, Oxford University Press, Oxford, 2012, pp. 244ss.

AUST, H.P., Complicity and the law of state responsibility, Cambridge University Press, Cambridge, 2011.

AUST, H.P., Complicity in international law, Oxford University Press, Oxford, 2015.

AUST, H.P., NOLTE, G., The interpretation of international law by domestic courts: Uniformity, diversity, convergence, Oxford University Press, Oxford, 2016.

AUST, H.P., Through the prism of diversity-the articles on state responsibility in the light of the ILC fragmentation report, in German Yearbook of International Law, 2006, pp. 277ss.

AVBELJ, M., KOMÁREK, J., Constitutional pluralism in the EU and beyond, Hart Publishing, Oxford & Oregon, Portland, 2012.

AZNAR GÓMEZ, M.J., Responsabilidad internacional del Estado y accion del Consejo de Seguridad de las Naciones Unidas, ed. Ministerio de Asuntos Exteriores, Madrid, 2000.

AZNAR, M.J., FOOTER, M.E., Select proceedings of the European Society of International Law, Hart Publishing, Oxford & Oregon, Portland, 2016.

BAARDE, B., MÜHREL, L., PETROV, A.O., International humanitarian law in areas of limited state hood: Adaptable and legitimate or rigid and unreasonable?, Nomos Verlag, Baden-Baden, 2018, pp. 222ss.

BADAR, M.E., The mental element in the Rome Statute of the International Criminal Court: A commentary from a comparative criminal law perspective, in Criminal Law Forum, 19 (3), 2008, pp. 477ss.

BADAR, M.W., The concept of mens rea in international criminal law. The case for a unified approach, Hart Publishing, Oxford & Oregon, Portland, 2013.

BAGIŃSKA, E., Damages for violations of human rights: A comparative study of domestic legal systems, ed. Springer, Berlin, 2015.

BAILLIET, C., MUJEZINOVIĆ LARSEN, K., Promoting peace through international law, Oxford University Press, Oxford, 2015.

BAIMU, E., PANOV, A., Responsibility of international organizations an the World Bank inspection panel: Parallel tracks unlikely to converge?, in The World Bank Legal Review, 2011, vol. 3, pp. 149ss.

BAKER, R.B., Customary International Law: A reconceptualization, in Brooklyn Journal of International Law, 41, 2016, pp. 442ss.

BAKIRCIOGLOU, O., Self-defence in international and criminal law: The doctrine of imminencce, ed. Routledge, London & New York, 2011, pp. 204ss.

BAKKER, C., Dual attribution of acts committed by a UN peacekeeping force: An emerging norm of customary international law? The Dutch Supreme

Court's judgments in Nuhanoviç and Mustafić, in Italian Yearbook of International Law, 23, 2013, pp. 288ss.

BANNER, C., THOMSON, A., Human rights review of state acts performed in compliance with EC law-Bosphorus Airways v Ireland, in European Human Rights Law Review, 6, 2005, pp. 650ss.

BANTEKAS, I., OETE, L., International human rights law and practice, Cambridge University Press, Cambridge, 2013, pp. 686ss.

BARBER, N.W., CAHILL, M., EKINS, R., The rise and face of the European constitution, Hart Publishing, Oxford & Oregon, Portland, 2019.

BARBERIS, J.A., Nouvelles questiones concernant la personalitè juridique internationale, in Recueil des cours, ed. Brill, Bruxelles, vol. 180, 1983, pp. 216ss.

BARBIER, S., Assurances and guarantees of non-repetition, in J. CRAWFORD, A. PELLET, S. OLLESON, The law of international responsibility, Oxford University Press, Oxford, 2010, pp. 554ss.

BARBOZA, J., State crimes: A decaffeinated coffee?, in L. BOISSON DE CHAZOURNES, V. GOWLLAND-DEBBAS, The international legal system in quest of equity and universality. Liber amicorum Georges Abi-Saab, Kluwer Law International, The Hague, 1998, pp. 164ss.

BARNES, S.H., The contribution of democracy to rebuilding post-conflict societies, in American Journal of International Law, 95 (1), 2000, pp. 1ss.

BARNICE, R.P., The due diligence principle under international law, in International Community Law Review, 8, 2006, pp. 81ss.

BARRAS, A.S., RYNGAERT, C., WOUTERS, J., International organizations and member state responsibility. Critical perspectives, ed. Brill, Bruxelles, 2016, pp. 130ss.

BARRETTE, B., Croyances et cooperation: Analyse du résau des acteurs de la Politique de sécurité et de défense commune de l'UE, in Swiss Political Science Review, 20 (1), 2014, pp. 118ss.

BARROS, A.S., Member states and the international legal (dis)order, in International Organizations of Law Review, 12, 2015, pp. 334ss.

BARROS, A.S., RYNGAERT, C., WOUTERS, J., International organizations and member State responsibility: Critical perspectives, ed. Brill, The Hague, 2016, pp. 154ss.

BARTHE-GRAY, C., Rèflexions sur la satisfaction en droit international, in Annuaire Français de Droit International, 49, 2003, pp. 54ss.

BASTID-BURDEAU, G., Le commerce international des armes: de la sécurité à la défense de l'éthique et des droits de l'homme?, in Journal du Droit International, 2 (4), 2007, par. 7.

BAUER, E.F., Die Völkerrechtswidrige Entführung, Duncker & Humblot, Berlin, 1968, pp. 92ss.

BAXTER, R.R., Multilateral treaties as evidence of customary international law, in British Yearbook of International Law, 41, 1965-1966, pp. 285ss.

BAXTER, R.R., Treaties and custom, in Recueil des cours, ed. Brill, The Hague, vol. 129, 1970, pp. 64ss.

BECKER, T., Terrorism and the state: Rethinking the rules of state responsibility, Bloomsbury Publishing, New York, 2006.

BECKER, Y., LANGE, F., Linien der Rechtsprechung des Bundesverfassungsgerichts: erörtert von den wissenschaftlichen Mitarbeiterinnen und Mitarbeitern, De Gruyter, Berlin, 2014.

BEDERMAN, D.J., Acquiescence, objection and the death of customary international law, in Duke Journal of Comparative and International Law, 21, 2010, pp. 32ss.

BEHAM, M.P., State interest and the sources of international law: Doctrine, morality and non-treaty law, ed. Routledge, London & New York, 2018.

BEHRENS, P., Diplomatic interference and the law, Hart Publishing, Oxford & Oregon, Portland, 2016.

BEHRENS, R., HENNAM, J., Elements of genocide, ed. Routledge, Taylor & Francis, Glass House Book, New York, 2013, pp. 194ss.

BEIGBEDER, Y., International Criminal Tribunals, ed. Palgrave, London, 2011.

BEKKER, P.H.F., Land and maritime boundary between Cameroon and Nigeria, in American Journal of International Law, 97 (2), 2003, pp. 388ss.

BELL, C.A., Reassessing multiple attribution: The International Law Commission and the Behrami and Saramati decision, in International Law and Politics, 42, 2010, pp. 352ss.

BELLAL, A., CASEY-MASLEN, S., GIACCA, G., Implications of international law for a future arms trade treaty, UNIDIR Resources, 2012, pp. 13ss.

BELLAMY, A.J., Libya and the responsibility to protect: The exception and the norm, in Ethics & International Affairs, 25 (3), 2011, pp. 263ss.

BELLAMY, A.J., Responsibility to protect, polity, Cambridge University Press, Cambridge, 2009.

BELLIER, S., Le recours à l'arbitrage par les organizations internationales, Harmattan, Paris, 2011, pp. 25ss.

BELLINGER III, J.B., VIJAY PADMANABHAN, M., Detention operations in contemporary conflicts. For challenges for the Geneva Convention and other existing law, in American Journal of International Law, 105, 2011, pp. 248ss.

BENADAVA, S., Derecho internacional pùblico, ed. Universitaria, Santiago, 2005.

BENDIECK, A., Due diligence in cyberspace, in Stiftung Wissenschaft und Politik German Institute for International and Security Affairs, ed. Palgrave Macmillan, London, 2016, pp. 12ss.

BENNOUNA, M., Le droit international entre la lettre et l'esprit. Cour gènèral de droit international public, in Recueil des cours, ed. Brill, Bruxelles, vol. 383, 2016, pp. 12ss.

BENVENISTI, E., NOLTE, G., Community interests across international law, Oxford University Press, Oxford, 2018.

BENVENISTI, E., The law of global governance, ed. Brill, The Hague, 2014, pag. 99,

BENVENUTI, P., Ensuring observance of the international humanitarian law: Function, extent and limits of the obligation to ensure respect for IHL, in

Yearbook of the International Institute of Humanitarian Law, 1989-1990, pp. 27ss.

BENVENUTI, P., Le respect du droit international humanitaire par les forces des Nations Unies: La circulaire de Secrètaire gènèral, in Revue Gènèrale de Droit International Public, 105, 2001, pp. 373ss.

BERBER, F., Lehrbuch des Völkerrechts, C.H. Beck, München, 1960, pp. 8ss.

BERGMANN, A., Zur Souveränitatskonzeption des Europäischen Gerichtshofs: Die Autonomie des Unionsrechts und des Völkerrecht, Mohr Siebeck, Tübingen, 2018.

BERKES, A., The Nagorno-Karabakh cases before the European Court of Human Rights: Pending cases and certain forecasts on jurisdiction and State responsibility, in The Military Law and Law of War Review, 52, 2013, pp. 415ss.

BERNER, K., Authentic interpretation in public international law, in Zeitschrift für äuslandisches öffentliches Recht, 76 (4), 2016, 848ss.

BERNHARDT, R., Art. 103, in B. SIMMA (ed.), The Charter of the United Nations: A Commentary, Oxford University Press, New York-Oxford, 2002, pp. 1293ss.

BERNHARDT, R., Decision of international courts and tribunals and international arbitrations, ed. Elsevier, Amsterdam, New York, Oxford, 2014.

BERNHARDT, R., International organizations in general universal international organization and cooperation, in Encyclopedia of Public International Law, 2014, pp. 147ss.

BERNHARDT, R., Interpretation and implied (tacit) modification of treaties-Comments on Arts. 27, 28, 29 and 38 of the ILC's 1966 Draft Articles on the Law of Treaties, in Heidelberg Journal of International Law, 27, 1967, pp. 492ss.

BERNHARDT, R., The Charter of the United Nations, a commentary. Article 103, vol. II, Oxford University Press, Oxford, 2002, pp. 1293ss.

BERRY, E., HOMEWOOD, M.Y., BOGUSZ, B., Complete European Union law. Texts, cases and materials, Oxford University Press, Oxford, 2013.

BESNÉ MAŇERO, R., El crimen internacional. Nuevos aspectos de la responsabilidad internacional de los Estados, Universidad de Deusto, Bilbao, 1999.

BESSELINK, L., CLAES, M., REESTMAN, J.H., A Constitutional moment: Acceding to the ECHR (or not), in European Constitutional Law Review, 11, 2015, pp. 2ss.

BESSON, S., La pluralitè d'États responsable. Vers une solidaritè international?, in Revue Suisse de Droit International et de Droit Europèen, 17, 2007, pp. 14ss.

BETTS, W.S., CARLSON, N., GISVOLD, G., The post-conflict transitional administration of Kosovo and the lessons-learned in efforts to establish a judiciary and rule of law, in Michigan Journal of International Law, 22, 2001.

BETTWY, D.S., The genocide Convention and unprotected groups: Is the scope of protection expanding under customary international law?, in Notre Dame

Journal of International and Comparative Law, 1 (1), 2011, pp. 102ss.
BIANCHI, A., PEAT, D., WINDSOR, M., Interpretation in international law, Oxford University Press, Oxford, 2015.
BIEHL, H., GIEGERICH, B., JONAS, A., Strategic cultures in Europe. Security and Defence Policies across the continent, ed. Springer, Wiesbaden, 2013.
BILLING, F.M.W., The right to silence in transnational criminal proceedings. Comparative law perspectives, ed. Springer, Berlin, 2016, pp. 323ss.
BILLON-GALLAND, A., QUENCEZ, M., Can France and Germany make PESCO work as a process toward EU defense?, in Policy Brief, n. 33, Washington, DC: German Marshall Fund of the United States, 2017.
BINDER, C., Die Grenzen der Vertragstreue im Völkerrecht: am Beispiel der nachträglichten Änderung der Umstände, ed. Springer, Berlin, 2013.
BINDSCHEDLER, R., International organizations, general aspects, in Encyclopdia of Public International Law, 1992, pp. 1299ss.
BINGHAM, T., The rule of law, Penguin Books, London, 2011, pp. 48ss, f Justice and the concept of state practice, in The University of Pennsylvania Journal of International Law, 31, 2009, pp. 295ss.
BISCOP, S., All or nothing? The EU global strategy and defence policy after Brexit, in Contemporary Security Policy, 37 (3), 2016, pp. 432ss.
BISSONNETTE, P.A., La satisfaction comme mode de rèparation en droit international, Imprimerie Granchamp, Genève, 1952.
BJORGE, E., MILES, C., Landmark cases in public international law, Hart Publishing, Oxford & Oregon, Portland, 2017.
BJORGE, E., The evolutionary interpretation of treaties, Oxford University Press, Oxford, 2014, pp. 83ss.
BLACK, J., HALl, A., COX, K., KEPE, M., SILVERSEN, E., Defence and security after Brexit: Understanding the possible implications of the UK's decision to leave the EU, Santa Monica: RAND Corporation, 2017.
BLAISE NGAMENI, H., La diffusion du droit international pènal dans les ordres juridiques africaines, ed. L'Harmattan, Paris, 2017.
BLECKMANN, A., Zur Festellung und Auslegung von Völkergewohnheitsrecht, in Zeitschrift für ausländisches Recht und Völkerrecht, 37, 1977, pp. 504ss.
BLOKKER, N.M., Preparing articles on responsibility of international organizations: Does the International Law Commission take international organizations seriously? A midterm view, in J. KLABBERS, A. WALLENDAHL (eds), Research handbook on the law of international organizations, Edward Elgar Publishers, Cheltenham 2011, pp. 313ss.
BLOKKER, N.M., SCHRIJNER, N.J., Immunity of international organizations, ed. Brill, The Hague, 2015.
BLUM, Y.Z., Eroding the United Nations Charter, Martinus Nijhoff Publishers, Leiden, 1993, pp. 252ss.
BOAS, G., Public international law. Contemporary principles and perspectives, Edward Elgar Publishers, Cheltenham, 2012.
BOBBIO, N., Nouvelles rèflexions sur les normes primaires et secondaries, in C. PERELMAN, La règle de droit, ed. Bruylant, Brussels, 1971, pp. 111ss.

BODANSKY, D., Customary (and not so customary) international environmental law, in Indiana Journal of Global Legal Studies, 3, 1995, pp. 106ss.
BODEAU-LIVINEC, P., Les faux-semblants de la lex specialis: l'exemple de la résolution 52/247 de l'assemblée générale des Nations unies sur les limitations temporelles et financières de la responsabilité de l'ONU, in Revue Belge de Droit International, 117, 2013, pp. 118ss.
BOGGERO, G., The legal implications of sentence no. 238/2014 by Italy's Constitutional Court for italian municipal judges: Is overcoming the "triepelian approach" possible?, in Zeitschrift für ausländisches öffentliches Recht und Völkerrecht, 76, 2016, pp. 204ss.
BOHOSLAVSKY, J.P., CERNIC, J.L., Making sovereign financing and human rights work, Bloomsbury Publishing, New York, 2014, pp. 125ss.
BOISON DE CHAZOURNES, L., ROMANO, C., MACKENZIE, R., International organizations and international dispute settlement: Trends and prospects, Martinus Nijhoff Publishers, New York, 2002, pp. 73-88.
BOISSON DE CHAZOURNES, L., FROMAGEAU, E., Le mècanisme de sanction de la Banque mondiale contre la fraude et la corruption. Le droit administratif global comme outil d'èlaboration et de consolidation d'une procèdure, in C. BORIES, Un droit administratif global?, A global administrative law? ed. Pedone, Paris, 2012, pp. 262ss.
BOISSON DE CHAZOURNES, L., KOHEN, M., International law and the quest for Its implementation. Liber Amicorum Vera Gowlland-Debbas, Martinus Nijhoff Publishers, Leiden, 2010, 73-84.
BOISSON DE CHAZOURNES, L., SANDS, P., International law, the International Court of Justice and nuclear weapons, Cambridge University Press. Cambridge, 1999, pp. 38ss.
BOISSON DE CHAZOURNES, L., Subsequent practice, practices, and "family-resemblance:" Towards embedding subsequent practice in its operative milieu, in G. NOLTE, Treaties and subsequent practice, Oxford University Press, Oxford, 2013, pp. 54ss.
BOIVIN, A., Complicity and beyond. International law and the transfer of small arms and light weapons, in International Review of the Red Cross, 94, 2012, pp. 255ss.
BOLLECKER-STERN, B., Le prèjudice dans la thèorie de la responsabilitè internationale, ed. Pedone, Paris, 1973, pp. 192ss.
BONAFÉ, B.I., The relationship between state and individual responsibility for international crimes, Martinus Nijhoff Publishers, The Hague, 2009.
BONN, K.E., New directions in responsibility: Assessing the International Law Commission's Draft Articles on the Responsibility of international organizations, in The Yale Journal of International Law, 37, 2011, pp. 4ss.
BONN, K.E., The role of lex specialis in the Articles on the responsibility of international organizations, in M. RAGAZZI, Responsibility of international organizations. Essays in memory of Sir Ian Brownlie, Martinus Nijhoff Publishers, Leiden, Boston, 2013, pp. 129ss.
BOON, E.K., The law of responsibility: A response to fragmentation, in Global

Business & Development Law Journal, 25, 2012, pp. 398ss.

BOON, K.E., The United Nations as good samaritan: Immunity and responsibility, in Chicago Journal of International Law, 17, 2016, pp. 361-362.

BOOTHBY, W.H., The law of targeting, Oxford University Press, Oxford, 2012, pp. 88ss.

BORCHARD, E.M., The diplomatic protection of citizens abroad. The law of international claim, Tha Banks Law Publishing Company, New York, 1914, pp. 217ss.

BORDIN, F.L., Reflections of customary international law. The authority of codification Conventions and ILC draft articles in international law, in International & Comparative Law Quarterly, 63 (3), 2014, pp. 537ss.

BORDIN, F.L., The analogy between and international organizations, Cambridge University Press, Cambridge, 2018, pp. 154ss.

BOS, A., The identification of custom in international law, in German Yearbook of International Law, 25, 1982, pp. 10ss.

BOSCHIERO, N., Jurisdictional immunities of the state and exequatur of foreign judgements: A private international law evaluation of the recent ICJ judgement in Germany v. Italy, in N. BOSHIERO, T. SCOVAZZI, C. RAGNI, C. PITEA, International courts and the development of international law. Essays in Honour of Tullio Treves, ed. Springer, The Hague, 2013, pp. 781ss.

BOSCHIERO, N., SCOVAZZI, T., PITEA, T., RAGNI, C., International courts and the development of international law. Essays in honour of Tullio Treves, Asser Press, The Hague, 2013, pp. 782ss.

BOSSUYT, M., VERRIJDT, W., The full effect of EU law and of constitutional review in Belgium and France after the Melti judgment, in European Constitutional Law Review, 7, 2011, pp. 356ss.

BOSTER, V., An introduction to transnational criminal law, Oxford University Press, Oxford, 2012, pp. 24ss.

BOTHE, M., Der Irak-Krieg und das völkerrechtliche Gewaltverbot, in Archiv des Völkerechts, 41, 2003, pp. 46ss.

BOTHE, M., Le droit de la guerre et le Nations Unies à propos des incidents armès au Congo, in Etudes et travauz de l'Institut Univeritaire des Haute Etudes Internationales, 5, 1967, pp. 208ss.

BOTHE, M., Peace-keeping, in B. SIMMA, The charter of the United Nations. A commentary, Oxford University Press, Oxford, 2002, pp. 648ss.

BOTHE, M., Peacekeeping forces, in Max Planck Encyclopedia of Public International Law, 2016, par. 51.

BOTTIGLIERO, L., Redress for victims of crimes under international law, ed. Springer, Leiden, 2004.

BOUTIN, B., Atttribution of conduct in international military operations. A causal analysis of effective law, in Melbourne Journal of International Law, 18, 2017, pp. 158ss.

BOUTIN, B., Responsibility of the Netherlands for the acts of Dutchbat in

Nuhanović and Mustafić: The continuous quest for a tangible meaning for "effective control" in the context of peacekeeping, in Leiden Journal of International Law, 25, 2012, pp. 522ss.
BOUVERESSE, A., RITLENG, D., L'effectivitè du droit de l'Union europèenne, ed. Larcier, Bruxelles, 2018.
BOVIN, A., Complicity and beyond. International law and the transfer of small arms and light weapons, in International Review of Red Cross, 87, 2005, pp. 468ss.
BOWETT, B.W., A legal study of United Nations practice, The Lawbook Exchange, London, 1964, pp. 484ss.
BOWETT, D., Reprisals involving recourse to armed force, in American Journal of International Law, 66 (1), 1972.
BOWETT, D., The court's role in relation to international organizations, in Fifty years of the International Court of Justice. Essays in honour of Sir Robert Jennings, Cambridge University Press, Cambridge, 1996, pp. 190ss.
BOWETT, D., The impact of Security Council Decisions on dispute settlement procedures, in European Journal of international law, 5, 1994, pp. 89-101.
BOWETT, D.W., Crimes of state and the 1996 report of the International Law Commission on state responsibility, in European Journal of International Law, 9, 1998, pp. 164ss.
BOWMAN, M.J., KRITSIOTIS, D., Conceptual and contextual perspectives on the modern law of treaties, Cambridge University Press, Cambridge, 2018, pp. 41, 165, 779ss.
BOYLE, A.E., State responsibility and international liability for injurious consequences of acts not prohibited by international law. A necessary distinction?, in International and Comparative Law Quarterly, 39 (1), 1990. pp. 5ss.
BOYLE, F.A., The entebbe hostages crisis, in Indian Journal of International law, 29 (1), 1982, pp. 20ss.
BRAIBANT, G., Le principe de proportionnalitè, in Mèlanges offerts à M. Waline. Le juge et le droit public, LGDJ, Paris, 1974, pp. 298ss.
BRAND, M.G., Institution-building and human rights protection in Kosovo in the light of UNMIK legislation, in Nordic Journal of International Law, 70, 2001.
BRANDES, M., "All's well that ends well" or "much ado about nothing?" A commentary on the arms trade treaty, in Goettingen Journal of International Law, 5 (2), 2013, pp. 399-429.
BRATSPIES, R., Transboundary harm in international law, Cambridge University Press, Cambridge, 2006.
BREAU, C., The constitutionalization of the international legal order, in Leiden Journal of International Law, 21, 2008, pp. 546ss.
BREGALDA, G., Direito internacional pùblico & direito internacional privado, ed. saràiva, São Paulo, 2014.
BRESLIN, A., Ensuring respect: The European Union's guidelines on promoting compliance with international humanitarian law, in Israel Law Review, 43 (2), 2010, pp. 382ss.

BRIERLY, J.L., The theory of implied state solicity in international claims, in The British Yearbook of International Law, 9, 1928, pp. 42ss.

BRIGGS, H.W., Nicaragua v. United States: Jurisdiction and admissibility, in American Journal of International Law, 79, 1985, pp. 374ss.

BRIGGS, H.W., The travaux préparatoires of the Vienna Convention on the Law of Treaties, in The American Journal of International Law, 65, 1971, pp. 705-712.

BROCKMAN-HAWE, B.E., Questioning the UN's immunity in the Dutch Courts: Unresolved issues in the Mothers of Srebrenica litigation, in Washington University Global Studies Law Review, 10, 2011, pp. 727ss.

BRÖLLMANN, C., The 1986 Vienna Convention on the law of treaties: The history of draft article 26 bis, in J. KLABBERS, R. LEFEBER, Essays on the law of treaties. A collection of essays in honour of Bert Vierdag, ed. Brill, The Hague, 1998, pp. 122ss.

BROLMANN, C., Member states and international legal responsibility. Developments of the institutional veil, in International Organizations Law Review, 12, 2015, pp. 358-381.

BRÖLMANN, C., The institutional veil in public international law. International organizations and the law of treaties, Hart Publishing, Oxford & Oregon, Portland, 2007, pp. 20ss

BRÖLMANN, C.M., Specialized rules of treaty interpretation: International Organizations, in D.B. HOLLIS, The Oxford guide to treaties, Oxford University Press, Oxford, 2012, pp. 508ss.

BROWER, H., Why the FTC notes of interpretation constitute a partial amendment of NAFTA article 1105, in Virginia Journal of International Law, 46, 2006, pp. 348ss.

BROWN WEISS, E., Invoking state responsibility in the twenty-first century, in American Journal of International Law, 96, 2002, pp. 798ss.

BROWNLIE, I., Brownlie's principles of public international law, Oxford University Press, Oxford, 2012, pp. 24ss.

BROWNLIE, I., International law and the use of force, Oxford University Press, Oxford, 1963, pp. 349ss.

BROWNLIE, I., Principles of public international law, Oxford University Press, Oxford, 2003, pp. 650ss.

BROWNLIE, I., Some problems in the evaluation of the practice of states as an element of custom, in International Law Studies in Honor of Gaetano Arangio Ruiz, vol. I, Editoriale Scientifica, Napoli, 2004, pp. 313-318.

BROWNLIE, I., State responsibility, Oxford University Press, Oxford, 1983.

BROWNLIE, I., System of the law of nations. State responsibility, Oxford University Press, Oxford, 1983, pp. 200ss.

BROWNLIE, I., The responsibility of states of the acts of international organizations, in M. RAGAZZI, International responsibility today. Essays in memory of Oscar Schachter, ed. Brill, Leiden, 2005, pp. 335ss.

BUCHAM, R., Cyber attacks: Unlawful uses of force or prohibited interventions?, in Journal of Conflict and Security Law, 17, 2012, pp. 214ss.

BUCHAN, R., Cyberspace, non-state actors and the obligation to prevent transboundary harm, in Journal of Conflict & Security Law, 21, 2016, pp. 430ss.

BUCHAN, R., UN peacekeeping operations: When can unlawful acts committed by peacekeeping forces be attributed to the UN?, in Legal Studies, 32 (2), 2012, pp. 284ss.

BUERGENTHAL, T., MURPHY, S.D., Public international law, West Group, Saint Paul, Minnesota, 2007.

BUGA, I., Modification of treaties by subsequent practice, Oxford University Press, Oxford, 2018.

BUIRETTE, P., Le droit international humanitaire, ed. La Dècouverte, Paris, 2019.

BURBER, M.D., HÖRNLE, T., The Oxford handbook of criminal law, Oxford University Press, 2014.

BURCKARDT, V., Die völkerrechtLiche Verantwortlichkeit der Staaten, ed. P. Hart, Bern, 1924, pp. 6ss.

BURKE, N., A change in perspective: Looking at occupation through the lens of the law of treaties, in International Law and Politics, 41 (1), 2008, pp. 104.

BUTKIEWITCZ, E., The premises of international responsibility of intergovenrnmental organization, in Polish Yearbook of International Law, 11, 1981-1982, pp. 132ss.

BUXBAUM, M., A legal history of international reparations, in Berkeley Journal of International Law, 23, 2005, pp. 315ss.

BUYSE, A., Lost and regained? Restitution as a remedy for human rights violations, in Heidelberg Journal of International Law, 68, 2008, pp. 132ss.

BÜYÜKBAY, C., ERTIN, D., EU-Skeptizismus am Bosporus?, in Zeitschrift für Internationale Beziehungen, 2017, n. 2.

BYERS, M., Conceptualizing the relationship between jus cogens and erga omnes rules, in Nordic Journal of International Law, 62 (2-3), 1997, pp. 4ss.

CAHIN, G., La varièté des fonctions imparties aux organizations internationales, in E. LAGRANGE, J.M. SOREL, Droit des organizations internationales, LGDJ, Paris, 2013, pp. 678ss.

CAHIN, G., Le coutume internationale et les organizations internationales: L'incidence institutionnelle sur le proessus coutumier, ed. Pedone, Paris, 2001.

CALVO-GOLLER, K., La procèdure et la jurisprudence de la Cour pènale internationale, ed. Lextenso, Paris, 2012.

CAMARGOS, L.A., A responsabilidade penal internacional dos individuos: Estudo do caso Darfur, in Revista de Direito Brasileira, 2013, pp. 199ss.

CAMERON, L., CHETAIL, V., Privatizing war: Private military and security companies under public international law, Cambridge University Press, Cambridge, 2013, pp. 162Ss, 205-208.

CAMMAERT, P.C., KLAPPE, B., Authority, command and control in United Nations-led peace operations, in T. GILL, D. FLECK (eds.), Oxford University Press's handbook of the international law of military operations,

Oxford University Press, Oxford, 2010, pp. 262ss.
CANAL-FORGUES, É., RAMBAUD, P., Droit international public, LGDJ, Paris, 2007.
CANAL-FORGUES, É., RAMBAUD, P., Droit international public, LGDJ, Paris, 2016.
CANÇADO TRINDADE, A., The application of the rule of exhaustion of local remedies in international law, Cambridge University Press, Cambridge 1983, pp. 46ss.
CANNIZZARO, E., A machiavallian moment? The UN Security Council and the rule of law, in International Organizations Law Review, 3, 2006, pp. 190ss.
CANNIZZARO, E., Is there an individual right to reparation? Some thoughts on the ICJ judgment in the jurisdictional immunities case, in D. ALLAND, V. CHETAIL, OP. DE FROUVILLE, J.E. VIÑUALES, Unity and diversity of international law. Essays in Honour of Professor Pierre-Marie Dupuy, Oxford University Press, Oxford, 2014, pp. 498.
CANNIZZARO, E., The European Union as an actor in international relations, The Hague-London-New York, 2002, pp. 219-230.
CANNIZZARO, E., The law of treaties beyond the Vienna Convention, Oxford University Press, Oxford, 2011.
CAPOTORTI, F., Cours gènèral de droit international public, in Recueil des cours, ed. Brill, Bruxelles, vol. 218, 1994, pp. 256ss.
CARDONA LLORENS, J., PUEYO LOSA, J., RODRIGUEZ-VILLASANTE PRIETO, J.L., (eds.) Estudios de Derecho Internacional y de Derecho Europeo en Homenaje al Profesor Manuel Pérez González, ed. Tirant lo Blanch, Valencia, 2012, pp. 168ss.
CARDWELL, P.J., Values in the European Union's foreign policy: An analysis and assessment of CFSP declarations, in European Foreign Affairs Review, 21 (4), 2016, pp. 602ss.
CARLEBACH, A., Le problème de la faute et sa place dans la norme du droit international, LGDJ, Paris, 1962, pp. 4ss.
CARTER, B.E., TRIMBLE, P.R., WEINER, A.S., International law, Aspen publishers, New York, 2007.
CARTER, B.E., WEINER, A.S., HOLLIS, D.B., International law, Wolters Kluwer, New York, 2018, pp. 706ss
CARTY, A., Doctrine versus State practice, in B. FASSBENDER, A. PETERS, The Oxford Handbook of the history of international law, Oxford University Press, Oxford, 2012, pp. 972.
CASSELLA, S., La nècessite en droit international: De l'ètat de nècessite aux situations de nècessitè, ed. Brill, Bruxelles, 2011, pp. 488ss.
CASSESE, A., A follow-up forcible humanitarian countermeasures and opinion necessitatis, in European Journal of International Law, 10 (4), 1999, pp. 792ss.
CASSESE, A., Ex iniuria ius oritur: Are we moving towards international legitimation of forcible humanitarian countermeasures in the world community?, in European Journal of international Law, 10 (2), 1999, pp. 23ss.

CASSESE, A., International law, 2nd edition, Oxford University Press, 2005, pp. 164ss.
CASSESE, A., Remarks on Scelle's theory of "role splitting" (dédoublement fonctionnel in international law), in European Journal of International Law, 1, 1990, pp. 210ss
CASSESE, A., The Geneva Protocols of 1977 on the humanitarian law of armed conflict and customary international law, in UCLA Pacific Basin Law Journal, 3, 1984, pp. 55ss.
CASSESE, A., The nexus requirement for war crimes, in Journal of International Criminal Justice, 10, 2012.
CASSESE, A., The Nicaragua and Tadić test revisited in light of the ICJ judgment on genocide in Bosnia, in European Journal of International Law, 18 (4), 2007, pp. 649-668.
CASSESE, Q., On the use of criminal law notions in determining state responsibility for genocide, in Journal of International Criminal Justice, 5, 2007, pp. 888ss.
CASTILLO DE LA TORRE, F., Tribunal constitucional (Spanish Constitutional Court), Opinion 1/2004 of 13 December 2004, in Common Market Law Review, 42, 2005, pp. 1170s
CASTILLO DE LA TORRE, V.F., Article 340 TFEU on contractual and non-contractual liability of the Union, in P.E. HERZOG, C. CAMPBELL, G. ZAGEL, Smit & Herzog on the law of the European Union, LexisNexis, New York, 2010, pp. 340-347.
CENGIC, A., Commentary, in A. KLIP, G. SLUITER (eds), Annotated leading cases of International Criminal Tribunals, Vol. XXIII, ed. Intersentia, Antwerp/Oxford, 2010, pp. 182-184.
CEPELKA, C., Les consèquences juridiques du dèlit en droit international contemporain, Prague, 1965.
CHAINOGLOU, K., Re-conceptualising self-defence in international law, Oxford University Press, Oxford, 2007.
CHARNEY, J.J., Universal international law, in American Journal of International Law, 87, 1993, pp. 532ss.
CHAUMONT, C., Cours gènèral de droit international public, in Recueil des cours, ed. Brill, Bruxelles, vol. 129, 1970-1971, pp. 495ss.
CHECHI, A., Judgment n. 238-2014 (IT. Const. Ct.), in International Legal Materials, 54 (3), 2015, pp. 472ss.
CHEN, Y., Structural limitations and possible future of the work of the ILC, in Chinese Journal of International Law, 9, 2010, pp. 478ss.
CHENG, B., United Nations Resolutions on outer space: "Instant" international customary law?, in The Indian Journal of International Law, 5, 1965, pp. 4ss.
CHERIF BASSIOUNI, M., Crimes against humanity: Historical evolution and contemporary application, Cambridge University Press, Cambridge, 2011, pp. 206ss.
CHERIF BASSIOUNI, M., Legal control of international terrorism, in Harvard International Law Journal, 43, 2002, pp. 84ss.

CHESTERMAN, S., Leading from behind: The responsibility to protect, the Obama doctrine, and humanitarian intervention after Libya, in Ethics & International Affairs, 25 (3), 2011, pp. 282ss.

CHESTERMAN, S., Rule of law, in Max Planck Encylcopedia of Public International Law, 2015, parr. 42ss.

CHETAIL, V., Permanence et mutation du droit des conflits armès, ed. Bruylant, Bruxelles, 2013

CHINKIN, C., Third parties in international law, Oxford University Press, Oxford, 1993, pp. 4ss.

CHINKIN, C.C., Crisis and the performance of international agreements: The outbreak of war in perspective, in Yale Journal of Public Order, 7, 1981-1982, pp. 177ss.

CHODOSH, H.E., Neither treaty not custom: The emergence of declarative international law, in Texas International Law Journal, 26, 1991, pp. 88ss.

CHUKWUEMEKE OKEKE, E., Jurisdictional immunities of states and international organizations, Oxford University Press, Oxford, 2018.

CIAMPI, A., Security Council targeted sanctions and human rights, in B. FASSBENDER, Securing human rights?: Achievements and challenges of the UN, Oxford University Press, Oxford, 2011, pp. 123ss.

CINKIN, C., KALDOR, M., International law and new wars, Cambridge University Press, Cambridge, 2017, pp. 367ss.

CIORCIARI, J.D., Request for interpretation of the judgment of 15 June 1962 in the Temple of Preah Vihear case (Cambodia v. Thailand), in American Journal of International Law, 108 (2), 2014, pp. 290ss.

CLARK, R.S., The mental element in international criminal law: The Rome Statute of the International Criminal Court and the elements of offences, in Criminal Law Forum, 12, 2001, pp. 296ss.

CLASS, W., Die Kausalität der Beihilfe, in G. SPENDE, Festschrift für Ulrich Stock. Studium zur Strafrechtswissenschaft, Holzner, Würzburg, 1966, pp. 116ss.

CLÊMENT-WILZ, L., Le rôle politique de la Cour de justice de l'Union europèenne, ed. Larcier, Bruxelles, 2019.

CLOSA, C., KOCHENOV, D., Reinforcing rule of law oversight in the EU, Cambridge University Press, Cambridge, 2016.

COHN, M.G., La thèorie de la responsabilitè internationale, in Recueil des cours, ed. Brill, Bruxelles, vol. 68, 1939, pp. 2010ss.

COLLINS, P.T., Civil-military "legal" relations: Where to from here? The civilian courts and the military in the United Kingdom, United States and Australia, ed. Brill, The Hague, 2018.

COLLINS, R., The institutional problem in modern international law, Bloomsbury Publishing, New York, 2016.

COLLINS, R., WHITE, N., (eds.) international organizations and the idea of autonomy. Institutional independence in the international legal order, ed. Routledge, London & New York, 2011, pp. 10ss.

COMAN-KUND, F., European Union agencies as global actors. A legal study of the European aviation safety agency, frontex and europol, ed. Routledge, London & New York, 2018.

COMBACAU, J., ALLAND, D., "Primary" and "secondary" rules in the law of state responsibility: Categorizing international obligations, in Netherlands Yearbook of International Law, 16, 1985, pp. 82ss.

COMBACAU, J., Obligations de résultat et obligations de comportement. Quelques questions et pas de rèponse, in Mélanges offerts à Paul Reuter: Le droit international: Unitè et diversitè, ed. Pedone, Paris, 1981, pp. 189ss.

CONDORELLI, L., BOISSON DE CHAZOURNES, C., Common article 1 of the Geneva conventions revisited: Protecting collective interests, in International Review of Red Cross, 82, 2000.

CONDORELLI, L., BOISSON DE CHAZOURNES, L., Quelques remarques à propos de l'obligation des Etats de "respecter et faire respecter" le droit international humanitaire "en toute circonstances," in C. SWINIARSKI, Études et essais sur le droit international humanitaire et sur le principes de la Croix-Rouge en l'honneur de Jean Pictet, Martinus Nijhoff Publishers, Genève, The Hague, 1984, pp. 18ss.

CONDORELLI, L., Conclusions Generales, in La soumission des organizations internationales aux normes internationales relatives aux droits de l'homme. Journée d'études de Strasbourg/Societe Francaise pour le Droit International. Institut International des Droits de l'Homme, ed. Pedone, Paris, 2009.

CONDORELLI, L., Customary international law: The yesterday, today, and tomorrow of general international law, in A. CASSESE, Realizing utopia: The future of international Law, Oxford University Press, Oxford, 2012, pp. 147, 150.

CONDORELLI, L., De la responsabilité internationale de l'ONU et/ou de l'État d'envoi lors d'actions de Forces de Maintien de la Paix: l'écheveau de l'attribution (double?) devant le juge néerlandais, in QIL-Questions of International Law, Zoom-in 1 (2014), pp. 3-15.

CONDORELLI, L., DE SENA, P., Les droits de l'homme à Guantanamo: en attendent la Cour suprême des Etats-Unis, in P. AMSELEK, Liberté, Justice, Tolérance. Mélanges en hommage au Doyen Gérard Cohen- Jonathan, ed. Brill, Bruxelles, 2001, pp. 450ss.

CONDORELLI, L., DIPLA, H., Solutions traditionnelles et nouvelles tendances en matière d'atttributon à l'État d'un fait internationalement illicite dans la convention de 1982 sur le droit de la mer, in A.A.V.V., Le droit international à l'heure de sa codificaton. Études à l'honneur de R. Ago, vol. III, ed. Giuffrè, Milano, 1987, pp. 66ss.

CONDORELLI, L., Imputation à l'Etat of an internationalement illicite: class solutions and nouvelles tendances, in Recueil des cours, ed. Brill, Brussels, vol. 189, 1984, pp. 186ss.

CONDORELLI, L., KRESS, C., The rule of attribution. General considerations, in J. CRAWFORD, A. PELLET, S. OLLESON, The law of international responsibility, Oxford University Press, Oxford, 2010, pp. 222ss.

CONDORELLI, L., L'imputation à l'Etat d'un fait internationalement illicite:

Solutions classiques et nouvelles tendances, in Recueil des cours, ed. Brill, Bruxelles, vol. 189, 1984, pp. 10ss.

CONDORELLI, L., L'évolution du Champ d'Application de la Protection Diplomatique, in La protection diplomatique: Mutations contemporaines et pratiques nationales: Actes de la journée d'études du 30 mars 2001 organisée à la mémoire de Georges Perrin, ed. Bruylant, Bruxelles, 2003, pp. 20ss.

CONDORELLI, L., La Cour pènale internationale. Un pas de gèant (pourvu qu'il soit accompli), in Revue Gènèrale de Droit International Public, 111, 1999, pp. 12ss.

CONDORELLI, L., La protection diplomatique et l'évolution de son domaine d'application, in Rivista di Diritto Internazionale, 2003, pp. 5ss.

CONDORELLI, L., Le Conseil de sécurité, les sanctions ciblées et le respect des droits de l'homme, ed. Brill, Bruxelles, 2010, pp. 78ss.

CONDORELLI, L., Le statut des forces de l'Onu et le droit international humanitaire, in Rivista di Diritto Internazionale, 1995, pp. 881ss.

CONDORELLI, L., MÉRIBOUTE, Z., Some remarks on the state of international law concerning military activities in outer space, in Indian Yearbook of International Law, 6, 1975, pp. 17ss.

CONWAY, G., European Union law, ed. Routledge, London & New York, 2015.

CONWAY, G., The limits of legal reasoning and the European Court of Justice, Cambridge University Press, Cambridge, 2012, pp. 156ss.

CONZE, A., Die völkerrechtliche Haftung der Europäischen Gemeinschaft, ed. Nomos, Baden-Baden, 1987, pp. 68ss.

CORREALE, F., Les origines de la "question du Sahara occidental:" enjeux historiques, défis politiques, in M. BALBONI, G. LASCHI (eds), The European Union approach towards Western Sahara, ed. Peter Lang, Bruxelles, 2017, pp. 34ss.

CORTEN, O., KLEIN, P., The limits of complicity as a ground for responsibility. Lessons learned from the Corfu channel case, in K. BANNELIER, T. CHRISTAKIS, S. HEATHCOTE, The ICJ and the evolution of international law. The enduring impact of the Corfu channel case, ed. Routledge, London & New York, 2012, pp. 315ss.

CORTEN, O., KLEIN, P., The Vienna Conventions on the law of treaties. A commentary, Oxford University Press, Oxford, 2011.

CORTEN, O., La "complicitè" dans le droit de la responsabilitè international. Un concept inutile?, in Annuaire Français de Droit International, 57, 2011, pp. 58ss.

CORTEN, O., The "unwilling or unable" test: Has it been and could it be, accepted?, in Leiden Journal of International Law, 29, 2016, pp. 794ss.

CORTEN, O., The law against war: The prohibition in the use of force in contemporary international law, Bloomsbury Publishing, 2010, pp. 250ss.

CORTEN, O., The obligation of termination, in J. CRAWFORD, A. PELLET, S. OLLESON, The law of international responsibility, Oxford University Press, Oxford, 2010, pp. 545ss.

CORTÉS MARTÍN, J.M., Las organizaciones internacionales: Codificación y desarrollo progresivo de su responsabilidad internacional, ed. Instituto Andaluz de Administración Pública, Sevilla, 2008, pp. 30ss.

COSTA, J.P., La Cour europèenne des droits de l'homme. Des juges pour la libertè, ed. Dalloz, Paris, 2017.

COSTELLO, C., The Bosphorus ruling of the European Court of Human Rights: Fundamental rights and blurred boundaries in Europe, in Human Rights Law Review, 6 (1), 2006, pp. 88ss.

COT, J.P., La conduite subséquente des parties à un traité, in Revue Générale de Droit International Public, 70, 1966, pp. 634ss.

COT, P., PELLET, M., FORTEAU, A., La Charte des Nations Unies. Commentaire article par article, vol. II, ed. Economica, Paris, 2006, pp. 2134-2147.

COUVEINHES MATSUMOTO, F., L'effectivitè en droit international, ed. Bruylant, Bruxelles, 2014.

COUVREUR, P., Reflexions sur la portèe et les effets de l'engagement conentionnel externe de la CEE, in Melanges Tryol Serra, Madrid, 1986, pp. 330ss.

CRAIG BARKER, J., International law and international relations, Bloomsburry Publishing, New York, 2000, pp. 127ss.

CRAWFORD, J., (ed. by), State responsibility. The general part, Cambridge University Press, Cambridge, 2014, pp. 487ss.

CRAWFORD, J., Brownlie's principles of public inter national law, Oxford University Press, Oxford, 2012, pp. 24ss.

CRAWFORD, J., Chance, order, change. The course of international law, ed. Brill, Bruxelles, 2014.

CRAWFORD, J., KOROMA, A., MAHMOUD, S., PELLET, A., The international legal order: Current needs and possible responses. Essays in honour of Djamchrd Momtaz, ed. Brill, Bruxelles, 2017.

CRAWFORD, J., Multilateral rights and obligations in international law, in Recueils des cours, ed. Brill, Bruxelles, vol, 327, 2007, pp. 325ss.

CRAWFORD, J., PELLET, A., OLLESON, S., PARLETT, K., The law of international responsibility, Oxford University Press, Oxford, 2010.

CRAWFORD, J., Responsibility to the international community as a whole, in Indian Journal of Global Legal Studies, 9, 2001-2002, pp. 304ss.

CRAWFORD, J., Revising the draft articles on state responsibility, in European Journal of International Law, 10 (2), 1999, pp. 444ss.

CRAWFORD, J., The identification and development of customary international law, Keynote Speech, Spring Conference of the ILA British Branch-Foundations and Future of International Law, 23 May 2014, a p. 13.

CRAWFORD, J., The international law introduction. Text and commentaries, Cambridge University Press, Cambridge, 2002, pp. 14ss.

CRAWFORD, J.R., Military and paramilitary activities in and against Nicaragua case (Nicaragua v. United States of America), in Max Planck Encyclopedia of Public International Law, 2011.

CREMONA, M., DE WITTE, B., EU foreign relations law-Constitutional

fundamentals, Oxford University Press, Oxford, 2008, pp. 65ss.
CREMONA, M., Implementation of the Lisbon treaty. Improving functioning of the EU: Foreign Affairs (Brussels: Policy Department C: Citizens' Rights and Constitutional Affairs, European Parliament, 2016.
CREMONA, M., SCOTT, J., European Union law beyond EU borders: The extratteritorial reach of European Union law, Oxford University Press, Oxford, 2019, pp. 79ss.
CROOK, J.R., The fiftieth session of the UN Commission on human rights, in American Journal of International Law, 90 (1), 1994.
CROQUET, N., The import of international customary law into the EU legal order: The adequacy of a direct effect analysis, in Cambridge Yearbook of European Legal Studies, 15, 2012-2013, pp. 48ss.
CROSS, M.K., The military dimension of European security: An epistemic community approach, in Millennium, 42 (10), 2013, pp., 47ss.
CROWE, J., WESTON-SCHEUBEL, K., Principles of international humanitarian law, Edward Elgar Publishers, Cheltenham, 2013, pp. 8, 149ss.
CRYER, R., FRIMAN, H., ROBINSON, D., WILMSHURST, E., An introduction to international criminal law and procedure, Cambridge University Press, Cambridge, 2010.
CURRIE, J.H., FORCESE, C., OOSTERVELD, V.L., International law, Irwin law, Toronto, 2007.
CZAPLIŃSKI, W., HLECZKOWSKA, A., Unrecognised subjects in international law, Scholar Publishing, Warsaw, 2019.
CZAPLINSKI, W., Sources of international law in the Nicaragua case, in The International and Comparative Law Quarterly, 38 (1), 1989, pp. 152ss.
D'AMATO, A., The concept of custom in international law, Cornell University Press, Ithaca, 1971, pp. 89-90.
D'AMATO, A., Trashing customary international law, in American Journal of International Law, 81, 1987, pp. 102ss.
D'ARGENT, P., La personnalitè juridique internationale de l'organization internationale, in E. LAGRANGE, J.M. SOREL, Droit des organizations internationales, LGDJ, Paris, 2013, pp. 439ss.
D'ARGENT, P., Les rèparations de guerre en droit international public. La responsabilitè internaitonale des États à l'èpreuve de la guerre, ed. Bruylant, Bruxelles, 2002.
D'ARGENT, P., Reparation, cessation, assurances and guarantees of non repetition, in A. NOLLKAEMPER, I. PLAKOKEFALOS, Principles of shared responsbibility in international law. An appraisal of the state of the art, Cambridge University Press, Cambridge, 2015, pp. 228ss.
D'ASPREMONT, D., BESSON, S., KNUCHEL, S., The oxford handbook of the sources of international law, Oxford University Press, Oxford, 2017.
D'ASPREMONT, J., Epistemic forces in international law, Edward Elgar Publishers, Cheltenham, 2015, pp. 118ss.
D'ASPREMONT, J., The idea of "rules" in the sources of international law, in British Yearbook of International Law, 84, 2014, pp. 106ss.

D'ASPREMONT, D., A European law of international responsibility? The Articles on the responsibility of international organizations and the European Union, in ACIL Research Paper (SHARES Series) n. 22, 2013, pp. 7-8.

D'ASPREMONT, J., The law of international responsibility and multilayered institutional veils: The case of authorized regional peace-enforcement operations, in SHARES Research Paper n. 24, 2013, pp. 9ss.

DAHLHOFF, D., International Court of Justice. Digest of judgments and advisory opinions, canon and case law 1946-2012, Martinus Nijhoff Publishers, The Hague, 2012, pp. 1657ss.

DAHM, C.G., DELBRÜCK, J., WOLFRUM, R., Völkerrecht, De Gruyter, Berlin, 2019.

DAHM, F., Völkerrecht, De Gruyter, Stuttgart, 1961, pp. 204ss.

DAHM, G., Völkerrecht, De Gruyter, Stuttgart, 1941, pp. 88ss.

DAHM, G., Völkerrecht, De Gruyter, Stuttgart, 1958, pp. 13ss.

DAILLER, P., Article 74 (Convention de Vienne de 1986), in O. CORTEN, P. KLEIN, Les Conventions de Vienne sur le droit des traitès. Commentaire article par article, ed. Bruylant, Bruxelles, 2006, pp. 2634ss.

DAILLER, P., FORTEAU, M., PELLET, A., Droit international public, LGDG, Paris, 2009, pp. 680ss.

DAILLER, P., PELLET, A., QUOC DINH, N., Droit international public, ed. LGDJ, Paris, 1999, pp. 745ss.

DALACOURA, K., Islamist movements as non-state actors and their relevance to international relations, in D. JOSELLIN, W. WALLACE, Non-state actors in world politics, ed. Palgrave, London, New York, 2001, pp. 236ss.

DAMNJANOVIC, V., Die Beteilingunsformen im deutschen und serbischen Stafrecht sowie in der ICTY-Rechtsprechung, BWN Berliner Wissenschafts Verlag, Berlin, 2013, pp. 246ss.

DAMROSCH, L., Multilateral disputes in the International Court of Justice, in L. DAMROSCH, The International Court of Justice as a crossroads, Transnational publications Inc., Dobs Ferry, New York, 1987, pp. 376ss.

DANIEL, D.C.F., HAYES, B.C., Beyond traditional peacekeeping, ed. Springer, Berlin, 2016, pp. 17ss.

DANILENKO, G.M., The theory of international customary law, in the German Yearbook of International Law, 31, 1988, pp. 12ss.

DANNENBAUM, T., Killings at Srebrenica, effective control, and the power to prevent unlawful conduct, in International and Comparative Law Quarterly, 62 (3), 2012, pp. 713-728.

DANNENBAUM, T., Translating the standard of effective control into a system of effective accountability: How liability should be apportioned for violations of human rights by member state troop contingents serving as United Nations peacekeepers, in Harvard Journal of International Law, 51, 2010, pp. 113ss.

DARCY, S., Collective responsibility and accountability under international law, ed. Brill, Bruxelles, 2007.

DASTOOR, N.F., The responsibility to refine: The need for a Security Council Committee on the responsibility to protect, in Harvard Human Rights Journal,

22, 2009, pp. 25ss.

DAUGIRDAS, K., How and why international law binds international organizations, Harvard International Law Journal, 57 (2), 2016, pp. 330ss.

DAUGIRDAS, K., Reputation and the responsibility of international organizations, in European Journal of International Law, 25 (4), 2014, pp. 994ss.

DAVID, E., Primary and secondary rules, in J. CRAWFORD, A. PELLET, S. OLLESON, The law of international responsibility, Oxford University Press, Oxford, 2010, pp. 29ss.

DAVID, E., Principles de droit des conflits armès, ed. Bruylant, Bruxelles, 2019.

DAVID, E., Principes de droit des conflicts armés, ed. ULB, Bruxelles, 2002, pp. 109ss.

DAWIDOWICZ, M., The obligation of non recognition of an unlawful situation, in J. CRAWFORD, A. PELLET, S. OLLESON, The law of international responsibility, Oxford University Press, Oxford, 2010, pp. 683ss.

DAWIDOWICZ, M., Third party countermeasures in international law, Cambridge University Press, Cambridge, 2017.

DE BAAERE, G., WOUTERS, J., The contribution of international and supranational courts to the rule of law, Edward Elgar Publishers, Cheltenham, 2015, pp. 268ss.

DE BRABANDERE, E., Immunity of international organizations in post-conflict international administrations, in International Organizations Law Review, 7, 2010, pp. 79ss.

DE FROUVILLE, O., Attribution of conduct to the State: Private individuals, in J. CRAWFORD, The law of international responsibility, Oxford University Press, Oxford, 2010.

DE HERT, P.J.A., KORENICA, F., The doctrine of the equivalent protection: Its life and legitimacy before and after the European Union's Accession to the European Convention on Human Rights, in German Law Journal, 13, 2012, pp. 884ss.

DE HOOGH, A., Australia and East Timor-rights erga omnes, complicity and non recognition, in American Journal of International Law, 93, 1999, pp. 79ss.

DE HOOGH, A., Obligations erga omnes and international crimes: A theoretical inquity into the implementation and enforcement of the international responsibility of states, Martinus Nijhoff Publishers, Brill, The Hague, Boston, London, 1996.

DE HOOGH, A.J.J., Articles 4 and 8 of the 2001 ILC articles on State responsibility, in British Yearbook of International Law, 72, 2001, pp. 278ss.

DE LA RASILLA DEL MORAL, I., Nihil novum sub soli since the South West Africa cases? On ius standi, the ICJ and community interests, in International Community Law Review, 10, 2008, pp. 172ss.

DE OLIVERIA MAZZUOLI, B., Direito internacional pùblico, ed. RT, São Paulo, 2005.

DE PAUW, M., The inter-American Court of human rights and the imperative method of external referencing regional consensus v. universality, in Y.

HAECK, O. RUIZ-CHIRIBOGA, V. CHERRERA, The inter-American Court of human rights: Theory and practice, present and future, ed. Intersentia, Antwerp, Oxford, 2016, pp. 4ss.156.

DE SENA, P., The notion of "contracting parties' jurisdiction" under Article 1 of the ECHR: Some marginal remarks on Nigro's paper, in Italian Yearbook of International Law, 20, 2010, pp. 75ss.

DE SENA, P., VITUCCI, M.C., The European Courts and the Security Council: Between dédoublement fonctionnel and balancing of values, in The European Journal of International Law, 20, 2009, pp. 193-228.

DE VATTEL, E., The law of nations or the principles of natural law applied to the conduct and to the affairs of nations and sovereigns, 1758, pag. 136.

DE VISSCHER, C., La responsabilitè des Etats, in Bibliotheca Visseriana, vol. II, ed. Brill, Leiden, 1924.

DE VISSCHER, C., Thèories et rèalitès en droit international public, ed. Pedone, Paris, 1970, pp. 312ss.

DE VRIES, S., BERNITZ, U., WEATHERILL, S., The EU Charter of fundamental rights as a binding instrument: Five years old and grooming, Hart Publishing, Oxford & Oregon, Portland, 2015, pp. 32ss.

DE WECK, D., Non refoulement under the European Convention of Human Rights and the UN Convention against torture, ed. Brill, The Hague, 2016, pp. 98ss.

DE WET, E., From Kadi to Nada: Judicial techniques favouring human rights over United Nations Security Council sanctions, in Chinese Journal of International Law, 12, 2013, pp. 787-808.

DE WET, E., The role of human rights in limiting the enforcement power of the Security Council: A principled view, in E. DE WET, A. NOLLAKAEMPER, Review of the Security Council by member states, Oxford University Press, Oxford, 2003, pp. 7ss.

DE WET, E., The governance of Kosovo: Security Council Resolution 1244 and the establishment and functioning of EULEX, in American Journal of International Law, 103 (1), 2009, pp. 85ss.

DE WITTE, B., Article 53, in S. PEERS et al. (eds.), The EU Charter of Fundamental Rights, A Commentary, Hart Publishing, Oxford & Oregon, Portland, 2014, pp. 1523-1538.

DECAUX, E., La rèciprocitè en droit international, LGDJ, Paris, 1980.

DEKKER, I.F., WERNER, W.G., Governance and international legal theory, ed. Springer, Berlin, 2014.

DEL MAR, K., The International Court of Justice and standards of proof, in K. BANNELIER, T. CHRISTAKIS, S. HEATHCOTE, The ICJ and the evolution of international law. The enduring impact of the Corfu channel case, ed. Routledge, London & New York, 2012, pp. 108ss.

DELBRÜCK, J., Proportionality, Encyclopedia of Public International Law, 1984, pp. 396ss.

DELBRÜCK, J., War, effect on treaties, in R. BERNHARDT, Encyclopedia of Public International Law, Amsterdam, 2000, pp. 1371ss.

DELGADO CASTELEIRO, A., The international responsibility of the European Union-The EU perspective: Between pragmatism and proceduralisation, in Cambridge Yearbook of European Legal Studies, 15, 2012-2013, pp. 564ss.

DEMAN, C., La cessarion de l'acte illicite, in Revue Belge de Droit International, 94, 1990, pp. 88ss.

DEN DEKKER, G., The law of arms control. International supervision and enforcement, Martinus Nijhoff Publishers, Dordrecht, 2001, pp. 50ss.

DENZA, E., Diplomatic law. A Commentary on the Vienna Convention on Diplomatic Relations, Oxford University Press, Oxford, 2008, pp. 189ss.

DENZA, E., Nationality and diplomatic protection, in Netherlands International Law Review, 65 (3), 2018, pp. 465ss.

DEPLANO, R., Assessing the role of resolutions in the ILC Draft conclusions on identification of customary law. Substantive and methodological issues, in International Organizations Law Review, 14 (2), 2017, pp. 224ss.

DERLÉN, M., LINDHOLM, J., The Court of Justice of the European Union. Multidiciplinary perspectives, Hart Publishing, Oxford & Oregon, Portland, 2018

DEUITCH, S.T., Putting the spotlight on "the terminator:" How the ICC prosecution of Bosco Ntaganda could reduce sexual violence during conflict, in William & Mary Journal of Women & Law, 23, 2016, pp. 656ss.

DEVISSER, M., Constitutional review in Europe: A comparative analysis, Hart Publishing, Oxford & Oregon, Portland, 2013.

DEYRA, M., Droit international public, LGDJ, Paris, 2007.

DEYRA, M., Droit international public, LGDJ, Paris, 2018.

DI STEFANO, F., Fait continu, fait composè et fait complexe dans le droit de la responsabilitè internationale, in Annuaire Français de Droit Internationl. 52, 2006, pp. 4ss.

DIACONU, I., La responsabilitè internationale des Etats. Quelques aspects rècents, in Revue Roumaine d'Études Internationales, 3, 1978, pp. 360ss.

DÍAZ BARRADO, C.M., El consentimiento, causa de exclusion de la ilicitud del uso de la forza, and derecho internacional, ed. Universidad de Zaragoza, Zaragoza, 1989, pp. 24ss.

DÍAZ-GONZÁLEZ, L., Fourth report on relations between states and international organizations (second part of the topic), UN Doc. A/CN/424/Corr.1., in Yearbook of International Law Commission, vol. II. pp. 153ss, par. 36.

DIEZ DE VELASCO, D., Instituciones de derecho internacional publico, ed. Tecno, Madrid, 2013, pp. 538ss.

DIJKSTRA, H., Policy-making in EU security and defense: An institutional perspective, ed. Palgrave Macmillan, Basingstoke, 2013.

DINSTEIN, Y., The interaction between customary international law and treaties, in Recueil des cours, ed. Brill, Bruxelles, vol. 322, 2006, pp. 244ss.

DINSTEIN, Y., The interaction between customary law and treaties, in Recueil des Cours, ed. Brill, The Hague, vol. 322, 2006, pp. 242ss.

DINSTEIN, Y., War, aggression and self-defence, Cambridge University Press,

Cambridge, 1988.
DINSTEIN, Y., War, aggression and self-defence, Cambridge University Press, Cambridge, 2017, pp. 184ss.
DIPLA, H., La responsabilitè de l'Etat pour violation des droits de l'homme: problèmes d'imputation, ed. Pedone, Paris, 1994.
DIREK, Ö.F. Responsibility in peace support operations: Revisiting the proper test for attribution conduct and the meaning of the "effective control" standard, in Netherlands International Law Review, 61, 2014, pp. 7ss.
DISTEFANO, G., Fundamentals of public international law: A sketch of the international legal order, ed. Brill, The Hague, 2019, pp. 621ss.
DISTEFANO, G., La pratique subséquente des États parties à un traité, in Annuaire Français de Droit International, 40, 1994, pp. 42ss.
DIXON, M., MCCORQODALE, R., WILLIAMS, S., Cases and materials on international law, Oxford University Press, Oxford, 2011, pp. 41ss.
DJEFFAL, C., Static and evolutive treaty interpretation-a functional reconstruction, Cambridge University Press, Cambridge, 2016, pp. 165ss.
DJEFFAL, C., Static and evolutive treaty interpretation. A functional reconstruction, Cambridge University Press, Cambridge, 2015.
DODGE, W.S., Customary international law and the question of legitimacy, in Harvard Law Review Forum, 120 2007, pp. 19ss.
DOEHRING, K., Unlawful resolution of the Security Council and their legal consequence, in Max Planck Yearbook of United Nations Law, 2, 1997, pp. 92ss, C. GRAY, Application of the convention on the prevention and punishment of the crime of genocide (Bosnia and Herzeovina v. Yugoslavia (Serbia and Montenegro)), orders of provisional measures of 8 April 1993 and 13 September 1993, in International and Comprative Law Quarterly, 43, 1994, pp. 704ss.
DOMINICÉ, C., Attribution of conduct to multiples states and the implication of a state in the act of another state, in J. CRAWFORD, A. PELLET, S. OLLESON, The law of international responsibility, Oxford University Press, Oxford, 2010, pp. 282ss.
DOMINICÉ, C., La responsabilitè internationale des Nations Unies, in J.P. COT, A. PELLET, M. FORTEAU, La Charte des Nations Uines-commentaire aricle par article, Economica, Paris, 2005, pp. 142ss.
DOMINICÉ, C., La satisfaction en droit des gens, in B. DUTOIT, E. GRISEL, L'ordre juridique international entre tradition et innovation. Mèlanges Perrin: Recueil de travaux offerts à Georges Perrin, ed. PUF, Paris, 1997, pp. 350ss.
DOMINICÉ, C., Observations sur le contentieux des organizations internationales avec les personnes privées, in Annuaire Français de Droit International, 45, 1999, pp. 623ss.
DOMINICÉ, C., The international responsibility of states for breach of multilateral obligations, in The European Journal of International Law, 10, 1999, pp. 360ss.
DOMINICÉ, C., The international responsibility of the United Nations for injuries resulting from non-military enforcement measures, in M. RAGAZZI,

Responsibility of international organizations. Essays in memory of Sir Ian Brownlie, Martinus Nijhoff Publishers, Leiden, Boston, 2013, pp. 367ss.

DON TAYLOR III, B,, Crimes against humanity in the Former Yugoslavia, in R. BELLELLI (ed. by), International criminal justice. Law and practice from the Rome Statute to its review, ed. Ashgate Publishing, Farnham, 2010, pp. 285-294.

DOPAGNE, F., La responsabilitè de l'Etat du fait des particuliers: les causes d'imputation par les articles sur la responsabilitè de l'Etat pour fait internationalement illicite, in Revue Belge de Droit International, 34, 2001, pp. 522ss.

ĐORĐESKA, M., The process of international law. Making: The relationship between the International Court of Justice and the International Law Commission, in International Comparative Law Review, 15 (1), 2015, pp. 14ss

DORMOY, D., Sanction ciblèes et respect des droits de l'homme: Quelques rèflections sur la responsabilitè des organizations internationales et de leurs ètats membres, in Revue Quebècoise de Droit International, 28 (2), 2015, pp. 8ss.

DÖRR, O., Article 31. General rule of interpretation, in O. DÖRR, K. SCHMALENBACH (a cura di), Vienna Convention on the Law of Treaties. A commentary, Springer, Heidelberg-New York 2012, pp. 536ss.

DOSWALD-BECK, L., Human rights in times of conflict and terrorism, Oxford University Press, Oxford, 2011, pp. 159ss.

DOSWALD-BECK, L., The legal validity of military intervention by invitation of the government, in British Yearbook of International Law, 56 (1), 1985, pp. 190ss.

DOWHERING, K., Unlawful resolutions of the Security Council and their legal consequences, in Max Planck Yearbook of United Nations Law, 1, 1997, pp. 92ss.

DOYLE, M., International ethics and the responsibility to protect, in International Studies Review, 13, 2011.

DOYLE, M.W., Dialectics of a global constitution. The struggle over the UN Charter, in European Journal of International Relations, 18 (4), 2011, pp. 602ss.

DOYLE, M.W., SAMBANIS, N., Making war and building peace: United nations peace operations, ed. Princeton, New Jersey, 2011.

DRAHOZAL, C.R., GIBSON, C.S., The Iran-US claims tribunal at 25, Oxford University Press, Oxford, 2007.

DRUMBL, M.A., Rule of law amid lawlessness: Counseling the accused in Rwanda's domestic genocide trials, in Columbia Human Rights Law Review, 29, 1998.

DUBOUT, E., Les règles ou principles inhèrented à l'identitè constitutionelle de la France: une supra-constituionnalitè, in Revue Française de Droit Constitionnel, 108, 2010, pp. 452ss.

DUDLEY, L., Until we achieve universal peace: Implications of the International

Law Commission's Draft Articles on the "effects of armed conflict on treaties, in American University National Security Law Brief, 2016, pp. 32ss."

DUFFY, H., Strategic human rights litigation: Understanding and maximinising impact, Bloomsbury Publishing, New York, 2018, pp. 154ss.

DUFFY, H., The war on terror and the framework of international law, Cambridge University Press, Cambridge, 2015.

DUGARD, J., Diplomatic protection, in Max Planck Encyclopedia of Public International Law, 2009.

DUMBERRY, P., The function and identification of rules of customary international law in international investment law, Cambridge University Press, Cambridge, 2018.

DUNBAR, N.H., The myth of customary international law, in the Australian Yearbook of International Law, 8, 1978-1980, pp. 4ss.

DUPUY, P.M., Action publique et crime international de l'Etat, in Annuaire Français de Droit International, 25, 1979, pp. 540ss.

DUPUY, P.M., A general stocktaing of the connections between the multilateral dimension of obligations and codification of the law of responsibility, in European Journal of International Law, 13, 2002, pp. 108ss.

DUPUY, P.M., Action publique et crime international de l'État. A propos de l'article 19 du projet de la commission du droit international sur la responsabilitè des États, in Annuaire Français de Droit International, 25, 1979, pp. 540ss.

DUPUY, P.M., Crime sans châtiment ou mission accomplie?, in Revue Gènèrale de Droit International Public, 111, 2007, pp. 247s

DUPUY, P.M., Droit des traitès, codification et responsabilitè internationale, in Annuaire Français de Droit International, 43, 1997, pp. 7ss.

DUPUY, P.M., FASSBENDER, B., SHAW, M.N., SOMMERMANN, K.P., Völkerrecht als Weltordnung. Festschrift für Christian Tomuschat, Engel Verlag, Kehl, 2006, pp. 308ss.

DUPUY, P.M., L'unitè de l'ordre juridique international. Cours général de droit international public, in Recueil des cours de l'Académie de Droit International de La Haye, ed. Brill, Brussels, vol. 296, 2002, pp. 413-427.

DUPUY, P.M., Le fait gènèrateur de la responsabilitè internationale des Etats, in Recueil des cours, ed. Brill, Bruxelles, 1984, pp. 12ss.

DUPUY, P.M., Obligations multilatèrales, droit impèratif et responsabilitè international de l'État, Paris, 2003, pp. 26ss.

DUPUY, P.M., Quarante ans de codification du droit de la responsabilitè intrnationale des Etats. Un bilan, in Revue Gènèrale de Droit International Public, 107, 2003, pp. 336ss.

DÜSTERHERF, I.K., GERLACH, A.I., The successes and failures of the interventions of the European Union, the African Union and neighbouring powers in Somalia, in Sicherheit und Frieden, 31 (1), 2013, pp. 19ss.

EAGLETON, C., International oganization and the law of responsability, in Recueil des cours, ed. Brill, Bruxelles, vol. 77, 1950, pp. 324ss.

EAGLETON, C., The responsibility of states in international law, New York University Press, New York, 1928, pp. 206ss.
ECKES, C., EU Counter-terrorist policies and fundamental rights, Oxford University Press, Oxford 2009, pp. 32ss.
ECKES, C., HOLLENBERG, S., Reconciling different legal spheres in theory and practice: Pluralism and constitutionalism in the cases of Al Jedda, Ahmed and Nada, in Maastricht Journal of European and Comparative Law, 20, 2013, pp. 218ss.
ECKHOUT, P.E., Opinion 2/13 on European union accession to the ECHR and judicial dialogue. Autonomy or autarchy, in Fordham International Law Journal, 38 (4), 2015, pp. 964ss.
EDWARDS, S.S.M., The European Court of Human Rights. Universalist aspirations of protection in the middle of the edge of occupation, in Denning Law Journal, 22, 2010, pp. 146ss.
EECKHOUT, P., The EU and its Member States in the WTO-Issues of responsibility, in L. BARTELS, F. ORTINO (eds.), Regional trade agreements and the WTO legal system, Oxford University Press, Oxford, 2006, pp. 450ss.
EECKHOUT, P., The EU's Common Foreign and Security Policy after Lisbon: From pillar talk to constitutionalism, in A. BIONDI, P. EECKHOUT, S. RIPLEY, (eds.), EU Law after Lisbon, Oxford University Press, Oxford, New York, 2012, pp. 265-291.
EGEDE, E., Politics of international law and international justice, Edinburgh University Press, Edinburgh, 2013, pp. 372ss.
ELAGAB, O.Y., The legality of non-forcible counter-measures in international law, Clarendon Press, Oxford, 1988.
ELGEBEILY, S., The rule of law in the UN security Council decision-making process. Turning the focus inwards, ed. Routledge, London & New York, 2017.
ELIAS, O., The relationship between general and particular customary international law, in African Journal of International & Comparative Law, 8, 1996, pp. 68ss.
ELLIS, M.S., DOUTRIAUX, Y., RYBACK, T.W., Justice and diplomacy resolving contradictions in diplomatic practice and international humanitarian law, Cambridge University Press, Cambridge, 2018.
ELLIS, M.S., The consequence of the Kosovo conflict on Southeastern Europe, in The International Lawyer, 34, 2000.
ELSDTRÖM, H., GYLLENSPORRE, D., Minding the gap between words and needs: Towards a new European Union strategy on security in, in European Foreign Affairs Review, 25, 2015, pp. 6ss.
EMANUELLI, C., Les conflits armès et le droit, ed. Wilson et Laflaeur, Montrèal, 2017.
ENGBERG, K., The European Union and military operations: A comparative analysis, ed. Routledge, London & New York, 2013, pp. 53ss.
ENGDAHL, O., Multinational peace operations forces involved in armed

conflict: Who are the parties?, in K.M. LARSEN, C. GULDAHL COOPER, G. NYSTUEN, Searching for a "principle of humanity" in international humanitarian law, Cambridge University Press, Cambridge, 2013, pp. 256ss.

ENGEL, S., "Living" international constitutions and the world Court (the subsequent practice of international organs under their constituent instruments), in International and Comparative Law Quarterly, 16, 1967, pp. 867ss.

ENGEL, S., Procedures for the de facto revision of the Charter, in American Society International Law Proceedings, 59, 1965, pp. 110ss.

ENGEL, S., The changing Charter of the United Nations, in G.W. KEETON, G. SCHWARZENBERGER, The Yearbook of World Affairs, ed. Stevens, London, 1953, pp. 72ss.

EPINEY, A., Nachbarrechtliche Pflichten im internationalen Wasserecht und Implikationen von "Drittstaaten," in Archiv des Völkerrechts, 39, 2001, pp. 49ss.

EPPS, V., GRAHAM, L., Examples and explanations for international law, Wolters Kluwer Law, Alphen aan den Rijn, 2014.

ESER, A., Mental elements-Mistake of fact and mistake of law, in A. CASSESE, P. GAETA, G.R.W.D JONES (eds.), The Rome Statute of the International Criminal Court: A Commentary, Oxford University Press, Oxford, 2002, pp. 890ss.

ESTREICHER, S., Rethinking the binding effect of customary international law, in Virginia Journal of International Law, 44, 2003, pp. 6ss.

EUSTATHIADES, C.T., Les sujets du droit international et la responsabilitè internationale. Nouvelles tendences, in Recueil des cours, ed. Brill, Bruxelles, vol. 84, 1953, pp. 460ss.

EVANS, M., International law, Oxford University Press, Oxford, 2014

EVANS, M., KOUTRAKOS, P., (eds.), The international responsibility of the European Union. European and international perspectives, Hart Publishing, Oxford & Oregon, Portland, 2013, pp. 6ss.

EVANS, M.D., International law, Oxford University Press, Oxford, 2018, pp. 103ss.

EVERILL, B., KAPLAN, J., The history and practice of humanitarian intervention and aid in Africa, ed. Springer, Berlin, 2013.

FAHRON-HUSSEY, C., Military crisis management operations by NATO and the European Union. The decision making process, ed. Spinger, Berlin, 2018.

FALK, R., The Iran hostage crisis: Easy answers and hard questions, in American Journal of International Law, 74 (2), 1980, pp. 411ss.

FARALL, J., Strengthening the rule of law through the UN Security Council, ed. Routledge, London & New York, 2016.

FARRAL, J.M., United Nations sanctions and the rule of law, Cambridge University Press, Cambridge, 2009, pp. 6ss.

FASOLI, E., Declaratory jurisdiction and official apologies as forms of reparation for the non-material damage suffered by the state. The Djibouti-France case, in The Law and Practice of International Courts and Tribunals, 7, 2008, pp.

178ss.

FAUCHALD, O.K., The legal reasoning of ICSID Tribunals-An empirical analysis, in European Journal of International Law, 2, 2008, pp. 302ss.

FEICHTER, L., Waiver, in Max Planck Encyclopedia of Public International Law, 2008.

FELDER, A., Die Beihilfe im Rect der völkerrechtlichen Staatenverantwortlichkeit, Shultheness, Zurich, 2007.

FELDMAN, A.M., Evolving treaty obligations: A proposal for analysing subsequent practice derived from WTO Dispute Settlement, in New York University Journal of International Law & Politics, 41, 2009, pp. 656ss

FENWICK, G., International law, Apleton Century Crofts inc., New York, 1965, pp. 328ss.

FERNÁNDEZ ARRIBAS, G., International responsibility of the European Union for the activities of its military operations. The issue of effective control, in Spanish Yearbook of International Law, 18, 2013-2014, pp. 58ss.

FERRARI BRAVO, L., Mèthods de recherche de la coutume internationale dans la pratique des États, in Recueil des cours, ed. Brill, Bruxelles, vol. 192, 1985, pp. 247ss.

FERRER MAC-GREGOR, A.E., Conventionality control and the new doctrine of the inter-American Court of Human Rights, in AJIL Unbound, 109, 2015, pp. 95ss.

FERSTMAN, C., International organizations and the fight for accountability. The remedies and reparations gap, Oxford University Press, Oxford, 2017, pp. 207ss

FIDELL, E.R., HILLMAN, E.L., SULLIVAN, D.H., Military justice: Cases and materials, Lexis Nexis, New York, 2012.

FIDLER, D.P., Challenging the classical concept of custom: Perspectives on the future of customary international law, in German Yearbook of International Law, 39, 1996, pp. 198ss.

FITSCHEN, T., Inventing the rule of law for the United Nations, in Max Planck United Nations Yearbook, 12, 2008, pp. 348ss.

FITZMAURICE, G., Environmental protection and the International Court of Justice, in LOWE, G. FITMAURICE, Fifty years of the International Court of Justice. Essays in Honour of Sir Robert Jennings, Cambridge University Press, Cambridge, 1996, pp. 294ss.

FITZMAURICE, G.G., The juridical clauses of peace treaties, in Recueil des cours, ed. Brill, Bruxelles, vol. 73, 1948, pp. 308ss

FITZMAURICE, G.G., The law and procedure of the International Court of Justice, in British Yearrbok of International Law, 23, 1952, pp. 28ss.

FITZMAURICE, M., ELIAS, O., MERKOURIS, P., Treaty interpretation and the Vienna Convention on the Law of Treaties: 30 Years on, Martinus Nijhoff Publishers, Leiden/Boston, 2010.

FITZMAURICE, M., International liability for injurious consequences of acts not prohibited by international law, in Polish Yearbook of International Law, 24, 1999-2000, pp. 48ss.

FITZMAURICE, M., SAROOSHI, D., Issues of state responsibility before international judicial institutions, Oxford University Press, Oxford, 2004.
FITZMAURISCE, M., Third parties and the law of treaties, in Max Planck Yearbook of United Nations Law, 2002, pp. 40ss.
FLAUSS, J., (a cura di), La protection diplomatique. Mutations contemporaines et pratiques nationales, ed. Bruylant, Bruxelles, 2003.
FLECK, D., The handbook of humanitarian law in armed conflicts, Oxford University Press, Oxford, 1995, pp. 40ss.
FLECK, D., The law of non-international armed conflict, in D. FLECK (ed. by), The Handbook of International humanitarian law, Oxford University Press, Oxford, 2013, pp. 581-610.
FLETCHER, G., Rethinking criminal law, Oxford University Press, Oxford, 2000, pp. 635ss.
FOCARELLI, C., Ahead to the past? Responsibility to protect and the global system, in Groningen Journal of International Law, 1, 2012, pp. 4ss.
FOCARELLI, C., Common article 1 of the 1949 Geneva Conventions: A soap bubble?, in European Journal of International Law, 21, 2010, pp. 126ss.
FOCARELLI, C., International law as social construct. The truggle for global justice, Oxford University Press, Oxofrd, 2012, pp. 178ss.
FOLEY, C., UN peacekeeping operations and the protection of civilians saving succeding generations, Cambridge University Press, Cambridge, 2017.
FOLK, R.A., Toward authoritativeness: The ICJ ruling on Israel's security wall, in American Journal of International Law, 99 (1), 2005, pp. 44ss.
FORD, C.M., WILLIAMS, W., Complex battlespaces: The law of armed concflict and the dynamics of modern warfare, Oxford University Press, Oxford, 2019.
FORLATI, S., The International Court of Justice. An arbitral tribunal or a judicial body?, ed. Springer, Berlin, 2014, pp. 148ss.
FORLIN, K., The accountability of armed groups under human rights law, Oxford University Press, Oxford, 2017.
FORREST, C., International law and the protection of cultural heritage, ed. Routledge, London & New York, 2012, pp. 51ss.
FORTEAU, M., Le droit applicable en matiere de droits de l'homme aux administrations territoriales gerees par des organizations internationales, in S.F.D.I., La soumission des organizations internationales aux normes internationales relatives aux droits de l'homme. Journée d'études de Strasbourg, ed. Pedone, Paris, 2009, pp. 14ss.
FORTEAU, M., Régime général de responsabilité ou lex specialis?, in Revue Belge de Droit International, 117 (1), 2013, pp. 147-160.
FORTIN, K., The accountability of armed groups under human rights law, Oxford University Press, Oxford, 2017.
FRANCIONI, F., Multilateralism à la carte: The limits to unilateral withholdings of assessed contributions to the UN budget, in European Journal of International Law, 11 (1), 2000, pp. 43ss.
FRANCK, T.M., Preemption, prevention and anticipatory self-defence: New law regarding recourse to force?, in Hastings International and Comprative Law

Review, 27, 2004, pp. 426ss.
FRANK, D., Verantwortlichkeit für die Verletzung der Europäischen Menshenrechtkonvention durch internationale Organizationen, Helbing & Lichtenhahn, Basel, 1999.
FREEDMAN, R., UN Immunity or Impunity: A human rights based challenge, in European Journal of International Law, 29 (4), 2014, pp. 4ss.
FREEMAN, A.V., The international responsibility of states, ed. Longman, London, 1970.
FRIEDE, W., Das Estoppel-Prinzip im Völkerrecht, in Zeitschrift für ausländisches Recht und Völkerrecht, 5, 1935, pp. 545ss.
FRIEDMAN, W., The changing structure of international law, Columbia University Press, Columbia, Princeton, 1973, pp. 198ss.
FRIEDMANN, W., The changing structure of international law, Stevens & Sons, London, 1964, pp. 10ss.
FRÖHLICH, M., WILLIAMS, A., The UN Secretary General and the Security Council. A dynamic relationship, Oxford University Press, Oxford, 2018.
FROWEIN, J.A., Recognition, in Max Planck Encyclopedia of Public International Law, 2010, par. 1
FRY, J.D., Coercion, causation and the fictional elements of indirect state responsibility, in Vanderbilt Journal of Transnational Law, 40, 2007, pp. 631ss.
FUENTES, I., Normative plurality in international law. A theory of the determination of applicable rules, ed. Springer, Berlin, 2016, pp. 234ss.
FURGLER, K., Grundprobleme der völkerrechtlichen Verantwortlichkeit der Staaten, Mohr Siebeck, Zürich, 1948, pp. 13ss.
GAETA, P., Gènocide d'Etat et responsabilitè penale individuale, in Revue Gènèrale de Droit International Public, 111, 2007, pp. 278ss.
GAETA, P., The UN genocide convention. A commentary, Oxford University Press, Oxford, 2009, pp. 283ss.
GAJA, G., A "new" Vienna Convention on treaties between states and international organizations: A critical commentary, in British Yearbook of International Law, 58, 1987, pp. 264ss.
GAJA, G., I have been specially affected when its nationals' human rights are infringed, in L.C. VORAH, Man's inhumanity to man. Essays in international law in honor of Antonio Cassese, Kluwer Law International, The Hague, 2003, pp. 394ss.
GAJA, G., Is a State specially affected when its nationals' human rights are infringed?, L.C. VORAH, Man's inhumanity to man. Essays in international law in honour of Antonio Cassese, Kluwer Law International, The Hague, 2003, pp. 376ss.
GAJA, G., Primary and secondary rules in the international law of state responsibility, in Rivista di Diritto Internazionale, 2014, pp. 982ss.
GAJA, G., Should all references to international disappear from the ILC draft articles on state responsibility?, in European Journal of International Law, 10 (2), 1999, pp. 366ss.

GAJA, G., Some reflections on the European Community international responsibility, in H.G. SCHERMERS, T. HEUCKLES, P. MEAD, Non-contractual liability of the European Communities, ed. Brill, Dordrecht, 1988, pp. 168ss.

GAJA, G., The concept of an injured state, in J. CRAWFORD, A. PELLET, S. OLLESON, The law of international responsibility, Oxford University Press, Oxford, 2010, pp. 942ss.

GAJA, G., The protection of general interest in the international community. General course on public international law, in Recueil des cours, ed. Brill, Bruxelles, vol. 364, 2012, pp. 10ss.

GAJA, R., Sould all references to international crimes disappear form the ILC draft articles on state responsibility?, in European Journal of International Law, 12, 1999, pp. 366ss.

GALBRAITH, J., What should the restatement (fourth) say about treaty interpretation?, in Brigham Young University Law Review, 2016, pp. 1467ss.

GALLAS, W., Strafbares Unterlassen im Fall einer Selbsttötung, in Juristen Zeitung, 15, 1960, pp. 686ss.

GANGALE, T., How high the sky? The definition and territorial airspace in international law, ed. Brill/Nijhoff, Leiden/Boston, 2018.

GARBEN, S., GOVAERE, I., The division of competences between the European Union and the member states. Reflection on the past, the present and the future, Hart Publishing, Oxford & Oregon, Portland, 2017.

GARCIA AMADOR, F.V., State responsibility in the light of the new trends of international law, in American Journal of International Law, 49, 1955, pp. 347ss.

GARCIA AMADOR, F.V., State responsibility. Some new problems, in Recueil des cours, ed. Brill, Bruxelles, vol. 94, 1958, pp. 370ss.

GARCIA, T., La reconnaissance du statut d'Etats à des entitès constestèes: Approches de droit international, règional et interne, ed. Pedone, Paris, 2018, pp. 64ss.

GARCIN, M., The haitian cholera victims complaints against the United Nations, in Zeitschrift für ausländisches öffentliches Recht und Völkerrecht, 75, 2015, pp. 680ss.

GARDAM, J., The contribution of the International Court of Justice to international humanitarian law, in Leiden Journal of International Law, 14, 2001, pp. 350ss.

GARDINER, R., The Vienna Convention rules on treaty interpretation, in D.B. HOLLIS, The Oxford guide to treaties, Oxford University Press, Oxford, 2012, pp. 475-48.

GARDINER, R., Treaty interpretation, Oxford University Press, Oxford, 2008, pp. 211ss.

GARVEY, J., Nuclear weapons counter proliferation. A new grand bargain, Oxford University Press, Oxford, 2013, pp. 58ss.

GASSER, H.P., International humanitarian law: An introduction, in H. HAUG (ed. by), Humanity for all. The International Red Cross and red crescent

movement, Paul Haupt, Berne, 1993, pp. 510ss.
GATTINI, A., A return ticket to communitarisme, please, in European Journal of International Law, 13, 2002, pp. 1182ss.
GATTINI, A., Breach of the obligation to prevent and reparation thereof in the ICJ's genocide judgment, in European Journal of International Law, 18, 2007, pp. 696ss.
GATTINI, A., La notion de faute à la lumière du projet de convention de la commission du droit international sur la responsabiloitè internationale, in European Journal of International Law, 3, 1992, pp. 254ss.
GATTINI, A., Les obligations des États en droit d'invoquer la responsabilitè d'un autre État pour violations graves d'obligations dècoulant de normes impèratives du droit international gènèral, in P.M. DUPUY, Obligations multilatèrales. Droit impèratif et responsabilitè internationale, ed. Pedone, Paris, 2003.
GATTINI, A., Smoking/no smoking: Some remarks on the current place of fault in the ILC Draft articles on state responsibility, in European Journal of International Law, 10, 1999, pp. 398ss.
GATTINI, A., Zufall und force majeure im System der Staatenvernatwortlichket anhand der ILC-Kodifikationsarbeit, Duncker & Humblot, Berlin, 1991.
GAZZINI, T., Personality of international oganizations, in J. KLABBERS, Å. WALLENDAHL, Research handbook on the law of international oganizations, Edward Elgar Publishers, Cheltenham, 2001, pp. 34ss.
GEERT, J., KNOOPS, J., Defenses in contemporary international law, The Martinus Nijhoff, The Hague, 2008, pp. 7ss.
GEISER, H.J., Les effets des accords conclus par les oganisations internationales, ed. PeterLang, Berne, Las Vegas, 1977, pp. 140ss
GENONI, M.M., Die Notwehr im Völkerrecht, Schulthess, Zürich, 1987.
GENSER, J., STAGNO UGARTE, B., The UN security Council in the age of human rights, Cambridge University Press, Cambridge, 2014.
GÉRARD, P., VERRIJDT, W., Belgian Constitutional Court adopts national identity discourse: Belgian Constitutional Court n. 62/2016, 28 April 2016, in European Constitutional Law Review, 13, 2017, pp. 182ss.
GERSON, A., Peace building: The private sector's role, in American Journal of International Law, 95, 2001.
GESLIN, A., Rèflexions sur la repartition de la responsabilitè entre l'organization internationale et ses États membres, in Revue Gènèrale de Droit International Public, 109, 2005, pp. 570ss.
GIEGERICH, T., Retorsion, in Max Planck Encycopedia of Public International Law, 2011, par. 4.
GIEGERICH, T., Wege zu einer vertieften Gemeinsamen Außen-und Sicherheits-politik: Reparatur von Defiziten als "kleine Lösung," in S. KADEBACH, Die Europäische Union am Scheideweg: mehr oder weniger Europa?, ed. Nomos, Baden-Baden, 2015, pp. 138ss.
GIL, A.G., Mens rea in co-perpetration and indirect perpetration according to article 30 of the Rome Statute. Arguments against punishment for excesses

committed by the agent or the co-perpetrator, in International Criminal Law Review, 14, 2014, pp. 87ss.

GILL, T., FLECK, D., (eds.), Oxford University Press's handbook of the international law of military operations, Oxford, 2010.

GILL, T.D., FLECK, D., The handbook of the international law of military operations, Oxford University Press, Oxford, 2011, pp. 523ss.

GINIFER, j., Beyond the emergency: Development within UN peace missions, Frank Cass, London, Portland, OR, 1997, pp. 85ss.

GINTHER, C., ZEMANEK, K., Völkerrecht zwischen normativen Anspruch und politischer Realität. Festschrift für Karl Zemanek zum 65. Geburtstag, Duncker & Humblot, Berlin, 1994, pp. 320ss.

GINTHER, K., international organizations, responsibility, in Ecyclopedia of Public International Law, 1983, pp. 162ss.

GLAD, B., DOLAN, V., Striking first. The pre-emption and preventive war doctrines and the reshaping of US foreign policy, ed. Springer, Berlin, 2016.

GLANVILLE, L., The responsibility to protect beyond borders, in Human Rights Law Review, 12, 2012, pp. 4ss.

GLASER, J., Abhandlungen aus dem Österreichischen Strafrecht, Verlag von Tendler & Comp., Wien, 1958, pp. 298ss.

GOLDIE, L.F.E., Liability for damage and the progressive development of international law, in International and Comprative Law Quarterly, 14, 1965, pp. 1190ss.

GOLDSMITH, J.L., POSNER, E.A., A theory of customary international law, University of Chicago Law School, John M. Olin Law & Economics Working Paper No. 63, 2000, pp. 1114ss.

GOLDSTONE, R.J., HAMILTON, R.J., Bosnia v. Serbia: Lessons from the encounter of the International Court of Justice with the International Criminal Tribunal for the Former Yugoslavia, in Leiden Journal of International Law, 21, 2008, pp. 96ss.

GOMEZ-ROBLEDO VERDUZCO, A., Concepto de responsabilidad internacional del Estado segùn Hans Kelsen, in Boletin Mexicano de Derecho Comparado, 62, 1985, pp. 66ss.

GONZÁLEZ-SALZBERG, D., The effectiveness of the inter-American human rights system. A study of the American States compliance with the judgments of the inter-American Court of human rights, in Revista Colombiana de Derecho Internacional, 15, 2015, pp. 116ss.

GOODRICH, L.M., HAMBRO, E.I., Charter of the United Nations, Columbia University Press, Boston, 1949, pp. 153ss.

GORDILLO, L.I., Interlocking constitutions: towards an interordinal theory of national European and UN law, Hart Publishing, Oxford & Oregon, Portland, 2012.

GORDON, G., The oil platforms opinion: An elephant in the eye of a needle, in Amsterdam Law Forum, 1 (2), 2009.

GORDON, G.S., Hate speech and persecution. A contextual approach, in Vanderbilt Journal of Transnational Law, 46, 2013, pp. 332ss.

GOULD, W.L., An introduction to international law, ed. Harper, New York, 1957, pp. 508ss.

GOUNELLE, M., Quelques remarques sur la notion de crime international et sur l'èvolution de la responsabilitè internationale de l'Etat, in Mèlanges Reuter: Le droit international: Unitè ed diversitè, ed. Pedone, Paris, 1980.

GOURGOURINIS, A., General/particular international law and primary/secondary rules: Unitary terminology of a fragmented system, in European Journal of International Law, 21, 2011, pp. 994ss.

GOUVEINHES, F., Retour sur un clasique: Le plaidioiries de Paul Reuter dans l'affaire du Temple de Prèah Vichear (Cambodge v. Thailand), in Revue Gènèrale de Droit International Public, 116 (2), 2012, pp. 468ss.

GOW, J., KERR, R., PAJIC, Z., Prosecuting war crimes, lessons and legacies of the International Criminal Tribunal for the Former Yugoslavia, ed. Routledge, Abington & New York, 2014.

GOWLLAND-DEBBAS, V., Collective responses to illegal acts in international law. United Nations action in the question of Southern Rhodesia, Martinus Nijhoff Publishers, Dordrecht, 1990, pp. 290ss.

GRABENWARTER C., European Convention on human rights: ECHR, C.H. Beck, München, 2014.

GRABITZ, E., Der Grundsatz der Verhältnismäßigkeit in der Rechtsprechung des Bundesverfassungsgerichts, in Archiv des öffentliches Recht, 98 (4), 1973, pp. 568ss.

GRAEFRATH, B., Complicity in the law of state responsibility, in Revue Belge de Droit International, 29, 1996, pp. 370ss.

GRAEFRATH, B., Die völkerrechtliche Verantwortlichkeit der Staaten-ein wichtiges Instrument zur Durchsetzung des Völkerrechts, in Neue Justiz, 1980, pp. 252ss.

GRAEFRATH, B., OESER, E., STEINIGER, P.A., Völkerrechtliche Verantwortlichkeit der Staaten, Duncker & Humblot, Berlin, 1977, pp. 310ss.

GRAEFRATH, B., OESER, E., Teilnahmeformen bei der völkerrechtlichen Verantwortlichkeit, in Staat und Recht, 1980, pp. 445ss.

GRAEFRATH, B., Responsibility and damage caused. Relationship between responsibility and damage, in Recueil des cours, ed. Brill, Bruxelles, vol. 185, 1984, pp. 62ss.

GRAMLICH, L., Diplomatic protection against acts of intergovernmental organs, in German Yearbook of International Law, 27, 1984, pp. 396ss.

GRAY, C., Is there an international law of remedies?, in British Yearbook of International Law, 56, 1985, pp. 27ss.

GRAY, C., International law and the use of force, Oxford University Press, Oxford, 2000, pp. 144ss.

GRAY, C., Judicial remedies in international law, Oxford University Press, Oxford, 1987, pp. 6ss.

GREEN, J.A., WATERS, C.P.M., Adjudicating international human rights. Essays in honour of Sandy Ghandi, Martinus Nijhoff Publishers, The Hague, 2014.

GREEN, L., The raw materials of international law, in International &

Comparative Law Quarterly, 29, 1980, pp. 188ss.
GREEN, N.A., International law. Law of peace, Macdonald & Evans, London, 1973, pp. 22ss.
GREENWOOD, C., Customary law status of the 1997 Additional Protocols, in A.J.M. DELISSEN, G.J. TANJA (ed. by), Humanitarian law of armed conflict, Martinus Nijhoff Publishers, The Hague, 1991, pp. 93ss.
GREENWOOD, C., International humanitarian law and United Nations military operations, in Yearbook of International Humanitarian Law, 1, 1998, pp. 18ss.
GREENWOOD, C., Scope of application of humanitarian law, in D. FLECK (ed), The Handbook of international humanitarian law, Oxford University Press, Oxford, 2008, pp. 45ss.
GRENFELL, K., Partnerships in UN Peacekeeping, in International Organizations Law Review, 13, 2016, pp. 55-73.
GREY, C.D., Remedies in international law, Oxford University Press, Oxford, 1990.
GREY, R., SHEPHERD, L.J., Stop rape now?: Masculinity, responsibility, and conflict-related sexual violence, in Men & Masculinities, 15, 2012, pp. 117ss.
GRILLER, S., The Court of Justice and the common foreign and security policy, in CJEU, The Court of Justice and the construction of Europe, T.M.C. Asser Press, Bruxelles, 2013, pp. 675ss.
GROUSSOT, X., LOCK, T., PECH, L., Adhésion de l'Union européenne à la Convention européenne des droit de l'homme: Analyse juridique du projet d'accord d'adhésion du 14 octobre 2001, in Fondation Robert Schuman/Question d'Europe, n. 218 (7 November 2011), pp. 5ss.
GROVER, L., Interpreting crimes in the Rome statute of the International Criminal Court, Cambridge University Press, Cambridge, 2014, pp. 426ss.
GROVER, L., UN human rights treaty bodies law and legitimacy, Cambridge University Press, Cambridge, 2012.
GROVER, S., The responsibility to protect: Perspectives on the concepts meaning, property application and value, ed. Routledge, London & New York, 2018.
GUILD, E., BIGO, D., GIBNEY, M., Extraordinary rendition: Addressing the challenges of accountability, ed. Routledge, London & New York, 2018.
GUTIÉRREZ ESPADA, C., La contramedidas de Estados "terceros" for the violation of the international laws, in Anuario Argentino de Derecho Internacional, 11, 2001-2002, pp. 30ss.
GUTIERREZ ESPADA, C., La responsabilidad internacional de las organizaciones internacionales a la luz del proyecto definitive de artículos de la Comisión de Derecho Internacional (2011), ed. Comares, Granada, 2012.
GUZMAN, A.T., MEYER, T.L., Customary international law in the 21st century, in R. A. MILLER, R. M. BRATSPIES, Progress in international law, Martinus Nijhoff Publishers, Leiden/Boston, 2008, pp. 199ss.
HACHEZ, N., WOUTERS, J., Promoting the rule of law: A benchmarks approach, KU Leuven Working paper No. 105, April 2013.
HAECK, Y., RUIZ CHIRIBOGA, O., HERRERA, C., The inter-American Court

of human rights: Theory and practice, present and future, ed. Intersentia, Antwerp, Oxford, 2016, 46ss.

HAFNER, G., Is the topic of responsibility of international organizations ripe for codification? Some critical remarks, in U. FASTENRATH et al. (ed. by), From bilateralism to community interest: Essays in honour of Judge Bruno Simma, Oxford University Press, Oxford University Press, Oxford, 2011, pp. 697ss.

HAFNER, G., Liability and compensation: “civil liability” and other forms of transnational accountability, in Yearbook of International Environment Law, 12, 1991, pp. 92ss.

HAFNER, G., Subsequent agreements and practice: Between interpretation, informal modification, and formal amendment, in G. NOLTE, Treaties and subsequent practice, Oxford University Press, Oxford, 2013, pp. 106ss.

HAHN, M.J., SCHUSTER, G., Le droit des Etats membres de se prèvaloir en justice d’un accord liant la Communqutè: l’invocabilitè du GATT dans l’affaire Rèpublique fèdèrale d’Allemagne contre Conseil de l’Unione europèenne, in Revue Gènèrale de Droit International Public, 99, 1995, pp. 378ss.

HAJJAMI, N., Que signifie l’expression “prendre toutes les mesures nécessaires” dans la pratique du Conseil de Sécurité des Nations Unies?, in Revue Belge de Droit International, 46, 2013, pp. 232ss.

HALBERSTRAM, D., “It’s the autonomy, stupid!”. A modest defense of opinion 2/13 on EU accession to the ECHR, and the way forward, in German Law Journal, 16, 2015, pp. 114ss

HALDEMANN, F., UNGER, T., The United Nations principles to combat impunity: A commentary, Oxford University Press, Oxford, 2018, pp. 32ss.

HALLESKOV STORGAARD, L.H., EU law autonomy versus European fundamental rights protection-On Opinion 2/13 on EU accession to the ECHR, in Human Rights Law Review, 15, 2015, pp. 485.

HALLESLOV STORGAARD, L., European Union law autonomy versus European fundamental rights protection. On opinion 2/13 on EU accession to the ECHR, in Human Rights Law Review, 15 (3), 2015, pp. 487ss.

HALMAI, G., The hungarian national(ist) constitutional identity, in Quaderni Costituzionali, 2017, pp. 152ss.

HAMONIC, A., Les relations entre l’Union europèenne et l’ONU dans le domaine de la gestion des crises, ed. Bruylant, Bruxelles, 2018.

HANDL, G., Liability as an obligation established by a primary rule of international law, in Netherlands Yearbook of International Law, 16, 1985, pp. 62ss.

HAPPOLD, M., EDEN, P., Economic sanctions and international law, Bloomsbury Publishing, New York, 2016.

HARAMOTO, S., SAKAI, H., SHIBATA, A., L’être situè. Effectiveness and purposes of international law. Essays in honour of Professor Ryuichi Ida, ed. Brill, Bruxelles, 2015, pp. 223ss.

HARLOW, C., LEINO, P., DELLA CANNANEA, G., Research handbook on EU administrative law, Edward Elgar Publishers, 2017. pp. 453ss.

HARRIS, C., Extraterritorial application of human rights treaties, Oxford University Press, Oxford, 2012.

HARRIS, D., O'BOYLE, M., WARBRICK, C., Law of the European Convention on Human rights, Oxford University Press, Oxford, 2014, pp. 372ss.

HART, H.L.A., HONORÉ, T., Causation on the law, Oxford University Press, Oxford, 1985, pp. 438ss.

HART, H.L.A., RAZ, J., The concept of law, Clarendon Press, London, 1961, pp. 95ss.

HARTKAMP, A., SIBURGH, C., DEVROE, W., Cases, materials and text on European Union law and private law, Hart Publishing, Oxford & Oregon, Portland, 2017, pp. 282ss.

HARTWIG, M., Die Haftung der Mitgliedstaaten für internationale Organizationen, ed. Springer, Berlin, 1993, pp. 290ss.

HARTWIG, M., International organizations or institutions. Responsibility and liability, in Max Planck Encyclopedia of Public International Law, 2013, pp. 4, par. 18.

HARTWIG, M., International Organizations or institutions. Responsibility and liability, in Max Planck Encyclopedia of Public International Law, 2011.

HATJE, A., TERHECHTE, J.P., MÜLLER-GRAFF, P.C., Europarechtswissenschaft, ed. Nomos, Baden-Baden, 2018.

HEATHCOTE, G., OTTO, D., Rethinking peacekeeping gender equality and collective security, ed. Springer, Berlin, 2014.

HEHIR, A., The responsibility to protect: Rhetoric, reality and the future of humanitarian intervention, Palgrave MacMillian, London, 2012.

HELFER, L.R., WUERTH, I.B., Customary international law: An instrument choice rerspective, in Michigan Journal of International Law, 37, 2016, pp. 564ss.

HELGESON, E., LAUTERPACHT, E., Iran-US claim tribunal, Cambridge University Press, Cambridge, 2000.

HELLER, K.J., Specially-affected States and the formation of custom, in American Journal of International Law, 112 (2), 2018, pp. 194ss.

HELLER, K.J., The Rome Statute of the International Criminal Court, in K.J. HELLER, D. DUBBER (eds.), The handbook of comparative criminal law, Stanford Law Books, Stanford, 2011, pp. 597ss.

HELMKE, B., Under attack: Challenges to the rules governing the international use of law, ed. Routledge, London & New York, 2016.

HENCKAERTS, J.M., DOSWALD-BECK, L., Customary international humanitarian law, Cambridge University Press, Cambridge, 2005, pp. 510ss.

HENCKAERTS, J.M., DOSWALD-BECK, L., Customary international humanitarian law. Vol. I: Rules, Cambridge University Press, Cambridge, 2009.

HENDERSON, C., Commissions of inquiry. Problems and prosepcts, Bloomsbury Publishing, New York, 2017.

HENNEBEL, L., The inter-American Court of human rights: The Ambassador of

universalism, in Quebec Journal of International Law, 57, 2011, pp. 58ss.
HENQUET, T., international organizations in the Netherlands: Immunity from the jurisdiction of the Dutch courts, in Netherlands International Law Review, 49, 2010, pp. 267ss.
HENRY, E., Alleged acquiescence of the international community to revisionist claims of international customary law (with special reference to the jus contra bellum regime), in Melbourne Journal of International Law, 18, 2017, pp. 264ss.
HERDEGEN, M., Interpretation in international law, in Max Planck Encyclopedia of International Law, 2010.
HERDEGEN, M., Principles of international economic law, Oxford University Press, Oxford, 2016, pp. 458ss.
HERDEGEN, M., The insolvency of international organizations and the legal position of creditors. Some observations in the light of the international Tin Council crisis, in Netherlands International Law Review, 37, 1988, pp. 142ss.
HERDEGEN, M., Völkerecht, C.H. Beck, München, 2019.
HERNANDEZ, G.I., Beyond the control paradigm? International responsibility and the European Union, in The Cambridge Yearbook of European Legal Studies, 15, 2012-2013, pp. 644ss.
HERZBERG, R.D., Die Unterlassung im Strafrecht und das Garantenprinzip, De Gruyter, Berlin, New York, 1972, pp. 2.
HERZOG, P.E., WESER, M., Civil procedure in France, ed. Springer, Berlin, 2014, pp. 162ss.
HERZOG, S., Revisiting the estonian cyber attacks: Digital threats and multinational responses, in Journal of Strategic Security, 4, 2011, pp. 52ss.
HESSBRUEGGE, J.A., The European Court of Human Rights: Catan and others v. Moldova and Russia, in International Legal Materials, 52 (1), 2013, pp. 219ss.
HEUSA VINAIXA, R., Algunas consideraciones sobre el Convenio de Viena de 1986 sobre Tratados celebrados entre Estados y organizaciones internaconales o entre organizaciones internacionales, in Revista Española de Derecho Internacional, 41, 1989, pp. 65ss.
HEXNER, E., Teleological interpretation of basic instruments of public international organizations, in S. ENGEL, R.A. MÉTALL, Law, State, and international legal order: Essays in honor of Hans Kelsen, University of Tennessee Press, Knoxville, 1964, pp. 120ss.
HIGGINS, R., Problems and process. International law and how we use it, in Oxford University Press, Oxford, 1994, pp. 47ss.
HIGGINS, R., WEBB, P., AKANDE, D., SLOAN, J., SIVAKUMARAN, S., Oppenheim's international law: United Nations, Oxford University Press, Oxford, 2017.
HILPOLD, P., (ed.), Responsibility to protect (R2P): A new paradigm of international law?, ed. Brill Martinus Nijhoff Publishers, Leiden-Boston, 2015.
HIRSCH, M., The responsibility of international organizations toward third

parties. Some basic principles, Martinus Nijhoff Publishers, Dordrecht, Boston, London, 1995, pp. 102ss.

HLAVAC, M., Less than a State, more than an international organizations: The sui generis nature of the European Union, in MPRA paper, 2010.

HOFFMANN, A., Zur Unterscheidung Verbrechen und Delikt im Bereich der Staatenvernatworlichkeit, in Zeitschrift für ausländisches Recht und Völkerrecht, 45, 1985, pp. 196ss.

HOFFMANN, J., NOLLKAEMPER, A., (eds.), Responsibility to protect: From principle to practice, Pallas, Amsterdam, 2012.

HOFFMEISTER, F., Bosphorus Hava Yollari Turizm ve Ticaret Anonim Sirket v. Ireland. App. No. 45036/98, in American Journal of international law, 100, 2006, pp. 447ss.

HOFFMEISTER, F., Litigating against the European Union and its Member States-Who responds under the ILC's Draft Articles on international responsibility of international organizations?, in European Journal of International Law, 21 (3), 2010, pp. 724ss.

HOFFMEISTER, L., Bosphorus Hava Yollari Turizm ve Ticaret Anonim Sirket v. Ireland. App. No. 45036/98, in American Journal of international law, 100, 2006, pp. 447ss.

HOIJER, O., La responsabilitè internationale des États, Les Éditions Internationales, Paris, 1930, pp. 31ss.

HOLDER, W.E., International organizations: Accountability and responsibility, in ASIL Proceedings, 97, 2003, pp. 232ss.

HOLLENBERG, S., The diverging approaches of the European Court of Human Rights in the cases of Nada and Al-Dulimi, in International and Comparative Law Quarterly, 64, 2015, pp. 454ss.

HOLLIS, D.B., The Oxford guide to treaties, Oxford University Press, Oxford, 2012, pp. 437ss.

HONG, M., Human dignity, identity review of the European Arrest Warrant and the Court of justice as a listener in the dialogue of Courts: Solange-II and Aranyosi: Bverfg 13 December 2015, 2 BvR 2735/154 Solange III and ECJ (Grand Chamber) 5 April 2006, joined cases C-404715 and C-659/15 PPU, Aranyosi and Căldăraru, in European Constitutional Law Review, 12, 2016, pp. 550ss.

HOOGH, A.J.J., Articles 4 and 8 of the 2001 ILC articles on state responsibility, the Tadić case and attribution of acts of Bosnian Serb authorities to the Federal Republic of Yugoslavia, in British Yearbook of International Law, 72 (1), 2001, pp. 256ss.

HORBACH, N.L., BEKKER, P.H., State responsibility for injurious transboundary activity in retrospect, in Nordic International Law Review, 72, 2003, pp. 328ss.

HOSS, C., Satisfaction, in Max Planck Encyclopedia of Public International Law, 2011, par. 10.

HOVELL, D., The power of process. The value of due process in Security Council of sanctions decision-making, Oxford University Press, Oxford, 2016.

HOWARD, J., Invoking state responsibility or aiding the Commission of international crimes-Australia, the United States and the question of East Timor, in Melbourne Journal of International Law, 2, 2001.

HOWORTH, J., Security and Defence Policy in the European Union, Palgrave Macmillan, Basingstoke, 2014.

HUMMELBRUNNER, S., PRICKARTZ, A.C., It's not the fish that stinks! EU trade relations with Morocco under the scrutiny of the General Court of the European Union, in Utrecht Journal of International and European Law, 84, 2016, 19ss.

HUNEEUS, A., Courts resisting courts: Lessons from the Inter-American Court's struggle to enforce human rights, in Cornell International law Journal, 44, 2011, pp. 520ss.

HUTCHINSON, D.N., Solidarity and breaches of multilateral treaties, in British Yearbook of International Law, 59 (1), 1988, pp. 152ss.

ILIOPOULOS STRANGAS, J., La responsabilitè de l'Etat en tant que lègislateur, in Revue Hellènique de Droit International, 51 (1), 1998, pp. 48ss.

IMSEIS, A., Critical reflections on the international humanitarian law aspects of the ICJ wall opnion in American Journal of International Law, 99, 2005, pp. 102ss. D. TURNS, Implementation and compliance, in E. WILMSHURST, S. BREAU, Pespectives on the ICRC study on customary international humanitarian law, Cambridge University Press, Cambridge, 2007, pp. 354ss.

IWASAWA, Y., IWATSUKI, N., Procedural conditions, in J. CRAWFORD, A. PELLET, S. OLLESON, The law of international responsibility, Oxford University Press, Oxford, 2010, pp. 1149ss.

JACKSON, M., Complicity in international law, Oxford University Press, Oxford, 2015.

JACOB, P., Les définitions des notions "d'organe et d'agent" retenues par la ILC sont-elles opérationnelles?, in Revue Belge de Droit International, 117, 2013, pp. 18ss.

JACOVIDES, A., International law and diplomacy. Selected writings by Ambassador Andrew Jacovides, ed. Brill, Bruxelles, 2011, pp. 49ss.

JACQUÉ, J.P., CJUE-CEDH: 2-0, in Revue Trimestrielle de Droit Européen, 40 (4), 2014 pp. 823ss.

JACQUÉ, J.P., La Cour de Justice de !'Union et !'application de la Charte dans les Etats membres: "Mehr Licht," in European Yearbook on Human Rights, 14, 2014 pp. 125-147.

JACQUÉ, J.P., The accession of the European Union to the European Convention on Human Rights and Fundamental Freedoms, in Common Market Law Review, 48 (4), 2011, pp. 995, 1005.

JAIN, N., Perpetrators and accessories in international criminal law: Individual modes of responsibility for collective crimes, Bloomsbury Publishing, New York, 2014, pp. 156ss.

JAKUBOWSKI, A., WIECZYŃSKA, K., Fragmentation vs the constitutionalisation of international law: A practical inquiry, ed. Routledge, London & New York, 2016.

JALLOH CHEVROR, C., MARONG A., Promoting accountability under international law for gross human rights violations in Africa. Essays in honour of prosecutor Hasan Bubacar Jallow, ed. Brill, The Hague, 2015.

JANIS, M.V., An introduction to international law, Aspen Law & Business, New York, 2008.

JANSEN, N., The making of legal authority. Non-legislative codifications in historical and corporating perspective, Oxford University Press, Oxford, 2010, pp. 8ss.

JANSSENS, C., The principle of mutual recognition in European Union law, Oxford University Press, Oxford, 2013, pp. 208ss.

JEFFREY, A., The American hostages in Tehran: the ICJ and the legality of rescue missions, in International and Comparative Law Quarterly, 30, 1981, pp. 718ss.

JENNINGS, R., The identification of international law, in B. CHENG, International law: Teaching and practice, ed. Stevens, London, 1982, pp. 4ss.

JENNINGS, R.Y., What is international law and how do we tell it when we see it?, in The Cambridge Tilburg Lectures, Kluwer, 1983, pp. 2ss.

JENSEN, D., LONERGAN, S., Assessing and restoring natural resources in post-conflict peacebuilding, ed. Routledge, London & New York, 2015.

JENSEN, E., State obligations in cyber operations, in Baltic Yearbook of International Law, 14, 2014, pp. 29ss.

JENSEN, E., TALBOT, E., Cyber sovereignty: The way ahead, in Texas International Law Journal, 50, 2015, pp. 276ss.

JESCHECK, H., WEIGEND, T., Lehrbuch des Strafrechts. Allgemeiner Teil, Duncker & Humblot, Berlin, 1996, pp. 686ss.

JESSUP, P.C., A modern law of Nations, Macmillan, New York, 1948, pp. 153ss.

JESSUP, P., A modern law of nations. An introduction, Macmillan, New York, 1958, pp. 94ss.

JEUTNER, V., Irresolvable norm conflicts in international legal dilemma, Oxford University Press, Oxford, 2017.

JIA, B.B., The relations between treaties and custom, in Chinese Journal of International Law, 9, 2010, pp. 82ss.

JIMENEZ DE ARECHAGA, E., International responsibility, in M. SØRENSEN, Manual of public international law, Macmillan & Co, London, New York, 1968, pp. 532ss.

JIMÉNEZ DE ARÉCHAGA, E., TANZI, A., La responsabilitè des Etats in M. BEDJAOUI, Droit international. Bilan et perspectives, ed. Pedone, Paris, 1991, pp. 368ss.

JOHANSEN, S.Ø., Accountability mechanisms for human rights violations by CSDP missions: Available and sufficient, in International & Comparative Law Quarterly, 66 (1), 2017, pp. 184ss.

JOHNSTONE, I., Law making through the operational activities of international organizations, in The George Washington International Law Review, 40, 2008, pp. 88ss.

JØRGENSEN, M.H.B., The obligation of cooperation, in J. CRAWFORD, A.

PELLET, S. OLLESON, The law of international responsibility, Oxford University Press, Oxford, 2010, pp. 696ss.

JØRGENSEN, N.H.B., The responsibility of states for international crimes, Oxford University Press, Oxford, 2000.

JOUANNET, E., Emer de Vattel et l'èmergence du droit international classique, ed. Pedone, Paris, 1998, pp. 407ss.

JOYNER, C.C., International law in the 21st century: Rules for global governance, Rowmann & Littlefield Publishers, Lanham, 2005.

JUNCOS, A.E., European Union foreign and security policy in Bosnia. The politics of coherence and effectiveness, Manchester University Press, Manchester & New York, 2015, pp. 145ss.

JUSS, S., SUNKIN, M., Landmark cases in public law, Hart Publishing, Oxford & Oregon, Portland, 2017, pp. 258ss.

KACZOROWSKA-IRELAND, I., Public international law, ed. Routledge, London & New York, 2015.

KADELBACH, S., Al-Dulimi and Montana management Inc v. Switzerlnd (ECtHR), in International Legal Materials, 55 (6), 2016, pp. 1023ss.

KADENS, E., YOUNG, E.A., How customary is customary international law?, in William & Mary Law Review, 54, 2013, pp. 886ss.

KADISH, H., Acts and omission, mens rea and complicity. Approaches to codificaton, in Criminal Law Forum, 1, 1989, pp. 65ss.

KADISH, S.H., Complicity, cause and blame. A study in the international of doctrine, in California Law Review, 73, 1985, pp. 323ss.

KALIMO, H., STAAL, T., "Softness" in international instruments-The case of transnational corporations, in Syracuse Journal of International Law & Commerce, 41, 2014, pp. 258ss.

KALSHOVEN, F., The year at the international humanitarian law, ed. Brill, Bruxelles, 1997, pp. 48ss.

KAMBER, K., Prosecuting human rights offences: Rethinking the sword function of human rights, ed. Brill, The Hague, 2017.

KAMMERHOFER, J., Orthodox generalists and political activists in international legal scholarship, in M. HAPPOLD, International law in a multipolar world, ed. Routledge, London & New York, 2012.

KAMMERHOFER, J., Uncertainty in the formal sources of international law, in European Journal of International Law, 15, 2004, pp. 524ss.

KANETAKE, M., The UN security Council and domestic actors: Distance in international law, ed. Routledge, London & New York, 2017.

KAPLAN, J., WEIBERG, R., BINDER, G., Criminal law. Cases and materials, Wolters Kluwer Law & Business, Aspen, 2012.

KARMS, M.P., MINGST, K.A., International organizations. The politics and processes of global governance, ed. Lynne Rienner, New York, 2009.

KATZ COGAN, J., HURD, I., JOHNSTONE, I., (eds), The Oxford handbook of international organizations, Oxford University Press, Oxford, 2016.

KAUFMANN-KOHLER, G., Interpretive powers of the Free Trade Commission and the rule of law, in E. GAILLARD, F. BACHAND, Fifteen years of

NAFTA Chapter 11 arbitration, ed. Juris Net, New York, 2011, pp. 181.

KAWASAKI, K., Draft articles on state responsibility adopted by the International Law Commission in 2001: A brief overview, in Hitotsubashi Journal of International Law, 29, 2002, pp. 49ss.

KEEFE, O., TAMS, C.J., TZANAKOPOLOS, A., The United Nations Convention on jurisdictional immunities of States and their property, Oxford University Press, Oxford, 2013, pp. 241ss.

KEINLEIN, T., Konstituutionalisierung im Völkerrecht: Konstruktion und Elemente einer idealischen Völkerrechtslehre, ed. Springer, Berlin, 2011, pp. 400ss.

KEITH, K., The processes of law-making: The law relating to international organization as an example, in M. RAGAZZI, Responsibility of International Organizations. Essays in memory of Sir Ian Brownlie, ed. Brill, Bruxelles, 2013, pp. 15ss.

KEITH, K.M.F., The mens rea of superior responsibility as developed by ICTY Jurisprudence, in Leiden Journal of International Law, 14, 2001, pp. 618ss.

KELIN, E., Beihilfe zum Völkerrechttsdelikt, in I. VON MÜNCH, Staatsrecht-Völkerrecht-Europarecht für Hans-Jurgen Schlochauer, De Gruyter, Berlin, 1981, pp. 434ss.

KELLERBAUER, M., KLAMERT, M., TOMKIN, J., Commentary on the European Union treaties and the Charter of fundamental rights, Oxford University Press, Oxford, 2019.

KELLY, M.G., The debate or genocide in Darfur, Sudan, in University of California, in Davis Journal of International Law & Policy, 19, 2012, pp. 208ss.

KELLY, M.J., The parameters of vicarious corporate criminal liability for genocide under international law, in A. BYRNES, C. HAYASHI-MICHAELSEN, International law in the age of globalization, ed. Brill, The Hague, 2013.

KELSEN, H., The draft declaration on rights and duties of states. Critical remarks, in American Journal of International Law, 44, 1950, pp. 272ss.

KELSEN, H., Unrecht und Unrechtsfolge im Völkerrecht, in Zeitscrhift für öffentliches Recht, 1932, pp. 482ss.

KENT, A., SKOUTARIS, N., TRINIDAD, J., The future of international courts. Regional, institutional and procedural challenges, ed. Routledge, London & New York, 2019.

KEPPLER, E., Preventing human rights abuses by regulating arms brokers: The US. Brokering amendment to the arms export control act, in Berkeley Journal of International Law, 19 (2), 2001, pp. 381-411, 386ss.

KERBAT, Y., Sanctions et contre-mesures: risques de confusion dans les articles de la ILC sur la responsabilité des organizations internationales, in Revue Belge de Droit International, 117, 2013, pp. 105ss.

KERBRAT, Y., The interaction between the forms of reparation, in J. CRAWFORD, A. PELLET, S. OLLESON, The law of international responsibility, Oxford University Press, Oxford, 2010, pp. 573ss.

KESSLER, B., Die Durchsetzung der genfer Abkommen von 1949 in nicht-internationalen bewaffneten Konflikten auf Grundlage ihres gemeinsamen Art. 1, Duncker & Humblot, Berlin, 2001, pp. 108ss.

KESSLER, B., The duty to "ensure respect" under the common article 1 of the Geneva conventions: Its implications on international and non-international armed conflicts, in The German Yearbook of International Law, 44, 2001, pp. 507ss.

KEWENIG, W.A., Der Internationale Zinrat. Ein Lehrstück des Wirtschaftsvölkerrechts, in Recht der internationalen Wirtshaft, 16, 1990, pp. 782ss.

KIHARA HUNT, A., Holding UNPOL to account: Individual criminal accountability of United Nations police personnel, ed. Brill/Martinus Nijhoff Publishers, Leiden, Boston, 2017.

KINCHIN, N., Administrative justice in the UN: Procedural protections, gaps and proposals for reform, Edward Elgar Publishers, Cheltenahm, 2018.

KINGSBURY, B., En guise d'ouverture-Views on the development of a global administrative law, in C. BORIES, Un droit administratif global?/A global administrative law?, ed. Pedone, Paris, 2012, pp. 16-17.

KIRBY, P., How is rape a weapon of war?, Feminist international relations, modes of critical explanation and the study of wartime sexual violence, in European Journal of International Relations, 18, 2012.

KIRGIS, F.L., Custom on a sliding scale, in American Journal of International Law, 81, 1987, pp. 148ss.

KIRGIS, F.L., Security Council Resolution 1483 on the rebuilding of Iraq, in American Journal of International Law, 97, 2003.

KIRKMAN, C.C., Fair and equitable treatment: Methanex v. United States and the narrowing scope of NAFTA Article 1105, in Law & Policy International Business, 34, 2002, pp. 344ss.

KISS, A., State responsibility and liability for nuclear damage, in Denver Journal of International Law and Policy, 35 (1), 2006, pp. 68ss.

KISS, A.C., La notion de patrimoine commun de l'humanitè, in Recueil des cours, ed. Brill, Bruxelles, vol. 175, 1982, pp. 243ss.

KITHARIDIS, S., The power of article 103 of the UN Charter on Treaty obligations. Can the Security Council authorise non-compliance of human right treaty obligations in UN peacekeeping operations?, in Journal of International Peacekeeping, 20 (1-2), 2016.

KJELDGAARD-PEDERSEN, A., The international legal personality of the individual, Oxford University Press, Oxford, 2018.

KLABBERS, J., Advanced introduction of the law of international organizations, Edward Elgar Publishers, Cheltenham, 2015, pp. 92ss.

KLABBERS, J., An introduction to international institutional law, Cambridge University Press, Cambridge, 2009, pp. 89ss.

KLABBERS, J., International Courts and Informal International Law, J. PAUWELYN, R. WESSEL, J. WOUTERS, Informal international lawmaking, Oxford University Press, Oxford, 2012, pp. 220ss.

KLABBERS, J., International organizations in the formation of customary international law, in E. CANNIZARO, P. PALCHETTI, Customary international law on the use of force, Martinus Nijhoff Publishers, The Hague, 2005, pp. 179-182.
KLABBERS, J., LEFEBER, R., Essays on the law of treaties: A collection of essays in honour of Bert Vierdag, Martinus Nijhoff Publishers, The Hague, 1998, pp. 31ss.
KLABBERS, J., Reflections on role responsibility. The responsibility of international organizations for failing to act, in European Journal of International Law, 28 (4), 2017, pp. 1138ss.
KLABBERS, J., The changing image of international organizations, in J.M. COICAUD, V. HEISKANEN, The legitimacy of international organizations, United Nations University Press, Tokyo, 2001, pp. 221-255.
KLABBERS, J., The transformation of international organizations law, in European Journal of International Law, 26, 2015, pp. 10ss.
KLABBERS, J., WALLENDAHL, A., (eds.) Research handbook on the law of international organizations, Edward Elgar Publishers, Cheltenham, 2011, pp. 314ss.
KLEIN, E., Beihilfe zum Völkerrechtsdelikt, in I. VON MÜNCH, Staasrecht, Völkerrecht, Europarecht Festschrift für Hans-Jurgen Schlochauer, De Gruyter, Berlin, 1981, pp. 425ss.
KLEIN, F., Die mittelbare Haftung im Völkerrecht, Klosrtermann, Frankurt, 1941.
KLEIN, K., Les articles sur la responsabilité des organizations internationales: quel bilan tirer des travaux de la CDI?, in Annuaire Français de Droit International, 58, 2012, pp. 15.
KLEIN, N., KLEIN, N.S., Litigation international law disputes: Weighting the options, Cambridge University Press, Cambridge, 2014, pp. 169ss.
KLEIN, P., La responsabilitè des organizations internationales dans le ordres juridiques internes et en droit des gens, ed. Bruylant, Bruxelles, 1998.
KLEIN, P., Le panel consultatif des droits de l'homme (human rights advisory panel) de la MINUK: une étape dans le processus de responsabilisation des Nations Unies?, in M. KOHEN, R. KOLB, D.L. TEHINDRAZENARIVELO, Perspectives du droit international au 21e siècle-Liber Amicorum Christian Dominicé, ed. Brill, Leiden/Boston, 2012, pp. 226ss.
KLEIN, P., Les compètences et pouvois de l'organization internationale, in E. LAGRANGE, J.M. SOREL, Droit des organizations internationales, LGDJ, Paris, 2013, pp. 721ss.
KLEIN, P., Panels, médiateurs et mécanismes informels de controle des activités des organizations internationales: entre accountability et responsibility, in Select Proceedings of the European Society of International Law, vol. 3, Oxford University Press, Oxford, 2010, pp. 228ss.
KLEIN, P., Responsabilitè pour les faits commis dans le cadre d'opèrations de paix et ètendue du pouvoir de contrôle de la cour europèenne des droits de l'homme: quelques considèrations critiques sur l'arrêt Behrami et Saramati, in Annuaire Français de Droit International, 53 (1), 2007, pp. 44ss.

KLEIN, P., The attribution of acts to international organizations, in J. CRAWFORD, A. PELLET, S. OLLESON, The law of international responsibility, Oxford University Press, Oxford, 2010, pp. 310ss.

KNOLL, B., Rights without remedies: The European Court's failure to close the human rights gap in Kosovo, in Zeitschrift für äuslandisches öffentliches Recht, 68, 2008, pp. 432ss.

KNOOPS, G.J., Defences in contemporary international criminal law, Transnational Publishers, New York, 2001, pp. 97ss.

KOCHENOV, D., PECH, L., Monitoring and enforcement of the rule of law in the EU rhetoric and reality, in European Constitutional Law Review, 12, 2015, pp. 514ss.

KOHEN, M.C., Individual reparation claims in instances of grave human rights violations: The position under general international law, in A. RANDELZHOEFER, C. TOMUSCHAT, State responsibility and the individual. Reparation in instances of grave violations of human rights, ed. Brill, The Hague, 1999.

KOHEN, M.G., Keeping subsequent agreements and practices in their right limits, in G. NOLTE, Treaties and subsequent practice, Oxford University Press, Oxford, 2013, pp. 34.

KOHEN, M.G., La pratique et la théorie des sources du droit international, in La pratique et le droit international, colloque de Genève de la Societe française pour le droit international, ed. Pedone, Paris, 2004, pp. 9, 81ss.

KOIVUROVA, T., Due diligence, in Max Planck Encyclopedia of Public International Law, 2010, par. 8.

KOK, E., The principle of complicity under international law. Its application to states and individuals in cases involving genocide, crimes against humanity and war crimes, in C. STAHN, L. VAN DEN HERIK, The diversification and fragmentation of international criminal law, Martinus Nijhoff Publishers, Leiden/Boston, 2012, pp. 558ss.

KOLB, A.S., The UN Security Council member's responsibility to protect a legal analysis, ed. Springer, Berlin, 2017.

KOLB, R., Does Article 103 of the Charter of the United Nations apply only to decisions or also to authorizations adopted by the Security Council?, in Zeitschrift fur äuslandisches öffentliches Recht und Völkerrecht, 64, 2004, pp. 21ss.

KOLB, R., Droit international et opèrations de paix internationales, Helbing & Lichtenhahn, Genève, 2002, pp. 20ss.

KOLB, R., GAGGIOLI, G., (ed. by), Research handbook on human rights and humanitarian law, Edward Elgar Publishers, Cheltenham, 2013, pp. 560ss.

KOLB, R., Ius in bello. Le droit internationale des conflits armès, Helbing & Lichtenhahn, Basel, 2003, pp. 244ss.

KOLB, R., La bonne foi en droit international public. Contribution à l'ètude des principes gènèraux de droit, ed. PUF, Paris, 2000, pp. 18ss.

KOLB, R., Peremptory international law: Ius cogens. A general inventory, Bloomsbury Publishing, New York, 2015, pp. 91ss.

KOLB, R., Reflections on due diligence duties and cyberspace, in German Yearbook of International Law, 58, 2015, 114ss.

KOLB, R., Selected problems in the theory of customary international law, in Netherlands International Law Review, 50, 2003, pp. 120ss.

KOLB, R., The International Court of Justice, Hart Publishing, Oxford & Oregon, Portland, 2013, pp. 762ss.

KOLB, R., The international law or State responsibility. An introduction, Edward Elgar Publishers, Cheltenham, 2017.

KOLB, R., Theory of international law, Hart Publishing, Oxford & Oregon, Portland, 2016, pp. 442ss.

KOMORI, T., Public international rules of international law: Towards effective implementation, ed. Routledge, London & New York, 2016, pp. 202ss.

KOMORI, T., WELLENS, J., Public interest rules of international law: Towards effective implementation, ed. Routledge, London & New York, 2016, pp. 203ss.

KONDOCH, B., The responsibility of peacekeepers, their sending States, and International Organizations, in T.D. GILL, D. FLECK, The handbook of the international law of military operations, Oxford University Press, Oxford, 2010, pp. 524ss.

KONSTADINIDES, T., The rule of law in the EU: The internal dimension, Hart Publishing, Oxford & Oregon, Portland, 2017.

KORENICA, F., The EU accession to the ECHR: Between Luxembourg's search for autonomy and Strasbourg's credibility on human rights protection, ed. Springer, Berlin, 2015, pp. 282ss.

KORHONEN, O., International governance in post-conflict situations, in Leiden Journal of International Law, 14 (3), 2001, pp. 3ss.

KORKEAKIVI, A., Consequences of "higher" international law: Evaluating crimes of state and erga omnes, in Journal of International Legal Studies, 2, 1996, pp. 82ss.

KOSKENNIEMI, M., From apology to utopia. The structure of international legal argument. Reissue with a new epilogue, Cambridge University Press, Cambridge, 2005, pp. 258ss.

KOSKENNIEMI, M., From the apology to utopia: The structure of the international legal argument, Cambridge University Press, Cambridge, 2006.

KOSKENNIEMI, M., Solidarity measures: state responsibility as a new international order ?, in The British Yearbook of International Law, 72, 2001, pp. 338ss.

KOSKENNIEMI, M., Sources of international law, ed. Routledge, London & New York, 2017, pp. 222ss.

KOTZUR, M., Intertemporal law, in Max Planck Encyclopedia of International Law, 24, 2008, par. 6.

KOUTRAKOS, P., EU international relations law, Hart Publishing, Oxford & Oregon, Portland, 2015.

KOUTRAKOS, P., Judicial review in EU's common foreign and security policy, Cambridge University Press, Cambridge, 2018.

KOUTRAKOS, P., The EU Common Security and Defence Policy, Oxford University Press, Oxford, 2013.

KRAHMANN, E., FRIESENDORF, C., The role of private security companies (PSCs) in CSDP missions and operation, European Parliament Directorate-General for External Policies, Policy Department, 2011, pp. 6-7.

KRENC, F., La Belgique "condamnée" pour la première fois par le Comité des droits de l'homme sur fond de lutte contre le terrorisme: cap sur Genève!, in Journal des Tribunaux, 2009, n. 6367 (24 oct. 2009), pp. 621 ss.

KRENN, C., Autonomy and effectiveness as common concerns: A path to ECHR accession after Opinion 2/13, in German Law Journal, 16 (1), 2015, pp. 147ss.

KRESS, C., Universal jurisdiction over international crimes and the Institut de Droit International, in Journal of International Criminal Justice, 4, 2006, pp. 561-585.

KRETZMER, D., Rethinking the application of international humanitarian law in non-international armed conflicts, in Israel Law Review, 42, 2009.

KRETZMER, S., The advisory opinion. The light treatment of international humanitarian law, in American Journal of International Law, 99, 2005, pp. 89ss.

KRIEG, A., Motivations for humanitarian intervention: Theoretical and empirical considerations, ed. Springer, Dordrecht, 2013.

KRIEGER, H., Addressing the accountability gap in peacekeeping. Law-making by domestic courts as a way to avoid UN reform?, in Netherlands International Law Review, 62, 2015, pp. 262ss.

KRIEGER, H., Common European Defence: Competition or compatibility with Nato?, in M. TRYBUS, N.D. WHITE (eds.), European security law, Oxford University Press, Oxford 2007, pp. 174-197.

KRÜCK, H., Völkerrechtliche Verträge im Recht der Europäischen Gemeinschaften, ed. Springer, Berlin, 1977, pp. 126ss.

KRUGER, H., WALTER, V., Self-determination and secession in international law, Oxford University Press, Oxford, 2014, pp. 214-220.

KRUMREY, J., Die Immunität der Vereinten Nationen: Verantwortlichkeit für Friedenswissenshaft, Mohr Siebeck, Tübingen, 2018, pp. 312ss.

KUHN, M., Verschuldens-oder Verursachungshaftung der Staaten im allgemeinen Völkerrecht, Frankfurt am Main, 1961, pp. 116ss.

KUIJER, M., The accession of the European Union to the ECHR: A gift for ECHR's 60th anniversary or an unwelcome intruder at the party?, in Amsterdam Law Forum, 4 (3), 2011, pp. 17-32.

KUIJPER, P.J., Introduction to the symposium on responsibility of international organizations and of (member) states: Attribute or direct responsibility or both?, in International Organizations Law Review, 7, 2010, pp. 22ss.

KUIJPER, P.J., The Court and Tribunal of the EC and the Vienna Convention on the Law of Treaties 1969, in Legal Issues of European Integration, 25, 1998, pp. 4ss.

KUNZ, J.L., The nature of customary international law, in American Journal of

International Law, 47, 1953, pp. 664ss.

KÜNZLI, A., Exercising diplomatic protection the fine line between litigation, demarches and consular assistance, in Heidelberg Journal of International Law, 66, 2006, pp. 329ss.

KUWALI, D., VILJOEN, F., By all means necesary: Protecting civilians and preventing mass atrocities in Africa, Pretoria University Law Press, Pretoria, 2017.

KWAKWA, E., Globalization and international organizations, ed. Routledge, London & New York, 2017.

LACCHI, C., The ECtHR's interference in the dialogue between National Courts and the Court of Justice of the EU: Implications for the preliminary reference procedure, in Review of European Administrative Law, 9 (1), 2015, pp. 96ss.

LACHENMANN, F., WOLFRUM, K., The law of armed conflict and the use of force. The Max Planck Encyclopedia of public international law, Oxford University Press, Oxford, 2017.

LACHMANN, P., The international legal personality of the European Communities: Capacity and competence, in Leiden Journal of International Law, 3, 1984, pp. 12ss.

LADENBURGER, C., Vers l'adhésion de l'Union européenne à la Convention européenne des droits de l'homme, in Revue Trimestrielle de Droit Européen, 47 (1), 2011, pp. 20-26.

LAGRANGE, P., Responsabilitè des Etats pour actes accomplis en application du Chapitre VII de la Charte des Nations Unies, in Revue Gènèrale de Droit International Public, 112, 2008, pp. 86ss.

LAIS, R., Die Rechtsfolgen völkerrechtlicher Delikte, Dunker & Humblot, Berlin, 1932.

LAMBRECHT, S., The sting is in the Tail: CJEU Opinion 2/13 objects to draft agreement on accession of the EU to the European Convention on Human Rights, in European Human Rights Law Review, 15 (1), 2015, pp. 185ss.

LAMMERS, G., New developments concerning international responsibility and liability for damage caused by environmental interferences, in The Hague Yearbook of International Law, 20, 2007, pp. 88ss.

LANDAU, J.L., Living law: Modern constitutionalism and its effect on emerging and dynamic democracies: Bridging governments: The role of international law in State government, in Willamette Journal of International Law and Dispute Resolution, 20 (1-2), 2012, pp. 50ss.

LANG, A.F., WIENER, A., Handbook on global constitutionalism, Edward Elgar Publishers, Cheltenham, 2017, pp. 362ss.

LANGFORD, M., VANDENHOLE, W., SCHEININ, M., VAN GENUGTEN, W., (ed. by), Global justice, State duties: The extraterritorial scope of economic, social and cultural rights in international law, Cambridge University Press, Cambridge 2013.

LANOVOY, V., Complicity and its limits in the law of international responsibility, Hart Publishing, Oxford & Oregon, Portland, 2016.

LANSING, R., The North Atlantic coast fisheries arbitration, in University of

Pennsylvania Law Review and American Law Register, 59 (3), 1910, pp. 122ss.

LARENZ, K., Methodenlehre der Rechtswissenschaft, ed. Springer, Berlin, 1975, pp. 251ss.

LARIVÉ, M.H.A., Debating European security and defence policy under standing the complexity, ed. Routledge, London & New York, 2016, pp. 197ss.

LARSEN, K.M., Attribution of conduct in peace operations: the "ultimate control and authority test," in European Journal of International Law, 19, 2008, pp. 522ss.

LARSEN, K.M., COOPER, C.G., NYSTUEN, G., Searching for a principle of humanity in international humanitarian law, Cambridge University Press, Cambridge, 2013.

LAUTERPACHT, E., The contemporary practice of the United Kingdom in the field of international law. Survey and comment, Cambridge University Press, Cambridge, 2008.

LAUTERPACHT, H., General rules of the law of peace, in E. LAUTERPACH, International law being the collected papers of Hersch Lauterpacht, vol. 1. The general works, Cambridge University Press, Cambridge, 1970, pp. 384ss.

LAUTERPACHT, H., The grotian tradition in international law, in British Yearbook of International Law, 17, 1946, pp. 4ss.

LAVAL, P.F., Les activitès opèrationnelles, du conseil à l'administration international du territoire, in E. LAGRANGE, J.M. SOREL, Droit des organizations internationales, LGDJ, Paris, 2013, pp. 767ss.

LAVIOLETTE, N., Commanding rape: Sexual violence, command responsibility and the prosecution of superiors by the international criminal Tribunals for the Former Yugoslavia and Rwanda, in The Canadian Yearbook of International Law, 36, 1998, pp. 94ss.

LAWSON, R.A., Life after Bankovic: On the extraterritorial application of the European Convention of Human Rights, in Extraterritorial application of the Human Rights Treaties, ed. Intersentia, Antwerp, 2004, pp. 83-123.

LEACH, P., Taking a case to the European Court of Human Rights, Oxford University Press, Oxford, 2011, pp. 55ss.

LEANDRO, A., Arms transfer and complicity in war crimes, in F. POCAR, M. PEDRAZZI, M. FRULLI (eds.), War crimes and the conduct of hostilities, Edward Elgar Publishers, Cheltenham, Northampton, 2013, pp. 225ss.

LEB, C., Cooperation, the law of transboundary water resources, Cambridge University Press, Cambridge, 2013.

LEBEN, C., Les contre-mesures inter-ètatiques et les rèactions à l'illicite dans la sociètè internationale, in Annuaire Français de Droit International, 28, 1982, pp. 10ss.

LEBEN, CH., Les sanctions privatives de droit ou de qualitè dans les organizations internationales spècialisèes, ed. Bruylant, Bruxelles, 1979, pp. 41ss.

LECK, C., International responsibility in United Nations peacekeeping operations. Command and control arrangements and the attribution of conduct, in Melbourne Journal of International Law, 10, 2009, pp. 346ss.

LECKOW, R., PLITH, E., Codification, progressive development or innovation? Some reflections on the ILC Articles on responsibility of international organizations, in M. RAGAZZI, Responsibility of International Organizations. Essays in memory of Sir Ian Brownlie, ed. Brill, Bruxelles, 2013, pp. 228ss.

LEE, L.T., Consular law, Oxford University Press, Oxford, 1991, pp. 112ss.

LEFEBER, R., Transboundary environmental interference and the origin of state liability, ed. Brill, The Hague, 1996.

LEISTENSCHNEIDER, N.A.A., La responsabilidad internacional de los estados por actos ilicitos, crimines internacionales y daňos transfronterizos, in Anuario Mexicano de Derecho Internacional, 12, 2012.

LENAERTS, K., Federalism and the rule of law: Perspectives from the European Court of Justice, in Fordham International Law Journal, 33, 2011, pp. 1338ss.

LENAERTS, K., MASELIS, I., GUTMAN, K., European Union procedural law, Oxford University Press, Oxford, 2014, pp. 133ss.

LENNARD, M., Navigating by the Stars: Interpreting the WTO agreements, in Journal of International Economic Law, 5, 2002, pp. 19ss.

LEONARD, E., RAMSAY, G., Globalizing Somalia: Multilateral international and transnational recpercussions of conflict, Bloomsbury Publishing, New York, 2013.

LESTER, S., MERCURIO, B., BARTELS, L., Bilateral and regional trade agreements. Commentary and analysis, Cambridge University Press, Cambridge, 2016.

LÉVY, J.P., De quelques "modifications" et nterprétations de la Convention sur le droit de la mer, in Revue Générale de Droit International Public, 111, 2007, pp. 408ss.

LIAKOPOULOS, D., Art. 275 TFUE, in P.E. HERZOG, C. CAMPBELL, G. ZAGEL, Smit & Herzog on the law of the European Union, ed. LexisNexis, New York, 2018.

LIAKOPOULOS, D., Conflits de normes à la Cour internationale de Justice: rôle du Conseil de sécurité des Nations Unies, in Juris Gradibus, 2017.

LIAKOPOULOS, D., Cooperation and coordination of arbitral proceedings in merger and acquisition transactions, in International and European Union Legal Matters, 2011.

LIAKOPOULOS, D., Die Hybridität des Verfahrens der Internationalen ad hoc Strafgerichtshöfe und die Bezugnahme auf innerstaatliches Recht in der Rechtsprechun, in International and European Union legal Matters, 2012.

LIAKOPOULOS, D., Equo processo nella Convenzione europea dei diritti dell'uomo e nel diritto comunitario, ed. Cedam, 2007.

LIAKOPOULOS, D., European integration and its relation with the jurisprudence of European Court of Human Rights and private international law of European Union, in Homa Publica. Revista Internacional de Direitos Humanos e Impresa, 2 (2), 2018.

LIAKOPOULOS, D., Evolutionary, dynamic or contemporary interpretation in WTO system?, in The Chinese Journal of Global Governance, 5, 2019, pp. 28ss.

LIAKOPOULOS, D., International Law Commission and protection of environment in times of armed conflict: The case of protection of international cultural heritage, in ArtPaths, 2012.

LIAKOPOULOS, D., Kritik an friedenserhaltenden/Peacekeeping Operationen und die Entwicklung des Konzepts der Souveränität im Völkerrecht, in International and European Union Legal Matters, 2011.

LIAKOPOULOS, D., L'ingerenza umanitaria nel diritto internazionale e comunitario, ed. Cedam, Padova, 2007, pp. 69ss.

LIAKOPOULOS, D., La tutela cautelare nella Corte internazionale di giustizia. Aspetti processuali e comparati, ed. AMON, Firenze, 2012.

LIAKOPOULOS, D., Parità di armi nella giustizia penale internazionale, vol. 1, ed. Libellula, Puglia, 2018.

LIAKOPOULOS, D., Protection of human rights between European Court of Human Rights and Court of European Union, in International and European Union Legal Matters, 2015.

LIAKOPOULOS, D., The function of accusation in International Criminal Court. Structure of crimes and the role of Prosecutor according to the international criminal jurisprudence, ed. Maklu, The Hague, Antwerp, New York, 2019.

LIAKOPOULOS, D., The legal system of climate change and the mechanism of control in the European Union, in International Journal of Environment and Health, 6, (1), 2011.

LIANG, J., Modifying the UN Charter through subsequent practice: Prospects for the charter's revitalisation, in Nordic Journal of International Law, 81, 2012, pp. 4ss.

LIEFLÁNDER, T.R., The Lubanga judgment of the ICC: More than just the First Step?, in Cambridge Journal of International and Comparative Law, 2012, pp. 191–212.

LIIVOJA, R., The scope of the supremacy clause of the United Nations Charter, in International and Comparative Law Quarterly, 57, 2008, pp. 583ss.

LINDAHL, H., Fault lines of globalization. Legal order an the politics of a-legality, Oxford University Press, Oxford, 2013.

LINDERFALK, U., On the interpretation of treaties. The modern international law as expressed in the 1969 Vienna Convention on the Law of Treaties, ed. Springer, Dordrecht, 2007.

LINDERFALK, U., State responsibility and the primary-secondary rules terminology. The role of language for an understanding of the international legal system, in Nordic Journal of International Law, 78 (1), 2009, pp. 54ss.

LINDROOS, A., Addressing norm conflicts in a fragmented legal system. The doctrine of lex specialis, in Nordic Journal of International Law, 74, 2005, pp. 45ss.

LINGAAS, C., Imagined identities: Defining the racial group in the crime of genocide, in Genocide Studies and Prevention: An International Journal, 9

(1), 2016, pp. 80ss.
LINNAN, D.K., Legitimacy, legal development and change: Law and modernization reconsidered, ed. Routledge, London & New York, 2016.
LIVOJA, R., The scope of the supremacy clause of the United Nations, in International and Comparative Law Quarterly, 57 (3), 2008, pp. 583-612.
LOCK, T., Beyond Bosphorus: The European Court of Human Rights case law in the responsibility of Member States of international organizations under the European Convention on Human Rights, in Human Rights Law Review, 10 (4), 2010, pp. 530ss.
LOCK, T., The ECJ and the ECtHR: The future relationship between the two European courts, in The Law and Practice of International Courts and Tribunals, 8, 2010, pp. 375-398
LOCK, T., The European Court of Justice and international courts, Oxford University Press, Oxford, 2015.
LOCK, T., The future of EU accession to the ECHR after Opinion 2/13: Is it still possible and is it still desirable?, in Edinburgh School of Law Research Paper Series, 2015.
LOOMER, K., Australia v. Japan: Is it possible for Japanese compliance?, in North Carolina Journal of International Law, 36, 2016, pp. 4, 9ss.
LORENZ, N.L.A., GROUSSOT, Z., PETURSSON, G.T., The European human rights culture. A paradox of human rights protection in Europe?, Martinus Nijhoff Publishers, Leiden, 2013.
LOVE, B., The International Court of Justice: Jurisdictional immunities of the state (Germany v. Italy: Greece intervening. Jurisdictional immunities of the state (Ger. v. IT. Greece intervening (ICJ), in International Legal Materials, 51 (3), 2012, pp. 564ss.
LOWE, V., International law, Oxford Univesity Press, Oxford, 2015.
LOWE, V., Precluding wrongfulness or responsibility. A plea for excuses, in European Journal of International Law, 10 (2), 1999, pp. 408ss.
LOWE, V., Responsbility for the conduct of other states, in Japanese Journal of International Law and Diplomacy, 101, 2002, pp. 4ss.
LUERS, W.H., Choosing engagement. Uniting the U.N with U.S interests, in Foreign Affairs, 79, 2000.
LUSA BORDIN, F., The analogy between States and international organizations, Cambridge University Press, Cambridge, 2018.
LYONS, T., European Union customs law, Oxford University Press, Oxford, 2018.
LYSÉN, J., State responsibility and internationaliability of states for lawful acts, ed. Justus, Uppsala, 1997.
MACAK, K., Decoding article 8 of the International Law Commission's articles on state responsibility: Attribution of cyber operations by non-state actors, in Journal of Conflict & Security Law, 16, 2016, pp. 406.
MACAK, K., International law and practice, from cyber norms to cyber rules: Re-engaging states as law-makers, in Leiden Journal of International Law, 30, 2017, pp. 883ss.
MACGIBBON, IC., Customary international law and acquiescence, in British

Yearbook of International Law, 33, 1957, pp. 116ss.
MACGIBBON, IC., Means for the identification of the international law: General Assembly Resolutions: Custom, practice and mixed identity, in B. CHENG, International law: Teaching and practice, ed. Stevens, London, 1982, pp. 12, 21ss.
MADDOCK DILLON, E., DEXTER, M., The Haitian revolution an the early United States: Histories, textualities, geography, University of Pennsylvania Press, Pennsylvania, 2016.
MAGGIO, A.R., Environmental policy, non product related process and production methods and the law of the World Trade Organization, ed. Springer, Berlin, 2017.
MAISSON, R., Justice pènale internationale, ed. PUF, Paris, 2017.
MAJOR, C., Towards an EU peacebuilding strategy: The effects of the Lisbon Treaty on the comprehensive approach of the EU in the area of civilian crisis management, in European Foreign Affairs Review, 18, 2014, pp. 46ss.
MALANCZUK, P., Zur Repressalie im Entwurf der International Law Commission zur Staatenverantwortlichkeit, in Zeitschrift für ausländisches Recht und Völkerrecht, 45, 1985, pp. 294ss.
MALINTOPPI, A., La fonction normative de l'OACI, in Revue Gènerale de l'Air, 10, 1950, pp. 1050ss.
MANACORDA, S., MELONI, C., Indirect perpetration versus Joint Criminal Enterprise: Concurring approaches in the practice of international criminal law?, in Journal of International Criminal Justice, 9 (1), 2011, pp. 165ss.
MANIN, F., Droit international public, ed. Masson, Paris, 1979, pp. 182ss.
MANIN, P.H., La Convention de Vienne entre Etats et organizations internationales ou entre organizations internationales, in Annuaire Français de Droit International, 32 (1), 1986, pp. 454ss.
MANN, F.A., The consequences of an international wrong in international and national law, in British Yearbook of International Law, 48 (1), 1975-1976, pp. 4ss.
MARAHAUN, G., MARAHAUN, T., ZIMMERMANN, A., (ed. by), Making treaties work. Human rights, environment, arms control, Oxford University Press, Oxford, 2007, pp. 267ss.
MARAHAUN, T., Dispute resolution, compliance control and enforcement of international arms control law, in G. ULFSTEIN T. MARAHAUN, A. ZIMMERMANN (ed. by), Making treaties work. Human rights, environment, arms control, Oxford University Press, Oxford, 2007, pp. 243ss.
MARCHADIER, F., Convention européenne des droit de l'homme et des libertès fondamentales, in Revue Critique de Droit International Privè, 193 (4), 2014, pp. 679-694.
MARHIC, G., Le règime de responsabilitè des opèrations de paix de l'unione europèenne. Quelles règles applicables?, in Revue Belge de Droit International, 46, 2013, pp. 137ss.
MARÍN-LÓPEZ, A., La responsabilidad internacional objetiva y la

responsabilidad internacional por riesgo, ed. Beramar B.L. Madrid, 1995.
MAROSSI, A.Z., BASSETT, M.R., Economic sanctions under international law. Unilateralism, multilateralism, legitimacy and consequences, ed. Springer, Berlin, 2015.
MÁRQUEZ CARRASCO, C., The applicability of human rights instruments to European Union's CSDP operations: Framing the challenges, in Cuadernos Europeos de Deusto, 53, 2015, pp. 60ss.
MARTHA, R.S.J., The financial obligation in international law, Oxford University Press, Oxford, 2015.
MARXSEN, C., Violation and confirmation of the law: The intricate effects of the invocation of the law in armed conflict, in Journal on the Use of Force and International Law, 5 (1), 2018, pp. 12ss.
MARXSEN, C., What do different theories of customary international law have to say about the individual right to reparation under international humanitarian law?, in Zeitschrift für äuslandisches öffentliches Recht, 78 (3), 2018.
MATHESON, M.J., United Nations governance of postconflict societies, in American Journal of International Law, 95, 2001.
MATHIAS, S., The work of the International Law Commission on identification of customary international law: A view from the perspective of the office of legal affairs, in Chinese Journal of International Law, 15, 2016, pp. 20ss.
MATSUCHITA, M., SCHOENBAUM, T.J., MAVROIDIS, P., The World Trade Organization: Law, practice and policy, Oxford University Press, Oxford, 2015, pp. 849ss.
MATZ-LÜCK, N., Treaties, conflict clauses, in Max Planck Encyclopedia of Public International Law, 2006, pp. 6ss.
MAZIAU, N., PECH, L., L'administration internationale de la Bosnie-Herzègovine: Un modale pour le Kosovo?, in Civitas Europa, 2000.
MAZZOCCHI, S., Humanitarian intervention in a post-Iraq, post-Darfur world: Is there now a duty to prevent genocide even without Security Council approval?, in Annual Survey of International Law & Comparative Law, 17, 2011, pp. 112ss.
MCCONNELL, F., MOREAU, T., DITTMER, J., Mimicking state diplomacy: The legitimizing strategies of unofficial diplomacies, in Geoforum, 43 (4), 2012, pp. 806ss.
MCCORQUODALE, R., Defining the international rule of law. Defying gravity?, in International and Comparative Law Quarterly, 65 (2), 2016, pp. 278ss.
MCCOUBREY, H., MORRIS, J., Regional peacekeeping in the post-colf war era, Kluwer Law International, The Hague, London, Boston, 2000, pp. 228ss.
MCDOUGAL, M.S., The hydrogen bomb tests and the international law of the sea, in American Journal of International Law, 49, 1955, pp. 358ss.
MCDOUGAL, M.S., The International Law Commission's Draft Articles upon interpretation: Textuality redivivus, in American Journal of International Law, 61, 1967, pp. 994ss.
MCGINLEY, G.P., Practice as a guide to treaty interpretation, in Fletcher Forum

of World Affairs, 9, 1985, pp. 211ss

MCGINNIS, J.O., The comparative advantage of customary international law, in Harvard Journal of Law and Public Policy, 30, 2006, pp. 7-12.

MCHENRY, J.R., The prosecution of rape under international law: Justice that is long overdue, in Vanderbilt Journal of Transnational Law, 35, 2002, pp. 1310ss.

MCINTRYE, J., The role of the dispute requirement in assessing jurisdiction and admissibility before the international court, in Melbourne Journal of International Law, 19 (2), 2018.

MCINTRYRE, S.H., Legal effect of world war II on treaties of the United States, ed. Springer, Berlin, 2012, pp. 160ss.

MCINTYRE, J., The declaratory judgment in recent jurisprudence of the International Court of Justice. Conflicting approaches to state responsibility, in Leiden Journal of International Law, 29 (1), 2016, pp. 180ss.

MCLACHLAN, C., The evolution of treaty obligations in international law, in G. NOLTE, Treaties and subsequent practice, Oxford University Press, Oxford, 2013, pp. 70ss.

MCNAIR, A.D., The law of treaties, Oxford University Press, Oxford, 1961, pp. 486, 697ss.

MCRAE, D., The work of the International Law Commission 2007-2011: Progress and prospect, Cambridge University Press, Cambridge, 2012, pp. 325ss.

MCWHINNEY, E., The illegal diversion of aircraft and international law, Sijthoff, Leiden, 1975, pp. 10.

MEDELLÍN URQUIAGA, X., The normative impact of the inter-American Court of Human Rights on Latin-america national prosecution of mass atrocities, in Israel Law Review, 46 (3), 2013, pp. 410ss.

MEDLONG, J., All other breaches: State practice and the Geneva Conventions' nebulous class of less discussed prohibitions, in Michigan Journal International Law, 34, 2013, pp. 830ss.

MELISCHEK, A., The relevant market in international economic law: A comparative antitrust and GATT analysis, Cambridge University Press, Cambridge, 2013, pp. 70ss.

MENDELSON, M., The definition of international organization in the International Law Commission's current project on the reponsibility of international organizations, in M. RAGAZZI, Responsibility of international organizations. Essays in memory of Sir Ian Brownlie, Martinus Nijhoff Publishers, Leiden, Boston, 2013, pp. 384ss.

MENDELSON, M.H., The formation of customary international law, Recueil des Cours, ed Brill, The Hague, vol. 271, 1998, pp. 156, 272ss.

MENDELSON, M.H., The International Court of Justice and the sources of international law, in V. LOWE, M FITZMAURICE, Fifty years of the International Court of Justice: Essays in Honour of Sir Robert Jennings, Cambridge University Press, Cambridge, 1996, pp. 86s.

MENDELSON, M.H., The subjective element in customary international law, in

The British Yearbook of International Law, 66, 1995, pp. 184ss.
MENG, W., Internationale Organizationen im Völkerrechtichen Deliktsrecht, in Zeitschrift für ausländisches Recht und Völkerrecht, 45, 1985, pp. 324ss.
MERIBOUTE, Z., Le facteur temps et la violation des obligations internationales, in Revue de Droit et des Sciences Diplomatiques, 62, 1984, pp. 186ss.
MERKET, H., The European Union and the seurity-development nexus briding the legal divide, ed. Brill, Leiden, Boston, 2016, pp. 130ss.
MERON, T., Revival of customary humanitarian law, in American Journal of International Law, 99, 2005, pp. 817ss.
MERON, T., The continuing role of custom in the formation of international humanitarian law, in American Journal of International Law, 90, 1996, pp. 238ss
MERON, T., The Geneva Conventions as customary law, in American Journal of International Law, 81, 1987, pp. 348ss.
MERON, T., The humanization of humanitarian law, in American Journal of International Law, 94, 2000, pp. 239ss.
MERRILLS, J.G., Interim measures of protection in the recent jurisprudence of the International Court of Justice, in International and Comparative Law Quarterly, 44, 1995, pp. 128ss.
MERRILLS, J.G., International dispute settlement, Cambridge University Press, Cambridge, 1999.
MERRILS, J.G., International dispute settlement, Cambridge University Press, Cambridge, V° ed., 2011, pp. 4ss.
MESSINEO, F., Attribution of conduct, in A. NOLLKAEMPER, I. PLAKOKEFALOS, Principles of shared responsbibility in international law. An appraisal of the state of the art, Cambridge University Press, Cambridge, 2015, pp. 71ss.
MEYER, D., Les contrats de fourniture de biens et services dans le cadre des opèrations de maintien de la paix, in Annuaire Français de Droit International, 42, 1996, pp. 79ss.
MEYER, F.C., From "Solange II to Forever I." The German Federal Constitutional Court and the European Arrest Warrant (and how the CJEU responded), in New Journal of European Criminal Law, 7, 2016, pp. 278ss.
MEYER, J., (ed.), Charta der Grundrechte der Europäischen Union, ed. Nomos, Baden-Baden, 2014, pp. 813-826.
MEZGER, E., Strafrecht. Ein Lehrbuch, Duncker & Humblot, Leipzig, 1933, pp. 413ss.
MICHIE, A., The law of arms control. International supervision and enforcement, in Journal of Conflict and Security Law, 10 (3), 2005, pp. 345-377.
MILANO, E., The Security Council and territorial sovereignty: The Case of Kosovo, in International Community Law Review, 12, 2010, pp. 172ss.
MILANOVIC, M., Extraterritorial application of human rights treaties, Oxford University Press, Oxford, 2011, pp. 136-142.
MILANOVIC, M., PAPIC, T., As bad as it gets: The European Court of Human Rights' Behrami and Saramati decision and general international law, in

International and Comparative Law Quarterly, 58 (2), 2009, pp. 268ss.
MILANOVIC, M., State responsibility for genocide: A follow-up, in European Journal of International Law, 18, 2007, pp. 670ss.
MILANOVIC, M., The Human Rights Committee's views in Sayadi v. Belgium: A missed opportunity, in Goettingen Journal of International Law, 3, 2009, pp. 520ss.
MILLER, R.A., BRATSPIES, R.M., Progress in international law, ed. Brill, Bruxelles, 2008.
MINOW, M., TRUE-FROST, C., WHITTING, A., The first global prosecutor: Promise and constraints, University of Michigan Press, Michigan, 2015.
MOECKLI, D., SHAH, S., SIVAKUMARAN, S., International human rights law, Oxford University Press, Oxford, 2010, pp. 598ss.
MOELLE, M.P., The international responsibility of international organizations. Cooperation in peacekeeping operations, Cambridge University Press, Cambridge, 2017, pp. 168ss.
MÖLDNER, M., Responsibility of international organizations-Introducing the ILC's DARIO, in Max Planck Yearbook of United Nations Law, 16, 2012, pp. 282ss.
MÖLER, B., European security. The roles of regional organizations, ed. Routledge, London & New York, 2016.
MOLOO, R., Changing times, changing obligations: The interpretation of treaties over time, in American Society International Law Proceedings, 106, 2012, pp. 262ss.
MOLOO, R., When actions speak louder than words, in Berkeley Journal of International Law, 31, 2013, p. 40ss.
MOMIROV, A., Dutch courts and Srebrenica: Ascribing responsibilities and defending legally relevant relationships, in Netherlands Yearbook of International Law, 43, 2012, pp. 233ss.
MOORMAN, W., Humanitarian intervention and international law in the case of Kosovo, in New England Law Review, 37, 2002-2003, pp. 776ss.
MORANO-FOADI, S., VICKERS, L., (eds.), Fundamental Rights in the EU-A matter for two Courts, Oxford University Press, Oxford, 2015.
MORISSE-SCHILBACH, M., HALFMANN J., (eds), Wissen, Wissenschaft und Global Commons: Forschungen zu Wissenschaft und Politik jenseits des Staates am Beispiel von Regulierung und Konstruktion globaler Gemeinschaftsgüter, ed. Nomos, Baden-Baden, 2012, pp. 134ss.
MORTENSON, J.D., The travaux of travaux. Is the Vienna Convention hostile to drafting history, in American Journal of International Law, 107 (4), 2013, pp. 782ss.
MOUTHAAN, S., Sexual violence against men and international law. Criminalising the unmentionable, in International Criminal Law Review, 13, 2013, pp. 668ss.
MOUTON, J.D., KOVÁCS, P., La concept de citoyennetè en droit international, ed. Brill, The Hague, 2019.
MRAZEK, Y., Prohibition of the use and threat of force: Self-defence and elf-help

in international law, in Canadian Yearbook of International Law, 2, 1989, pp. 82ss.

MUJEZINOVI Ć LARSEN, K., Attribution of conduct in peace operations: The "ultimate authority and control" test, in European Journal of International law, 19 (3), 2008, pp. 512ss.

MUJEZINOVIĆ LARSEN, K., The human rights treaty obligations of peacekeeping, Cambridge University Press, Cambridge, 2012.

MÜLLER, W., WTO agreement on subsidies and countervailing measures. A commentary, Cambridge University Press, Cambridge, 2017

MÜLLERSON, R., The Interplay in K. WELLENS, International Law: Theory and practice-Essays in Honor of Eric Suy, Martinus Nijhoff Publishers, The Hague, 1998, pp. 162ss.

MURPHY, C.C., EU counter terrorism law: Pre-emption and the rule of law, Hart Publishing, Oxford & Oregon, Portland, 2012.

MURPHY, S.D., Codification, progressive development, or scholarly analysis? The art of packaging the ILC's work product, in M. RAGAZZI (ed.), Responsibility of international organizations-Essays in Memory of Sir Ian Brownlie, Martinus Nijhoff Publishers, Leiden, Boston, 2013, pp. 29-40.

MURPHY, S.D., Humanitarian intervention. The United Nations in an evolving world order, University of Pennsylvania Press, Pennsylvania, 1966, pp. 106ss.

MURPHY, S.D., The relevance of subsequent agreement and subsequent practice for the interpretation of treaties, in G. NOLTE, Treaties and subsequent practice, Oxford University Press, Oxford, 2013, pp. 84ss.

MUSA, S., Victim reparation under the ius post bellum. An historical and normative perspective, Cambridge University Press, Cambridge, 2019.

NADYA SADAT, L., Seeking accountability for the unlawful use of force, Cambridge University Press, 2018, pp. 50ss.

NAERT, F., International law aspects of the EU's security and defence policy with a particular focus on the law of armed conflict and human rights, ed. Intersentia, Antwerp, Oxford, Portland, 2010.

NAGY, K., Le problème de la lègitime dèfense en droit international, in Acta juridica et Politica, Szeged, 42, 1992.

NAHAPETIAN, K., Confronting state complicity in international law, in UCLA Journal of International Law and Foreign Affairs, 7, 2002-2003, pp. 100ss.

NASU, H., The UN Security Council's responsibility and the "responsibility to protect," in Max Planck Yearbook of United Nations, 15, 2011, pp. 379ss.

NEBESAR, D.A., Gender-based violence as a weapon of war, in U.C. Davis Journal of International Law and Policy, 4, 1998, pp. 148ss.

NEDESKI, A., NOLLKAEMPER, N., Responsibility of international organizations "in connection with the acts of States," in International law Review, 9 (1), 2012

NEFRAMI, E., Les accords mixtes de la Communautè Europèenne aspects communautaires et internationaux, ed. Bruylant, Bruxelles, 2007, pp. 562ss.

NEGRELIUS, J., KRISTOFFERSSON, E., Human rights in contemporary

European law, Hart Publishing, Oxford & Oregon, Portland,2015, pp. 17ss.
NEUHOLD, H., Die Pflicht zur Zusammenarbeit zwischen den Staaten: Moralisches Postulat oder völkerrechtliche Norm?, in H. MIEHSLER, E. MOCK, B. SIMMA, I. TAMMELLO, Ius Humanitas. Festschrift zum 90. Geburtstag von Alfred Verdross, Duncker & Humblot, Berlin, 1980, pp. 578ss.
NEUMANN, G.L., Inter-American Court of Human Rights (IACtHR), in R. WOLFRUM, The Max Planck Encyclopedia of Public International Law, Oxford University Press, Oxford, 2012.
NEWCOMBE, A.P., PARADELL, L., Law and practice of investment treaties. Standards of treatment, Kluwer Law International, The Hague, 2009, pp. 527ss.
NICOLA, F., DAVIES, B., European Union law stories, Cambridge University Press, Cambridge, 2017.
NIETONAVIA, R., Responsabilidad internacional del Estado por genocidio. La sentencia de la Corte Internacional de Justicia en el caso de Srebrenica, International Law, in Revista Colombiana de Derecho Internacional, 22, 2010, pp. 18ss.
NOLLAEMPER, A., PLAKOKEFALOS, I., The practice of shared respnsibility in international law, Cambridge University Press, Cambridge, 2017.
NOLLAKAEMPER, A., Dual attribution: Liability of the Netherlands for conduct of Dutchbat in Srebrenica, in Journal of International Criminal Justice, 9, 2011, pp. 1144ss.
NOLLKAEMPER, A., Dual distribution, in Journal of International Criminal Justice, 9, 2011, pp. 1144ss.
NOLLKAEMPER, A., Issues of shared responsibility before the International Court of Justice, in E. RIETER, H. DE WAELE, Evolving principles of international law. Studies in honor of Karel v. Wellens, ed. Brill, Leiden, Boston, 2011, pp. 219ss.
NOLLKAEMPER, A., JACOBS, D., SCHECHINGER, J.N.M., Distribution of responsibilities in international law, Cambridge University Press, Cambridge, 2015, pp. 283ss.
NOLLKAEMPER, A., JACOBS, D., Shared responsibility in international law. A conceptual framework, in Michigan Journal of International Law, 34, 2013, pp. 36.
NOLLKAEMPER, A., PLAKEFALOS, I., Principles of shared responsibility in international law, Cambridge University Press, Cambridge, 2014.
NOLLKAEMPER, A., PLAKOKEFALOS, I., Principles of shared responsibility in international law. An appraisal of the state of the art, Cambridge University Press, Cambridge, 2015.
NOLLKAEMPER, A., REINISCH, A., JANIK, R., International law in domestic courts. A case book, Oxford University Press, Oxford, 2019.
NOLLKAEMPER, A., The duality of shared responsibility, in Contemporary Politics, 24 (5), 2018, pp. 528ss.
NOLLKAEMPER, A., The internationalized rule of law, in Hague Journal on the

Rule of Law, 1, 2009, pp. 76ss.

NOLLKAEMPER, A., The power of secondary rules to conneect the international and national legal orders, in T. BROUDE, Y. SHANY, Multisourced equivalent norms in international law, Hart Publishing, Oxford & Oregon, Portland, 2011, pp. 45ss.

NOLTE, G., AUST, H.P., Equivocal helpers. Complicity states, mixed messages and international law, in International and Comparative Law Quarterly, 58, 2009, pp. 14ss.

NOLTE, G., The International Law Commission facing the second decade of the twenty first century, in U. FASTENRATH et al., From bilaterism to community interests, Oxford University Press, Oxford 2011, pp. 782ss.

NOLTE, G., Third Report for the ILC Study Group on Treaties over time: Subsequent agreements and subsequent practice outside of judicial or quasi-judicial proceedings, in G. NOLTE, Treaties and subsequent practice, Oxford University Press, 2013, pp. 310ss.

NOLTE, G., Treaties and subsequent practice, Oxford University Press, Oxford, 2013.

NOORTMANN, M., Enforcing international law: From self-help to self-contained regimes, ed. Routldge, London & New York, 2016.

NORTMANN, M., REINISCH, A., RYNGAERT, C., Non state actors in international law, Bloomsbury Publishing, New York, 2015, pp. 172ss.

NOUTE, G., Treaties and subsequent practice, Oxford University Press, Oxford, 2013, pp. 224ss.

NOVÁKY, N.I.M., European Union military operations: A collective action perspective, ed. Routledge, London & New York, 2018.

NOVOSSELOFF, A., United Nations-European Union. Cooperation in the field of peacekeeping. Challenges and prospects, in Global Governance Institute, Analysis Paper, June 2012.

NOYES, J.E., SMITH, B.D., State responsibility and the principle of joint and national liability, in Yale Journal of International Law, 13, 1988, pp. 234ss.

NTUBE NGANG, S., The position of witnesses before the International Criminal Court, ed. Brill, The Hague, 2015.

NYSTEN, C., CASEY-MASLEN, S., GOLDEN BERSAGEL, A., Nuclear weapons under international law, Cambridge University Press, Cambridge, 2014.

O'KEEFE, R., World cultural heritage: Obligations to the international community as a whole?, in International and Comparative Law Quarterly, 53, 2004, pp. 190ss.

O'MEARA, N., A more secure Europe of rights? The European Court of Human Rights, the Court of Justice of the European Union and EU Accession to the ECHR, in German Law Journal, 12, 2011, pp. 1813-1832.

O'KEEFE, R., Universal jurisdiction: Clarifying the basic concept, in Journal of International Criminal Justice, 2, 2004, pp. 735-760.

OBERMATT, J., The development of customary international law by international organizations, in International & Comparative Law Quarterly, 66 (2), 2017, pp. 494ss.

OCHOA RUIZ, N., Las cláusulas compromisorias de las convenciones de derechos humanos de las Naciones Unidas a la jurisdicción de la ICJ Internacional de Justicia: ¿un mecanismo jurisdiccional de protección de los derechos humanos?, in Anuario Espaňol de Derecho International, 19, 2003, pp. 263ss.

OCHOA-RUIZ, N., SALAMANCA-AGUADO, E., Exploring the limits of international law on the use of force, in European Journal of International Law, 16 (3), 2005, pp. 500ss.

ODELLO, M., PIOTROWIC, R., International military missions and international law, ed. Brill, Bruxelles, 2011, pp. 136ss.

ODENDAHL, K., Article 30, in K. SCHMALENBACH, O. DÖRR, Vienna convention on the law of treaties. A commentary, ed. Springer, Berlin, Berlin, Heidelberg, 2012, pp. 512ss.

ODRIOZOLA GURRUTZAGA, M., Responsabilidad penal por crìmenes internacionales y coautoria medita, in Revista Electrònica de Ciencia Penal y Criminologia, 17, 2015, pp. 7ss.

OHLIN, J.D., GOVERN, K., FINKELSTEIN, C., (eds.), Cyber war, law and ethics for virtual conflicts, Oxford University Press, Oxford, 2015, pp. 130ss.

OHLIN, J.D., Targeting and the concept of intent, in Cornell Law Faculty Publications, paper 774, 2013, pp. 84ss.

OLALEKAN YUSSUF, E., A critical evaluation of the UN Security Council's power in form of article 39 of the United Nations Charter: Interpretation, invocation and the morder threat to international peace and security, in Independent Student Journal Law, 2018 (1), pp. 7-9.

OLIVECRONA, K., Law as fact, Oxford University Press, Oxford, 1939, pp. 130ss.

OLSON, P.M., A NATO perspective on applicability and application of international humanitarian law to multinational forces, in International Review of Red Cross, 95, 2013, pp. 654ss.

OOSTHUIZEN, G.H., Playring the devil's adovacte: The United Nations Security Counil is unbound by law, in Leiden Journal of International Law, 12, 1999, pp. 562ss.

OPPENHEIM, L., International law. A treatise, Longmann Green & Co., London, 1955, pp. 354ss.

ORAKHELASHVILI, A., Division of reparation between responsible entities, in J. CRAWFORD, A. PELLET, S. OLLESON, The law of international responsibility, Oxford University Press, Oxford, 2010, pp. 648ss.

ORAKHELASHVILI, A., International public order and the international court's adivosry opinion on the construction of a wall in the ocupied palestinian territory, in Archiv des Völkerrechts, 43, 2005, pp. 248.

ORAKHELASHVILI, A., Peremptory norms in international law, Oxford University Press, Oxford, 2006.

ORAKHELASHVILI, Q., Division of reparation between responsible entities, in J. CRAWFORD, A. PELLET, S. OLLESON, The law of international

responsibility, Oxford University Press, Oxford, 2010, pp. 658ss.
ORAKHELASHVILL, A., Jurisdictional immunities of the state (Germany v. Italy; Greece intervening), in American Journal of International Law, 106 (3), 2012, pp. 610ss.
ORENTLICHER, D., Some kind of justice. The ICTY's impact in Bosnia and Serbia, Oxford University Press, Oxford, 2018, pp. 376ss.
ORFORD, A., Jurisdiction without territory: From the holy roman empire to the responsibility to protect, in Michigan Journal of International Law, 30 (3), 2009, pp. 982ss.
ORREGO VICUÑA, F., Le règime d'exploration et d'exploitation, in R.J. DUPUY, D. VIGNES, Traitè du nouveau de la mer, ed. Economica, PaResolution Bruxelles, 1985, pp. 552ss.
ORTIZ, P.J.C., EU treaties and the judicial politics of national courts: A law and politics approach, ed. Routledge, London New York, 2015.
OSSENBÜHL, F., Rechtliche grundfragen der Erteilung von Schulzeugnbissen, Duncker & Humblot, Berlin, 2019, pp. 51ss.
OSTOJIC, M., Between justice and stability: The politics of war crimes prosecutions, Ashgate Publishing, Farnham, 2014.
OSWALD, B., DURHAM, H., BATES, A., Documents on the law of UN peace operations, Oxford University Press, Oxford, 2010, pp. 52ss.
OUDE ELFERINIC, A.G., HENRIKSEN, T., VEIERUD BUSCH, S., Maritime boundary delimitation: The case law: Is it consistent and predictable?, Cambridge University Press, Cambridge, 2018.
OUDE ELFERINK, A.G., The delimitation of the continental shelf between Denmark, Germany and the Netherlands, Cambridge University Press, Cambridge, 2014.
PAASIVIRTA, E., KUIJPER, P.J., Does one size fit all? The European Community and the responsibility of international organizations, in Netherlands Yearbook of International Law, 36, 2005, pp. 169-226.
PADDEU, F., Justification and excuse in international law. Concept and theory of general defences, Cambridge University Press, Cambridge, 2018.
PADDEU, F.I., Countermeasures, in Max Planck Encyclopedia of International Law, 2015.
PAJUSTE, T., The evolution of the concept of immunity of international organizations, in East West Studies, 8, 2017.
PALCHETTI, P., Attributing the conduct of dutchbat in Srebrenica: The 2014 Judgment of the District Court in the Mothers of Srebrenica Case, in The Netherlands International Law Review, 62, 2015, pp. 279-294, 283-285.
PALCHETTI, P., Can State action on behalf of victims be an alternative to individual access to justice in case of grave breaches of human rights?, in Italian Yearbook of International Law, 24, 2014, pp. 53ss.
PALCHETTI, P., Exploring alternative routes: The obligation of members to enable the organization to make reparation, in M. RAGAZZI, Responsibility of international organizations. Essays in memory of Sir Ian Brownlie, Martinus Nijhoff Publishers, Leiden, Boston, 2013, pp. 303ss.

PALCHETTI, P., Litigating member state responsibility. The Monetary Gold principle and the protection of absent organizations, in International Organization Law Review, 12, 2015, pp. 468ss.

PALCHETTI, P., The allocation of responsibility for internationally, committed in the course of multinational operations, in International Review of the Red Cross, 95, 2013, pp. 727-742.

PALM, T., The changing character of EUFOR Althea: Power politics or learning?, in Cambridge Review of International Affairs, 30 (1), 2017, pp. 68ss.

PALMISANO, G., Les causes d'aggravation de la responsabilitè des États et la distinction entre "crimes" et "dèlits" internationaux, in Revue Gènèrale de Droit International Public, 98, 1994, pp. 629ss.

PALWANKAR, U., Applicability of international humanitarian law to United Nations peacekeeping forces, in International Review of Red Cross, 81, 1993, pp. 228.

PANARA, C., The sub-national dimension of the EU: A legal study of multilevel governance, ed. Springer, Berlin, 2015.

PAPARINSKIS, M., Procedural aspects of shared responsibility in the International Court of Justice, in Journal of International Dispute Settlements, 4 (2), 2013, pp. 310ss.

PAPASTAVRIDIS, E., Interpretation of Security Council Resolutions under Chapter VII in the aftermath of the Iraqi crisis, in International and Comparartive Law Quarterly, 56 (1), 2007, pp. 84ss.

PARRY, J., (Review): Ways and means of making the evidence of customary international law more readily available: Preparatory work within the purview of article 24 of the statute of the International Law Commission (Memorandum submitted by the Secretary-General), in International Law Quarterly, 3, 1950, pp. 462ss.

PARRY, J., The political theory of treaties in the restatements of foreign relations law, Brigham Young University Law Review, 2016, pp. 1618ss.

PATTERSON, D., SÖDERSTEN, A., European Union law and international law, ed. Wiley Blackwell, New York, 2016.

PAUST, J.J., The U.N. is bound by human rights: Understanding the full reach of human rights, remedies, and non immunity, in Harvard International Law Journal, 51, 2010, pp. 4-9.

PAVONI, R., Human rights and the immunities of foreign states and international organizations, in E. DE WET, J. VIDMAR, Hierarchy in international law: The place of human rights, Oxford University Press, Oxford, 2012, pp. 71ss.

PAYÁ MARTÍNEZ, I., Derecho internacional pùblico: teorìa y casos pràcticos, Murcia, Madrid, 2008.

PAYNE, T., Teaching old law new tricks: Applying and adapting state responsibility to cyber operations, in Lewis & Clark Law Review, 20, 2016, pp. 686ss.

PEAY, J., Mental incapacity and criminal liability: Redrawing the fault lines?, in International Journal of Law and Psychiatry, 42, 2015, pp. 4ss.

PECK, C., The United Nations as a dispute settlement system. Improving mechanisms for the prevention and resolution of conflict, Kluwer Law International, The Hague, London, Boston, 1996.

PEEL, J., Notice of claim by an injured state, in J. CRAWFORD, A. PELLET, S. OLLESON, The law of international responsibility, Oxford University Press, Oxford, 2010, pp. 1032.

PEERS, S., The EU's Accession to the ECHR: The dream becomes a nightmare, in German Law Journal, 16, 2015, pp. 213, 222.

PEGORIER, C., Ethnic cleansing: A legal qualification, ed. Routledge, London, New York, 2013.

PEJIC, J., The protective scope of common article 3: More than meets the eye, in International Review of the Red Cross, 93, 2011, pp. 5-7.

PELLET, A., International Organizations are definitely not States, in M. RAGAZZI, Responsibility of International Organizations. Essays in memory of Sir Ian Brownlie, ed. Brill, Bruxelles, 2013, pp. 41ss.

PELLET, A., L'imputabilitè d'èventuels actes illicites. Responsabilitè de l'OTAN ou des États membres, in C. TOMUSCHAT, Kosovo and the international community: A legal assessment, ed. Brill, The Hague, 2002, pp. 194ss.

PELLET, A., Les articles de la CDI rur la responsabilité de l'État pour faits internationalement illicite suite-et fin ?, in Annuaire Français de Droit International, 48, 2002, pp. 17.

PELLET, A., Shaping the future of international law: The role of the world court in law-making, in M. H. ARSANJANI, Looking to the future: Essays on International Law in Honor of W. Michael Reisman, Martinus Nijhoff Publishers, The Hague, 2011, pp. 1066ss.

PELLET, A., Vive le crime! Remarques sur les degrès de l'illicite en droit international, in International law on the eve of the twentieth century, views from the international law commission, United Nations Publications, New York, 1997, pp. 288ss.

PERELMAN, C., Le raisonnable et le dèraisonnable en droit, in Archives de Philosphie du Droit, 29, 1978, pp. 35ss.

PEREZ GONZALEZ, M., Les organizations internationale et le droit de la responsabilitè, in Revue Gènèrale de Droit International Public, 92, 1988, pp. 67ss.

PERNICE, I., Die Haftung internationaler Organizationen und ihrer Mitarbeiter-dargetellt am "Fall" des internationalen Zinnrates, in Archiv des Völkerrechts, 26, 1988, pp. 419ss.

PEROVA, N., Disentangling "effective control" test for the purpose of attribution of the conduct of UN peacekeepers to the State and the UN, in Nordic Journal of International Law, 86 (1), 2017, pp. 32ss.

PERRET, R.L., De la faute et du devoir en droit international, Polygraphischer Verlag, Zürich, 1962, pp. 1506ss.

PERRIN, G., L'agression contre la lègation de Roumanie à à Berne et les fondements de la responsibilitè internationale dans les dèlits d'omission, in Revue Gènèrale de Droit International Public, 61, 1957, pp. 410ss.

PERSONNAZ, J., La rèparation du prèjuice en droit international public, ed.

Sirey, Paris, 1939.
PERUGINI, N., GORDON, N., The human right to dominate, Oxford University Press, Oxford, 2015.
PESCATORE, P., Les relations extèrieurs des Communautès europèennes, in Recueil des cours, ed. Brill, Bruxelles, 1961, pp. 134ss.
PETCULESCU, I., Droit international de la responsabilitè et droits de l'homme, in Revue Gènèrale de Droit International Public, 109, 2005, pp. 590ss.
PETERS, A., International organizations: Effectiveness and accountability, in Max Planck International Law Research Paper Series, No. 2016-01, p. 10.
PETERS, A., Subsequent practice and established practice of International Organizations: in Göttingen Journal of International Law, 3/2, 2011, pp. 618ss.
PETERS, A., The responsibility to protect and the permanetnt five-the obligation to give reasons for a veto, in J. HOFFMANN, A. NOLLAEMPER, Responsibility to protect. From principle to practice, Palas Publication, Amsterdam, 2012, pp. 205ss.
PETERS, A., The Security Council's responsibility to protect, in International Organizations Law Review, 8, 2011, pp. 4ss.
PETERSEN, N., Customary law without custom? Rules, principles, and the role of State practice in international law creation, in American University International Law Review, 23, 2008, pp. 276ss.
PETITE, M., The battle over Strasbourg: The protection of human rights across Europe has suffered a setback, thanks to the Court of Justice of the European Union, in Competition Law Insight, 2015, pp. 10ss.
PETROV, P., Early institutionalisation of the ESDP governance arrangements: Insights from the operations Concordia and Artemis, in S.VANHOONACKER, D. HYLKE, M. HEIDI (eds). Understanding the role of bureaucracy in the European Security and Defence Policy, in European Integration online Papers, 14 (1), 2010.
PETSCHE, M., Jus cogens as a vision of the international legal order, in Penn State International Law Review, 29 (2), 2010, pp. 242ss.
PFANNER, T., Various mechanisms and approaches for implementing international humanitarian law and protecting and assisting war victims, in International Law Red Cross, 91, 2009, pp. 280ss.
PHELAN, W., What is sui generis about the European Union? Costly international cooperation in a self-contained regime, in International Studies Review, 14 (3), 2012, pp. 368ss.
PICCOLO, I., The crime of rape in international criminal law, International Courts Association, 2013.
PICHON, J., The principle of complementarity in the cases of the sudanese nationals Ahmad Harun and Ali Kushayb before the ICC, in International Criminal Law Review, 8 (1-2), 2008.
PICOD, F., La Cour de justice a dit non à l'adhésion de l'Union européenne à la Convention EDH, in La Semaine Juridique, Édition Générale, 2015, pp. 230, 234.

PINGEL-LENUZZA, I., Remarques sur le procèdure dans l'affaire de la dèlimitation maritime et des questions teritoriales entre Quatar et Bahrèn. Cour Internationale de Justice, arrêts du 1er juillet 1994 et du 15 fèvrier 1995, in Revue Gènèrale de Droit International Public, 101, 1996, pp. 180ss.

PISILLO MAZZESCHI, R., Access to justice in constitutional and international law: The recent judgment of the Italian Constitutional Court, in Italian Yearbook of International Law, 24, 2014, pp. 9-23.

PISILLO MAZZESCHI, R., Impact on the law of diplomatic protection, in M.T. KAMMINGA, M. SCHEININ, The impact of human rights law on general international law, Oxford University Press, Oxford, 2009, pp. 219ss.

PISILLO MAZZESCHI, R., International obligations to provide for reparation claims?, in A. RANDELZHOFER, C. TOMUSCHAT, State responsibility and the individual. Reparation in instances of grave violations of human rights, ed. Brill, The Hague, 1999, pp. 159ss.

PISILLO MAZZESCHI, R., Reparation claims by individuals for state breaches of humanitarian law and human rights: An overview, in Journal of International Criminal Justice, 1 (3), 2003, pp. 339-347.

PISILLO MAZZESCHI, R., The marginal role of the individual in the ILC's articles on State responsibility, in Italian Yearbook of International law, 14 (1), 2004, pp. 44ss.

PITSCHAS, C., Die volkerrechtliche Verantwortlichkeit der Europaischen Gemeinschaft und ihrer Mitgliedstaaten, Duncker & Humblot, Berlin, 2001.

PLAKOKEFALOS, I., Causation in the law of state responsibility and the problem of overdetermination. In search of clarity, in European Journal of International Law, 26, 2015, pp. 472ss.

PLENGE, A., The special tribunal for Lebanon. Decision on the disclosure of materials from the criminal file of Mr El Sayed, in International Legal Materials, 50 (6), 2011, pp. 1099ss.

PODESTÁ COSTA, L.A., Derecho internacional publico, Editora Argentina, Buenos Aires, 1955, pp. 414ss.

POELLE, M.P., The international responsibility of international organizations in peacekeeping operations, Cambridge University Press, Cambridge, 2017, pp. 168ss.

POHLREICH, E., Das rechtliche Gehör im Strafverfahren, Mohr Siebeck, Tübingen, 2016, pp. 148ss.

POLAKIEWICZ, J., EU law and the ECHR: Will the European Union's accession square the circle?, in European Human Rights Law Review, 6, 2013, pp. 592-605.

POLITIS, N.S., The problème des limitations de la souverainetè and the théorie de la abus de droits dans les rapports internationaux, in Recueil des cours, ed. Brill, Brussels, vol. 6, 1925, pp. 10ss.

POMERANCE, M., The ICJ's advisory jurisdiction and the crumbling wall between the political and the judicial, in American Journal of International Law, 99, 2005, pp. 28ss.

POMMIER, B., The use of force to protect civilians and humanitarian action: The case of Lybia and beyond, in International Review of the Red Cross, 93, 2011, pp. 1063ss.

PORRO, S., Risk and mental element: An analysis of national and international law on core crimes, ed. Nomos, Baden-Baden, 2014.

PORTMANN, R., Legal personality in international law, Cambridge University Press, Cambridge, 2010, pp. 233ss.

POSTEMA, G.L., Custom in international law: A normative practice account, in A. PERREAU-SAUSSINE, J. B. MURPHY, The nature of customary law: Legal, historical and philosophical perspectives, Cambridge University Press, Cambridge, 2007, pp. 280ss.

POTTEAU, A., Quelle adhésion de l'Union Européenne à la CEDH pour quel niveau de protection des droits et de l'autonomie de l'ordre juridique de l'UE?, in Revue Générale Droit International Public, 115, 2011, pp. 77-111.

POWELL, C., You have no God: An analysis of the prosecution of genocidal rape in international criminal law, in Richmond Public Interest Law Review, 20, 2017, pp. 26ss.

PROELLS, A., Article 34, K. SCHMALENBACH, O. DÖRR, Vienna convention on the law of treaties. A commentary, ed. Springer, Berlin, 2012, pp. 622-642.

PROELSS, A., United Nations Convention on the law of the sea. A commentary, H. Beck/Hart Publishing, München/Oxford & Oregon, Portland, 2017, pp. 970ss.

PROST, M., The concept of unity in public international law, Hart Publishing, Oxford & Oregon, Portland, 2012.

PROULX, V.J., An uneasy transition?, in M. RAGAZZI, Responsibility of International Organizations. Essays in memory of Sir Ian Brownlie, ed. Brill, Bruxelles, 2013, pp. 112ss.

PROULX, V.J., Institutionalizing state responsibility, Oxford University Press, Oxford, 2016.

PROVOST, R., State responsibility in international law, ed. Routledge, Aldershot, 2002.

PROVOST, R., State responsibility in international law, ed. Routledge, London & New York, 2017.

PRZETACZNIK, F., La responsabilitè internationale de l'Etat à raison des prèjudices de caractère moral et politique causès à un autre Etat, in Revue Gènèrale de Droit International Public, 78, 1974, pp. 943ss.

QUENEUDEC, J.D., La responsabilitè internationale de l'Etat pour les fautes personnelles de ses agents, LGDJ, Paris, 1966, pp. 252ss.

QUIGLEY, J., Complicity in international law. A new direction in the law of state responsibility, in British Yearbook of International Law, 57, 1986, pp. 78ss.

QUIGLEY, J., Responsabilitè internationale, ed. Pedone, Paris, 1987.

QUIGLEY, J., State responsibility for ethnic cleansing, in University of California Davis Law Review, 32, 1999, pp. 342ss.

QUIGLEY, J., The International Law Commission's crime-delict distinction: A toothless tiger?, in Revue de Droit International de Sciences Diplomatiques et Politiques, 65, 1987, pp 118ss.

QUIRILO, O., The international responsibility of the European Union. A basic interpretive pattern, in Hungarian Yearbook of International and European Law, 63, 2013.

QUISPE-REMÓN, D.J.L., El debido proceso en el derecho internacional y en el sistema interamericano, ed. Tirant lo Blanc, Valencia, 2010.

RABI, U., International intervention in local conflicts. Crisis management and conflict resolution in the cold war, I.B. Tauris Publishers, London & New York, 2010.

RAGAZZI, M., International responsibility today, Martinus Nijhoff Publishers, Leiden, 2005.

RAGAZZI, M., Responsibility of International Organizations. Essays in memory of Sir Ian Brownlie, Martinus Nijhoff Publishers, Leiden, 2013.

RAGAZZI, M., The concept of international obligations erga omnes, Clarendon Press, Oxford, 1997, pp. 43-72.

RAGNI, C., The contribution of Special Tribunal for Lebanon to the notion of terrorism: Judicial creativity or progressive development of international law, in N. BOSCHIERO, T. SCOVAZZI, C. PITEA, C. RAGNI, International courts and the development of international law. Essays in Honour of Tullio Treves, T.M.C. Asser Press-Springer, The Hague, 2013, pp. 671ss.

RAINEY, B., WICKS, W., OVEY, C., Jacobs, White and Ovey: The European Convention on Human Rights, Oxford University Press, Oxford, 2017.

RAMA MONTALDO, M., International legal personality and implied powers of international organizations, in The British Yearbook of Inernational Law, 44, 1970, pp. 112ss.

RANJEVA, R., L'environnement, la Cour Internationale de Justice et la chambre spèciale pour les questions de l'environnement, in Annuaire Français de Droit International, 40, 1994, pp. 434ss.

RANK, R., Modern war and the validity of treaties: A comparative study, in Cornell Law Quarterly, 38 (1), 1952-1953, pp. 321ss.

RAO, P.S., Comments on article 19 of the draft articles on state responsibility adopted by the International Law Commission, in Indian Journal of International Law, 37, 1997, pp. 694ss.

RASHKOW, B., Remedies for harm caused by UN peacekeepers, in AJIL Unbound, 108, 2014, pp. 125ss.

RAUBER, J., Struktur Wandel als Prinzipien Wandel: Theoretische, dogmatische und methodische Bausteine eines Prinzipien modelles des Völkerrechts und seiner Dynamik, ed. Springer, Berlin, 2017, pp. 22ss.

RAVASI, E., Doctrine of equivalent protection in human rights protection by the ECtHR and the ECJ, ed. Brill, The Hague, 2017, pp. 24ss.

RAYFUSE, R., War and the environment. New approaches to protecting the environment in relation to armed conflict, Martinus Nijhoff Publishers, The Hague, 2014, pp. 180ss.

RAZ, J., ALEXY, R., BULYGIN, E., Un discusiòn sobre la teorìa del derecho, Marcial Pons, Madrid, 2007, pp. 100ss.

REIBSTEIN, E., Völkerrecht-Eine Geschichte seiner Ideen und Praxis, Alber

Verlag, Freiburg-München, 1958, pp. 338ss.
REICHARD, M., The European Union-NATO relationship: A legal and political perspective, ed. Routledge, London & New York, 2016, pp. 247ss.
REICHEL, P., ALBANESE, J., Handbook of transnational crime and justice, Sage Publications, New York, 2013.
REICHLER, P., The impact of the Nicaragua case on matters of evidence and fact-finding, in Leiden Journal of International Law, 25 (1), 2012, pp. 152ss.
REINALDA, B., BERBEEK, B., Autonomous policy making by international organizations, ed. Routledge, London & New York, 1998, pp. 4ss.
REINISCH, A., Aid or assistance and direction and control between states and international organizations in the commission of internationally wrongful acts, in International Organization Law Review, 7, 2010, pp. 64ss.
REINISCH, A., Developing human rights and humanitarian law accountability of the Security Council for the imposition of economic actions, in American Journal of International Law, 95, 2001, pp. 852ss.
REINISCH, A., international organizations before national courts, Cambridge University Press, Cambridge, 2000.
REINISCH, A., KNAHR, C., From United Nations administrative tribunal to the United Nations appeals tribunal-Reform of administration of justice system within the United Nations, in Max Planck Yearbook of United Nations Law, 12, 2008, pp. 447ss.
REINISCH, A., The privilege and immunities of international organizations in domestic courts, Oxford University Press, Oxford, 2013, pp. 324ss.
REINISCH, A., Veerfahrensrechtliche Aspekte der Rechtskontrolle von Organen der Staatengemeinschfat in R. HOFMANN, A. REINISCH, T. PFEIFFER, S. OETER, A. STADLER, Berichte der Deutschen Gesellschaft für Völkerrecht: Die Rechtskontrolle von Organen der Staatengemeischaft; Vielfalt der Fericht-Einheit des Prozessrecht?, C.F. Müller, Heidelberg, 2007, pp. 44ss.
REINOLD, T., The responsibility to protect-much ado about nothing?, in Review of International Studies, 36, 2010.
REISMAN, W.M., Kosovo's antinomies, in American Journal of International Law, 93 (4), 1999.
REISMAN, W.M., Nullity and revision, Yale University Press, New Haven, 1970, pp. 329ss.
REISMAN, W.M., The cult of custom in the late 20th century, in California Western International Law Journal, 17, 1987, pp. 134ss.
REISMAN, W.M., The democratization of contemporary international law-making processes and the differentiation of their application, in R. WOLFRUM, V. RÖBEN, Developments of international law in treaty making, ed. Springer, Berlin, 2005, pp. 16.
REITZER, L., La rèparation comme consèquence de l'acte illicite en droit international, ed. Sirey, Paris, 1938, pp. 134ss.
RENSMANN, T., Die Humansierung des Völkerrects durch das ius in bello. Von der Marten'schen Klausel zur Responsibility to protect, in Zeitschrift für

ausländisches Recht und Völkerrecht, 68, 2008, pp. 120ss.
RENZIKOWSKI, J., Teilnahme, in R. MAURACH, K.H. GÖSSEL, H. ZIPF, Strafrecht, allegemeiner teils. Teilband 2: Erscheinungsformen des Verbrechens und Rechtsfolgen der Tat, ed. Springer, Heidelberg, 2014, pp. 531ss.
REUTER, P., Droit international public, ed. Brill, Bruxelles, 1983, pp. 224ss.
REUTER, P., La responsabilitè internationale. Droit international public, ed. Thèmis, Paris, 1956, pp. 56ss.
REUTER, P., Sixième rapport sur la question des traitès conclus entre États et organizations internationales ou entre deux ou plusiers organizations internationales, UN Doc. A/CN. 4/298, in Anuaire de la Commission du Droit International, 1977, vol. II, p. 127ss, par. 25.
REUTER, P., Trois observations sur la codification de la responsabilitè internationale des Etats pour fit illicite, in Mèlanges Virally, ed. Pedone, Paris, 1991.
REYNOLDS, R., Human rights in the line of fire: Al-Skeini v. United Kingdom, in Judicial Review, 16, 2011, pp. 340ss.
RID, T., BUCHANAN, R., Attributing cyber attacks, in The Journal of Strategic Studies, 38, 2015, pp. 7ss.
RIDDERVOLD, M., ROSÉN, G., Trick and treat: How the Commission and the European Parliament exert influence in EU Foreign and Security Policies, in Journal of European Integration 38 (6), 2016, pp. 688ss.
RIDEAU, J., GREWE, C., BALMOND, L. ARCARI, A., Sanctions ciblèes et protection juridictionnelle des droit fondamentaux dans l'Union europèenne. Équilibre et dèsèquilibre de la balance, ed. Anthemis, Bruxelles, 2010.
RIGAUX, F., International responsibility and the principle of causality, in M. RAGAZZI, International responsibility today. Essays in memory of Oscar Schachter, Martinus Nijhoff Publishers, Leiden, Boston, 2005, pp. 88ss.
RIPHAGEN, W., Cinquième rapport siur le contenu, les formes et les degrès de la responsabilitè internatonale (deuxième partie du projet d'articles), Annuaire de la Commissione de Droit International, 1984, II, p. 1ss, p. 4.
RIPHAGEN, W., Quatrème rapport sur le contenu, les formes et le degrès de la responsabilitè internationale (deuxième partie du projet d'articles), in Annuaire de la Commission de Droit International, 1983, II, 1, p. 4ss.
RIPHAGEN, W., Sixth report on the content, forms an ddegrees of international responsibility (part two of the draft articles) and "implementation" (mise en oeuvre) of international responsibility and the settlement of disputes (part three of the draft articles), Doc. A/CN.4/389 and Corr. 1&2, in Yearbook of International Law Commission, 1985, vol. II, p. 3ss.
RIPHAGEN, W., The international concern for the environment as expressed in the concepts of the "common heritage of mankind" and of "shared natural resources," in M. BOTHE, Trends in environmental policy and law, Gland, Switzerland, 1980, pp. 343ss.
RITTER, J.P., La protective diplomatique à l'egard d'une organization internationale, in Annuaire Français de Droit International, 8, 1962, pp. 445ss.

ROBERT, E., The jurisdictional immunities of International Organizations: The balance between the protection of the organizations interest and individual rights, in Mélanges en l'honneur de Jean Salmon, ed. Bruylant, Bruxelles, 2007, pp. 1445ss.

ROBERTS, A.E., Traditional and modern approaches to customary international law: A reconciliation, in American Journal of International Law, 95, 2001, pp. 758ss.

ROBERTS, F.R.J., ARAUJO, S.J., Implementation of the ICJ advisory opinion. Legal consequences of the construction of a wall in the occupied Palestinian territory. Hences (do not) make good neighbors?, in Boston University of International Law Journal, 23, 2004, pp. 358ss.

ROBERTS, I., Satow's diplomatic practice, Oxford University Press, Oxford, 2017, pp. 314ss.

ROBINSON, P.H., GRALL, J.A., Element analysis in defining criminal liability: The model penal code and beyond, in Stanford Law Review, 35, 1983, pp. 685ss.

RODENHÄUSER, T., Organizing rebellion: Non-state armed groups under international humanitarian law, human rights and international criminal law, Oxford University Press, Oxford, 2018.

RONZITTI, N., NATO's intervention in Libya: A genuine action to protect a civil population in mortal danger or an intervention aimed at regime change?, in Italian Yearbook of International Law, 21, 2011, pp. 4ss.

ROONEY, J.M., The relationship between attribution and jurisdiction after Jaloud v. Netherlands, in Netherlands International Law Review, 62, (3), 2015, pp. 407.

ROSAS, A., Balancing fundamental rights in EU law, in Cambridge Yearbook of European Legal Studies, 16, 2014, pp. 348ss.

ROSCINI, M., Cyber operations and use of force, Oxford University Press, Oxford, 2014, pp. 34ss.

ROSCINI, M., Evidentiary issues in international disputes related to state responsibility for cyber operations, in Texas International Law Journal, 50, 2015.

ROSENBERG, S.P., Responsibility to protect: A framework for prevention, in Global Responsibility to Protect, 1, 2009, pp. 442ss.

ROSENNE, S., State responsibility and international crimes further reflections on article 19 of the draft articles on state responsibility, New York Journal of Law & Policy, 30, 1998, pp. 146ss.

ROSENNE, S., The law and practice of the international Court, ed. Brill, Dordrecht, Boston, 1985, pp. 324ss.

ROSENSTOCK, R., The ILC and state responsibility, in American Journal of International Law, 96, 2002, pp. 794ss.

ROSS, A., A textbook of international law, general part, The Lawbook Exchange Ltd., London, 1947 and reprinted edition of 2013.

ROSENTRETER, D., Article 31 (3) c) of the Vienna convention on the law of treaties and the principle of systemic integration in international investment law and arbitration, ed. Nomos, Baden-Baden, 2015, pp. 217ss.

ROTH, A., Das völkerrechtiche Delikt vor und in den Verhandlungen auf der Haager Kodificationskonferenz 1930, Robert Noske, Leipzig, 1932, pp. 54ss.

ROUSSEAU, C., La responsabilitè internationale, in Cours de droit international public, ed. Pedone, Paris, 1959-1960, pp. 8ss.

ROXBURGH, R.F., International conventions and third states, Longmans Green, London, 1917.

ROXSTRUM, E., GIBSON, M., EINARSEN, T., The NATO bombing case (Banković et al. v. Belgium et al.) and the limits of western human rights protection, in Boston University International Law Journal, 23, 2005, pp. 58ss.

RUSSO, D., The Injured individual's right to compensation in the law on diplomatic protection, in Rivista di Diritto Internazionale, 2016, pp. 725ss.

RUYS, T., CORTEN, O., HOFER, A., The use of force in international law. A case based approach, Oxford University Press, Oxford, 2018, pp. 538ss.

RUZIÉ, D., Droit international public, Dalloz, Paris, 2015.

RYNGAERT, C., Apportioning responsibility between the UN and member states in UN peace-support operations: An inquiry into the application of the effective control standard after Behrami, in Israel Law Review, 45, 2012, pp. 152ss.

RYNGAERT, C., BUCHANAN, H., Member state responsibility for the acts of international organizations, in Utrecht Law Review, 7, 2011, pp. 132ss.

RYNGAERT, C., The European Court of Human Rights approach to Member States responsibility in connection with acts of International Organizations, in International and Comparative Law Quarterly, 60 (4), 2011, pp. 1000ss.

RYNGAERT, C., The responsibility of Member States of International Organizations. Concluding observations, in International Organization Law Review, 12, 2015, pp. 516ss.

RYNGAERT, C., WOUTERS, J., Impact on the process of the formation of customary international law, in M.T. KAMMINGA, M. SCHEININ, The impact of human rights law on general international law, Oxford University Press, Oxford, 2009, pp. 112ss.

RYNGAERT, S., DEKKER, I.F., WESSEL, R.A., Judicial missions on the law of international organizations, Oxford University Press, Oxford, 2016, pp. 325ss.

RYNIKER, A., L'application du droit international humanitaire et les opèrations militaires organisèes en vertu de la Charte des Nations Unies, in International Review of Red Cross, 86, 1999, pp. 796ss.

SADURSKA, R., CHINKIN, C.M., The collapse of the international tin council: A case of state responsibility?, in Virginia Journal of International Law, 30, 1989-1990, pp. 845ss.

SALINAS DE FRÍAS, A.M., SAMUEL, K., WHITE, N., Counter terrorism. International law and practice, Oxford University Press, Oxford, 2012.

SALMON, J., Dictionnaire du droit international public, ed. Bruylant, Bruxelles, 2001, pp. 587.

SALMON, J., La fait ètatique complexe: une notion contestable, in Annuaire Français de Droit International, 28, 1982, pp. 710ss.

SALMON, J., Les accords Spaak-U Thant du 20 fevrier 1965, in Annuaire Français de Droit International, 11, 1965, pp. 479ss.

SALMON, J., Les circonstances excluant l'illiceitè, in J. SALMON, K. ZEMANEK, La responsabilitè internationale, ed. Pedone, Paris, 1987, pp. 90ss.

SALVIOLI, G., La responsabilitè des États et la fixation des dommages-intèrêts par les tribunaux internationaux, in Recueil des cours, ed. Brill, Bruxelles, vol. 28, 1929, pp. 238ss.

SAMSO, M., High hopes, scant resources: A word of scepticism about the anti-fragmentation function of article 31(3)(c) of the Vienna Convention on the Law of Treaties, in Leiden Journal of International Law, 24, 2011, pp. 5ss.

SAMUEL, K.L.H., WHITE, N.D., Counter-terrorism and international law, ed. Routledge, London & New York, 2017.

SÁNCHEZ REVERTE, R.S., Referencia al crimen de genocidio aprocimation genocide crime, in Revista de Estudios Juridicos, 16, 2016.

SANDHOLTZ, W., WHYTOCK, C.A., Research handbook on the politics of international law, Edward Elgar Publishers, Cheltenham, 2017, pp. 379ss.

SANDS, P., KLEIN, P., Bowett's law of international institutions, Sweet & Maxwell, London, 2009.

SARI, A., Jurisdiction and international peace support operations. The Behrami and Saramati cases, in Human Rights Law Review, 8 (1), 2008, pp. 154ss.

SARI, A., UN peacekeeping operations and article 7 ARIO: The missing link, in international organizations Law Review, 9 (1), 2012, pp. 77-85.

SARI, A., WESSEL, R.A., International responsibility for EU military operations: Finding the EU's place in the global accountability regime, in B. VAN VOOREN, S. BLOCKMANS, J. WOUTERS (eds.),The EU's role in global governance: The legal dimension, Oxford University Press, Oxford 2013, pp. 128ss.

SARKIN, J., Is the responsibility to protect an accepted norm of international law in the post-Libya era? How its third pillar ought to be applied, in Groningen Journal of International Law, 3, 2012, pp. 12ss.

SARKIN, J., The responsibility to protect and humanitarian intervention in Africa, in Global Responsibility to Protect, 2, 2010, pp. 371ss.

SAROOSHI, D., (ed.), Remedies and responsibility for the actions of international organizations, Martinus Nijhoff Publishers, The Hague, 2014, pp. 444ss.

SAROOSHI, D., International organizations and state responsibility, in M. RAGAZZI, Responsibility of international organizations. Essays in memory of Sir Ian Brownlie, Martinus Nijhoff Publishers, Leiden, Boston, 2013, pp. 86ss.

SAROOSHI, D., La responsabilité des organizations internationales: un état des lieux à l'issue des travaux de la Commission du droit international des Nations Unies, in Revue Belge de Droit International, 217, 2013.

SAROOSHI, D., Remedies and responsibility for actions of international organizations, ed. Brill, The Hague, 2014.
SASSÓLI, M., State responsibility for violations of international humanitarian law, in International Review of Red Cross, 84, 2002, pp. 414ss.
SAUER, F., System des Völkerrecht, V & R Unipress, Bonn, 1952, pp. 432ss.
SAUL, B., KINLEY, D., MOWBRAY, J.,The International Covenant on Economic, Social and Cultural Rights: Commentary, cases and materials, Oxford University Press, Oxford, 2014.
SAVARESE, E., Complicitè de l'État dans la perpètration d'actes de gènocide: les notions contiguës et la nature de la norme. En marge de la dècision application de la convention sur la prèvention et la rèpression du crime de gènocide (Bosnie-Herzègovine v. Serbie-et-Montenegro), in Annuaire Français de Droit International, 53, 2007, pp. 286ss.
SCHABAS, A.W., The European Convention on Human Rights: A commentary, Oxford University Press, Oxford, 2015, pp. 1755ss.
SCHABAS, W.A., Genocide and the International Court of Justice: Finally, a duty to prevent the crime of crimes, in Genocide Studies and Preventions, 2, 2007, pp. 101ss.
SCHABAS, W.A., Genocide law in a time of transition: Recent developments in the law of genocide, in Rutgers Law Review, 40, 2008-2009, pp. 162ss.
SCHABAS, W.A., The European Convention on Human Rights: A commentary, Oxford University Press, Oxford, 2015, pp. 1755ss.
SCHACHTER, O., Entangled treaty and custom, in Y. DINSTEIN, International law in a time of perplexity: Essays in Honor of Shabtai Rosenne, Martinus Nijhoff Publishers, Leiden/Boston, 1989, pp. 718ss.
SCHACHTER, O., Interpretation of the charter in the political organs of the United Nations, in S. ENGEL, Law, state and international legal order. Essays in Honor of Hans Kelsen, University of Tennesse Press, US, 1964, pp. 274ss.
SCHACHTER, O., New custom: Power, opinio juris and contrary practice, in J. MAKARCZYK, Theory of international law at the threshold of the 21st Century, Kluwer Law International, The Hague, 1996, pp. 532ss.
SCHACHTER, O., Self-defense and the rule of law, in American Journal of International Law, 83, 1989, pp. 26.
SCHACKELFORD, S., Holding States accountable for the ultimate human rights abuses: A review of the ICJ's Bosnian genocide case, in Human Rights Brief, 2007.
SCHARF, M.P., Accelerated formation of customary international law, in ILSA Journal of International & Comparative Law, 20 (2), 2014, pp. 310ss.
SCHARF, M.P., How the Tadić appeals chamber decision foundamentally altered customary international law, in M. STERIO, M. SCHARF, The legacy of ad hoc tribunals in international criminal law. Assessing the ICTY's and the ICTR's most significant legal accomplishments, Cambridge University Press, Cambridge, 2019.
SCHEININ, M., The Italian Constitutional Court's judgment 238 of 2014 is not another Kadi case, in Journal of International Criminal Justice, 13 (3), 2016,

pp. 616ss.

SCHERMERS, H.G., BLOKKER, N.M., International institutional law. Unity within diversity, ed. Brill, Dordrecht, Bruxelles, 2011, par. 1579.

SCHERMERS, H.G., International insitutional law, ed. Brill, Leiden, 1980, pp. 780ss.

SCHERMERS, H.G., Liability of international organizations in Leiden Journal of International law, 1 (1), 1988, pp. 4ss.

SCHERMES, H.G., BLOKKER, N.M., International institutional law. Unity within diversity, ed. Springer, Leiden, Boston, 2003, pp. 26ss.

SCHIELE, S., Evolution of international, environmental regimes. The case of climate change, Cambridge University Press, Cambrdige, 2014, pp. 83ss.

SCHINDLER, D., Die erga-omnes Wirkung des humanitären Völkerrecths, in U. BEYERLIN, M. BOTHE, R. HOFMANN, Recht zwischen Umbruch und Bewährung. Festschrift für Rudolf Bernhardt, ed. Springer, Berlin, 1995, pp. 200ss.

SCHINDLER, D., The different types of armed conflicts according to the Geneva Conventions and Protocols, in Recueil des Cours de l'Académie de Droit International, vol. 163, 1979, pp. 131ss.

SCHLÜTTER, B., Developments in customary international law, ed. Brill, Bruxelles, 2010, pp. 113ss.

SCHMALENBACH, K., Article 2, in K. SCHMALENBACH, O. DÖRR, Vienna convention on the law of treaties. A commentary, ed. Springer, Berlin, Heidelberg, 2012, pp. 45ss.

SCHMALENBACH, K., Die Haftung Internationaler Organizationen im Rahmen von Militäreinsätzen und Territorialverwaltungen, ed. Peter Lang, Frankfurt am Main, 2004, pp. 249.

SCHMALENBACH, K., DÖRR, O., Vienna convention on the law of treaties. A commentary, ed. Springer, Berlin, 2012, pp. 622-642.

SCHMALENBACH, K., Preserving the gordian knot: UN legal accountability in the aftermath of Srebrenica, in Netherlands International Law Review, 62, 2015, pp. 313ss.

SCHMITT, M.N., In defence of due diligence in cyber space, in Yale Journal Law Forum, 24, 2015, pp. 79ss.

SCHMITT, M.N., The development and principles of international humanitarian law, ed. Routledge, New York, 2017.

SCHNABEL, A., Kosovo and the challenge of humanitarian intervention: Selective indignation, collective action and international citizenship, United Nations University Press, Tokyo, 2000.

SCHÖN, P., Die völkerrechtliche Haftung der Staaten aus unerlaubten Handlugen, Breslau, Kern, 1917, pp. 34ss.

SCHRIJVER, N.J., The use of economic sanction by the UN Security Council: An international law perspective, in H.G. POST, International Economic Law and Armed Conflict, ed. Brill, Bruxelles, 1994, pp. 125ss.

SCHRÖDER, E., Die Grenzen der staatlichen Verantwortlichkeit für Handlungen von Staats-Organen im völkerrectkichen Verkehr, Zürich, 1939, pp. 22ss.

SCHÜTZE, R., TRIDIMAS, T., Oxford principles of European Union law, Oxford University Press, Oxford, 2018.

SCHWABACH, A., Yugoslavia v. NATO, Security Council Resolution 1244 and the law of humanitarian intervention, in Syracuse Journal of International Law and Commerce, 27 (1), 2000, pp. 92ss.

SCHWARTZBERG, J.E., Transforming the UN system designs fore a workable world, Brookings Institution Press, Tokyo, New York, Paris, 2016.

SCHWARZE, J., BECKER, V., HATJE, A., SCHOO, J., EU-Kommentar, ed. Nomos, Baden-Baden, 2019.

SCHWARZENBERGER, G., A manual of international law, Cambridge University Press, Cambridge, 1967, pp. 192ss.

SCHWARZENBERGER, G., Myths and realities of treaty interpretation: Articles 27-29 of the Vienna Draft Convention on the Law of Treaties, in Virginia Journal of International Law, 9, 1968, pp. 2ss.

SCHWARZENBERGER, J., International law, Stevens & Sons, London, 1957, pp. 348ss.

SCOBBIE, I., The invocation of responsibility for the breach of "obligations under peremptory norms of general international law," in European Journal of International Law, 13, 2002, pp. 1210.

SCOTT, G.L., CARR, L., Multilateral treaties and the formation of customary international law, in Denver Journal of International Law and Policy, 25, 1996, pp. 72ss.

SCOTT, J., The new EU extraterritoriality, in Common Market Law Review, 52, 2015, pp. 1343ss.

SCOVAZZI, T., Within and beyond mutatis mutandis, in M. RAGAZZI, The responsibility of international organizations. Essays in memory of Sir Ian Brownlie, Martinus Nijhoff Publishers, Leiden, Boston, 2013, pp. 122ss.

SEAMAN, P.J., International bounty hunting. A question of state responsibility, in California Western International Law Journal, 15, 1985, pp. 408ss.

SEAMAN, K., UN-tied Nations: The United Nations, peacekeeping and global governance, ed. Routledge, London & New York, 2016.

SEIBERT-FOHR, A., VILLIGER, M.E., Judgments of the European Convention of Human Rights. Effects and implementation, ed. Nomos, Baden-Baden, 2017.

SEIDL HOHENVELDERN, I., Responsibility of members states of an international organization for acts of that organization, in Studi in onore di R. Ago, III, ed. Giuffrè, Milano, 1987, pp. 415ss.

SEIDL-HOHENVELDER, I., Die völkerrectiche Haftung für Handlungen internationaler organizationen im Verhältnis zu Nichtmitgliedstaaten, in Österreichische Zeitschrift für öffentliches Recht, 11, 1961, pp. 498ss.

SEIDL-HOHENVELDERN, I., L'ordre public international et la fraude à la loi- Luer importance en droit international public, in Mèlanges offerts à Jacques Maury, ed. Sirey, Paris, 1960, pp. 475ss.

SEIDL-HOHENVELDERN, I., Liability of member states for acts or omissions of an international oganization, in S. SCHLEMMER-SCHULTE, K.U.

TUNG, Liber amicorum F.I. Shihata. International finance and development law, ed. Springer, The Hague, Boston, New York, 2001, pp. 732ss.
SEIDL-HOHENVELDERN, I., LOIBL, G., Das Recht der Internationalen Organizationen entischliesslich der Supranationalen Gemeinschaften, Heymanns Verlag, Köln, 2000, pp. 4ss.
SEIDL-HOHENVELDERN, I., Responsible of member states of an international organization for acts of that organization, in A.A.V.V., Le droit international à l'heure de sa codification. Études à l'honneur de R. Ago, ed. Giuffrè, Milan, 1987, pp. 416ss.
SEIDL-HOHENVELDERN, I., Völkerrecht, C. Heymanns, Berlin, Bonn, 1986, pp. 366ss.
SENDER, O., WOOD, M., A mystery no longer! Opinio juris and other theoretical controversies associated with customary international law, in Israel Law Review, 50 (3), 2017, pp. 300ss.
SEYERSTED, F., United Nations forces in the law of peace and war, A.E. Sijthoff, Leyden, 1966, pp. 194ss.
SHACKELFORD, S., State responsibility for cyber attacks: Competing standards for a growing problem, in Conference on Cyber Conflict Proceedings, 2010.
SHACKLEFORD, S., RUSSELL, S., KUEHN, A., Unpacking the international law on cybersecurity due diligence: Lessons from the public and private sectors, in Chicago Journal of International Law, 16, 2016, pp. 8ss.
SHAHABUDDEEN, M., Does the principle of legality stand in the way of progressive development of law?, in Journal of International Criminal Justice, 2, 2004, pp. 1007ss.
SHARP, D.N., Rethinking transitional justice for the twenty-first century: Beyond the end of history, Cambridge University Press, Cambridge, 2018.
SHAW, M.N., International law, Cambridge University Press, Cambridge, 2008, pp. 120ss.
SHAW, M.N., International law, Cambridge University Press, Cambridge, 2014.
SHAW, M.N., International law, Cambridge University Press, Cambridge, 2017, pp. 81ss.
SHELTON, D., International law and domestic legal systems: Incorporation, transformation and persuasion, Oxford University Press, Oxford, 2011, pp. 330ss.
SHELTON, D., Reparation, in Max Planck Encyclopedia of Public International Law, 2015.
SHEPSON, S., Jurisdiction in complicity cases. Rendition and refoulement in domestic and international courts, in Columbia Journal of Transnational Law, 54, 2015-2016, pp. 713ss.
SIBERT, M., Traitè de droit international public, ed. Dalloz, Paris, 1951, pp. 316ss.
SICILIANOS, A.L., Les rèactions dècentralisèes à l'illicite. Des contremesures à la lègitime dèfense, LGDJ, Paris, 1990.
SICILIANOS, A.L., Sanctions institutionnelles et contre-mesures: tendances rècentes, in L. PICCHIO FORLATI, A.L., SICILIANOS, Les sanctions

èconomiques en droit internatonal-economic sanctions in international law, Leiden, Boston, 2004, pp. 58ss.

SICILIANOS, A.L., The classification of obligations and the multilateral dimension of the relations of international responsibility, in European Journal of International Law, 13, 2002, pp. 1137ss.

SICILIANOS, L.A., L'innovation de la lègitime dèfense face aux activitès d'entitès non-ètatiques, in Hague Yearbook of International Law, 2, 1989, pp. 150ss.

SICURELLI, D., The European Union's Africa policies: Norms, interests and impact, ed. Routledge, London & New York, 2016.

SIEKMANN, R.C.R., National contingents in United Nations peace-keeping forces, ed. Springer, Dordrecht, 1991, pp. 112ss.

SILANDER, D., WALLACE, D., International organizations and the implementation of the responsibility to protect, ed. Routledge, London & New York, 2015.

SILVERBURG, S., International law. Contemporary issues and future developments, ed. Routledge, London & New York, 2018.

SIMMA, B., ALSTON, P., The sources of human rights law: Custom, human rights and general principles, in Australian Yearbook of International Law, 5, 1988 pp. 88ss.

SIMMA, B., Das Reziprozitätelement im Zustandekommen Völkerrecht Verträge, Ducker & Humblot, Berlin, 1972.

SIMMA, B., From bilateralism to community interest in international law, in Recueil des cours, ed. Brill, Bruxelles, vol. 189, 1994, pp. 302ss.

SIMMA, B., GEIGER, R., KHAN, D.E., VON SCHORLEMER, S., From bilaterism to community interest: Essays in honour of judge Bruno Simma, Oxford University Press, Oxford, 2011.

SIMMA, B., Genocide and International Court of Justice, in C. SAFFERLING, W. CONZE (eds.), The genocide convention sixty years after its adoption, T.M.C. Asser Press, The Hague, 2010, pp. 259-264.

SIMMA, B., Grundfragen der Staatenverantwortlichkeit in der Arbeit der International Law Commission, in Archiv des Völkerrechts, 53, 1985, pp. 358ss.

SIMMA, B., KHAN, D.E., NOLTE, G., PAULUS, A., WESSENDORF, N., The Charter of the United Nations, a commentary. Oxford University Press, Oxford, 2012, pp. 1293-1301.

SIMMA, B., Miscellaneous thoughts on subsequent agreements and practice, in G. NOLTE, Treaties and subsequent practice, Oxford University Press, Oxford, 2013, pp. 46ss.

SIMMA, B., PULKOWSKI, D., Leges speciales and self-contained regimes, in J. CRAWFORD, A. PELLET, S. OLLESON, The law of international responsibility, Oxford University Press, Oxford, 2010, pp. 141ss.

SIMMA, B., Reciprocity, in Encylopedia of Public International Law, 1984, pp. 29ss.

SIMMA, B., Reciprocity, in Max Planck Encyclopedia of Public International

Law, 2008, par. 91.

SIMMA, B., Reflections on article 60 of the Vienna Convention on the law of treaties, in Österreichische Zeitschrift für öffentliches Recht, 20, 1970, pp. 11ss.

SIMMA, B., Universality of international law from the perspective of a practitioner, in European Journal of International Law, 20, 2009, pp. 280ss.

SIMMA, D., PULKOWSKI, D., Of planets and the universe: Self-contained regimes in international law, in European Journal of International Law, 17, 2006, pp. 494ss.

SIMMONDS, R., Legal problems arising from the United Nations military operations in the Congo, ed. Springer, Berlin, 1968, pp. 238ss.

SIMMS, B., TRIMM, D., (ed.), Humanitarian intervention: A history, Cambridge University Press, Cambridge, 2011.

SIMÓN, L., No mighty, no right: Europeans must rediscover military power, in Real Instituto Elcano, European Global Strategy Project, EGS 2/2013, 19 March 2013.

SIMONDS, S., Conventional warfare and environmental protection: A proposal for international legal reform, in Stanford Journal of International Law, 29, 1992, pp. 190ss.

SINCLAIR, I., The impact of the unratified codification Convention, in A. BOS, H. SIBLESZ, Realism in law-making: Essays on International Law In Honour of Willem Riphagen, Martinus Nijhoff Publishers, Leiden, 1986, pp. 211.

SLOSS, D.L., The death of treaty supremacy. An invisible constitutional change, Oxford University Press, Oxford, 2016, pp. 357ss.

SLUITER, G., FRIMAN, H., LINTON, S., VASILIEV, S., ZAPPALÁ, S., International criminal procedural principles and rules, Oxford University Press, Oxford, 2013, pp. 373ss.

SMITH, L.V., Sovereignty at the Paris peace conference of 1919, Oxford University Press, Oxford, 2018, pp. 67ss.

SMITH, M.E., Europe's common security and defence policy: Capacity-building, experimental learning and institutional change, Cambridge University Press, Cambridge, 2017.

SOBENES OBREGON, E., SAMSON, B., Nicaragua before the International Court of Justice: Impacts on international law, ed. Springer, Berlin, 2017.

SÖFKER, C., Durch die Besatzungsmacht geprägte Neuordnungen besetzter Staaten: Welche Auswirkungen haben Völkerrechtlich verbotene Angriffsriege und die Reichweite der Kompetenzen von Besatzungsmächten Untersucht am Beispiel des Irak-krieges, H. Utz Verlag, München, 2014.

SOHN, L.B., "Generally accepted" international rules, in Washington Law Review, 61, 1986, pp. 1073ss.

SOHN, L.B., Sources of international law, in Georgia Journal of International and Comparative Law, 25, 1995-1996, pp. 399ss.

SOHN, L.B., Unratified treaties as a source of customary international law, in A. BOS, H. SIBLESZ (eds.), Realism in law-making: Essays in international law in Honour of Willem Riphagen, Martinus Nijhoff Publishers, The Hague, 1986, pp. 232s.

SOLIS, G.D., The law of armed conflict: International humanitarian law in war, Cambridge University Press, Cambridge, 2010.

SOMMARIO, E., Responsibility under international law for human rights violations committed by UN peacekeepers: Reconsidering issues of attribution, in A. DE GUTTRY, E. SOMMARIO, L. ZHU (eds.), China's and Italy's participation in peacekeeping operations: Existing models, emerging challenges, Lexington Books, London, 2014, pp. 369-397.

SOREL, J.M., BORÉ EVENO, V., Article 31. General rule of interpretation, in O. CORTEN, P. KLEIN, The Vienna Convention on the law of treaties. A commentary, Oxford University Press, Oxford, 2011, pp. 806ss.

SOREL, J.M., L'avenir du "crime" en droit international à la lumière de l'expèrience du jus congens, in Polish Yearbook of International Law, 23, 1997-1998, pp. 70ss.

SPAVENTA, E., A very fearful Court? The protection of fundamental rights in the European Union after Opinion 2/13, in Maastricht Journal of European and Comparative Law, 22, 2015, pp. 51ss.

SPERDUTI, G., Responsibility of states for activities of private law persons, in Encyclopedia of Public International Law, vol. IV, 2000, pp. 216ss.

SPIELMANN, D., L'adhésion de l'Union européenne à la Convention européenne des droits de l'homme, (Réunion conjointe de la Cour de justice de l'Union européenne et de la Cour européenne des droits de l'homme-Réseau des présidents des Cours suprêmes judiciaires de l'Union européenne, Helsinki 6 septembre 2013.

SPIJKERS, O., The evolution of United Nations peacekeeping in the Congo: From ONUC, to MONUC, to MONUSCO and its force intervention brigade, in Journal of International Peacekeeping, 19 (1), 2015, pp. 90ss.

SPIJKERS, O., The immunity of the United Nations in relation to the genocide in Srebrenica in the eyes of a Dutch District Court, in Journal of International Peacekeeping, 9, 2009, pp. 197ss.

SPIROPOULOS, J., Die Haftung der Staaten für "indirekten Schaden" aus völkerrechtlichen Delikten, in Niemeyers Zeitschrift für Völkerrecht, 35, 1925-1926, pp. 60ss.

SPRIK, L., Protection of civilian and individual accountability: Obligations and responsibilities of military commanders in UN peacekeeping operations, ed. Routledge, London & New York, 2019.

STAHN, C., EASTERDAY, J.S., IVERSON, I., Jus post bellum, Oxford University Press, Oxford, 2014, pp. 121ss.

STAHN, C., International territorial administration in the former Yugoslavia: Origins, development and challenges ahead, in Zeitschrift für ausländisches öffentliches Rechts und Völkerrecht, 61, 2001.

STAHN, C., VAN DEN HERIK, L., The diversification and fragmentation of international criminal law, Martinus Nijhoff Publishers, Leiden/Boston, 2012, pp. 34ss.

STARKE, J.G., An introduction to international law, Butterworth & Co., London, 1963, pp. 409ss.L. CAFLISCH, The effect of armed conflict on treaties, in BOSCHIERO N., PITEA C., RAGNI C., SCOVAZZI T., International Courts and the development of international law, ed. Springer, The Hague, 2013, pp.

STARSKI, P., Right to self-defence, attribution and the non-State actor. Birth of the "unable" of "unwilling" standard?, ion Zeitscrhift für ausländisches und öffentliches Recht und Völkerrecht, 75, 2015, pp. 456ss.

STARSKI, P., Silence within the process of normative change and evolution use of force: Normative volatility and legislative responsibility, in Journal of Use of Force & International Law, 14, 2017, pp. 248ss.

STEIN, T., BUTTLAR, C., KOTZUR, M., Völkerrecht, F. Vahlen Verlag, München, 2017.

STEIN, T., Kosovo and international community. The attribution of possible internationally wrongful acts: Responsibility of NATO or of its member states?, in C. TOMUSCHAT, Kosovo and the international community: A legal assessment, ed. Brill, The Hague, 2002, pp. 182ss.

STEIN, T., The approach of the different drummer: The principle of the persistent objector in international law, in Harvard International Law Journal, 26, 1985, pp. 458ss.

STERN, B., A plea for "reconstruction" of international responsibility based on the notion of legal injury, in M. RAGAZZI, International responsibility today. Essays in memory of Oscar Schachter, Martinus Nijhoff Publishers, Leiden, Boston, 2005, pp. 104ss.

SCHMITT, M.N., PEJIC, J., International law and armed conflict exploring the facultlines. Essays in honour of Yoram Dinstein, Martinus Nijhoff Publishers, 2007, The Hague, 2007, pp. 67ss.

STERN, B., Custom at the heart of international law, in Duke Journal of Comparative & International Law, 11, 2001, pp. 89ss.

STERN, B., The elements of an internationally wrongfull acts, in J. CRAWFORD, A. PELLET, S. OLLESON, The law of international responsibility, Oxford University Press, Oxford, 2010.

STEWART, J.G., The end of "modes of liability" for international crimes, in Leiden Journal of International Law, 25 (1), 2012, pp. 168ss.

STILLMUNKES, P., Le "forum prorogatum" devant la court permanente de justice internationale e la court internationale de justice, in Revue Gènèrale de Droit International Public, 35, 1964, pp. 676ss.

STRUPP, K., Das völkerrechtliche Delikt, Mohr Siebeck, Stuttgart, 1920.

STRUPP, K., Grundzüge des positiven Völkerrechts, L. Rohrscheid, Bonn, 1972, pp. 120ss.

SUBOTIĆ, J., Legitimacy, scope, and conflicting claims on the ICTY: In the aftermath of Gotovina, Haradinaj and Perišić, in Journal of Human Rights, 13(2), 2014, pp. 172ss.

SUR, S., Interpretation en droit international public, LGDJ, Paris, 1974, pp. 164ss.

SUR, S., Les organizations internationales. Dynamiques et dèsenchantement, in Revue Gènèrale de Droit International Public, 116, 2012, pp. 668ss.

SUZUKI, E., Responsibility of international organizations, in Michigan Journal of International Law, 27, 2005, pp. 178ss.
SZABÓ, M., International legal responsibility of the European Union according to the Draft Articles of the International Law Commission, in M. SZABÓ (ed.), State responsibility and the law of treaties, Eleven International, The Hague, 2009, pp. 186ss.
SZASZ, P.C., The law and practices of the International Agency for Atomic Energy, Wien, 1970, pp. 989ss.
TALMON, S., A plurality of responsibile actors. International responsibility for acts of the coalition provisional authority in Iraq, in P. SHINER, A. WILLIAMS, The Iraq war and international law, Bloomsbury Publishing, New York, 2008, pp. 186ss.
TALMON, S., Determining customary international law. The ICJ's methodology between induction, deduction and assertion, in European Journal of International Law, 26 (2), 2015, pp. 422ss.
TALMON, S., Jus cogens after Germany v. Italy: Substantive and procedural rules distinguished, in Leiden Journal of International Law, 25 (4), 2012, pp. 979.
TALMON, S., Kollektive Nichtanerkennung illegaler Staaten: Grundlagen und Rechtsfolgen einer internationaler koordinierten Sanktion dargestellt am Beispiel der Türkischen Republik Nord-Zypern, Mohr Siebeck, Tübingen, 2006, pp. 334ss.
TALMON, S., The responsibility of outside powers for acts of secessionist entities, in International and Comparative Law Quarterly, 58, 2009, pp. 498ss.
TAMS, C.J., All's well that ends well. Comments on the ILC's articles on state responsibility, in Zeitschrift für ausländisches Recht und Völkerrecht, 62, 2002, pp. 759ss.
TAMS, C.J., Countermeasures against multiple responsible actors, in A. NOLLKAEMPER, I. PLAKOKEFALOS, Principles of shared responsbibility in international law. An appraisal of the state of the art. An appraisal of the state of the art, Cambridge University Press, Cambridge, 2015, pp. 312ss.
TAMS, C.J., SLOAN, J., The development of international law by the International Court of Justice, Oxford University Press, Oxford, 2013, pp. 118ss.
TAMS, C.J., ZIMMERMANN, A., The federating shall occur to agreements providing for general, comprehensive and compulsory international arbitration. The German optional clause declaration of 1 May 2008, in German Yearbook of International Law, 51, 2008, pp. 392ss.
TAMS, J., The continued relevance of compromissory clauses as a source of ICJ jurisdiction, in T. GIEGERICH, A wiser century? Judicial dispute settlement, disarmament and the laws of war 100 years after the second Hague peace conference, Duncker & Humblot, Berlin, 2009, pp. 461ss.
TANAKA, Y., The peaceful settlement of international disputes, Cambridge University press, Cambridge, 2018, pp. 55ss.
TANCREDI, A., Enforcing WTO law, in A. JAKAB, D. KOCHENOV, The

enforcement of EU law and values. Ensuring member states' compliance, Oxford University Press, Oxford, 2017, pp. 342ss.

TANZI, A., Is damage a distinct condition for the existence of an international wrongful act?, in M. SPINEDI, B. SIMMA, United Nations codification of state responsibility, Oceana Publications, Dobbs Ferry, New York, Rome, 1987, pp. 4ss.

TASIOULAS, J., In defence of relative normativity: Communitarian values and the Nicaragua case, in Oxford Journal of Legal Studies, 16, 1996, pp. 88ss.

TASIOULAS, J., Opinio juris and the genesis of custom: A solution to the "paradox," in Australian Yearbook of International Law, 26, 2007, pp. 200ss.

TAVERNIER, J., La responsabilité des Etats au regard de la Convention européenne des droits de l'homme pour la mise en oeuvre de résolutions adoptées dans la cadre du chapitre VII de la Charte des Nations Unies, in Revue Générale de Droit International Public, 117, 2013, pp. 102ss.

TEHINDRAZANARIVELO, D.L., Targeted sanctions and obligations of states on listing and de-listing procedures, in L. BOISSON DE CHAZOURNES, M. KOHEN, International law and the quest for its implementation. Liber Amicorum Vera Gowlland-Debbas, ed. Brill/Martinus Nijhoff Publishers, Leiden, 2010, pp. 127-171.

TEITGEN COLLY, C., La Convention europèenne des droits de l'homme: 60 ans et après?, ed. LGDJ, Paris, 2013.

THAKUR, R., MALEY, W., (ed.)., Theorising the responsibility to protect, Cambridge University Press, Cambridge, 2015.

THALLINGER, G., The rule of exhaustion of local remedies in the context of the responsibility of international organizations, in Noridc Journal of International Law, 77, 2008, pp. 414ss.

THIRLWAY, H., Human rights in customary law, in Leiden Journal of International Law, 28, 2015, pp. 496ss.

THIRLWAY, H., Responsibility of international organizations. What role for the International Court of Justice?, in M. RAGAZZI, Responsibility of international organizations. Essays in memory of Sir Ian Brownlie, Martinus Nijhoff Publishers, Leiden, Boston, 2013, pp. 354ss.

THIRLWAY, H., The International Court of Justice, Oxford University Press, Oxford, 2016, pp. 578ss.

THIRLWAY, H., The law and procedure of the International Court of Justice 1960-1989 (part eleven), in The British Yearbook of International Law, 72, 2001, pp. 72ss.

THIRLWAY, H., The law and procedure of the International Court of Justice, in British Yearbook of International Law, 60, 1989, pp. 143ss.

THIRLWAY, H., The sources of international law, in M. D. EVANS, International law, Oxford University Press, Oxford, 2018, pp. 95ss.

THOUVENIN, J.M., Responsibility in the context of the European legal order, in J. CRAWFORD, A. PELLET, S. OLLESON (eds.), The law of international responsibility, Oxford University Press, Oxford, 2010, pp. 861ss.

THYM, D., The intergovernmental constitution of the EU's foreign security &

defence executive, in European Constitutional Law Review, 11 (3), 2011, pp. 453ss.

TIMMERMANS, F., Fundamental rights protection in Europe before and after accession of the European Union to the European Convention on Human Rights, in Liber amicorum Pieter Van Dijk, M. Van Roosmalen and others (eds.), Intersentia, Antwerp, Oxford, 2013, pp. 225ss.

TITTEMORE, B.D., Belligerents in blue helmets: Applying international humanitarian law to United Nations peace operations, in Stanford Journal of International Law, 33, 1997, pp. 80ss.

TIZZANO, A., Les Cours européennes et l'adhésion de l'Union à la CEDH, in Il Diritto dell'Unione Europea, 2011, pp. 12ss.

TOMKA, P., Custom and the International Court of Justice, in The Judge and International Custom, CAHDI, Council of Europe, 19-20 September 2012, The Law and Practice of International Courts and Tribunals, 12, 2013, pp. 28ss.

TOMUSCHAT, C., Article 36, in A. ZIMMERMANN, C. TOMUSCHAT, K. OELLRS-FRAHM, The statute of the International Court of Justice. A commentary, Oxford University Press, Oxford, 2006, pp. 602ss.

TOMUSCHAT, C., Die internationale Gemeinschaft, in Archiv des Völkerrechts, 33, 1995, pp. 25ss.

TOMUSCHAT, C., Human rights between idealism and realism, Oxford University Press, Oxford, 2011.

TOMUSCHAT, C., Human rights between idealism and realism, Oxford University Press, Oxford, 2014.

TOMUSCHAT, C., Individual reparation claims in instances of grave human rights violations: The position under general international law, in A. RANDELZHOFER, C. TOMUSCHAT, State responsibility and the individual. Reparation in instances of grave violations of human rights, ed. Brill, The Hague, 1999.

TOMUSCHAT, C., International crimes by states: An endangered species?, in E. SUY, K. WELLENS, International law: Theory and practice. Essays in honour o Eric Suy, Martinus Nijhoff Publishers, The Hague, 1998.

TOMUSCHAT, C., Reparation in favour of individual victims of gross violations of human rights and international humanitarian law, in M.C. KOHEN, Promoting justice, human rights and conflict resolution through international law. Liber Amicorum Lucius Caflisch, ed- Brill, Leiden, 2007, pp. 569-590.

TOMUSCHAT, C., Specificities of human rights law and international humanitarian law regarding state responsibility, in R. KOLB, G. GAGGIOLI, Research handbook on human rights and humanitarian law, Edward Elgar Publishers, Cheltenham, 2013, pp. 198ss.

TOMUSCHAT, C., The European Court of Human Rights and the United Nations, in A. FØLLESDAL, B. PETERS, G. ULFSTEIN, Constituting Europe: The European Court of Human Rights in a national, european and global context, Cambridge University Press, Cambridge, 2013, pp. 334ss.

TOMUSCHAT, C., The international responsibility of the European Union, in E.

CANNIZZARO, The European Union as an actor in intrnational relationa, Wolters Kluwer, Deventer, 2002, p. 178ss.
TÖRBER, G., The contractual nature of the optional clause, Bloomsbury Publishing, New York, 2015.
TORRES PEREZ, A., Too many voices? The prior involvement of the Court of Justice of the European Union? in European Journal of Human Rights, 40, 2013, pp. 565-583.
TOURNIER, A., De Brunsbüttel a Kinshasa. Le droit de la rèparation dans la jurisprudence des cours mondiales à l'aune de l'arrêt Diallo, in Annuaire Français de Droit International, 58, 2012, pp. 210ss.
TOWNSEND, G., State responsibility for acts of de facto agents, in Arizona Journal of International and Comparative Law, 14, 1997, pp. 662ss.
TRAPP, K.N., MILLS, A., Smooth runs the water where the brook is deep: The obscured complexities of Germany v. Italy, in Cambridge Journal of International and Comparative Law, 1, 2012, pp. 154ss.
TRAVISS, A., Temple of Preah Vihear. Lessons on provisional measures, in Chicago Journal of International Law, 13, 2012, pp. 327ss.
TREBILCOCK, J., Waiver, in Encyclopedia of Public International Law, 2000, pp. 1327ss.
TRIEPEL, H., Völkerrecht und Landesrecht, Verlag Von G.L. Hirscefeld, Leipzig, 1899, pp. 333ss.
TRIMBLE, P., Beyond verification: The next step in arms control, in Harvard Law Review, 102, 1989, pp. 885-912.
TSAGOURIAS, N., BUCHAN, R., International law and cyber space, ed. Edward Elgar Publishers, Cheltenham, 2015, pp. 66ss.
TSAGOURIAS, N., The responsibility of international organizations for military missions, in M. ODELLO, R. PIOTROWICZ (eds.) International military missions and international law, Martinus Nijhoff Publishers, The Hague, 2011, pp. 246ss.
TSAGOURIAS, N., MORRISON, A., International humanitarian law: Cases, materials and commentary, Cambridge University Press, Cambridge, 2018.
TUCKER, R.W., Principles of international law, Holt, Rinehart and Winston, New York, 1966, pp. 16ss.
TUNKIN, G.I., Remarks on the juridical nature of customary norms of international law, in California Law Review, 49, 1961, pp. 422ss.
TURAN, G., Responsibility to prosecute in an age of global governamentality: The International Criminal Court, in Cooperation and Conflict, 50, 2015.
TÜRK, A.H., Judicial review in European Union law, Edward Elgar Publishers, Cheltenham, 2010.
TZANAKOPOULOS, A., Disobeying the Security Council, Oxford University Press, Oxford, 2011.
TZENG, P., Jurisdiction and applicable law under UNCLOS, in Yale Law Journal, 126, 2016-2017.
TZEVELEKOS, V.P., Reconstructing the effective control criterion in extraterritorial human rights breaches. Direct attribution of wrongfulness,

due diligence and concorrent responsibility, in Michigan Journal of International Law, 35, 2014, pp. 129ss.

ULESTEIN, G., Les activitès normatives de l'organization internationale, in E. LAGRANDE, J.M. SOREL, Droit des organizations intrnationales, LGDJ, Paris, 2013, pp. 746ss.

ULFSTEIN, G., MARAHAUN, T., ZIMMERMANN, A., (ed. by), Making treaties work. Human rights, environment, arms control, Oxford University Press, Oxford, 2007, pp. 3ss.

USHAKOV, N., Statement at the 1518th meeting of the International Law Commission, in Yearbook of International Law Commission, 1999, pp. 398ss.

USHERWOOD, J., PINDER, S., The European Union. A very short introduction, Oxford University Press, Oxford, 2018.

VADI, V., Cultural heritage in international investment law and arbitration, Cambridge University Press, Cambridge, 2014, pp. 100ss.

VALLEJO FRANCO, B.E., La responsabilidad de proteger. Una nueva dimensión de la soberanía, in Oasis, 15, 2011, pp. 8ss.

VAN AAKEN, A., MOTOC, I., The ECHR and general international law, Oxford University Press, Oxford, 2018, pp. 194ss.

VAN CALSTER, G., VANDENBERGHE, W., REINS, L., Research handbook on climate change mitigation law, Edward Elgar Publishers, Cheltenham, 2015.

VAN DAMME, I., Treaty interpretation by the WTO Appellate Body, in European Journal of International Law, 21, 2010, pp. 606ss.

VAN DEN BOSSCHE, P., ZDOUC, W., Law and policy of the World Trade Organization, Cambridge University Press, Cambridge, 2013, pp. 140ss.

VAN DEN HERIK, L., Research handbook on UN sanctions and international law, Edward Elgar Publishers, Cheltenham, 2017, pp. 218ss.

VAN DER HAVE, N., The prevention of gross human rights violations under international human rights law, ed. Springer, Berlin, 2018.

VAN HOUTTE, H., International law and community treaty-making, in Northwestern Journal of International Law & Business, 3, 1981, pp. 633ss.

VAN RAEPENBUSCH, S., La convergence entre les régimes de responsabilité extracontractuelle de l'Union Européenne et des États Membres, in ERA Forum, 12 (4), 2012, pp. 672ss.

VAN SLIEDREGT, E., Pluralism in international criminal law, in Leiden Journal of International Law, 25 (4), 2012, pp. 849ss.

VANDENBROUKE, F., BARNARD, V., DE BAERT, G., A European social union after the crisis, Cambridge University Press, Cambridge, 2017.

VARGAS CARREŇO, E., Derecho internacional pùblico, Editorial Jurìdica, Santiago de Chile, 2007.

VENTURA, M.J., The duty to investigate Zimbabwe crimes against humanity (torture) allegations: The Constitutional Court of South Africa speaks on universal jurisdiction and the ICC act, in Journal of International Criminal Justice, 13, 2015, pp. 861-889.

VENZKE, I., How interpretation makes international law. On semantic change and normative twists, Oxford University Press, Oxford, 2012, pp. 38ss.

VENZKE, I., The role of International Courts as interpreters and developers of the law: Working out the juris generative practice of interpretation, in Loyola of Los Angeles International & Comparative Law Review, 34, 2011, pp. 100ss.

VERDIRAME, G., Breaches of the European Convention on Human Rights resulting from the conduct of international organizations, in European Human Rights Law Review, 8, 2008, pp. 220ss.

VERDIRAME, G., The UN and human rights: Who guards the guardians? Cambridge University Press, Cambridge, 2011, pp. 225ss.

VERDROSS, A., Règles gènèrales de droit de la paix, in Recueil des cours, ed. Brill, Bruxelles, vol. 30, 1929, pp. 272ss.

VERDROSS, A., SIMMA, B., Universelles Völkerrecht. Theorie und praxis, Duncker & Humblot, Berlin, 1984, pp. 413ss.

VERDROSS, A., Theorie der mittelbaren Staatenhaftung, in Österreichische Zeitschrift für öffentliches Recht, 2, 1948, pp. 410ss.

VERDROSS, A., Völkerrecht, ed. Springer, Wien, 1964.

VERHOEVEN, J., The law of responsibility of the law of treaties, in J. CRAWFORD, A. PELLET, S. OLLESON, The law of international responsibility, Oxford University Press, Oxford, 2010, pp. 106ss.

VERLAGE, V., Responsibility to protect: ein neur Ansatz im Völkerrecht zur Verhindernung von Völkerrechtmord, Kriegsverbrechen und Verbrechen gegen die Menschlkichkeit, ed. Mohr Siebeck, Tübingen, 2009.

VEZZANI, S., Countermeasures by member states against international organizations, in M. RAGAZZI, Responsibility of international organizations. Essays in memory of Sir Ian Brownlie, Martinus Nijhoff Publishers, Leiden, Boston, 2013.

VEZZANI, S., Prior exhaustion of internal remedies in cases involving the international responsibility of the European Union, in Italian Yearbook of International Law, 22, 2012, pp. 61-89.

VILLALPANDO, S., Codification light. A new trend in the codification of international law at the United Nations, in Brazilian Yearbook of International Law, 10, 2013, pp. 118ss.

VILLALPANDO, S., L'èmergence de la communautè internationale dans la responsabilitè des États, ed. PUF, Paris, 2005.

VILLALPANDO, S., On the International Court of Justice and the determination of rules of law, in Leiden Journal of International Law, 26, 2013, pp. 248ss.

VILLIGER, M.E., Commentary on the 1969 Vienna Convention on the Law of Treaties, Martinus Nijhoff Publishers, The Hague, Boston, 2009, pp. 432ss.

VILLIGER, M.E., Customary international law and treaties, Kluwer Law International, The Hague, 1997, pp. 39ss.

VILLIGER, M.E., The rules on interpretation: Misgivings, misunderstandings, miscarriage? The "crucible" intended by the International Law Commission, in E. CANNIZZARO, The law of Treaties beyond the Vienna Convention, Oxford University Press, Oxford, 2011, pp. 106s.

VIOLINI, L., BARAGGIA, A., The fragmented landscape of fundamental rights protection in Europe, Edward Elgar Publishers, Cheltenahm, 2018, pp. 95ss.

VIRALLY, M., Definition and classification of international organizations, in G. ABI-SAAB, The concept of international organization, UNESCO, Paris, 1981, pp. 50ss.

VIRALLY, M., La notion de fonction dans la thèorie de l'organization internationale, in G. ABI-SAAB, La communautè internationale. Mèlanges offerts à Charles Rousseau, ed. Pedone, Paris, 1974, pp. 278ss.

VIRALLY, M., Le principle de rèciprocitè dans le droit internatonal contemporain, in Recueil des cours, ed. Brill, Bruxelles, vol. 122, 1967, pp. 54ss.

VIRALY, M., La valeur juridique des recommanations des organizations internationales, in Annuaire Français de Droit International, 2, 1956, pp. 66ss.

VIRZO, R., INGRAVALLO, I., (eds.), Evolutions in the law of International Organizations, ed. Brill, Leiden-Boston, 2015.

VISSER, L., May the force be with you: The legal classification of intervention by invitation, in Netherlands International Law Review, 66 (1), 2019, pp. 22ss.

VOENEKY, S., NEUMAN, G.L., Human rights democracy and legitimacy in a world of disorder, Cambridge University Press, Cambridge, 2018, pp. 216ss

VOGLER, J., The global commons: Environmental and technological governance, Wiley, New York, 2000.

VOJDIK, V.K., Sexual violence against men and women in war: A masculinities approach, in Nevada Law Journal, 15, 2014-2015, pp. 925ss.

VON ARNAULD, A., Völkerrecht, C.F. Müller, Heidelberg, 2016.

VON ARNAULD, A., Völkerrecht, C.F. Müller, Tübingen, 2014.

VON BOGDANDY, A., DANN, P., GOLDMANN, M., Developing the publicness of public international law. Towards a legal framework for global governance, in German Law Journal, 9, 2008, pp. 1381ss.

VON BOGDANDY, A., General principles of international public authority: Sketching a research field, in A. VON BOGDANDY, R. WOLFRUM, J. VON BERNSTORFF, M B. DANN, M. GOLDMANN, The exercise of public authority by international institutions, ed. Springer, Berlin. pp. 733ss.

VON BOGDANDY, A., IOANNIDIS, M., Systemic deficiency in the rule of law: What it is, that has been done, what can be done, in Common Market Law Review, 51, 2014, pp. 60ss.

VON BOGDANDY, A., KOTTMANN, M., ANTPÖHLER, C., DICKSCHEN, J., HENTREI, S., SMRKOLJ, M., Reverse Solange-protecting the essence of fundamental rights against the Member States, in Common Market Law Review, 49, 2012, pp. 490ss.

VON BOGDANDY, A., VENZKE, I., International judicial law making, ed. Springer, New York, London, 2012.

VON BURI, M., Über Kausalität und deren Verantwortung, J.M. Gebhardt's Verlag, Leipzig, 1873.

VON HIPPEL, R., Lehrbuch des Strafrechts, ed. Springer, Berlin, 1932, pp. 99ss.

VON LUDEN, FH., Abhandlungen aus dem gemeinen deutschen Strafrecht, vol.

II, Göttingen, 1840.

VON MÜNCH, I., Das Völkerrechtliche Delikt in der Modernen Entwicklung der Völkerrechtsgemeinschaft, P. Keppler Verlag, Frankfurt, 1963, pp. 170ss.

VON MÜNCH, I., Völkerrecht, De Gruyter, Berlin, New York, 2019.

VÖNEKY, S., HÖFELMEIER, A., Article 139, in A. PROELS, United Nations Convention on the law of the sea. A commentary, C.H. Beck, Hart Publishing, München/Oxford, Oregon & Portland, 2017, pp. 968ss.

VÖNEKY, S., A new shield for the environment: Peacetime treaties as legal restraints of wartime damage, in Review of European Community and International Environmental Law, 9 (1), 2000, pp. 20ss.

VÖNEKY, S., Analogy in International Law, in Max Planck Encyclopedia of Public International Law, 2008.

VÖNEKY, S., Implementation and enforcement of international humanitarian law, in D. FLECK, The handbook of international humanitarian law, Oxford University Press, Oxford, 2013, pp. 648ss.

VOULGARIS, N., Allocating international responsibility between member states and international organizations, Bloomsbury Publishing, New York, 2019.

VOULGARIS, N., Rethinking indirect responsibility: A study of article 17 of the Draft Articles on the Responsibility of International Organizations, in International Organizations Law Review, 11, 2014, pp. 8ss.

WAGNER, E., The rule of law and its application to the United Nations: Conference report, in Max Planck United Nations Yearbook, 18, 2014, pp. 347ss.

WÄHLISCH, M., Peace making power-sharing and international law. Imperfect peace, Hart Publishing, Oxford, Oregon, Portland, 2019.

WAIBEL, M., Demystifying the art of interpretation, in The European Journal of International Law, 22 (2), 2011, pp. 572ss.

WALKER N., Intimations of global law, Cambridge University Press, Cambridge, 2014, pp. 66ss.

WALKER, H., Modern treaties of friendship, commerce and navigation, in Minnesota Law Review, 42, 1957-1958, pp. 805ss.

WALLACE, R., International law, Sweet & Maxwell, London, 1986, pp. 160ss.

WALTER, C., VON UNGERN-STERNBERG, A., ABUSHOV, K., (eds), Self-determination and secession in international law, Oxford University Press, Oxford, 2014, pp. 262ss.

WALTER, C., VON UNGERN-STERNBERG, A., ABUSHOV, K., Self-determination and secession in international law, Oxford University Press, Oxford, 2014.

WARNER, D., Human rights and humanitarian law. The quest for universality, Martinus Nijhoff Publishers, The Hague, Boston, London, 1997.

WATSON, K.W., Behrami v. France: Constructive blue helmets protect KFOR nations from accountability, in Tulane Journal of International and Comparative Law, 16, 2007-2008, pp. 576ss.

WATSON, R., The "wall" decisions in legal and political context, in American Journal of International Law, 99, 2005, pp. 27ss.

WATTS, A., The international rule of law, in German Yearbook of International Law, 36, 1993, pp. 15ss.

WEBB, P., International judicial interpretation and fragmentation, Oxford University Press, Oxford, 2013, pp. 140ss.

WECKEL, P., Convergence du droit des traitès et du droit de la responsabilitè internationale, in Revue Gènèrale de Droit International Public, 102 (3), 1998, pp. 648ss.

WEIBUST, I., MEADOWCROFT, J., Multilevel environmental governance. Managing water and climate change in Europe and North America, Edward Elgar Publishers, Cheltenham, 2014.

WEIGEND, T., Intent, mistake of law, and co-perpetration in the Lubanga Decision on the confirmation of charges, in Journal of International Criminal Justice, 8, 2008, pp. 476ss.

WEIL, P., Droit international en quête de son identitè, Recueil des cours, ed. Brill, Bruxelles, vol. 237, 1996.

WEIL, P., Towards relative normativity in international law?, in American Journal of International Law, 77, 1983, pp. 41ss.

WEILER, J.H.H., The geology of international law. Governance, democracy and legitimacy, in Zeitschrift für ausländisches Recht und Völkerrecht, 64, 2004, pp. 548ss.

WEINER, P., The evolving jurisprudence of the crime of rape in international criminal law, in Boston College Law Review, 54, 2013, pp. 1210ss.

WEISBURD, A.M., Customary international law: The problem of treaties, in Vanderbilt Journal of Transnational Law, 21, 1988, pp. 2ss.

WEISBURD, A.M., International crimes of states. The decay of an idea, in Polish Yearbook of International Law, 23, 1997-1998, pp. 52ss.

WEISS, N., THOUVENIN, J.M., The influence of human rights on international law, ed. Springer, Berlin, 2015, pp. 61ss.

WELER, T., NAFTA investment arbitration and the growth of international economic law, in Business Law International, 158, 2002, pp. 180ss.

WELLENS, K., International Law: Theory and Practice Essays in the Honor of Eric Suy, Martinus Nijhoff Publishers, The Hague, 1998, pp. 161ss.

WELLENS, K., Remedies against international organizations, Cambridge University Press, Cambridge, 2002, pp. 14

WELLENS, W., Remedies against international organizations, Cambridge University Press, Cambridge, 2004, pp. 30ss

WELLER, M., SOLOMOU, A., RYLATT, J.W., The oxford handbook of the use of force in international law, Oxford University Press, Oxford, 2015, pp. 645ss.

WELLER, M., The oxford handbook of the use of force in international law, Oxford University Press, Oxford, 2015, pp. 724ss.

WENDEL, M., Exceeding judicial competence in the name of democracy. The German Federal Constitutional Court's OMT reference, in European Constitutional Law Review, 10, 2014, pp. 264ss.

WENGLER, W., Recours judiciaire à instituer contre le dècisions d'organes internationaux: Rapport et projet de rèsolution, in Annuaire de l'Institut du Droit International, 1952, pp. 224ss.

WENGLER, W., Völlkerecht, ed. Springer, Berlin, Heidelberg, 1964, pp. 178ss.

WENZEL, N., Das Spannungsverhältnis zwischen Gruppenschutz und Individualschutz im Völkerrecht, ed. Springer, Berlin, 2007.

WERLE, G., JESSBERGER, F., Principles of international criminal law, Oxford University Press, Oxford, 2014.

WERLE, G., JESSBERGER, F., Unless otherwise provided: Article 30 of the ICC Statute and the mental element of crimes under international criminal law, in Journal of International Criminal Justice, 3, 2005, pp. 37ss.

WESSEL, R.A., BLOCKMANS, S., (eds.) Between autonomy and dependence. The EU legal order under the influence of international organizations, T.M.C. Asser Press, The Hague, 2013, pp. 14ss.

WESSEL, R.A., Division of international responsibility between the EU and its member States in the area of foreign polict, security and defence policy, in Amsterdam Law Forum, 3 (3), 2011, pp. 44.

WESSEL, R.A., ŁAZOWSKI, A., When Caveats Turn into Locks: Opinion 2/13 on Accession of the European Union to the ECHR, in German Law Journal, 16, 2015, pp. 179ss.

WESTON, B.H., FALK, R.A., CHARLESWORTH, H., International law and world order. A problem-oriented course-book, West Academic, Saint Paul, Minnesota, 2006.

WHEELER, C.H., The right to be present at trial in international criminal law, ed. Brill, Bruxelles, 2018.

WHITE, N., The law of international organization, Manchester University Press, Manchester, 2005.

WHITE, N.D., The law of international organizations, Oxford University Press, Oxford, 2016.

WHITEMAN, M.M., Digest of international law, Washington, 1970, pp. 509ss.

WHITTLE, D., The intervention brigade, Monusco, and the application of international humanitarian law to UN forces, in Georgetown Journal of International Law, 6, 2014-2015, pp. 838ss.

WIERZBOWSKI, M., GUBRYNOWICZ, A., International investment law for the 21st century, Oxford University Press, Oxford, 2015.

WILDE, R., The legal space or espace juridique of the European Convention on Human Rights: Is it relevant to extraterritorial State action?, in European Human Rights Law Review, 2, 2005, pp. 116ss.

WILLIAMSON, J.A., Some consideration on command responsibility and criminal liability, in International Review of the Red Cross, 90, 2008, pp. 306ss.

WILLIAMSON, R.L., Jr., Is international law relevant to arms control? Hard law, soft law and non-law in multilateral arms control: Some compliance hypotheses, in Chicago Journal of International Law, 4, 2003, pp. 59ss.

WILLMOT, H., WELLER, M., MAMIYA, R., SHEERAN, S., The protection of civilians, Oxford University Press, Oxford, 2016, pp. 238ss.

WILLS, S., Protecting civilians: The obligations of peacekeeping, Oxford University Press, Oxford, 2009.
WILMSHURST, E., BREAU, S., Perspectives on the ICRC study on customary international humanitarian law, Cambridge University Press, Cambridge, 2008, pp. 43ss.
WILMSHURTS, E., (ed. by), International law and the classification of conflicts, Oxford University Press, Oxford, 2012.
WITTBERGER, V., ZANGL, B., KRUCK, A., International organization, ed. Palgrave Macmillan, London & New York, 2012.
WITTICH, S., Joint tortfeasors in investment law, in C. BINDER, U. KRIEBAUM, A. REINISCH, S. WITTICH, International investment law for the 21st century, Oxford University Press, Oxford, 2009, pp. 708ss.
WOLF, J., Gibt es im Völkerrecht einen einheitlichen Schadensbegriff?, in Zeitschrift für ausländisches Recht und Völkerrecht, 49, 1989, pp. 444ss.
WOLF, J., Zurechnungsfragen beim Handlungen privatpersonen, in Zeitschrift für ausländisches Recht und Völkerrecht, 45, 1985, pp. 232ss.
WOLFKE, K., Custom in international law, Martinus Nijhoff Publishers, Leiden/Boston, 1993, pp. 162ss.
WOLFKE, K., Some persistent controversies regarding customary international law, in Netherlands Yearbook of International Law, 24, 1993, pp. 4ss.
WOLFKE, K., Treaties and custom: Aspects of interrelation, in J. KLABBERS, R. LEFEBER, Essays on the Law of Treaties: A collection of Essays in Honour of Bert Vierdag, Martinus Nijhoff Publishers, The Hague, 1998, pp. 32ss.
WOLFRUM, J., Reparation of internationally wrongful acts, in Encyclopedia of Public International Law, 2000, pp. 178ss.
WOLFRUM, R., RÖBEN, E., Developments of international law in treaty making, ed. Springer, Berlin, 2005, pp. 16ss.
WOLFRUM, R., The principle of the common heritage of mankind, Zeitschrift für ausländisches Recht und Völkerrecht, 53, 1983, pp. 314ss.
WOLTAG, J.C., Military cyber warfare: Cross-border computer network operations under international law, ed. Intersentia, London/Antwerp, 2014, pp. 274ss
WOOD, B., International initiatives to prevent illicit brokering of arms and related materials, in Disarmament Forum, 2009, n. 3, pp. 5-16.
WOOD, M., "Weighing" the articles on responsibility of international organizations, in M. RAGAZZI, Responsibility of international organizations. Essays in memory of Sir Ian Brownlie, Martinus Nijhoff Publishers, Leiden, Boston, 2013, pp. 55ss.
WOOD, M., SENDER, O., State practice, in Max Planck Encyclopedia of International Law, 2014, par. 16.
WOOD, M., The General Assembly and the International Law Commission: What happens to the Commission's work and why?, in I. BUFFARD et al., International law between universalism and fragmentation, Martinus Nijhoff Publishers, The Hague, 2008, pp. 373ss.

WOOD, M., The present position within the ILC on the topic: Identification of customary international law, in The Chinese Journal of International Law, 15, 2016, pp. 3-14.
WOODS, L., WATSON, P., Steiner & Woods European Union law, Oxford University Press, Oxford, 2017, pp. 37ss.
WOUTERS, J., BREMS, E., SMIS, S., SCHMITT, P., Accountability for human rights violations by international organizations, Oxford University Press, Oxford, 2010.
WOUTERS, J., RYNGAERT, C., RUYS, T., DE BAERE, G., International law. A european perpective, Bloomsbury, New York, 2018.
WOUTERS, J., VERHOEVEN, S., "Desuetudo," in Max Planck Encyclopedia of International Law, 2011.
WOUTERS, J., VERHOEVEN, S., The prohibition of genocide as a norm of ius cogens and its implications for the enforcement of the law of genocide, in International Criminal Law Review, 5, 2005, pp. 401ss.
WUERTH, I., Treaty interpretation, subsequent agreements and practice, and domestic constitutions, in G. NOLTE, Treaties and subsequent practice, Oxford University Press, Oxford, 2013, pp. 154ss.
WYLER, W., PAPAUX, A., The different forms of reparation. Satisfaction, in J. CRAWFORD, A. PELLET, S. OLLESON, The law of international responsibility, Oxford University Press, Oxford, 2010, pp. 625ss.
XIONG, P., An international law perspective on the protection of human rights in the TRIPS agreement: An interpretation of the TRIPS agreement in relation to the right of health, Martinus Nijhoff Publishers, The Hague, 2012.
YASSEEN, M.K., L'interprétation des traités d'après la Convention de Vienne sur le Droit des Traités, ed. Brill, Recueil des Cours, ed. Brill, Bruxelles, vol. 151, 1976, pp. 48ss.
YEE, S., A reply to Sir Michael Wood's Response to AALCOIEG's Work and I report on the ILC project on the identification of customary international law, in Chinese Journal of the International Law, 15, 2016, pp. 34ss.
YEE, S., Report on the ILC Project on "identification of customary international law," in Chinese Journal of International Law, 14, 2015, pp. 385ss.
YEE, S., Towards an international law of co-progresiveness, Martinus Nijhoff Publishers, The Hague, 2014.
ZABALZA, G.O., The principle of systemic integration. Towards a coherent international legal order, LIT Verlag, Münster, 2017.
ZACKLIN, R., Beyond Kosovo: The United Nations and the humanitarian intervention, in Virginia Journal of International Law, 41, 2001.
ZACKLIN, R., The amendment of the constitutive instruments of the United Nations and Specialized Agencies, A.W. Sijthoff, Leiden, 1968, pp. 172ss.
ZAGEL, G., Responsibility of international organizations for international law, in Sudebnik, 11, 2006, pp. 652ss
ZARKA, J.C., Droit international public, Dalloz, Paris, 2013.
ZARKA, J.C., Droit international public, ed. Ellipses, Paris, 2015.
ZEEGERS, K., International criminal tribunals and human rights law. Adherence

and contextualization, ed. Springer, Berlin, 2016, pp. 17ss.
ZEMANEK, K., General course on public international law, in Recueil des Cours de l'Académie de Droit International, ed. Brill, Bruxelles, vol. 158, 1977, pp. 230ss.
ZEMANEK, K., The legal foundations of the international legal system, in Recueil des cours, ed. Brill, Bruxelles, vol. 270, 1997, pp. 272ss.
ZEMANEK, K., What is "state practice" and who makes it ?, in U. BEYERLIN and others, Festschrift für Rudolf Bernhardt, ed. Springer, Berlin, 1995, pp. 289ss.
ZHUANG, W., Intellectual property rights and climate cchange. Interpeting the TRIPS agreement for environmentally sound technologies, Cambridge University Press, Cambridge, 2017.
ZICCARDI CAPALDO, G., International Court of Justice, legal maxims: Summaries and extracts from selected case law, in The Global Community Yearbook of International Law Journal, 1, 2001, pp. 159, 182ss.
ZICCARDI CAPALDO, G., The pillars of global law, Ashgate Publishing, London, 2013, pp. 295ss.
ZIMMERMANN, A., TAMS, J., OELLERS-FRAHAM, K., The statute of the International Court of Justice. A commentary, Oxford University Press, Oxford, 2019.
ZIMMERMANN, A., The obligation to prevent genocide: Towards a general responsibility to protect?, in U. FASTENRATH et al. (eds.), From bilateralism to community interest. Essays in honour of judge Bruno Simma, Oxford University Press, Oxford, 2011, pp. 629ss.
ZIPPERLE, N., European Union internatonal agreements: An analysis of direct effect and judicial review pre and post-Lisbon, ed. Springer, Berlin, 2017, pp. 69ss.
ZOLLER, E., Peacetime unilateral remedies, Martinus Nijhoff Publishers, Dobbs Ferry, New York, 1984.
ZOLLER, E., Quelques rèflexions sur les contre-mesures en droit international public, in Etudes offèrts à C.A. Colliard, ed. Pedone, Paris, 1984, pp. 362ss.
ZRILIC, J., The protection of foreign investment in times of armed conflict, Oxford University Press, Oxford, 2019, pp. 216ss.
ZWANENBURG, M., Accountability of peace support operations, Martinus Nijhoff Publishers, Leiden, Boston, 2005.
ZWANENBURG, M., The duty to respect international humanitarian law during European Union-led operations, in CLEER Working paper, 2012/6. pp.24ss.
ZWANENBURG, M., The duty to respect international humanitarian law during European union-led operations, in A. SARI, R.A. WESSEL, Human rights in EU crisis management operations. A duty to respect and to protect?, T.M.C. Asser Institute, The Hague, 2012.
ZWANENBURG, M., Toward a more mature ESDP: Responsibility for violations of international Humanitarian Law by EU crisis management operations, in S. BLOCKMANS (ed.), The European Union and crisis management. Policy and legal aspects, T.M.C. Asser Institute, The Hague, 2008, pp. 395ss.

ZWOLSKI, K., The European Union and international security: Developing a comprehensive approach, in C. KAUNERT, S. LÉONARD (eds) European security, terrorism and intelligence, ed. Palgrave Macmillan, London, 2013.

ZYBERI, G., The development and interpretation of international human rights and humanitarian law rules and principles through the case-law of the International Court of Justice, in Netherlands Quarterly of Human Rights, 25, 2007, pp. 118ss.

ZYBERI, G., Enforcemenet of international humanitarian law, in G. OBERLKEITNER, International human rights institutions, tribunals and courts. International human rights, ed. Springer, Berlin, 2018.

www.ingramcontent.com/pod-product-compliance
Lightning Source LLC
LaVergne TN
LVHW070743240926
848802LV00001B/3

A THEORY OF WONDER

Evolution, Brain and the Radical Nature of Science

by

Gonzalo Munévar
Lawrence Technological University

Series in Philosophy of Science
VERNON PRESS

www.vernonpress.com

In the Americas:
Vernon Press
1000 N West Street, Suite 1200,
Wilmington, Delaware 19801
United States

In the rest of the world:
Vernon Press
C/Sancti Espiritu 17,
Malaga, 29006
Spain

Series in Philosophy of Science

Library of Congress Control Number: 2021936397

ISBN: 978-1-64889-197-7

Cover design by Vernon Press using elements designed by starline / Freepik.

Dedicated to the memory of Paul K. Feyerabend and in honor of the celebration of his 100th birthday on January 13, 2024

"A Theory of Wonder" is a wonderful book. Professor Munévar, an original philosopher of science, challenges logical empiricism, falsificationism (critical rationalism), scientific realism, Bohr's epistemology, and the philosophy of science of Kuhn, Feyerabend and Lakatos. Thus he creatively explores the evolutionary relativism: a novel and "dynamic" philosophy of science on the basis of evolutionary biology and neuroscience with a focus on living organisms. By contrast, the old and "static" philosophies of science are almost entirely based on physics that focuses on inanimate objects. The author provides a biologically based theory of relative truth, and thereby holds that truth is relative to a frame of reference, and that success explains truth, not the other way around. Creative and germinal is his view of science: "Science as Part of Nature", and "Science as Radical Knowledge". In sum, this thought-provoking work brings forth a new field in philosophy of science. In order to develop and complete this new field, further inputs from philosophers and scientists are much needed.

Yuanlin Guo
Professor of Philosophy
Center for Science, Technology and Society
Tianjin University, China

Gonzalo Munévar's "Theory of Wonder" provides a detailed, well organized journey through the controversies animating 20th century philosophy of science between those looking for a logic of science that captures its method, and those such as Thomas Kuhn and Paul Feyerabend who take the history of scientific practice seriously. Munévar makes this history come alive for scientists and intelligent laypersons, rather than just professional academic philosophers. It is a sophisticated and very engaging account on both a personal and professional level. He presents an innovative exploration of an alternative for the 21st century in which a naturalistic perspective on biological evolution and cognitive neuroscience can shape our understanding of scientific inquiry. His clever arguments and his scholarship reflect a broad interdisciplinary understand of science and its history.

He punctuates his lively discussion with a large variety of scientific examples and observations that show a masterful command of the literature and a well-focused analysis and criticism—a tour de force. Munévar holds that science is an extension of our sense of wonder, but holds that the nature of science described by much of 20th-century academic philosophy of science actually baffled practicing scientist and blunted their curiosity. He offers instead a new, optimistic vision of the field in which science is seen as part of nature, and the nature of science can only be adequately understood if the insights of science itself (particularly evolutionary biology and cognitive neuroscience) are taken into account. This is a large task, but Munévar makes an admirable start in doing so.

The book should be especially valuable to an international audience drawn to the work of Paul Feyerabend as we approach the centenary of his birth. Feyerabend was Munévar's mentor and friend, who shaped his view of science and launched him on the path that has led to it.

David W. Paulsen
Professor emeritus
The Evergreen State College

Mr. Munévar's manuscript addresses what can be considered the main issue that arises about science from a philosophical reflection, that is, what is the nature of science. The philosophy of science as an autonomous discipline originated around this question and other more specific ones that derive from it at the end of the 19th century and developed more systematically throughout the last century and the last two decades.

Understanding what scientific progress consists of and explaining its success are two central specific questions about the nature of science. The most dominant answers to these two questions have been, respectively, that scientific progress lies in the application of the scientific method and that the success of science is due to discovering the truth about the world, that is, it achieves a true knowledge of how this is, regardless of our state of knowledge and our cognitive abilities.

The manuscript focuses on these two problems, that of progress (scientific method) and that of success (scientific realism), taking them from the answers given in the first half of the 20th century to the most current proposals, and to finally expose and argue the personal solutions given to these by Munévar. This is done masterfully, exposing each of the main points of view precisely and clearly and how they are overcome among themselves: inductivism present in positivists or logical empiricists, falsification in its various variants (radical, Popper and Lakatos), and the historicist turn favored mainly by Kuhn and Feyerabend. As for the original solutions that Munévar proposes, these are based on the findings of the historicist school (so that Munévar recognizes the intellectual debt that he owes to Feyerabend), but it goes further by enriching this historical perspective with the scientific one that considers evolutionary biology and neuroscience in the context of evolution. Munévar calls "evolutionary relativism" to the solution he proposes, to the point of view he develops, because science seen from history and evolutionary biology cannot be understood as a cumulative or progressive process in which a conception or point of view is consolidated, but rather as a process in which science undergoes drastic changes and in which different conceptions of the world can be given that can be equally correct, and even so it is possible to speak of progress in science.

Munévar's work, while in principle it is aimed at specialists in philosophy of science, given the general problem with which it deals and the way it exposes itself, it may also be of importance for philosophers in general, concerned with the central problems of epistemology. Even because of the centrality of the philosophical problems dealt in the work, I consider that this could be a good tool in university courses, specialized and introductory on philosophy, and much better in philosophy of science.

I believe that the main impact that the work could have lies in the original idea that it displays to understand the nature of science, the evolutionary relativism. Although it is a controversial thesis, as the author himself acknowledges, the exposition and the justification made are clear and precise, supported by arguments from the history of science and evolutionary biology, including elements of neuroscience. Besides, it seems to me that the work could also be welcomed by specialists and a wider audience, cultured, because of the way it is written, starting from the historical context of the problem up to its current state. Although technical, all this with a clear and precise language is accompanied by illustrations that are very appropriate to the subject matter, which allows non-specialists to follow the line of argument.

Germán Guerrero Pino
Professor, Department of Philosophy
Universidad del Valle, Colombia

Gonzalo Munévar is an internationally recognised philosopher of science and among the most important interpreters of the work of Paul Feyerabend, a philosopher of science renowned for encouraging a deep sense of wonder at our abundant reality. He is superbly placed to offer a powerful reflection on the nature of wonder - a complex concept and experience with, I think, a deep role in human life. Munévar argues that the sciences, properly understood, can enrich our sense of wonder - a theme rooted not only in his work on Feyerabend but his recent research in neuroscience and space exploration. Perhaps more than any other sciences, they are apt to evoke a sense of wonder. Munévar is certainly unique in being capable of philosophical reflection on both human consciousness and the cosmos.

Dr. Ian Kidd
Professor, Department of Philosophy
University of Nottingham

TABLE OF CONTENTS

LIST OF FIGURES

ACKNOWLEDGEMENTS

Over several decades many people have made contributions to help me develop the ideas presented in this book. Already in graduate school, I had invaluable conversations with Paul Feyerabend and Carl Hempel. It was Hempel, whose teaching assistant I was, who inspired some of the figures in Chapter 2 against induction. Indeed, I owe much gratitude to the many artists who have contributed drawings to the manuscript. Beginning with unnamed staff members of the University of Nebraska at Omaha research office; continuing, many years later, with Nicole Ankeny, at Lawrence Technological University; with Leonardo Falaschini, from Cambridge, and finally with my former student Ruoyu Huang. Then there are all those students who reacted to earlier versions of the manuscript. Students in graduate seminars at the University of Washington in Seattle and at the University of California at Irvine, as well as advanced undergraduates at several schools, including the University of Nebraska at Omaha, Evergreen, and Lawrence Technological University. Their many questions have provided useful guideposts. As for my writing the final draft of the book, I am very grateful for their computer help to my colleague, Dr. Matthew Cole, and to my former student Phillip McMurray, who has gone well beyond the call of duty in improving the appearance of the manuscript by formatting the text and images of the book. And last, I also wish to mention the many improvements owed to the proofreading and encouraging comments from my wife, Dr. Susan Greenshields. I do apologize to all those not acknowledged here because of the failings of my memory.

PREFACE

About a year ago, I walked around the beautiful campus of the University of California at Berkeley. Inevitably my steps took me to the manicured lawns by the Campanile, to the green grass where a long time ago I sat with other students, term after term, in Paul K. Feyerabend's graduate seminar. It was the early seventies, when Feyerabend was slowly putting together the manuscript of his greatest work, *Against Method*, the culmination of the revolution in philosophy of science that he and Thomas Kuhn had begun in 1962.

Standing there, in the very spot where we used to sit around him over forty years ago, I could almost feel his presence, the force of his incomparable personality again. I begin this book with these very personal remarks, because this book is the culmination of a very long personal journey, regardless of how intellectual it might have also been. And in both the personal and intellectual aspects of the journey, Feyerabend had a great influence, not by having me become his "follower"—he would have found the thought repulsive—but by challenging my ideas while encouraging me to develop my own thoughts.

Feyerabend was born in Vienna in 1924. During World War II, three Russian bullets left him crippled for the rest of his life (he called himself a cripple and would make fun of euphemisms like "handicapped"). After the war, he recovered enough to study physics and astronomy at the University of Vienna. In those days, Vienna was still a city of geniuses. Feyerabend had a great voice, good enough to sing at the Vienna Opera House, and at one time Bertolt Brecht asked him to be his assistant. Feyerabend also met Konrad Lorenz, who also asked him to be his assistant. Although it was obvious that he had many talents, he ended writing his doctoral thesis in philosophy, under Victor Kraft. After meeting Ludwig Wittgenstein, Feyerabend made arrangements to work with him in Cambridge, but Wittgenstein's death forced him to end up as Karl Popper's assistant instead. All those Viennese figures influenced the young Feyerabend significantly, and in the long run, that influence played an important role in the intellectual revolution that he forged with Kuhn in the sixties and seventies.

I met him in Berkeley in early 1973, during the second year of my doctoral studies. I showed up in his seminar, thinking that I would just sit in it—being cautious just in case the many students who dreaded his critical mind were right. "What will be topic of your presentation?" he asked me after he sat down. "I am just sitting in," I answered. "If you want to stay you will have to give a presentation," he insisted. "But all my ideas are bizarre," I said. "Par for the course," he answered, taking his schedule book out. "When are you going to present them?"

During my presentation, weeks later, I experienced in my own flesh how disconcerting his criticism could be – something I would have wished on my worst enemy, or on myself if I had really believed that criticism was the main source of progress. Feyerabend questioned everything; he would argue against, and even make fun of what appeared to be obvious claims. In a conversation with him no idea could be taken for granted. That day I was as critical of his remarks as he was of mine, but left the classroom fearing that I had made a fool of myself. Afterwards, however, he was very friendly and invited me to lunch at the Golden Bear, an outdoor restaurant on campus. That would be the first of many meals, not only at the Golden Bear, but at many other restaurants in the San Francisco Bay area and in Europe; meals in which his perceptive comments would jump from philosophy and science to music, or art, or theater, and back to philosophy again; the first of many discussions in which we would talk about women and make fun of each other.

Feyerabend was as mesmerizing in conversation as he was during his lectures. It was difficult then to notice his metal crutch or the constant pain and bad health that he had to overcome during his adult life. Before the great fame, or notoriety, that *Against Method* brought him, he was already an intellectual giant. Standing in the grass by the Campanile a year ago, I vividly remembered his animated face, his contagious laughter, and that extraordinarily sharp mind that delighted his students, his colleagues, his friends – a mind worthy of the greatest admiration.

Someone wrote in the famous journal *Nature* that Feyerabend was the worst enemy of science. But, on the contrary, what Feyerabend did was demonstrate how complex and human science can and should be. Of his many contributions, perhaps the most important is that there is no method or rule that can capture the nature of science. Even the most excellent idea about the practice of science must allow for exceptions. And when we examine the history of science, we discover not only that the great scientists violated the so-called "empirical method," in all its main incarnations, but they had to violate it, for otherwise the great accomplishments by which we know them today would not have come to pass.

Some intellectuals, particularly analytic philosophers in the English speaking world, felt that Feyerabend was insane, or at best, the court jester in philosophy of science. But many people around the world who have read his works, published in many languages, have thought very highly of those works. Over the years, I had doctoral students and post-docs from Europe, China and Africa come to work with me on Feyerabend. I felt honored to be able to guide them. Not that I refrained from criticizing him; surely no less than when I used to sit across a restaurant table from him, or on the grass at Berkeley, with the Campanile looming large behind him.

Even if my main philosophical view, evolutionary relativism, which I will discuss in this book, may go well beyond Feyerabend's body of work, he was glad that I went my own way. *A Theory of Wonder* is one more book in a long series of books I have published. It may be the last. As I share it with you, I wish to honor someone who showed me the way no less by his example than by his writing and his teaching.

It is only fair that I devote this preface to Paul K. Feyerabend. After all, he wrote the foreword to my very first book, *Radical Knowledge*.

FOREWORD

by David Lamb

A Theory of Wonder is a tribute to the legendary Paul Feyerabend of whom the author was a student. It outlines philosophy of science as it appeared before Feyerabend and advances to the author's well-developed theory of evolutionary relativism, first outlined in his groundbreaking book, *Radical Knowledge*, in 1981, which argued that since both perception and scientific knowledge depended on the brain, and since evolution could create different kinds of brains (or equivalents of the central nervous system), the notion of grasping the naked truth of the world, so to speak, was unsustainable. This book was followed by his *Evolution and the Naked Truth* in 1998, a collection of essays that elaborated his original ideas. Among those original ideas was the suggestion that Munévar's evolutionary relativism can be seen as overlapping with Feyerabend's principle of proliferation. When seen from an evolution inspired perspective, Munévar's approach leads to a social conception of scientific rationality. These ideas are further developed here in close connection to an insightful account of the revolution in the philosophy of science brought about by Kuhn and Feyerabend, with particular emphasis on Feyerabend.

A Theory of Wonder is also influenced by the large amount of work that Munévar has published, and helped publish, concerning the philosophy of his mentor and PhD Dissertation Director at Berkeley, Paul Feyerabend. He edited highly regarded collections of essays on Feyerabend, such as *Beyond Reason* (Kluwer 1991) and *The Worst Enemy of Science?* (Oxford, 2000, co-edited with John Preston and David Lamb).

Munévar accomplishes two tasks in this contribution to the history and philosophy of science. The first is a critique of twentieth-century philosophy of science, outlining its successes and shortcomings; and the second is the development of the author's own theory of evolutionary relativism. In the early chapters, Munévar critiques the so-called scientific method or received view, where observations are said to support theories and are in some way distinct from them. According to the received view, the scientific method consists in having observation pass judgment on theory, either by supporting it or by rejecting it. Practically every introductory science textbook devotes a good portion of its first chapter to emphasize the importance of the scientific method and to give credit to its inventor, Galileo. But whilst the founder of the scientific method is said to be Galileo, an examination of his science reveals that his approach actually ran counter to claims regarding the distinction between observation and theory.

Two aspects of the standard empiricist account of the scientific method, inductivism and falsificationism associated with Sir Karl Popper, are covered in the early chapters. Rejecting both aspects of the standard empiricist account of the relationship between observations and theory, both Kuhn and Feyerabend drew attention to the actual history of science rather than appeals to the scientific method. They published their initial versions of a historical approach to the comprehension of science in 1962, thus igniting a revolution in the philosophy of science. Nevertheless, there were major differences in their respective standpoints. According to Kuhn, the basic concepts and practices of a scientific community are located within paradigms, which are held until anomalies build up and force a scientific revolution or paradigm shift. To this end, Kuhn defended dogmatism in his principle of tenacity, holding that a paradigm is held dogmatically as long as it holds the promise that it will prove the best way to conceive of the world until it is overcome by a crisis brought on by anomalies. In contrast, Feyerabend held that rather than dogmatically holding to a paradigm we ought to create more crises, and therefore more fruitful change, in Kuhn's own terms, by providing a mechanism to strengthen the anomalies. To accomplish this goal, science should be organized so as to require the continuous generation of alternatives. This is what Feyerabend called the principle of proliferation.

Of considerable interest, and well covered here, is Imre Lakatos's theory of competing research programmes, which involved Lakatos's objective to make Kuhn and Feyerabend's insights cohere into a rational pattern. Lakatos's model of research programme aims to combine Popper's adherence to empirical validity with Kuhn's appreciation for conventional consistency. In essence, his idea is that the proper mix of the principles of tenacity and proliferation leads to the growth of science and would portray the history of science as rational. Lakatos's theory of competing research programmes is covered here in considerable depth, and Munévar argues that the methodology of research programs is not able to overcome Feyerabend's objections because when we look at the actual practice of science, we see that in order to progress scientists sometimes had to violate the most cherished methodological rules—rules as basic as "do not advance hypotheses that conflict with the facts." This is what Copernicus, Galileo, Newton, Einstein and many others had to do, even when they preached otherwise, as in the case of Newton. What is at stake is not the simple-minded point that people of great insight may take shortcuts, but rather that the methodology of science advocated by many philosophers may be incompatible with scientific success.

According to Feyerabend, when scientists consider alternative views, they may change theoretical assumptions, and as a result, also change what counts as evidence. This was elaborated in *Against Method* and most of Feyerabend's subsequent work. Nevertheless, Munévar takes Feyerabend's insights much further by looking at science through neuroscience in the context of evolutionary biology. In addition to the achievements of the historical school of Feyerabend and Kuhn, Munévar adds an important scientific perspective, arguing that science is produced by biological creatures, so accordingly, biology is applied to investigate the nature of science: evolutionary biology first, and then neuroscience in the context of evolution.

According to Munévar, evolutionary relativism holds that an organism's view of the world depends on its mind, that mind depends on biology, that biology supports a logically impeccable form of relativism, and that success explains truth, not the other way around. This approach is consistent with the history of science and with the science most relevant to understanding the pursuit of knowledge.

The scope and depth of insight make it difficult to think of comparable attempts. The originality of Munévar's findings and his scholarship in the several philosophical and scientific fields he brings to the table make those findings very significant. That significance, furthermore, is likely to have a great impact, for *A Theory of Wonder* is written in a clear language accessible not only to professional philosophers but to students and to those members of the general public curious about the nature of scientific knowledge. It should also appeal greatly to the many people whose interest in Feyerabend is greatly increasing as we approach the celebrations for his Centennial in early 2024.

CHAPTER 1

INTRODUCTION

We take our first steps and the world around us assaults our senses with excitement and fires our imaginations with mystery. As we grow up, an enigmatic universe teases our curiosity, and often infects us for life with an overwhelming sense of wonder. In our civilization that sense of wonder has evoked a systematic response: science. This science of ours studies what intrigues us about nature, and in weaving its wondrous tales, it becomes itself a most fascinating object of study. Science thus becomes itself a source of wonder.

The purpose of this book is to determine the best way science can continue to satisfy our sense of wonder by exploring the world. Now, it is presumably well known that the reason science succeeds is because it follows the scientific method, which consists in having observation pass judgment on theory, either by supporting it or by rejecting it. Practically every introductory science textbook devotes a good portion of its first chapter to emphasize the importance of the scientific method and to give credit to its inventor, Galileo. This view of how scientific knowledge does, and should, work is called "empiricism" (for the priority it gives to experience). If perchance the students who were so introduced to science happen to read what Galileo actually wrote and did, they would be shocked to find out that he instead drives a dagger through the heart of empiricism: He strikes down the distinction between theory and observation.

Now, a most famous description of the scientific method as inductive reasoning was given by Newton in his classic *Principia Mathematica*, in the section titled "Rules for Reasoning in Philosophy." Today it would be called "Rules for Reasoning in Science," but at that time science was still part of philosophy. We will discuss the basic insights and difficulties of induction as the method of science in Chapter 2. And we will pay particular attention to Newton's inductive rules in Chapter 3. Newton spoke of standing on the shoulders of giants, with Galileo particularly in mind. But had Galileo not violated Newton's rules, the Copernican Revolution, which removed the Earth from the center of the universe and placed it in motion, would have failed, and *Principia Mathematica* most likely would have never been written.

In Chapter 3, we will consider the proposal that falsification is the method of science, i.e. that scientists should test their theories against the facts, and if those theories conflict with the facts, then they should be rejected. There are several problems with this apparently sensible suggestion. The worst is that, if Galileo was right and theory and observation are not naturally distinct, there is no reason to assume that experience (through observation) must always take precedence over theory. Indeed, as we will see, progress in science may require scientists to follow Galileo's example, from time to time, and replace the body of accepted facts with a radically different one. Science would thus be a form of radical knowledge.

In Chapter 4, we will consider a more sophisticated version of falsificationism attributed to Karl Popper, the one 20th Century philosopher of science to meet with general approval within the scientific community. Over much of history, the most prominent philosophers—e.g., Plato, Aristotle, Descartes, Kant—made insightful comments on the nature of science and exerted considerable influence on the directions taken by science. We might say they were the philosophers of science of their day. In today's academic circles, or at least in philosophy departments, it is supposed that just as science constructs theories about the universe, philosophy of science constructs theories about science. Thus, it should seem surprising that the philosophy of science is nowadays far more obscure to the intelligent lay reader than the nature of black holes, while exciting far less curiosity. It may seem even more surprising that trained scientists do not fare better in this respect. What can account for this situation?

Part of the problem is simply that most scientists have been baffled by the linguistic and "logical" concerns of the analytic philosophers who dominated philosophy of science during much of 20th Century, as well as by their impenetrable jargon. But apart from its being unintelligible, logical positivism, the main analytic view, amounted to a dead end as a philosophy of science. Fortunately, it was challenged by thinkers trained in science who paid great attention to the history and practice of science. It was people like Thomas Kuhn and Paul Feyerabend, then, who turned our attention to Galileo's actual views, and who cast very serious doubts on all the most familiar views on method. We could call them and others with similar approaches the historical school. In very revealing remarks, Carl Hempel, one of the most important analytic philosophers of science, pointed out correctly that the historical school of thought "rejects the idea of methodological principles arrived at by purely philosophical analysis" (1978, 292).

The logical school insists on such principles, however, since it is heir to a tradition that holds that the job of philosophy is to determine the foundations of empirical knowledge. In this sense, philosophy is intellectually prior to science (it tells science where it may tread). Thus considerations from the actual practice of science would seem to be of little relevance. In the eyes of the logical school of thought, Hempel continues, "The methodology of science... is concerned solely with certain logical and systematic aspects of science which form the basis of its soundness and rationality—in abstraction from, and indeed to the exclusion of, the psychological and historical facets of science as a social enterprise" (1978, 291).

It is not surprising that scientists might tend to find this arm-chair theorizing about science rather presumptuous, but the main problem is that the "logical aspects" involved require both the inductive and the deductive "logics" of the analytic philosophers. In Chapter 2 we will learn of the resounding failure of the so-called "inductive logic." And in Chapter 6 we will see that the "deductive logic" of analytic philosophy is based on very bad reasoning and applies neither to science nor to what most human beings would like to call "real life."

But before getting too far ahead of myself, I should mention that in Chapter 5 we will discuss Kuhn's ideas about scientific "paradigms," his distinction between revolutionary and normal science, and his thesis about the incommensurability in the meaning of scientific terms (that the meanings of the same terms might be different in two paradigms). We will also become acquainted with Feyerabend's version of such a thesis. I will also suggest there that the issue of incommensurability need not pertain to meanings at all.

In Chapter 6, we will move on to Feyerabend, the man called an "irrationalist" by a great many philosophers and others who have misread his main works. He has been accused, for example, of claiming that in science "anything goes." What he did say is that, when confronted with the actual practice and history of science, a "rationalist" (the run-of-the-mill philosopher) will conclude in horror that in science "anything goes." But Feyerabend does not agree with such a characterization, let alone recommend it. Much to be recommended, however, is his Principle of Proliferation, as I will point out. In addition, I will present my argument that the "logic" of philosophers is irrelevant to science in crucial ways.

In Chapter 7 we will take a look at the very clever attempt by Imre Lakatos to incorporate several of Kuhn and Feyerabend's main ideas into a system of competing "research programs" that, he hoped, would paint the history of science as rational. For all his cleverness, however, Lakatos' methodology of research programs is not able to overcome Feyerabend's objections.

Now, what the historical school shows is that the so-called scientific method does *not* always work. Not that we cannot *prove* that it works, even though it does. But that it does *not* always work. These philosophers argue that we have been taken in by a historical fiction. When we look at the actual practice of science, we see that in order to progress scientists sometimes had to violate the most cherished methodological rules—rules as basic as "do not advance hypotheses that conflict with the facts." This is what Copernicus, Galileo, Newton, Einstein and many others had to do. Even when, as in the case of

Newton, they preached otherwise. What is at stake is not the simpleminded point that people of great insight may take shortcuts, but rather that method may be incompatible with scientific success.

Imagine that a staircase permits hikers to go from the top of a cliff to the beach below. Someone of extraordinary agility—and luck—may dismiss the steps, leap from the top, and land on her feet. But she could have taken the staircase to reach the same destination, albeit in not so spectacular a fashion. What the new philosophy of science claims, though, is that the staircase of method may well keep science from getting to the bottom of things. Such is the lesson that Kuhn, Feyerabend and others have drawn from the most significant episodes of the history of science. Furthermore, in such episodes, it was often the losing side—the one our ahistorical present derides—that put up the good fight for methodological propriety. To traditional empiricist ears it must be at least jarring to hear Galileo say, "There is no limit to my astonishment when I reflect that Aristarchus and Copernicus were able to make reason so to conquer sense that, in defiance of the latter, the former became mistress of their belief" (*Dialogue Concerning the Two Chief World Systems*, 381).

In a war of ideas, it is not uncommon to see the warring factions give way to a completely new vision of the field. And this book may be seen as an attempt to develop such a vision. What is at stake is our understanding of the nature of science. It will make use of the findings of the historical school. But it will add a scientific perspective as well, in Chapters 8-10. Science is produced by biological creatures, so we will apply biology to investigate the nature of science: evolutionary biology first, and then neuroscience in the context of evolution.

One of the issues to be discussed In Chapter 8 concerns the degree to which science can be said to be adaptive. Although that subject has a history of pitfalls, I think that a case can be made along those lines. And it will be seen that the downfall of method actually facilitates, such a case. It will also be seen that when science is taken as a social enterprise, it exhibits certain structural features that permit us to call it rational. Some readers may detect a possible connection with evolutionary epistemology. Indeed, there is. But whereas evolutionary epistemology mostly suggests analogies to evolution, I argue not that science is like nature, but that it is part of nature. Along the way, we will realize that thinking of science as a cumulative, progressive process, as suggested by some historians of science and some scientific realists, is undermined both by history and by evolutionary considerations about the nature of science.

In Chapter 9, we will discuss the realist argument that the success of science can make sense only if we assume that science discovers the truth about the world. We will see, however, that a proper application of evolutionary biology, in combination with neuroscience, defeats realism and leads to the realization that science is not only open to radical transformation, as history indicates, but that it should be so. That will be an important topic of this chapter and the next. This chapter will pay particular attention to how distortion and exaggeration may often lead us to more successful interactions with the world than veridical perceptions would.

In Chapter 10, we will consider that there might exist "brains" with structures very different from ours, but which may nonetheless serve those other species as well as our kind of brain serves our own species. It would then be highly arbitrary to insist that whatever science our brains develop best resembles the God's Eye point of view. It is clear that different species often do experience the world differently. Those different ways of experiencing the world, including conceiving of the world, are relative to what we may call frames of reference determined by biology. And we may speak of a "complementarity," at least potentially, that is in some way reminiscent of Niels Bohr's epistemology. This evolutionary relativism is the last nail in the coffin of realism, at the level of science. The chapter will then expose the reasoning blunders in the best-regarded objections against relativism. And it will also suggest a reasonable theory of relative truth. Furthermore, instead of leading to a view of science as irrational, thinking of science as radical knowledge, as biology and the history of science suggest, makes us recognize that drastic changes may occur at any level of our scientific enterprise and yield scientific progress.

When all is said and done, this book will settle for a new and optimistic vision of science. I hope that scientists and intelligent lay readers, who have been left out of the proceedings for too long, will wish to join this journey to understand the organized response to our sense of wonder.

REFERENCES

Galileo. (2001). *Dialogue Concerning the Two Chief World Systems.* Stillman Drake, trans. *The Modern Library.* First published in 1632.

Hempel, C. (1978). "Scientific Rationality: Normative vs. Descriptive Construals," in *Wittgenstein, the Vienna Circle and Critical Rationalism.* Proceedings of the 3rd International Wittgenstein Symposium.

CHAPTER 2

THE TRIALS AND TRIBULATIONS OF INDUCTION

Galileo is to be commended, wrote Richard Rorty, a prominent philosopher, "for preferring his eyes to his Aristotle."[1] Rorty assumes, as many others do, that Galileo succeeded because he did not allow theoretical speculation to taint his careful observations of the world. Indeed, most people, many scientists included, are under the impression that science is successful, unlike religion and magic, because scientists ultimately judge the worth of their ideas by the evidence of the senses.

This insight is the heart of empiricist philosophy. Now, there are two main ways in which our observations – our experience of the world – can be used to pass judgement upon scientific theories, and thus two main kinds of empiricism. The first one is simply that experience may give evidence in favor of a theory. The second is that experience may give evidence against a theory. In this chapter, I will concentrate on the first, on evidence that supports a theory directly. This is the province of an empiricist view of science called **inductivism**, according to which science uses a special kind of reasoning called **induction,** which presumably has the great Isaac Newton as a patron saint.

The main version of inductivism in the 20th Century was Logical Positivism, and his main proponent was Rudolf Carnap. A rather extensive bibliography of his most pertinent publications is enclosed. Nonetheless, the discussion of inductivism in the 20th Century and before will be kept brief. It is no longer a popular or promising view. Karl Popper wrote that *"Induction, i.e. inference based on many observations, is a myth. It is neither a psychological fact, nor a fact of ordinary life, nor one of scientific procedure" (1963, 53).*[2] The most important issues of this book will be properly introduced in connection with falsificationism in Chapter 3.

For many empiricists, our theories should have the maximum support possible, although some support is better than none. But for some philosophers nothing

---

1 Richard Rorty. *Philosophy and the Mirror of Nature* (Princeton: Princeton University Press, 1979), p. 246.

2 See also his *Logic of Scientific Discovery* (1959).

short of the ideal is acceptable: they demand that theory be *proved* by fact. Now, what is a proof? For philosophers, to prove something means to put it beyond doubt. The classical example of this sort of philosophical rigor was set by the French philosopher, mathematician and scientist Rene Descartes (1596-1650).[3] This demand for proof, when coupled with the empiricist ideal that experience be the ultimate judge of theory, leads to something like the following account, which Descartes, himself not an empiricist, would not have favored.

To build a true science we must begin with a solid foundation: nature itself. The world should have a say on what ideas scientists accept. But the world, or nature, can speak only through our experience of it. Unfortunately, even sensory experience can be distorted by intellectual prejudice and bias, as the English philosopher Francis Bacon (1561- 1626) argued.[4] We may, for example, fail to see those aspects of nature that do not agree with the theories that are dear to our heart. Hence, before looking at nature, we must cleanse our minds of all bias, or theoretical influences, so our experience can be undistorted and thus trustworthy. Science starts with a process of purification, with a search for objectivity, to ensure that when we read the book of nature we report truly what is writ in it and no more. As the British astronomer John Herschel (1831) put it, science requires "the absolute dismissal and clearing the mind of all prejudice. . . and the determination to stand and fall by the result of a direct appeal to the facts. . . ."[5]

Second, from this foundation we *derive* the rest of scientific knowledge (science requires, that is, in Herschel's words, "the *strict* logical derivation from the [facts]"). Only logically or mathematically valid derivations can constitute *proof* because only they can transmit the truth of the foundations. That is, only valid inferences guarantee at every step that we do not go from a truth to a falsehood (indeed, the definition of a valid inference is one in which it is impossible for all the premises to be true and the conclusion false).

By fulfilling these two requirements we will presumably ensure that our ideas about nature be justified by nature itself.

This empiricist account of science has taken a terrible beating over the years. But before moving on to more sophisticated versions of empiricism, it pays to examine why this form of inductivism fails, so that we may better appraise the virtues of those other versions.

---

[3] Rene Descartes, *Discourse on Method* (1637) and *Principles of Philosophy* (1644).

[4] Francis Bacon, *Novum Organum* (1620).

[5] John Herschel's *Preliminary Discourse of Natural Philosophy* (1831).

OBJECTIONS TO THIS IDEAL OF EMPIRICISM

The challenge to the empiricist ideal has two parts, one per each of the empiricist requirements for proving theories. First, the empiricist requires observations of nature untainted by theory (pure experience); and second, he requires that the truth of those observations be passed on to the theories without loss. The foundation must be firm and the structure erected upon it must be flawless. This is, of course, an ideal. It is not an objection against it that since we are imperfect we cannot really get rid of all bias or avoid all mistakes in reasoning. What we want to determine is whether scientists ought to be guided by it.

An extreme version of this ideal, if correct, might make it possible to put science in the hands of robots. A complete lack of bias seems to suggest that scientists should treat all data equally, for to assign greater importance to some of the data implies a bias. Thus, in the far future perhaps, we could program a robot to collect all the data pertaining to some question of scientific interest. The robot would then derive the correct scientific answer to the question.

Some simple considerations, however, demonstrate the implausibility of such a mechanical way of doing science. As the Austrian philosopher Karl Popper (1902-1994) emphasized, the collection of facts cannot succeed without at least some prior guesses or hypotheses as to what the answer to our quest might be like. The scientist is asked to observe (and carefully at that). But if a scientist, say Niels, is asked to observe, what is he expected to do?

If Niels has really cleansed his mind of all preconceived ideas, of all prior expectations, and he goes into a chemical laboratory where an experiment is going on, what observations would he report? Would he describe the clock on the wall? The smell on the benches? The patterns formed by the light as it comes through the window? No. He would presumably zero in on the experiment. But he is likely to do that only because of his prior knowledge, from which he gets clues as to what is most important in the room. Observing requires some sort of direction. Without it, the task soon becomes unwieldy (he might, for example, examine instead the quality of the wood on the benches and the porosity of the wall). We must narrow our field of observations, or else science cannot even begin.[6]

The suggestion that Niels should restrict his observations to those relevant to the problem will not help much. Problems do not normally come with tags as to what is relevant to observe. And when they do, it is only because they have been posed against a background of prior knowledge that directs our attention

---

[6] See Popper's critiques in the works referenced.

to certain aspects of those problems. Let us take an example. Right before the sun sets, it seems to grow larger. Why? In order to answer this question, we immediately narrow the domain of observation. We would not send a spaceship to keep tabs on the sun, for we do not believe it actually gets larger. No. The scientific knowledge we already have leads us to hypothesize instead that perhaps it is an optical illusion similar to the *Moon illusion,* for the Moon also gets larger near the horizon, and thus proceed using the techniques of perceptual psychology. The point is that we decide that certain things are worth checking into or not, depending on our tentative solutions to the problem.

By contrast, a true "inductive machine," or robot, that treats all data equally would be overwhelmed by them. Science cannot be mechanically generated from mere experience.

Nevertheless, this result is devastating only to an extreme version of inductivism. A more reasonable inductivist might argue that scientists are only obligated to ensure that the hypotheses they make prior to observing an aspect of the world do not distort those observations. In the next chapter, I will discuss whether even such "unbiased" experience is really possible, even in principle. But for the time being, let us assume that our scientific efforts will reward us with a fine collection of relevant facts or "data." Can we use these data to prove theories?

The answer is no. Strictly speaking, a *proof* must contain *no* steps in which it is *possible* to go on from truth to falsehood. It seems difficult, however, to avoid such faulty steps when the conclusions (in our case, the scientific theories) have a greater content than the evidence supporting them. The laws of rocket propulsion (or rather a theory about what the laws of propulsion are) should apply to all rockets we can think of, not only to the relatively few rockets that we have flown. The view that theories can be proved by the facts suffers from this logical difficulty on two levels.[7]

First, inductive rules, or rules for generalizing from the data, cannot lead by themselves to concepts not encountered in the data. At first sight, this is just as it should be, for a good scientist presumably never goes beyond the evidence. The problem is that when we look at the history of science, we notice that in many instances progress required the introduction of new concepts not present in the available data.

As an illustration, let us consider an important hypothesis advanced by Torricelli, one of Galileo's pupils. Galileo and many other scientists, or natural

[7] Hume was particularly influential in getting this point across. See his works referenced in this chapter.

philosophers as they were then called, had been intrigued by the fact that suction pumps could not raise water more than 34 ft. over the surface of the well. It occurred to Torricelli that the suction pump created a vacuum; this vacuum would offer no resistance to the pressure exerted upon the water by a sea of air that surrounded the Earth (the atmosphere). The water rises only 34 ft. because the column of air pushing the water weighs only so much. Pascal used Torricelli's hypothesis to conjecture that this column of air would also support a column of mercury (a much shorter one, obviously, since mercury is considerably heavier than water). This is how the barometer was born. Pascal also conjectured that the height of the column of mercury would decrease as the barometer was carried to higher altitudes, for the simple reason that the column of air exerting pressure upon the liquid would be shorter. In a famous experiment, Pascal's brother-in-law, Perier, confirmed Pascal's conjecture by carrying a barometer up the Puy-de-Dome while a control barometer at the foot of the mountain remained unchanged.

The moral of the story is that no generalization or mathematical deduction from all the data about suction pumps would have produced Torricelli's sea of air. Progress sometimes requires creative, not mechanical intelligence. We may also note that what made Torricelli's such a good scientific hypothesis is precisely that it went beyond the evidence: Pascal extended it to cover the behavior of columns of mercury at different altitudes, surely a matter on which no evidence had been gathered.

This point leads to a similar difficulty at a *second* level. It was pointed out by the Scottish philosopher David Hume (1711-1776) that if science is supposed to be based on experience, then we seem destined to make claims about a large class of unexamined cases on the basis of a (relatively) few examined cases.[8] Scientific theories normally have a much more general scope than the finite and limited body of facts available to scientists, as we saw in the case of rocket propulsion. Thus, there is greater content in the conclusion than in the evidence. This means that parts of the conclusion cannot be warranted by the evidence, and thus that it is possible to move from a truth to a falsehood. As a consequence, no valid mathematical or logical derivation is possible.

Scientific reasoning, as described by inductivism, is then invalid.

This is the famous problem of induction, which at one time, the German philosopher Immanuel Kant (1724-1804) called the "scandal of philosophy." A special case of this problem occurs when we conclude that a theory is true because it has led to accurate predictions. In this case, the evidence from which

---

[8] Hume. Mainly in his *Treatise,* Book I (1740).

we "induce" the truth of the theory is admittedly of small scope, but somehow it is also very impressive. Thus, for example, if Albert Einstein's General Theory of Relativity is correct, light rays should bend around large masses such as stars. Since light rays do bend around stars, we think that we have evidence in favor of General Relativity. Our intuition tells us that there must be something right about this point. But unfortunately, our intuition does not also come with an explanation of how successful predictions alone can, in general, guarantee the truth of the hypothesis or theory in question. To see why let us look at a passage from Mark Twain's *Huckleberry Finn*:

> I've always reckoned that looking at the new moon over your left shoulder is one of the carelessest and foolishest things a body can do. Old Hank Bunker done it once, and bragged about it; and in less than two years he got drunk and fell off of the shot tower, and spread himself out so that he was just a kind of a layer, as you may say, and they slid him edgeways between two barn doors for a coffin, and buried him so, so they say, but I didn't see it. Pap told me. But anyway it all come of looking at the moon that way, like a fool.

The fallacy in this reasoning comes from supposing that since the hypothesis (looking at the moon over your left shoulder is bad for you) led us to expect that something awful would happen to Hank Bunker, then the hypothesis is the *only way* of accounting for Hank's untimely death. In the case of scientific hypotheses, we tend to be so impressed because we cannot think of anything else that could have brought about the same event. But that may only indicate the shortcomings of our imagination. In any event, a mode of reasoning that is fallacious in real life (or literature) is not transformed into good reasoning as soon as it enters the laboratory. Let us see some examples.

According to a hypothesis by the Scottish physician John Hunter (18th Century), syphilis and gonorrhea are caused by the same agent and are, thus, basically the same disease, except that the symptoms of gonorrhea appear when a mucous membrane is infected, and those of syphilis develop when the skin is infected instead. We should expect, accordingly, that advanced cases of gonorrhea would develop into cases of syphilis. In order to check the hypothesis, it would be crucial to see whether patients who suffer from gonorrhea for some time eventually develop the symptoms of syphilis. As it turned out, the "confirming" instances came in great numbers. If we were to apply the proposed mode of inference, then we should conclude that Hunter's hypothesis had been proved by the facts (or validated or confirmed). But the hypothesis is actually false. It just so happens that victims of one disease often contract the other, both being risks of a certain life style, although the symptoms of syphilis may not appear until much later.

Another illustration is provided by Van Helmont's experimental "proof" of the claim that water was the sole constituent of vegetative matter (1662). After questioning the prevalent Aristotelian predilection for mixtures of the four basic elements (earth, water, air and fire), Helmont reported as follows:

> I took an earthen vessel, in which I put 200 pounds of earth that had dried in a furnace, which I moystened with Rain-water, and I implanted therein the Trunk or Stem of a Willow Tree, weighing five pounds; and at length, five years being finished, the Tree sprung from thence did weigh 269 pounds and about 3 ounces. But I moystened the Earthen Vessel with Rain-water, or distilled water (always when there was need), and it was large and implanted into the Earth, and lest the dust that flew about should be co-mingled with the Earth, I covered the lip and mouth of the vessel, and there were found the same 200 pounds, wanting about 2 ounces. Therefore 264 pounds of Wood, Barks and Roots arose out of the water only.[9]

If Van Helmont's hypothesis about water were correct, then the results of the experiment would be exactly as those actually observed. But the problem is that they would also be so if the hypothesis were false and some very different one true (e.g., a hypothesis involving photosynthesis and a few other processes not known in his time). This is the problem we face every time we apply the fallacious mode of reasoning under discussion.

Einstein had supposed that the great mass of the sun would change the geometry of space-time in its vicinity in such a way that the rays of light from other stars would be deflected so they would look closer to the sun than they should be expected to be in the night sky (for a more detailed explanation see Chapter 7). Scientists did look for other possible explanations. According to Newton's theory of light, particles of light have mass. It follows then that rays of light passing near the sun would feel a strong gravitational pull towards the sun. But the predicted Newtonian deflection was far less than observed, and we do not believe today that photons (Einstein's particles of light) have mass. Other alternative theories without these drawbacks, although with others, have been proposed since Einstein's (see Chapter 4). Moreover, Einstein's General Relativity could also explain why Mercury's perihelion (the closest point to the sun in Mercury's orbit) was off 43" from expectation. As the years went on, and particularly since the beginning of space exploration, more and more predictions from General Relativity are coming true. Any competing theory—and some are offered from time to time—has a lot to overcome. But the point

---

[9] Quoted in Toulmin S. and Goodfield J.'s *The Architecture of Matter* (1962, pp. 152-153).

is that a plausible, nay, convincing case may be offered for Einstein's theory on the basis of its prediction, but that being convincing, even overwhelmingly convincing, is not the sort of proof this type of inductivism was after.

ATTEMPTS TO JUSTIFY INDUCTION

We might have hoped for a mechanism that would crank out knowledge about the world, a scientific discovery machine, as long as we were pure of scientific mind and steady of mathematical hand. But unfortunately, we cannot collect all the facts nor avoid prior hypotheses. To get around this frustrating situation, some empiricists decided to emphasize the *justification* of theories instead of their *discovery*. Thus Rudolf Carnap (1891-1970), the most prominent figure of the famous Vienna Circle, says that the task of finding "a law for the explanation of given phenomena...cannot be solved by any mechanical procedure or by fixed rules; it is rather solved through the intuition, the inspiration, and the good luck of the scientist." A consequence of this distinction is that since in discovering a theory "such nonrational factors as intuition or the inspiration of genius play a decisive role," discovery can no longer be the province of philosophy (for presumably philosophy deals only with the rational). The job of philosophy of science consists of developing a rational procedure for examining theories once they are proposed. As Carnap says, "the relation between a theory and the observational evidence available is, strictly speaking, not that of *inferring* the one from the other but rather that of *judging* the theory of the basis of the evidence when both are given."[10]

The reader may wonder, however, how such a move can get around Hume's objection to the effect that the mode of inference of "induction" is fallacious; for there does not seem to be a way to avoid generalizing from a limited body of observational evidence to a conclusion of general scope.

1. *The Uniformity of Nature*

One way of countering this objection is to suggest that nature is uniform, and that, consequently, unobserved events will be very much like those we have already observed. Many scientists do feel that without the belief in the uniformity of nature it would make no sense to practice science, for presumably the alternative to a regular cosmos would be chaos, and if chaos reigns there is no regularity to discover. But these scientists' feelings aside, can this suggestion of the uniformity of nature save the day for inductivism?

---

[10] Cited by Lakatos in *Mathematics, Science and Epistemology* (1980, 146).

The merit of this suggestion is presumably that if nature is uniform, the scientific mode of reasoning will be valid. If the hypothesis under test agrees with the evidence in the section of nature we have already examined, and if we assume that the rest of nature will be like that section, it follows that the hypothesis will be true everywhere. That is, we have proved our hypothesis, for we have gone from true premises to a conclusion that cannot be false.

But is the assumption of the uniformity of nature true? In some clear sense, nature is not uniform. Whereas water boils at a certain temperature in New York City, it will not do so in Quito, Ecuador. Early European explorers of the North were greeted with derision when they spoke of the midnight sun. Nature looks different, feels different as we move from place to place. But perhaps what is meant by the uniformity of nature is that the same laws operate everywhere. Thus, according to Einstein, for example, even though every region of space-time may be different from all others, it still conforms to his theory of General Relativity. Assuming the uniformity of nature may also prove useful. Paleontology, for example, is supposed to have advanced by assuming that the same forces of nature that operate on the fauna and flora of today also operated on extinct species. Thus, by comparing a few salvaged dinosaur bones with those of living species, say iguanas, 19th Century paleontologists thought they could make reliable guesses about what the dinosaurs were like.

Whether this principle is a useful guide to research is an interesting issue. But the question at hand is one of justification, of whether the principle of the uniformity of nature can help us prove, now or in the future, that our scientific theories are true.

Right away, we face the problem that no one knows how to prove that the principle itself is true; so it seems that we have to take it on faith. Perhaps this is not a grave transgression, for the principle is only one step in our more general proof; and even though we have to accept it on faith, this little bit of faith can go a long way in science.

This concession is unnecessarily generous, however, for the principle of the uniformity of nature does not do the job expected of it. When it comes to proving the truth of theories, this principle is either contradictory or useless.

Let us first see why it may be contradictory. In examining raw data, we presumably look for patterns that make the data cohere, that make them manageable. In a limited sample, however, it is in principle possible to find more than one pattern consistent with the data. The problem is that when we gather more data the patterns (or functions) may now conflict, as we can see illustrated in **Figures 2.1-2.5**. Since we assume the uniformity of nature, we have to expect that future data will conform to the same patterns. Since the two patterns accounted for the data in the limited sample, we must expect that the data will continue to cohere **with both patterns** as the sample expands. We can see in **Figures 2.1-2.5**, however, that as the sample expands, the two patterns give us different expectations as to what the future data will be like. That is, given the uniformity of nature, the data has to conform to two **different**, **now conflicting** patterns at the same time (in the expanded sample). This is impossible, though. In order to conform to one pattern, the data must avoid conforming to at least some parts of the other pattern. Applied without restrictions, then, the principle of the uniformity of nature leads to a contradiction.

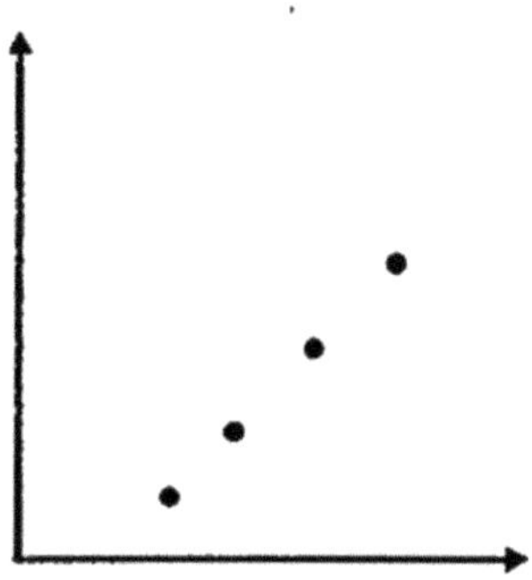

Figure 2.1.
Data points. Author.

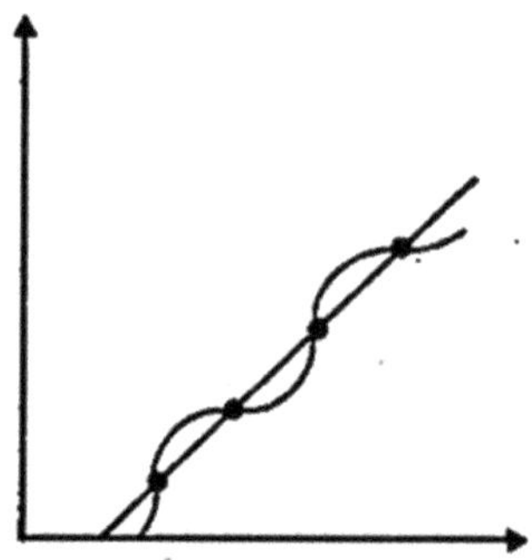

Figure 2.2.
Functions consistent with data. Author.

The data from Figure 2.1 can be accounted by either of the two functions drawn in Figure 2.2. But according to the principle of uniformity of nature, future data will conform to the patterns (the functions) already established.

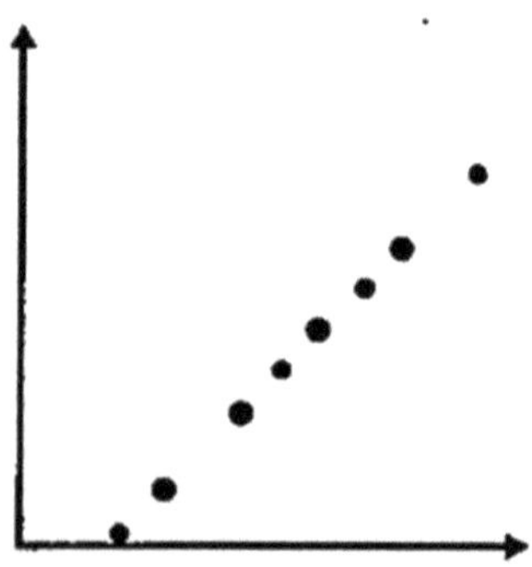

Figure 2.3.
Additional data for first function. Author.

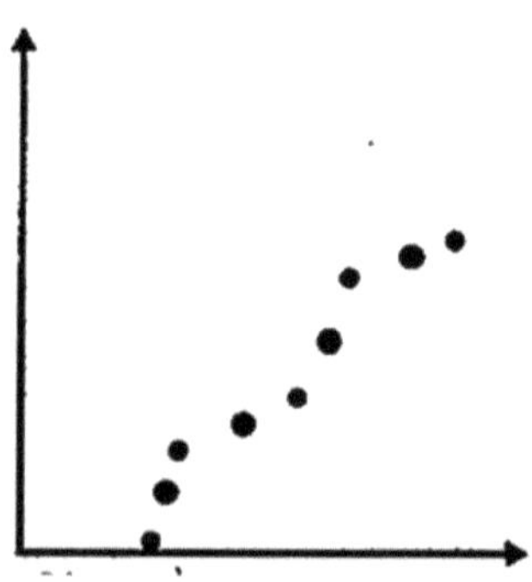

Figure 2.4.
Inconsistent additional data for second function. Author.

That is, we must expect the distribution of data to be in accordance with Figure 2.3. But we must also expect it to be in accordance with Figure 2.4! The principle leads to contradictory expectations, and is, therefore, a contradictory principle.

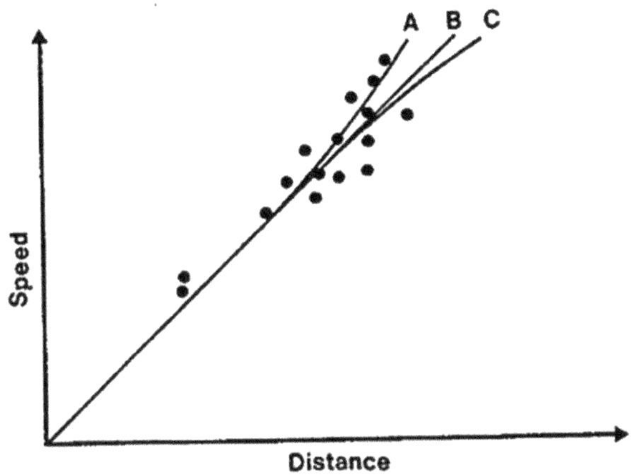

Figure 2.5. The Hubble Law extended to great distances. Author.

The Hubble Law extended to great distances. The shape of the universe affects how the Hubble Law looks when we include data for the most distant galaxies. Curve A corresponds to a positively curved universe, curve B to a flat universe, and curve C to a negatively curved universe.

To avoid this contradiction, inductivists may require that our samples be representative. Surely, if a sample is representative, those patterns that agree within it will continue to agree as the sample expands (that is part of what being representative means). But here comes a big problem. To say that a sample is representative is to say that the rest of nature (or the aspect of it we are investigating) is just like our sample in all the important respects. Thus, it is not enough to say that nature is uniform; we need nature to be uniform in just this way. Therefore, even if the principle is true, we still have to determine that the sample in question is representative. Knowing that nature is uniform tells us nothing about whether any given sample is representative or not. This makes the principle useless.

The point can be expressed in a variety of ways. Suppose that nature is uniform at the level of laws. We still cannot be assured that the laws of our science are true, since we may have been misled by local phenomena into thinking that we have gotten hold of a law of nature. For example, an isolated tropical society may develop the notion that climate is very uniform, say, in terms of temperature, since that society has never experienced the change of the seasons. Thus, even if the principle of the uniformity of nature is true, it is useless. For it may always happen that what we now think is the order of nature may turn out to be nothing but the peculiar landscape of our cosmic neighborhood.

It is not surprising, then, that we have given up so many views of the world, so many laws of which at one time we felt very certain. Of course, nature may be uniform at the *next* deeper level, or at the one after that. But what we need to know is whether our present theories are at the appropriate level. To know that nature is uniform is of no use unless we know that our theories have captured that uniformity. Only that sort of knowledge can make valid the reasoning of the inductive method, and thus only that knowledge will permit us to speak of proof in science. But to have that knowledge is to know that our theories tell us what the world is really like, *that they are true.* That is, the principle of the uniformity of nature will permit us to prove that our theories are true only if we already know beforehand that they are true!

To summarize the argument: even if nature is uniform, it may be uniform in a way different from what our theories tell us it is. In that case, the principle of the uniformity of nature does not help us one iota in trying to prove the theories we have. On the other hand, to show that nature is uniform just in the way that our theories tell us it is, we need to show first that our theories are correct. But in this case, the principle of the uniformity of nature does not help us either.

At first sight, the principle led to contradictory expectations. To correct that, we had to take steps that made it useless instead. On the first horn of this dilemma we impale the principle as false (since a principle that leads to a contradiction is presumably false). On the second horn, we let the principle be true, but we impale it nonetheless because it cannot help us show that our theories are true. Either way, the principle does not live up to the hopes it has raised.

If Einstein is correct, then, the laws of his General Theory of Relativity will apply in every region of spacetime. But the question of how to determine such correctness is still open. As for paleontology, a field where the principle of the uniformity of nature appeared useful, anatomical comparisons with living species have often proved wildly misleading. Indeed, from a tooth that looked just like that of an iguana, some concluded that its ancient owner, the iguanodon, must have been way over a hundred feet long! Richard Owen, the originator of the term "dinosaur" (terrible lizard), thought that those comparisons were a scandal, and provided a more sensible approach. The extinct monsters are still monsters, but surely not of Godzilla's proportions. And Owen's methods have in turn been checked by the introduction of physiological and other types of considerations. In **Figures 2.6-2.9** we can see how some of these considerations changed radically the way the "terrible lizards" were supposed to look. Today paleontologists discuss ideas about the biology of dinosaurs that are more radical still (e.g., whether dinosaurs were warm-blooded, perhaps even social animals).

2. *The Future will Resemble the Past*

It was felt for a long time that there were two forms of reasoning: deductive and inductive. Induction was our means for thinking about the world; thus, if induction was inherently invalid, our reasoning about the world was hopelessly irrational. This result was understandably discomforting to the many who had long associated science with rationality.

Figure 2.6. Megalosaurus as described by Owen in *Geology and inhabitants of the ancient world*, London 1854.

Figure 2.7. Megalosaurus as conceived two decades later. Image by Contry CC BY-SA 3.0.

Figure 2.8. Iguanodon as described by Owen. Drawing by Samuel Griswold Goodrich (public domain Image).

Figure 2.9. The iguanodon as envisaged by later paleontologists. Painting by Joseph Smit (public domain image).

Nonetheless, annoyance rather than intellectual despair has met the objection in some quarters. Taking the bull by the horns, some thinkers have claimed that induction is the method of the sciences and it works, so there! Of course, we generalize from (relatively) small samples to all cases. But it takes sophistry to find anything wrong with that! This feeling has been aptly captured by the former Harvard professor of chemistry E. B. Wilson:

> Practical scientists who rashly allow themselves to listen to philosophers are likely to go away in a discouraged frame of mind, convinced that there is no logical foundation for the things they do, that all their alleged scientific laws are without justification, and that they are living in a world of naive illusion. Of course, once they get out into the sunlight again, they know that this is not so, that scientific principles do work, bridges stay up, eclipses occur on schedule, and atomic bombs go off.[11]

In general, the heart of this response is that as a matter of fact the inductive method has always worked in the past, therefore we should trust it. But before we cast philosophy aside and give full inductive steam to our scientific engines, we should consider the following counter reply: The response is question begging. According to the inductive method, if the many cases we have examined exhibit a certain property, then all cases (of that sort) that we

[11] *E. Bright Wilson Jr.* (1952), p.293.

examine in the future will exhibit the same property. Thus, if something has been reliable in the past, it will continue to be so. This is what the methodology tells us to do. And what justifies the methodology? What makes us find it **reliable**? The fact that is has been reliable in the past! Such "justification" has all the advantages circularity has to offer.

Someone who already finds philosophy suspect is unlikely to be impressed by this sort of counter-reply. It is just one more argument purporting to show that he cannot demonstrate what he feels in his bones is right.

I must point out, incidentally, that such inductive ossification is even more prevalent among philosophers than among scientists. Far from being the exasperating skeptics that E. B. Wilson imagines, many philosophers see their job as that of justifying the claims to knowledge made by the empirical sciences. Indeed, philosophers tend to share Wilson's mistrust of the skeptical line of reasoning, and to suspect that there is something fishy about it. As a not uncommon 20th Century argument would have it, since inductivism provides our standard of rationality, questions about it are actually pseudo-questions, for they cannot be asked reasonably without a standard of comparison in mind! A philosophy so remarkably willing to turn off its powers of reasoning surely deserves to be called accommodating!

In any event, we must realize that skepticism is not the issue. Not only is this defense of induction circular, it accepts without examination the thesis that the classical method has always worked in the past. But many historical examples, including those of Hunter's hypothesis and Van Helmont's tree experiment, as we have seen, testify otherwise. Not only has the method led people astray, its violation was clearly required for scientific progress to come about (for example in the case of Torricelli, since he had to introduce an idea, a sea of air, that could not have been derived from the data). Thus, the most stinging attack against "strict" inductivism is not that we cannot prove it—even if it is right—but that it is not the guide for science that it claims to be.

3. *A Retreat from Truth to Likelihood*

In the face of logical disaster, the heirs of inductivism have tried to make do with a less strict sense of "proof." Instead of demanding that the evidence show our theories to be true, we should require only that they be likely—or to be more "precise," that they be probable, in the sense of the calculus of probability.

On passing, this move to probability seems to make eminent sense. One should expect that better theories are more likely to be in agreement with the evidence than inferior theories. Just as the detective bets on the most likely suspect, the scientist pursues the most likely "hunch."

But can the clues we find in nature really tell us what views are most likely to be true? If I know that in a box there are seven black balls and three white ones, I can say that in a random drawing I am more likely to get a black ball. Indeed, in this case I can also say that the probability of my getting a black ball is 7/10 or .7. The probability is determined by dividing the number of possible favorable outcomes by the total number of possible outcomes (I have seven chances out of ten to get a black ball). But the problem with theories is that I do not know what proportion of outcomes in the entire universe are favorable to them.

It seems that at best I can estimate the probability of theories with respect to the evidence already available. This could be done, for example, by means of what is called "frequency probability," in which we measure the frequency of favorable outcomes in a given sample. As the size of the sample increases (in a presumably representative sample) we may feel more confident that we are approaching the true probability. Unfortunately, we have no assurance that further evidence will agree with the theories to the same degree. That is, all the problems of the previous sections apply to the probability version of induction as well — we can't prove that our theory will remain just as likely as it now appears, a point Hume made over two centuries ago. We cannot even show that it is *likely* that our theory will remain as likely as it now appears, and so on.[12]

Is not this, however, another case of philosophical punctiliousness? After all, do we not use probabilities and statistics in science with great success?

There is a significant difference, however, between determining the probability of an event, as we do in science all the time, and estimating the probability of general hypotheses and theories. It is this second task—which some conceived as the objective of an "inductive logic"—that concerns us now. When looking at history with this approach in mind, we should expect that the Copernican system was superior to Ptolemy's (which put the Earth at the center of the universe) because it had a higher probability. But nothing of the sort has ever been shown. Nor has anyone ever conceived of a way to assign probabilities to Newton's dynamics or to the Copenhagen interpretation of quantum physics, or to any other law or theory for that matter. One simply does not expect to find in a scientific textbook the probability values of the formulas that appear within its pages.

Nevertheless, the aim of inductive logic is to determine the probability of theories on the basis of the evidence. While what we actually *do* in scientific practice is pretty much the converse: We use scientific theories to determine the probability of events. We can do this because scientific theories tell us what

---

[12] Also in his *Treatise (1740)*.

the world is like (the equivalent of telling us that there are seven black and three white balls in the box), or at least guess what the world is like. Of course, sometimes we think that the amazing reliability of some probability estimates, just as that of predictions in general, gives support to the relevant theories (and just as failure of the same is thought to count against the theories). But the problem is how to go from this amazement to a method for determining how likely those theories are.

The prospects are not very good. Even die-hard inductivists conceded practically at the start that the probability value of any universal hypothesis would be zero. This may sound like a paradox; but let us consider that one of the aims of science, according to the empiricist, is to be as comprehensive as possible. A theory that can explain a whole range of phenomena is higher on the pecking order than another that explains less, all other things being equal. Now, in the probability calculus we determine the probability of a conjunction (e.g., A and B) by multiplying the individual component probabilities (P(A) x P(B)). Thus, the more claims we make (the more components the conjunction has), the lower the resulting probability of the whole. Suppose that we have a theory made up of two hypotheses, each with a probability value of 1/2. The combined probability of the two hypotheses will be 1/2 x 1/2 = 1/4. Now, if the theory makes three claims about the world instead, its probability will be 1/2 x 1/2 x 1/2 = 1/8. The more the theory tells us about the world the lower its probability then. But surely, we want our theories to be as comprehensive as possible. *Therefore, we should want our theories to approach 0 probability!*

There may be some inductivists who wish to turn this absurdity to advantage (as a way of identifying good theories). Unfortunately, the probability of false (but comprehensive) theories would also approach zero.

The point of scientific method, according to empiricism, is to devise a way for experience to pass judgment upon theory. We started this chapter with the intuition that worthwhile scientific theories would be *supported* by experience (facts, data, evidence). And by "supported" we meant at first that the theories should be *proved* by experience; or in failing that, we thought that scientific theories should at least be shown by experience to be highly likely (sometimes philosophers talk of "validation" or "confirmation" respectively). Given the chronic failure of the ideas of inductivism so far presented, we could wash our hands of method. Or we could follow a different path to understand scientific method.

One of our options is to devise much more sophisticated inductive logics. A lot of the work in philosophy of science in the 20th Century attempted to do just that. In looking back over the meager results, the resolve of the analytic philosophers who have taken on the task seems very surprising. In pointing out some of the reasons for optimism, the philosopher Wesley Salmon has said that just as it took thousands of years before deductive logic could be systematized by Gottlob Frege and Bertrand Russell towards the end of the 19th century, perhaps the key to inductive logic is right around the corner of hard work and ingenuity.

It is true that symbolic (deductive) logic has become so respectable that a course in it may satisfy the mathematics requirement at some universities. But symbolic logic is largely the formalization of patterns of reasoning that were intuitively found valid for thousands of years. The problem lay in the formalization itself. The problem for inductive logic, on the other hand, lies in showing that what has been considered fallacious can be turned into a proper calculus by further refinement. In any event, a characterization of inductive logic (or of a "logic of confirmation," as it is also called) is rather difficult. In Appendix I will consider some such characterizations and advance reasons for pessimism on the subject. And, to add insult to injury, in Chapter 6 I will explain why the deductive logic used by philosophers fails to apply to science, and even to real life, for that matter.

A second option, however, is to argue that the inductivists had scientific method all wrong. The role of evidence is not to support theories directly but something else altogether. The role of evidence may be, for example, to disprove theories instead. I turn to this second option in the next chapter.

REFERENCES

Bacon, F. (1620). *Novum Organum.*

Carnap, R. (1939). *Foundations of Logic and Mathematics* in *International Encyclopedia of Unified Science,* Vol. I, No. 3. University of Chicago Press.

Carnap, R. (1945a). "On Inductive Logic," in *Philosophy of Science,* Vol. 12.

Carnap, R. (1945b). *The Two Concepts of Probability* in *Philosophy and Phenomenological Research,* Vol. 5, No. 4.

Carnap, R. (1947). "On the Application of Inductive Logic" in *Philosophy and Phenomenological Research,* Vol. 8.

Carnap, R. (1956). (1947). Meaning and Necessity: A Study in Semantics and Modal Logic. University of Chicago Press.

Carnap, R. (1950). *Logical Foundations of Probability.* University of Chicago Press.

Carnap, R. (1952). *The Continuum of Inductive Methods.* University of Chicago Press.

Carnap, R. (1963). "Intellectual Autobiography," in Schlipp, P.A (ed.) *The Philosophy of Rudolf Carnap, Library Of Living Philosophers* Vol. XI, Open Court.

Carnap, R. (1966). *Philosophical Foundations of Physics.* Martin Gardner, ed. Basic Books.

Carnap, R. (1971). *Studies in Inductive Logic and Probability, Vol. 1.* University of California Press.

Descartes, R. (1911). *Discourse on Method* in *The Philosophical Works of Descartes, E.S. Haldane and G.R.T. Ross, trans. Cambridge University Press.* Originally published in 1637.

Descartes, R. (1983). *Principles of Philosophy.* V.R. and R.P. Miller, trans. Reidel. Originally published in1644.

Herschel, J. (1831). *Preliminary Discourse of Natural Philosophy.*

Hershey, D. (2003). "Misconceptions about Helmont's Willow Experiment." *Plant Science Bulletin.* The Botanical Society of America. Vol: 49, No. 3.

Hume, D. (1967). A Treatise of Human Nature. Oxford University Press. Originally published 1740.

Hume, D. *(1777). [1748]. An Enquiry Concerning Human Understanding. London: A. Millar.*

Lakatos, I. (1980). *Mathematics, Science and Epistemology.* Philosophical Papers. Vol: 2. Cambridge University Press.

Popper, K. (1959). *The Logic of Scientific Discovery,* translation of *Logik der Forschung.* Hutchinson.

Popper, K. (1963). *Conjectures and Refutations: The Growth of Scientific Knowledge.* Routledge.

Rorty, R. (1979). *Philosophy and the Mirror of Nature.* Princeton University Press.

Toulmin, S. and Goodfield, J. (1962). *The Architecture of Matter.* Harper & Row.

Wilson, E. B. (1952). *An Introduction to Scientific Research. McGraw-Hill.*

CHAPTER 3
THE PERILS OF DISPROVING THEORIES

FIRST VERSION OF FALSIFICATIONISM

Millions of predictions follow easily from Newton's law of gravitation. For example, if I pick up a book and let go of it, the book will fall to the ground. But the fall of the book will not provide much evidence in support of Newton's law. The reason is that many other theories, or just plain common sense, could have also predicted that the book would fall to the ground. A real test of Newton's law takes place when we use it to make interesting or bold predictions, predictions that its competition would be hard pressed to match. For example, Halley used Newton's law of gravitation, as well as other parts of Newton's physics, to calculate that a certain comet, now called Halley's Comet, would return every 76 years. Since at that time it was not widely accepted that comets were astronomical phenomena, let alone that they returned, only Newtonian physics could make the scheduled reappearance of the comet anything less than an astonishing coincidence.

In this respect, Newton's theory sticks its neck out where others do not, it is testable in areas where others are not, and it tells us things about the world that others cannot. This experiment, and many others just as interesting, properly impressed the physicists of the day (or natural philosophers as they called themselves). But notice that by making bold predictions Newton's theory also ran a greater chance of clashing with experience, and thus, some say, of being proved wrong.

It is tempting to draw two lessons at this point. The first is that even though facts cannot prove theories, they can disprove them. If a theory clashes with the facts, it is false. Around this insight we can presumably build a more sensible version of scientific method: come up with theories that make bold predictions, and that tell us more about the world than their competitors. If the predictions fail, reject your theory and look for another one. The second lesson is that the support we give to our theory is only tentative, no matter how successfully it passes our toughest tests. After all, Newton's view was eventually rejected in favor of Einstein's.

The aim of the scientist, according to this account of method, is to develop theories that can be tested, and testing is nothing but a way of putting a theory in a risky situation where it may be shown to be false. A theory that fails the test is said to have been falsified, hence this account of method is called falsificationism. Ruthless testing cuts fat and weakness out of science. Gone is the inductivist timidity, the fear of moving out of the shade of the facts. Only by taking risks shall we understand nature. To learn from experience is to learn from our mistakes.

Some scholars feel uneasy about falsificationism because they think it does not offer enough support to technology. They feel that technology needs to use those parts of science that can be considered reliable; it cannot afford to try questionable principles in the design of its commercial airplanes or in the equipment used at the operating table. The boldest hypothesis hardly seems the most appropriate basis for the safety of passengers, patients, and consumers in general. Inductivism, by contrast, aims at determining the degree of support; if it fails, we are apparently left without the foundation needed for technology.

Nevertheless, the falsificationist may point out that his method is, in fact, quite superior in this respect to the inductivist's. After all, he gives his tentative support only after the most stringent tests have been taken, only after he has used great ingenuity and effort in devising ways to show that the hypotheses and theories in question are false. Only when his earnest attempts at falsification have failed does he give his approval. This happens to be precisely the sort of approach favored when technological reliability is at a premium. The design of a spaceship, for example, should involve consideration of all the things that could go wrong; prototypes are put to the most rigorous, and sometimes imaginative, tests; simulations are carried out on the actual vessel as much as possible, etc. We try to make things fail, from the first blueprint to shortly before the spaceship takes off. Only after working hard and ingeniously to that end do we feel rather confident that the spaceship is as dependable as we need — as long as it has met all the tests. Even then, our confidence is only tentative — we realize that in spite of our efforts we may have overlooked some possible way for disaster to occur. Just as in the scientific realm, it is the ruthless search for failure that allows for (temporary) acceptance in technology. When we forget this lesson, we court disaster.

Apparently, that was precisely what happened in the explosion of the Space Shuttle Challenger, which killed seven astronauts and brought the U.S. space program to a halt. If NASA officials had preserved their long-standing policy, they would have insisted that certain components could not be trusted until they were tested in conditions in which they were yet to show their reliability, and in which the engineers suspected there was a good chance of failure (the infamous "O" rings, which were supposed to seal the hot gases inside the solid-fuel boosters, but which lost their elasticity during very cold weather and thus permitted the escape of flames that blew up the main tank). Instead, those officials demanded that the engineers give them reasons, without the testing, for why the components could not be trusted. When reasons came forth, the NASA officials did not find them all that alarming. A few experiments might have been more persuasive, but unfortunately, the officials had lost patience for that sort of thing. Instead, they had to settle for a full-scale test during the actual flight itself. The price could not have been higher.

Having discussed this symmetry of approach in science and technology, let us return to how the scientist applies the method of falsification. It is not necessary, according to falsificationism, that only hypotheses that reflect standard practice be proposed, although those hypotheses may have a higher plausibility at first. In this view, any hypothesis or theory can be proposed for consideration as long as it is testable. Its origin does not matter, for it is the testing that finally will decide the fate of the theory or hypothesis. Scientific ideas can come from dreams, visions, trial and error, educated guesses, even generalizations from the facts. But acceptance is an entirely different matter. Only those theoretical structures that have survived the fire of rigorous falsification are kept — not because they are true, for testing cannot show this, but because we have failed to show that they are false.

Let us take a particle physicist, Lisa, for example. Suppose Lisa finds a puzzling interaction between two kinds of sub-atomic particles. It may occur to her, following standard practice in her field, that a third kind of particle may be responsible for the puzzling phenomena; and so, she postulates the existence of a new particle with just the right properties to provide an explanation. She would thus articulate her hypothesis by estimating the charge, mass, spin, and so on of her particle. And then she would set out to look for it. A good way to do this might be to examine bubble chamber photographs of reactions in which the new particle might appear (**Figure 3.1**). A bubble chamber is a vessel filled with a super-heated liquid. As the charged particles travel through the liquid, they ionize the molecules. The resulting string of bubbles marks the path of the particle. And from the path the physicist is able to determine the charge, mass and other characteristics of the particles that result from the reaction. The more massive a particle is, say, the less it will be deflected by magnetic fields in the chamber. For the hypothesis to be tentatively accepted, there should appear in the bubble chamber photographs traces with the angle, direction, and duration predicted for the new particle. Otherwise, the hypothesis should be rejected. The scientist proposes and Nature disposes.

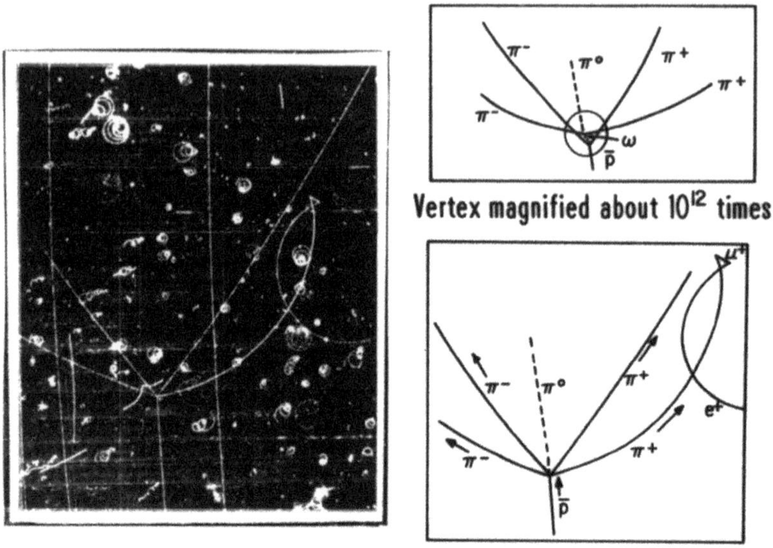

Figure 3.1. Courtesy of the Lawrence Berkeley National Laboratory. © 2010-2019. The Regents of the University of California, Lawrence Berkeley National Laboratory.

There may be occasions in which two competing hypotheses seem to be consistent with the available facts. The scientist must then elaborate them until some of their predictions conflict. In that case, we perform a *crucial experiment* to decide between the two. At the beginning of the 19th century, there were two main views on the nature of light. According to the Newtonians, light was corpuscular; according to their opponents, light consisted of transversal waves. The corpuscular theory of light predicted that the speed of light would increase in water, whereas the wave theory predicted just the opposite. The French physicist Foucault determined by experiment that the speed of light decreases in water, thus presumably refuting the corpuscular theory. (That the wave theory was itself abandoned in the first part of this century only serves to emphasize once again that theories can be accepted only tentatively.)

Falsificationism restores to our view of science the romance of adventure: daring creativity coupled with ruthless questioning. Our scientist is an explorer of the unknown. Lisa is open-minded, for she is willing to entertain the boldest of suggestions; but she is also tough-minded, for she is prepared to throw out the harvest of her own efforts if it does not withstand the criticism of experience. In addition, this method appears to have two clear advantages over the method of induction. One problem with the method of induction is that the majority of theories ever proposed have been rejected, even though many of them presumably had been advanced in accordance with the "scientific" method. With the method of falsification that historical problem looks less awesome: theories are held only tentatively; testing will eventually force us to give them up. Another problem was that the mode of inference of induction was fallacious. Not so with falsification. Let us take the last example as an illustration.

> If light is corpuscular then it will travel faster in water than in air.
>
> Light does not travel faster in water.
>
> Therefore, light is not corpuscular.

The structure of this argument is perfectly valid. Indeed, this mode of inference is employed in practically every logic textbook (under the Latin name *modus tollens*).

Just as the method of falsification gives our scientist advice on what to do, it also gives Lisa advice on what not to do. If criticism is at the heart of scientific rationality, the worst sin a scientist can commit is to present her views in such a way that they cannot be criticized (tested). Thus, it should not be permissible to modify any hypothesis for the specific purpose of saving it from refutation (a move called *ad hoc*). Until the discovery of oxygen (by Lavoisier and others), some scholars clung to the old view of combustion. According to a version of that view, things have a substance called phlogiston which is separated at the time of combustion. A piece of wood that is burned for a long time loses a lot of phlogiston and consequently shrinks down to ashes. It was found, however, that at certain temperatures, metals become oxidized and gain weight. But some phlogiston theorists preferred to *ad hoc* than to worry: The phlogiston in metals has a negative weight, they said, and so when a metal loses its phlogiston in combustion it gains weight. Appeal to this kind of saving move may forever shield the theory from the verdict of experience.

CRITIQUE OF FALSIFICATIONISM

This method appeals to the intuitions of many working scientists. But at least in this version, it is untenable, as a little probing will make clear. Let us reconsider the example of Halley's Comet. Halley made a detailed record of the path of the comet. On the basis of this path and Newton's physics, he was able to calculate the orbit of the comet and to predict when it would be back. But what was relevant to his calculations? Among other things, he took into account the gravitational influences of other bodies on the comet, mainly the Sun's, since the forces that move the comet in its orbit are gravitational. The comet and those other bodies together form a system. From a certain state of that system, Halley was able to predict what a future state of the system would be like. But notice that the prediction does not follow unless we assume that *nothing interferes* with the system, as Imre Lakatos pointed out (1970).

Let me explain. Comets typically have very long orbits that take them to the outer reaches of the solar system. In its long journey, comet Halley might have passed near Neptune and this would have falsified Halley's prediction. Neptune's gravity would have thrown comet Halley off its orbit because Neptune is a very big planet and comet Halley barely a few miles across. But Halley could not have taken this into account for the simple reason that Neptune had not yet been discovered. There were many other possible factors that, with a bit of bad luck, would have kept the comet from its famous appointed round. And the point is that the prediction would have failed then even though Halley's hypothesis – that the comet would behave in accordance with Newton's physics – was correct.

It is clear that Halley's prediction must assume that nothing other than the factors he considered will affect the future state of the system. That is, the prediction requires that the system be closed to outside interference. This is the case for most scientific predictions. We expect a certain event on the basis of a theory, *all other things being equal.* But this is a simple point, so what is the problem for the method of falsification? The problem is that when the prediction fails we cannot blame the theory, for things might not have been equal: Something might have interfered with the system.

Suppose Neptune had thrown comet Halley off its regular orbit. Halley's prediction would have failed, but his hypothesis should not be blamed. Falsificationism's mode of inference cannot then be as straight forward as we supposed earlier.

Three things come together to make the prediction:

If (1) the comet behaves according to Newton's physics

And (2) the path of the comet through the solar system in 1682 has been properly described, and

And (3) only the sun and the (then known) planets will affect the orbit of the comet

Then (4) the comet will be back in December of 1758.

But if (then unknown) Neptune had interfered, the comet would not have returned on that date.

Therefore, something would be false. But what? Pointing the finger at the theory surely would be arbitrary. And wrong. In this case, the failure was caused by the violation of requirement (3).

We can see now that when it comes to the practice of science, the presumed valid mode of reasoning of falsificationism, *modus tollens*, does not really apply. Thus, the apparent advantage over Inductivism vanishes.

These simple points complicate matters for falsificationism to no end. Let us go back to our crucial experiments to decide between two competing theories. In a famous dispute between Pasteur and Pouchet, appeal was made to a crucial experiment. Pasteur held that living matter could come only from living matter, whereas Pouchet thought that the addition of oxygen to inert matter would lead to living organisms (those were the days when some people believed that worms sprung from putrid meat and rats from garbage.) The disputants agreed to take hay in a sealed flask to a point high in the Alps, where the flask would be opened, and its contents would be able to react with pure air. It was thought that at that altitude, there would be little dust, thus reducing the chance that living matter carried by dust would contaminate the experimental set-up. The substance chosen, dry hay, was considered dead matter, and had been carefully boiled so as to kill any living organisms attached to it. The experiment was carried out, and after some time mold was found in the flask! Pouchet's side claimed victory, of course. But Pouchet was wrong. There were two important auxiliary hypotheses involved in the design of the experiment. One concerned the amount of dust at the chosen altitude; the other required that hay be inert. As it turns out, hay contains spores, and spores are the sort that may survive boiling water only to be triggered by oxygen under the conditions of the crucial experiment. Crucial experiments may not be so decisive after all.

The falsification advice to scientists on what to do turns out to be too simple-minded. So does the advice on what not to do. The falsificationist believes that nothing could be further from the scientific spirit than *ad hoc* moves to safeguard a theory that conflicts with experience. But let us see how this falsificationist advice would have served the makers of scientific history. According to the Copernican view, for example, the Earth orbits around the sun. If this is so, the famous 15th Century observer Tycho Brahe reasoned, the positions of the stars relative to one another should change as seen from the Earth at different points in its orbit. In other words, the stars should exhibit what is called "parallax motion." But neither Tycho Brahe nor anyone else was able to detect such motion for another 150 years (and then only with far more powerful instrumentation). Such failure led Brahe to reject the Copernican system. His conclusion accords with the method of falsification: Parallax motion is a logical consequence of the heliocentric view (see **Figure 3.2**), but it cannot be found, therefore the view is refuted. The same objection had been directed against Aristarchus, a Greek precursor of Copernicus, almost two millennia earlier.

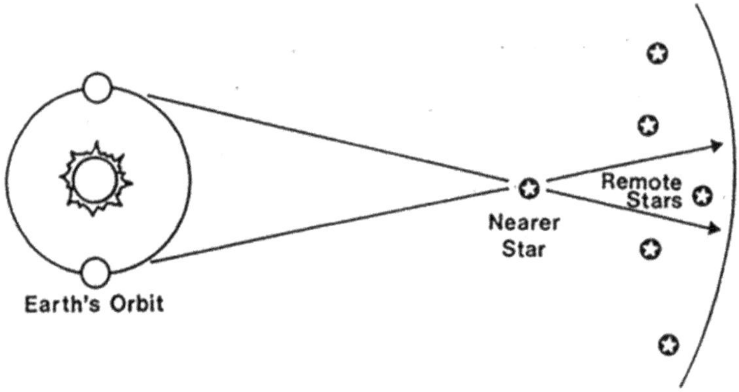

Figure 3.2. Parallax motion.

The position of the near star relative to the remote stars will change (as seen from Earth) depending on the Earth's orbit from which the observation is made. A similar argument can be made even if all the stars are supposed to be fixed on the shell of the same sphere.

How did the Copernicans preserve their view from refutation? They advanced the notion that the universe was far larger than Tycho had assumed. Immensely larger, for if the parallax motion of the stars went undetected, then the size of the earth's orbit would be insignificant compared to the distance to the fixed stars—just as a man walking in circles around his desk in his study can notice the relative changes of position of the chairs and bookcases in the room, but cannot detect any such changes in a line of trees that he can see far away through his window. We now believe that the Copernicans were right. But at the time, the idea seemed inconceivable to Tycho, for by the standards of his day the proposed axis of the Earth's orbit was an extraordinary distance already. Moreover, and this is the most important point, he could not see any motivation for advancing this notion except to save the Copernican view from refutation. Tycho could tell an *ad hoc* move when he saw one.

To clinch the matter, Tycho Brahe also argued that if the universe were of Copernican size the stars could not be seen! His argument was based on a relationship between the size of stars and their apparent brightness. Today we know that Tycho was wrong in assuming that the perceived brightness of a point of light against a dark background can tell us much about the size of its source. But as far as anyone could tell at that time, Tycho was right. The Copernicans had no convincing rebuttal to offer. In time their hunch was justified. But their chance had to be purchased at the price of flouting the falsificationist ideal of science. *Ad hoc* moves saved the Copernican view from refutation, and thus gave it the breathing room it needed to develop and eventually show its superiority.

These objections are devastating, but nagging doubts remain. Are not *ad hoc* moves just plain wrong sometimes? And is it not clear, at least on occasion, that some views should be rejected? Have we taken the method of falsification too literally? Perhaps with a few sensible modifications, it will do the job it was intended for. But before modifying the method, let us take stock of the most formidable obstacle it has to overcome.

THE BREAKDOWN OF THE DISTINCTION BETWEEN THEORY AND FACT

The method of falsification is above all empiricist: It shares with Inductivism the belief that theory should be subjected to the judgment of experience. Facts may prop up or demolish theories; that is presumably the very heart of science. To figure out how is the bread and butter of philosophy of science. To place theory ahead of fact is to sin against science and philosophy.

But why should this be so? Why should experience sit in judgment of theory? Apparently, because experience can be reliable, whereas it is well known that unchecked theorizing more often than not will lead us astray. Of course, it is also well known that our experience is often mistaken. People see extraterrestrial witches fly over sleepy towns and monsters stir at the bottom of lakes. And it has been recognized for a long time that prejudice may distort observation. But it is assumed that a normal observer under normal conditions will give reports of the world that are reliable enough, as Aristotle thought thousands of years ago. Reliable enough, that is, to demand that theory conform to them. Whether they are reliable because they are true representations of the world or because they satisfy some other sophisticated sense of reliability is a matter of dispute. Certainly, the normal observer must also be unbiased, careful, and so on. As I pointed out in Chapter 2, empiricism begins with an act of purification. We may also demand that the reports be intersubjective (i.e., made by a variety of observers). In any event, such observational reports constitute the solid empirical basis against which theories must be measured.

It is precisely on this point that the new, historical philosophy of science has launched its greatest attack against empiricism. What Thomas Kuhn, Paul Feyerabend and others have done is to undermine the solidity of the empirical basis. But their attack must not be confused with traditional skepticism. The new challenge cannot be as safely ignored as the traditional epistemological concerns have been.

Such traditional concerns sometimes have the air of mere intellectual pastimes. Practically everyone who wanders into an introductory philosophy class soon learns all sorts of arguments to the effect that we cannot "trust" our senses. Many such arguments generalize from observations made under abnormal conditions and are thus apparently irrelevant to a position that considers observations made by normal observers under normal conditions a solid empirical basis for science. Nevertheless, the skeptics' arsenal is formidable, and the inquiry about the justification for our reports about the world continues unabated. Philosophers have suggested a wide array of solutions: from the kindness of Descartes' God, who could not bear to have us deceived about the world when we are doing our Cartesian best, to an equally kind evolution that has adapted our perceptual faculties to the world. Generation after generation of philosophers have brought up the dragon of skepticism only to spear its heart with reason. But the next generation of philosophers finds that it must slay the same dragon all over again.

Should this controversy be of interest to the scientist, except perhaps as a harmless intellectual exercise? The scientist may sensibly argue that it should not. The skepticism that worries philosophers holds that it is logically possible that the most solid claims about the world are false, where "logically possible" does not mean "reasonable to suppose" but merely that there is no contradiction in so imagining.

As Descartes pointed out (1641), even the plain realization that he is in his study, reading in front of the fire, could be mistaken because he might only be *dreaming* that he is in his study, reading in front of the fire. But then it seems that the scientists can let the philosophers lose sleep over this worry. Murray Gell-Mann, say, would have found it ludicrous to argue that a particular hypothesis about quarks had not really been disconfirmed because it is *logically possible* that he is not actually reading the negative results of a crucial particle collision experiment but only dreaming them!

The doubts raised by the new philosophy of science against the solidity of the empirical basis are of a very different sort. Empirical methodologies seem to assume that there is a clear natural distinction between theory and observation. Without such a distinction, it would be hard to imagine why one should have priority over the other. And without the priority of observation, empiricism would collapse. But is not the distinction between theory and observation perfectly obvious? Careful observation is the means by which experience becomes fact. If the distinction does not hold, we might just replace the facts that contradict our pet theory with other "facts" more to our liking, and that sounds just plain absurd.

Perhaps so. Nonetheless, let us take a close look, following roughly the highlights Feyerabend suggests in his *Against Method* (1978), at the way this distinction played itself out in the scientific revolution carried out by Copernicus and Galileo, allegedly the first great triumph of empiricism.

The view that the Earth moves may seem commonsensical to many of us today. But that is only because we are the heirs to a revolution in scientific thought. When the battle was fought, victory was by no means easy. Among the many telling objections against the movement of the Earth perhaps the Tower Argument, presented by Aristotle, in his *On the Heavens*, almost 2,000 years earlier, was the strongest of all. It goes as follows. Suppose that you let go of a stone from the top of a tall tower (see **Figure 3.3**). If the world moves, by the time the stone hits the ground, the tower being stuck in the Earth, will have moved considerably (back then, the velocity of rotation of the Earth would have been calculated to be about 1,000 miles per hour). Thus, there will be a perceptible difference between the initial and final distances from stone to tower. But when we actually look, there is practically no difference at all! We plainly see the stone fall straight down. For the distance to remain constant, if the Earth did move, the stone would have to fall in a parabolic path that any fool with even less than average sight can see is not so. Therefore, it is as plain as plain can be that the Earth does not move. The idea that it does makes no sense.

It does no good to talk about gravity and the like, for the appropriate concepts were not developed until years later, and then partly as a result of Galileo's success. Presented with the Tower Argument what could Galileo say? First, in "The Second Day" of his *Dialogues Concerning the Two Chief World Systems* (1632), he made the argument against his view as strong as possible. For example, equal cannons shooting east and west will send their cannonballs pretty much the same distance, but if the Earth moved, the cannon shooting East should go a lot further. If you shoot a cannon straight up, and the Earth moves, by the time the cannonball falls to the ground, the cannon should have moved a great distance and the cannonball will hit the ground far from it; but obviously that is not so: the cannonball will fall back straight down towards the cannon. Galileo then acknowledges that *all the experiments* are on Aristotle's side! This greatly pleases Simplicio, Aristotle's representative in the dialogue, who admiringly tells Salviati, Galileo's representative, that it would appear to be "an impossible feat to contradict such palpable experiences." If these experiments were false, Simplicio asks, "…what true demonstrations were ever more elegant?" (73).

That is quite an admission by someone who is introduced as the inventor of the empirical or scientific method in the first chapter of many science textbooks, because of his presumed insistence that observation and experiment are to have precedence over theory. According to Newton's (1687) *Third Law for Reasoning in Philosophy* (in those days people made no distinction between science and philosophy), the qualities of bodies determined by experiment ought to be considered universal, therefore the good (natural) philosopher does not consider alternative accounts of the phenomena: "We are certainly not to relinquish the evidence of experiments for the sake of dreams and vain fictions of our own devising." (146)

Nevertheless, Galileo does entertain hypotheses contrary to such powerful experimental results (contrary to Rule III) and without having produced any "other phenomena" (as Rule IV requires), i.e. no new observations or experimental results. What did Galileo do instead? *He offered a theoretical argument.* He begins by asking what may seem to be a silly question: How do we know that the rock falls vertically? We see it, obviously, as Simplicio points out ("by means of the senses"). But what if the Earth did rotate? How would the rock move then? Galileo's move here anticipates Feyerabend's advice to imagine "*a dream-world in order to discover the features of the real world we think we inhabit*" (1993, 32). Salviati gives the answer: The motion would then be a compound of two motions, "one with which it measures the tower, and the other with which it follows it" (77). The real motion would thus be a compound of a vertical and a circular motion (see **Figure 3.4**). Of course, this is implied: we only observe the vertical motion, since we share, with the rock and the tower, the motion of the Earth. A few pages earlier Galileo had pointed out that any motions that may be attributed to the Earth "must necessarily remain imperceptible to us... for as inhabitants of the earth, we consequently participate in the same motions" (69).

It follows, then, that from *seeing* the motion of the stone "you could not say for sure that it described a straight and perpendicular line, *unless you first assumed the earth to stand still*" (77, my italics). But whether the Earth stands still is precisely what is in question. The evidence adduced to show that the earth stands still *assumes* that the earth stands still! Aristotle, the great logician, has committed the fallacy of *petitio principii* (77). His "facts" assumed the theory in question.

In a few pages, then, and without providing one single piece of new empirical evidence, Galileo disposes of the main objection against the very possibility that the Earth rotates, thus creating the stage for the eventual triumph of the Copernican Revolution. By relinquishing the evidence of experiments for the sake of a dream of his own devising, he was able not only to discover important features of the world we thought we inhabited, but eventually to show that such a world was itself a dream.

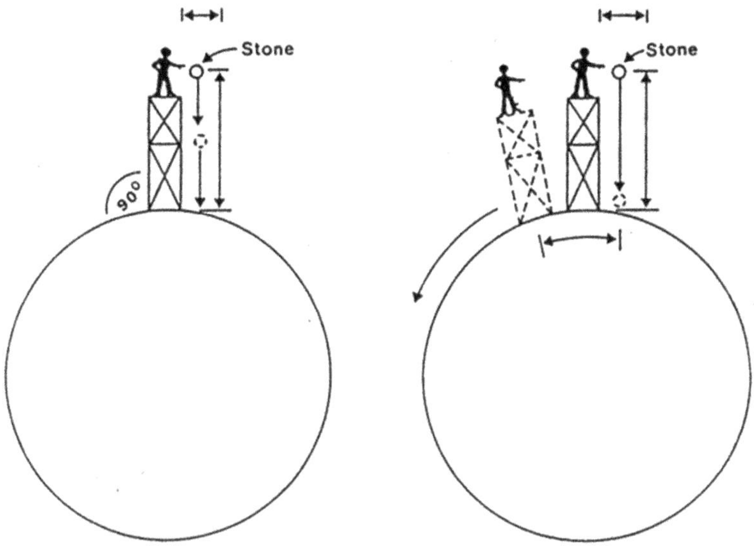

Figure 3.3. If the Earth moves, the stone lands far from the bottom of the tower.

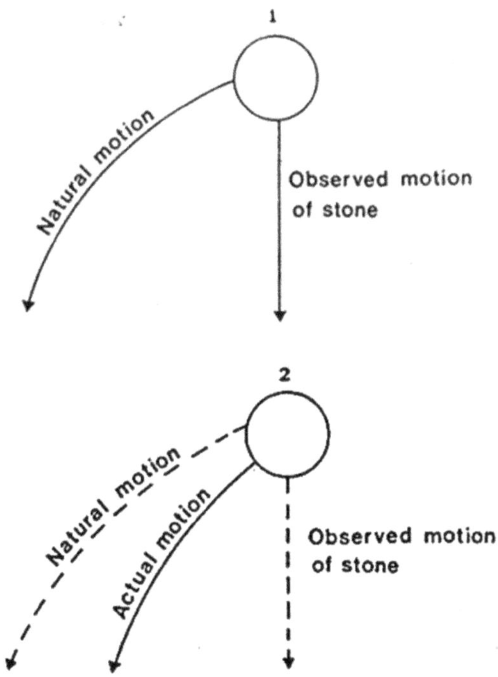

Figure 3.4. The new natural interpretation of the motion of the stone.

Galileo could say, and did, that the stone does not fall straight down, plain as it may be. The stone only *seems to move so; its real motion* is far more complicated than that. But this makes no sense, people thought. Motion is *observed* motion. Not so, said Galileo. Shared motion goes unobserved (motion is relative). He made the point in the following dialogue:

> Salviati:...imagine yourself in a boat with your eyes fixed on a point of the sail yard. Do you think that because the boat is moving along briskly, you will have to move your eyes in order to keep your vision always on that point of the sail yard and follow its motion?
>
> Simplicio: I am sure that I should not need to make any change at all; not just as to my vision, but if I had aimed a musket I should never have to move it a hairsbreadth to keep it aimed, no matter how the boat moved.
>
> Salviati: And this comes about because the motion which the ship confers upon the sail yard, it confers also upon you and upon your eyes, so that you need not move them a bit in order to gaze at the top of the sail yard, which consequently appears motionless to you. (And the rays of vision go from the eye to the sail yard just as if a cord were tied between the two ends of the boat. Now a hundred cords are tied at different fixed points, each of which keeps its place *whether* the ship moves or remains still. (Modern Library edition, p. 289).[1]

The reason why the stone falls at that distance from the tower is that, as we have seen, its real motion has two components: the first is straight down and we notice it, the second (circular inertia) is shared with the Earth, the tower, and the observer (us). That is why we do not notice it; but it is there all the same. Just as the tower moved laterally, so did the stone. When we are in an airplane flying smoothly, we do not perceive that the passenger sitting next to us and the magazine on our lap are traveling at 450 miles an hour, even if we know they both are. We do perceive the motion of the flight assistant up and down the aisle and of the drink spilling on the sleepy man to our left. We perceive those motions that we do not share but fail to notice those that we do. In this manner, Galileo neutralized the objection against the Copernican view.

What conclusions can we draw about the Tower Argument then? According to Feyerabend (69-98), people noticed a phenomenon and *interpreted* it in what they thought was the most *natural* way, i.e., the stone *moves* only straight down. It was

---

[1] I have used above the Hackett edition because M. R. Mathews excerpted the most essential passages of Galileo's crucial critique of Aristotle's Tower Argument. Passage cited by Feyerabend in *Against Method* (83).

this "natural" *interpretation* of the phenomenon, not the phenomenon itself, which contradicted the Copernican view. Galileo did away with the contradiction by providing a *different set of interpretations.* Galileo, then, constructed a new empirical basis! This new empirical basis, furthermore, is constituted by a *new theory of interpretation.* It is fair to conclude, then, that when confronting facts that refuted his theory, Galileo changed the facts!

On the surface, we had a clash between theory and fact, for clearly that the stone falls straight down looked like a fact if anything did. What we did really have was a clash between a rather explicit theory (i.e., Copernicus') and a covert theory of interpretation. After close analysis, it turns out that instead of theory vs. fact, we have theory vs. theory. In any event, the main moral of the story is that observations make theoretical assumptions, and thus it is arbitrary to go along *always* with the judgment of experience, no matter how careful, inter-subjective, and so on (again, all those requirements were met in the case of the Tower Argument).

It does no good to empiricism to claim that since the "facts" were replaced then they could not have been *real* facts. In the first place, we have no way to tell the real ones from good imitations. That the stone falls straight down looked like a real one. In the second place, what brought Galileo the real facts, if we can grant for the sake of argument that there are real facts, was not more careful observation, or a purer experience, or anything of the sort. What permitted the change of empirical basis was a change in theoretical assumptions. More specifically, as I see it, Galileo changed the concept of motion. Motion had been supposed by his opponents, the Aristotelians, to be only observable motion, i.e., it involved observable change of position over time. In the jargon of analytic philosophy of science, we might say that the Aristotelians had an operationalist concept of motion (i.e., that a phenomenon would count as motion only if it could be expressed in terms of observable changes). But Galileo introduced into motion components that could not be observed in principle, since shared motion was not observable for him. And in the particular case of the Tower Argument, one of those components was circular inertia, which the observer shared with the tower and the Earth (Munévar, 2015).

Nor do we help empiricism by suspecting that there is something terribly peculiar, unrepresentative about the case of the Tower Argument. For the thesis of the distinction of fact and theory can admit of no exceptions. And this case shows that what looked like solid observations (and thus empirical "facts") are embedded in theory, by means of an actual example. As long as it is possible to overthrow the judgment of experience, a theory is never proven to be false. There is no disproof in science any more than there is proof.

Moreover, the history of science offers many similar instances in which theoretical breakthroughs made short work of the most careful of observations—

instances in which presumably solid facts are shown to be an illusion. According to Prout's theory (circa 1840), atomic weights should be whole numbers (since they are multiples of 1, the atomic weight of hydrogen). But the most refined techniques of the century showed unequivocally that the atomic weights of some substances were not whole numbers—chlorine was 35.5, for example. With the advent of Bohr's atomic theory, almost a century later, we learned that the atomic weights of elements are determined by the total weights of protons and neutrons in the nucleus of the atom. The number of neutrons in an element may vary, however. Thus, different variations of the same element, named isotopes, will have different weights. In the case of chlorine, the isotopes will weigh respectively 35 and 36 (which, given their mix in nature, will result in a reading of about 35.5 if the standard 19th-century techniques are applied). Here we have one more case in which a theory clashed with the facts, for surely the careful observations in question were as "factual" as any observations have a right to be. Nevertheless, theoretical developments gave us a new way to interpret the troublesome observations and Prout's hypothesis was rehabilitated. The atomic weight of each isotope of chlorine *is* a whole number. In this case, the new theory of interpretation came from a different field—an esoteric branch of physics some eighty years after the birth of Prout's hypothesis. But once this view was taken up in chemistry, the entrenched observations were replaced by others in agreement with the new theory. Once more, theory overturns the negative verdict handed down by experience. Lakatos also pays special attention to Prout's case (beginning in 128).

Returning to the Tower Argument, it is perhaps ironic that the Aristotelians, the losers, are now seen as sticking to the facts, demanding operationalist concepts, and on the whole defending the "empirical method." What can we say now of the philosopher's praise of Galileo for preferring his eyes to his Aristotle?

By all means, let us talk about the relation between Galileo's views and Galileo's eyes. Galileo was a Copernican. The central thesis of Copernicus stated that the Earth was one more planet in orbit around the sun. The evidence of the eyes, unfortunately, refuted this Copernican thesis. As we well know now, the Earth and Venus are sometimes on the same side of the sun, and thus rather close to each other; and sometimes they are on opposite sides of the sun and thus very far from each other. The same can be said for Mars, except that Mars gets much farther from the Earth. It seems commonsensical then that Venus and Mars should look brighter when they are close and dimmer when they are far. But the magnitude of Venus barely changes, and that of Mars does not change as much as it should.

Nevertheless, Galileo's admiration for Copernicus did not decrease, even though Copernicus "with reason as his guide...resolutely continued to affirm what sensible experience seemed to contradict"(Modern Library, 381). Reason, it appears, can overturn the verdict of experience. In Galileo's case, as Feyerabend reminds us (103), he came upon "the existence of a superior and better sense than natural and common sense": the telescope, which then joins "forces with reason" (381). Indeed, his telescopic observations of Mars gave magnitudes much more in agreement with Copernicus' thesis. And the telescope showed that Venus has phases. When Venus is farthest from us, we see its full face illuminated by the sun. When it is closest, most of the face that it shows to us is dark. Thus, the amount of light that reaches us from Venus remains constant enough for our eye to perceive little change in magnitude.

In this situation, we find an outright conflict between natural and artificial sense. Galileo surely thought of it that way. He resolved the conflict by *denying the testimony of his eyes* and siding with the sense that agreed with Copernicus, the telescope. This conflict between senses should dispel any illusions to the effect that scientific instruments merely amplify and sharpen our senses. But some empiricists may feel relieved that it was telescopic *experience* after all that decided the matter. Nevertheless, such relief is unjustified unless they can show that the telescopic experience was without question superior to that of the eye, as far as the observers of that day were concerned, *and* that the choice of the telescope over the eye does not require theoretical assumptions.

Empiricists will have difficulties on both counts. The first difficulty comes from the role of learning in observation. A beginning observer using a telescope or microscope often fails to observe anything. When the telescope is directed at the moon, the observer will notice nothing, or perhaps a light, or several, not in front of his line of sight but almost out of the corner of his eye. This was, in fact, a common complaint by those Galileo sought to impress with his primitive telescope. Some of the reports of the period express even frustration on the matter. As reported by Feyerabend, Horky wrote to his teacher Kepler the following account of a demonstration Galileo gave to twenty-four professors at the house of his opponent Magini:

> I never slept on the 24th or 25th of April, day or night, but I tested the instrument of Galileo's in a thousand ways, both on things here below and on those above. Below it works wonderfully; in the heavens it deceives one, as some fixed stars are seen double...I have as witnesses most excellent men and noble doctors... and all have admitted the instrument to deceive...This silenced Galileo and on the 26th he sadly left quite early in the morning...not even thanking Magini for his splendid meal... (123).

This situation is not all that surprising. Perception makes use of many background clues in order to fix distance, shape, color, and movement.

Suppose, for example, that you paint a big dot on your wallpapered wall. You see that dot fixed at a particular location relative to the designs in the wallpaper. But suppose now that you had used fluorescent paint and that you turn the lights off. Lisa comes into the completely darkened room and stares at the dot on the wall. She will see the dot moving. The motion of the dot is due to the motion of the eyes themselves. Normally this motion, as well as the many motions of the body that change the position of the head and thus of the eyes, are discounted by the brain. But to fine-tune its operation the brain uses many clues. In this case, without the points of reference provided by the wallpaper design, the brain has no particular reason to conclude that the spot of light is fixed. All kinds of perceptual illusions can arise when the normal sorts of background clues are absent. This is why Jupiter shining through clouds low on the horizon is one of the most common UFOs. And it is also why astronauts have trouble estimating how far objects are in space. Coming back to Galileo, the telescope could work well below because the clues would still be there. But looking at the heavens was a different story. To make matters worse, Galileo's primitive telescope was focused for his eyes (unlike today's telescopes, whose focus can be adjusted).

Nor was Horky the only one to complain about Galileo's telescope. Many other similar reports prompted Kepler to write to Galileo:

> I do not want to hide it from you that quite a few Italians have sent letters to Prague asserting that they could not see those stars (the moons of Jupiter) with your own telescope. I ask myself how it can be that so many deny the phenomenon, including those who use a telescope. Now, if I consider what occasionally happens to me, then I do not at all regard it as impossible that a single person may see what thousands are unable to see.... (124).

Students of astronomy do not have as many problems today. But it is clear that it takes some training before one can become a proficient observer. A person untrained in biology will make little sense of what he sees through an electron microscope for the first time (even a novice biologist will have trouble). The eye needs to be educated to distinguish what is important from the background. Of course, some observers did see through the telescope what Galileo saw, and some of them were not sympathetic to his views. The point is, nonetheless, that the reliability of the telescope for observing the heavens was by no means obvious in Galileo's day. Good empiricists would have found it reasonable to trust the testimony of the eye instead.

The second, and major, difficulty for empiricism, as Feyerabend points out, is that Galileo's trust in the telescope required the granting of several *theoretical* assumptions. Images from the heavens would travel immense distances, enter a different medium upon hitting the Earth's atmosphere, work their way through the telescope, and finally be handled by a brain that had never perceived anything like them. To be assured that those images were not significantly distorted, Galileo needed supporting theories about optics, about the nature of light, about the atmosphere, about the interaction between light and a variety of gases, about the telescope, and about perception. We may realize, then, that it was not Galileo's telescopic *observations* that challenged the geocentric view of the universe, but Galileo's observations together with a host of assumptions from many supporting or auxiliary sciences that had not yet been invented; and were thus only theoretical guesses at that time. The crucial question was: could experience alone have reconciled the magnitudes of the planets with Copernicus' thesis? If by experience we mean sensory experience, the answer is no. If we allow telescopic experience, then we should remember that such experience could be taken as reliable only if interpreted on the basis of certain theories. The answer again is no.

To make matters worse, most of the auxiliary sciences in question were not within Galileo's reach. Some of them took hundreds of years of development before they could fully back Galileo's hunches. Thus, to a good empiricist of the day, many of Galileo's theoretical assumptions should have seemed unwarranted.

If we take a more flexible approach, however, the situation does not look so dismal. We have seen that the telescope could be trusted only if we made certain theoretical assumptions. But the same analysis that leads to this result applies to the eye as much as it does to the telescope. From the discussion of the brain and the perception of the fluorescent dot we may discern that the eye is also an instrument. Visual perception is a complex process in which the brain takes into account not just the "input" from the retina but also from the inner ear and hundreds of skeletal muscles (to determine the position of the body) *and* from the other senses. Think of how vague images suddenly come into focus when we smell the particular scent of a flower in a forest or hear the growling of a dog in a dark street.

The brain does not merely "copy" or "process" the shapes and colors that objects imprint on the retina, as we can easily tell by noticing how often in our visual perception shape and color remain constant. Once we have identified an object as a red apple, we tend to see it that way even if we look at it from an odd angle and in a yellow light (so the frequency of the light bouncing off the apple and hitting the retina is not that of red). And as we will see later, the brain also uses memory and imagination in making its "pictures" of the world.

That perception should work in these and other complex ways is the result of the history of adaptations of the brains of our ancestors to a variety of environments. And as extensive as that ancestral history has been, it is quite limited compared to the range of situations that science considers. The extent to which the senses can be "trusted" is thus not a matter for philosophy alone to determine. Psychology tells us of the richness and complexity of perception; neuroscience may help reveal the structures that make such richness and complexity possible; and evolutionary biology may explain how those structures arose and give us clues about where they apply. See Chapters 9 and 10.

Trying to decide between the eye and the telescope is a very complicated affair that involves a host of theoretical assumptions then. Of course, Galileo did not know anything about neuroscience, let alone evolutionary biology. But he did realize that his opponents' assumption about the reliability of the senses had to be backed up by some view of the relation between the world and the senses. Indeed, that view was Aristotle's theory of perception, according to which an undisturbed mind will take on the "form" of an object as long as that form has traveled through an undisturbed medium. That is how a normal observer under normal conditions would gain knowledge of the world (*De Anima* II 5 and III 2,). Thus, behind the clash of the senses there was a clash of theories, whether those theories were explicit or not. Galileo chose to side with the theories that promised him the most exciting discoveries.

That senses may so clash, it seems to me, does away with a cherished dream of analytic philosophers: neutral observations (or neutral observation languages, as they would put it). Diehard empiricists may have suspected throughout this discussion that some of the theoretical assumptions at issue would be better than others because eventually experience (observation) would back them up. To avoid the problem of whether at this point, those observations could themselves be challenged by theory, it is necessary that they be entirely neutral, i.e., free of theoretical taint. The most popular candidates are "immediate' sensory reports such as dial readings and color patches in our field of vision. Surely a dial reads seven or it does not, regardless of what theory one assumes. And the observer sees red or he does not. But let us apply these notions to the case of the Galilean telescope. On the one hand we have the pure sensory observations that refuted the Copernican thesis, on the other hand, we have those (telescopic) observations that *agreed* with the Copernican thesis. How are we to choose between them? Color patches from naked-eye observation conflict with color patches (or whatever) from telescopic observations. Achieving "neutrality" does not resolve the conflict. And even if perchance both sides agree on a single set of color patches or dial readings, those neutral observations still have to be *interpreted.* But remember that in the Tower argument both sides could agree that the stone *seems* to fall straight down, while disagreeing as to its real motion and what it implies about the motion of the Earth.

It is important to notice that Galileo did not merely take methodological shortcuts. It is not as if his hunches had led him more quickly to results that more patient methodologists would have achieved eventually. Not at all. If method requires the priority of experience, method would have forever closed the door on a view that could not be established without overthrowing accepted experience. If, in pursuing a theory that had been refuted by experience, Galileo committed a sin against science and philosophy, we should love not only the sinner but the sin.

We should notice also that the breakdown of the separation between theory and fact does occur in not only the empiricist methods we have considered so far, but *any* empiricist method whatsoever. As long as empiricism gives absolute priority to experience over theory, the problem cannot be avoided. This is not to say, however, that theory is always overturning the verdict of experience. Nevertheless, it is to say that it *may*. And this is, on occasion, all the encouragement we need to break the siege of the security policy of method. For method is just the working out of the way in which experience can pass final judgment on theory. But now we know that the judge can suddenly become the convict. Thus, we should not be startled upon hearing that Einstein, or some other brilliant scientist, showed little concern about the results of apparently crucial experiments or observations. At one such time, when Einstein was asked what he would have thought if an important experiment (discussed in Ch. 7) had disconfirmed his theory of general relativity, he answered, "Then I would have to be sorry for dear God. The theory is correct."

REFERENCES

Aristotle. (1995). *On the Heavens* II, Ch. 14, 296b7-24. Leggat, S., trans. Liverpool University Press. Written around 350 BCE.

Aristotle. (1987). *De Anima* II 5 and III 2. Lawson-Tancred, H., trans. Penguin, Random House. Written around 350 BCE.

Descartes, R. (1980). "First Meditation" in *Discourse on Method and Meditations on First Philosophy.* Hackett Publishing Company. First published 1641.

Feyerabend, P. (1978). *Against Method.* Verso. First published by New Left Books in 1975.

Galileo (1989) *Dialogues Concerning the Two Chief World Systems.* In Mathews, M.R. (Ed.), *The Scientific Background to Modern Philosophy.* Hackett Publishing Company, pp. 61-81. (First published in 1632). Published in full by *The Modern Library,* 2001.

Lakatos, I. (1970). "Falsification and the Methodology of Scientific Research Programmes." In Lakatos, I. and Musgrave, A., eds., *Criticism and the Growth of Knowledge,* Cambridge University Press, pp. 91-196.

Munévar, G. (2015). "Historical Antecedents to the Philosophy of Paul Feyerabend," *Studies in History and Philosophy of Science.*

Newton, I. (1989). *Principia.* Excerpted in *The Scientific Background to Modern Philosophy;* Matthews, M.R., Ed.; Hackett Publishing Company, pp.137-153. First published in 1687.

Popper, K. (1972). *Objective Knowledge.* Oxford University Press.

CHAPTER 4

SCIENCE AS A DARING ENTERPRISE: CHOOSING BY CONVENTION

A REACTION AGAINST FEYERABEND

John Preston in his book *Feyerabend* claims that Feyerabend's case in *Against Method* works only against the Popperians but not against the inductivists. Preston believes that Feyerabend's presumed demonstration that Galileo brought about scientific progress by breaking rules such as Newton's "Do not entertain hypotheses which contradict well-established and generally accepted experimental results" succeeds only against the universal rules of the falsificationists. Because of his Popperian ancestry (early in his career, Feyerabend was Popper's assistant), Feyerabend presumably could not "accept that any rule could really work unless it is made exceptionless." (1997, 174) Thus, and only because of such ancestry, "does Feyerabend think he can refute methodological monism [that there is only *one* method of science] by demonstrating that methodological rules have been profitably violated." (174). But, Preston, following William Newton-Smith, claims that "This strategy is obviously bankrupt," for it "fails to address any other rationalist position."

Feyerabend's strategy allegedly fails to address inductive rules that, by being probabilistic, should be expected "to lead us astray on some occasions." We cannot rule out, "these exceptions notwithstanding," says Newton-Smith, "that our chance of progress is greater if we employ the rule" (Preston, 175). According to Preston (and Newton-Smith) "wise methodological monists will endorse inductive rules, rules which will advise us which of a pair of theories to adopt in the face of available evidence."

This is all sheer fiction, however, an inductivist's pipe dream.[1] Newton-Smith is not talking about rules that have been explicitly formulated and employed with great success in actual science (and some of which Galileo may have violated). If such rules had existed, most of the philosophy of science of last century would have been a futile exercise, pre-empted by a scientifically and philosophically satisfactory methodology, and surely Popper would not have been taken seriously by a majority of those scientists who have given any

---

[1] The following remarks on Preston are taken from my1999 comments to his book on Feyerabend.

importance to the philosophy of science. Newton-Smith is talking about the Promised Land of Induction. A promised land, by the way, against which much independent argument has been directed, from Hume on down, as we saw in Ch. 2. Thus, Preston's wise methodological monists are all imaginary, or, at best, true believers waiting for their Moses to show them the way.

But let that pass. After all, what concerns Preston is whether Feyerabend can rule out all possible forms of methodological monism (including those of questionable plausibility). It seems to me that Feyerabend has indeed ruled out all such that may be fairly called empiricist, and that he has surely ruled out the kind of inductive monism favored by Preston and Newton-Smith.

The structure of Feyerabend's argument is rather simple. An analysis of the history of science shows that, in significant episodes, scientists had to violate methodological rules in order for scientific progress to result. Scientists have to choose, then, between being "rational" (by always adhering to the rules) and moving science forward. The choice is obvious, much to the distress of the philosophers.

Notice again that Galileo is doing at least two important things. One, he is introducing a body of facts that accords with what would be the case if the Earth indeed rotates (*Dialogues*). Second, in order to accomplish that task, he changes the concept of motion (Munévar 2000, 60). Instead of the highly empiricist concept of the Aristotelians (motion is observable change of position over time), he suggests a concept of motion with components that are in principle non-observable (since the observers share them). Today, of course, out of the context of the scientific dispute in Galileo's time, we could in principle observe the parabolic motion of the stone (from a spaceship, for example). Galileo, incidentally, as Feyerabend quotes him (1978, 101), is quite conscious of what is at stake. Time and again he praises Copernicus for resisting the verdict of experience. "With reason as his guide [Copernicus] resolutely continued to affirm what sensible experience seemed to contradict." And "there is no limit to my astonishment," Galileo writes, "when I reflect that Aristarchus and Copernicus were able to make reason so conquer sense that, in defiance of the latter, the former became mistress of their belief" (*Dialogue*, 328)

Now, any methodology that can be fairly called empiricist needs to specify the means by which experience will pass judgement on theory. If the "facts" can be overthrown, however, all methodologies may fail from time to time. This result thus applies to all empiricist methodologies. Probabilistic inductive rules are no exception. For it is not a question of the rule failing to *guarantee* a conclusion (being probabilistic) but rather of the rule *failing to apply* because the evidence on which the probability estimates were to be based has been taken away (that is, we are *unable* to apply the rule). Even if an inductivist Moses found the Promised Land, there would be no rule to give us guidance in the case of Galileo, for the Aristotelians would apply the rule to one body of evidence (vertically falling stones) and the Copernicans to another (parabolically falling stones).

Since probabilities are estimated on the basis of the available data, Preston and Newton-Smith's rules are simply inapplicable across the divide between camps with inconsistent sets of data. If you buy 100 tickets, out of 150, for the church raffle at Easter, you still run a chance of not getting the prize. But if your 100 tickets are for the raffle held the previous Christmas, you are not even in the contest.

Moreover, it is clear from Feyerabend's analysis (*pace* Preston) that there is nothing peculiar about Galileo's case. Scientific progress will occasionally require the overthrow of the "empirical basis" and thus the violation of *all* empiricist rules worth the name (AM).

An objection apparently similar to Preston's and Newton-Smith's is made by Larry Laudan:

> ... when we endorse a rule, we are asserting our belief that following that rule is more likely to realize [our] goals than violating it will. What makes a rule acceptable as a rule is our belief that it represents the *best strategy* we can imagine for reaching a certain desired end; but it need not be, and commonly will not be, either a necessary or a sufficient condition for reaching that end.[2]

Laudan's point is that methodological rules are like rules of thumb, not exceptionless, universal rules of reason. Therefore, a notion of rationality based on adherence to methodological rules cannot be defeated by case studies showing that Galileo or Einstein violated this or that rule, or even that such a violation was necessary for scientific progress. Any sensible methodologist will thus realize that Feyerabend is merely attacking a straw man.

Notice, however, that at this level of generality Laudan is not objecting but actually agreeing with Feyerabend: All methodological rules must allow for exceptions, otherwise scientific progress will suffer. As for attacking a straw man, "sensible" methodologists at the time when Feyerabend wrote his work *did* require universal rules of method. All Feyerabend needs is to congratulate Laudan for coming to see the light. Nevertheless, once we get down to particulars this harmony of views may not be very enlightening. For recognizing that rules have limits is not the same as explaining, as Feyerabend does by means of the case studies, *why* they have such limits.

---

[2] Laudan, L. *Beyond Positivism and Relativism*, 1996, p. 103.

Moreover, there is an additional sense in which the shortcomings of the standard rules of rationality become quite embarrassing. The favorite rules of methodologists fail precisely in instances in which scientists should have received the most guidance from them (when they should have served as the *best strategies*). That is, the rules seem to have failed (had to be violated) precisely when science took its greatest strides forward. As Robert Farrell remarks, the episodes Feyerabend selects are not just any old counterexamples, but rather those that until recently were presented by "Rationalists" as "paradigmatic cases of rationality."[3] In Farrell's words, in those episodes the considerations that led to the scientists' decisions "were completely inexplicable in terms of 'Rationalist' theses," and in fact were arrived at in a manner "demonstrably contrary to the whole program of 'Rationalist' philosophy" (2003, 17).

Thus, Laudan's looser and more sophisticated approach does not quite do historical and philosophical justice to Feyerabend's remarks on method. As we will see later in this book, some of Laudan's main contributions actually complement those of Feyerabend.

In the rest of this chapter, I will consider two possible avenues to bypass the problems presented by Feyerabend's analysis of Galileo's case. They both have in common the recognition that there is a certain conventional element in the practice of science.

MATURE FALSIFICATION

The first possibility stems from the belief that the practice of science is a lot like falsificationism. If the aim is to be faithful to the practice of science, perhaps it pays to consider whether the falsificationist picture presented earlier is too simpleminded. Perhaps the key resides in interpreting the falsificationist view of science in a way that keeps in mind the complexities of actual scientific practice.

As it happens, Lakatos (1970) gave such an interpretation of Popperian methodology (although he himself did not subscribe to it). I will consider it in this section. To begin with, let us recognize that it was perhaps too naive to think that careful observations were a completely solid empirical basis, that theories could be shown to be false if their predictions fail, and so on. It is time then to outgrow fairy tales and face up to the responsibilities of a mature methodology. Of course, observations are fallible. Of course, the elimination of hypotheses may be a very complicated affair. But experience still plays a critical

---

[3] Feyerabend had anticipated this point. "My aim," he said, "was to show that some very simple and plausible rules and standards which both philosophers and scientists regarded as essential parts of rationality were violated in the course of episodes... they regarded as equally essential." (*Science in a Free Society*, NLB, 1978, p. 13).

role in the direction scientific knowledge must take. The scientist still has the obligation to present only testable theories. And the elimination of alternatives, though fraught with difficulties, still is characteristically ruthless. Such is the kernel of the methodology that Imre Lakatos has taken from the writings of Karl Popper.

A mature approach would be mindful of several things. First, the mature falsificationist separates rejection from disproof, for the clash with observation does not imply that the theory is false, as we have seen in Ch. 3. Nonetheless, he thinks that a theory may be eliminated under certain conditions of conflict with observation. To that end, second, some steps must be taken to ensure that the blame for the failure of predictions can be placed squarely on the theory or hypothesis under test. As an illustration, consider the following account of a "crucial experiment."

The first astronauts to set foot on the Moon installed a special reflector for a laser beam sent from Earth. As the beam bounced back to Earth, it enabled a group of scientists to measure very carefully the distance between the Earth and the Moon. More reflectors were installed later, and a series of measurements was carried out for a long while. The point of the measurements was to decide between Einstein's and Dicke's theories of gravitation. In the few areas in which Einstein's General Relativity had been tested until then, it had gained the upper hand over its predecessor (Newton's). But Dicke had suggested an alternative theory, according to which gravity grows weaker as the universe expands. If Dicke were correct, the Moon's orbit would fall toward the sun, and this would lead to small but systematic variations of the distance between the Earth and the Moon (extremely small, which called for extremely precise measurements, hence the laser). No such variations were found, so the experiment can be said to have ruled against Dicke's theory (See **Figure 4.1**).

It should be obvious that astronomic observations based on the use of lasers (and reflectors and receiving telescopes) involve many assumptions. These assumptions span many fields of science: optics, atomic and molecular physics, electromagnetism, meteorology, and so on. And it would be very surprising to have the scientists in the group claim that those sciences could hardly be mistaken or, worse, that those sciences are indeed infallible. Short of that infallibility it makes little sense to say that the observations could not be wrong. But fallible as they may be, these observations are grounded on scientific work that has endured more prolonged and severe testing than the gravitational views in question, at least in the context of the experiment. And thus, it seems reasonable to let the observations count *against* Dicke's theory and give some (tentative) *support* to Einstein's.

In other words, scientists decide what is to count as the observation (or interpretation) theory for every testing situation. They try to make this decision intelligently (e.g., they prefer to use as observation theories those that have already survived rigorous testing, etc.) But scientists may make a mistake: they may reject a theory that is actually true and (tentatively) accept a false one instead. That is just a risk that as mature methodologists they must accept if they are to have a procedure for preferring some views to others. When we cast an adult eye upon the practice of science, we realize that, far from having a firm foundation, it is like "driving piles into a swamp," as Popper says (1992, 94). Rejection does not amount to disproof. It is purely a matter of methodological decision — or rather, of several types of methodological decisions.

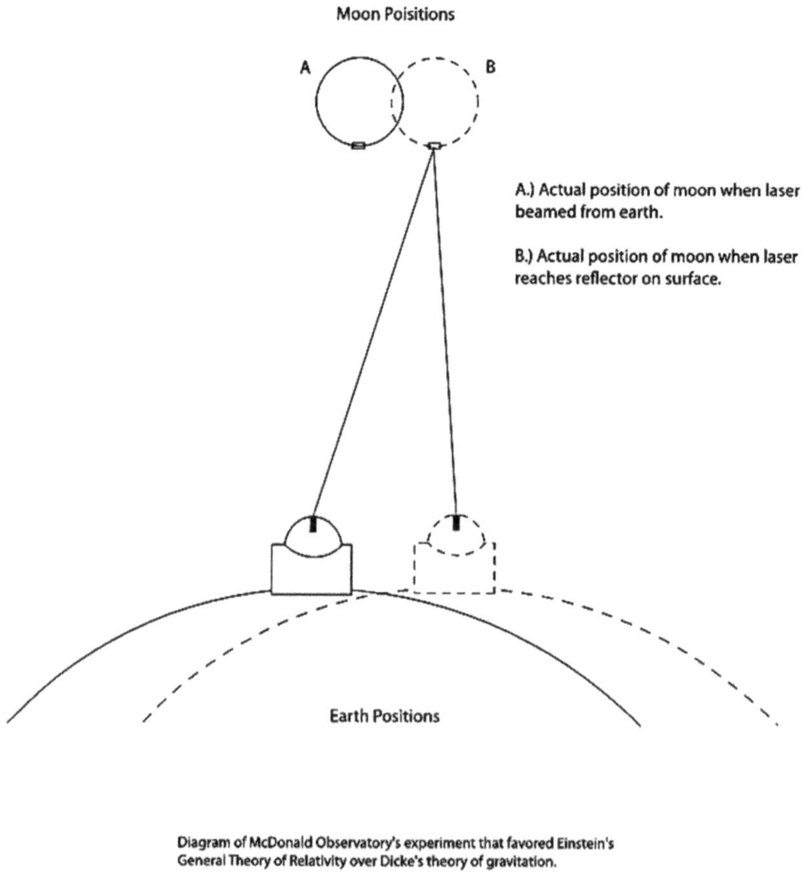

Figure 4.1. Lunar Laser Crucial Experiment on Gravitation. Drawing by Nicole Ankeny.

One type of decision, according to Lakatos, is determining what will constitute the observation theory in any one particular experiment or test of a hypothesis. In making this determination the conventional wisdom of the discipline will play a large role. The parts of science that can reasonably be taken for granted will form the proper background knowledge in that testing situation. After that, the conventional wisdom will also dictate what procedures are to count as correct applications of that background knowledge (e.g., after taking the contemporary theory of electromagnetism "for granted," we must still follow certain steps before concluding that we have a "correct" reading of current or voltage). In some cases, this decision—which need not be explicit—may be rather simple. But in many other cases it could be quite complicated (think of biochemical testing for example: Was the bacteria strain pure? Could there have been contamination of the culture? Did the staining fail to reveal some important feature of the affected cells? The list could be very long.) The demands of the conventional wisdom may seem extremely rigorous at times. Consider, for instance, the gravitational experiment mentioned above, based on the account by Nigel Calder (1979).

Laser beams bouncing off the reflectors made it possible to measure the distance to the Moon to within a few inches. The experiment used the 107-inch telescope at the McDonald Observatory in Texas starting in 1969 and collaborated with about ten other laboratories. As Calder tells us:

> The ordinary astronomical observations at the McDonald Observatory are frequently interrupted when the telescope swings toward the Moon for a 45-minute "run" of laser ranging. It is fascinating to watch because the observer must continuously aim the big telescope and the emergent laser beam precisely at one of the retroreflecting panels—and the target is moving. "It's a sporting occasion," says Eric Silverberg, who oversees these operations at McDonald.
>
> Every three seconds the laser fires a very brief pulse of light, only three feet long. At about the expected moment of return, the detection system is activated, and it admits a single particle of light. It may be stray light, but an atomic clock times its arrival to better than a billionth of a second and a computer compares the timings for successive particles of light. When an incoming particle of light arrives at the appropriate instant, it is judged to be from the reflector on the Moon, and a bell rings to let the observer know that he is on target (97-98).

A mature falsificationist methodology recognizes that these decisions must be made in order to have an empirical basis at all. And it also recognizes one more crucial type of decision if the title of "empirical science" is to be maintained. Since nothing goes more against the falsificationist grain than ad hocness, no methodology could be called falsificationist that did not find some way to preserve the injunction against the "unscientific" modification of hypothesis. We have already seen that once the predictions disagree with the (fallible) empirical basis, the finger of refutation is pointed not at the hypothesis alone — that would be arbitrary — but against a conjunction of hypothesis, initial conditions, and *ceteris paribus* clause. Mature falsification directs the scientist to isolate the hypothesis, so its refutation is far less arbitrary. The way to achieve such isolation is to:

(a) Make further hypotheses to the effect that the initial conditions have been incorrectly reported (e.g., if a voltage reading is unusual, we check the magnitude setting in the voltmeter, then we might use a different voltmeter, and so on). If those hypotheses fall, we accept the report of the initial conditions.

(b) We must then suppose that the *ceteris paribus* clause was violated (i.e., we must suppose that the system was not closed), suggest how the violation could have come about (i.e., what other factor may be affecting the system), and test the suggestion. The process must be done as many times as the situation warrants, until our ingenuity is reasonably exhausted. For example, if a planet's orbit does not accord with Newtonian predictions, we postulate the presence of another planet that would account for the perturbations. If the predicted planet is found, we conclude that the *ceteris paribus* clause had indeed been violated. If not, we propose another way in which the system was open or one of the auxiliary hypotheses was false — and check it. If we cannot show that the clause was violated, then the only reasonable culprit for the failure of the original prediction seems to be the hypothesis in question. Therefore, we *reject* it.

As Popper puts it: "In general we regard an intersubjectively testable falsification as final.... A corroborative appraisal made at a later date...can replace a positive degree of corroboration by a negative one, but not *vice versa.*" (1934, Section 82).

Popper's view is a bit too strong, however, for if we were to find out, years after the logical isolation and consequent elimination of a theory, that one of the auxiliary hypotheses was false — that we should have pursued our testing of the *ceteris paribus* clause further — it would be perplexing not to take back the rejection of the theory (as in fact happened with Prout's view).

The mature falsificationists realize that science is a complicated adventure fraught with peril. Unlike their naive counterparts, the mature falsificationists recognize that their testing procedures are very fallible, but still insist on constructing an empirical basis against which to test their views of the world. Thus, they share with their predecessors two important concerns:

(1) The obligation to state a theory in such a way that predictions follow from it (to force the theory to stick its neck out).

(2) A preparedness to eliminate the theory if the predictions do not come through.

They differ from their predecessors in that they recognize that observation is fallible, that hidden auxiliary hypotheses and not the theory under test may be the culprits in the failure of a prediction, and that it is thus necessary to separate rejection from disproof. As a result, they specify the three main types of decision scientists must make in the hope of bringing progress to their discipline:

(1) As to what is unproblematic background knowledge (choice of observation theory).

(2) As to the procedures by which a claim will qualify as an observation statement.

(3) As to when the Initial conditions and the *ceteris paribus* clause have been checked sufficiently, so as to leave the theory as the only victim of (informal) *modus tollens*; or, in other words, as to when the theory under test is to be blamed for the negative result of the experiment or observation.

It is worth remarking once again that these choices are not left up to the individual scientist's discretion, says Marie. What is always in question is whether she has lived up to the most rigorous standards of observation and criticism that her discipline may demand of her. And when we speak of acting in accordance with the collective wisdom, we have in mind the temporary state of the art that results from the relentless elimination of error by a community of critical explorers of the universe. As a consequence of such communal work, we may sometimes speak of some theories as being well corroborated. This notion of corroboration is properly applied only when we at least:

(1) Repeat the tests (replication)

(2) Use a variety of tests under widely different conditions

(3) Test new implications of the theory suggested by the present tests

(4) Determine how well our theory fits with other well-tested theories[4]

---

[4] If some of those theories are more general, our theory may receive so-called "support from above."

It would be a mistake to think that the three types of decision so far discussed are always clearly distinct and made separately. Consider the following example. Suppose that we want to test the effectiveness of a drug to cure the common cold. The normal procedure is to try the drug on a sample of the population intended, and then to extrapolate the results to the entire population by means of statistics. The sample is divided into two groups: one of them will actually take the drug (the experimental group), the other will instead take a placebo, i.e., a substance not presumed to have any curative powers at all (the control group). It is also normal procedure to run the test *double blind.* This means that the patients in the control group do not know that they are taking a placebo and not the drug, and that the doctors who examine the patients do not know who has taken the drug and who has not.

The first blind ensures that there is a comparison between the effects of the drug and the benefits of simply being under treatment (the placebo effect, which can be considerable in many people). The second blind ensures that the researchers' possible bias in favor of the hypothesis (that the drug works) does not distort the data yielded by the test (for example, by deciding that a patient who has taken the drug but is still sniffling a little has gotten over his cold, whereas some other examiner may hesitate to place the patient in the "cured" category). Great precautions should also be taken to ensure that the experimental and the control group are equivalent in all relevant respects (half men, half women in both groups, for example), as well as representative samples of the intended population (are their members, for example, too young on the whole, or too old? do most of them live in cities, the country, or an appropriate mix of both?) There are many factors that could increase or diminish the effectiveness of the drug in a certain specific group. But if those factors are not present in the same proportion in the intended larger population, the results of the test are going to be misleading.

It may appear that all such precautions are taken in order to ensure that the data (i.e., the observations) that will decide the fate of the hypothesis are "correctly" gathered. This is one type of decision. But all this activity can also be interpreted as trying to ensure that if the prediction fails (that the drug has a statistically significant effect), then it will be reasonable to blame, and thus to reject, the hypothesis. This is another type of decision. Nonetheless, even if there are cases in which the different types of decision may be hard to pull apart, the mature methodologist can still rest assured of the construction of an empirical basis and of the logical isolation of the hypothesis under test.

OBJECTIONS TO MATURE FALSIFICATIONISM

If we think about what scientists *do*, we should conclude that they often carry out the sorts of activities envisioned by the mature falsificationist. Indeed, previous methodologies may appear too literal and simple-minded by contrast. Nevertheless, some bothersome discoveries come to mind when reviewing the history of science.

First of all, we should remind ourselves of the case of Prout. The conventional wisdom had chosen carefully a theory of observation. Unfortunately for Prout, that theory of observation conflicted with his hypothesis. Furthermore, the measurements were careful and precise. Nor could the failure of his predictions (e.g., the atomic weight of chlorine), be easily excused. On the contrary, all the mature falsificationist steps were apparently taken. Thus, it was proper, from this methodology's point of view, to reject Prout's hypothesis. The decision had to be reversed almost a century later, however. But if a decision can be reversed, it can also be ignored. Einstein, for example, was not concerned by Miller's careful replication of the Michelson-Morley experiment, in which Miller concluded that there was an ether wind after all. Miller's conclusion was in direct conflict with Einstein's theory of special relativity, and no one could determine what was wrong with Miller's experiment. But Einstein simply assumed that Miller had to be mistaken—and eventually the mistake was discovered. In this case the conventional hunch was with Einstein: Miller was ignored. The point is, however, that if the discipline had followed the mature falsificationist procedures, it would have ruled against Einstein. It is difficult to say that we have a method when the conventional wisdom is not dictated by the presumed conventional procedures. Fair is fair: Miller had played by the rules.

There is also the glaring case of the perihelion of Mercury. (The details will be discussed in a later chapter.) Suffice it to say for now that the predictions about Mercury's orbit were erroneous. When the anomaly was detected, the scientists involved did behave like mature falsificationists at first. Many ingenious ideas were put forward to explain how the *ceteris paribus* clause might have been violated — some unknown force had to be acting on Mercury. There could be an extra planet between Mercury and the Sun—it was baptized "Vulcan"—or perhaps the sun was considerably flattened at the poles. Indeed, all the decisions required by the mature falsificationist were properly and exhaustively taken; Newtonian gravitational theory was logically isolated, but it was not given up in spite of this clear predictive failure.

At times it pays for a scientist to buck the tide of conventional wisdom even when the canons of mature falsificationism are obeyed by the discipline. And some other times the conventional wisdom does not follow such canons. And a good thing, too: On more than one occasion there lay open the door for spectacular progress in science. Thus, it appears that mature falsification has some severe shortcomings.

Nevertheless, a mature falsificationist may wonder at the propriety of using historical objections to assail his methodology. After all, a methodology deals with norms, with what the scientists ought to do. Why should a description of actual practice be the basis of criticism? Could we likewise point to the high incidence of murder throughout history as evidence that the prescription against murder is wrong? Complete adherence to a methodology would be possible only if humans were perfectly rational. So, it is not surprising that actual scientific practice falls short of the methodological ideal.

This reply will not do, however. Living up to the standards of methodology makes sense only because doing so would increase the chances of success in science. And we know the record of the methodology in this regard from the practice of science. But if it turns out that the methodology would actually get in the way of that success, then we face a choice between method and success. Method, being subordinate to success, is the clear loser. This is why history can be used to evaluate methodologies.

The point is not, then, that mature falsification is sometimes at odds with the practice of science, but rather that scientific success requires from time to time the violation of the standards of mature falsificationism. This means that if one had followed the falsificationist precepts one could not have achieved what is now considered a great advance. Thus, we are not merely talking about cases where we fell short of falsificationist perfection, but rather in which falsificationist perfection was an obstacle to the growth of science.

According to mature falsificationism, a theory must agree with the empirical basis or else be rejected. Admitting that the empirical basis is fallible and a matter of conventional wisdom makes our position more flexible and enlightened. And yet it is not enough. For we should remember that Galileo took on such an empirical basis and replaced it with another more convenient to a Copernican program. And the lesson we draw from Prout is essentially the same. It seems that there are times when the growth of science needs to take turns far more radical than the sensible falsificationist is able to accommodate.

The analysis of historical cases presented here seems to have covered all the bases: Experience cannot serve as the *decisive* judge of theory, even with qualifications. Those that equate method with scientific rationality must be aghast. How could science not be rational? But the same argument holds for rationality, so understood, as it did for method. Scientific rationality is of use only if it yields progress in science. If it gets in the way of progress, too bad for rationality.

SIMPLICITY

In light of all this, how are we to proceed in science? If facts can neither prove nor disprove theories, how can we ever choose between two alternatives? And if experience is not to guide our choice, in what sense can science be called "empirical"? One suggestion is that some ways of accounting for experience may be simpler or more elegant than others. Pierre Duhem, one of the main proponents of this suggestion, argued that a scientist's function is to "save the phenomena," that is, to modify his theory until it is no longer in conflict with observation (1908).

Duhem wants to forget about the truth or falsity of theories and to concentrate instead on the ease with which the theory accounts for the experience. Many competing views can be saved by all sorts of stratagems, even *ad hoc* moves, as we have seen in the previous chapter. But if Duhem is right, we should agree to choose the simplest or most elegant alternative. This would make the choice of scientific theories a matter of convention; but perhaps a reasonable convention at that, for it keeps us out of idle disputes about what is real and permits us to spend our time and efforts on improving the theoretical buildings into which we house the phenomena of our experience. Some theories become so complicated in their efforts to "save the phenomena" that they turn unmanageable. After excessive patch-up work and repairs, the building crumbles of its own weight.

The classic historical example is presumably Ptolemy's system, whose machinery of epicycles and equants was finally too cumbersome to warrant even further refinements. The conventionalist claim is, then, that the Copernican system should have been preferred because it was simpler.

It is best to keep in mind that Duhem need not argue that simplicity is evidence of truth, although there are some who believe that it is so. Those scholars may even find encouragement in quotes from great scientists. "Nature loves simplicity," said Copernicus. Einstein added: "God is subtle but not malicious." Whether Copernicus and Einstein took simplicity as evidence of truth may be a matter for debate. But it would be difficult to see what argument supports such a position. Of course, sometimes the simplicity of a view may lead a scientist to adopt it, and then since he accepts it he also thinks that it is true. But the truth of the view does not follow from its being the simplest view. If I arrive home without my key, the simplest thing is to check to see if the door is unlocked. On failing that, I will ring the bell in hopes there is someone in. Only after the simplest alternatives have been exhausted should I attempt to pry open a window, or even worse to break it. If a scientist sees an alternative as the simplest, he is most likely to see it also as the easiest to put into effect. But truth is a different matter altogether.

In any event simplicity is too difficult to define. Do we choose the theory that is simpler mathematically, experimentally, ontologically? These need not, and often do not, coincide. Moreover, simplicity seems relative to the context, and to the researcher's point of view. It may also depend on a complex array of purposes. (These matters will be treated in the next chapter). Nor is the historical record all that clear in favor of the conventionalist. According to Stephen Toulmin and June Goodfield (179),

> [Copernicus'] methods of astronomical computation were not, in principle, any more accurate than Ptolemy's: in practice, they were sometimes less so. Nor were they, in the end, appreciably simpler than the earlier methods. Even the outstanding merit of the system—the recognition that retrograde motion was an optical illusion—was obscured by the time the theory was completely worked out; in the end, the constructions used to compute the planetary motions reintroduced elements from the Earth's own motion, by way of the "moving center" of the Earth's circular orbit. (See **Figures 4.2-4.3**).

If simplicity may be in the eye of the beholder, and if the historical record does not show the clear example we were promised, the plausibility of conventionalism is quite reduced. In addition, some strong considerations suggest that conventionalism in general is not an acceptable position.

It may seem possible to modify a view so it will keep in agreement with experience, so it will "save the phenomena." And both the followers of Ptolemy and Copernicus might have done so for their respective views. But as a matter of practice, we can at best be sure that the two competing alternatives fit the facts *within a limited domain.* What happens, though, when the domain is extended to entirely new areas? It is not clear, for example, how the Ptolemaic system would have handled all that is now known about the size, dynamics, and configuration of the universe. The outer sphere of stars would have to go, for example, to say nothing of black holes, neutron stars and galaxies.

What is clear in this "exemplary" historical case is that the Ptolemaic system was given up before ingenuity had to stretch beyond the borders of credulity. As we can see in figures 1 and 2, the winner was not all that straightforward and simple. Copernicus thought that planetary orbits were circular and was forced to use epicycles for his calculations. Perhaps when Newton accepted Kepler's ellipses, the heliocentric Copernican view became clearly simpler; but by then the Copernicans had already won the revolution. Thus, it seems that some crucially important decisions in science have to be taken without an appeal to simplicity, or at least, long before simplicity has been clearly established. This does not mean that simplicity may not on occasion serve as the criterion that shows one view's superiority over another. But it indicates that oftentimes something else is afoot.

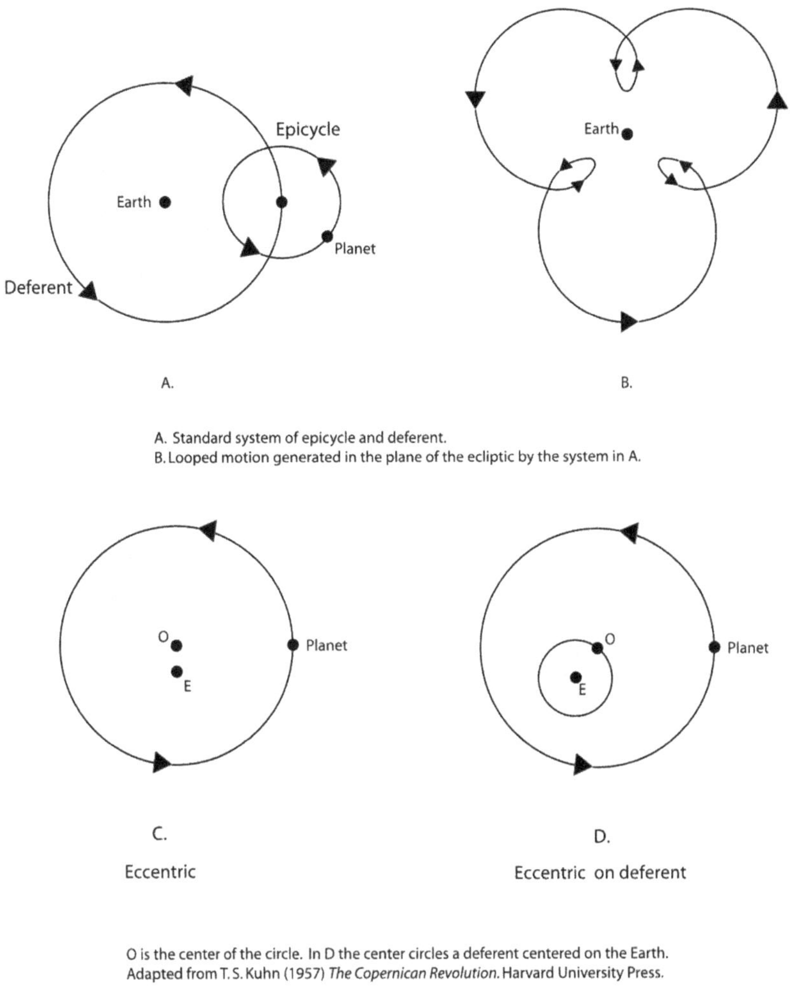

Figure 4.2. Complexities of Greek Astronomy. Drawings by Nicole Ankeny.

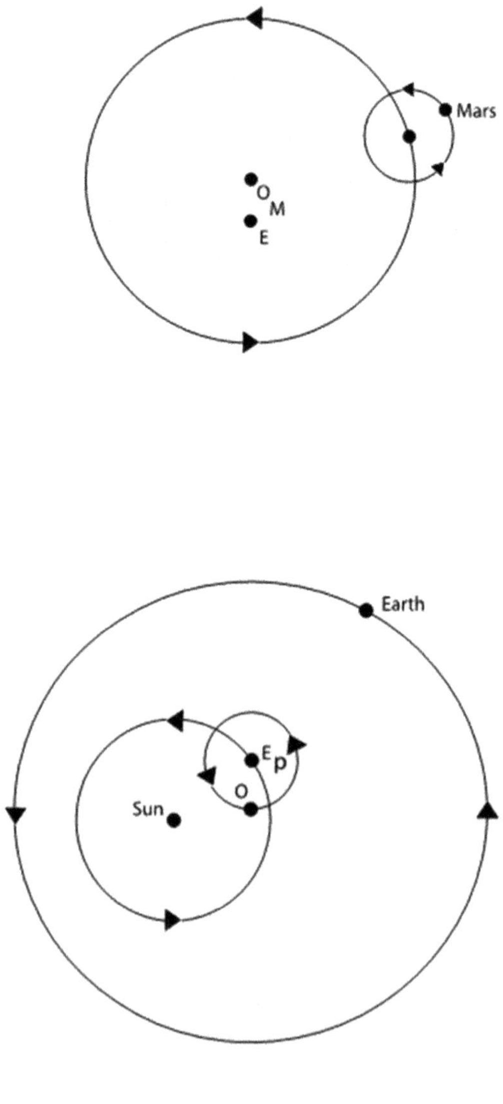

The Copernican account: The Earth revolves around a point in an epicycle that itself revolves around a point eccentric to the sun. E_p is the center of Earth's epicycle. O is the center of Earth's orbit.
Adapted from T. S. Kuhn (1957) *The Copernican Revolution.* Harvard University Press.

Figure 4.3. Complexities of Fully Developed Copernican Account.
Drawings by Nicole Ankeny.

In the second place, there are times in which simplicity is not only not used as a criterion of choice, but in which *it could not be so used.* Those are cases in which it is simply inapplicable, except perhaps strictly as a matter of taste. We must remember that the separation between observation and theory has been questioned. Therefore, in a clash of theories the empirical basis may vary (the sides may prefer different "observation theories"). But if there is not a unique body of "facts," of phenomena, it makes little sense to claim that both alternatives save the phenomena just as well, or that one does it better than the other.

Let us examine next the work that was largely responsible for the reconceptualization of the epistemology of science: Thomas Kuhn's *The Structure of Scientific Revolutions.*

REFERENCES

Calder, N. (1979). *Einstein's Universe.*Viking.

Duhem, P. (1908). *Sauver les Phénomènes. Essai sur la Notion de Théorie Physique de Platon à Galilée.* A. Hermann (*To Save the Phenomena*).

Farrell, R. (2003). *Feyerabend and Scientific Values: Tightrope-Walking Rationality.* Springer.

Feyerabend, P. K. (1978a). *Against Method.* Verso.

Feyerabend, P. K. (1978b). *Science in a Free Society.* Verso.

Galileo (1989). *Dialogues Concerning the Two Chief World Systems.* In Mathews, M.R. (Ed.), *The Scientific Background to Modern Philosophy.* Indianapolis: Hackett Publishing Company, pp. 61-81. (First published in 1632). Published in full by *The Modern Library,* New York, 2001

Galileo. (1989). *The Assayer.* In *The Scientific Background to Modern Philosophy,* Matthews, M.R., Ed.; Hackett, 1989; pp. 56–61. First published in 1623.

Kuhn, T. S. (1957). *The Copernican Revolution.* Harvard University Press.

Lakatos, I. (1970). "Falsification and the Methodology of Scientific Research Programmes." In Lakatos, I. and Musgrave, A., eds., *Criticism and the Growth of Knowledge,* Cambridge University Press, pp. 91-196.

Laudan, L. (1996). *Beyond Positivism and Relativism: Theory Method and Evi-dence.* Westview Press.

Munévar, G. (1999). My comment on Preston in G. Courvalis, ed. "Radical fallibilism vs conceptual analysis: The significance of Feyerabend's Philosophy of science." *Metascience* 8(2):206-233. DOI: 10.1007/BF02913264.

Munévar, G. (2000). "A Réhabilitation of Paul Feyerabend." In Preston, J, Munévar, G. and Lamb, D. (eds.) *The Worst Enemy of Science? Essays on the Life and Thought of Paul Feyerabend.* Oxford University Press.

Musgrave, A. (eds.), *Criticism and the Growth of Knowledge.* Cambridge University Press.

Popper, K. (1992). *The Logic of Scientific Discovery.* Routledge.

Popper, K. (1934). *Logik der Forschung.* Springer. *Translated as The Logic of Scientific Discovery.*

Preston, J. (1997). *Feyerabend: Philosophy, Science and Society.* Polity Press.

Toulmin, S. and Goodfield, J. (1965). *The Fabric of the Heavens: The Development of Astronomy and Dynamics.* Harper & Row.

CHAPTER 5

DOGMATISM IN SCIENCE: KUHN AND SCIENTIFIC REVOLUTIONS

In spite of all the arguments offered, some degree of puzzlement must remain. Even if induction and falsification fail to provide *the* reliable guide for science, and even if the (apparently) most obvious rules of method must be sacrificed to progress every so often, we may still feel that those ideas capture some important insights about what science ought to do. Furthermore, we may hope that Kuhn and Feyerabend's critique of science will afford us some understanding of what those insights might be.

Of course, it may turn out that all Kuhn and Feyerabend have to offer is a "demolition" view of science: "Science is not the magnificently rational institution it was supposed to be—the hell with it." Some of the post-modernist figures involved in the recent "science wars" have been suspected of precisely such an attitude, but that is clearly not so in the case of Kuhn and Feyerabend, even though at one point Feyerabend was identified in the journal *Nature* as "the worst enemy of science" (Theocharis and Psimopoulos,1987)

The prevailing view for most of the century approached theories, and even observations, in terms of sentences (or propositions), or more formally in terms of sets of sentences (or propositions). With Kuhn we begin to forge a new way of thinking about science.

To introduce this new way, let me draw an analogy to perception with the help of **Figure 5.1**. Scientific views, for Kuhn, are indeed that, views of the world. These views of the world are, furthermore, held by communities of scientists. As R.L. Gregory put it: "Science is the cooperative perception of the universe" (1966, 226). Visual perception, however, is not limited to the "processing" of visual information. What we see is not a mere summary or construction of patterns formed originally on the retina of the eye. The contribution of the eyes is often made to fit in with expectations derived from the other senses, including the proprioceptors (body position) and other internal senses. We look into a bush and see nothing but branches and leaves. But as soon as we hear chirping, a portion of the bush is almost instantly transformed into the image of a small bird. Previous experience and expectation are often needed as well in order to disambiguate our perceptual and conceptual "pictures of the world."

Prior interaction with the world provides the setting into which the new perception has to fit, and subsequent interactions may modify such perception. Think of the fine-tuning of a bow-and-arrow hunter's visual perception made possible by his successes and failures. Consider also **Figure 5.2**, F.P. Kilpatrick's distorted-room experiments, in which he made some walls longer or taller than others. Just looking through a peephole, subjects initially saw a distorted room as rectilinear. When trying to touch a drawing of a bug on the opposite wall with a long stick, the subjects fell short at first. By going further, the target was finally reached. Next the subjects looked at a rectilinear room but saw it as distorted, according to their previous interaction. The first effort to touch the bug stubbed the wall too fast. New and increasingly successful interactions led to viewing the room differently: as distorted (1961).

In **Figures 5.1 and 5.2** we can perceive each of the drawings in two alternative ways. This ambiguity of perception sometimes affects us also when looking at the pictures in a magazine or when viewing an unfamiliar scene. The perceptual apparatus disambiguates in normal circumstances by providing contextual clues that favor one of the alternative perceptual hypotheses (in the manner described above). In **Figure 5.3** we can see how failure and success alter perception. Such analogies may serve to introduce Kuhn's conception of scientific views.

Figure 5.1. E. G. Boring's object-ambiguous mother-in-law.

She is seen sometimes as a young girl, at other times as an old woman. These are the two most probable object interpretations of this figure, which are entertained in turn.

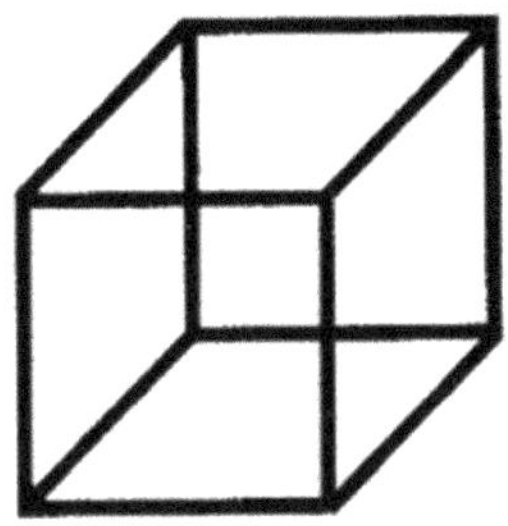

Figure 5.2. The Necker Cube.

This is the plane projection of a cube as seen from a great distance. There is no perspective size change. The figure is seen in spontaneously reversing depth. Evidently, there are two equally probable solutions to the perceptual problem: 'What is the object out there?' The brain entertains each of its hypothetical solutions in turn – and never makes up its mind.

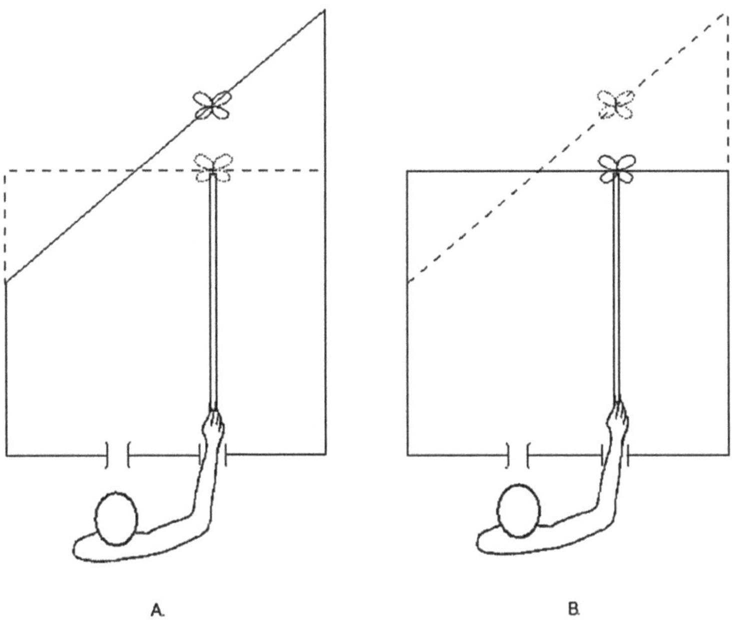

Figure 5.3. E. G. Two stages of F. P. Kilpatrick's distorted-room experiment.

Picture A: Man looking through peephole sees distorted room according to his expectations (i.e., a square room). His attempts to touch the bug on the wall with the stick come up short.

Picture B: After competing A, man looks now at a square room. He sees it as distorted, though, and hits the bug on the wall earlier than he expects.

Drawings by Nicole Ankeny.

First, a scientific view such as Copernican astronomy or Newtonian dynamics amounts to more than the usually expected "representation" of nature (think instead of a counterpart to the visual image). A scientific view must also involve a commitment to several modes of interaction with the world. For Kuhn (1970, 181-188) those commitments would involve (1) models that have a fruitful role in the way theories are constructed: "the electric circuit may be regarded as a steady-state hydrodynamic system; the molecules of a gas behave like tiny elastic billiard balls in random motion." Such models supply the scientific group with "preferred or permissible analogies and metaphors." Those commitments also include (2) the concrete problem-solutions that scientists encounter throughout their education and later in their careers. These concrete problem-solutions—which Kuhn calls "exemplars"—are more than illustrations of theory. If anything, by making them second nature the scientist apprentice finally comes to master the theory. Such problem-solutions range from those found in textbooks, examinations and laboratories to those found in the technical literature for specialists.

The scientists who belong to a group will of course also share (3) theories, i.e., symbolic generalizations (in the case of the physical sciences) such as f = ma, which may "function in part as laws but also in part as definitions of some of the symbols they deploy." Another important category of shared commitment is that of (4) values like simplicity, consistency, and agreement with prediction.

A way of viewing the world is, in a sense, a way of approaching the world. It involves a host of theoretical, experimental, and methodological commitments (in this last case, of the standards expected of proposed questions and solutions).

And now we come to the second part of the analogy with perception. We tend to "see" specific parts of the world in certain ways because those ways are in accordance with the commitments involved in our views of the world—which Kuhn first called "paradigms" and later "disciplinary matrices."[1] But sometimes we have a clash between two general ways of viewing the world. What *may* happen then is that we have no way to disambiguate the figures. This is so because each alternative "gestalt" already incorporates all the clues that it will permit us to use when viewing the figure (the world). That is, the alternatives may give different directions on how to look at the clues—for all practical purposes, they will give us then different sets of clues. Each alternative gestalt specifies an alternative context, and thus—without a common context—a

---

[1] Under the pressure of some linguistic objections he moved away from the term "paradigm," unnecessarily, I think.

change of worldview is not unlike the gestalt switch that we experience when we look at the drawings in **Figures 1 and 2**, first one way and then another.

The analogy would make scientific views into spectacles with which scientific communities see the world. Although of necessity this account is oversimplified, it already suggests two important consequences. The first is that the distinction between fact and theory is internal to the guiding scientific view. Different commitments lead to different ideas as to what can be considered secure parts of experience (hence the "conventional" character of the empirical basis proposed by the mature falsificationist). But then major changes of view may well lead to changes in the empirical basis also. This account of science therefore leads us to expect that the empirical basis will be overthrown during some episodes of struggle between alternative views. Thus, a major difficulty in the traditional epistemology of science is now seen as perfectly natural within the new philosophy of science.

A second consequence is that insofar as a paradigm—to use Kuhn's earlier term—constitutes the spectacles through which we see the world, to give up the paradigm without replacing it is to go blind. We may switch to an alternative, but if we simply abandon our paradigm, we stop doing science. This consequence may well explain why Newtonians did not consider their theory of gravitation refuted even in the face of the prolonged failure to account for the anomalous perihelion of Mercury. They thought of the universe in Newtonian terms. To give up Newton's theory of gravitation was to give up thinking about the universe. So, the anomaly was taken as a challenge and not as a refutation. Such was the situation until a rival paradigm, Einstein's general theory of relativity, provided an explanation of Mercury's perihelion within an alternative way of thinking about the universe. Once again, numerous episodes of the history of science that mystify the empiricist (cf. the historical problems of mature falsificationism in the previous chapter) make perfectly good sense to the new philosophers.

Kuhn and Feyerabend published their initial versions of this account of science in 1962, thus igniting a revolution in the philosophy of science. Even though both generally agree on many of the points made so far, there are, nevertheless, significant differences in their ideas about the nature and value of science. We will begin an examination of those ideas by considering in more detail Kuhn's *The Structure of Scientific Revolutions* (1970).

THE ESSENTIAL DOGMATISM OF SCIENCE

Kuhn's evaluation of science within its historical context undermines the standard picture of scientists as objective, open-minded explorers of the unknown who continually tests their view in order to add to the cumulative growth of knowledge. Instead Kuhn concludes that scientists are dogmatic, do not normally test their theories, and seldom search for the unknown. Moreover, dogmatism is essential to the nature of science.

Such theses perhaps sound less startling if we realize that scientific training creates a deep commitment to one view of the world and of the practice of science, to the exclusion of all others. To understand Kuhn's position, it is necessary to study the sort of view that could command such a strong commitment from the scientific community. The normal practice of science, Kuhn claims, is "research firmly based upon one or more extraordinary achievements that implicitly define the legitimate problems and methods of a field of endeavor." Such achievements, or paradigms, are "sufficiently unprecedented to attract an enduring group of adherents away from competing modes of scientific activity." They must also be "sufficiently open-ended to leave all sorts of problems for the redefined group of practitioners to resolve" (10).

Paradigms tell the scientist:

(1) what things there are in the universe
(2) how those things behave
(3) what questions may be properly asked about nature
(4) what techniques may be used in answering such questions.

Paradigms include law, theory, application, and instrumentation together. It is upon comprehensive models of this sort that scientists build entire traditions of research (e.g., Ptolemaic astronomy, Newtonian physics, wave optics). A crucial point is that Kuhn does not find that theories are the basic units of science. The basic units are complexes that constitute our ways of thinking about the world, of perceiving it in a communal sense. Theories, as normally understood, can be thought of as elaborations of some of the central ideas derived from the paradigm.

Normal science is research carried out in accordance with the models, the theories, and the exemplary solutions provided by the paradigm. Consider, for example, a classical physics dominated by a model of the world in which the constituents are corpuscles colliding with each other. This billiard-ball model will, of course, lead to great concern about the preservation of momentum during collisions, will consider as an ideal case perfectly elastic collisions, and will force the search for mechanisms that connect different aspects of experience in terms of such collisions of corpuscles. The resulting accounts will, furthermore, be stated in terms of the mathematical laws developed by Newton, Huygens, and others.

This program of research leads to many small problems to be solved—more in the nature of puzzles, Kuhn points out—and to some big ones: how to account, among other things, for Newton's own law of gravitation, which seems to be a case of action at a distance. Much ingenuity was spent unsuccessfully on this endeavor, until finally action at a distance was grudgingly granted a seat at the table of science (only to be driven out by Einstein eventually). Once this final adjustment in the model is made, Newton's view dominates physics completely, it becomes a paradigm, and from then on practically all research is based on it.

This does not mean that all research must be carried out in accordance with rules. Oftentimes, the paradigm simply sets an *example* of how a view of nature can be applied. Indeed, a student of science learns how to attach the symbols in the laws and formulas to nature by learning to see new problems as being like problems that he has already encountered. The point of his training is to have him come to view "the situations that confront him as a scientist in the same gestalt as other members of his specialists' group." When he achieves this, he has "assimilated a time-tested and group-licensed way of seeing" (189). It is perhaps helpful at this point to consider a concrete historical illustration of how the solution to a problem may serve as an example for solving other apparently very different problems.

Galileo discovered that balls rolling down an inclined plane and up another come up to the same vertical height. And this behavior of balls reminded him of a pendulum with a point mass for a bob. This discovery inspired Huygens to calculate the center of oscillation of a physical pendulum by thinking of it (the extended part) as being made up of Galilean point-pendula that rose and fell as balls in inclined planes, given their collective center of gravity. This in turn inspired Bernoulli to think of the flow of water from an orifice in a tank as resembling Huygens' pendulum. As the center of gravity of the water in the tank and orifice descends it imparts a rebounding velocity in the individual particles of water, so that the descent of the center of gravity of the water in the tank and orifice will equal the ascent of the center of gravity of the individual particles. Given this account, we can then calculate the speed of efflux.

Normal science is then made possible by a commitment to a single view of the world, to a paradigm, *to the exclusion of all others.* But even though normal science is most of science, there are periods of paradigm change, periods of revolution. The problem for Kuhn now is to show that such a single-minded commitment leads to progress first through normal science and then through revolutions. Only then can it make sense to say that dogmatism is essential to science.

DOGMATISM LEADS TO PROGRESS THROUGH NORMAL SCIENCE

In the absence of a paradigm, research must always begin from the foundations up. Scientific effort is directed at arguing with competitors and not with nature.

But once the scientists have confidence in one way of thinking about the world, they can do extremely concentrated, sometimes esoteric, research in one area. A paradigm thus channels the scientists' energies in one direction, thereby leading to fruitful research.

During periods of normal science, the function of the scientist is to actualize the promise made by the extraordinary achievement that has become a paradigm. It is clear that, as Kuhn says, "the success of a paradigm...is at the start largely a promise of success," and that paradigms gain their status "because they are more successful than their competitors in solving a few problems that the group of practitioners has come to recognize as acute." Normal science, according to Kuhn, "consists in the actualization of that promise, an actualization achieved by extending the knowledge of those facts that the paradigm displays as particularly revealing, by increasing the extent of the match between those facts and the paradigm's predictions, and by further articulation of the paradigm itself" (23-24).

Although Kuhn does not draw a sharp distinction between fact and theory, he finds it convenient for narrative purposes to divide research into factual and theoretical. The emphasis in *theoretical research* is often placed on the mathematical developments that will permit the comparison of paradigm and world. On other occasions what is called for is the reformulation of the paradigm theory in order to make it more amenable to testing or to extend it to new areas. In any event, the categories of theoretical research closely parallel those of factual research described immediately below.

Normal factual research will be devoted to:

(1) Facts revealing of the nature of things (e.g., stellar position and magnitude in astronomy, fundamental particles in physics).

(2) Facts interesting solely because they can be compared with predictions from the paradigm theory (e.g., bending of light by the sun's gravity, from the general theory of relativity; stellar parallax, from the heliocentric view of the universe which requires building telescopes powerful enough to observe it).

It should be noted that research of these two types is undertaken solely because of the paradigm: of type (1) because the paradigm tells us that those facts are fundamental and thus, we are given the motivation to build synchrotrons, radio telescopes, and what not—to look for them. Research of type (2) would make no sense without a paradigm. The existence of the paradigm sets the problem to be solved.

(3) Empirical work undertaken to articulate the paradigm theory. In this category we find:

(a) The determination of physical constants (e.g., the universal gravitational constant, Avogadro's number, coefficients, etc.);

(b) The determination of quantitative laws (e.g., Boyle's law).

There is striking resemblance between these two last types of factual research and inductivism. Boyle, for example, took measurement after measurement until he was satisfied with having a basis broad enough for his famous generalization that the pressure and the volume of a gas are inversely proportional. But even in such cases we should note how the paradigm directs the enterprise of fact collection, for Boyle's research made little sense unless his paradigm had first assured him that air was a fluid to which he could apply the elaborate concepts of hydrostatics.

Since these two types of research comprise so much of normal science, it is not surprising that many have taken them as characteristic of the nature of science. But whereas in inductivism the emphasis is placed on the justification that such investigations provide for the theories of science, in Kuhn's scheme they play no such role. The paradigm is not in question. On the contrary, if it were not assumed, these investigations with the inductivist air would make no sense. Apparently, by examining science in its historical context, we not only gain a new understanding of its nature but also come to understand some of the fixations in the history of the *philosophy* of science.

With this application in mind, let us consider one last type of factual research aimed at articulating the paradigm:

(c) Experiments designed to choose between alternative ways of extending a paradigm to areas closely related to the area of success of the paradigm, but where the paradigm gives no specific direction as to the most fruitful approach. There were, for example, many plausible ways of extending the caloric theory of heat, e.g. chemical combination, friction, compression, etc.

Hypotheses are then made, tested, and rejected if they conflict with experience. And in the experiments to choose between the different alternatives we can see a strong resemblance to the crucial experiments of the falsificationist. But this is at best a case of in-house falsificationism. The paradigm, once again, is not in question. What is in question is merely a particular proposal to extend or articulate the paradigm. Nevertheless, in this and other aspects of normal science we can find the roots of the tendency to see the testing of hypotheses as *the* fundamental characteristic of science. This tendency is reinforced by the spectacular disputes during revolutionary periods (extraordinary science), during which alternatives are openly sought and paradigms do come into question. I will discuss such periods in the next section.

At any rate, we can realize how some philosophers could look at science and see inductivism in it, whereas others—in part spurred by the epistemological failures of the inductivists—could find falsification of the essence. But when looking at science through Kuhn's spectacles we see that what resembled inductivism and falsificationism were merely expected functions of the normal practice of a mature science, that is, of research based on a paradigm.

If this picture is correct, if the scientist is normally engaged in no activity other than those described by Kuhn, we can see that the scientist is not really an explorer of the unknown. Lisa is really after the kind of phenomena her paradigm tells her to expect. Normal research is in fact very similar to puzzle-solving, Kuhn claims, for, as in a puzzle, the paradigm tells the scientist what the "picture" that results from her research ought to look like (by telling her, for example, what ought to count as a solution).

Nor is the scientist attempting to falsify her paradigm theory through rigorous testing. Failure to achieve a match between the paradigm and the world is a personal failure, a reflection on the lack of skill or the insufficient effort of the investigator, not a failure of her general view of the world, just as the failure to solve a game puzzle is not a failure of the promise of a particular picture on the cover of the puzzle box. The scientist who blames her paradigm, Kuhn says, is like the carpenter who blames her tools. It is possible to see how dogmatism leads to the concentrated effort, and how concentrated effort leads to much of the splendid empirical harvest that has so amazed our civilization.

But something seems to have been left out. Science is, after all, in the business of discovery. Kuhn would not want to deny that many features of the world that we take for granted today, say galaxies and electrons, were simply unimagined not long ago. On the contrary, Kuhn thinks that his view can account well for discovery. To begin with, a paradigm is a human invention, and thus it would be extremely surprising if the promise implicit in it could be strictly kept—our "comprehensive perceptions" of the world are bound to fall short of perfection. In such cases we are confronted with anomalies. It is very crucial to realize, however, that the awareness of those anomalies require the prior presence of a paradigm, for only someone who knows what to expect will notice that something has gone wrong. It is precisely the class of anomalous instances that provide the scientist with the most fruitful opportunities to articulate his paradigm. But the recognition of anomaly does not amount to a discovery: the scientist, Caleb, say, must first be able to explain the anomaly within his paradigm. That is, by articulating his paradigm to account for the anomaly he assimilates it into his scientific framework.

As an example, we may consider the discovery of X-rays. It began when Roentgen noticed an unexpected glow at some distance from his cathode ray tube. (The big tube in a television set is a cathode ray tube.) It was clear that the radiation that produced the glow was coming in straight lines from the cathode ray tube, that it cast shadows, and that it could not be deflected by a magnet. After seven weeks of work Roentgen was sure that he had discovered a new form of radiation. It must be noted, first, that only a scientist who knew what to expect may have sensed that there was something out of the ordinary with the glow behind his apparatus. Indeed, X-rays violated the entrenched expectations of the experimental physicists of the time. As Kuhn points out, "If Roentgen's apparatus had produced X-rays, then a number of other experimentalists must for some time have been producing those rays without knowing it.... Previously completed work on normal projects would now have to be done again because earlier scientists had failed to recognize and control a relevant variable" (59).

Important discoveries are made, then, against an understandable background of resistance. There is a loathing of re-tooling unless it is strictly necessary—too much work goes out of the window when a major articulation of the paradigm is required. But then only until that articulation is carried out and the anomaly has been assimilated do we have a new discovery. In these two respects, detection and assimilation, discoveries require a paradigm. Once again, we encounter the payoff of the single-minded commitment to one view of the world. Insofar as that commitment is characterized as dogmatism, dogmatism is essential to the practice of science.

REVOLUTIONS IN SCIENCE

Some anomalies prove far too recalcitrant in the long run, however—so recalcitrant that the failure to assimilate them within the theoretical, experimental and methodological commitments of the paradigm becomes a failure of the discipline as a whole. When the best minds have tried their hand at the puzzle, when the puzzle is in a particularly significant area (dealing with the fundamental entities of the system, for example), when the attempt to assimilate it has been very prolonged, the general confidence in the promised picture begins to wane. Scientists still may not give up their paradigm, for it constitutes the pair of spectacles with which they perceive the world. Simply to abandon their paradigm is to abandon their perception of the world, to give up science. But there comes a point at which the general failure brings about a complete crisis of confidence. At this stage the paradigm loses its stronghold over the discipline, scientists begin to argue again about fundamentals, and some start to think of different ways of perceiving the world, i.e., they start the search for a new paradigm while grudgingly holding on to the old one. If the search for a new way of possible looking at nature also produces one achievement generally recognized as extraordinary, a new paradigm and a new stage of normal science may have been born.

It must be understood, however, that those anomalies which provoke the crisis cannot be properly said to have refuted the paradigm. There is no reason in principle why a crisis cannot be overcome. Thus, even those anomalies do not constitute counterevidence to the paradigm unless they can be successfully made part and parcel of a competing approach to the science in question. Once so integrated, the allegiance of the scientific community may switch to the challenger and the old view will have been defeated. We have seen previously that the anomalous perihelion of Mercury was not generally considered to be counterevidence to the Newtonian paradigm until it was assimilated within the rival paradigm provided by Einstein's General Theory of Relativity. The only scientific way to reject a paradigm is to replace it.

THE REVOLUTIONARY NATURE OF PARADIGM CHANGE

A new paradigm redefines the discipline's view of the world: It speaks of new fundamental entities, of new sorts of relations between whatever entities there may be, of new standards for problem-solving, and it makes new experimental and methodological commitments. But these "new" things that the paradigm brings to the scientific community are not just additions to the accomplishments of the old view: they often *replace* such accomplishments. To change paradigms may well involve a change in sets of facts about the world as well. Thus, the growth of science need not be cumulative. A revolution in science, Kuhn says, has the nature of a gestalt-switch, of a change of perception about the universe (in the particular field involved). It would be unusual for it to be otherwise, since what used to be seen as a recalcitrant anomaly in one paradigm is now seen as straightforward, perhaps even obvious, in the new one. The choice between paradigms, Kuhn claims, "proves to be a choice between incompatible modes of community life" (94).

If all this is correct, then it does not seem possible to give reasons that are logically or probabilistically compelling for why the new paradigm is better than the old one. It is rather a question of providing a clear exhibit of what the new scientific practice will be like. And this exhibit can be extremely persuasive, persuasive enough to encourage the adherents of old ways of doing science to step into the new circle and evaluate its supporting evidence in its terms.

Within research based on a paradigm, i.e., within normal science, the paradigm supplies the standards for evaluating the merits of competing claims. But when the paradigm itself is in question (thus when the standards themselves are in question), there is no higher authority to which appeal can be made. A successful scientific revolution, then, brings about the establishment of a new scientific order.

Dogmatism in science thus leads to progress through normal science, through discovery, and finally through the creation of a crisis of confidence that brings about a new tradition of normal science. Even though this account implies that the growth of scientific knowledge is not cumulative, it can also be seen how a paradigm sets the stage, so to speak, for the next one. The milieu in which a new candidate for paradigm develops is most likely to depend on the paradigm that it may eventually replace. Thus, the scientific revolutionary may often (though not always) owe a debt to his predecessors.

THE NON-CUMULATIVE GROWTH OF SCIENCE: A CHALLENGE TO SCIENTIFIC RATIONALITY? THE PROBLEM OF INCOMMENSURABILITY

Kuhn's thesis that the growth of science is not cumulative, also defended by Feyerabend, has been met with dismay by many philosophers of science. According to these philosophers, rationality in science requires that changes of points of view may be justified. And this justification must be made by showing that the winner is superior to the loser. But without common standards by which to measure the alternatives it is not possible to show such superiority. Thus, if Kuhn and Feyerabend are right, it cannot be shown that science is a rational enterprise. Of course, even if this argument is correct, the critics have not shown that Kuhn and Feyerabend are wrong. The irrationality of science may just turn out to be an unpleasant discovery of great merit. But whether such discovery is really a consequence of this thesis of *incommensurability*, as it has been called, we will see later. Let us first discuss the direct case against the noncumulative thesis.

Leading the list of counterexamples in strength and historical distinction is the account of Newtonian physics as a special case of the theory of relativity. Now, here we have a case in which, according to Kuhn, the two views are fundamentally incompatible: "Einstein's theory can be accepted only with the recognition that Newton's was wrong" (98). But Newton's physics is widely thought to have a limited validity and is in fact still much in use by engineers and even many scientists. What Einstein did, according to Kuhn's critics, was to draw the proper boundaries for classical mechanics. Within those boundaries Newton's theory is essentially correct. Furthermore, taken within those boundaries (e.g., low velocities) it can be shown to be derived from relativistic mechanics. The point is that the 20th Century's revolution in physics did not replace what preceded it but rather *added to it*; therefore, knowledge in physics has grown by accumulation.

At first glance the conceptual changes brought about by Einstein's special theory of relativity are overwhelming. Take a very simple example. If I am piloting a glider, my velocity with respect to an observer sitting on the ground is 100 km/h, whereas the jet flying in the same direction overhead has a velocity of 500 km/h with respect to me, 600 km/h with respect to the sitting observer, and 1200 km/h with respect to another jet flying in the opposite direction. It would seem that the velocity of light would likewise change as measured in different frames of reference. But according to Einstein, the sitting observer, I, and the pilots of the two jets should all get the same result! The speed of light is a constant.

This drastic rethinking extends to the most basic concepts employed in physics. Take mass, for instance. In Newton's mechanics, mass is conserved. A body may win or lose mass only by interaction with another system. A snowball rolling down a snowy hill will gain mass; but were it to roll into the proverbial hell, fire would evaporate the entire ball eventually. Let us now throw the same original snowball in space, let it interact with nothing, and then calculate its mass. Well, the snowball will have different velocities for me in the glider, for the sitting observer, and for the two jet pilots. According to Einstein, we should all calculate different masses! As it turns out, in the special theory of relativity the mass of an object depends on its velocity. The mass of a starship that approached the speed of light would approach infinity—both mass and velocity as measured, say, with respect to mission control back here on Earth. Length, on the other hand, contracts as the velocity increases. The conceptual discrepancy between the two theories seems to be great indeed.

Nevertheless, Kuhn's critics insist that Newton's theory can be derived from Einstein as a special case. To see more clearly the nature of the derivation involved, let us consider the formula for relativistic mass.

$$m = m_0 / \sqrt{1 - v^2 / c^2}$$

Where m is the relativistic mass, m_0 is the rest mass (which we could equate with the initial or Newtonian mass), v is the velocity of the object in question, and c is the speed of light. At very low velocities the expression v^2/c^2 approaches o, for the speed of light is immense. The formula then, becomes:

$$m = m_0 / \sqrt{(1 - \approx 0)}$$

and thus:

$$m \approx m_0$$

Since in these cases the relativistic mass and the presumably Newtonian mass have the same values for all practical purposes, all Newtonian claims about mass are identical with the relativistic ones. That is, at low velocities they yield practically the same numbers. Thus, we see that Newtonian mechanics is a special case of the theory of relativity. And, of course, only extravagant claims by Newtonians, about their theory applying at very high velocities, for example, can be shown by Einstein to be wrong. But those claims supported by previous evidence have not been overthrown.

This position is not acceptable, however, for as Kuhn points out, any theory would be immune to criticism as long as it does not venture beyond its accomplishments. But scientists do want constantly to extend the range of application of their theories, as well as to increase the degree of precision beyond previous practice. Otherwise, that would mean the end of normal science, which has precisely the function of extending the paradigm to new areas and degrees of precision.

Moreover, the alleged derivation of Newtonian mechanics from Relativity is spurious. A necessary condition for the validity of any derivation is that the terms preserve their meanings throughout (otherwise we commit the logical fallacy of equivocation). Both classical and relativistic mechanics employ concepts of space, time, mass, etc. But according to Kuhn, "The physical referents of [the] Einsteinian are by no means identical with those of the Newtonian concepts that bear the same name" (102). Newtonian mass is conserved, Einsteinian is convertible with energy. In a similar fashion Feyerabend also questions the attempt to identify classical mass with the *rest* mass of Special Relativity (so m_0 should not be interpreted as Newtonian mass in the equation above). And relativistic length, Feyerabend adds, "involves an element that is absent from the classical concept and is in principle excluded from it. It involves the *relative velocity* of the object concerned in some reference system." He concludes that "different magnitudes based on different concepts may give identical values on their respective scales without ceasing to be different magnitudes" (1970, 221-222). Where the terms involved have different meanings, then, no derivation is possible. Since this situation will occur in all those cases where a new comprehensive view of the world is born out of conflict, scientific revolutions are marked by the incommensurability of the theories (or paradigms) involved.

Some critics have suggested that it is possible to provide a "common dictionary," so it is possible to compare, say, the predictive successes of two competing views of the world. And there is a clear sense in which that is indeed possible. In fact, the present example provides an illustration. The laws that give such good agreement in numbers with Einstein's at low velocities are not really Newton's laws, as he would have understood them, but rather a relativistic version of them. They are Newton's laws transposed into Einstein's Special Theory of Relativity with limits and parameters on them that would have been inconceivable to Newton himself. Of course, if we take those laws and Einstein's as well, as mere instruments for the management of data, the meanings of the crucial terms may remain the same. But then we forget that those terms acquire meaning for scientists only as their training makes it second nature for them to attach such to the world in ways guided by the view of the world accepted by their discipline.

As long as the way a term is used has nothing to do with its meaning, then we do not have *this* problem of incommensurability. On the other hand, if we do think that the use of the term has something to do with its meaning, then we must consider how our view of the world influences that use. If Kuhn is correct in thinking that normal research is research based on a paradigm, that influence is considerable. And if that is so, it should be expected that changes in world view may lead to changes in the meaning of scientific terms.

There are, incidentally, two recurrent themes in analytic philosophy of science with respect to the meaning of scientific terms (Hempel 1966). At one extreme we find Bridgman's operationism, according to which the meanings of scientific terms should be determined by operations (e.g., length is defined by specified ways of measuring with rods and so on). This makes meaning sound very empirical but leads to serious conceptual problems. One is, of course, that we have a diversity of operations for every concept (e.g., measuring length by the use of rods, by triangulations, or by bouncing of radar signals off an object). It would seem bizarre to say that we have not one concept of length but many. At the other extreme we find the view, favored by Hempel, that scientific terms have what he calls "theoretic import," which means roughly that the meaning of a term depends in part on the role it plays in a theory; meaning is therefore affected by its relations to other terms also used in the theory. Whatever extreme we tend to favor, or a suitable combination of both, we have the ingredients for cooking the cake of incommensurability. When we change paradigms we obviously may change the relevant "operations," for the new paradigm may offer new and different experimental and instrumental commitments. And if we are inclined towards Hempel's view, it seems that drastic theoretical change may surely lead to change in meaning as well.

There is also a fixation in some circles that the meaning of "theoretical terms" has to be determined by prior "observational terms" (this is inductivism imported into semantics, i.e., the equivalent of "theories have to be derived from the facts"). But then the meaning of observational terms would be prior and thus could not be changed by changes in the meaning of theoretical terms. It seems, however, that among the many assumptions made in such an argument, most of them very questionable, special prominence must be given to the distinction between theory and observation. But if this view of meaning needs such a distinction to even get off the ground, to advance it against those who question the distinction is to beg the question. Even though critics often concentrate their attacks on what they call Kuhn and Feyerabend's "holistic theory of meaning," it is not clear that Kuhn and Feyerabend need commit themselves to any particular theory of meaning.

In any event, Einstein's *use* of the terms "mass" and "length" precludes Newton's. According to Feyerabend, to say that Einstein's and Newton's theories (or paradigms) are incommensurable is to say that the principles for constructing concepts in one *suspend* the principles of the other. That is, the relativistic ideas used to understand mass, length, etc., do not permit the use of the alternative Newtonian ideas (1978, 267-285). This is similar to the perceptual situation in **Figure 1**, where seeing the young lady does not permit the simultaneous perception of the drawing as an old hag (the same point applies to the Necker Cube). And surely, since concepts like "mass" and "length" are used to determine what counts as facts in physics, we may conclude that presenting Einstein's facts means suspending principles assumed in the construction of Newtonian facts.

This last way of putting the matter can bring us out of an issue over which philosophers have burned up much slobber for little profit. The problem of incommensurability has been understood as a problem about change in meanings. Perhaps this emphasis was natural because analytic philosophy, the dominant approach in the English-speaking world, has so often acted on the credo that most philosophy can be reduced to the philosophy of language, whether formal or natural language. If we could just be straight and rigorous about meaning, our philosophical problems would either be solved or just fall by the wayside. At any rate, incommensurability simply means that there are no common standards for measurement. And as the previous paragraph indicates, the bottom line is that there may be no common sets of facts to judge one theory or paradigm superior to another. But when we put the matter this way, we realize that we are just talking about the possibility of overthrowing the empirical basis. And this we have done without semantic mirrors in Chapter 3.

The extrapolation of the case made in Chapter 3 to the conceits of linguistic epistemology may have been all to the good. But the essential points can be made without such distracting battles. This is not to deny that the air of paradox surrounds the issue of incommensurability and that a rather distinct odor of skepticism clings to it. If our paradigm or basic theory determines, among other things, the constituents of the world, one may say that "the world changes when basic theory changes." Or as Kuhn puts it: "after a revolution scientists are responding to a different world." "It is rather," he adds, "as if the professional community had been suddenly transported to another planet where familiar objects are seen in a different light and are joined by unfamiliar ones as well" (111).

There are some who find this an exciting discovery about the nature of science. But others feel that we are confronted with a new skeptical problem. If the furniture of the world is relative to our world view, then it seems that there is no *proof* that a revolution in science does not bring about a change of furniture. Duddley Shapere, for example, argues that, even if scientific terms change meanings, the important thing is that they still refer to the same objects (1964). But on this point Feyerabend can be most irksome. How can we assert that the terms used by both sides refer to the same object or situation when they never make sense together (because the use of one interpretation precludes the other)?

In a sense the insistence on the same objects and identity of reference only worsens the situation. It is difficult to deny that, as Kuhn so thoroughly illustrates, the terms "element" and "mixture" have referred to different objects at different times in the history of chemistry. As for the furniture of the world, Feyerabend points out, our epistemic activities have made gods disappear and replaced them by heaps of atoms in empty space. Nevertheless, it is felt that we have a skeptical problem in that "we know in our bones that the world has not changed even though we cannot prove it." This in a nutshell is the ontological problem of incommensurability for some philosophers. Insofar as it is stated in this fashion, the average scientific practitioner is not bound to be much impressed. This is one more question of justification that he may view as separate from his concerns as a scientist.

Feyerabend put the matter in perspective by adding that incommensurability may be a problem for philosophers but not for scientists. The reason is that (analytic) philosophers demand that meanings be the same in the premises and the conclusion of an argument (or derivation), whereas when scientists try to explain a situation, they are prepared both to follow rules and to change them. Thus, they are flexible when it comes to meanings (1988, 272).

Even for philosophers the issue of (semantic) incommensurability should have decreased in importance, even though the meaning of scientific terms does change from time to time. It seemed urgent once, when analytic philosophy of science favored the view that logical derivation was an essential component of scientific explanation and that logical reduction was the right model for the growth of scientific knowledge.

We will see later, however, that the assumption that the world is independent of our system of knowledge can be quite a bone of contention in trying to determine the nature of quantum physics, one of the great scientific disputes since the early 20th Century. At that point we will consider whether Kuhn and Feyerabend's thesis of incommensurability can be considered a proper extension of Bohr's interpretation of quantum mechanics; and if so, whether my own approach, which is drawn from biology, can throw some light on both.

FURTHER APPRAISALS OF KUHN'S WORK

The problem of the rationality of science will be set aside for the moment. For before proceeding we need to understand the differences between Kuhn's view of science and that advanced by Feyerabend. Once we understand these differences, we may also understand why whereas Feyerabend proclaims that science needs to proceed by "irrational" means, Kuhn finds Feyerabend's position "vaguely obscene."

REFERENCES

Feyerabend, P. K. (1970). "Consolations for the Specialist." In Lakatos, I. and Musgrave, A.E. (Eds.), *Criticism and the Growth of Knowledge.* Cambridge University Press.

Feyerabend, P. K. (1978). *Against Method: Outline of an Anarchistic Theory of Knowledge.* Verso. First published by New Left Books in1975.

Feyerabend, P. K. (1988). *Farewell to Reason.*Verso.

Hempel, C. G. (1966). *Philosophy of Natural Science.* Prentice Hall.

Ittelson, W. H., & Kilpatrick, F. P. (1961). *The monocular and binocular distorted rooms.* In F. P. Kilpatrick (Ed.), *Explorations in transactional psychology* (p. 154–173). New York University Press. https://doi.org/10.1037/11303-008

Kuhn, T. (1970). *The Structure of Scientific Revolutions* (2nd. Edition). Chicago University Press.

Shapere, D. (1964). "The Structure of Scientific Revolutions," *Philosophical Review*, 73.

Theocharis, T. and Psimopoulos, M. (1987). "Where Science has Gone Wrong." *Nature*, Vol. 329.

CHAPTER 6
FEYERABEND AND SCIENTIFIC ANARCHY

KUHN VS. FEYERABEND

Paul Feyerabend, who shares many of Thomas Kuhn's views, disagrees most vehemently on the value of dogmatism in science. Kuhn, as we have seen, believes that a single-minded commitment to one paradigm eventually forces us to search for a replacement, not by abstract discussions of possibilities, but by procedures in close contact with nature, "and therefore, in the last resort," writes Feyerabend, "by nature itself" (1970, 201-202).[1]

Kuhn correctly claims that a comprehensive view is abandoned not because it has anomalies, but because it is replaced by an alternative. Anomalies thus do not refute a paradigm, but they may bring a crisis about if they are thought to be important enough (for then the failure to assimilate them gains great significance). And Feyerabend largely agrees (202).

No anomaly, however, Feyerabend points out, is as important as one which a competitor claims to have explained—no anomaly, that is, accentuates more the loss of confidence in the paradigm. The reason is that, as Kuhn believes, a paradigm is accepted on the promise of future performance, on the promise, that is, that it will prove the best way to conceive of the world (1970, 23-24 157-158). When a competing would-be paradigm seems to be doing better, our faith in the *promise* of our anomaly-besieged paradigm may falter. Thus, Feyerabend thought, we will create more crises, and therefore more fruitful change, in Kuhn's own terms, by providing a mechanism to strengthen the anomalies. To accomplish this goal, science should be organized so as to require the *continuous generation of alternatives.* This Feyerabend calls the *principle of proliferation* (197-230).

Kuhn's case for dogmatism thus will be made only if it is shown that the tenacious commitment to one point of view is the best way of bringing about revolutionary change, let alone the only way. This is now in question.

---

[1] Much of the content of this chapter has been heavily influenced by my books *Radical Knowledge* (1981) and *Evolution and the Naked Truth* (1998), as well as by my (2000) and (2015) papers, listed in the References.

Now, expectation can cut two ways: It permits us to see, but it may also keep us from seeing. Can we do better? Yes, if we have more than one set of expectations to draw from. That is Feyerabend's point. Of course, it may be difficult for the same individual to hold alternative sets of expectations. On the other hand, in a discipline where proliferation is not ruled out, some individuals may develop a different world view, and may thus be in a position to point out areas of difficulty that the other members of the discipline may be unlikely to notice. That is the first step.

The second step is that in the very areas the standard view faces anomalies, the rival may claim to have explained those very anomalies. If so, it may be far more difficult for the practitioners of the standard view to regard the anomalies as mere oddities that could be taken care of at a later date. The failure to articulate the paradigm may then acquire great significance precisely because of the pressing possibility that the paradigm's categories may not provide the best box into which to file the experience in question. And this suspicion of doom grows larger in proportion to the ease demonstrated by the rival view.

Two resolutions are then made available: (1) the defenders of the standard view do manage to assimilate the anomaly, or (2) a crisis ensues that may result in a paradigm shift. Either resolution is prompted by the presence of a rival. Without the competition by that rival there would have been no motivation for worry in the first place. That is, even according to Kuhn's own specifications, the scientific discipline would not have done as well. The point is not really all that intricate. It is possible to discover one's own faults through introspection. But the great majority of us learn of our faults thanks to all those around us who are plain delighted to point them out.

On the other hand, from Kuhn we have learned—against falsificationism—that a view should not be dropped merely because some of its predictions fail. A view should be given time to develop, to bear out its original promise. Thus, commitment to a view is crucial to science (Feyerabend calls this the *principle of tenacity*). Where Kuhn goes too far is in his insistence that the *entire discipline* be dedicated to only one view. It is more fruitful for science, Feyerabend says, to have several competing groups working on those ideas that they find particularly promising. It is also a more humanitarian outlook, for instead of authoritarian enforcement of a dominant view, it allows for the individual scientist's pursuit of happiness through his scientific work.

In this regard, Feyerabend makes use of two simple notions. First, people work best at those things they like best. Thus, scientists should be encouraged to develop those views of nature that for any reason have caught their fancy. Second, the quality of work improves when strong challenge points the way in a direction that could use improvement. Without such challenge we become complacent, and even if we want to keep on our toes we may fail to see the flaws in our pet theories because we are too close to them, or because we lack enough imagination, or for many other reasons. Thus, competition aids us in our pursuit of excellence.

The principle of proliferation, and within its action, the principle of tenacity, leads to greater human happiness. Those two principles also create the conditions for fruitful change and improvement. Therefore, both humanity and science are better for their presence. Kuhn's insistence on the restriction of the principle of tenacity to only one view is the sort of dogmatism that gets in the way of what Kuhn himself considers advantageous. On the other hand, the falsificationist's rigid quest for rejection robs science of the depth tenacity offers to it—without contributing to individual happiness, for scientists are obliged to give up what may well intrigue them. It seems that Feyerabend is offering us the opportunity to have our scientific cake and eat it too.

As a historical illustration Feyerabend reminds us of the tension between competing views of matter in the 19th Century: the mechanical, the view connected with the invention of the phenomenological theory of heat, and the view implicit in Maxwell's electrodynamics. The tension brought about the troubles that led to the special theory of relativity and to the kinetic theory of heat (both developed mainly by Einstein). It is not necessary to dispute the merits of this particular illustration because strictly speaking no illustration is necessary. In order to show that dogmatism is not essential one need only show that science could proceed without it. Feyerabend even improves on this: science *may* do better without it.

Feyerabend does not claim that science in fact progresses. He thinks that his position on incommensurability precludes that. So why claim that the picture he presents is the most fruitful approach for science? Because he leaves the evaluation of progress up to each individual (or each individual group). He only tells the different parties how they can best bring about their own goals by adhering to the principles of tenacity and permitting the functioning of the principles of proliferation. If by continuous confrontation with competing views Marie is spurred to improve her own view – where improvement is measured by her own standards – then her work has benefitted. If, on the other hand, she finds that the competition has gotten the best of her – again, for whatever reasons – she abandons her view and takes up the other. In this case her work has also benefitted. The appropriate mix of the principles of tenacity and proliferation increases the scientist's chance of scientific profit *as seen from her own methodological point of view.*

This is just one variation on Feyerabend's grand theme of scientific anarchy. His tune against Kuhn's dogmatism is an adaptation of a general approach that he developed against the standard methodologies. "Anarchism," Feyerabend writes at the outset of his *Against Method*, "while perhaps not the most attractive *political* philosophy, is certainly excellent medicine for *epistemology* and for the *philosophy of science*" (1978a, 17). What Feyerabend wants to show is that even the most obvious methodologies have their limitations. To empiricism, for instance, it makes no sense to use hypotheses that contradict well-confirmed theories, and even less sense to use hypotheses that contradict well-established experimental results. But we saw in Chapter 3 how Feyerabend shows that such hypotheses may be used to the great advantage of science. But why? How can we advance science by proceeding counter-inductively?

The reason, as we may have surmised from Feyerabend's case against Kuhn's dogmatism, is that those counter-inductive hypotheses give us evidence that cannot be obtained in any other way. Prejudice is often discovered not by analysis but by contrast. If, as we have seen, every fact is already viewed in a certain way, and to progress often requires viewing facts in a different way, then we simply need alternative ways of seeing. As for the conflict between those counter-inductive hypotheses and the facts—and it is that conflict that presumably makes them counter-inductive—we should remember that no theory ever agrees with all the facts in its domain. We have already seen why this should be so (e.g., Kuhn's account of how a paradigm is a promise of results and not a collection of them). If such conflict is grounds for throwing out a theory, then we should throw out all theories. The main reason for not trembling in the shadow of the facts, as we saw in Chapter 3, is that facts are constituted by older ideologies, and thus a clash between facts and theories may actually be an indication of progress. An indication that our probe is coming in contact with some of the principles assumed in familiar observational notions.

It is often said that we cannot step outside science to see whether it represents the world. This simple point is supposed to dog the idea that truth is correspondence to reality. And maybe it does. But we may still observe the relationship between our science and the world by comparing our science with an alternative interpretation of what the world is like. As Feyerabend says, "*we need a dream-world in order to discover the features of the real world we think we inhabit* (and which may actually be just another dream-world)" (32). In this Feyerabend echoes John Stuart Mill (1859). If our present views are right, by criticizing them from another vantage point we come to understand them better. And if they are not right, we gain the opportunity to replace them.

If this is so, however, we come to realize that any idea, no matter how ancient or absurd, is capable of improving our knowledge. This sounds at first preposterous. For example, we finally got rid of all that Aristotelian nonsense in science. Why bring it back? But then, many of the central ideas of modern science were once considered preposterous. Consider, to name only three, heliocentrism, held by Aristarchus; atomism, held by Democritus; and evolution, held by Lamarck and before him by even more disreputable characters. Of course, the modern versions of those ideas are quite different. But the fact of the matter is that thinkers like Copernicus, Dalton, and Darwin found promise in those discredited ideas and took the trouble to develop them. To those thinkers we owe in large part the glory of modern science. Here we find in action both the principles of proliferation and of tenacity.

The operation of these last two principles makes science appear far more "sloppy" and "irrational" than its methodological image. But as we have seen, the attempt to make science conform to that methodological image, the attempt, that is, "to make science more 'rational' and more precise is bound to wipe it out." For, as Feyerabend argues, "what appears as 'sloppiness', 'chaos' or opportunism when compared with such [image] has a most important function in the development of those very theories which we today regard as essential parts of our knowledge of nature" (179). But then from the methodologist's point of view nothing can be ruled out, *anything goes*. And if methodology is equated with reason, science is and must be an irrational enterprise.

Feyerabend arrives at this position not by the mere examination of historical cases, but by a historical examination backed by "an analysis of the relation between idea and action." Or as Einstein once put it: "The external conditions which are set for [the scientist] by the facts of experience do not permit him to let himself be too much restricted, in the construction of his conceptual world, by the adherence to an epistemological system. He therefore must appear to the systematic epistemologist as a type of unscrupulous opportunist..." (1951, 68 3f).

The situation is then as follows. According to the rationalist, alias methodologist, alias systematic epistemologist, certain events in the history of science constitute progress. But, Feyerabend points out, for those events to come about some scientists have to be opportunistic enough to adopt "whatever procedure seems to fit the occasion." This means that even the best of methodological rules *must* be violated from time to time. This inherent limitation of all rules implies that nothing can be excluded once and for all. To a methodologist this amounts to an admission that *anything goes*. Therefore, *from the methodologist's point of view*, anarchy will be occasionally essential to science.

HOW FAR DOES SCIENTIFIC ANARCHY GO?

This principle of "anarchy" is the only principle that does not inhibit progress, according to Feyerabend. But can it really be the case that anything goes in science? Although Feyerabend sometimes points out how ideas that today are considered preposterous have much to offer, he does this partly for rhetorical purposes and partly to annoy his educated opponents. For he does not argue that all ideas and procedures fit all circumstances equally well. On the contrary, in the case of Galileo and others he illustrates how some specific ideas and procedures were particularly helpful. "Anything goes" not from his point of view, but from the point of view of one who thinks that only certain ideas or procedures are admissible. Anarchy is thus in the eye of the rationalist beholder. If anarchy means ignoring the rationalist's rules from time to time, then science requires anarchy. This is not to say that the rules never apply. If anything goes, "reason" sometimes goes too. Nor is this simply a bromide to the effect that since science is a human activity it *cannot* be perfectly rational. The point is rather that science *must not,* if it is to achieve progress.

Nor is Feyerabend putting forth a new methodology (a counter-inductive methodology, for example: Advance theories inconsistent with the facts, and so on). What we cannot do is precisely to specify in advance whether the inductive or the counter-inductive rules will apply. This would not change even if, somehow, we could foresee the context that scientists will face. For the different choices they might make when faced with a new context may themselves change that context in many different ways. When Dalton imported into chemistry his notions of simple ratios, he changed, as a consequence, the concepts of mixture and compound, as well as the standards of chemical explanation.

It is nevertheless uncanny that Feyerabend seems to be blessed with such special knowledge about what is good and what is bad in science. He certainly seems to have no qualms about using words like "progress," "advance," "improvement," and so on. Is there perhaps at least a rational way of appraising episodes in the history of science? But Feyerabend does not have to figure out whether some episode or other *really* constituted progress. He is just pointing out that a dose of "anarchy" made a difference in those cases scientists tend to agree constituted progress.

Are there not some limits within which science must operate if it is to remain science? Or, since Feyerabend is trying to beat the methodologist at his own game, are there not some conditions that cannot be violated if we are to have progress in the standard sense? Let us grant Feyerabend that the traditional methodological rules developed by inductivists and falsificationists will not serve in that role. But are there no other rational conditions? Let us see what they may be. One obvious candidate, especially to someone trained in philosophy, is that science must not violate the rules of logic. The other, perhaps equally obvious, is that scientific practice must be free of political interference. Let us take them in turn. But before doing so, we must keep in mind that we are only trying to see now how far Feyerabend's brand of scientific anarchy may go. Even if these two conditions prove exceptionless, they will not be enough to bring universal method back from the grave.

LOGIC AS A LIMIT

I will not blame the main points made in this section on Feyerabend, although I sort of remember that he cast a kind eye on them when I published them (1982).

Surely, some critics of Feyerabend may feel, science must conform to the dictates of logic. But why should it? Science cannot be asked to obey all the laws that logicians find intuitive. Supergravity theories, for example, use numbers that do not obey the law of commutation (A X B = B X A); in fact, some vector operations do not obey that law either. Perhaps what those critics ask instead is that science not be marred by inconsistency. Contradiction is the mark of absurdity in matters intellectual. Science, the queen of intellect, must avoid it like the plague. Or so it would seem.

Nevertheless, one finds in the practice of science that inconsistencies are constantly discovered, and in the history of science we find some very important breakthroughs that have been accused of blatant inconsistency. One of the most famous is Bohr's initial atomic theory. As the story goes, the electrons were supposed to be in orbit around the nucleus. But since the electrons are charged, they should radiate energy in accordance with Maxwell's laws of electrodynamics. Unfortunately, as the electrons radiate, they should lose energy, and thus their orbits should decay and eventually collapse. But the model required stable orbits, as it should since atoms are not in the habit of imploding. Thus, the theory, it is said, was built on inconsistent foundations. Moreover, everyone concerned was aware of the problem but forged ahead, nonetheless. Now this atomic theory was a great breakthrough. So, what are we to make of it? To have thrown out the theory at the outset because of the contradiction would show, as Feyerabend puts it, that the attempt to remove contradictions may remove also "either important factual statements, or the ability of the theory to grow, or its fertility in the treatment of concrete problems" ("In Defense of Aristotle," 1978b, 154). Similar remarks may be made about several attempts to axiomatize, and thus render logically flawless, certain parts of quantum physics.

Lakatos suggests that it is possible for a theory (a research program in his scheme) to progress on inconsistent foundations. But the scientists know that eventually they must face up to the inconsistency and remove it (1970). Nevertheless, if the inconsistency is permitted because the science with that inconsistency in it is progressing, why should it be removed later? Only, it seems, if the inconsistency finally gets in the way of progress. And some surely do. If the very statement of the theory is contradictory, one would not know what to make of it. If at a crucial point in research the theory leads to contradictory expectations, a consistent reformulation of the theory will have to be sought. Otherwise there seems to be no reason, other than philosophical punctiliousness, to stop research that is producing a good harvest. Of course, it *may* happen that removing the inconsistency would provide further stimulation. In that case, removing it is worth a try. All these maneuvers sound quite reasonable. But let us pay some attention to *what* sounds reasonable. How much concern an inconsistency should draw seems to depend on what else the scientist has to give up. Thus, the striving for consistency, even though obvious in many situations, has limitations, not unlike the previous methodological rules discussed by Feyerabend.

Ludwig Wittgenstein made a similar point about mathematics: "If a contradiction were now actually found in arithmetic—that would only prove that an arithmetic with *such* a contradiction in it could render very good service; and it will be better for us to modify our concept of the certainty required, than to say that it would really not yet have been a proper arithmetic" (1967, 181e). As far as science goes, such a result should be expected. Many theories are gerrymandered, grafted on other views, as indeed Bohr's atomic theory was. Those that are quite original are at some time embryonic and must be developed. And those that are quite revolutionary are likely to be out of phase with the prevailing auxiliary theories (cf. Chapter 3). Thus, science is built up of many different parts and those parts are bound to be in conflict with others. Inconsistencies seem therefore practically inevitable. Whether and how to remove the inconsistency is a function of many considerations. To let the logician impose hard and fast rules on this score would bring to science a severe case of logic-induced anemia.

The horror of contradiction arises largely from the well-known dictum that if a theory contains a contradiction it entails anything whatsoever and is therefore worthless. But we have seen that in the actual practice of science this need not be so. For one thing, deriving significant logical consequences in science is not all that easy. For another, determining what to make of a contradiction is often not easy either. Furthermore, the scientist may still recognize that contradictions are bad news without letting the logician lead him by the nose.

In any event, why do contradictions entail anything whatsoever? Because, the logician claims, an inference is valid if it is impossible for all its premises to be true and the conclusion false. Thus, the following inference:

All Latins are great lovers
I am Latin
Therefore, I am a great lover

is logically valid. Whether the two premises are actually true or not is beside the point. The point is instead that *if* the two premises are true, the conclusion cannot fail to be true. The argument is therefore valid. If the premises are actually true, the conclusion will be actually true as well. In that case the argument is said to be sound as well as valid.

Notice now that two contradictory premises cannot both be true. It cannot be the case that Feyerabend was born in Austria and that he was not born in Austria. But then an inference from contradictory premises will always be valid, since it will be impossible for all the premises to be true while the conclusion is false. Thus, from the contradiction about Feyerabend's birth we can logically conclude that dragons exist. And we can just as well conclude that dragons do not exist. If perchance some poor layperson (or student) feels confused about calling such inferences valid, we hasten to point out that they are valid but not sound. In this manner the odd instances are rendered harmless.

The story does not end there, however. Every inference (or argument, if we prefer) has what is called a corresponding conditional (i.e., an "if...then..." sentence). The conditional: "If all Latins are great lovers and I am Latin, then I am a great lover" corresponds to the inference given above. Now, an inference is valid if and only if its corresponding conditional is a logical truth. To say that a sentence is a logical truth is to say that it comes out true no matter what the actual truth values (true and false) of its components. Take for example the sentence "I am Martian or I am not." This sentence is true if I am Martian and true if I am not, since both possibilities are covered. There are no more possibilities; thus, the sentence will be true no matter what.

Valid inferences are then required to have logical truths as corresponding conditionals. The problem is that the conditionals of logic are very peculiar. Indeed, they are not equivalent to those of the sciences or of real life. A conditional of logic, called a "material conditional," has an antecedent (the sentence that follows the "if") and a consequent (the sentence that follows the "then"), just as real conditionals. It also shares another property with real conditionals: whenever the antecedent is true and the consequent false, the entire conditional is considered false (e.g., "If China has a lot of people, the Chinese are free of disease").

Here the similarity ends. For material conditionals are true under all other conditions. For example, in the logic of logicians, the following is true: "If the moon is made of cheese, the human population problem is due to an overproduction of storks." The reason is simply that the antecedent is false, and all material conditionals with false antecedents are automatically true. There need be no connection at all between antecedent and consequent. By contrast, in the conditionals of science we often find a causal connection between antecedent and consequent (e.g., "if the mass of that star is 100 times that of the sun, it will eventually become a black hole").

The consequence of this line of thought is that material conditionals do not apply in science. And one of the main reasons is precisely that they can be made true simply by having a false antecedent. But, and here we come to the crucial point: A presumably valid inference must have a corresponding conditional that is always true. The determination of such truth must be made, for the logician, in terms of his definition of the material conditional. That is, that determination will give a value of true in all cases in which the antecedent is false. Of course, these cases will include antecedents with contradictions in them—precisely the conditionals that correspond to the puzzling valid inferences. But these cases are inadmissible in science! And since the notion of logical validity is tied to that of the material conditional, such a notion of validity is also inadmissible in science! In other words, the logic of logicians does not apply to science (at least not fully).

This result is not a bad reflection on science, I believe. If anything, it just points out the limitations of standard logic. As for the horror of contradiction, we can now place it in a more proper perspective. The reason for such horror can no longer be that a contradiction entails anything whatsoever. This is so only if one adopts a certain definition of validity. But that definition does not apply in science. Those who argue that science must conform to the dictates of logic or otherwise face promiscuous entailments, assume that logic does apply to science. They assume, that is, the very thing in question.

These two lines of attack, the first based on the way scientific views develop, the second on the peculiarities of logic, should make us realize that even the standard of consistency has some limitations.

We may also notice, incidentally, that the logic of philosophers does not apply to what most humans would see as real life, since in real life we also expect the antecedents and consequences of our conditionals to be related by their subject matters.

THE POLITICAL AUTONOMY OF SCIENCE AS A LIMIT

Probably dearer to the heart of many scientists is the notion that science should be free from political intervention. This is perfectly understandable. The history of science makes all too clear what religious zealots with political power can do to the practice of science. Similarly, self-righteous Marxist pressures against Russian scientists produced many shameful episodes and led to serious setbacks for Russian genetics and computer science. Political considerations interfere with the satisfaction of intellectual curiosity and are therefore inimical to the pursuit of science.

This may be too narrow a view of the matter, however. According to Feyerabend, the scientific establishment may become so pervasive and powerful that contrary views and scientific practices are denied a hearing and an opportunity to develop, let alone to compete in the marketplace of ideas. So entrenched can become the scientific powers-that-be that only an outside agency can restore intellectual freedom. Sometimes, that is, proliferation must be enforced by political intervention. I think that this is a good theoretical point as far as it goes. But whether it applies to any actual situations is a different matter altogether.

Feyerabend does claim that science has become a sacred cow. But even if he is wrong on that, his main point about the limits of the principles of the political autonomy of science is not affected. We must always guard against inflicting on others the intellectual tyranny that science has had to endure so often in its history. It pays nonetheless to consider now one of Feyerabend's illustrations. According to him, Mao's forces acted properly in forcing the medical establishment in China to accept a partnership of sorts with traditional medicine (herbal medicine, acupuncture, and so on). Scientific medicine had pretty much strangled alternative practices, and so it was correct on Mao's part to give those alternative practices the opportunity to show what they had to offer. The resulting proliferation had some very good consequences for medicine as a whole, according to Feyerabend. And, indeed, the medical horizons were broadened in many respects. But this illustration cannot be taken as a blanket endorsement of Mao, and even less as encouraging political intervention in science no matter what the circumstances. Nor should it be denied that some very silly techniques of traditional medicine were put into effect in China—swallowing tadpoles as contraceptives, for example (for an extensive critique see my 1991). As J.S. Mill pointed out a long time ago, however, only in the open can the shortcomings of ideas be properly exposed.

OBJECTIONS TO THE NEW PHILOSOPHY OF SCIENCE

Many of the standard objections against Kuhn and Feyerabend have already been discussed in the last two chapters. I have saved for the very end some burning questions that a few people apparently find decisive. The hottest one concerns the nature of the very evidence that Kuhn and Feyerabend have used against the standard views in philosophy of science. Kuhn and Feyerabend have used history to make their points. But how do they know that the history of science can be trusted to that extent? How is it that the "facts" of physics, astronomy and chemistry can be overthrown but we must show reverence for the "facts" of history? Kuhn and Feyerabend cannot have it both ways. Indeed, it seems more reasonable to suppose that physics is more reliable than history. Therefore, if Kuhn and Feyerabend's thesis against the theory-observation distinction is granted, their evidence is not worth all that much.

Several important points must be considered in reply. The first is that when the objection is aimed against Feyerabend it misunderstands the structure of his argument. To see this more clearly it pays to consider first a similar objection. According to this other objection, Feyerabend argues against reason in science. But in order to establish his conclusion, Feyerabend has to use reason. If reason is no good, Feyerabend's means for establishing his conclusion are no good either. Thus, Feyerabend must be committed to the correctness of reason. Unfortunately for him, this consequence invalidates his conclusion.

What this objection misses completely, however, is that Feyerabend does not need to be committed to the correctness of reason, whether as rational argument or methodological rules. As he says again and again, his argument is a *reductio ad absurdum* (reduction to absurdity), and a rather simple one at that. In a *reductio* one assumes *for the sake of argument* the opponent's position, and then derives a conclusion unacceptable to that opponent (that is, reduces his position to absurdity). This is so straightforward and common a technique of reasoning that the raising of this objection by professionals should be viewed with sheer amazement. As he says, for example, "An Anarchist is like an undercover agent who plays the game of Reason in order to undercut the authority of Reason" (32-33).

Of course, if reason is no good Feyerabend has no argument; but he does not need one, since the conclusion is already established (see my 2000).

Now we can consider the initial objection. How can Feyerabend trust the "facts" of history after undermining the apparently far more solid "facts" of physics, astronomy, chemistry, and the like? Furthermore, is Feyerabend now arguing that methodologies are refuted by facts and thus have to go? But did he not argue against this very way of dispensing with views? But all Feyerabend does, all he has to do, is provide the rationalist with statements that he will be highly inclined to accept, given his rationalist frame of mind, and at the same time will create serious problems for some favorite rationalist view or another.

Take the view that observations should not be tainted by theoretical assumptions, one of the key beliefs of Empiricism. Then Feyerabend can point out that Galileo, presumably one of the great heroes of Empiricism, wrote that the vertical fall of stones from a tall tower, which provided crucial evidence against the Copernican view, had to assume that the Earth did not move, the very point in question (Ch. 3). That if we assume that the Earth did move, then the stones would not fall straight down, but only seem to. Thus the "facts," whether stones fall vertically or parabolically, make theoretical assumptions. It was, thus, Galileo, who made the argument that destroys Empiricism. Feyerabend merely brings it to the attention of the empiricist, bringing him to intellectual distress.

After Fresnel's work in the early 1800s, many experiments made an overwhelming case for the wave theory of light. But in spite of all that evidence, Einstein wrote his paper on the photoelectric effect, in which he argued, theoretically, for a particle theory of light (photons). Was Einstein a clueless fellow trying to do science? Some scientists did think so at the time, although they were perhaps even more hostile towards the theory of relativity. Eventually he won the Nobel Prize for that one paper. And now even the strictest methodologist is likely to agree that Einstein was one of the great scientists of all time.

It is not clear, however, that Kuhn also intends to offer a *reductio*. But the objection does not work against him either. In the first place, Kuhn does not claim that conflict with historical facts makes it obligatory to abandon traditional epistemology of science.

> The contrary historical facts] by themselves...cannot and will not falsify that philosophical theory, for its defenders will do what we have already seen scientists doing when confronted by anomaly. They will devise numerous articulations and *ad hoc* modifications of their theory in order to eliminate any apparent conflict. (1970, 78).

Such historical anomalies can then at best "help to create a crisis or, more accurately, to reinforce one that is already very much in existence." Their main contribution to the epistemology of science is that they make possible "the emergence of a new and different analysis of science within which they are no longer a source of trouble" (78). This is, incidentally, the sort of development that we have seen in the previous chapter.

The key point at issue is the overthrow of the empirical basis. If it can be done for physics, it can surely be done for history as well. But then views of science that take such historical facts seriously can have the rug pulled from under their feet no less than theories in physics or astronomy. This a socio-historical or naturalistic approach must acknowledge. Nevertheless, we do not have much of an objection. After all, the task at hand would require the overthrow of the present socio-historical empirical basis that has been used by Kuhn and Feyerabend. Theories of science are thus in the same boat with scientific theories: They can be replaced by alternatives that change the "facts" on them. But that possibility does not diminish their worth. There will be no decisive objection along the present lines, therefore, unless the empirical basis of the naturalistic view of science in question is actually overthrown. The ball is then in the opponents' court—and what a difficult play it is!

This response to the objection has some very significant consequences for the philosophy of science. It very often happens in philosophy that pointing out that a view *could be* mistaken is tantamount to showing that it *is* mistaken. The reason is that philosophy is construed as a purely conceptual, indeed *aprioristic* discipline. This means that what philosophers do is logically prior, and therefore independent of empirical considerations. Given this presumed independence, the realm of philosophical analysis or investigation is not unlike that of mathematics. Once concepts are properly understood and relations between them identified, such relations are not just so, they *must* be so (e.g., bachelors must be unmarried; minds must be distinct from bodies). Thus, in philosophy to point out how a view could be mistaken is often all it takes to defeat the view, or at least to advance a very serious objection against it (e.g., that brains and minds *may* be identical).

Mainstream philosophy of science in the last century has proved no exception. According to this "logical" approach, the specific task of philosophy of science is, in Carl Hempel's words,

> ...to exhibit, by means of 'logical analysis' or 'rational reconstruction', the logical structure and the rationale of scientific inquiry. The methodology of science, thus understood, is concerned solely with certain logical and systematic aspects of science which form the basis of its soundness and rationality—in abstraction from, and indeed to the exclusion of, the psychological and historical facets of science as a social enterprise (1978, 291).

By purely conceptual and logical investigation the philosopher of science is supposed to discover the method of science. Once established, the principles of the methodology can then serve as

> conditions for the rational pursuit of empirical inquiry, as criteria of rationality for the formulation, test, and change of scientific knowledge claims (291).

In this manner philosophy of science may set itself in Lakatos' words, "as a watchdog of scientific standards" (1978, 226)

Nevertheless, we have discovered in this essay that the historical and psychological facets of science do make a great difference; indeed, we have seen that the tides of historical investigation have washed away the castles that philosophy built on the sands of logic. We must remember that the appeal of method was that it paid for scientists to follow it, for presumably their chances to achieve success were thereby increased. But then philosophical method seemed applicable only to the extent that it abstracted from the practice of science those features that proved particularly helpful. This suggests that philosophical analysis has to be as empirical about science as science is about the world. A good view of science would result from a complex interplay of idea and experience (in the terms that we have discussed previously). In looking back over the history of philosophy of science, Hempel recognizes this point. He recalls that "explication in the sense of analytic empiricism has been guided to a considerable extent by close attention to salient features of actual scientific procedures and the logical means required to do justice to them" (298-99). And Lakatos, who argues in favor of what he calls "statute law" in science, openly says that demarcationists—his kind of philosophers—"reconstruct *universal* criteria which explain the appraisals which great scientists have made of particular theories or research programmes" (226).

It seems then that though analytic philosophy of science denigrated history in public, it could not help trying to bed her on the sly. In any event, the pitfalls of theorizing about science are not unlike the pitfalls of theorizing about the world. One may have a view that works for the time being, perhaps forever, but that is unlikely. That view will have to be amended under the pressure of discoveries about the practice of science and may have to be replaced for many different reasons. One of those reasons, in the case of the new philosophy, would be the overthrow of the socio-historical empirical basis on which it is partly built. Therefore, there is neither pretension nor need to hold eternal and exceptionless theses. This is a significant change in the standards of philosophical procedure.

Be that as it may, many of the historical claims made by Kuhn and Feyerabend can be questioned by the methodologists only at the price of their own embarrassment (more on this later). This is not to say that they should not be questioned. Notice, however, that serious consideration of the practice of science compromises the very purity of philosophical analysis. For philosophical investigations are to be settled, to some degree, by "dirty" empirical findings. Even if Kuhn and Feyerabend are mistaken on many specific points of history, the game is already lost for traditional philosophy. If Kuhn and Feyerabend are mistaken, for this or other reasons, the view of science that should emerge may differ greatly from theirs. But a return to the logical virginity of yesteryear seems most unlikely. Once lost, it is hard to see how that state of innocence can be regained.

This pretty much concludes my exposition of the positive views put forth by Kuhn and Feyerabend on the nature of science. Of course, some of the important consequences must still be examined, and will be examined in the chapters that follow. The one standing point that should still be mentioned in this chapter is that of scientific rationality. Kuhn has reacted with distress at the accusation that he is an irrationalist. For him change of paradigms is not irrational because it involves reasons. Those reasons, furthermore, are of the sort that scientists (and philosophers) find unobjectionable: accuracy, simplicity, fruitfulness and the like. The problem, as he sees it, is that the weight given to each of these values cannot be uniquely determined in each situation. Thus, the proponent of the new paradigm may emphasize fruitfulness over accuracy, whereas the defender of the old paradigm may do just the opposite. But the problem is greater than Kuhn recognizes, for given his own account, those who refuse to step into the circle, as he would say, need not even recognize that the proposed new paradigm has greater fruitfulness, for example (or that it solves the problems it claims to solve—cf. Chapter 5—or that it has greater consistency).

Since the rationalist insists that we must be able to show that change in science is for the better, his requirement is bound to be frustrated by Kuhn's scheme. Even religious zealots may give reasons in arguing for their particular faiths. The difficulty is that such reasons are acceptable only to the converted. Thus, though the reasons involved in paradigm change may be of a higher pedigree, it is still not possible to make an *impartial* determination of improvement in the case of paradigm change. Kuhn has to face it: The rationalist requires that the standards by which change will be measured have to be specified. Kuhn attacks the idea that such standards exist (or rather, those he allows are much too flexible and circular to suit the rationalist's purposes). Thus, if Kuhn is correct, science cannot be a rational enterprise. Feyerabend grants the point and cheerfully uses it to give rationalists and other respectable people a hard time. But the main difference between Feyerabend and Kuhn on this issue, it seems to me, is chiefly one of attitude.

Nonetheless, attitude is not a matter of small importance. Feyerabend goes on to draw the inference that science has too privileged a position in society, that its power should be curbed. We will discuss this thesis later. Kuhn on the other hand goes on to suggest that:

> if history or any other empirical discipline leads us to believe that the development of science depends essentially on behavior that we have previously thought to be irrational, then we should conclude not that science is irrational, but that our notion of rationality needs adjustment here and there (1971, 144).

Feyerabend actually is sympathetic to this Kuhnian attitude. Anarchy, irrationality, even propaganda, are so only from the point of view of the self-appointed rationalists. This is not to say, however, that either Kuhn or Feyerabend do provide a different notion of rationality, nor that their views suggest one. But as I will argue later, their views, seen from a naturalistic perspective, give us some strong hints of a new conception of rationality.

REFERENCES

Einstein, A. (1951). *Albert Einstein: Philosopher Scientist.* Schilpp, A., ed. *Library of Living Philosophers.*

Feyerabend, P. K. (1970). "Consolations for the Specialist," in Lakatos I. and Musgrave, A. (eds.), *Criticism and the Growth of Knowledge.* Cambridge University Press.

Feyerabend, P. K., (1978a). *Against Method.* Verso.

Feyerabend, P. K. (1978b). "In Defense of Aristotle: Comments on the Condition Of Content Increase", in Radnitsky, G. and Anderson, G. (eds.), *Progress and Rationality in Science,* D. Reidel Publishing Co, 1978.

Hempel, C. (1978). "Scientific Rationality: Normative vs. Descriptive Construals," in *Wittgenstein, the Vienna Circle and Critical Rationalism.* Proceedings of the 3rd International Wittgenstein Symposium.

Kuhn, T. (1970). *The Structure of Scientific Revolutions.* 2nd Edition. Chicago University Press.

Kuhn, T. (1971). "Notes on Lakatos." In Cohen, R. S. and Buck, R. C., eds. Boston Studies in the Philosophy of Science, Vol. VIII, 144.

Lakatos, I. (1970). "Falsification and the Methodology of Scientific Research Programmes." In Lakatos, I. and Musgrave, A., eds., *Criticism and the Growth of Knowledge,* Cambridge University Press, pp. 91-196.

Lakatos, I. (1978). "Understanding Toulmin." Reprinted in his *Mathematics, Science and Epistemology.* Worrall, J. and Currie, G., eds., Cambridge University Press.

Mill, J.S. (2005). *On Liberty.* In Morgan, M. L. (Ed.). *Classics of Moral and Political Theory* (4th Edition). Hackett Publishing Co (first published in 1859).

Munévar, G. (1981). *Radical Knowledge: A Philosophical Inquiry into the Nature and Limits of Science.* Avebury Publishing Co. and Hackett Publishing Co.

Munévar, G. (1982). "Allowing Contradictions in Science," *Metaphilosophy,* January.

Munévar, G. (1991). "Science in Feyerabend's Free Society," English version in G. Munévar, ed., *Beyond Reason: Essays on the Philosophy of Paul K. Feyerabend,* Vol. 132, *Boston Studies in the Philosophy of Science,* Kluwer Academic Publishers. First published in German as "Die Wissenschaft iun Feyerabend's freier Gesellschaft," in *Versuchungen Aufsatze zur Philosophie Paul Feyerabends.* Duerr, H.P., ed., Suhrkamp, 1980.

Munévar, G. (1998). *Evolution and the Naked Truth.* Ashgate Publishing Ltd.

Munévar, G. (2000). "A Réhabilitation of Paul Feyerabend." In Preston, J., Munévar, G. and Lamb, D., eds., *The Worst Enemy of Science? Essays on the Life and Thought of Paul Feyerabend.* Oxford University Press.

Munévar, G. (2015). *"Historical Antecedents to the Philosophy of Paul Feyerabend." Studies in History and Philosophy of Science, December.*

Wittgenstein, L. (1967). *Remarks on the Foundations of Mathematics,* G. H. von Wright, R. Rhees, G. E. M. Anscombe (eds.). G. E. M. Anscombe (trans.). The M.I.T. Press), p. 181e.

CHAPTER 7

ONE LAST PLEA FOR "RATIONALITY": RATIONALITY AND THE GROWTH OF SCIENCE

One of Imre Lakatos' main goals was to make Kuhn and Feyerabend's insights cohere into a *rational pattern* (1970). In essence, his idea is that the proper mix of the principles of tenacity and proliferation leads to the *growth* of science. Maurie is entitled to stick to her view (tenacity), to modify it on the face of adverse predictions, and so forth, as long as her saving moves offer predictions of new phenomena. When, in developing her view, she opens up new avenues for investigation (at least theoretically), she contributes to the growth of knowledge, and thus her view is said to be progressing. But if she limits the modifications of her view to saving face (ad hoc moves), then her research program is stagnating (or degenerating). Proliferation is also essential to science, according to Lakatos, for it raises the "problem fever" of scientific research – thus leading to more rapid growth – and provides the only acceptable way to reject theories: replacement.

The history of science, then, should be one of struggle between competing views (which he calls research programs). Such a history should pay due attention to the points raised by Kuhn and Feyerabend; but at the same time the structure provided by Lakatos' methodology of research programs should permit us to see the rational character of science. This he thinks he will achieve by conflating the notions of scientific rationality and growth.[1]

According to Lakatos, any modification in one's theory, or any change from theory A to theory B is warranted as long as the following criteria are fulfilled:

1. B has excess empirical content over A: that is, it predicts *novel* facts, that is facts improbable in the light of, or even forbidden by, A.
2. B explains the previous success of A, that is, all the *unrefuted* content of A is included (within the limits of observational error) in the content of B. And
3. Some of the excess content of B is corroborated (116).

---

[1] Lakatos developed his ideas in "Falsification and the Methodology of Scientific Research Programmes." (1970) and *History of Science and its Rational Reconstructions* (1971). My job in this chapter is to explain and critique them briefly.

Since there is no falsification without replacement, in Lakatos' scheme, to say A is falsified is to say that another theory B has been proposed which meets these criteria.

Suppose, however, that the proponents of A do not wish to give up their point of view. They may then elaborate (modify) A so as to take into account the novel facts predicted by its rival, and by doing so predict some novel facts of their own. Theory A, so elaborated, may have the advantage now. But then the sympathizers of B may respond in kind and regain the upper hand. The outcome of the story is that we do not really pit one isolated theory against another, but that we appraise rather *series* of theories. Now theories belong to a series only if there is some sort of *continuity* among them. This continuity is provided in mature science by two factors: (a) a common core that expresses a point of view about the world, and (b) a set of directions (a heuristic) as to how the series is to be constructed. A series of theories so produced constitutes the appropriate unit of evaluation in the philosophy of science. It is also what Lakatos calls a research program.

Feyerabend's principle of tenacity comes into play in that any setbacks of the program do not affect the core directly but only the most recent theory of the program. The core is simply not open to refutation (as Lakatos would say, the negative heuristic deflects the arrow of *modus tollens* away from the core). As an example, take a simplified version of the Newtonian program. The core would be comprised of Newton's three laws of motion and his law of gravitation. Together these laws give us a certain picture of the physical universe: The physical elements of the world are of a certain type, they interact with each other in certain ways, and there is also a certain new proper way to ask and answer theoretical and experimental questions about such elements and their interactions (e.g., by formulations within the calculus of infinitesimals). If this sounds very much like Kuhn's paradigms, it is because it is very much like Kuhn's paradigms. One difference is presumably that Lakatos' scheme allows for proliferation as well as tenacity. Another difference is that the fine structure of Lakatos' research programs is expected to make us see science as a rational enterprise.

Tenacity holds, then, because when trouble starts, we do not give up our research program but rather modify the theory that presently bears its standard. Furthermore, trouble is always expected—any research program is always born in a sea of anomalies, and most have progressed in such an environment. Let us see why. In the case of Newton's gravitational program, the positive heuristic roughly tells us that the planets are to be treated as spinning tops revolving in elliptical orbits around the sun, much in accordance with Kepler's laws. The first theory of the series, A_1, will treat only the sun and one planet, say Earth, and those only as mass points. Such a theory will generate predictions, but obviously we expect many of them to be incorrect. We must develop sophisticated methods which will consider the perturbation in the system caused by a second planet (or perhaps by the moon). This would be our second theory of the series, A_2. We then include solutions for a group of three-body problems by bringing in the rest of the known planets, A_3, A_4, and so on. We understand that later we will have to treat the members of the solar system as extended bodies, A_k, and then as rotating, A_{k+1}. Because we, the Newtonian theoreticians, know in advance that we will eventually have to work out the details according to a full-blown positive heuristic, we also know that many anomalies should not worry us yet – worrying about them will have to be postponed until the appropriate member of the series is constructed. In a mature science the positive heuristic tells us, in some sense, of the order in which we will have to tackle the anomalies.

In a matter resembling Kuhn's paradigms, Lakatos' research programs give us a *promise* of future performance, while leaving most problems still to be resolved within a certain framework. Unlike Kuhn, we now have a good idea of how we are going to fulfill the promise. And—most important of all—what corresponds to Kuhn's articulation of a paradigm can now be seen as rational as long as the taking of every step in the development of the series generally leads to the prediction of novel facts (theoretical progress) and some of those facts are corroborated (empirical progress).

In a struggle between competing research programs what we evaluate, then, is the form in which they shift over time. If one series $B_1 \ldots B_n$ shifts on the whole by offering novel predictions, whereas its rival, $A_1 \ldots A_n$, can only react after the fact, barely able to incorporate the new content but without making any new predictions in the wake of its development, we should say that $B_1 \ldots B_n$ is *progressing* whereas $A_1 \ldots A_n$ is *degenerating*. The test of progress or degeneration is whether the development of the program leads to content increase or to mere reinterpretation. It may also be helpful to think of the matter in terms of momentum, or lack of it.

Lakatos agrees with Kuhn and Feyerabend that there is no counterevidence without an alternative. And he agrees with Feyerabend that the struggle between research programs raises the "problem fever" of science. It is often only the rival program that will predict the troublesome fact that will spur us to the development and growth of our program. Now, just as theories can be replaced in accordance with Lakatos' three-point criteria, research programs themselves may be replaced along similar lines.

Let us consider an example. Einstein's research program (General Relativity) overthrew Newton's. The crucial reason, in Lakatos' scheme, is that Einstein's view of the universe was both unusual and fruitful (it made amazing predictions and some of them were corroborated). Einstein thought, unlike Newton, that the geometry of space and time is affected by the amount of mass (mass-energy). "Spacetime" (Einstein's term) has properties, and those properties depend to a large extent on the amount and distribution of mass in its vicinity. **Figure 7.1** serves to illustrate the contrast between the two views. The distance between two points on a regular coffee cup is independent of the amount of coffee in the cup (**Figure 7.1a**). But that is so only if the cup is made of a relatively rigid material. If the cup is made of, say, thin rubber, its shape—its "geometry"—will change in accordance with the amount of coffee in it. In this case the shortest distance between the same two points on the surface of the cup will definitely be affected, as shown by the lines drawn between such points in **Figure 7.1b** (and not only the length is affected; its curvature also changes). **Figure 7.1c** shows that the same principles illustrated in **Figure 7.1b** occur with any type of elastic cup.

In an analogous manner, Einstein's spacetime is made to curve by the mass-energy it contains. Light rays, which travel in the easiest possible path, will then follow the "contours" of space-time. We might say that a strong gravitational source (e.g., a star) carves a basin out of space-time (**Figure 7.2**), or that it "stretches" it so. As a result, a light ray coming close to a star would be slowed down and deflected by it (think of what would happen to the trajectory of marbles that fall into a curved basin) (**Figure 7.2**). It should then be observed that the stars very close to the sun in our visual field should appear shifted. A solar eclipse is a very good occasion to make such an observation; and, indeed, an expedition in 1920 did just that (**Figure 7.3**), not long after Einstein made his prediction. Today we can check the matter more routinely because the point applies to all electromagnetic radiation (of which visual light is only one kind). Thus, radio sources directly behind the sun can be tracked by radio telescopes, and spaceships passing on the other side of the sun can send signals that allow us to make the appropriate measurements of deflection or delay.

Figure 7.1a. Rigid cup. Author.

The distance between the two points in the cup is not affected by the amount of coffee in the cup.

Figure 7.1b. Elastic cup. Author.

However, if the cup were made of an elastic material, the amount and distribution of the coffee would make a big difference to the distance between the two points. Likewise, in Einstein's view, matter "tells" the universe how to curve.

Figure 7.1c. Very elastic cup. Author.

Another elastic cup. The same principles apply no matter what shape the cup takes.

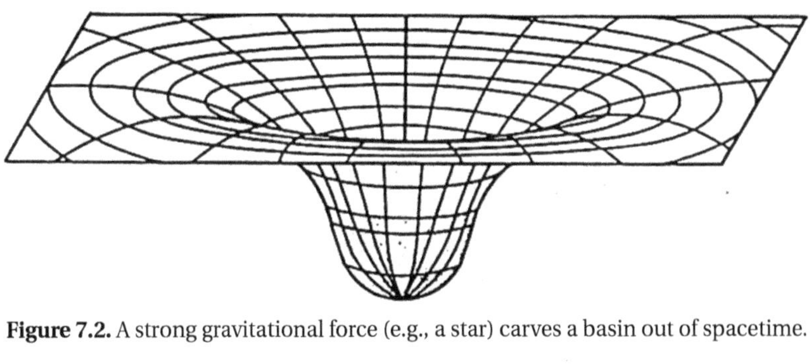

Figure 7.2. A strong gravitational force (e.g., a star) carves a basin out of spacetime.

We should realize that the stronger the gravitational source, the greater the curvature of the basin. A light ray that is following the shape of the basin will thus be so much more delayed (it will have longer to go). In some cases, the gravitational source is so strong that the basin actually becomes a hole without a bottom, and light entering it cannot climb out again. Such is the nature of the infamous black holes. Moreover, just as light is delayed, time is slowed down. Thus, in the presence of a strong gravitational field, time passes more slowly. By using atomic clocks at the top and the basement of very tall buildings (and in some experiments using airplanes flying in circles), this very strange prediction of Einstein's general theory of relativity has been confirmed.

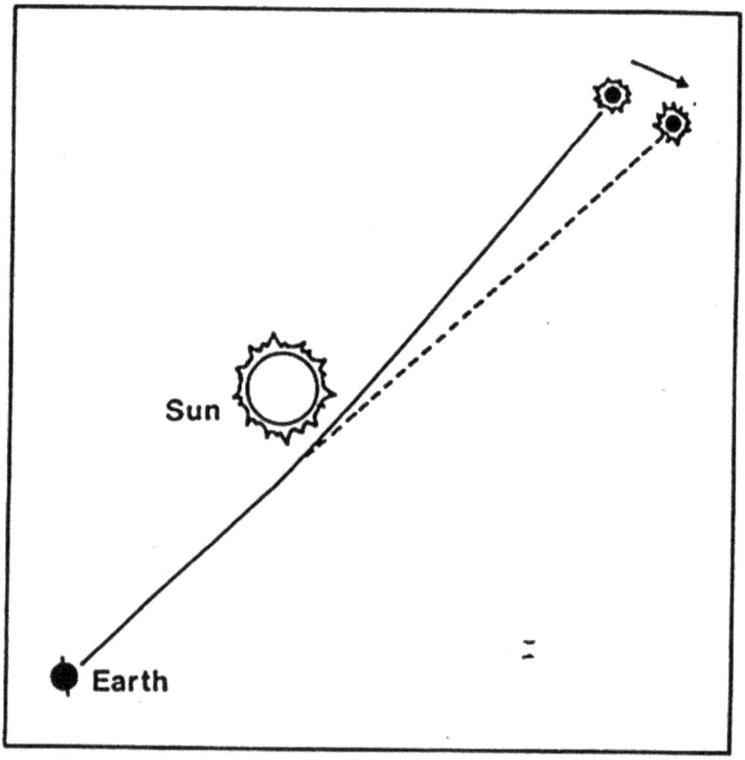

Figure 7.3. Deflection of a light ray by the gravitation of the sun. Drawing by Nicole Ankeny.

Incidentally, Einstein's ideas can also be used to account for the anomalous perihelion of Mercury that was so troublesome for the mature falsificationist. According to Lakatos we may now see why the Newtonians were in no hurry to abandon their gravitational program on the basis of this recalcitrant anomaly. For the perihelion of Mercury did not become counter-evidence for 85 years, not until it was explained within a rival program, the general theory of relativity (see **Figure 7.4**).

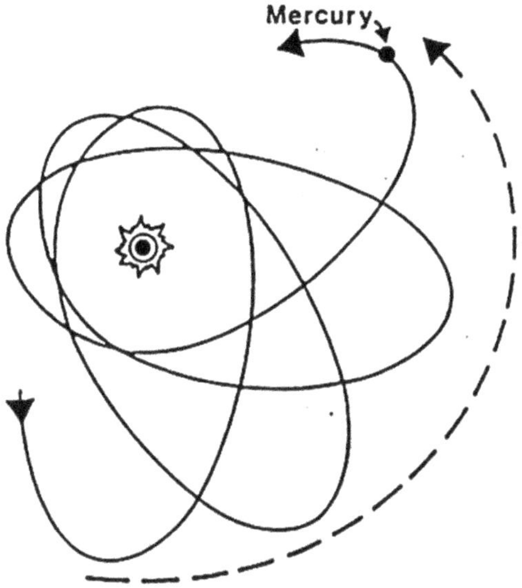

Figure 7.4. Effect on Mercury's orbit (exaggerated). Drawing by Nicole Ankeny.

The startling predictions made by Einstein were certainly novel from the Newtonian point of view. Thus, Einstein's general relativity program led to *theoretical progress*, for it opened up new areas of investigation and confronted us with the possibility of new and unusual characteristics of the universe. Furthermore, those predictions were well corroborated, thereby leading to *empirical progress*.

Some attempts have been made to accommodate these findings within a Newtonian framework, but without much empirical success. (Recall that empirical character and growth have been soldered into one by Lakatos). We should then say that Einstein's program is progressing while Newton's is degenerating. This presumably justifies the shift of allegiance that has taken place within physics.

In this manner Lakatos accounts for change in science. It is worth noting that he places no strict requirements on the core – not even a demand that it be an exemplary achievement. The core may be so vague as to be considered metaphysical. But as long as the series of theories that articulate the vision of the core is progressing, the decision to preserve the core untouched is rational. On the other hand, Lakatos tempts us to think that the core of any program may crumble, whether metaphysical or not, because of prolonged degeneration in the research program. The reasons are logical and empirical: the pervasive lack of novel facts or appropriate corroborations. They have little to do with "aesthetic" feelings of simplicity, elegance, or what not. The emphasis must be on "prolonged," however, for any program can presumably make a come-back. A degenerating shift may be due to temporary dearth of able supporters and not to inherent shortcomings of the program *vis a vis* the world.

A problem with Lakatos' proposal is found in his second requirement for the development of a series of theories (and in general for replacement): B explains the previous success of A, that is, all the *unrefuted* content of A is included (within the limits of observational error) in the content of B. But as Lakatos has told us, a theory in a series or a research program is refuted only when it is replaced by a better theory (or research program). In that case, the *unrefuted content* of a theory or research program that has been replaced by another is nothing more than the content that *has not been replaced.* Thus, Lakatos second requirement is trivial and pointless: "Preserve the portion (of a replaced theory) that you preserve" (Munévar, 1981, 100). The same reasoning applies to refuted (replaced) research programs.

Otherwise, Lakatos' methodology will succeed only if two conditions are met. First, he must show that his methodology can live up to the demands of historical examination. Of course, he seems to have set out to meet just this goal. That is the principal merit of his attempt to read Kuhn and Feyerabend's results in a rationalistic light. And the second condition is that what he proposes must indeed be rational. Should we really accept that the growth of science is tantamount to rationality? The answer to this last question will be postponed until later in the chapter. Let us now discuss the first condition.

It must be mentioned at the outset that the historical performance of Lakatos' methodology of research programs remedies some of the most glaring difficulties of mature falsificationism, the most sophisticated of the methodologies we had studied previously. In fact, it seems to have been designed with that very purpose in mind.

(1) The methodology of research programs eliminates the arbitrary element represented by the nature falsificationists' third type of decision. We no longer have to worry about whether we have tested the ceteris paribus clause exhaustively enough, whether the main hypothesis has been logically isolated and can now be eliminated. Lakatos' directive is to attempt to replace *all* components. Whenever we are able to do this successfully, we will consider the appropriate ingredient "falsified." That is, we do not eliminate the main hypothesis until we are in a position to replace it according to his criteria. A qualification is in order here, however. It would be preposterous to hold on to every low-level hypothesis because no replacement is in the wings. Think of a detective who would refuse to give up the hypothesis that the wife did it, even though he has determined beyond reasonable

doubt that she has been paralyzed for weeks and could not have fired that fatal shot, just because he has no other suspects in mind.

(2) The methodology of research programs also reduces the conventionalist element involved in the first two types of decision (those related to the background knowledge and proper observation procedure). Suppose that a new research program fails to fit the world as represented by the "unproblematic" background knowledge (which is determined by the conventional wisdom of the discipline at the time). Whereas, with previous methodologies we had no choice but to give up our view, Lakatos realizes that Feyerabend had a point in saying that the conflict is between the new view and a *theory of interpretation that could be changed* (as Galileo did, see Ch. 3). Lakatos therefore provides an *appeal procedure.* The proponents of a research program in empirical trouble can always challenge the accepted theory of observation, by proposing another one of their own design, or by simply turning the tables on the establishment and using the program in trouble as "unproblematic"). If the result of the challenge is a progressive shift, the research program in trouble will have been rescued from the jaws of a now degenerating conventional wisdom. (In addition to Galileo's case consider Prout's).

What constitutes unproblematic background knowledge and proper observational procedures will depend on the conventional wisdom of the practitioners. But the conventional element is reduced by the existence of this appeal procedure.

These advantages reduce the areas of conflict with history that were so devastating for mature falsificationism. Presumably we can now see why scientists were rational even though they held on to their views in the face of clear contrary evidence, or conversely why they switched allegiance so quickly on other occasions. In addition, Lakatos does more justice to the feeling scientists often have that they should *support* a view because of the interesting outcome of an experiment or a theoretical breakthrough. Of course, the support given by corroboration, in Lakatos' sense, is merely that of a signpost that things are turning out according to plan, and that the research program is thus progressing, not the support of old-fashioned inductivism.

Nonetheless, can Lakatos really expect a nearly perfect fit between his methodology and the practice of science (as instantiated in the history of science)? This would require that all scientists at all times have proceeded according to (Lakatos') rational plan. Such a concession is by no means an admission of defeat, however, for if falsificationism is not an appropriate critical tool at the level of scientific theories, why should we bend to its demands at the level of methodologies? Lakatos is not about to hang himself with a rope he has already cut. If there are no good reasons for falsificationism at the methodological level, then we must simply search for more fruitful strategies of criticism.

And he has a most promising candidate to offer: a version of his methodology of research programs, now adapted to the explanation of history. Of several competing methodologies, he proposes, choose the one that explains history best. A methodology no longer needs a perfect fit with history any more than a scientific view needs to be free from anomalies (remember, scientific research programs may progress in a sea of anomalies). And what constitutes a better explanation of history? One that makes more sense of history, i.e. that makes more of history seem rational. A methodology, thus used as a historiography, will be progressing whenever it (1) suggests new discoveries about history, and (2) some of those discoveries are corroborated. Of course, Lakatos wants to claim that his methodology will come out on top. To support this claim, he carried out several clever and interesting studies of crucial episodes in the history of science.

There are two clear assumptions here. The first is that science is rational, and that as a consequence the job of the philosopher is to figure out just what makes science rational. Lakatos' own approach to the task is to "reconstruct *universal* criteria which explain the appraisals which great scientists have made of particular theories or research programmes." We will discuss this assumption and Lakatos' approach later. The second assumption is that methodologies can *explain*. The problem is this: methodologies are normative, whereas explanation is a descriptive business. In Hempel's model of explanation, for example, one explains by reference to general laws. In other accounts of explanation, causes are the crucial elements of explanations. Most views on scientific explanation, in any event, seem to require reference to true empirical statements of some sort (to some sort of description, that is). The once attractive suggestion that explanation is provided by an account of the agent's reasons may be more amenable to Lakatos' position. Unfortunately, Hempel has already argued that this appeal to reasons confuses justification and explanation. How can normative positions, then, *explain* the history of scientific practice?

Lakatos states that only internal history (rationally reconstructed history) is relevant to the understanding of science, and that the best historiography is the one that makes more of science appear rational. (The internal history of an episode is a tale about how that episode would have developed if it had been a textbook case of rational scientific behavior. The external history deals with those events that had non-rational influence on the actual outcome – e.g., love affairs, illnesses, political upheavals that kept the scientists in question from developing their research program in accordance with perfect theoretical blueprints.) This is, again, Lakatos' assumption that science is largely rational and that to give understanding of the history of science is to show how it is (largely) rational. But it is plausible to think that understanding science may be different from understanding its history, regardless of how both kinds of understanding may affect one another. A normative account may perhaps provide a grasp of ideal science as a rational enterprise. And to this grasp perhaps the external history of science would be irrelevant.

But in order to explain the practices of science we also need an account of those events that did not go according to rational plan. And that (to use Lakatos' jargon) must be provided by the external history. Lakatos is aware of this point, and so he describes how the internal history sets the problems for the external. If we know what ought to have happened, but it did not, then we also know where factors external to the rationality of science may have been of crucial importance. In this way relevant directions are set even for the external historical inquiry. Moreover, a historiography cannot be said to be progressing unless its associated external history progresses whenever the internal history lags. Again, his notion of progress is basically the same as that for research programs: theoretical positing of new facts and empirical corroboration of some of them. And it is worth emphasizing that when a historiography progresses externally the credit goes to the normative account, for even external history depends on it.

Let us grant Lakatos that the fruitfulness of a historiography springs from the methodology at its core. Still, it does not follow that the methodology explains history. Even if rational reconstructions may be the *starting points* in our search for explanations of the history of science, they are not the *explanations.* For we want to know what *actually* happened and how and why it happened. That is, we want accounts that must involve what Lakatos calls external history (since it is clear that the practice of science could not be completely rational). Those accounts, if any, would be the explanations. And even if they depend on rational reconstruction, they are distinct from it. This is not much of an objection in the long run, but it helps clarify what Lakatos' accomplishment on this topic is supposed to be.

According to Lakatos, we begin with a rational reconstruction that provides a sketch, an outline to be checked against actual history. When gaps occur in the normatively-generated sketch, a progressive historiography will give direction to the external attempt to fill the gaps. The resulting account will be a combination of internal and external history. It is that account which may explain the actual practice of science. What methodologies do is generate the account. So even if methodologies cannot, strictly speaking, explain the history of science, they may be the source of the explanations. And that is all the ground we need to make comparisons between competing methodologies.

Unfortunately, it is not enough to say that the norms of a methodology will lead to a descriptive account that may explain some significant episode in the history of science. For such an account to be explained successfully, the rational reconstruction which produced it must meet certain conditions of relevance. We must show, for example, that it had the commitment of the scientists of the age in question – otherwise both the internal and histories used in the construction of the account would be off-target. Such a commitment need not be explicit, or even suspected. Indeed, the scientists of the period in question may have paid lip service to some other methodology, or perhaps even sincerely believed that the other was *the* method of science (Newton, for example, believed himself to be an inductivist, but, if Lakatos is correct, he wasn't.) It is what scientists do, not what they say, that shows where their methodological commitments lie. Still, in the long run we come back to a position much in agreement with the spirit of Hempel's: it is not the norms that explain but rather the knowledge of the commitment to those norms.

This requirement of relevance, however, brings up the question of whether the scientific standards of rationality have been different at different times. It also suggests that to explain best some historical episodes, historians *may* need to construct the internal history with a methodology that they *believe to be wrong*. It is not *prima facie* implausible that science took certain turns because of adherence to, say, inductivist methodologies. And even if that adherence was mistaken, it is important to recognize it in order to explain those turns.

These considerations drive a wedge between rationality and the history of science, at least insofar as Lakatos' plan is concerned. A methodology that progresses at a terrific pace (as a historiography) – that is, a methodology that "explains" more of history, that makes more of it rational – may explain too much, may in fact require the outright distortion of history by hanging from the necks of some scientists a rationality that never encumbered them. Of course, Lakatos may lower his aim. The best methodology is not the one that makes more of science look rational, but the one that makes more of *successful* science look rational. This move may work for several views of science, but unfortunately it does not work for Lakatos'. His methodology of research programs is after all a way of viewing the interplay of Feyerabend's principles of proliferation and tenacity as rational. But if the principle of tenacity is in operation, scientists may hold on to a degenerating research program for a long time. Thus, part and parcel of Lakatos' methodology of research programs is that scientists are rational even when holding on to science that is not successful. This leads to several problems. The most pressing is the divorce of rationality from successful science, a problem that by itself defeats his use of history as a tool for deciding between conflicting methodologies of science.

In short, Lakatos' appeal to history backfires because of one of two reasons. Either some methodologies have first rights in some periods, even if they are mistaken, because they actually had the adherence of the scientists of that period (so the "rationality" of history will not help decide which methodology is best); or else, if the domain of explanation is restricted to successful science, we wipe out the advantages that Lakatos' methodology of research programs seemed to offer by incorporating the principles of tenacity and proliferation.

So even though the importance of the history of science for the philosophy of science is undeniable, it seems that we need more than history alone to understand the nature of science. This conclusion is not based entirely on the failure of Lakatos' imaginative proposal to connect history and philosophy, as will be seen in the next chapter. But can Lakatos' methodology of scientific research programs still be salvaged? If it does indeed provide for the interplay of the principles of tenacity and proliferation, it is not likely to get in the way of scientific success the way standard methodologies did. Thus, it will not suffer the fate that the others did at the hands of Feyerabend's *reductio* arguments. And since it has an appeal procedure, it can rationally account for those instances in which theory overturns the verdict of experience—it does not succumb to the main problem of empiricism, i.e., the possibility of alternative bodies of evidence.

All these are considerations for not just rejecting Lakatos' methodology, as long as it can deliver what it promises. But, unfortunately, it may deliver too much. And here we come to an objection that parallels one of the points made against Lakatos' proposals about history. Feyerabend has pointed out in several occasions that Lakatos' methodology gives no directions for the elimination of research programs, for even a degenerating research program can always make a comeback. But if this is so, anything goes, and thus Lakatos' position is indistinguishable from epistemological anarchy. Feyerabend presses the point: Lakatos' kind of standards "have practical force only if they are combined with a *time limit* (what looks like a degenerating problem shift may be the beginning of a much longer period of advance)." For if you "are permitted to wait, why not wait a little longer?" And then, longer still (1981, 148). If so, Lakatos' notions of "progression" and "degeneration" are little more than verbal ornaments.

Of course, Lakatos would not have cherished the title of "fellow anarchist," bestowed upon him by Feyerabend. But the point is not Lakatos' feeling on the matter, but rather whether his "methodology" does commit him to a position close to Feyerabend's. Lakatos' attempted line of defense is unfortunately disappointing and inconsistent with his general philosophy. At one point, Lakatos states that, even though it is rational for someone to work on a degenerating program, it is also rational on the part of the scientific community to deny him all support (publications, employment, etc.). One can almost hear Feyerabend's quip that whereas Kuhn held that some views finally lose when all its proponents die off, Lakatos would hurry things up by starving them to death.

Lakatos remarks that "...it is rational to play a risky game, what is irrational is to deceive oneself about the risk" (1971, 104). The view we should, then, seek to develop amounts to something like the following. The rational scientist and the charlatan may have in common the work on programs with a bad record. But they differ in that the rational scientist, Joseph say, recognizes the bad record (with some qualifications), although he also holds that further work on his program promises to be at least theoretically fruitful. Joseph has, or thinks he has, a perhaps undeveloped "picture" which may successfully articulate insights that have not been harvested properly so far. His is a "hunch," of course, but hunches of that sort have played a very important role in science (e.g., in the development of atomic theory). The charlatan, on the other hand, generally acts as if the previous performance of his approach were at least as good as that of more reputable science, and as a result fails to show how his program could begin to progress.

Rationality would then be in the last instance a matter of honesty. But Feyerabend is not impressed. Even if confession is really good for the soul, how can it make the initial actions (what one confesses) any more rational? Is the husband who cheats on his wife any less of a cheat because he tells her every time? (Some may call him a sadistic brute in addition.)

Are these the dying gasps of the attempt to show that science is rational? In one respect they are not, since many philosophers of science are now tripping over each other to proclaim what was heresy not long ago. Thus, the breakdown of the fact-theory distinction is pretty much commonplace, although there is always much care in coupling this breakdown with emphasis on some aspect of science that offers, if only for the moment, some claim to the mantle of rationality. But most of such work is seldom more than a thinly disguised variation on the themes stressed by Lakatos or even Kuhn himself. This is not to say incidentally, that Kuhn and Feyerabend have now become highly respected members of the philosophy of science community. Chances are the devil will get credit before they do. Not that they deserve any better. The loss of logical innocence, like that of all innocence, is very difficult to forgive.

REFERENCES

Feyerabend, P. K. (1978). *Against Method.* Verso.

Feyerabend, P. K. (1981). *Problems of Empiricism: Philosophical Papers.* Vol: 2. Cambridge University Press.

Lakatos, I. (1970). "Falsification and the Methodology of Scientific Research Programmes." In Lakatos, I. and Musgrave, A., eds., *Criticism and the Growth of Knowledge,* Cambridge University Press, pp. 91-196.

Munévar, G. (1981). *Radical Knowledge: A Philosophical Inquiry into the Nature and Limits of Science.* Avebury Publishing Co. and Hackett Publishing Co.

Musgrave, A. (eds.), *Criticism and the Growth of Knowledge.* Cambridge University Press.

CHAPTER 8

EVOLUTION AND SCIENCE

At the beginning of this book, we saw the philosophy of science devote itself to the main task of theory of knowledge of the past three hundred years: an attempt to find a satisfactory answer to skepticism. We knew that science worked but we could not prove it. We could not prove it because scientific theories could not be proved by experience. The steps that took us from the facts, from the data, to our favored theories involved fallacious reasoning. Arguing that the facts merely "justify" the theories (or our belief in them) did not help, nor did the notion that experience merely tells us which theories are most probable. We then examined Popper's claim that the problem was misstated, for science did not work by induction. But his suggestion that scientific rationality lies in our attempt to falsify theories, although intuitively more appealing, also faltered under criticism by Kuhn, Feyerabend, and Lakatos. Other suggestions, such as simplicity and the capacity for problem-solving fared no better in our search for a demonstration of the rationality of science.

In the process, the very problem with which we began has been transformed in the following way. Science was supposed to proceed by adherence to methodological rules that specified the means by which experience passed judgment on theory (e.g., providing inductive support for a particular theory, or falsifying it, and so on). But through the work of Kuhn, Feyerabend, and others, it has become apparent that no such rules are to be found, at least not general methodological rules. We should not take this to mean that no rationale can ever be given for preferring one scientific view to another, but rather that such rationale cannot be given by a set of rules of general application. Now, Kuhn's work, as well as Polanyi's, suggests not just that the rationale will vary from case to case, but also that only those who are experts in the discipline will be able to tell whether the correct decision has been made. According to Lakatos, this result would leave scientific rationality in the hands of an elite. And the trouble with an elite is that its procedures may degenerate because of overconfidence or many other reasons.

The new problem of rationality then is how to build a scientific practice that increases our chances to come up with rules, standards, methods, or procedures appropriate to specific cases, without having to depend entirely on the judgment of a possibly stagnant elite.

It seems to me that in trying to solve this problem we should move away from outmoded conceptions of human nature. It is high time to acknowledge, in the first place, that human beings are part of nature and that, when analyzing their conceptions of themselves and the world, we should take seriously the lessons that Darwin began to teach us in 1859 with the publication of his *Origin of Species.* In this vein, it pays to recall that science is a product of intelligence, that intelligence is an instrument of adaptation and itself the result of evolution. Now, what distinguishes intelligence from other chemical and neural mechanisms of interaction with the world is that intelligence transcends the ability to respond to the immediate demands of the environment, as Piaget made clear (1972). It is this freedom of response that permits intelligence to form sweeping views of the world and the means to criticize them. Science is, of course, a communal enterprise that involves division of labor and is carried out in a social milieu. Science is thus, to speak perhaps metaphorically, but not inaccurately, a social application of intelligence to understand our world, a world of which we ourselves are part.

I am not the first to argue that we should try to understand science in an evolutionary context. Mach, Poincare, Lorenz, Popper, Campbell, Toulmin, Hull, and many others have made a variety of attempts – for an account see Chapter 6 of my (1981). Even Kuhn claimed that we could understand progress in science by analogy to the theory of evolution, and Feyerabend occasionally tied his ideas to evolutionary biology. Moreover, the famous American philosopher W.V.O. Quine argued for the naturalization of epistemology, dropping the word "evolution" here and there.

Although normally it is good practice for a writer simply to say what he wants to say, this time, in order to avoid confusions, it is best for me to begin by pointing out what I do not want to say. The reason is that the work produced by several of the thinkers I have just named has been called "evolutionary epistemology" or (in the case of Quine) "naturalized epistemology." References to evolution may, thus, incline some readers to categorize my words as belonging to either field (or both) and to read them with certain expectations in mind, a process that is very likely to produce misunderstandings.

The view I will argue for is not like the analogical evolutionary epistemology of Popper, Campbell, Toulmin, and Hull. Nor is it like Quine's naturalized epistemology. Interesting and valuable though all this body of work may be, it has some decisive shortcomings. In presenting the analogical view, for example, the epistemologist tries to show that the development of science closely parallels the evolution of species according to neo-Darwinism. Populations of scientific ideas, say, shift in response to the pressures placed upon them by the intellectual environment (which may serve as the equivalent of natural selection). What the epistemologist wants is, of course, to show that science is a rational enterprise. Now, let us suppose that he succeeds in forging a close analogy. What follows from that? Surely not that science is rational. Being like the evolution of life, which is not itself rational, cannot suffice. Thus, the very approach seems wrongheaded. To make matters worse, all such proposed analogies have broken down upon close inspection. This matter, as well as those mentioned in the next two paragraphs, is supported by argument in my original paper on this subject (1986).

A second problem with most, if not all analogical approaches, is that they cheat. The epistemologist wants to account for the history of science as a rational process, and thus he takes his cue from the great success of neo-Darwinism in explaining natural history. That is, he uses the prestige of neo-Darwinism to get a hearing. But once he has made a few plausible comparisons, he rushes to announce that biological evolution is the responsibility of only one part of a much more comprehensive theory of evolution – a theory that includes such niceties as the coupling of variation and selection or the inheritance of acquired characteristics, which cultural evolution is supposed to exhibit (since the ideas acquired by one generation can be passed on to the next). In other words, the epistemologist brings back the very notions that neo-Darwinism had to discard in order to earn the prestige it enjoys today. Under close examination, thus, the analogical approach offers little in the way of justification or motivation. This is not to say that some analogies to evolution cannot be put to good use in epistemology, but that is a different story.

A third problem, at least in the eyes of most philosophers, is that an epistemology based on the history of science can only be descriptive, whereas a true epistemology has to be prescriptive. That is to say, the history of science presumably can only tell us what science is like, not what it ought to be like. It is the business of epistemology to do the second, not the first. Now, some philosophers have reacted to this argument by throwing up their hands and declaring that a descriptive epistemology is good enough. Hence Quine proposed that we should make epistemology a chapter of psychology. He thought that this amounted to a naturalization of epistemology. Again, the details do not bear out the sensational announcement, for Quine's idea of psychology was the behaviorism of B.F. Skinner, which, apart from its many internal difficulties, by making the mind a black box ruled out neuroscience and, therefore, the search for mechanisms through which natural selection can ground psychology. Granted that Quine was right in suggesting that, since the positivists' logical reconstructions of science were dismal failures, it made more sense simply to inquire into how science is actually generated. But his actual proposal would not only keep epistemology from understanding epistemic values, it would keep *psychology* from being naturalized.

There is no reason, however, for the epistemology of science to fear the distinction between describing and prescribing. We have already seen Hempel's acknowledgement that the norms of scientific method "explicated" by the logical positivists were actually drawn with an eye to the practice of science after all (Chapter 6). And earlier we saw that Popper's claim that the business of epistemology was to tell us how science ought to be done, not how it is actually done, which puts rationality and progress at odds, and that progress will win out in that confrontation (Chapter 4). In this chapter I will go even further and sketch a biological view of scientific rationality, a view more in line with the spirit, and occasionally with the word, of Lorenz's thought.

I do not wish to say that science is like nature, but rather that it is part of nature. Let me return to my account of the genesis of science. I claimed earlier that science is a social expression of intelligence in dealing with the world. A characteristic aspect of intelligence, Piaget tells us, is that it allows organisms to transcend the immediate demands of the environment so that they may behave to their greater advantage at a more convenient time and place. This indirect action of intelligence permits us, for example, to evaluate alternative courses of action on the basis of prior experience and to rehearse future actions in the imagination. Piaget found intelligence to be a powerful instrument of adaptation. His insight is buttressed by an analysis of the neural basis of intelligence. As the complexity of the central nervous system increases, so does the flexibility of its response. Information from the senses can now be rerouted, delayed, and stored; it can be compared with information from other sense modalities, as well as with previous information, and with expectation. As the complexity of the central nervous system increases, so does the number of modes of indirect action. Intelligence, of course, has many facets, but there is one in particular that suggests how adaptability may be increased. I am referring to curiosity.

Jacob Bronowski once said that curiosity liberates us from plain animalhood (1973). But as Konrad Lorenz pointed out (1971), curiosity exists in rats and ravens, as well as in many other animals, not just in humans. Curiosity is best seen as a form of play (with the environment) and as such it arises in situations that do not demand immediate attention to the environment. Animals play, or exhibit curiosity, not to satisfy hunger or sex drives directly, but because play (and curiosity as a form of it) provides a motivation of its own: It is enjoyable. In trying to satisfy its curiosity, an animal rehearses a wide range of skills, and of combinations of skills, that will later enable it to deal more effectively with the environment. For those skills, cognitive skills in this case, will permit the animal to either know its environment better or devise strategies by which to accomplish that goal (by knowing the environment better I mean developing means of dealing with the environment that lead to a more successful response). Through curiosity, others can adapt to environments for which their species have not been "designed," and still others, who preserve much of their playful character throughout their lives, can adapt to changing environments.

In the American Midwest, where I live, the cold temperatures alone would make it impossible for humans to survive year round, were it not for the fact that humans have applied their intelligence to produce clothing and shelter, to invent fire, and to protect themselves from the inclement weather in many other ways. To do even better than that, humans have applied their science and technology to transportation, and are thus able not only to live comfortably but to seek occasional respite from their environment in the benign climates of countries like Mexico and Australia.

The evolutionary justification of curiosity, and of play in general, can be found in the increased range of abilities that become useful later in life. But there is a cost to the individual. When playing with others or with the physical environment, an organism is not eating, it is not mating, and it is not doing anything of immediate use. To make matters worse, the organism is distracted by its play and may fail to notice the approach of a predator, or some other danger. The payoff is often long in the future. This postponement of material satisfaction is a wonderful illustration of the indirect action that intelligence permits. In any event, my suggestion is that we can find the origins of science at the juncture where human curiosity about the world becomes social.

Just as we came to hunt in groups – an exercise of another form of social intelligence –now we try to satisfy our curiosity in groups. There are two main reasons why this should be so. The first is simply that to explore our environment in great depth often requires the cooperation of others. An experiment in gravitational physics may have to be carried out beyond the Earth's atmosphere and will involve fields as diverse as rocketry, metallurgy, superconductors, chemistry and orbital dynamics, as well as the general theory of relativity. Even in the same field some projects are much too large to be taken up by a single investigator. At a certain level of sophistication, division of labor becomes of the essence.

The second reason is that the very attempt to satisfy one's curiosity in a specific way may well require the prior existence of an institution devoted to such a goal. One cannot just decide to study the interactions between hadrons and leptons unless one has entry into a society committed to a program of research in elementary particle physics – likewise, one cannot just decide to become a milkman in a continent where placental mammals do not exist.

Once it becomes social, the attempt to satisfy our curiosity about the world gains extraordinary power, and so do the skills that result from it. Now, if this general account is correct, we should expect that such a social enterprise (science) would allow us to:

(a) Have a more thorough interaction with the environment.

(b) Increase the number of environments to which we can adapt.

And (c), adapt to a changing environment.

As I have suggested, science does indeed provide such advantages (e.g., contemporary living in the Midwest). I do not mean to suggest also that in every case when a human skill takes on a social character it thereby becomes more effective. It was so in the case of hunting in the environments our ancestors faced until about ten thousand years ago. And it seems to me that is so in the case of science, too. What science has to offer, then, is a more thorough interaction with the environment and an increasing number of environments, including changing environments, to which we can adapt. This is the function that science may perform for us, if we choose to engage in it.

Not that curiosity guarantees survival. Because of its ability to deal with a greater range of environments, a species may move into a particularly rich environment. But subsequent changes in that environment may be so drastic that this particular species becomes extinct, in spite of its flexibility. Groups and individuals undergo similar tribulations. Because of curiosity, many animals will later accrue great advantages, even though at an early stage some of them will die because of perils that must be blamed on their curious nature. What curiosity increases, then, is the capacity for adaptation, even at the cost of increasing immediate risks.

It would be a mistake to think that organisms incapable of curiosity, let alone of developing science, cannot also be very adaptable. What increases adaptation (or the potential for adaptation) in one type of organism depends on the sorts of interactions organisms of that type can have with the environment. An opposable thumb may be of great value to animals that exhibit a certain skeletal structure and development of their central nervous system, e.g., humanoids, in many but not all environments. But to other types of animals, say horses or cockroaches, an opposable thumb would be disadvantageous or useless in most typical environments (**Figure 8.1**). Likewise, with intelligence: The increase in metabolism that would go hand in hand with an increase in the complexity of the central nervous system carries a price tag that may be too high for many organisms. A move in the direction of high intelligence, let alone its social telescoping into science cannot even begin.

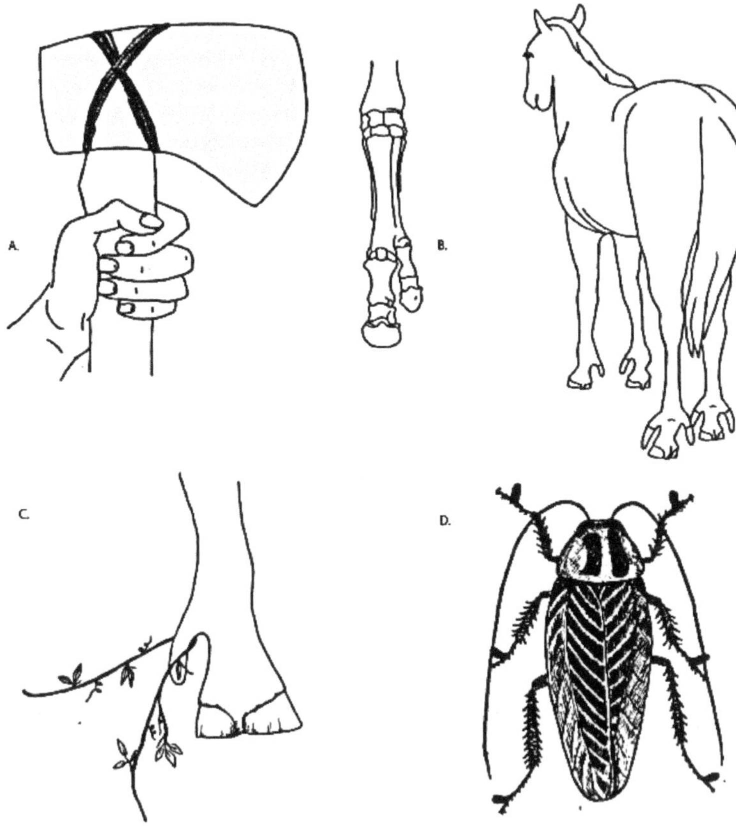

A. An opposable thumb gave our ancestors an evolutionary advantage.
B. A simliarly protruding digit became a hindrance for ancient horses, and it would be fatal to modern horses.
C. Vine trips horse
D. Where would a cockroach put a thumb?

Figure 8.1. An Opposable Thumb is not Advantageous for all Species. Drawings by Nicole Ankeny.

Nor should one think that every product of science, or every scientific skill or technique must be clearly adaptive. Surely, the model of science as arising out of curiosity does not entail such a conclusion. After all, not every skill that an animal develops in its play with the environment will later prove to be of the greatest usefulness. Some of them will be of no use at all. And others will be put to use indirectly. If science is play, as I suggest, we are likely to devise all sorts of games in exploring our world. And some of those games are bound to be very abstract and intricate. A few of those may greatly facilitate the development of some skills that will prove useful in our dealing with one or several environments (e.g., by providing for conceptual, mathematical, or instrumental elaborations of our theories). As it is, Kuhn already pointed out that much scientific work goes into the articulation of the main views we hold.

With this account of the genesis and nature of science in mind, let me now turn to the problem of rationality. Given that science is a communal enterprise with division of labor, the question of the rationality of science should be asked of science as a whole. This point goes directly against the typical manner in which philosophers have approached the question of rationality: They look at whether this or that great scientist, or research group, adhered to this or that set of methodological rules. But it seems to me that to approach the question in this manner is to commit a logical mistake. In trying to determine whether a football (soccer) team is good, we cannot merely look at whether its players are individually good. We wish to know instead the social and structural relations that the team exhibits during its games, whether, in short, it can play as a team. When a player creates space into which another can move to receive the ball and score, the social unit is working well. Even brilliant individual action often depends on good positioning by teammates that keep the defense guessing about what the next play is going to be. In any event, to ascribe the properties of the individual members to the whole team would be a mistake. And it seems to me that the same is true in science.

I propose that the question, "What would it take for science to be rational?" should be thought equivalent to the question, "How should science be structured so as to perform its function?" My evolutionary account forces us to pose the question in this way, and it also suggests how to answer it. To determine how science should be structured or organized so as to perform its function is to determine what it would take for science to enable us to adapt to new environments or to a changing environment, and so on.

We may then easily realize that scientific views are often designed to make sense of a particular environment: that of our experience. But success in one environment, or in one context, does not guarantee success in others. If the environment or context is likely to change, it pays to have a strategy for generating alternative points of view. That is, an organizational requirement of science is that it should allow dissension and the generation of alternatives. This requirement of intellectual freedom must be accompanied by another: Scientific views must be given a chance to develop. They have to begin like all ideas: small and almost certainly vague. But if we see some promise in them, we should not abandon them just because they are in conflict with the evidence. We may do so, but we should not have to. Otherwise, ideas would never blossom into glorious scientific achievements. Let us recall a key reason why counter-evidence need not be always decisive: Observation and experiment always have to be interpreted, but the interpretation that makes them into counter-evidence may depend on theories that the very development of the new ideas would expose as inadequate.

These two requirements of intellectual freedom, that science must be organized so as to permit and perhaps encourage the generation and development of new ideas, must be met by science as a whole, not necessarily by individual scientists. Some scientists will generate new approaches, others will develop them in a very stubborn fashion, and still others will reject all but the accepted views of the time. Some scientists will be open-minded and some will not. It does not matter, as long as there is enough room in science for all kinds. If there is, if science does employ a strategy for accepting and developing new ideas, then science will be in a better position to adapt flexibly to new challenges. It will thus permit us to deal with new or with changing environments. If so, it will perform its function, the function suggested by my biological account. And in a very straightforward means-ends analysis of rationality, we should conclude that science would then be a rational enterprise.

Notice that this means-ends analysis also provides a recipe for solving the contemporary problem of scientific rationality. Two demands were placed upon the epistemologist. The first was that science should proceed in such a manner that its practitioners generate opportune methods and procedures. When viewed from the perspective of my social conception of rationality, science offers precisely a general strategy to improve the chances of accomplishing the desired goal. The second demand is that the first should be met without tying science to the dangers of being ruled by a stagnant elite. The two requirements of freedom under the social conception will reduce such dangers.

After determining what science ought to be like, however, we still need to know whether science is actually rational. I think that it is largely so. Even under the most challenging description of the history of science, i.e., Feyerabend's, we can see that science exhibits the required strategies. Indeed, what I have called the two requirements of intellectual freedom overlap to a great extent with Feyerabend's principles of proliferation and tenacity (Chapter 6). What looks like anarchy under a conception that equates rationality with adherence to methodological standards, now looks like the very sort of organizational structure that science ought to have. With the shift to a social conception, we also shift from looking for rationality in the choice of theory to finding rationality in the ability to reach certain goals. As it happens in science itself, the solution of a problem takes place within a transformation of outlook in the field.

I do not mean to say, incidentally, that irrationality at the level of the individual becomes rationality at the social level. My point is rather that the concept of scientific rationality no longer should be applied to individual scientists. Social properties are social properties. Nevertheless, there are many other ways in which the question of individual rationality may still come up. For example, once a certain view of the world is found promising, by a scientist or group of scientists, procedures are devised for developing it further and for testing it. Many goals and subgoals must then be reached, and some means may be more effective in reaching those goals. Once more we would use a means-ends analysis of rationality.

In the transformation of epistemology that ensues from taking seriously the idea that science is part of nature, not everything is entirely new. Many readers will no doubt have already noticed the similarity between my requirements of intellectual freedom and the conditions for the growth of science put forth by other philosophers, Toulmin (1972) for example. The crucial difference is that whereas for Toulmin such conditions lead to the evolution of populations of ideas, for me they lead to an increase in the adaptability of the human societies that practice science. This shift to a truly naturalistic epistemology can better place the work of many other epistemologists with social and naturalistic inclinations. For we all wish primarily to understand science, not to draw philosophical distinctions that protect the autonomy of epistemology at the price of keeping the nature of science beyond our grasp.

Once upon a time, such a distinction, between description and prescription, seemed to doom naturalistic approaches to something less than a genuine epistemology. But now we can brush this qualm aside and get on with our naturalistic programs. One task that still must be done in much greater detail is the determination of the social, organizational, or institutional dynamics by which science can best perform its function. For example, the interplay between the two requirements of intellectual freedom, striking out for novelty and sticking to one's point of view, is not restricted to big groups of scientists at odds with other groups. Such interplay takes place in many ways, and some of them are described, for example, in several papers in *Issues in Evolutionary Epistemology*, edited by K. Hahlweg and C.A. Hooker (1989). In that book, Hooker, to name one author, tells us about hierarchical levels, or layers, with a variety of feedback loops. In his model, individual scientists will fill one or several institutional roles, but in doing so they will find themselves sometimes in cooperation and sometimes at odds with other scientists with different institutional roles. For instance, a team of physicists working on the same project may well represent different areas of expertise within physics. In his institutional role, or in his role within the group, the plasma physicist should push his particular perspective as to what is important, and so should the particle physicist. The mathematical physicist will have other concerns that the group may face sooner or later. Hooker is right in suggesting that we will find some overlap as well as some different ideas on what to do and how to interpret what has been done. When the research group interacts with another research group, as Kuppers tell us, I imagine that we will find many other opportunities for variation and recombination, as well as for preserving the view initially favored by the group. I purposely chose a biological analogy here, for I think that in tasks such as these analogical reasoning has its greatest role to play. I have in mind, for example, the work of David Hull (1978). In particular, I find very useful his accounts of the way in which rewards in science help achieve cooperation and keep the discipline honest. We must bear in mind, however, that even though analogies suggest hypotheses about the mechanisms that determine the social dynamics of science, those hypotheses will eventually have to stand on their own.

Traditional philosophy is not very likely to take kindly to my approach. I cannot attempt to refute every conceivable objection in the space of one chapter, but let me go over one of the main sources of discontent: the feeling that I am treating rationality as the product of an invisible hand mechanism and that there is something terribly wrong about doing so. One way to express this feeling is that on my account scientific rationality would not be the product of conscious deliberation (since science as a whole seldom deliberates), and thus it is inappropriate to speak of rationality. If a means-end analysis is to be employed, we had better know what the ends are supposed to be and how the means will get them for us. Nevertheless, it seems to me instead that this very demand for conscious deliberation is inappropriate. Philosophers of science have been trying to determine for centuries what scientists ought to do, or what they do when behaving close to ideally. But these philosophers have been seldom deterred by what scientists announced their method is, for often scientists say one thing and do another – and they may do the wrong thing anyway. The "real" scientific method was then not part of the public domain, surely not a matter of conscious deliberation. As Lakatos (1978) put it, the philosopher's job is to discover the universal criteria that great scientists applied sub- or semi-consciously in their evaluation of particular cases. I do not believe there are any such universal criteria, but the point is that mainstream philosophy of science has always found it comfortable to speak of rationality in the absence of conscious deliberation. If this is an objection to my view, then it is an objection against doing mainstream philosophy of science at all.

A second way of expressing the nagging feeling is that if science is part of nature then it is somehow inevitable; and if it is inevitable, what is the point of talking about rationality? It seems to me, however, that our natural talents may or may not be developed: We often choose what to do about them. As basic a skill as eating may or may not be properly exercised (just look at practically any crowd of human beings in any Western city); or we may choose not to exercise it at all and starve ourselves to death out of spite or political passion. That our ability to produce science is a product of natural history need not prevent our choosing whether to practice it more, less, or not at all. We may be lazy or not daring enough. Moreover, science would be one of many social skills. In many social situations, science would not arise because it would conflict with and bring into question the society's mechanisms for preserving the cohesion of the group (e.g., religion). And there may be other conflicts as well. Once we see science as part of nature, however, we can understand it better, and we may also frame better questions about its rationality and its worth.

This brings us to a very important point. I speak of science as rational because the ends it permits us to achieve are presumably worth achieving. I have spoken of how science permits us to deal with new or changing environments, of adaptability in short. Given my naturalistic account, it seems that science has some worthwhile function to perform for us. But is that function truly worthwhile? Should adaptability take precedence over other goals that human beings may also have? The question of the rationality of science thus leads very naturally into questions about values, not just epistemic values but also social and moral values. Hard-nosed epistemologists may find this result a matter of despair. It is bad enough to worry about the rationality of science without also having to fight our way out of the morass of value. But I think that the situation is much more encouraging than that. With the standard inferential models with which philosophers have tackled questions of value, we could not get very far. But I have proposed elsewhere a causal theory of value in which knowledge and value form an intricate network that can be criticized in a variety of ways (1998). In any event, a naturalistic account thrives not by ignoring the normative aspect of human thought, but by joining that aspect with the rest of our nature.

I trust that what has been said so far establishes evolutionary epistemology as a genuine epistemology. I would like to mention briefly other areas of epistemology where a truly evolutionary approach has important contributions to make. One of them is the issue of realism, in which evolutionary considerations can be powerful philosophical tools. As I see it, a truly evolutionary epistemology commits us to a very sophisticated relativism. This will be the topic of the following two chapters.

A second area is in our understanding of the origins and motivations of science. It is a commonplace for philosophers to say that science has its origin in problem-solving. Popper (1972) and others have stressed this point throughout their work. But this commonplace can be misleading. As I have argued, and as scientific intuition often demands, science has its origin instead in curiosity, in our play with the world. Science is essentially play, a game. Within games there are always problems to solve, but it seems to me that to speak of problem solving, in this sense, is not very informative.

A third area directly affects some of the concerns expressed by contemporary evolutionary epistemologists. For many decades now, epistemologists have been trying to explain the history of science as rational, with mixed results, to be charitable. To some, evolutionary theory appears full of promise in tackling this task. But if we take evolution seriously enough to see science as part of nature, the epistemological task may begin to look like an unnecessary compulsion: For science should then be seen as part of the human phenotype, as other behavior surely is. Consider organisms as simple as bacteria. In a poor environment, one type of bacteria will prey on their competitors. If the environment becomes rich in nutrients, the bacteria will change their behavior radically: they will move away instead. We can explain their behavior by reference to their internal organization, their past history, and so on. But this explanation must go beyond an account of the two phenotypic states, of the history of the behavior itself. The second behavior does not "follow" from the first in a logical or rational way. The organism simply undergoes a radical change of posture toward the environment. What allows us to make sense of the change is the knowledge of the nature of the organism and the character of its interaction with the environment. And it appears to me that we cannot exclude the same kind of considerations in the case of human science.

If science is part of the human phenotype, there need not be logical or rational continuity from one stage of its history to the next. In that sense of "rational" science will often not be rational, for satisfying our curiosity about the world may demand, on occasion, a radical change in our approach to the game. The behavior of the small infant need not be continuous with that of the older child, although the change from one to the other may be explained by Piagetean considerations about ontogeny. In a similar fashion, the content of our science at a certain stage in development need not be continuous with that which follows it (although in many actual cases there could be quite a bit of continuity). For under radical pressures or the excitement of truly radical new ideas, science may switch just as radically from one point of view to another. The rationality of science should not depend, then, on the logical continuity of its content. We may find it instead outside of that history: in the mechanisms that bring about science and in the function that they allow it to perform.

REFERENCES

Bronowski, J. Television series: *The Ascent of Man*, 1973.

Hahlweg, K., Hooker, C.A. (1989). Eds., *Issues in Evolutionary Epistemology*, Volume 3, No. 2, SUNY Press.

Hull, D. (1978). "Altruism in Science: A Sociobiological Model of Co-operative Behavior Among Scientists", *Animal Behavior*: 26.

Lakatos, I. (1978). "The Problem of Appraising Scientific Theories", in his *Mathematics, Science and Epistemology*. Cambridge University Press.

Lorenz, K. (1971). *Studies in Animal Behavior*. Harvard University Press.

Munévar, G. (1981). *Radical Knowledge: A Philosophical Inquiry into the Nature and Limits of Science*, Avebury Publishing Co. and Hackett Publishing Co.

Munévar, G. (1998). "The Morality of Rational Ants." Chapter 10 of *Evolution and the Naked Truth*, Ashgate Publishing Ltd.

Piaget, J. (1972). *The Psychology of Intelligence*. Littlefield, Adams & Co.

Popper, K. (1972). *Objective Knowledge*. Oxford Univ. Press.

Quine, W.V.O. (1969). "Epistemology Naturalized," in his *Ontological Relativity and Other Essays*. Columbia University Press.

Toulmin, S. (1972). *Human Understanding*, vol. 1. Princeton University Press.

CHAPTER 9
EVOLUTIONARY RELATIVISM

The view that science is typically a cumulative, progressive process, as suggested by some historians of science and some scientific realists, is undermined both by history and by evolutionary considerations about the nature of science. The attempts to use evolutionary biology to portray scientific development as continuous are based on unfortunate analogies to the evolution of life, as we saw in the previous chapter. Non-evolutionary approaches for the historical continuity of science, such as Lakatos', do not fare much better, as we saw in Chapter 7. A proper application of evolutionary biology, in combination with neuroscience, defeats the case for realism and leads to the realization that science is not only open to radical transformation, as history indicates, but that it should be so. That will be an important topic of this chapter and the next.

Scientific Realism is the view that the world has a certain structure, and that it is the function of science to try to find that structure. One important version of scientific realism holds that this view is supported by the success of science, because, as Richard Boyd says (1992), truth is the only reasonable explanation of that success. In this he follows Hilary Putnam (1975, 79), who argued that realism "is the only philosophy that doesn't make the success of science a miracle." Such a position has been elaborated from then until the present by a variety of authors, with comments from J. Brown (1982), P. Lipton (1994), S. Psillos (1999), E.C. Barnes (2002), T. D. Lyons (2003), J. Busch (2008), G. Frost-Arnold (2010), and F. Dellsén (2016).

By contrast, *Evolutionary Relativism* holds that an organism's view of the world depends on its mind, that mind depends on biology, that biology supports a logically impeccable form of relativism, and that success explains the truth, not the other way around (1998). This approach is consistent with the history of science and with the science most relevant to understanding the pursuit of knowledge.

INTRODUCTION

There are two particular intuitions that afflict many philosophers. One is that realism must be right – even if they cannot prove it. Another is that relativism must be wrong – and they think they can easily show this. An important purpose of this chapter is to argue that these intuitions are misguided.

Behind the first intuition is the feeling that if realism is not right, pursuing science makes little sense. After all, the business of science is presumably to investigate what is *out there.* If talking about what is out there is pointless (e.g., because realism is false or nonsense) then science has no particular significance. Popper, for instance, talks about realism as a metaphysical presupposition of doing science (1972, 203). Of course, trying to show that realism is true has been such a messy affair that many philosophers, particularly in the 20th century, achieved great sophistication in washing their hands of the issue. Nevertheless, realism seems to come as standard equipment for most philosophers. According to Richard Boyd, as we have seen, only realism can explain why scientific success is not a mystery (1992).

ABSOLUTE TRUTH VS. SUCCESS

Popper and Boyd notwithstanding, when we look into the history of science, we find a disturbing separation between "absolute truth" and success. Greek astronomy postulated a universe with two basic spheres: The Earth in the center and the sphere of stars on the outer edge. This model has been an excellent guide to navigation. Only in the last century did modern science surpass it (with the help of electronic inventions, e.g., satellites that indicate position, etc.). That is, during more than two thousand years a completely false point of view has had great success in an area of great importance to the survival and welfare of human beings.

Boyd's claim that only realism can explain the success of science thus seems less than compelling. To make matters worse for him, the most successful scientific field of the last century is quantum physics, and quantum physics in its orthodox interpretation is decidedly anti-realist. At least that is what Niels Bohr, the foremost thinker in the field, said explicitly: "...an independent reality in the ordinary physical sense can neither be ascribed to the phenomena nor to the agencies of observation" ("The Quantum Postulate and the Recent Development of Atomic Theory," in *The Philosophical writings of Neil's Bohr,* Ox Bow, 1987, 54). By "phenomena" Bohr does not mean the sense data of philosophers but the *measured* subatomic objects. Phenomena are always the result of specific interactions with specific measuring equipment; but we should not thus conclude that they are two separate things, one of which gives us information about the other, for Bohr insists in the "*impossibility of any sharp separation between the behavior of atomic objects and the interaction with the measuring instruments which serve to define the conditions under which the phenomena appear*" ("Discussion with Einstein," in *Albert Einstein: Philosopher Scientist,* P. Schilpp, ed, Open Court, 1982, 210).

This interactionist view has many unpleasant philosophical consequences. One of them results from the fact that some measuring arrangements exclude others.

In some an electron will behave as a wave, in others as a particle, but never as both. It all depends on what kind of experimental arrangement we employ, and thus we end up with *complementary* descriptions, as happens in the Two-Slit Experiment (**Figure 9.1**). *Real* things, however, supposedly cannot behave this way. If we are realists, we want to know *the* way the electron really is. These complementary descriptions, moreover, cover the gamut of Heisenberg's uncertainty relations. One experiment arrangement allows us to measure the momentum of a particle, but it brings about an uncertainty in its position, and so on. Given all of these considerations it seems unjustified to ascribe an independent reality to those subatomic objects. Furthermore, insisting on their independent reality requires doing away with the complementary of arrangements (and therefore of descriptions) that is inconsistent with that reality. But then we rule out discovering important aspects of the subatomic "realm." As Bohr puts it, "In fact, it is only mutually exclusive of two experimental procedures, permitting the unambiguous definition of complementary physical quantities, which provides room for new physical laws, the coexistence of what might at first sight appear irreconcilable with the basic principles of science" ("Can Quantum Mechanical Description be Complete?" in S. Toulmin, ed., *Physical Reality*, Harper & Row, 1970, 139).

Bohr thus made it clear that realist explanations in quantum physics preclude the ability to predict successfully in that area. That is, realism does not only fail to explain the success of quantum physics but the appeal to it hinders that success. In Bohr's words: "...radiation in free space as well as isolated material particles are abstractions, their properties on the quantum theory being definable and observable only through their interaction with other systems" (*Philosophical Writings*, 56-7). Indeed, for the reasons previously stated, such interactions entail "the necessity of a final renunciation of the classical idea of causality and a radical revision of our attitude towards the problem of physical reality" ("Can Physical..., 132).

Whereas many philosophers find Bohr's words are very unintuitive, great sympathy has instead greeted the realist position defended by Einstein, Bohr's main opponent in the dispute concerning the interpretation of quantum mechanics. This is not the place for an analysis of that dispute. But it is a good place to begin an examination of the metaphysical urgency so many feel in favor of realism. Presumably, the success of science is an extraordinary event that clamors for an explanation; and only realism gives science its due. Science works because either it gets at the truth about the world or at least approximates such truth. Let us take, then, a further look at realism, even though, as the history of science shows us, the required connection between truth and success is rather doubtful.

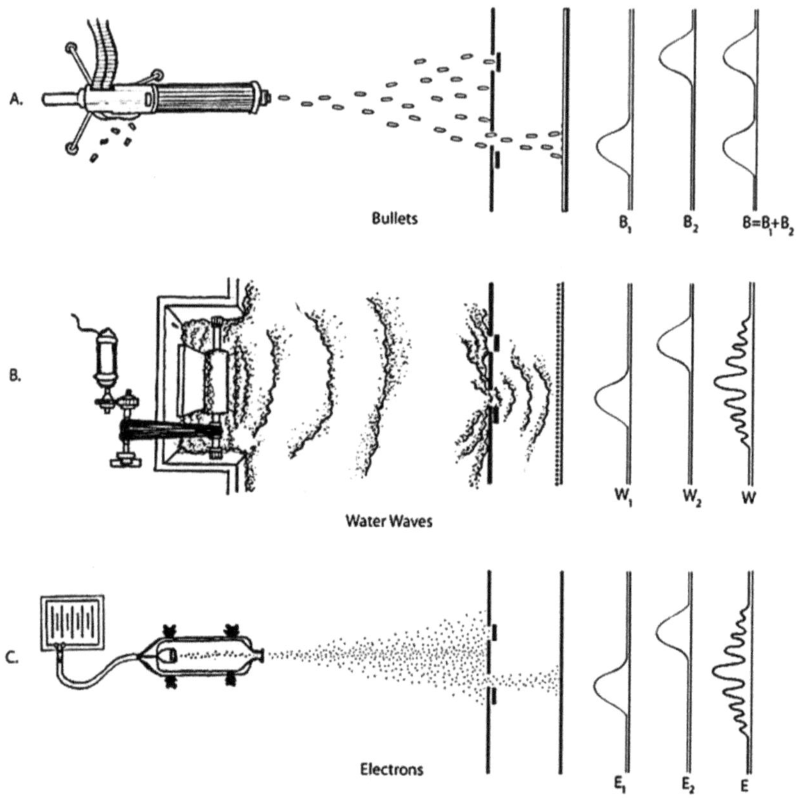

Figure 9.1. Double-Slit Experiment. Drawing by Nicole Ankeny.

A: When bullets pass through one slit, they leave a distribution of traces in front of the slit. When the two slits are open, the final distribution is simply the superimposition of the two independent slit distributions.

B: Analogous experiment with water waves. Observe the interference pattern when the two slits are open.

C: When photons or electrons pass through either one of the slits, their distribution resembles that of bullets. But when the two slits are open, the final distribution exhibits an interference pattern, which is what should be expected of waves passing through two slits. Drawing by Nicole Ankeny, adapted from H.R. Pagels (1982) *The Cosmic Code.* Simon and Schuster.

NATURAL SELECTION, PERCEPTION AND REALISM

Some may think that evolution supports scientific realism, for even at the level of perception it seems clear that (approximately) true or veridical perceptions give an organism a greater chance to survive. Organisms with false perceptions, instead, are likely doomed. And by truth they mean correspondence to the way things really are.

Considerations from evolutionary biology, neuropsychology, and other scientific fields, however, make implausible the claim that veridical ideas or perceptions are required to explain evolutionary success. In what follows I will informally present a sketch of an argument I have given elsewhere (1981, 1998), but my main intent is to present a series of scientific findings, influenced by evolution, that support my attempt to undermine the impulse to realism.

Given our previous discussion of Galileo, his comments on perceptual realism should not come as a surprise:

> ...tastes, odors, colors, etc., so far as their objective evidence is concerned, are nothing but mere names for something which resides exclusively in our sensitive body... so that if the perceiving creatures were removed, all of these qualities would be annihilated and abolished from existence" (1623).

What may surprise some is that Galileo's attitude, albeit with an evolutionary turn, is quite common today among scientists whose work must take perception into account. As the neuroscientist V.S. Johnston tells us (1999), we must abandon the common-sense view of reality, because:

> ...although the external environment is teeming with electromagnetic radiation and air pressure waves, without consciousness it is both totally black and utterly silent. Conscious experiences, such as our sensations and feelings, are nothing more than evolved illusions generated within biological brains.

Consider an example: The color spectrum is linear; our experience of the spectrum is not. Perceptually, red and green are "opposing" colors, but the wavelength difference between them is barely 1 / 150,000,000,000 m. Why do we perceive such an extraordinarily small difference then? Evolution gives us the reason: Green "corresponds" to a band of frequencies reflected in normal white light by chlorophyll molecules, whose detection would have given an evolutionary advantage to our remote ancestors. Perception of other colors such as red and blue helps fix the detection of chlorophyll at dawn and dusk and in cloudy days. In a different place where vital resources depend on different chemical compounds, evolution may bring about a different perceptual parceling of the color spectrum. This means that the "normal" color experiences of creatures on Earth and on Carnap II (a yet to be discovered planet in Andromeda) may be quite different, even at the hypothetical level of the "sense data" so beloved by the logical positivists.

BRAIN AND TRUTH: DOUBTS

Visual paradoxes

To understand this anti-realist position on perception, let us begin by considering the peculiarities of visual perception to which Donald D. Hoffman (1998) draws our attention. In accordance with his remarks, when looking at **Figure 9.2** we see clearly a three-dimensional image. But we know it is a two-dimensional drawing. When I project it on a screen, I run my hand up and down and sideways over it. My hand confirms what my intellect affirms: It is not three dimensional. But try as we might, we see it as three dimensional. That is, we see it as it is not. Of course, there are reasons why our visual mechanism works this way, and one of them is that, as we will see below, there are evolutionary advantages, at least on occasion, for perceiving falsely.

Figure 9.2. Drawing courtesy of Ruoyu Huang.

We are similarly baffled by **Figure 9.3**, the Kanizsa Triangle, created by Italian psychologist and artist Gaetano Kanizsa (1976). Though the figure contains no actual triangles, the contours and careful positioning of the shapes produce perceptions of two triangles. The center negative space is viewed as a triangle, which "pops out" at the viewer. The triangle appears brighter than the background, though the background has the same luminosity as the center.

Figure 9.3. Image by Fibonacci CC BY-SA 3.0.

Vision produces images that are perplexing or false, but also some that are downright inconsistent, as we can appreciate in Oscar Reutersvard's "Impossible Triangle" (**Figure 9.4**). This is no mere "paper trick." Our visual mechanism can produce such images in the "real world," as Richard Gregory showed by constructing out of wood the sort of object we see in **Figure 9.5**. When viewed from a certain angle, the image will be that of the Impossible Triangle.

Figure 9.4. Impossible Triangle. Image by Phillip McMurray. Model created by samtimes CC BY 4.0.

Figure 9.5. R. Gregory's wood construction seen as the Impossible Triangle from the right angle. Image by Phillip McMurray. Model created by samtimes CC BY 4.0.

Perceptual illusions are quite common. In "change blindness," for example, we fail to notice that important features of the scene have changed or disappeared (e.g., in watching what we take to be two copies of the same picture of a man sitting at his computer, we fail to notice that in the second "copy" the keyboard is missing!). And in one experiment at Cornell, two men carrying a large door interrupted the conversation (the subject was being asked for directions) by walking between the experimenter and the subject. While the two men walked by with the door, the experimenter was replaced by someone else, who continued the conversation, but the subject didn't realize it –"inattentional blindness" (Blackmore, 2002). It appears that perception often works to give us the "gist" of the scene rather than a feature-by-feature representation.

The extraordinary complexity of the brain mechanisms that produce our perceptions contrasts starkly with the ready-to-be-used character of the perceptions they produce. Instead of the realist impulse, it seems more sensible to suppose that the brain constructs perceptions that will allow us to interact promptly and successfully (at least much of the time) with our environment. Thus, when we look at a scene full of snow (or dots, or letters) but there is a different feature in our blind spot, we do not see the feature: Instead, our brain fills the blind spot with more of the same – snow, or dots, or letters (Blackmore, 2002). This construction by the brain is more than a bet on what is most likely to be in front of us. Indeed, the brain takes the direct response of its own neurons to sensory input and transforms it into a meaningful perception that is in important respects different from that response. As Edelman and Tononi (2000) point out:

> ...the activity of many neurons in sensory...pathways can be correlated with rapidly varying details of a sensory input...but do not seem to map to conscious experience. For example, patterns of neural activity in the retina and other early visual structures *are in constant flux* and correspond more or less faithfully to spatial and temporal details of the rapidly changing visual input. However, *a conscious visual scene is considerably more stable*, and it deals with properties of objects that are *invariant* under changes in position or illumination, properties that are easily recognized and manipulated. (My italics)

Hoffman's remarks on illusions show how far the brain may go in constructing perception. In **Figure 9.2**, for example, we know that the perception is radically different from the sensory input. Perceptions, he explains with a very apt metaphor, are like the icons that appear on user-friendly computer screens. The actual software and hardware those icons "stand for" are complicated and beyond the knowledge of most computer users. The colorful, easy-to-identify icons constructed by the programs are not like anything in particular – they are not like the programs, certainly – but they are convenient "symbols" for them. The relation is arbitrary, since the symbols could have been quite different. Similarly, the relation between our perceptions and those "real" objects they are supposed to be about (and that, in some accounts, produce them) is arbitrary. They could have been quite different also. Let us consider the case of color.

EVOLUTION: PRAGMATISM, NOT TRUTH (AS CORRESPONDENCE)

Evolution and Contrast

As we have seen, even creatures somewhat similar to terrestrial land mammals may chromatically divide the world differently from the way we do and might thus experience different colors when looking at our "green" grass and "red" apples. But we need not travel to other planetary systems. Right here in the Earth's ocean we find shrimp with as many as eleven primary colors (Koch, 2004), instead of our three primary colors (red, green and blue) which combine to produce the others, according to Young and Helmholtz's trichromatic theory of color vision. The biological basis for this theory is provided by the relative activation of our three types of cones (Koch, 2004). Some women actually have four types of cones and are thus likely to make more color discriminations than men. The shrimp mentioned earlier may share our planet, but their "world" is quite different from ours, and so are their environmental challenges and opportunities. It should not be surprising, then, that their color experience should be different as well. And there are also the better-known cases of birds, snakes, and insects that *see* portions of the electromagnetic spectrum that remain dark to us (ultraviolet or infrared). Being able to do so is clearly advantageous to them.

These considerations suggest that the "reason" for perception is pragmatic and that there is nothing intrinsic about "greenness" or "redness" (in corresponding to essential "features" of the world).

Some perceptions are useful abstractions. For example, Hoffman reminds us of the work of the ethologist Niko Tinbergen. In **Figure 9.6** we see some of the "icons" that permit ducklings to make instant decisions on which their lives may depend. The two images are crosses. If the cross is seen moving in the direction of its long end, it is a harmless "goose." But if it is seen moving in the direction of its short end, it is a dangerous "hawk" and the ducklings run for cover. In amusing experiments, Timbergen fooled the ducklings with cardboard figures. But in their regular environment such perceptions are crucial to the ducklings' survival.

Figure 9.6. Tinbergen's cardboard figure. Image by Phillip McMurray.

False Color and Exaggeration

The present evolutionary line of thought is strengthened by the discovery that perception works through exaggeration, particularly when small differences of degree are perceived as drastic differences in kind. This process of radical, false contrast is the same as that employed by space science in its observation of other worlds (and of our own planet, for that matter). I have in mind so-called "false color," in which arbitrary bands of electromagnetic frequencies can be assigned colors arbitrarily (or rather, for pragmatic reasons). In **Figure 9.7** we see examples of false color that help us determine at a glance patterns of global temperatures. We can also photograph contiguous regions made of materials of slightly different hues of brown and show them instead in clear-cut patterns of, say, purple and gold.

Figure 9.7. False color helps us see world temperatures. Photo Courtesy of NASA.

Perception works similarly: Without exaggeration and contrast it would be very difficult to make the distinctions we need to make (and to make quickly oftentimes) in order to survive. **Figure 9.8** gives us another example of the value of contrast and exaggeration. In a certain sense, we might quip, the more false (exaggerated) the perception, the more likely it is to succeed.

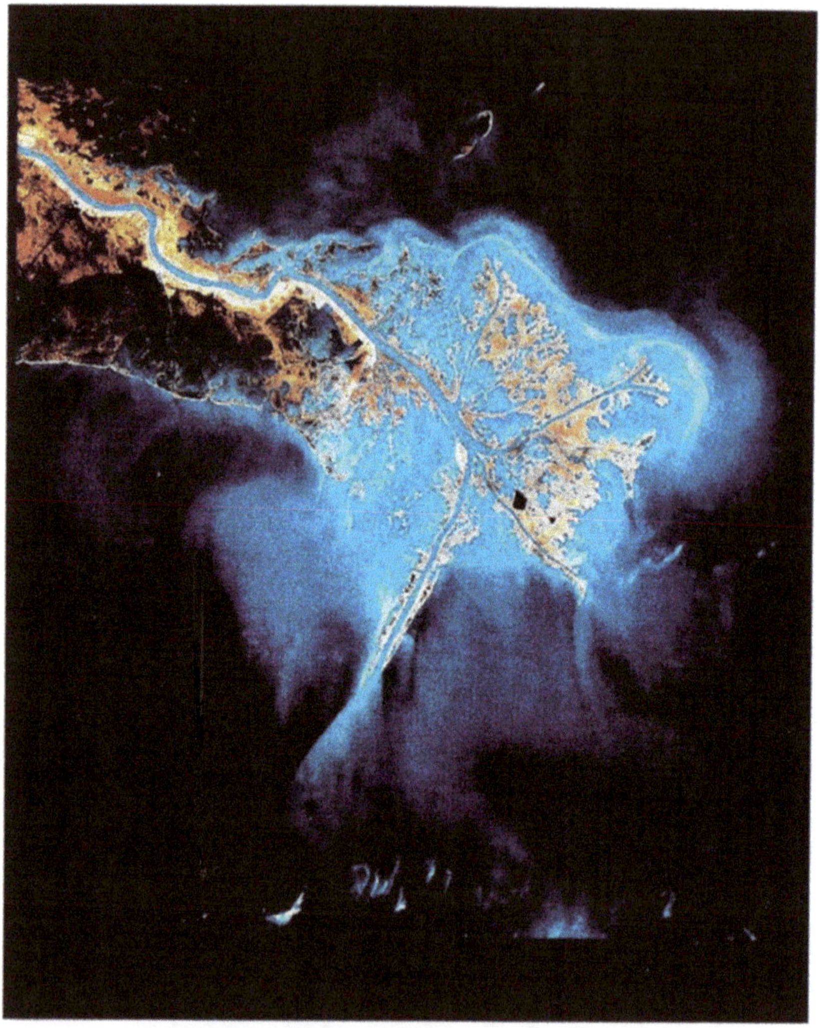

Figure 9.8. Sediment Transport by the Mississippi River into the Gulf of Mexico. Picture by the Landsat Thematic Mapper. Courtesy of NASA.

Useful contrast is the key to perceptual success, not faithful resemblance. In **Figures 9.9** and **9.10** we see radar images of Venus. In **Figure 9.9** we have a picture taken by NASA's Magellan spacecraft in which we benefit from the contrast provided by false color. In **Figure 9.10** we have the same picture but without color. In **Figure 9.11** and **Figure 9.12** we encounter another contrasting set. Thanks to false color, **Figure 9.12** reveals important tectonic features of Earth.

Figure 9.9. False color radar of Venus revealing features of the surface. Courtesy of NASA.

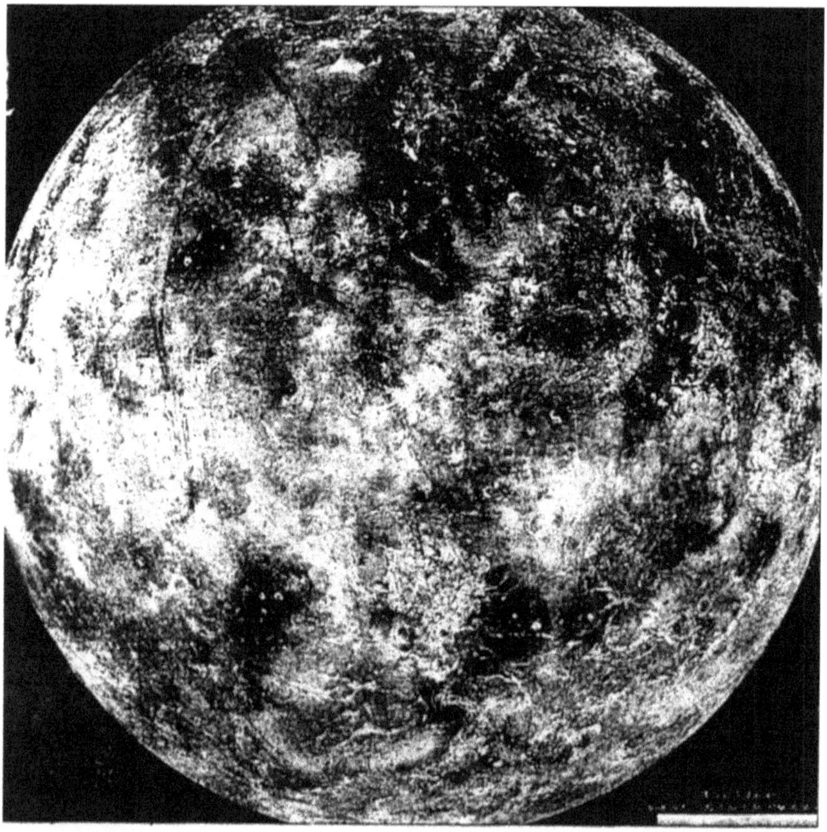

Figure 9.10. Same as Fig. 9.9 but without false color. Courtesy of NASA.

Figure 9.11. Atlantic Ocean without color. Courtesy of NASA.

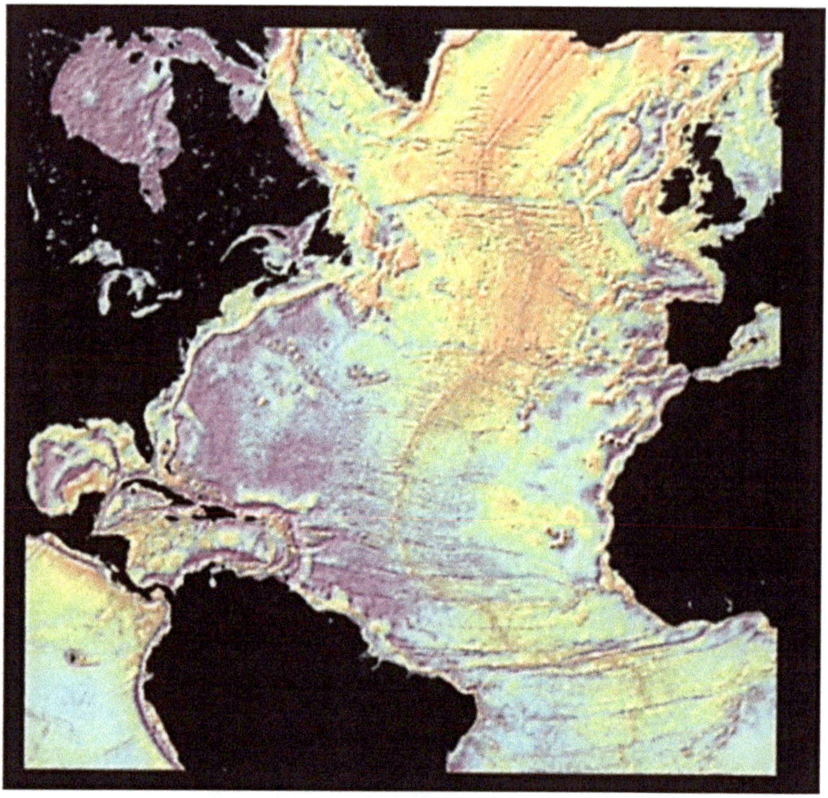

Figure 9.12. False-color picture of important tectonic features in the Atlantic Ocean. Courtesy of NASA.

We are thus led again to the reasonable hypothesis that the assignment of a particular color experience to the perception of objects that reflect the light of a certain frequency is quite arbitrary, this time in the sense that vision depends on the photo-chemicals that were around when primitive organisms began to take advantage of the color spectrum. In a different place that had different photo-chemicals at hand when the need arose, "red" may well look like who knows what, even when the discrimination is made exactly over the wavelength of our red. From the perspective of natural history, the point is (1) to be able to use some chemical compounds that allow for the discrimination of the color of objects that are key to survival and reproduction, and (2) to be able to experience them in a way that allows the organism to discriminate between them.

The Role of Memory and Emotion in Perception

The myriad reflections that hit our retina could be interpreted by the brain in a great many ways. Perhaps the biggest problem the brain faces is how to resolve ambiguity or vagueness. But it resolves them often enough, otherwise the organism would be unlikely to manage in the world. The mammalian brain, in particular, has evolved an appropriate structure. As Paul Churchland (1995) explains it, the lateral geniculate nucleus (LGN), for example, "projects a massive cable of ascending axons forward to your visual cortex. Curiously, the neurons in your visual cortex project ten times as many descending axons to make synaptic connections within the LGN." As he says, this pattern is "widespread throughout the brain." "Higher" centers in the cortex can, thus, by means of these descending axons, affect "lower" LGN neurons' response to stimuli with previous information, concerns, etc. What this means is that previous states of the brain partially determine your present perception, often by tilting the arrangement of the otherwise confusing patterns of light hitting your retina in favor of one interpretation found meaningful on the basis of previous experience.

Perception is also often influenced by evolutionary considerations, many of which do their work in subcortical areas. Francis Crick (1984) suggested the thalamic reticular nucleus plays a big role in the processing or filtering of potential perceptual consciousness, a suggestion vindicated recently. M. Halassa and his team (Wimmer et al., 2015) individuated a complicated neural circuit that also includes the basal ganglia. Most of the activity of this circuit concerning perception is the massive inhibition of incoming signals. In addition, the signals that are favored involve movement, size, and bright coloring, as well as other properties that would be relevant to being able to survive or adapt to the environment. For example, Tadin et al. (2019) found inhibition of the detection of large objects in favor of the perception of the motion of small objects.

This construction of perception through brain structure makes use of many neuronal networks, including those that involve emotions. Emotions can, of course, interfere with useful perception, but they may also provide the key to resolving perceptual ambiguities. The reason they can do so is that they provide us with what Edelman and Tononi call "value systems." In neuronal terms, of several possible interpretations, emotions will tilt the perceptual system towards those that are most significant for, say, our survival (so a tiger's face will suddenly stick out of the jungle's canopy). Not unlike perception itself, emotions also work by exaggeration, by tending to react very strongly to subtle differences in the situations in which we find ourselves (Johnston, 2000). Once again, exaggeration and contrast, rather than "true" representation are the keys to success.

Emotions motivate us to action. They do so by exaggeration, by tending to react very strongly to subtle differences in the situations in which we find ourselves. In this, the brain adapts us to the world as it does with perception. Nevertheless, wise people advise us to let reason prevail over emotion. To prevent the interference of emotion, we are urged to deliberate with a cool, logical head. One of the most popular examples of the rational man was a fictional alien: Mr. Spock, in the television series "Star Trek," whose control over his emotions was truly extraordinary.

Neuroscience, however, suggests that Mr. Spock would not have been a very effective starship officer. Antonio Damasio, in his *Descartes' Error* (1994), describes how some patients with severe frontal lobe damage do well in intelligence tests but are unable to function properly: They become incapable of making practical decisions at work and in their personal lives. It seems that their thinking gears just spin pointlessly, that they reason without a proper context and cannot bring their thinking to a decision to act. The explanation seems to be that the damage to their frontal lobe affects the interface between emotion and reasoning. The outcome is that their reasoning is not guided by emotion, and particularly by biologically-based emotion, which no longer influences the weight those patients give to their deliberations. Bereft of a sense of relevance, their reasoning wanders aimlessly.

The reasonable conclusion is that emotion plays a role in effective reasoning, at least when it comes to practical reasoning. A better understanding of that role is being forged both at the neuropsychological and evolutionary levels by researchers such as Joseph LeDoux (1998). LeDoux's work shows, for example, that the amygdala is crucial to the fear response in reptiles, birds, and mammals, even though their responses themselves are often unique to the species, and that the inputs (e.g., startling noises) that cause the fear response will be effective even in the absence of conscious awareness. Since intelligence is, thus, affected by emotion, a fruitful understanding of intelligence will have to depend on an aspect of the brain that works, in part, by exaggeration and contrast. And there is no reason, just as with perception, why only certain types of emotion may rise in all evolutionary lines. That is the same arbitrary element we encountered in perception.

The question still outstanding is whether at a deeper level intelligence corrects towards "truth" the deviations to which it is subjected by perception and emotion. After all, in this chapter I have often referred to scientific findings in order to lend credence to the connections between evolution and an organism's sensory experience of its environment. As we will see in the next chapter, similar connections exist between evolution and a species' conception of its universe.

REFERENCES

Barnes, E. C. (2002). "The Miraculous Choice Argument for Realism." *Philosophical Studies,* 111(2): 97–120; doi:10.1023/A:1021204812809

Blackmore, S. (2002). *Consciousness.* Oxford University Press.

Bohr, N. (1970). "Can Quantum Mechanical Description be Complete?" In Toulmin, S., Ed., *Physical Reality.* Harper & Row.

Bohr, N. (1982). "Discussion with Einstein." In Schilpp, P., ed. *Albert Einstein: Philosopher Scientist.* Open Court.

Bohr, N. (1987). "The Quantum Postulate and the Recent Development of Atomic Theory." In *The Philosophical writings of Neil's Bohr,* Ox Bow.

Boyd, Richard (1992). "On the Current Status of Scientific Realism," in Boyd, et al, eds., *The Philosophy of Science,* MIT Press.

Brown, J. R. (1982). "The Miracle of Science." *Philosophical Quarterly,* 32(128).

Busch, J. (2008). "No New Miracles, Same Old Tricks." *Theoria,* 74(2).

Churchland, P. (1996). *The Engine of Reason, the Seat of the Soul.* MIT Press.

Crick, F. & Koch, C. (2003). "A framework for consciousness." *Nature Neuroscience,* 6(2), 119 126.

Damasio, A. (1994). *Descartes' Error.* Putnam.

Dellsén, F. (2016). "Explanatory Rivals and the Ultimate Argument." *Theoria,* 82(3).

Edelman, G. and Tononi, G. (2000). *A Universe of Consciousness.* Basic Books.

Frost-Arnold, G. (2010). "The No-Miracles Argument for Realism: Inference to an Unacceptable Explanation." *Philosophy of Science,* 77(1).

Galileo. (1989). *The Assayer.* In Michael R. Matthews, ed. *The Scientific Background to Modern Philosophy.* Hackett. First published in 1623.

Hoffman, D. (1998). *Visual Intelligence.* W.W. Norton.

Johnston, V. S. (1999). *Why We Feel.* Perseus Books.

Kanizsa, G. (1976). "Subjective Contours." *Scientific American, 234*(4).

Koch, C. (2004). *The Quest for Consciousness.* Roberts & Co.

LeDoux, J. (1996). *The Emotional Brain.* Simon & Schuster.

Lipton, P. (1994). "Truth, Existence, and the Best Explanation." In Derksen, A. A., ed. *The Scientific Realism of Rom Harré.* Tilburg University Press.

Lyons, T. D. (2003). "Explaining the Success of a Scientific Theory." *Philosophy of Science,* 70(5).

Munévar, G. (1981). *Radical Knowledge.* Hackett.

Munévar, G. (1998). *Evolution and the Naked Truth.* Ashgate.

Popper, K. (1972). *Objective Knowledge.* Cambridge University Press.

Psillos, S. (1999). *Scientific Realism: How Science Tracks Truth.* Routledge.

Putnam, H. (1975). *Mathematics, Matter and Method.* Cambridge University Press.

Tadin, D., Park, W.J., Dieter, K.C., Melnick, M.D., Lappin, J.S. & Blake, R. (2019) "Spatial Suppression Promotes Rapid Figure-Ground Segmentation of Moving Objects." *Nature Communications*, 10:2732.

Wimmer, R.D., Schmitt, L.I., Davidson, T.J., Nakajima, M., Deisseroth, K., & Halassa, M.M. (2015). "Thalamic Control of Sensory Selection in Divided Attention." *Nature* 526, 705-709.

CHAPTER 10

ALTERNATIVE WAYS OF PERCEIVING THE UNIVERSE

OTHER POSSIBLE NATURAL HISTORIES

Evolutionary biology treats realism even more unkindly than history does, for reasons that to some degree resemble Bohr's epistemology. The most basic perceptual and conceptual equipment of organisms depends, at least in part, on their biology. An amoeba's perception of its environment depends on an interaction between its biology and that environment. A bird's perceptions depend on a central nervous system that results from two kinds of histories: the history of its own ancestors as they coped with a long sequence of environments, and its own individual history which fine-tuned its central nervous system. Our modes of thought also depend to a significant extent on our brains: People with unusual brain structures conceive of the world differently from most of us, as we can easily appreciate, for example, in Judith Ford's research on the neuroscience of schizophrenia (Whitford et al., 2012). But in the brains of different species, structures wildly different from ours might be advantageous.

An intelligent bat that had never seen birds or flying insects may think that his method of flight is *the* way to fly, nature's crowning glory. But wider experience – meeting hawks and honeybees, and reading Bat Darwin's *The Origin of Species* – soon convinces him that natural history not only could but has indeed produced alternative methods of flying that are equally as "good" (in terms of allowing the corresponding species to adapt to their environments).

The same intelligent bat might have also thought that his way of thinking about the world was *the* way of thinking about the world, until his new wisdom concerning different modes of flight cues him about the possibility of different modes of thought. The possibility, that is, that there might exist brains with structures as different from his as his flight mechanism is from those of birds and insects, but which nevertheless may serve those other species as well as his kind of brain serves his own species.

Our intelligent bat may then realize that his way of "viewing the world," his empirical science, even if it is the best that the collective efforts of batkind can produce, may be no more successful than the possible "best" empirical sciences that those other species might develop. And then a terrible thought occurs to him: His science at its best was supposed to "represent" the world as it really was – that is presumably why it was so successful. But the truth of such representation of the world depended on its being a *unique* representation. He had imagined that any alternative view that could be considered true was not a true alternative but rather an *equivalent* representation (either logically, conceptually, or theoretically, in some cases also mathematically, equivalent). He becomes aware, though, that views of the world based on different biological frames of reference may exist which are as good as his although fundamentally different from his, as was the case of the bird's and insect's modes of flying.

OTHER SENSES

Let us consider how the situation described above may come about. First, even on this planet many animals have senses that are quite different from ours. The luna moth, for example, sees in the ultraviolet. To human eyes, the male and female moths look pretty much alike. But the moths themselves detect some very vivid patterns that distinguish them.

Other animals perceive the world through even more drastically different senses: vipers detect heat, bats navigate with sonar, and some fishes' main interactions with the world are based on electric fields. Electroreceptors are particularly interesting. They work by analyzing the distortions of the returning electric waves or pulses the fish sends out. The fish needs a sophisticated system to distinguish its own returning signals from those emitted by other fishes, particularly members of its own species, for the latter could be rivals or possible mates. Entire social and courtship rituals depend on the proper manipulation of the fields (e.g., turning them down in the presence of a friendly fish). The world appears very different to them than it does to us. We depend, for instance, on the perception of surfaces that reflect light, which to the fish may not be an important consideration (those surfaces may be transparent to the electroreceptor), while the changes in mood that are given away by changing electric fields may well be.

The important lesson, for my purposes in this chapter, is that such different senses are likely to require different brain structures. As intelligence develops, it follows the paths open to it by the structures with which the animal interprets the world, including its social world, and which the animal uses to cope with that world. This is not a mere theoretical point. We can see such difference in structure in **Figure 10.1** (standard fish brain) and **Figure 10.2** (brain of fish that perceives using electric fields), inspired by *Sensory Exotica*, a very interesting work by Howard C. Hughes (1999). Notice in particular the clear segregation between relay cells and pacemaker cells in **Figure 10.2**. We see a different type of brain. An intelligent creature whose main sensory modality is electric rather than visual would have patterns of thought completely foreign to us.

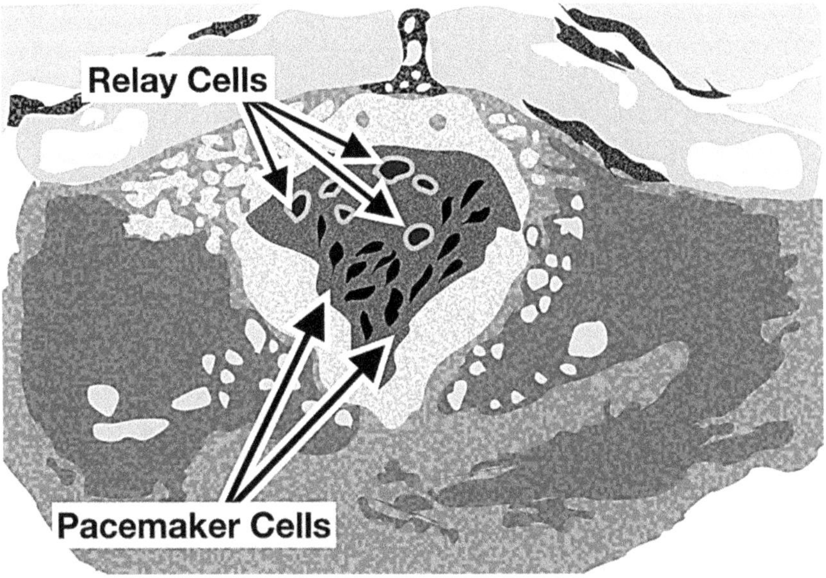

Figure 10.1. In many brains relay cells and pacemaker cells are found in the same region. Illustration by Leonardo Falaschini.

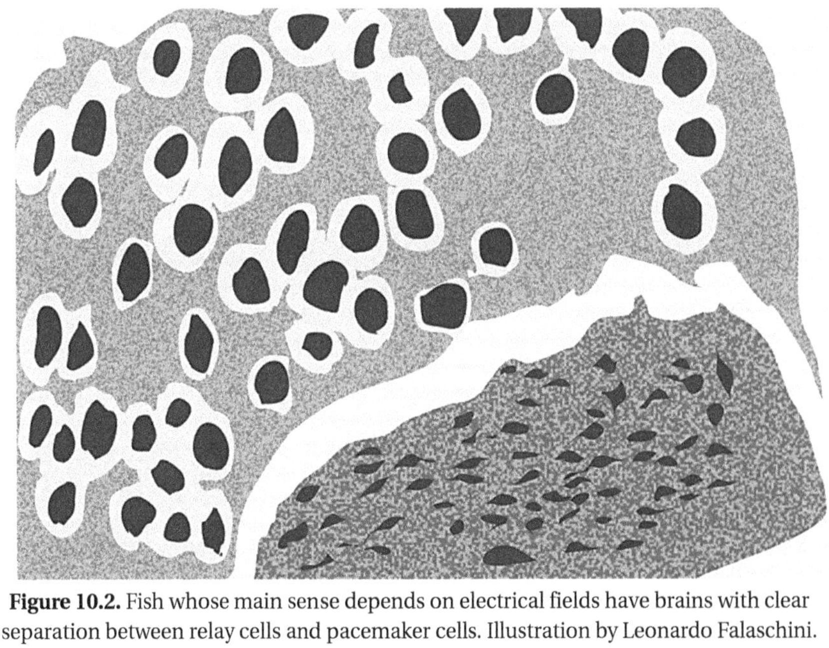

Figure 10.2. Fish whose main sense depends on electrical fields have brains with clear separation between relay cells and pacemaker cells. Illustration by Leonardo Falaschini.

Matters look even worse to our bat when he ponders the contingencies of the *social* history of bat science – contingencies that greatly magnify the relativistic conclusions that already concern him, for the possibility is raised that even within the confines of bat science several directions could have been followed successfully. It is more proper, then, to think of the frames of reference as biologic-historical, although the epistemological lessons can be drawn from the simplified (i.e., mainly biological) account.

RELATIVISM

The most alarming consequence of this entire line of reasoning is that realism is wrong: Science does not give us absolute truth, nor does it approximate absolute truth, nor can it aim to approximate the absolute truth.

Before analyzing this consequence in greater detail, it pays to comment further on two aspects of the argument. What our bat's line of reasoning establishes is not that *all* (perceptual and conceptual) frames of reference are equally good, but rather that, no matter how good a frame is, there may be some others that are equally good. Given that, it would be arbitrary to say of any one frame that it gives us *the way the world really is.* If it turns out that as a matter of fact there is only one frame that is good, we still cannot say that its view of the world is *the* correct way of viewing the world, for it is a mere accident that natural history did not bring about different but equally good frames. For the bat's view to capture the way the world really is, the world itself must cooperate by being one way and not many. But we have seen that many non-equivalent ways might represent "the world." The suspicion arises, then, that there is no truth of the matter to be represented here, since there can be no unique representation of the world. This last point is reinforced by the realization that the difficulty is not due to lack of information. For there is no new information that added to any one view could turn it into the unique representation of the world. And when every possible view will fail to represent "the world" correctly, we seem to face a dilemma: Either the world is un-representable, or else the expression "the world" is a mere convenience—there is no truth of the matter there.

Again, the first horn of the dilemma, that the world is un-representable, means not that the world cannot be represented at all, but that it cannot be represented "correctly" or "truthfully", at least as long as we understand such terms in their absolutist sense. Nevertheless many philosophers of science will hold on to their realist instincts. They may argue, for example, that the case for different modes of thought is not like the case for different modes of flight. As suggestive as the analogy is, they may say, it does not rule out the principle that the very best frames will turn out to be equivalent, or, more subtly, that the job of the scientist-philosopher, as Clifford Hooker (1991) would put it, is to discover the invariants between those frames. After all, their very success, and the fact that they are about equally successful (even if each does in its own way), cries out for an explanation. What other explanation can there be but that they all have captured some all-pervasive features of the world?

This reply may be found unsatisfactory on several levels. To begin with the presumed need for an explanation, the worth of a frame is a function of the performance (or potential performance), but that two frames may be just as good in this respect without agreeing on the content. The beginnings of human science offer us a good example in this regard. As we have seen, the two-sphere universe of the Greeks led to an extraordinary advance in navigational technology that sailors have preserved to this day. That is, in the area of navigation the performance of the Greek model was as good as that of Newtonian cosmologies. But the Greek model placed a stationary Earth at the center of the universe, two key beliefs denied by the Newtonian cosmologies. It is far from obvious, then, that overlap in success needs to be explained by overlap in content, by the "truth" the two views hold in common. As we will see below, it is success that explains truth instead.

Second, the realist may nonetheless wish to put the onus of the argument on me. How can I rule out a potential theory of invariants between the sciences developed within different biological frames of reference? Now, with the reader's indulgence, I would like to include a personal note at this point. This was the very objection that Paul Feyerabend wrote to me in a postcard when I was in my last year of doctoral studies. Carl Hempel was visiting at Berkeley that year, and I was his teaching assistant while Feyerabend was traveling. I had found the postcard in my mailbox right before one of Hempel's lectures and could not resist reading it during Hempel's terrific presentation. Nor could I resist writing my reply on the margins of the postcard (which I expanded in Ch. 3 of my *Radical Knowledge* and later publications, particularly 1998). That reply is essentially this: Such a theory of invariants would be possible, if at all, within a cognitive (biological) frame of reference. There could be, therefore, some other, quite different, theories of invariants developed within alternative cognitive (biological) frames of reference. A meta-theory of invariants would suffer the same fate, as would a meta-meta-theory, and so on....

Third, the realist seems to have missed the point altogether. If the bat's reasoning is correct, alternative frames based on significantly different brain structures are possible which may nevertheless allow the species in question to perform no less well. This is not merely a logical possibility: it follows directly from considering how natural history builds perceptual and conceptual frames. To deny this point is to assume that evolutionary biology is either incorrect or irrelevant – hardly the tack one would expect from a realist who is taking a scientific approach to epistemology.

COMPLEMENTARITY

Let us return to Ch. 9's discussion of Niels Bohr's notion of complementarity: At the subatomic level there are mutually exclusive phenomena (waves and particles) that separately give important information about the world, and in this sense *complement* each other. Recall the image where we see three versions of the double slit experiment. In (a) we notice that when either slit is open, a bell distribution of bullets will appear on the screen behind it. If both slits are open, then we will notice two bells in perfect juxtaposition of the single-slit results. In (b) we notice that when water waves go through only one slit we get a single bell distribution, but when the two slits are open we get an interference pattern instead. In (c), whether with photons or electrons, the results are the same as with water. The results in (c) show that when we set the experimental apparatus to get a particle answer (single slit open), we get the electron or photon to behave like a particle. But when we have two slits open we then get a wave answer.

What kind of answer we get depends on how the experimental setup interacts with the world: particle interactions give particles; wave interactions give waves. But neither interaction is somehow the preferred interaction, and therefore neither the particle answer nor the wave answer takes precedence over the other, neither is more "real" or "true." Although each experimental setup excludes the other, and thus getting one answer excludes the means of getting the other, each is valid in its own context and provides information about the world that the other does not.

The skeletal and other arrangements that enable the bat to fly are incompatible with those that enable birds and insects to fly. Likewise, some cerebral structures enable certain modes of thought while ruling out others. Of course, humans or bats whose cerebral structures vary significantly from those of the rest of their species may have an extreme difficulty trying to manage in the world. They are deviant. But in another species those structures, or even more unusual ones, may fit very well with the other characteristics of the species and thus be extremely adaptive and successful – just as skeletal structures or modes of respiration that would be great handicaps, if not outright lethal, in humans may well be extremely adaptive in birds or fishes. The views of "the world" produced by different frames may thus be *complementary* in a sense akin to Bohr's. It is possible then to produce information in one frame that is not logically, conceptually, theoretically, or mathematically equivalent to any produced in another, even if it is presumably about the same aspect of "reality" (they are "equivalent" only when that word is understood as a synonym of "analog", which is not the relevant sense here). As Bohr pointed out, the wave and the particle descriptions are in no relevant sense *equivalent.* An analogous situation (as in quantum physics) may thus obtain between descriptions of the "world" produced in mutually exclusive frames of reference.

It is worth emphasizing that there is nothing common to waves and particles for us to discover so as to provide a more complete description of the subatomic realm. So there is no information we lack: Failure to arrive at "reality" is a consequence of complementarity, not of ignorance on our part. My suggestion is, not surprisingly, that since analogous conditions obtain in the case of the different conceptual frames, we should arrive at the same sort of conclusion: Our talk of reality is misplaced – there is no truth of the matter "out there."

BRAIN DEVELOPMENT

In the *Birth of the Mind* (2004), Gary Marcus explains how relatively few genes (around 25,000) can create as complex an organism as ours, with trillions of cells. A smaller number "manufacture" the brain. That human brain that we see in **Figure 9.3** is of course a mammalian brain, and as such it has much in common with the brain of other mammals. Conscious states, incidentally, are also within the province of evolution and neuroscience. For my own theory of how the brain creates such states, you may consult Munévar (2020).

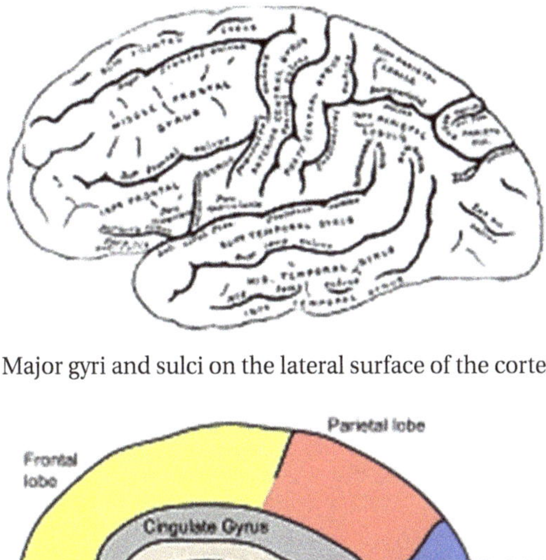

Major gyri and sulci on the lateral surface of the cortex

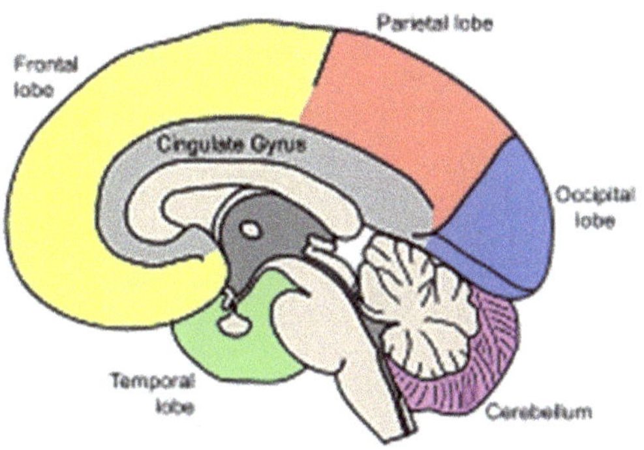

Lobes of the brain

Figure 10.3. The Human Brain. Top image public domain. Bottom image by NEUROtiker CC BY-SA 3.0.

Not all brains are equal. Some are better at some tasks than others, depending, of course, on what structures they have and how those structures function alone and in concert with other brain structures. How do those structures come about? In a variety of ways. While still in the mother's womb, for example, neurons grow in the new brain led by their growth cones, which are attracted to certain chemicals and move in the direction of the strongest signal. A slight difference in genes can alter the balance of those chemicals in the new brain and thus the structures that result. In **Figure 10.4**, we see how area V1 (a visual area in the occipital cortex) is emphasized considerably in an animal for whom quick and sharp appraisals of three-dimensional structures are crucial aspects of their environments (flying fox) and not so developed in the mouse. There is some overlap of structure in these cases, but we can imagine easily that as perceptual structures dominate the brain to a large extent, they affect the overall function of the brain. It also happens that, in the development of the brain, to emphasize a structure (or function) means to make a choice at the expense of others. Furthermore, as natural selection slowly shapes the evolution of the brain, a change in emphasis, which leads to a change in structures, provides a different context, a different niche. And given a different evolutionary context, other new structures are more likely to arise, creating even larger differences. For example, when an organism acquires the ability to react to small amounts of chemicals in the atmosphere or oceans (smell) then several new structures will be favored over others (neurons to carry the information, connections to combine it with the sense of taste, others to synchronize it with an internal sense of position, still others to allow the organism to act on the perception of those chemicals quickly, etc.).

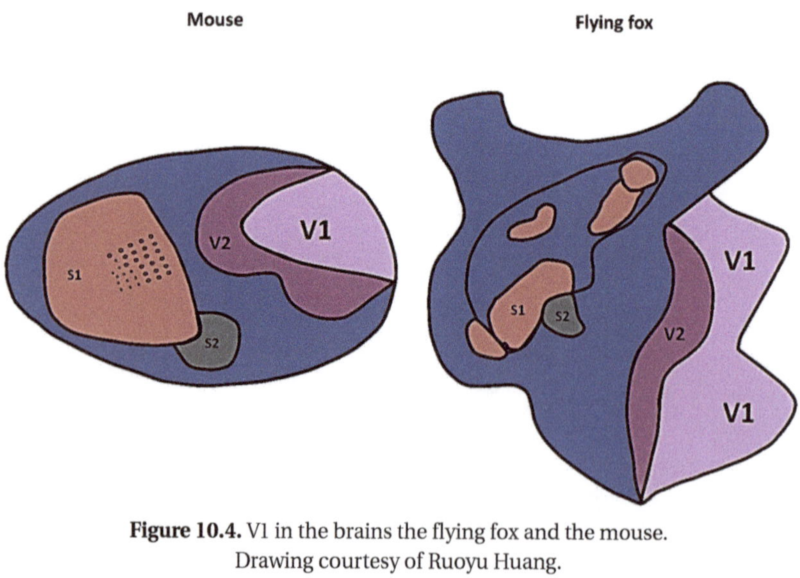

Figure 10.4. V1 in the brains the flying fox and the mouse.
Drawing courtesy of Ruoyu Huang.

Complementarity and Relativity

To do things one way, then, begins to exclude doing things another way. At appropriate phylogenetic distances, e.g., between humans and electric fishes, the brains have several incompatible structures and functions. At even larger evolutionary distances, one type of intelligence will be mutually exclusive with certain others. Their resulting approaches in dealing with the world will thus also be mutually exclusive (we even experience that within our own species: Interpreting a situation in terms of waves excludes interpreting it in terms of particles). But they both may give equally fruitful information about the world. They are thus "complementary" in a sense akin to Bohr's.

Neither the uncertainty relations nor the notion of complementary are due to ignorance on our part. These are precisely the conditions described earlier, conditions that led to the conclusion that, since "real" objects could not behave this way, we should not speak of "reality" in the subatomic world. My suggestion is, not surprisingly, that since analogous conditions obtain in the case of the different conceptual frames, we should arrive at the same sort of conclusion: Our talk of reality is misplaced—there is no truth of the matter "out there."

This is the view to which I arrived many years ago as a result of my failed attempt to develop an interactionist epistemology along the lines of Popper's scientific realism. It was Paul Feyerabend who first drew my attention to the similarity between my evolutionary relativism and Bohr's epistemological position regarding quantum mechanics, a position that I had not fully appreciated until then. I do not mean to suggest, though, that Bohr's epistemology is on the whole similar to mine. The views of his that I favor were clearly confined by him to the description of the behavior of atomic objects, and he might have very well looked unsympathetically upon a generalization of those views to the entire field of empirical knowledge. He did try to extrapolate the concept of complementarity to a few other areas of experience, without much acceptance anywhere. The significant difference, it seems to me, is that the principle of complementarity made eminent sense where the classical notion of reality was found wanting by the quantum phenomena. In the philosophical view that I propose, the classical notion of reality is found wanting even for the macroscopic phenomena. This finding requires a certain amount of reflection, and in that reflection an analog of Bohr's principle of complementarity helps us understand the possibility of equally worthy and yet non-equivalent frames.

It appears to me that the main reason Bohr's view was found so counter-intuitive was precisely that scientific realism was deeply entrenched in our general epistemology and scientists (and philosophers) were loath to make an exception in the realm of the very small. As Einstein (1982) argued, no one is inclined to give up the program of scientific realism in the "macroscopic" realm, but, as he put it, "the 'macroscopic' and the 'microscopic' are so inter-related that it appears impracticable to give up this program in the 'microscopic' alone." If, however, it turns out that for independent reasons we must give up the program of scientific realism in the "macroscopic" realm after all, and to give it up in favor of an epistemology congenial to Bohr's view about quantum mechanics, then it seems that Bohr's epistemology ends up looking very sensible indeed.

Ironically enough, the reasoning I have employed is analogous to the reasoning used by Einstein concerning some important conceptual consequences of his Special Theory of Relativity. In evolutionary relativism we can show that (a) our perceptions and conceptualizations of the world are relative to a biological frame of reference (or rather, to a biologic-social frame of reference). And (b) we can also show that there is no preferred frame. Likewise, in the Special Theory of Relativity, (a) mass, length and time are relativized to an inertial frame of reference, and (b) there is no preferred inertial frame of reference. From the fulfillment of these two conditions, (a) and (b), we conclude that mass, length and time are relative properties and, thus, cannot have absolute values. I trust I have used the same mode of reasoning to establish the relativism of perception, intelligence and science.

TRADITIONAL OBJECTIONS AGAINST RELATIVISM

Nevertheless, the reader may ask, did not Plato demonstrate that relativism is incoherent? And, in the last 2,300 years, have not philosophers added new demonstrations to the same effect? Not so. Plato's "demonstration" is based on a very serious logical error: that the denial of absolute truth commits the relativist to the claim that all points of view are equally valid. From this premise it follows that absolutism is also valid. But absolutism implies that relativism is false. Therefore relativism is both valid and invalid. And this, clearly, is incoherent. Now, Plato was a great philosopher, but his logical blunder is not any smaller for that. The negation of the claim that there can be only one true view of the world does not imply that all points of view are equally valid: It only implies that there may be more than one. That is exactly what evolutionary relativism says: that several points of view *may* be equally valid.

As for the other well-regarded "demonstrations" against relativism, I am afraid that they are also based on logical blunders. For example, a favorite argument of philosophers is that a relativist has to accept at least one truth: that relativism is a true view. Those philosophers then conclude that at the meta-level relativism has to rely on an absolute truth. Thus absolutism triumphs in the end. But this is a fallacious argument, an instance of begging the question.

When doubt is cast upon absolute truth, philosophers demand that no alternative should be taken seriously unless it is offered as an absolute truth!

According to others, relativism entails that the universe would not exist without observers. If the way the world is, reality, is relativized to a conceptual frame of reference, we are tying the existence of the world to a frame of reference. But surely, as Tuomela (1985), arguing in favor of realism, puts it, "...at least some real objects may exist in the world even if...all mankind is destroyed and even if there had never been any human beings." Objections of this sort are sometimes discussed by physicists concerned with the relativistic implications of quantum theory. The universe must be independent of any frames of reference. If it were not, then it would not come into existence until it could be described within the point of view of some observer or other (presumably the sort of thing that I mean when I talk of describing the universe within a frame of reference), and it would go out of existence when there are no longer any observers to describe it. Clearly, this line of thought reduces relativism to absurdity. But this objection misses the point of evolutionary relativism. The frames of reference in question need not be actual frames. Relativism requires only potential frames of reference; therefore the objection does not apply. I would like to explain the point by means of an analogy to the special theory of relativity once more. The equivalent objection, with respect to absolute, real mass, would run something like this: you say that mass is relative to a frame of reference; are we to conclude that if no one were around to measure mass, objects would have no mass? Of course that would not be so. The frames of reference, or measurement, in question may all be potential.

A NEW THEORY OF TRUTH

To review what has been suggested so far, we may consider Figures 10.5 and 10.6. In **Figure 10.5** we see two different perceptions of the world by Little Green Man and a member of another species, Papaya Man. Little Green Man sees the world as dots, whereas Papaya Man sees it as edges (drawn on top of where the Little Green Man's dots would be). Given such perceptual mechanisms, what kinds of intelligence will their brains generate to act in concert with them? Let us imagine that the best way to account for Little Green Man's perceptual experience is to provide a grid to keep track of the perceptual dots, as illustrated in **Figure 10.6**. For Papaya Man, however, such a grid would be not only useless but incomprehensible. A far more suitable, curvy grid is seen in the bottom half of **Figure 10.6**.

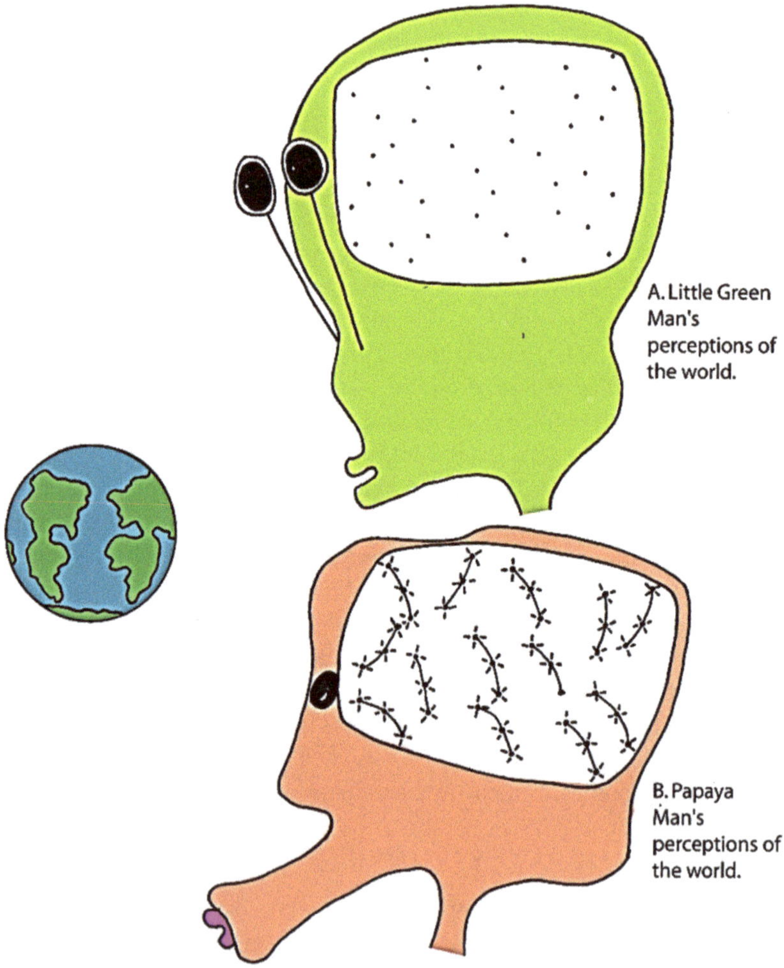

Figure 10.5. Drawing by Nicole Ankeny.

It is quite possible, of course, that in terms of performance neither is superior to the other. That means that neither neuro-biological frame is to be preferred. And of course, their perceptions and the intellectual mechanisms that arise from them (in the sense that newer phylogenetic structures will be, so to speak, built around them) will be relative to such frames. Not only are, thus, perceptions and modes of thought relative, but in this particular example we see that they are mutually exclusive: To develop one kind of brain (and so one particular way of interacting with the world) is to rule out developing the other kind of brain (and so that particular way of interacting with the world). The products (e.g., perception, intelligence, conceptual categories) of different neuro-biological frames may be complementary in Bohr's sense. In this particular example the two frames are.

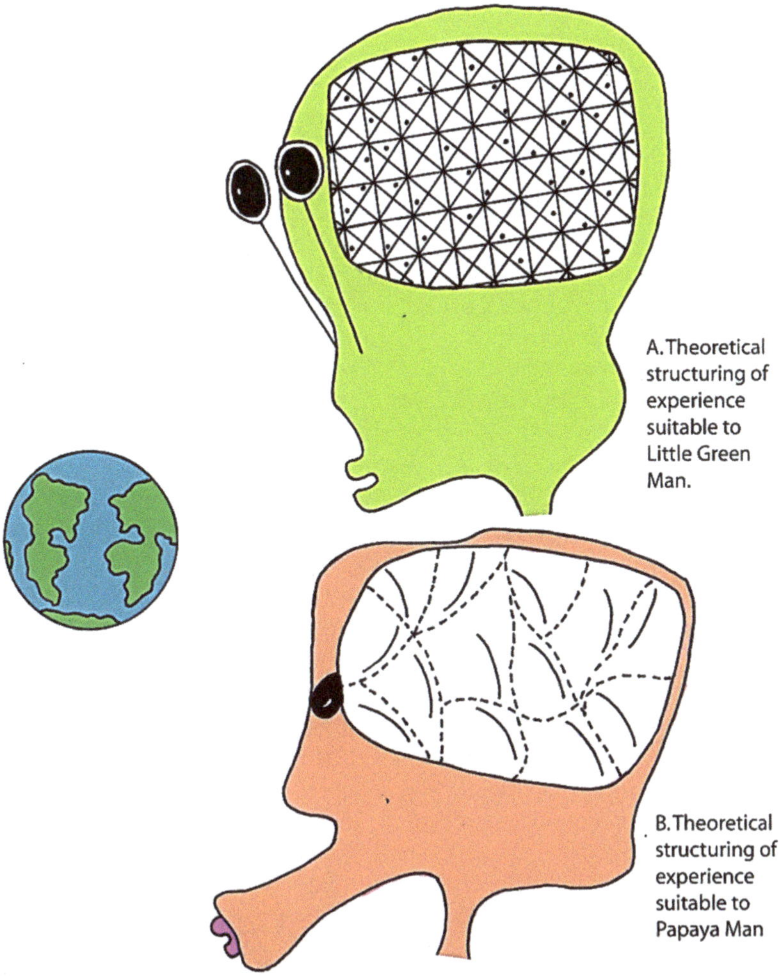

Figure 10.6. Drawing by Nicole Ankeny.

Is there no truth then? Or at least, is there no truth as correspondence? I think it is still useful to think of truth, albeit of relative truth, as I have explained in other work (1998). I will offer a brief sketch with the help of **Figures 10.7** and **10.8**.

In the bat's hypothetical comparisons between frames of reference, when two frames led to similar levels of performance, he found it arbitrary to make either one a preferred or absolute frame. This indicates that the notion of performance can be fruitfully tied to the notion of understanding, particularly to that of scientific understanding. Such a connection between performance and understanding suggests a biological theory of relative truth. I will introduce that theory by means of an illustration.

Let me suppose that when I perceive a mango, I see it as golden-red, taste it as juicy and delicious, and find it beautiful enough to make it the subject of a still-life painting. Successful perceptions of the mango lead me to suppose that they serve me best to deal with that section of the world (the mango). Imagine now that beings of a very different kind have perceptions of the mango different from mine, though just as successful as mine. Upon coming to know of these beings' perceptions, should I stop trusting my perception of the mango? Should I replace it by the perceptions those beings have? The answer in both cases is "no." For I have already said that this is the best way I can perceive that section of the world. Thus, learning of the other beings' perceptions would lead me to conclude that I do not perceive "the way the mango really is," simply because doing so would require me to claim my frame of reference as the preferred one, and that would be arbitrary. Nonetheless, this conclusion does not obligate me to change my perceptions of the mango, which after all are the best I can have.

In this example, my perceptions best exploit the resources of my genotype (or rather, of the genotype of beings like me) in dealing with a typical environment. Whenever the resulting performance is as satisfactory as in the case of the ideal perceptions of the mango, we tend to think that the world must be just as we perceive it. It is then that we feel entitled to speak of true representations. Our talk of truth then is warranted by the successful interaction with the world, given our frame of reference. Little Green Man, however, can also have successful interactions with the mango, but since his frame of reference is drastically different from ours, his perceptions will be different also (**Figure 10.7**). Nevertheless, that success will entitle him just as much to speak of truth.

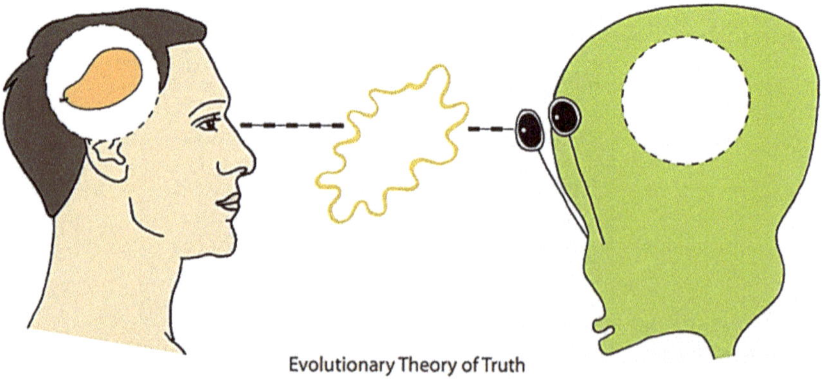

Figure 10.7. Both the human and the LGM from Andromeda perceive the mango differently, but their perceptions are equally successful. Neither one can thus be said to capture the way the mango "really is." Drawing by Nicole Ankeny.

Of course, in our conceptualizations of the world—e.g., in our scientific views—we seldom, if ever, reach the level of sufficiency or satisfaction given in the case of the mango. But when we do approach it we speak of truth. Human science is ultimately a variety of human behavior, and human behavior is part of the human phenotype. Although, at least in the case of humans, we should speak of phenotypes, since the plasticity of human behavior is such that there could be many expressions of the genotype even in the same environment. It seems to me also, that some phenotypic expressions exploit better the resources of our genotype in a given environment. Likewise, some scientific viewpoints (with their complex machinery of practices, experimental procedures, and so on) permit us to exploit better the resources of our genotype in a given environment (e.g., in dealing with the dynamics of bodies). In other words, some viewpoints enable us to realize more of our potential for performance. In this biological context, a viewpoint is said to be relatively true when it approaches the limits of the resources of the genotype. When a theory allows us to deal with the world in a great variety of ways, when thinking that the world accords with the theory leads to continuing success, when this capacity for performance clearly surpasses that of its competitors, then we come to think that the world must be so. And in a limited domain we may not be able to conceptualize the world any better. We conceptualize the world as powerfully as in the earlier example we perceive the mango. It is then that we may speak of truth.

This account explains why it may be worthwhile to make distinctions between true and untrue. In my account we would say that a viewpoint is true because the interaction (with the world) that results is of great quality (or seems to be) and very superior to its alternatives. This is not to say that we have finally arrived at the way things really are, but merely that our "picturing" of the world approaches the level of quality exemplified earlier by our perception of the mango. This "picturing", however, just as that perception, is relative to a frame of reference, and thus the truth involved is relative truth.

Many realists have tried to explain the success of science in terms of truth. A viewpoint was successful either because it was true or because it approached truth. My account of relative truth turns the tables. The relative truth (or seeming absolute truth) of a viewpoint depends on its success, not the other way around. Certain views hold us in a strong grip because they permit a strong, successful interaction with the world. I suggest that it is that grip under those conditions of successful interaction that seems to have a special character – such character is what philosophers have been trying to explain with correspondence theories of truth.

Some qualifications are in order. Few views are so successful that they are accepted on the basis of a clearly superior record. They are accepted because in a few instances the success achieved is felt to be so striking that many members of the discipline find the way of doing things extremely promising. That is, they are accepted on the basis of a promise of performance rather than on total performance. After a group takes up a way of thinking about the world, and elaborates it to the point that its performance begins to approach the limit of the potential of the genotype in the relevant environments, then its truth seems "evident" to all those concerned. There are also cases in which that limit is not approached but the scientists committed to the point of view are unable to think about the world in any other way, and so they keep on feeling that the truth must lie somewhere along the path they have undertaken.

There are, in addition, cases in which a point of view, if developed, would have exploited better the resources of the genotype; and so, years later we feel that an opportunity has been missed. And I suppose there are cases in which the superiority of a point of view goes unrecognized. All the sensible things that philosophers wanted to convey with the old correspondence notions can be conveyed with this relativistic and evolutionary notion.

It is in this sense that I accept the truth of evolutionary theory, neuroscience, and other scientific views I am sympathetic to as relative truths. To alien beings elsewhere, engaged in completely different modes of interaction with the universe, evolutionary thinking, say, of any kind resembling ours might not make sense within the bounds of their conceptual equipment. But to beings like us it does. Or so I believe. I would say similar things about the truth of my philosophical position, if called upon to do so; and I would adduce as evidence precisely the evolutionary and other scientific arguments I have provided so far.

The notion of ideal truth implicit in this evolutionary relativism has some features in common with a pragmatist's ideal truth (the approaching of a limit). But they differ in that in the evolutionary account the limit may well be a horizon that recedes. There are several reasons for this. The exploitation of the resources of the genotype depends on the environment, or environments, involved in the interaction. The environment is not static, however: it may simply change, in which case the phenotypes that might have been quite adequate before may now be challenged successfully by a different approach more in consonance with the new circumstances. The relevant environment may also change as a result of the interaction with a successful phenotype. That is, the environment may be transformed. Moreover, success in one environment may lead the organisms in question to venture into other environments that will offer challenges of a different sort. And finally, the influx of new ideas changes the conditions of interaction with the universe; and that change of conditions opens the door to different approaches.

These considerations make the relativistic ideal of truth a changeable one. Perhaps we can now understand why scientists so often feel that they are pretty much in possession of the truth, while at the same time allowing that others who had similar feelings in the past were "wrong," and even that others in the future may feel just as strongly about ideas that seem perfectly obvious to us now. At times, we may come close to the truth with respect to a certain environment, just as some species may come close to equilibrium with a given environment: but as conditions change, other ideas will be more appropriate and thus considered true. **Figure 10.8**, thus, illustrates the difference between the traditional notion of truth as correspondence – our mind somehow captures approximately the way the world really is – and this theory of relative truth born from an evolutionary approach to intelligence.

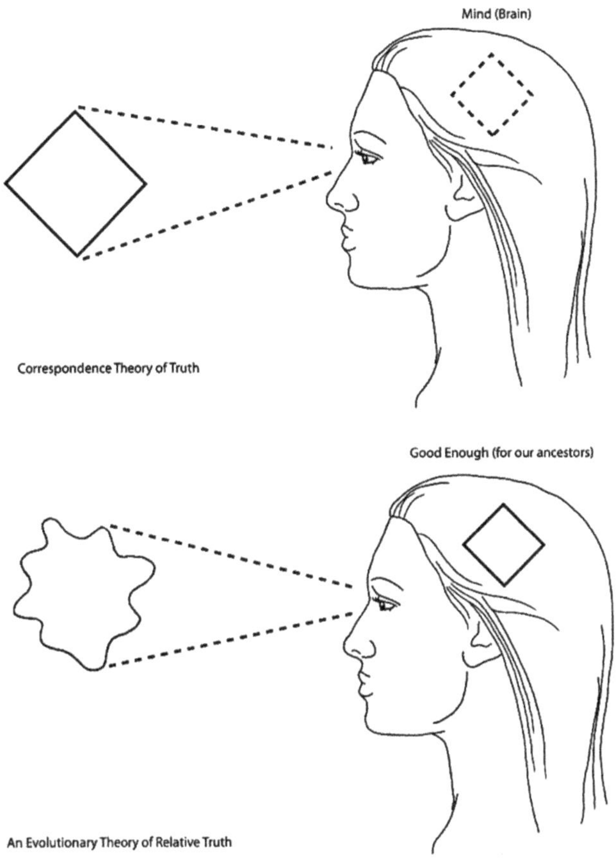

Figure 10.8. Drawing by Nicole Ankeny.

SCIENCE AS RADICAL KNOWLEDGE

Treating science as human behavior, i.e. as part of the human phenotype, allows us to put in perspective the question of its rationality, as we saw in Chapter 8. Organisms as simple as bacteria may change their behavior radically as their environments change, say from being impoverished to being rich in nutrients (from preying on their competitors to avoiding them instead). The second phenotype does not "follow" from the first in a logical or rational way. The organism simply undergoes a radical change of posture toward the environment.

Similarly, our scientific views at a point in time need not be continuous with those that replace them, although in some cases there might be quite a bit of continuity. A radical new idea (e.g., changing the body of physical facts, as Galileo did) may open the way for a far more suitable way to approach our world (environment). No less than in the case of the bacteria, as we have seen, the rationality of science should not be tied to the logical, theoretical, or empirical continuity of its content.

We discussed in the earlier chapters some of Kuhn valuable contributions to the topics covered in this book. His main disagreement with Feyerabend was about the latter's insistence on the proliferation of theories and the role that proliferation plays on radical changes in science that bring about progress (as future generations so judge). On that point Galileo's arguments make it clear which side history favors. When you consider alternative views, you change theoretical assumptions, and as a result you also change what counts as evidence. Points all that Feyerabend elaborated in *Against Method* and most of his subsequent work. I much admire Feyerabend's keen insight and skillful use of the history of science to help us understand how to approach the pursuit of science. Nevertheless, it has seemed to me that his insights must be supplemented by looking at science through neuroscience in the context of evolutionary biology.

A proper job required showing, as I did in Chapter 8, that evolutionary biology undermines the analogy between the "evolution" of scientific ideas and the evolution of species, and that insofar as evolutionary biology gives us insights about the brain and the nature of science, it also undermines scientific realism, and consequently the support some hoped it would provide to the notion of the gradual or continuous growth of science. In the process, I have marshalled many resources from biology, particularly about perception and intelligence, to support evolutionary relativism; I have dealt with the most important objections to relativism; and, finally, I have provided a biologically based theory of relative truth. I trust these proposals go beyond the well-known arguments of post-Kuhnian historicist philosophy of science. I hope the reader will find them worthy of consideration.

"Radical Knowledge" is not a mere "theoretical" thesis within the philosophy of science. It is intended rather as a description both of the history of science and of the sort of activity that we should expect from a social extension of intelligence to the exploration of nature. The knowledge that results is not "radical" merely in some abstract or theoretical sense. On the contrary, as we saw with Galileo and Prout, it describes not only theoretical changes in science but changes of the body of facts. Rocks do not fall vertically from towers, even though our eyes tell us that they do. They fall in a parabolic motion. To think of science as "Radical Knowledge" recognizes that very drastic changes may occur at any level of our scientific enterprise and that pursuing them may yield scientific progress. This "Radical Knowledge" also generates and drives the sense of wonder that nature inspires in us when we pursue science.

REFERENCES

Einstein, A. (1982). *Albert Einstein: Philosopher Scientist*; Schilpp, P., ed. Open Court.

Feyerabend, P. (1999). *Conquest of Abundance: A Tale of Abstractness versus the Richness of Being*. University of Chicago Press.

Hooker, C. A., (1991). "Between Formalism and Anarchism: A Reasonable Middle Way." In Munévar, G. ed. *Beyond Reason: Essays on the Philosophy of Paul Feyerabend*. Kluwer.

Hughes, H. C. (1999). *Sensory Exotica*. MIT Press.

Marcus, G. (2004). *The Birth of the Mind*. Basic Civitas Books.

Munévar, G. (1981). *Radical Knowledge*. Hackett.

Munévar, G. (1998). *Evolution and the Naked Truth*. Ashgate.

Munévar, G. (2020) "A Cellular and Attentional Network Explanation of Consciousness." *Consciousness and Cognition* 83.

Tuomela, R. *Science, Action and Reality*; Reidel: Dordrecht, Holland, 1985.

Whitford, T.J., Ford, J.M., Mathalon, D.H., Kubicki, M., and Shenton, M.E. (2012). Schizophrenia, Myelination, and Delayed Corollary Discharges: A Hypothesis. *Schizophrenia Bulletin* vol. 38 no. 3 pp. 486–494. doi:10.1093/schbul/sbq105

APPENDIX: THE FATE OF INDUCTIVE LOGIC

The belief in induction dies hard. Over the middle decades of the 20th Century, several saving moves were tried by Rudolf Carnap and other leading inductivists.[1] A rather popular one was to argue that we may obtain a theory's "degree of confirmation" or of "rational support" from the reliability of the theory in making predictions. The more reliable a theory is (the better its track record) the more confident we are that its next prediction will come true. In the case of law, the more reliable it is, the more confident we are that its next instance will conform to past experience. And somehow the reliability of a theory is indicated precisely by our confidence in it (that is, by the confidence that experts have in it). This confidence can be expressed by the degree to which we are willing to bet in the theory's (or law's) favor. We may not know whether the sun will always rise, but we can safely bet that it will rise tomorrow.

We only need to remember now that the probability calculus was developed precisely to cash our betting intuition in mathematical terms. So once we have determined a ranking scale for betting on different theories ("betting quotient"), we can express those rankings in terms of probability. Thus this probability estimate will represent a numerical betting quotient, which in turn will express our degree of confidence in the theory. The hope is that starting from the track record of the theory we can arrive at an estimate of the probability of each individual prediction it makes. And that probability estimate, which results from the reliability of the theory, is the degree of confirmation of the theory. This is one way in which we could produce a logic of confirmation, or inductive logic, along the lines of the probability calculus.

This is not the only possible way in which we can bring about a logic of confirmation. But many such attempts do have to establish similar relationships between the notions of confirmation, reliability, and so on. Unfortunately, as the Hungarian philosopher Imre Lakatos argued, those kinds of relationships are suspect. "Degree of confirmation", for example, normally means the degree to which the theory has been shown to be true or correct. But then the degree of confirmation of a theory may be incompatible with its degree of reliability. As Lakatos points out, the degree of reliability of the hypothesis that all tosses of a

---

[1] A good book to consult on these activities is The Philosophy of Rudolf Carnap (1963).

coin will come up heads is 50%, but its degree of confirmation must be zero, since it is obviously false.

Desperate moves are perhaps called for at this point. Perhaps we should give up on the truth or likelihood of laws and theories. Do not think of theories as true descriptions of the world, but merely as instruments for prediction. As the poet Robinson Jeffers wrote: "The mathematicians and the physics men have their mythology; they work alongside the truth, never touching it; their equations are false but the things *work*."

Let us try the following suggestion then: Forget about confirmation. Simply identify the degree of rational support for a theory with its degree of reliability. But this suggestion flounders precisely because of the presumed connection between reliability and probability. The problem is that the more comprehensive a theory is, the more rational it would be to support it. But we have already seen that the more comprehensive a theory is, the lower its probability. Thus whereas reliability and probability go hand in hand, degree of rational support and probability seem to be inversely proportional. How can reliability and degree of rational support be equated then?

Nevertheless, can't the suggestion be saved? Why couldn't we say that the more comprehensive a theory is, the more confident we feel about it, and therefore the more we are willing to bet on its predictions (the greater the probabilities we assign to them)? This amounts to solving the problem by fiat, but there is a certain merit in that. The key here seems to be the use of so-called subjective probabilities as the basis of our inductive logic. Let us simply take into account all the factors that influence our confidence in a certain theory, even if some of them are not explicit. Of course, the "we" in this case cannot be anyone who wishes to proffer an opinion on the worth of a theory: such judgments perhaps should be limited to scientists who are already experts on the matter and who are in a position to make educated guesses about it. *The* definitive probability estimate must then somehow be a composite of the probability estimates made by many experts.

Inductivists may find this a charming line of thought. But it is beset by serious problems. The most important problem, for our present concerns, still is the original problem: a comprehensive theory makes a lot of claims about the world. This is a problem because the more claims a theory makes about the world, the riskier it has to be (picking the top three horses in a race, in the right order, is a longer shot than picking only the winner); but the greater the risk, the lower the probability. No inductive fiat can rescue us here.

What is the situation for inductive logic, then? We thought that in some sense confirmation = degree of rational support = reliability = probability (via betting quotients). But we had to drop confirmation. And now we have to drop degree of rational support. Without this connection the measure of reliability left does not seem worth much.

Nonetheless, some believe that the ship of inductivism may remain afloat if we are willing to jettison even more of our intellectual baggage. First, we gave up on proving theories. Then we gave up on confirming them. What is left? We can give up on theories altogether!

But how could we have science without theories? The radical proposal, sometimes favored by Carnap and others, is to change the goal of inductive logic from the appraisal of theories and laws to that of particular predictions. As Frank Ramsey put it:

> ... we can agree that inductive generalization need have no finite probability, but particular expectations entertained on inductive grounds undoubtedly do have a high numerical probability in the minds of all of us.... If induction ever needs a logical justification it is in connection with [such probabilities].[2]

To hold this radical inductivism, we must claim that theories are not strictly necessary for the task of estimating the probability of individual events. They may be useful for that task, but not necessary. At the present time, of course, we do need theories; but eventually, when an inductive logic is developed, we will be able to dispense with them (and with laws) although we may still find them convenient. Theories and laws would then be like some little rhymes that help children remember certain rules of grammar, though in principle they could learn the rules without the rhymes.

This is tough-minded empiricism indeed! But we must remember that the very soul of empiricism was weaned on suspicion of theoretical speculation. Thus, it is not surprising that a sober empiricist like Carnap would come to see things this way. "... the use of laws is not indispensable for making predictions," he says; though he is careful to add: "nevertheless it is expedient, of course, to state universal laws in books on physics, biology, psychology, etc." (1945, 93).

Nevertheless, here we come to the end of the road for inductive logic. In order to estimate the probabilities of events we need to know what is relevant to such events, what is causally connected to them, what brings them about. That is, we need some idea of what nature is like. And surely different ideas about nature, i.e., different theories, would give different answers to all these questions. Therefore, different theories would yield different probability estimates. As Lakatos says, "... in a language separating celestial from terrestrial phenomena, data about

---

[2] Consult Ramsey's *Philosophical Papers* (1990) for his development of this and other ideas on induction.

terrestrial projectiles may seem irrelevant to hypotheses about planetary motion. In the language of Newtonian dynamics they become relevant and change our betting quotients for planetary predictions" (1980, 152). And, of course, as soon as we try to determine the best theories, we are back to where we started. The inductive method has yet to take us anywhere.

More recently, inductivists have focused their attention on Bayesian methodology. This is a version of subjective probability that appears plausible, at least at first sight. Informally the idea is something like this: Whatever your initial degree of confidence in a hypothesis (initial probability), as you begin to test the hypothesis you also begin to reassess your degree of confidence in it. When the test is positive, your confidence goes up. When the test is negative, your confidence goes down. After continuous testing, in the long run the hypothesis will come to be assigned a degree of confidence pretty close to what it deserves. The initial probability will wash out in a large number of tests.

When I was the South American equivalent of a sophomore in a U.S. high school, history, anatomy, and other classes were graded according to the following system. The instructor would ask a question of the student sitting upfront and furthest to his right. If the student did not know the answer, or hesitated, the instructor moved on to the student sitting directly behind him, and continued moving up the column of students, and to the beginning of the next column if necessary, until someone gave the correct answer. That student then would move up to the desk where the question had been originally asked, and every student who had failed would move one desk back. The questioning would resume at the point where the question had been answered. I used to sit at the end of the last column, but since I had a good memory for the kinds of facts asked about, I never worried, for I was confident that by the end of the month I would be sitting right in front of the teacher. After hundreds of questions, the initial position would wash out, so to speak. Will this approach solve the problem of the initial probability of hypotheses and theories? Will it then lead to a genuine logic of confirmation?

Let us see. Scientific theories and hypothesis are often, if not always, universal. That leads to two familiar kinds of problems. The first problem is that we just do not know how long the long run is, especially for a universal hypothesis. The second problem depends on the actual formulation of Bayes' theorem, which is derived from the definition of conditional probability:

$$pr(h|e\&b)=(pr(h|b)xpr(e|h\&b))/pr(e|b)$$

where h is the hypothesis, e is the evidence, and b is the background knowledge. Presumably we can then determine numerically the probability of a hypothesis as the evidence mounts in its favor. Multiplication being what it is, though, notice that if the initial probability of a hypothesis (with respect to the background) is 0, then it will not matter what e does (for 0 times any other value still yields 0). But we have seen that universal hypotheses appear to have a probability of 0. So we have to assume that the initial probability is not 0. Some observers find that assumption just plain arbitrary.

It seems to me, however, that the critics sometimes confuse universal and infinite. Universal hypotheses are infinite only if their domains are infinite. But in the actual universe, it seems that the domain of our scientific hypotheses will be extraordinarily large but finite. An infinite domain would yield a probability of 0. A very large, but still finite, domain would yield a probability that approaches 0 but is larger than 0. Thus, given an extraordinarily long run, Bayes' theorem may yet work to justify induction without arbitrary assumptions (as it does in limited domains). Of course, this move places us back at the point where we must wonder when a long run is long enough.

The most significant drawback, however, is that we have no mathematical function by which to determine how much a test should increase or decrease our degree of confidence in the hypothesis in question (or the probability estimates for any of the factors in Bayes' formula). And as we have seen throughout this book, such determinations depend on a myriad of factors and can reasonably yield contradictory results for different observers. Even at this point we should realize that the hope of an inductive calculus remains a chimera. The Bayesian methodology is a best a qualitative tool of great limitations for inductive logic, precisely because in real situations (whether life or science) it has no system for assigning numerical values. It can do so only in artificial, formal scenarios. Of course, Bayesian statistics can be a pragmatic help in a variety of actual scientific studies, as other statistics may also be.

REFERENCES

Carnap, R. (1945). "On Inductive Logic." Philosophy of Science, Vol. 12, No. 2. University of Chicago Press.

Carnap, R. (1963). *The Philosophy of Rudolf Carnap.* Schilpp, A., ed., *The Library of Living Philosophers.* Cambridge University Press.

Lakatos, I (1980). "Changes in the Problem of Inductive Logic." In *Mathematics, Science and Epistemology,* Vol. 2. *Philosophical Papers.* Cambridge University Press.

Ramsey, F. (1990). *Philosophical Papers.* Cambridge University Press.

INDEX

G

H

I

J

K

L

M

www.ingramcontent.com/pod-product-compliance
Lightning Source LLC
LaVergne TN
LVHW070743240926
848802LV00005B/10/J
* 9 7 8 1 6 4 8 8 9 1 9 7 7 *